Technology and Economic Development

Technology and Economic Development: The Dynamics of Local, Regional and National Competitiveness

Second Edition

Edward J. Malecki

LONGMAN

Addison Wesley Longman Limited
Edinburgh Gate, Harlow
Essex CM20 2JE
England

and Associated Companies throughout the world

First edition published 1991
Reprinted 1994, 1995, 1996
This edition published 1997

ISBN 0 582 27723 X

British Library Cataloguing in Publication Data
A catalogue record for this book is
available from the British Library

Library of Congress Cataloging-in-Publication Data
A catalog entry for this title is
available from the Library of Congress

Set by 34 in 11/12pt Adobe Garamond
Produced through Longman Malaysia, GPS

To Cindy and Mike

Contents

Preface

This book is a synthesis of the many literatures that address the topics of economic development and technology. It draws from the wide range of research which informs investigations of economic development – from disciplines such as economics, geography and planning, but also interdisciplinary areas, such as management and entrepreneurship studies, regional science, and science and technology policy.

About one-half of the material is new in this second edition. New chapters include those on large firms (Chapter 6), and on developing countries (Chapter 8). A great deal has changed in Chapters 2, 4, 5 and 7, and all the others have been revised and updated substantially. I sometimes fear that, instead of reflecting deeply about a few central readings, I only read more. The outpouring of research – in articles, books and research reports – is already so great that no one can expect to have time to read it all. I have tried to synthesize many of the most significant streams for students and other researchers.

I have been fortunate during the past several years to travel to many parts of the world, and to see firsthand much of the interaction of technology and economic development. I also have been fortunate to work with some wonderful colleagues and students. My thinking reflects to a large degree our discussions and joint work. These include Susan Bradbury, Sharon Cobb, Sergio Conti, Nancy Ettlinger, David Mulkey, Päivi Oinas, Dona Stewart, Franz Tödtling, Deborah Tootle, Eirik Vatne, Marlies Veldhoen and Betty Waldron. Discussions over the years with John Britton have always clarified my thinking on innovation policy.

Finally, this book is dedicated once again to my wife, Cindy, and our son, Mike, who have seen it grow from idea to reality and who keep me firmly grounded in our reality.

Acknowledgements

We would like to thank the following for permission to reproduce copyright material:

Richard J. Samuels and *Technology Review* for figure 3.1 from Samuels & Whipple (1989); Cartermill International Ltd for figure 4.2 from Kaplinsky (1984)

Whilst every effort has been made to trace the owners of copyright material, in a few cases this has proved impossible and we take this opportunity to offer our apologies to any copyright holders whose rights we may have unwittingly infringed.

List of abbreviations

ASEAN	Association of Southeast Asian Nations
BRITE	Basic Research in Industrial Technologies
CAD	computer-aided design
CERN	Conseil Européan pour la Recherche Nucléaire
CNC	computer numerically controlled
CIM	computer-integrated manufacturing
CRADA	Cooperative Research and Development Agreement
CRITT	Centre régional pour l'innovation et le transfert technologique
DRAM	dynamic random-access memory
EC	European Community
EMU	European Monetary Union
EPZ	export processing zone
ERDF	European Regional Development Fund
ESA	European Space Agency
ESPRIT	European Strategic Programme for Research and Development in Information Technologies
EU	European Union
EUREKA	European Research Coordinating Agency
EVIT	eight vehicles for industrial transformation
FDI	foreign direct investment
FMS	flexible manufacturing system
FYR	former Yugoslavian Republic
GDP	gross domestic product
GNP	gross national product
HCI	heavy and chemical industries
HPAEs	high-performing Asian economies
IBJ	Industrial Bank of Japan
ICETT	International Centre for Environmental Technology Transfer
IMD	International Institute for Management Development
IMF	International Monetary Fund
ISO	International Standards Organisation
IT	information technology
JIT	just-in-time
LCD	liquid crystal display
mbps	megabits per second

MCC	Microelectronics and Computer Technology Corporation
MIT	Massachusetts Institute of Technology
MITI	Ministry of International Trade and Industry
MSR	mode of social regulation
NGOs	nongovernmental organizations
NICs	newly industrializing countries
OECD	Organisation for Economic Co-operation and Development
POTS	plain old telephone service
R&D	research and development
RA	research association
RACE	R&D in Advanced Communication Technologies for Europe
RITE	Research Institute of Innovative Technology for the Earth
RTD	research and technology development
SAP	structural adjustment programme
SEMATECH	Semiconductor Research Corporation
SEZ	special economic zone
SME	small and medium-sized enterprise
SOE	state-owned enterprise
TEC	training and enterprise council
TFP	total factor productivity
TNC	transnational corporation
UK	United Kingdom
UN	United Nations
UNCTC	United Nations Centre on Transnational Corporations
UNCTAD	United Nations Conference on Trade and Development
UNDP	United Nations Development Programme
UNEP/ITEC	United Nations Environment Programme/International Environmental Technology Centre
USA	United States of America
USSR	Union of Soviet Socialist Republics
VCR	video cassette recorder
ZERI	Zero Emissions Research Initiative

Chapter 1

Economic growth and development at the local, regional and national levels

The dynamics of the capitalist economic system are more influential at the end of the twentieth century than ever before. Capitalism 'won' the Cold War conflict with socialism, with late hangers-on only in North Korea and Cuba. Within capitalism, corporations and entrepreneurs carry out their tasks, their decisions profoundly affecting people and places. The capitalist system is global, and has given rise to a growing competition among places, where people attempt to attract investment and shape their local circumstances. At the same time, capitalism is not monolithic but exhibits significant variations from place to place, suggesting both a resilience and a challenge for firms and nations trying to compete (Saunders 1995; Zysman 1994). Some of the variation is cultural, influencing the meaning found in work, attitudes toward stakeholders, styles of managing employees, and negotiation tactics (Hampden-Turner and Trompenaars 1993; Saunders 1995).

On a world scale, the 'Triad' economies of East Asia, Europe and North America are the dominant entities (Ohmae 1985; UNCTC 1991), and competition among them is a recurrent theme of the 1990s (Hart 1992; OTA 1991; Stopford and Strange 1992; Thurow 1992; see D. Henderson (1993) for a perspective that excludes East Asia). Fears of triadic regional trade blocs are not borne out by analyses of trade data since 1968, however. Japanese trade has been dispersed widely rather than concentrated in Asia, although US and German trade has increased in the neighbourhood regions of those countries (O'Loughlin and Anselin 1996).

The demise of communism presents a dramatic new style of economic competition. Regions and people isolated for decades from capitalist competition have been thrust into an economic environment where capitalist rules themselves change frequently. A region's position in the world economy is based on 'how it fits in to the international division of labour' (Bryan 1995; Radice 1995: 283). Trade – especially exporting – has become essential for nations and localities alike. But trade relies largely on far-flung corporate networks which control 'global factories' and commodity chains that shift goods and components from country to country. Strategic alliances and other coalitions of giant firms continue to strengthen both the technological and geographical scope of large enterprises. In contrast to the theoretical basis for studies of economic growth through the 1960s and 1970s, which tended to assume that growth and development would inevitably occur, if only the correct policies were chosen and

1

the proper economic factors were available (Landes 1989; Reynolds 1983), a vast variety of policies now springs up from localities and regions with little central control. Decentralization and local entrepreneurial governments are a major part of the competition for investment at national, regional and local scales. Efforts to promote development have become more local, enough so that Ohmae (1995) has hailed it 'the end of the nation state' as regions become players, competing for global investment. Whether or not nation-states are obsolete (Guéhenno 1995), the rise of local and regional states as active participants in development is among the major phenomena of the 1990s (Kanter 1995; Leitner 1990; Wilson 1995).

Countries, as well as regions and localities, face two imperatives in a capitalist world. First, they must be concerned with employment. Job creation, a principal indicator of economic growth, is fundamental to an economy's (and its people's) well-being. The second imperative is the ability to *develop* the economy. Development includes two related processes: structural change and productivity improvement. Structural change includes the large-scale sectoral shifts or structural changes from agriculture to manufacturing to services, as well as what Flammang (1990) has called 'niche changing'. This covers the set of Schumpeterian categories of innovation: new products, new techniques and new niches. Technology and the international financial system are two fundamental driving forces of contemporary change (Stopford and Strange 1991). In this book, we focus on technology, because it arguably has been the facilitator of financial system integration, together with regulatory changes (Corbridge 1994; Corbridge, Martin and Thrift 1994; Leyshon and Tickell 1994).

New forms of production organization, such as flexible specialization, economies of scope, strategic alliances among firms, and widespread subcontracting, have transformed economic activities into new forms that directly challenge theories and policies of all types (Harrison 1994; Sayer and Walker 1992). Flexible production systems are radically different from the mass-production assembly line, relying mainly on unskilled workers and routine tasks, on which critiques have focused (Braverman 1974; Sayer 1985; Scott 1988a). Most importantly, technology and product innovation are central elements in these complex new patterns of corporate activity and make any simple explanation less tenable. Globalization (or transnationalization) is particularly evident in a financial context. The breakdown of the Bretton Woods system in the 1970s was the culmination of a process that ended US hegemony, signs of which had been evident a decade earlier (Bluestone and Harrison 1982). The new financial order is extremely complex and dynamic, and plagued by financial flows that elude both accounting and regulation (Kester 1995).

The rise of the newly industrializing countries (NICs) to economic powerhouses has been especially remarkable (OECD 1988a; World Bank 1993). The NICs include a first tier, all located in Asia, also known as the 'four tigers' (Hong Kong, South Korea, Singapore and Taiwan), and a larger, more diverse group, which includes China, India, Malaysia, the Philippines and Thailand in Asia, Brazil and Mexico in Latin America and, in some lists, Israel and South Africa; for some issues on defining NICs, see Ingalls and Martin (1988) and D. Lorenz

(1989). Although NIC manufacturing began in unquestionably low-tech products such as textiles, clothing and shoes, more technology-intensive products, such as electrical and electronic products and transport equipment, are now common (Dicken 1992; J. Henderson 1989; OECD 1988a).

Cores and peripheries

The new spatial division of labour which has grown out of global corporate activity has produced three broad types of regional economies: (1) those with a highly technological environment; (2) those with a significant proportion of skilled personnel but lacking a diversified and modern industrial structure; and (3) those with reserves of unskilled labour which are either surplus to farming and rural occupations or redundant to declining industries (Hamilton and Linge 1983: 24). These correspond to the core–semi-periphery–periphery structure of the capitalist world system, which may well be too strict in practice (Knox and Agnew 1994; Lipietz 1986; W. Martin 1990; Wallerstein 1979). Between the core (where skilled tasks are done) and the periphery (usually single-product economies) is the *semi-periphery*, composed of countries that have regressed from core status through undergoing a process of deindustrialization, and those heading for core status as they experience rapid industrial development (So and Chiu 1995; Wallerstein 1979). Southern Europe is a frequent illustration of semi-development, resting uneasily between the core economies of northern Europe and the periphery of the Third World (Arrighi 1985; Hudson and Lewis 1985; Seers, Schaffer and Kiljunan 1979). Other countries, such as Canada and Ireland, resist easy classification as either core or semi-periphery (Grant and Lyons 1990; Niosi 1990). Nemeth and Smith (1985) provide a classification that includes Canada as one of nine core nations (the others are Belgium, France, Germany, Italy, Japan, the Netherlands, the UK and the USA), and they divide the semi-periphery into strong and weak components.

The world-system perspective sees the core–periphery structure as dynamic rather than static, as the rapid rise of Japan and the NICs suggests. The world-system view also maintains that 'core' and 'periphery' are not areas, regions or states, but spaces where core or peripheral *processes* dominate. 'In simple terms, core processes consist of relations that incorporate *relatively* high wages, advanced technology and a diversified production mix whereas periphery processes involve low wages, more rudimentary technology and a simple production mix' (P. J. Taylor 1989: 17). The semi-periphery is the dynamic category within the world-economy, through which regions rise and fall (W. Martin 1990). Shifts in the relative status of nations in international competition are frequent observations from many perspectives (Cohen and Zysman 1987; Ettlinger 1991; Kennedy 1987; Pavitt 1980; Porter 1990; Prestowitz 1988; So and Chiu 1995).

The *core–periphery* dichotomy, or dualism, remains one of the 'dominant metaphors' of regional development (Friedmann 1966; Santos 1979; Strassoldo 1981). Economically, the core is a set of regions where complexity, technology and control are the norm, and where linkages to other nodes and the global

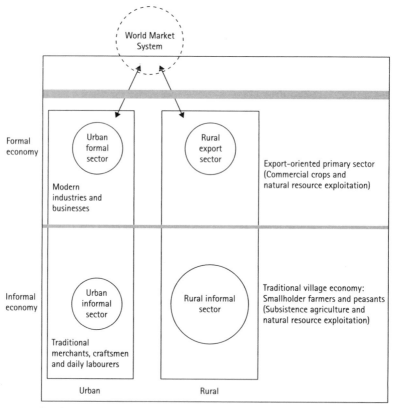

Figure 1.1 Dualism between formal and informal, urban and rural sectors. Source: modified from Lo, Salih and Douglass (1981).

system are common. Culturally and politically also, core regions are dominant and peripheral regions are dependent (Bivand 1981). The global system continues to be marked by deep disparities between core and periphery, both between nations and between regions within nations. The situation in the developing world is considerably more complex than the core–periphery model is able to capture (Lo, Salih and Douglass 1981). The concept of dualism, however, captures effectively the interrelationships – and lack of relationship – between different groups in an economy (Figure 1.1). In particular, Figure 1.1 illustrates the contrast between the formal sector, linked to the world economy through trade and commerce, and the informal sector, where modern technology rarely surfaces, in cities or in rural areas.

A major dimension of peripheral areas, and of their relationship to core regions, is the technological underdevelopment of not only rural areas, but of entire countries dating from colonial times. Colonialism in Asia and Africa was technological as well as political and cultural (Headrick 1988). A set of important inventions – steamships, railways, firearms and the telegraph – allowed Europeans to conquer inland sections previously impenetrable, and permitted control to be imposed over large territories. Industrialization in Western nations stimulated a growing demand for products of the tropics, which were easily shipped as transport costs fell. These included cotton, indigo, palm oil, copper, gutta-percha, tin, rubber, coffee, tea, sugar and cocoa. Technology transfer to Asia and Africa increased production at lower production costs by means of Western industrial and scientific methods (Braudel 1982).

An increase in demand for Western manufactured products was prompted by their introduction into Asia and Africa. 'Motor vehicles, television, and modern weapons have become irresistible but barely affordable temptations for people of poor countries' (Headrick 1988: 7). Nearly all the technological changes which affected relations between the West and the tropics originated in the West from the work of Western scientists and engineers, for the benefit of Western society (Colombo 1988). The response to goods in short supply was a heightened effort to find substitutes (e.g. aniline dyes for indigo and other natural colourings, petroleum for palm oil, synthetic rubber for natural rubber, synthetic fibres for silk) (Headrick 1988: 8).

For much of the Third World, then, technological underdevelopment has been the rule. Colonialism brought education, medical care and mechanical equipment to the colonies, but did not pass on essential skills and knowledge to the indigenous populations. When former imperial possessions attained political independence, their people and firms lacked the skills and experience to sustain the infrastructure left by the colonial powers or to build on and develop from this base (Fransman and King 1984; Headrick 1988; Stewart 1978; Weitz 1986). Saunders (1995) believes that neither the legacy of colonialism nor the world capitalist system are the major barriers to Third World development. Along with others, he places the blame on 'the inability or unwillingness of some Third World governments to take advantage of the opportunities which this system offers' (Saunders 1995: 51).

Technology, regions and economic development

The dynamics of technological change provide the focus of this book. Technology is central to regional change, positive and negative, and to economic change, job-creating and job-destroying. It is the most obvious cause and effect of the cumulative wealth of rich nations (Ayres 1988; Foray and Freeman 1993; Rosenberg, Landau and Mowery 1992). Technology also promises, more than any other phenomenon, to bring poor nations out of poverty. As a 'chronic disturber' of comparative advantage, it has provided the principal source of change for firms, regions and nations alike (Chesnais 1986). The concept of technology in this book encompasses knowledge in all its forms, from simple and routine procedures of everyday life, to the methods of organization and management in enterprises large and small, from the machines that produce in enormous quantities what formerly required many workers, to the complex scientific investigations that create ever newer inventions and products.

However, it is not an easy task to 'transfer' technology to places where it is not already entrenched. Among the biggest challenges for developing countries is the creation of jobs for the urban unemployed and its root cause, population growth

(Adriaansen, Storm and Waardenburg 1992; Rondinelli and Kasarda 1993). In the absence of job creation, an economy consists of little other than subsistence agriculture with little market activity. As agricultural productivity improves, a household can produce a surplus over and above its needs, bringing the surplus to market. The cash thus obtained is available for other market needs. One of the primary uses of cash among households in Haiti is for schooling for children (Parafina 1993). In the Central African Republic, wild animal hunting above subsistence brings money for necessities such as manioc, salt, tobacco, clothing and school fees, as well as newer economic 'needs' such as radios, cassette players, sunglasses and watches (Noss 1995: 311). As agricultural productivity rises higher, there is no opportunity for all children in a household to follow in the parents' footsteps as farmers. Continued subdivision of family plots in order to give each child a piece of land in fact lowers productivity, since it prevents taking advantage of economies of scale in the numerous technologies that raise agricultural output: herbicides, pesticides, fertilizer, irrigation and machinery.

The 'surplus labour' from agriculture typically moves to the 'bright lights' of the city (Rosenzweig 1988; Williamson 1988; Yap 1977). The growth of megacities is one of the greatest problems for the twenty-first century, since all will be in the less-developed world, where fewer jobs are available than the new urban residents can fill (Adriaansen, Storm and Waardenburg 1992; Dogan and Kasarda 1988). Table 1.1 shows that there are expected to be 27 cities in 2015 with populations of over 10 million people – all but three of them outside Europe and North America. This compares with only one city of that size in 1950 (New York) and six in 1980 (United Nations 1995). Rural-to-urban migration is a very rational decision in the light of minimal prospects in the rural area and at least an array of informal-sector opportunities in the urban area (Bhattacharya 1993). Low-wage manufacturing is a good choice for reasons beyond job creation. Linkages are higher from labour-intensive industries than from capital-intensive industries, and there are learning effects which allow an economy to shift to more sophisticated and higher-wage production (Adelman and Robinson 1989; Verbruggen 1992).

Productivity enhancement – or, more generally, technological change – is the only way to make the shift (or structural change) from agriculture and/or low-wage manufacturing to higher-wage and higher-skill products. Even within agriculture, as mentioned above, technological inputs are essential to raising production (Goldman 1993; Timmer 1988). Such technological changes have been behind the ability of India to move from being a grain importer to being a grain exporter in recent years (Jordan 1996a). Even more important is technological change in manufacturing. Manufactured goods are more complicated in several respects, not least of which is that they must appeal to buyers whose standards of price, quality, delivery and service must be met (Rhee 1990; Salais and Storper 1992). Beyond these characteristics, which apply to existing products, firms must find new ways to 'add value' and to innovate. New products – filling new niches – are the best way to do this. The creation of new niches in the form of new firms and new sectors is not unusual. The aerospace industry is a product of the twentieth century, as are the computer and many elec-

Table 1.1   World's largest cities 1950, 1980 and 2015 (projected).

	1950			1980			2015	
Rank	Urban agglomeration	Population (millions)	Rank	Urban agglomeration	Population (millions)	Rank	Urban agglomeration	Population (millions)
1	New York	12.3	1	Tokyo	21.9	1	Tokyo	28.7
2	London	8.7	2	New York	15.6	2	Bombay	27.4
3	Tokyo	6.9	3	Mexico City	13.9	3	Lagos	24.4
4	Paris	5.4	4	São Paulo	12.1	4	Shanghai	23.4
5	Moscow	5.4	5	Shanghai	11.7	5	Jakarta	21.2
6	Shanghai	5.3	6	Osaka	10.0	6	São Paulo	20.8
7	Essen	5.3	7	Buenos Aires	9.9	7	Karachi	20.6
8	Buenos Aires	5.0	8	Los Angeles	9.5	8	Beijing	19.4
9	Chicago	4.9	9	Calcutta	9.0	9	Dhaka	19.0
10	Calcutta	4.4	10	Beijing	9.0	10	Mexico City	18.8
11	Osaka	4.1	11	Paris	8.9	11	New York	17.6
12	Los Angeles	4.0	12	Rio de Janeiro	8.8	12	Calcutta	17.6
13	Beijing	3.9	13	Seoul	8.3	13	Delhi	17.6
14	Milan	3.6	14	Moscow	8.1	14	Tianjin	17.0
15	Berlin	3.3	15	Bombay	8.1	15	Manila	14.7
16	Mexico City	3.1	16	London	7.7	16	Cairo	14.5
17	Philadelphia	2.9	17	Tianjin	7.3	17	Los Angeles	14.3
18	St Petersburg	2.9	18	Cairo	6.9	18	Seoul	13.1
19	Bombay	2.9	19	Chicago	6.8	19	Buenos Aires	12.4
20	Rio de Janeiro	2.9	20	Essen	6.3	20	Istanbul	12.3
21	Detroit	2.8	21	Jakarta	6.0	21	Rio de Janeiro	11.6
22	Naples	2.8	22	Manila	6.0	22	Lahore	10.8
23	Manchester	2.5	23	Delhi	5.6	23	Hyderabad	10.7
24	São Paulo	2.4	24	Milan	5.3	24	Osaka	10.6
25	Cairo	2.4	25	Teheran	5.1	25	Bangkok	10.6
26	Tianjin	2.4	26	Karachi	5.0	26	Lima	10.5
27	Birmingham	2.3	27	Bangkok	4.7	27	Teheran	10.2
28	Frankfurt	2.3	28	St Petersburg	4.6	28	Kinshasa	9.9
29	Boston	2.2	29	Hong Kong	4.6	29	Paris	9.6
30	Hamburg	2.2	30	Lima	4.4	30	Madras	9.5

Source: United Nations (1995: 130–1).

tronic products. Indeed, the presence of the entire information technology (IT) sector has opened up opportunities for improvement in other sectors.

These examples show that capitalist firms profit from new products as much as, if not more than, from new, labour-saving processes, although far more attention has been paid to the latter (Sayer 1985; Webber, Sheppard and Rigby 1992). The neoclassical model, however, has not dominated in Japan and other East Asian countries as it has in much of the West. East Asian approaches to competition and to industrial policy have been based on the work of Austrian economists such as Schumpeter (1934) and List (1909), who focus not on the allocation of scarce resources (the neoclassical definition of economics), but on the creation of new resources through innovation (for reviews, see Chang 1995a; Fallows 1995; Freeman 1987).

Conventional theories and policies regarding regional development focus in one way or another on the capital–labour 'production function' and responses by the state via various policies. Early policies derived almost directly from the neoclassical model, which 'is an ideology, a religion' on which virtually all post-war economic policies have been grounded (Vining 1987). However, this 'religion' is losing ground somewhat to broader theories that incorporate technology and competition in more realistic ways. Labour is especially problematic, since it is seen by firms as an input to production and by governments as an outcome of economic growth. Labour skills and wages vary tremendously and these greatly influence location decisions of firms and the ultimate spatial division of labour. The interplay between capital, labour and the state (or public sector) is fundamental to the dynamics of economic development (Storper and Walker 1989).

Most of the concerns of neoclassical analysis and Schumpeterian variants have been combined in the prominence of economic competitiveness as a priority for firms, regions and nations. While Bryan (1995) criticizes competitiveness for its sport metaphor (rankings, teamwork), it remains the predominant image of capitalism at the end of the twentieth century. Porter's (1990) work epitomizes the approach, and his model of the factors underlying national competitiveness has been analysed for many other nations and regions. The crux of his model is a set of determinants of national advantage or competitiveness (Figure 1.2). The first set, factor conditions, closely captures the usual neoclassical or basic factors of production – physical, capital and human resources – but is extended to explicitly include advanced factors: knowledge resources and infrastructure. The second set, demand conditions, refers to the conditions of the home market for an industry's products or services. In particular, sophis-

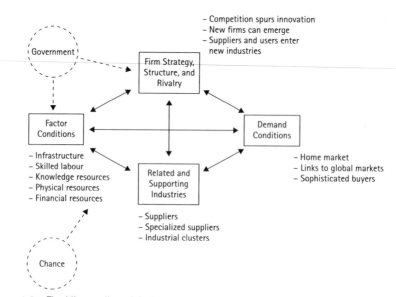

Figure 1.2 The 'diamond' model of competitiveness. Source: based on Porter (1990).

ticated and demanding buyers stimulate firms to meet high standards of product features, quality and service. The third set of determinants is the cluster of related and supporting industries, which, if they are internationally competitive, are able to transmit that quality throughout the network of linkages. The fourth element is the legal, cultural and institutional framework that determines firm strategy, structure and rivalry, i.e. the size and competition among a country's firms and the opportunities for competitors from elsewhere. Porter also adds chance and government as two additional variables that are 'necessary to complete the theory' (Porter 1990: 73). Chance events include inventions, wars and major shifts in foreign demand. Government policies, regulations, investments and purchases greatly determine national advantage or disadvantage.

Porter's framework has had a profound influence on policy at the local level, where local studies have emulated his analysis (Healey and Dunham 1994; Kaufman *et al.* 1994; Kresl 1995). At the national level, research has been more critical and has proposed new considerations to take into account trade, globalization, transnational enterprises, service industries and technology (Bellak and Weiss 1993; Cartwright 1993; Dunning 1993a; Narula 1993; Rugman and Verbeke 1993; Tan 1995). National 'competitiveness' has become an aspiration for most economies, bolstered in part by the *World Competitiveness Report*, issued annually by two Swiss organizations, the World Economic Forum and the International Institute for Management Development (IMD). In 1996, the two groups themselves decided to compete in rankings of countries by their competitiveness. The World Economic Forum ranked Singapore, Hong Kong, New Zealand, the USA and Luxembourg as the top five; the IMD's top five were the USA, Singapore, Hong Kong, Japan and Denmark (*The Economist* 1996a). There is controversy over the concept of international competition (Dunn 1994; Krugman 1994a). Fagerberg (1988), for example, shows that increasing labour costs do not jeopardize a country's competitiveness. Generally, however, a nation's policies influence its productivity growth in many ways, and this ultimately determines national living standards.

The roots of competitive advantage extend very deeply – into the history of any place. Ettlinger (1991), for example, examining the roots of competitive advantage in California and Japan, sees the development of both regions as very long-term processes, encompassing investments and improvements in human resources, local sources of capital, entrepreneurship, and an avoidance (whether purposely or by chance) of dependent links with other places. It is not just by chance that competitiveness develops, as Porter's model stresses. Auty (1991) sees the 'creation' of competitive advantage in South Korea through distinctive industrial policies that favoured several heavy (steel, shipbuilding) and chemicals (including plastics) sectors when they were infant industries. The development of these sectors provided the possibility to nurture downstream linkages, rather than to develop dependent links.

Porter (1990: 543–73) also proposes a model of economic development with four stages: (1) factor-driven development, based on basic (rather than advanced) factors of production; (2) investment-driven development, when investment improves factor conditions and utilizes technology but does not enhance it; (3) innovation-driven development, when firms create new technology and compete globally. The fourth stage, wealth-driven development, ultimately leads to decline, because attention turns from enhancing advantage to merely preserving it. Narula (1993) has criticized this model of development as static and proposes an enhanced model to take into account the accumulation of technological capability.

Regions: the arena of economic change

This book uses the framework of *regional development* to encompass economic dynamics at all spatial scales: national, regional and local. Some will be unfamiliar with the designation of region. Regions are subnational spaces, especially of large countries, as well as aggregates of several nations. The regional trading blocs, such as the European Union (EU) and the Association of Southeast Asian Nations (ASEAN), are commonly referred to as regions. Regions change and 'membership' in a region can be sought after; witness the countries of central and eastern Europe that aspire to join the EU. The flexibility of definition of a region is not imprecision; rather, it reflects the various geographic scales at which economic change occurs. Ohmae (1995) describes 'region states' as powerful engines of development, whose primary orientation is toward – and whose primary linkage is with – the global economy. As a result of linkages connecting local nodes with global networks of economic activity, each node and its region interacts with the global economy (Amin and Thrift 1994; Camagni 1995a; Conti 1993).

Regions such as the EU and ASEAN are *political* regions, not *homogeneous* with respect to some physical, social or economic characteristic, or *nodal* around a central urban place – the traditional types of regions in regional economic analysis (Boudeville 1966; Meyer 1963; Preto 1995). None of the three types – homogeneous, nodal or policy-oriented – addresses fully the internal economic and cultural dynamics of regions. Regions often are not well defined by political boundaries; instead they evolve through changes in economic and social relations (Markusen 1987; Massey 1995; Smith and Dennis 1987). The transformations of South Wales in the UK and of the New England region in the USA have identified these regions as places where labour has largely defined and moulded the regions and their processes of change (Cooke 1985a; Hall *et al.* 1987; Harrison 1984; Morgan and Sayer 1985; Sayer and Morgan 1986).

Regions are not static, but 'evolutive' and 'as mutable and malleable as the economic and social relations that comprise them and that they comprise' (Preto 1995; Smith and Dennis 1987: 169). During the twentieth century, industrial shifts have taken place in response to massive technological changes, such as dramatically lower transportation costs, standardization of production, and increased minimum efficient scale of plants. The result is that regions have become not only subsets of national space, but units of international space. Comparisons of costs, wages and work conditions – in every region – have shifted from being made on merely a local or regional basis to being made internationally. This internationalization, although recognized somewhat in terms of the global arena of finance and production investment, has markedly changed 'the scale at which regions are constituted as coherent and integrated economic units' (Smith and Dennis 1987: 171; see also Graham *et al.* 1988). Other regions have evolved in a manner that has reinforced their innovativeness. These innovative regional milieus stand out in the intensity of social and economic interaction which takes place within them, as well as in their openness to flows of knowledge and other inputs from outside (Hansen 1990, 1992). The specialization of urban regions has taken precedence in recent years over their hierarchical position (Camagni and Salone 1992; Preto 1995).

As Jensen and Leijon (1996: 29) put it, 'You can't see a region, because it is an interpretation of events.' Seen as a social construction, regions are 'the concrete articulation of *relations of production* in a given time and place' (Gilbert 1988: 209). Regions are also defined and differentiated by *local culture*, by which people are linked through communication processes which enhance their collective way of thinking about places and space. A third perspective sees the region as the setting for *social interaction* of all types, but particularly those which create or enforce domination and dependence (Gilbert 1988). The interactions between the capitalist system and localities and regions (the local–global linkages) define the region and its process of economic development (Amin and Thrift 1992; Preto 1995).

Regions and nations undergo similar processes of change which are at work in all spatial scales (Smith 1984). The division of labour within and between large firms, and dominance and dependence relationships between firms and between places, are common mechanisms that affect regions of all sizes. In particular, peripheral areas at different spatial scales – national, regional and local – exhibit similar structural and qualitative impacts, and side-effects of traditional economic development mechanisms have taken place (Stöhr 1982). Comparisons of differences in economic activity across nations are often dubious, given the vast differences in population, land area, resources and history (Perkins and Syrquin 1989; Walsh 1987), but the commonalities within the global economy or world-system suggest that much more is similar than different (Drucker 1989; Gereffi and Korzeniewicz 1994; P. J. Taylor 1989).

In one respect, however, regions are significantly different from nations. Regional units within nations are more 'open' than are national economies; that is, a larger proportion of a region's economy depends on flows of imports from and exports to other regions. These flows are notoriously more difficult to measure, because the usual restrictions on commerce via customs barriers, immigration control, exchange controls and trade quotas do not exist, and thus even the most rudimentary data on flows are either unavailable or superficial (Richardson 1973).

Growth or development?

Optimism prevailed in the immediate post-colonial era. Rostow's (1960) 'stages of economic growth' encapsulated the economic thinking at the time (Heilbroner 1963). Growth and development were considered synonymous, and a simple 'iron law' of economic growth held that, so long as the amount of savings, coupled with the fruitfulness of those savings, results in a rate of growth of output that is greater than the rise of population, cumulative economic growth would take place (Heilbroner 1963: 86). Rostow suggested that all societies could be identified as lying economically within one of five categories or stages of growth: (1) the traditional society, (2) the preconditions for take-off, (3) the take-off, (4) the drive to maturity, and (5) the age of high mass-consumption. The progression from one stage to another had to follow a rather precise formula or recipe: the rate of productive investment must rise from about 5 per cent of national income to over 10 per cent; one or more substantial manufacturing sectors must emerge to become 'leading sectors' in growth; and the political and social framework is modified to exploit the impulses to expansion in the modern sector (Rostow 1960: 39).

Needless to say, few if any countries were able to meet these demands, based on the experience of Western countries. Rostow's stages model was the ultimate attempt on the part of post-war economic planners to devise something like a 'development-vending machine: you put in the money, press the button, and get growth' (Brookfield 1975: 29). The challenge was to find the button – where to put the money and effort to get growth started. The problem was circular. Underdeveloped countries were not underdeveloped because of a lack of scope for investment; they were underdeveloped for want of capital; capital was lacking for want of savings, and savings were lacking for want of development (Brookfield 1975: 34). Suggestions ranged from a 'big push' in a single sector, to 'balanced growth' through investment across a number of sectors, to public investment in 'social overhead capital'. Landes (1989: 24) concluded of the impact of Rostow's optimistic model: 'We have been disappointed since' its publication. Economic development has not responded well to the injections of capital alone. The reasons for growth in some places and not in others may boil down to an as yet unknown combination of social and human requisites, including 'obstacles of a managerial and administrative nature' (de Oliveira Campos 1982; Mason 1982). Culture, for instance, seems to matter more than a colonial past; thrift and hard work make the simple concepts of capital and labour go farther in some places, such as East Asia, than in others, like Africa (Crook 1989; Landes 1989).

More importantly, we now know that external, or exogenous, inputs are not as effective for understanding growth processes as internal, or endogenous, processes such as learning and technological change. The proponents of 'high development theory' were unable to model adequately the interactions they had described (Krugman 1994b, 1995). Recent contributions of the 'new growth theory' (on which more discussion is found in Chapter 2) have incorporated several important processes, including increasing returns to scale and imperfect competition, essentially helping us to grapple with the ideas of the 1950s and 1960s (Krugman 1994b; Romer 1994). Development is more interdisciplinary than economics is able to comprehend, and more cumulative than simple models are able to capture (Streeten 1980). Policy and its implementation are of more than little importance, but have not been adequately dealt with in the correct sequence to bring success in all cases. Stiglitz (1991), recounting the successes of economics during the past century, admits to pessimism regarding the discipline's ability to bring 'even a reasonable hope of success' to the world's poorest countries. The plight of much of sub-Saharan Africa has led to research on economic *regress*, rather than only on progress (Sen 1994). Regress occurs not only as a result of war and famine, but also as a result of what Stern (1989) and Krueger (1990) have called 'government failure', the counterpart to 'market failure'. More effort is being placed in this direction, and this topic will be returned to in Chapter 8. The neoclassical or neoliberal resurgence has made some suggest that we simply leave it to 'the market' to bring about development, whereas others see the market as working best when compatible policies are in place (Amsden, Kochanowicz and Taylor 1994; Chang 1995a; Evans 1995). Corbridge (1990) notes that asymmetries of power and wealth continue in the face of faith in markets.

Despite the intertwining of growth and development, the two are very dissimilar in the degree to which they are understood. Economic growth in the developed world is 'unambiguous in its meaning', whereas development 'has meant almost all things to all men and women' (Arndt 1987: 6; Sen 1988; Wallerstein 1994). Economic development is different from economic growth. Growth – increases in population within a specific area, or increases in the quantity or the value of the goods and services produced in a local economy – does not necessarily lead to qualitative improvements in life. However, it is just such measures which have been conventionally used to gauge regional and national prosperity (Malizia 1990; Power 1988). Gross national product (GNP) or gross domestic product (GDP), common measures for economic growth, do not adequately measure the concept of development or its several dimensions (Cobb, Halstead and Rowe 1995). Horvath (1994) documents national 'paths' along several dimensions of development, including health, affluence, freedom and environmental sustainability. Sen (1988) summarizes the nature of development as 'the freedom to choose'. Each of these builds on the larger interpretation of development represented by the United Nations Development Programme (UNDP) *Human Development Report* (UNDP annual; ul Haq 1995). Hettne (1990) and Ingham (1993) provide excellent reviews of alternative concepts of development. Table 1.2 lists data for selected countries on what the UNDP uses to derive a human development index.

While development can be measured by quantitative indicators, development also refers to improvements in the quality of life associated with changes – and not necessarily increases – in the size and composition of the population, the quantity and nature of local jobs, and the quantity and prices of goods and services produced locally (Conroy 1975). 'Economic development is a process of structural change, implying something different if not something more' (Flammang 1979: 50). The growth process is primarily 'niche filling' and can be done in small increments that are easily modelled. Development involves 'niche changing', i.e. changing from one niche of economic activity to another (Flammang 1990).

Structural change focuses attention on issues of *structure*, a factor that affects

Table 1.2   Selected countries ranked by basic indicators of human development.

Rank	Country	Human Development Index	Life expectancy at birth, 1992	Mean years of schooling, 1992	Real GDP per capita (US$), 1991
1	Canada	0.932	77.2	12.2	19 320
2	Switzerland	0.931	77.8	11.6	21 780
3	Japan	0.929	78.6	10.8	19 390
4	Sweden	0.928	77.7	11.4	17 490
5	Norway	0.928	76.9	12.1	17 170
6	France	0.927	76.6	12.0	18 430
7	Australia	0.926	76.7	12.0	16 680
8	USA	0.925	75.6	12.4	22 130
9	Netherlands	0.923	77.2	11.1	16 820
10	United Kingdom	0.919	75.8	11.7	16 340
11	Germany	0.918	75.6	11.6	19 770
22	Italy	0.891	76.9	7.5	17 040
38	Chile	0.848	71.9	7.8	17 060
52	Mexico	0.804	69.9	4.9	7 170
54	Thailand	0.798	68.7	3.9	5 270
63	Brazil	0.756	65.8	4.0	5 240
68	Turkey	0.739	66.7	3.6	4 840
94	China	0.644	70.5	5.0	2 946
99	Philippines	0.621	64.6	7.6	2 440
105	Indonesia	0.586	62.0	4.1	2 730
134	Ghana	0.382	55.4	3.5	930
135	India	0.382	59.7	2.4	1 150
146	Bangladesh	0.309	52.2	2.0	1 160

Source: ul Haq (1995: 62–6).

not only the quantitative level of the economy of a place, but also its stability (Conroy 1975). In his classic work on urban economies, Thompson (1965: 1) proposed three goals for local economies, but which fit other scales as well: affluence, equity and stability. These goals address growth, distribution and structure simultaneously. Definitions which focus on total or per capita income tell us about increases, but not about change. They measure growth more than development, although structural change may have accompanied growth or made it possible. Flammang (1979: 51) elaborates:

> Is this not the same thing as saying that development (structural change) is necessary to keep overall production increasing? . . . Development supports growth by phasing out the old and bringing in the new, and growth supports development by supplying many (if not most) of the resources the newer sectors require. Alternating processes? Yes. But both are occurring at the same time, most of the time, and so mask each other to some degree.

Development dynamism is the product of change involving all infrastructures of society – economic, spatial, institutional and social – and is a phenomenon that can restructure a nation's socioeconomic base (Weitz 1986). These are the sorts of changes evoked by most authors assessing the technological transformation of the Third World (Patel 1993). The process of economic development is complex, especially in the long run, as the technological skills of a population and the technological capability of firms and institutions allow them to adapt to competition and change.

Development as qualitative or structural change includes dimensions that go beyond measurable indicators. It involves the changes necessary in social relations and in cultural orientation to stimulate in a cumulative fashion a greater diversity and specialization in the division of labour. Diversity and specialization, in turn, prompt a creative capacity in these regions (Sweeney 1987). Development also entails modifications in the system of values, leading to creativity; creativity, as part of the development process itself, demands values that promote, encourage and reward creativity rather than those that sustain the status quo (Weitz 1986). A focus on *structure* poses different problems for understanding economic and social change. Social or cultural factors have been seen mainly as obstacles to development, or as an explanation of last resort to account for success and failure in economic development (Landes 1989). Economists typically acknowledge that some non-economic factors are important, but they are ignored in most analyses in favour of more familiar variables such as capital and labour (Doeringer, Terkla and Topakian 1987; Weitz 1986). This is becoming less true, in part because of historical research by scholars such as Abramovitz (1986). Development studies in the Marxist tradition, including the regulation approach, treat culture largely within the concept of the *mode of regulation* – the system of 'norms, habits, laws and regulating networks' (Lipietz 1986: 19; Peck and Tickell 1994). Many of these norms, habits and networks are *institutions* operating outside the scope of formal policy but profoundly affecting the development process (Doeringer and Streeten 1990; Killick 1995a; Nelson 1995; Zysman 1994).

The traditional competitiveness of a regional economy: the economic base

The concern with growth at the national level corresponds to concern at the regional level, where a great deal of research has taken place to determine the *economic base* of a region and to measure its linkages with other regions. Although exports and a positive balance of payments serve as common indicators of competitiveness at the national level, measurement of regional economies has relied on a set of models that measure the 'impact' of changes in a regional economy. These models include the simple economic base model, and input–output and econometric models, more complex sets of tools that require large amounts of data and generate large amounts of information in return.

The economic base and regional multipliers

For economies that have made the shift to a non-agricultural or non-mining sector, the question becomes: in which sector should the economy specialize? All urban economies fall into this group, and many early studies of regional and urban economics concerned the 'urban economic base'. The economic base model attempts to answer the question of 'which economic base is best?' by calibrating the multiplier of the regional economy. Because no region is isolated from the rest of the world, demand for a region's products and services substantially determines whether that place grows economically or declines. This export orientation suggests that the economic base of a region lies in what it is able to export to other places (Jacobs 1984; Krueger 1983; Tiebout 1962).

At the local and regional scales, in particular, economic growth is fundamentally a process of multiplier effects. The production and distribution of goods and services create local employment and other income-earning opportunities which attract and keep people in a city or region. The *multiplier effect*, or the number of jobs generated, supported or 'created' by the basic jobs, is the standard means of estimating local economic impacts of export activity and forecasting future effects; in effect, it is a simple measure of competitiveness. As workers spend their incomes on local services and firms purchase supplies and other inputs, additional jobs are supported by these expenditures. New economic activity and its multiplier effect expand the service (or tertiary) sector, as local growth increases the size of the economy sufficiently to meet the threshold for new service activities (Figure 1.3). Increases in population in turn can spark a secondary multiplier effect as new investment enters the economy to serve expanded demand (Keeble 1967; Myrdal 1957; Pred 1977). This *circular and cumulative causation* process captures the dynamics of regional growth. Conceptually, the multiplier effect captures the process whereby sectors are linked through flows of money and jobs. The effects therefore are primarily, if not exclusively, concerned with growth – measured by income, capital flows and (especially) employment – rather than development (Watkins 1980).

Linkages of all sorts – for administrative information, material inputs for pro-

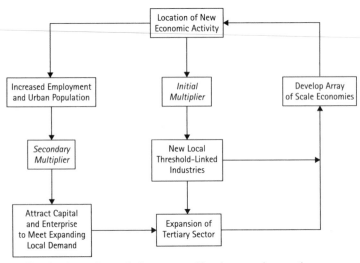

Figure 1.3   The circular and cumulative nature of local economic growth.

duction, finance, transport services, data processing and information transfer services – generate these multiplier effects, and the issue is to what extent these are local or flow to other places. This interregional growth transmission may be channelled within firms or organizations (including governmental organizations) or between different organizations as linkages (Pred 1977). In essence, profitable economic opportunities in a region or locality initiate a flow of revenues and employment that may disperse widely from their point of origin. At the places where the multiplier effects (in the form of purchases and profits) end up, local employment and income are increased. This non-local effect has become much more prominent in the context of foreign ownership and production in branch manufacturing plants. For example, *maquiladora* plants in Mexico near the US–Mexican border have strikingly low levels of linkage for inputs within Mexico (Sklair 1989). Chapter 6 returns to linkages and the impacts of large firms on local economies.

The economic base model traditionally classifies all economic activity into either of two sectors: *basic*, or export, activity (B) and nonbasic, or *service*, activity (S). The export sector produces in response to exogenous or external demand, and the service (or local or nonbasic) sector depends entirely on the size and performance of the basic sector. As a demand-driven model, the economic base model emphasizes the dependence of a regional economy on demand elsewhere for the goods and services produced within it, and assumes that the supply of factors of production – the inputs needed to produce the exported goods and services – is infinitely elastic. The economic base model can be adjusted for 'leakages' caused by consumers who spend a portion of their incomes outside the region, including purchases at nonlocally owned establishments, and the purchase of inputs outside the region by producers of goods and services (Archer 1976). The attraction of the economic base model is that it provides a simple means, with relatively low data requirements, of analysing a regional economy and of estimating impacts of gains or losses of basic activity. However, it is extremely difficult to know for certain how much of an activity is actually sold outside an arbitrary region, i.e. exported, without undertaking time-consuming and expensive survey research (Gibson and Worden 1981; Hewings 1977), and even that might not provide accurate results (Farness 1989).

A central issue is how to divide the economy; that is, which economic activities comprise the 'basic' sector? Three approaches have been taken: (1) the 'assumption method', which simply allocates all primary and secondary sectors as basic; (2) the location quotient approach, which attempts to identify the sectors which have employment in excess of average national levels; and (3) the minimum requirements approach, which determines the minimal level of a sector in an economy of a given size, which means that all additional employment is basic. The most common solution has been simply to postulate that primary and secondary economic activities (agriculture, extractive industries and manufacturing) are basic and that all others are nonbasic. This assumption method will yield a value for the regional multiplier, but the error involved 'can be enormous' (Tiebout 1962: 47). For example, some manufacturing is locally oriented, especially for certain types of firms such as bakeries and printing and publishing. Perhaps more importantly, the traditional allocation of primary activities and manufacturing as basic, and services as dependent, contradicts the shift in economic activity to services and the propulsive and basic nature of many services.

In order to avoid this problem, two alternatives to the assumption method for the delineation of the export sector have come into use. The first, *location quotients*, or coefficients of specialization, calibrates the importance of a sector in a region's economy against its importance nationally (Isserman 1977; Mayer and Pleeter 1975). The location quotient method is unable to adjust for product mix or the increasingly common situation of establishments that produce highly specialized products, such as computer components or automobile parts, rather than a bundle of goods that more or less mirrors the national economy (Tiebout 1962). The *minimum requirements* method is a variation on the location quotient technique, determining local self-sufficiency based on regression analysis of the actual minimum for a large set (more than 100 in most cases) of cities or regions (Isserman 1980; Ullman and Dacey 1960). This is the method of choice for multiplier estimation in developing countries (Brodsky and Sarfaty 1977) and a 'quick and dirty' method in developed countries (Erickson, Gavin and Cordes 1986; Moore 1975; Moore and Jacobsen 1984). Mulligan and Gibson (1984) have found that it provides quite accurate multipliers for small communities, especially if government transfer payments are also taken into account.

In addition to describing economic activity, multipliers are used to predict population, housing, schools and other impacts arising from new economic activity (Lewis 1986; Oppenheim 1980). Critical issues in impact analysis include the value of the multiplier and the time lag over which change takes place. Multiplier values vary tremendously, depending on the region, the basic industry analysed, and the method of analysis used (Bender 1975; Mellor and Ironside 1978). Isolated areas where tourism or large projects are located tend to have a high degree of leakage because supplies must be imported from elsewhere (Archer 1976; Glasson, van der Wee and Barrett 1988). For example, little local oil supply industry has developed near Aberdeen, Scotland, the base for most of the drilling activity in the North Sea (Hallwood 1988). Multiplier effects do not take place all at once, but 'kick in' over time. The time lag before a multiplier effect is complete is rarely addressed, but it is a central finding in research that has considered it (Ashcroft and Swales 1982; Gerking and Isserman 1981; Martin and Miley 1983; McNulty 1977).

Even though it is a simple model, the economic base model is difficult to utilize in practice. Fundamental data such as regional employment may not be known, especially categories such as full-time, part-time and seasonal employees. In Arizona, part-time and seasonal workers accounted for as much as 40 per cent of all employment (Gibson and Worden 1981). Adjusting for in- and out-commuting, wage-level differences across industries, and – perhaps most importantly – transfer payments (including those for unemployment, old age pensions and low incomes) resulted in lower multipliers by about 20 per cent. Gibson and Worden's study also demonstrates the value of survey studies for economic base research; they found that a 21 per cent sample of firms resulted in fairly reliable (± 10 per cent) estimates of multipliers, compared with a 100 per cent survey, as long as small firms (5–10 employees) are also included. Studying large firms alone yielded significantly larger errors. The best estimates of multipliers come from a detailed knowledge of the firms and industries in a community, and their degree of intraregional linkages (Pfister 1976). Multipliers remain an important concept for the flow of money and other benefits within and between places. Richardson (1985, 1988) suggests that the burden (and benefits) of a survey are great enough that one should eschew an economic base framework entirely in favour of a regional input–output model. Krikelas (1992) concludes that the economic base model is simply inadequate as a theory of regional growth.

Input–output analysis

While the economic base model simplifies reality to a two-sector economy, input–output analysis expands economic base and Keynesian multiplier analysis to focus on many interindustry linkages, in which each sector's output either is purchased by another sector or is used in final consumption by households or government. This 'social accounting system' is able to measure disaggregated and indirect effects of change in the output of a given industry (Hewings 1977, 1985; Leven 1964; Robinson 1989). Surveys of firms provide the raw input–output data, but short-cut estimating procedures and an array of applications in many regions and countries have accumulated (Hewings 1985; Hewings and Jensen 1986; Miller and Blair 1985; Richardson 1972, 1985).

In an input–output framework, each sector's output is another sector's input, and vice versa. Since not all transactions take place within a region, purchasers outside the producing sectors provide closure to the system. These final demand sectors include households, government and foreign trade. 'Demoeconomic' models combine income growth, migration and labour supply into the input–output framework (Batey 1985; Isserman 1985). Multi-regional input–output models trace not only flows between the sectors within a region, but also between sectors across regions (Miller and Blair 1985: 69–85). Input–output models, however, are based on an assumption of linear production functions for each industry. Changes in technology, the addition of new industries, and changes in the location of purchases are generally difficult to incorporate into the model (Pleeter 1980).

As with economic base analysis, a typical objective of input–output analysis is a set of multipliers that can be used to forecast economic activity (Miller and Blair 1985: 100–48). Their advantage over economic base multipliers is that input–output multipliers are disaggregated and, thus, vary according to the specific sector which experiences the initial change in activity and expenditure (Richardson 1972: 31). One can estimate effects on outputs of the sectors in an economy on value added, on income earned by households, and on employment, and these estimates provide information that can be used to simulate or forecast the impacts on a region (Beyers 1983; Pullen and Proops 1983).

Although this variety of multipliers might seem advantageous, it 'may sometimes constitute overkill . . . the typical set of tables from an input–output model run can be confusing or even misleading' (Stevens and Lahr 1988: 95). A comparison of impacts from several models shows wide variation in estimates of employment impact (Brucker, Hastings and Latham 1990).

The information in any input–output table, even if derived from painstakingly gathered surveys, loses accuracy over time as an economy changes. Among the changes are modifications in the techniques of production as a result of several factors (Miller and Blair 1985: 267):

1. technological change;
2. increased economies of scale;
3. new products and entirely new sectors;
4. relative price changes;
5. annual variations in the actual products of an aggregated sector, along with the inputs used to produce them; and
6. increased imports, meaning that the inputs of the goods purchased (and their multiplier effects) are shifted to the place of production. These changes are not easily incorporated, although progress is seen (Hewings, Sonis and Jensen 1988; Martin and Holland 1992).

The literature on economic base and input–output models, estimation and updating is large and quite technical (Hewings and Jensen 1986; Richardson 1985). It is sufficient for our purposes to point out that all such models are an aggregation; they cannot fully measure the activities of individual firms (unless a firm dominates a sector in a region). Nevertheless, the input–output model became, early on, a standard tool of regional analysis and was widely used in the context of policy. It allows for the identification of clusters of linked industries, 'key sectors', growth centres, and industrial complexes (Beyers 1976; Czamanski 1974; Czamanski and Czamanski 1976, 1977; O'hUallachain 1984; Steenbakkers 1991). Recent applications include the potential impacts of climate change (Johnson and Stabler 1991) and of an electric vehicle manufacturing complex in Los Angeles (Wolff *et al.* 1995), and industrial clusters in Japan (Okumura and Yoshikawa 1994). 'Extended' input–output models, incorporating demographic, labour market and income distribution, approach econometric models in comprehensiveness (Batey and Rose 1990).

Econometric models

The interrelationships among sectors and variables in a regional economy can be quite complex, and this complexity can be incorporated in econometric, or multiple-equation, models of an economy. Particularly for forecasting purposes, these models allow a researcher to estimate the impact of a change in any of the variables that affect the economy, such as employment, output, wages, prices, income, population, retail sales, construction activity, and so on. The typical interactions incorporated in these models include the effects of migration on labour supply and the effects of income, prices and investment on industries in the region. Regional econometric models are constructed specific to each region, and employ time-series data to estimate the hypothesized relationships by means of regression analysis (Pleeter 1980). These models can be very large – the Philadelphia Region Econometric Model contained 228 equations (Glickman 1971) – but need not be overly large or complex to be reasonably accurate. They should contain an appropriate degree of 'simultaneity' or interaction between the components of the economy, especially local labour-market conditions that affect population, employment and income (Taylor 1982).

Econometric models can be constructed 'top-down' or 'bottom-up' (Bolton 1982; Klein and Glickman 1977). In the 'top-down' approach, the regional model is designed as a satellite system, attached in some consistent way to a system for the national economy as a whole. At the opposite extreme, the ultimate 'bottom-up' approach would be to establish models for each region in a nation and combine the various relationships into a national aggregate. In practice, relatively accurate models exist for many regions, usually with a combination of 'bottom-up' local relationships and 'top-down' equations. Similar concerns surround efforts to model links between regions and subregional areas (Charney and Taylor 1983, 1986). Although covered only briefly here, the topic is a major area of research in regional science and regional economics (Bell 1993; Bolton 1985; Glickman 1977; Nijkamp, Rietveld and Snickars 1986; West 1995).

Which economic base is best?

Any industrial sector can act as the economic base or engine of a regional economy. Exports are the standard economic base, including goods and services sold outside the region, as well as goods and services provided locally to people who travel to the community and capital flows (such as pensions, loans and other investments) which bring income to a region. In addition to primary activities and manufacturing, therefore, a wide variety of economic activities qualify as 'basic', such as hospitals, airports, universities, large regional shopping centres, and banks, insurance and other financial firms. Tourists and retirees also comprise an economic base, since they represent money inflows to a region (Gibson 1993; Mulligan 1987; Reeder *et al.* 1993; see Stallmann and Siegel (1995) for cautions about retirees as an economic base). In remote economies, such as Alaska and French Polynesia, government transfer programmes may be the dominant source of income (*The Economist* 1994a; Knapp and Huskey 1988). Although primary activities, such as mining, forestry, fishing and agriculture, together with manufacturing, are customary economic bases for analysis, several other sectors have risen to prominence as potential foundations for regional economies. Tourism, high technology and services represent three very different economic bases for regions and nations.

Tourism

Tourism is a growing focus of economic development policy in regions and nations where employment creation through other forms of investment is difficult to attract (Pearce 1995). Tourism creates employment, because it is labour-intensive and shows little potential for substitution by capital (Gershuny and Miles 1983; Williams and Shaw 1988). Locations with special natural, cultural or historical attractions are exports since they attract revenue from residents of other places in the same way as export production. The World Heritage List includes 411 sites in 95 countries, representing the best cultural and natural tourism locations in the world (Vellas and Bécherel 1995).

Tourism also is increasingly 'created' by the construction of convention facilities and shopping outlets in urban locales, which, along with hotels and restaurants, comprise the destinations of most tourist expenditure (Patton 1985). These places are marketed vigorously to attract tourists (Ashworth and Goodall 1990; Heath and Wall 1992). It also is currently fashionable to promote 'hallmark events' to secure the attention of the tourism market for a short, defined period of time, in contrast to regular or seasonal attractions. Intense competition for the Olympic Games and the creation of other infrequent sporting events, international expositions or world fairs are international examples (S. Britton 1991; Hall 1989; Syme *et al.* 1989).

Tourism is a problematic sector to identify, however, since a tourism industry is rarely defined in official statistics and simple combinations of tourist attractions, hotels and restaurants do not do a very good job of representing a tourism sector (Stevens and Lahr 1988: 94). However, tourism provides entrepreneurial opportunities that can supplement income from the other jobs held by local residents. Tourism is an industry with particularly low entry requirements, as seen in the various 'Mom and Pop' hotels, shops and restaurants found both in developed tourist centres and in smaller locales where national and international chain establishments see insufficient market to warrant their investment. In either setting, employment in the tourist industry is known to be largely female, as well as part-time and seasonal (Ball 1989; Cater 1988; Shaw and Williams 1988; UNCTC 1982; Williams and Shaw 1995). Seasonality is a problem in most mountain and beach resorts, but increasingly 'constructed' tourism, including large 'theme parks' such as the Disneylands, is able to attract tourists year-round (Fjellman 1992; Richter 1989; Urry 1987: 21).

Whether the benefits of tourism as an economic base are equivalent to those of other sectors depends on the degree of linkage within or leakage from the regional economy (Sinclair and Sutcliffe 1988). Multipliers from tourism typically are greatly reduced (by up to 50 per cent and more of tourism receipts) by leakages and imports in some small economies (Archer 1976; Vellas and Bécherel 1995: 229–44). Moreover, wage levels tend to be low (Gibson 1993). In major urban areas, tourism multipliers may be larger, especially during hallmark events, but urban tourists rarely justify local investment in convention centres and sports arenas (Fenich 1994). Plans to improve national competitiveness in tourism in the face of international competition are common in older regions such as Mediterranean Europe (Marchena Gómez 1995). The unpredictability of tourism flows, especially internationally, is a continuing constraint for those economies dependent on tourists (Mansfield 1990).

Despite uncertainties over benefits, tourism is an alluring source of income to struggling countries attempting to revive their economies by permitting international hotel chains to establish resorts along beaches and near historical and archeological attractions. Infrastructure shortages of all kinds, including transportation, sanitation and energy, must be overcome to lure tourists (Cater 1988; Stabler 1988; Vellas and Bécherel 1995). Luxury hotels in developing nations require excessive financial support and disproportionate water, energy, food, land and construction materials – all items in scarce supply. In some island destinations, reefs are dynamited and fishing destroyed so that beaches can be widened and swimming improved (Richter 1989). The dominance of large hotel chains and international tour companies contributes to unpredictability and reduces the income that any tourist region actually receives (Borrus and Maremont 1988; Debbage 1990; Ioannides 1995; McKee 1988; UNCTC 1982). Holiday Inn's parent firm, Holiday Corp., owned 1867 hotels in 1989 (Debbage 1990: 517). Concentrated 'enclave tourism', found in many island nations, is also vulnerable to competition from other locations, and the mix and quality of services expected by tourists (e.g. golf courses and 'nightlife' activities) tend to increase over time (D. Harrison 1992). 'Ecotourism' has become a favoured label for tourism attracted to 'untouched' ecosystems in many parts of the world, including remote areas of Central America and parts of Asia (Bottrill and Pearce 1995; Schillinger 1995; Tenenbaum 1995). Whether ecotourism is sustainable in the face of increased demand is not clear (Steele 1995; Wild 1994). Each of these represents a 'flexibility' of places in attempting to respond to demand factors beyond their control and to supply factors controlled by giant firms (Debbage 1992; Hjalager 1994; Poon 1993).

High-technology industry

High technology (high tech) is the opposite of tourism in its close connection to technological change, but it has a similar problem of definition (Malecki 1984). High tech has great allure as an economic base for three reasons. First, because of its reliance on highly paid scientists and engineers, the multiplier impacts due to consumption tend to be relatively high. Second, high-tech industries are inherently more innovative than other sectors and this, in turn, should be related to above-average rates of growth. Third, high tech is counter-cyclical, growing when most other manufacturing sectors are in decline (Thompson 1988a). A large portion of high tech is related to military production, a connection not always noted when high technology is sought.

High-technology industry is misunderstood and overrated as a solution for local economies. Even over the long term, its probable direct employment generation is relatively low, with employment in high-tech firms unlikely to exceed 10 per cent of the US workforce, and at most 15 per cent in a few states, such as California and Massachusetts. Service industries – of which only a few, such as computer software and information processing, are high-tech – will account for the lion's share of future employment (Browne 1983; Riche, Hecker and Burgan 1983). The decline of the military funding which has supported high technology has shifted concern to dual-use and other ways of transferring technologies from civilian to military applications (Chapter 7).

At the same time, high-tech industries are the most probable source of innovations, of successful entrepreneurs, of new firms and of new industries. Although this is not a universal truth (van Hulst and Olds 1993), high tech is an important employment generator. Industries newly created since World War II, such as electronics, computers and biotechnology, now employ many people. It is the job-creation potential of high technology which attracts the interest of policy-makers (Brahm 1995). Based on the experience of such places as 'Silicon Valley' in northern California and 'Route 128' surrounding Boston, many regions have attempted to recreate the dynamism of technological and entrepreneurial 'fever' (Miller and Coté 1987; Rogers and Larsen 1984). Many of the jobs created by high tech end up in other locations, rather than where the research activities take place. Indeed, it is not at all clear that high tech is a dependable economic base, or one that can be 'created' in regions which lack agglomeration economies and other dynamics common to high-tech centres (Castells and Hall 1994; Gittell and Flynn 1995; Malecki 1987; Miller and Coté 1987). It may well be better for places to devote their energies and resources to the more common low-tech economic activities.

Diversification of the economic base

Any specialization – even high technology – is vulnerable to unpredictable and perhaps abrupt changes in demand for a region's exports. This problem is especially acute for Third World nations which rely heavily, perhaps exclusively, on a primary commodity for which demand and market price might shift suddenly and dramatically. When a single corporation, the Coca-Cola Company, reformulated its principal soft drink in 1985, it brought about a large drop in demand for the vanilla bean crop of Madagascar, which produced at the time about 80 per cent of the world's vanilla beans. Evidently, 30 per cent of the world's annual crop was purchased by Coca-Cola for its soft drink. Subsequent reformulation of 'Classic Coke' brought about a partial revival of demand for vanilla, an ingredient that apparently is used in that product but not in 'New Coke' (Mufson 1985).

Dependence on a natural resource, and the distortions this creates in the wider economy, has been called the 'resource curse' (Auty 1993). Auty suggests that a natural resource is the weakest economic base possible, and that such a base is beneficial only if the proceeds from exporting it are used to diversify the economy into other sectors. The oil-rich countries have benefited perhaps more than those based on other minerals (Davis 1995). The general impression of natural resources is very different from that of not so many years ago:

> There was a time when being well-endowed with natural resources was considered a distinct advantage. That was before the mineral-poor land-scarce East Asian NICs outperformed everyone, including the oil-exporting countries. Conventional

wisdom was then turned on its head – lucky is the country that has no mining sector and few farmers (Riedel 1988: 23).

In small regions and countries, the export sector represents a significant portion of total economic activity. Smaller regions tend to export more in order to import and satisfy the demands of inhabitants for items not produced locally. Urban regions and diverse economies with many different industries, on the other hand, produce a larger proportion of local requirements. In general, then, large regions and nations are better able to weather economic fluctuations because, even if the demand for the products of some industries declines, this is unlikely to affect all industries at the same time.

The economies of larger regions usually encompass a greater number of firms in a variety of exporting and supplier industries. However, this is not always the case, and concentration in a small number of sectors plagues large as well as small regions. The 'company town' with a single major employer is the extreme case of dependence on not simply a narrow range of economic activity, but on the fortunes of a single firm and sector. A dominant plant can wield a great deal of control over wage rates and unionization, and effectively dominate an area's economy (Clark, Gertler and Whiteman 1986; Sloan 1981). Fluctuations in unemployment rates are greater in labour markets dominated by single plants, even when controlling for industry and region (Lever 1979). Entrepreneurship also tends to be at low levels in company towns (Hjalager 1989).

Industrial diversification of a regional economy has a long history as a policy recommendation (Conroy 1975; Lande 1982, 1994). The size of a region's multiplier tends to be larger where control, information and diversity are found, such as in higher levels of the urban hierarchy (Olfert and Stabler 1994). Multipliers are smaller in smaller places and when regional structure is limited or narrow, as when branch facilities predominate. Thompson (1965) had argued strongly that city (or region) size, on average, decreases cyclical instability, in large part because of greater industrial diversity, and Marchand (1986) provided some evidence for the argument. The diversity–size relationship, however, is overly simplistic, since cities and regions of the same size vary (Conroy 1975). More recently, it has become clear that it is not industrial diversity alone that is the answer, but the actual mix of industries: some industries are better (more stable) than others (Browne 1978; Grossberg 1982; Howland 1984; Pollard and Storper 1996).

The occupational structure of a region, based on its place within corporate hierarchies and spatial divisions of labour – whether it specializes in research, decision-making or production – is also significant from a long-term perspective (Pedersen 1978; W. Thompson 1987). Thompson (1995) recently said that it might not be the diversity of a place that matters most, but its adaptability; national perspectives on this idea are found in Killick (1995a). A large portion of a place's adaptability derives from its external links, which continually bring new ideas, people and opportunities (Amin and Thrift 1993; Preto 1995). Industrial diversity has advantages. For example, it appears to be related to higher rates of new firm formation in several recent studies (J. J. Friedmann 1995; Reynolds, Miller and Maki 1993).

The service sector: engine of growth?

Part of the historical process of economic development entails the transition from one economic activity to another, as new industries arise and old ones fail to provide an adequate economic base for a region's population. The conventional way of presenting this change at an aggregate level is to consolidate economic activities into a small number of more general sectors. The *primary* sector, consisting of extractive activities such as agriculture, mining, forestry and fishing, comprises the traditional activities on which preindustrial people relied, but which are now performed by a wide range of techniques, from traditional labour-intensive systems to highly mechanized capital-intensive methods. *Secondary* activities are manufacturing or processing sectors, which, again, include both traditional and modern practices. *Tertiary*, or service, sectors have commonly been the residual category after primary and secondary activities are delineated. More recently, services have been separated into those which involve a substantial information content (*quaternary* services) and those which do not (tertiary services). For example, the 'knowledge-intensive' or information-based sector, defined by Machlup (1962) as consisting of education, research, publishing and broadcasting, accounted for 31 per cent of the US workforce in 1958. The composition of the 'information society', developed in the mid-1970s, is slightly broader (Porat 1977). In this conceptualization, information workers are defined as those engaged in creating or processing information, in three categories (Katz 1988: 5):

1. those whose final product is information;
2. workers whose main activity is informational in nature, including information creators ('knowledge workers'), information transmitters and information processors;
3. workers who operate information technologies (Katz 1988: 5).

The diverse nature of the service sector has led some to propose a fifth 'quinary' sector which represents control functions and not routine information-processing activities (Harper 1982).

Throughout history, primary activity has absorbed the largest fraction of the labour force in primitive economies. Exports of staple commodities and, later, of primary manufactured products, are typical of frontier regions, whose markets are in other, often distant, regions (Hayter 1986). Simple processing, such as sawing logs into milled lumber, can evolve into further production of plywood, veneers and, finally, wood and paper products such as furniture and newsprint. Some extractive exports are more likely than others to promote desirable linkages and processing; coal and other mining fosters few local linkages, leading to the 'resource curse' (Auty 1993; Lewis 1989). 'The export sector must grow and maintain flexibility, shifting commodities, markets and production techniques. . . . Lacking flexibility, regions may be forced into the staple trap, eking out a marginal existence by means of uncertain returns from the same old staples' (Gilmour

1975: 62). The US economy has shifted its principal products from cotton tex-tiles, lumber, and boots and shoes in 1860 to motor vehicles and equipment, air-craft parts, and computers and office equipment in 1987 (Spulber 1995: 163).

The shift among advanced economies from primary economic activities to manufacturing and, more recently, to services became part of the received and largely unquestioned wisdom in the 1930s (Fisher 1933). The 'Clark–Fisher hypothesis' (Clark 1957) became a standard model of economic development, and the study of structural change remains central to development economics (Syrquin 1988). Table 1.3 illustrates this shift; as one moves down the table to the more advanced economies, the percentage of the workforce in agriculture declines, and the percentage in services increases. In some developing countries, the historical progression seen in Europe and North America and represented in the Clark–Fisher model has not been occurring in the expected manner (Casetti and Pandit 1987; Pandit and Casetti 1989). Instead, the shift has been directly from agriculture to services, and manufacturing has remained at a relatively low level. Of the countries in Table 1.3, Israel and Nigeria exemplify this shift most. Selya (1994) suggests that Taiwan, which is typically seen as a manufacturing economy, is actually reliant on services.

Manufacturing is considered 'special' and appears to drive the economic growth process at both the regional and the national scale (Cohen and Zysman 1987; Gertler 1986; Harris 1987; Park and Chan 1989; Sass 1994). Services have undoubtedly become the dominant sector of economic activity in many economies, at least in employment. If broadly defined as all non-goods-producing industries, they account for over 70 per cent of total employment and over 50 per cent of GNP in most developed countries (Daniels 1993; Illeris 1989; Ochel and Wegner 1987: 105). The numerical importance of the service sector reinforces long-standing criticisms of the basic/service division on which economic base analysis relies (Massey 1973; Tiebout 1962; Watkins 1980). In Blumenfeld's (1955: 131) words: 'It is . . . the "secondary", "nonbasic" indus-tries . . . which constitute the real and lasting strength of the metropolitan economy.' The sectoral shift to services is fundamental to the 'post-industrial society' (Bell 1973; Power 1988; Stanback *et al.* 1981).

The difficulty with services is that, unlike manufactured goods, they are difficult to define. Examples of services are easy to come by: a shoe shine, a heart transplant, a wedding (or divorce), a computer program, a memo to the files, a tennis lesson, a burial, a car wash, a crop dusting (Cohen and Zysman 1987: 51). But what do these have in common? Gershuny and Miles (1983: 3) iden-tify the service industry as 'all those firms and employers whose major final output is some intangible or ephemeral commodity.' Grubel (1987) shows that all internationally traded services – whether consumed abroad by tourists, film producers or medical patients, or produced abroad by construction workers, teachers, artists or investors – are embodied in some way in people or products. Not all intangibles are services, because many have their end result in tangible goods, such as architectural services in buildings, product design in products, and shipping in stocks of goods (Cohen and Zysman 1987: 51–2). Non-storability is another trait frequently attributed to services, but on-line

Table 1.3   Workforce by sector in selected countries, as a percentage of the total.

Country	Year	Agriculture	Industry	Services
Bangladesh	1989	65.5	15.5	19.6
Central African Republic	1988	80.2	3.3	16.5
China	1993	61.0	18.0	21.0
Ghana	1984	61.0	12.8	26.2
India	1991	63.2	14.2	22.6
Indonesia	1993	50.4	15.8	33.8
Thailand	1989	66.3	11.9	21.8
Egypt	1989	42.5	20.7	36.8
Nigeria	1986	45.0	6.6	48.4
Philippines	1991	45.3	16.0	38.7
Guatemala	1989	49.9	18.3	31.8
Malaysia	1988	30.6	22.6	46.7
Turkey	1991	48.8	20.1	31.0
Brazil	1988	24.2	23.4	52.4
Chile	1991	19.1	26.3	54.6
Costa Rica	1991	25.0	26.9	48.0
Dominican Republic	1981	23.6	18.1	58.3
Greece	1990	23.2	27.7	49.0
Mexico	1990	22.6	27.8	49.6
Poland	1988	17.9	36.3	35.9
Ireland	1990	14.9	28.4	56.8
Korea	1991	16.7	35.6	47.7
Australia	1991	6.3	24.4	70.4
Canada	1991	3.5	24.4	74.1
France	1991	5.7	28.8	65.5
Israel	1990	5.3	8.3	86.4
Italy	1991	8.4	32.0	59.5
Japan	1991	6.7	34.5	58.8
Netherlands	1991	4.5	25.3	70.3
Norway	1991	5.7	23.7	70.6
Sweden	1991	3.2	28.2	68.5
United Kingdom	1990	2.1	28.7	69.3
United States	1991	2.9	25.8	71.3

Source: World Bank (1995a: 147–8, Table A–2).

databanks and computer tapes and disks belie this distinction. In many cases, products and services are interchangeable. A home washing machine (a product) can substitute for the use of a laundromat (a service), and a frozen dinner can replace a restaurant meal (Quinn, Baruch and Paquette 1987). Daniels (1993: 3) classifies services on the basis of the utility provided: some yield immediate if short-term utility (fast-food restaurant, cinema, laundry, etc.); others offer medium-term or semi-durable utility (automobile repair, tax advice, dental treatment, etc.); yet others provide longer-term, almost durable utility (life insurance, mortgage financing, pension plans, etc.).

Services play a central role by facilitating and stimulating economic growth in all sectors. This *infrastructural role* of services, particularly for communication and information, is perhaps their most important function (Cohen and Zysman 1987; Riddle 1986). In retailing, for example, infrastructural services (transport and communications) link the producer with the market (Nusbaumer 1987a). These roles played by services exemplify the way in which services 'permeate the value chain' of every firm (Porter 1990: 241). Likewise, services are integral to the clustering process which creates competitive advantage, by providing skills, technologies and support to other industries (Porter 1990: 267).

In order to simplify the variety of services, they are frequently divided into three general types (Marshall *et al.* 1988: 11–29):
1. *consumer services*, including retail and household services;
2. *producer services*, which itself includes three categories:
    (a) information processing, including R&D, consulting, engineering, legal services and purchasing;
    (b) goods-related services, such as transport and waste disposal; and
    (c) personnel support, including welfare, cleaning, security, travel and accommodation; and
3. *government services*, including education, welfare and defence.

These also involve different production processes, transforming physical objects (e.g. catering and repairs), people (e.g. barbers and health care), and codified information (e.g. banking and entertainment) (Miles 1994).

It is perhaps more common to exclude government services from the service sector, in order to separate public and private services (Waite 1988: 2). Recently, a category of *advanced producer services* has been put forward, to capture the 'complex knowledge-intensive business services designed as direct inputs to firms' (Moulaert and Tödtling 1995: 102). This is essentially the same as type 2(a) above. Yet another typology of sectors incorporates the growing inter-dependence between services and production, in which services comprise the circulation, distribution and regulation (all non-production) activities (Bailly *et al.* 1987; Bailly, Maillat and Coffey 1987). As privatization of government services has spread, the nongovernmental organizations (NGOs) or 'not-for-profit' sector has become more significant (Hammack and Young 1993; Oster 1995; Reiner and Wolpert 1981; Wolch and Geiger 1986).

'Mixed' activities serve both consumer and producer markets, thus raising definitional problems. Examples include transport, telecommunications, delivery and postal services, banking, and insurance. Some services, such as advertising, marketing, and research and development, are more easily classified as producer services, whereas recreation, education, health, welfare and personal services are primarily if not wholly consumer services. It is financial and commercial activities which are the hardest to categorize, for they are *circulation* services, not intermediate or final demand services, and they depend on velocity of turnover rather than an identifiable demand (Allen 1988).

The level of service activity is a response to a set of demand and supply factors (Daniels 1982). The level and distribution of income, along with the relative propensity to consume services, affects the consumption of consumer or distribution services (Kellerman 1985; Stanback *et al.* 1981). Retailing establishments and jobs increase in number in order to help provide the desired goods and services, such as automobiles, refrigerators, washing machines, and meals away from home. The size of the government sector affects the degree to which employment is found in public administration and related regulation activities. Population growth, rising incomes, and increased participation of women in the labour force have increased demands for certain services, such as medical care, personal banking and financial services, and child care. Changes in the composition of the population also account for substantial portions of increased service sector growth, e.g. demand for nursing home and related health industry outputs has grown as a population ages. Supply factors, such as mass production and new technology, also have greatly increased the types and variety of services possible (Kellerman 1985; Waite 1988). This is especially evident in producer (circulation) services, where new financial services and global transactions have proliferated in recent years, but it also a major factor in consumer services (Miles 1988). A final reason for the growth of the service sector is that government statisticians tend to include services in the value of the manufactured goods if they are performed internally, but to report them separately as services if they are purchased from another firm (Waite 1988). Thus, services as measured have expanded as the 'make or buy' decision has moved increasingly toward subcontracting and 'outsourcing' as firms obtain data-processing, management advice, transport, and cleaning services from outside providers (Quinn, Doorley and Paquette 1990).

Employment growth in services has been concentrated in relatively few sectors. In the USA, the greatest growth in employment has been in wholesale and retail trade (12 000 000 new jobs from 1959 to 1985) and services (15 000 000 new jobs), a category that includes repair, business services, hotels and private medical care. These two major sectors grew from 50 per cent of total job growth in 1959–69 to almost 99 per cent of 1979–85 job growth (Kutscher 1988: 26). When disaggregated, it is seen that just four industries – eating and drinking places, other retail trade, business services, and medical services– have accounted for 43 per cent of the 1959–85 growth and 65 per cent of the more recent (1979–85) job growth (Kutscher 1988: 28). Data for 1987 to 1992 show that these trends have continued (Du, Mergenhagen and Lee 1995).

Similar dualism is seen among occupations, with the largest increases occurring at the two extremes: among professional, technical and kindred workers, and managers and administrators at one end, and clerical workers at the other. The main beneficiaries of new service jobs are likely to be female, part-time and young employees, especially in clerical and sales occupations (Rajan 1987; Townsend 1986). In part because of the proliferation of low-wage jobs in services, manufacturing cities have higher multipliers in economic base studies (Mulligan and Fik 1994). Whether services can play a propulsive role depends almost entirely on which service jobs a place has. The 'dualistic nature' of services means that producer services are likely to be a solid economic base, whereas routine, consumer-oriented services are not (Glasmeier and Howland 1994).

Producer services

Producer services, or business services, have been especially prominent in the recent rise of the service sector (Daniels 1993; Marshall *et al.* 1988). These range from routine services, such as window-washing and janitorial services, to advanced producer services, such as management consulting and research and development. Advanced producer services – those which have high knowledge and innovation content – are closely tied to the technological changes taking place both in manufacturing and in services themselves (Moulaert and Tödtling 1995). Producer services form part of the modern regional infrastructure (Begg 1993).

Internal or external 'sourcing' of services is but one of several *linkages* with other firms that influence the size of the regional multiplier. Coffey and Polèse (1987a) surveyed a large number of Montreal firms to see which services are most often provided within the firm, purchased from local firms, or provided by distant firms or establishments. Several services are typically purchased rather than provided internally: consulting, personnel services, computer services, advertising, architecture, engineering and scientific services, and royalties/patents. If there is no local service infrastructure providing these services, then they are obtained from the firm's headquarters, even if located far away.

In many respects, producer services are the most important of services. They are frequently exported outside the region, thus constituting an economic base similar to the traditional role of manufacturing (Beyers and Alvine 1985; Hansen 1994). They are prominent in the dominant regional economies, and are concentrated in the seats of economic power (Borchert 1978; Moulaert and Gallouj 1993). Together with corporate headquarters, non-profit institutions and the public sector, non-consumer services account for roughly two-thirds of the labour force in 'world cities' such as New York (Noyelle and Stanback 1983; Shachar 1995b). In fact, it is this counterbalancing of employment gain in producer services during a period of deindustrialization that has led to conclusions that they are the principal economic base of contemporary economies (Daniels 1993; Hansen 1994; Illeris 1989; Stanback *et al.* 1981). Moreover, stable and prosperous regional economies are more likely to be based on producer services (Hansen 1993; Kirk 1987). Rural areas are least likely to benefit from this sector, despite its growing significance (Glasmeier and Howland 1994; Porterfield and Sizer 1995). At the international scale, the disparity in service activities is even more pronounced, and many countries are simply left out of the picture in organizational location decisions as 'world cities' attract the bulk of corporate investment (Friedmann 1986; Moulaert and Tödtling 1995; Sassen 1994). Advertising firms and design firms are among the most concentrated in major cities (Daniels 1993, 1995a,b; Leslie 1995). We return to the role of world cities in Chapter 6.

Services are commonly exported, even from very small urban and non-metropolitan areas of the Canadian Prairies (Stabler and Howe 1988), although this is not always true, as Townsend (1995) has found in the case of Edinburgh. Moreover, services embodied in goods exports add to the significance of service exports and service growth (Stabler and Howe 1993). Because services are strongly urbanized in location, exports are more common among urban areas. In a large study in the US Pacific Northwest, nearly all exporting service firms were located within the metropolitan agglomeration of Seattle (Beyers and Alvine 1985). In general, the concentration of producer services is continuing, even if decentralizing somewhat from urban core to suburban periphery (Hessels 1994; van Dinteren and Meuwissen 1994). Proponents of services as a viable, if not a superior, economic base typically cite the decline of manufacturing employment during the 1970s and 1980s and the rapid rise of service employment, particularly in producer services (Gillis 1987; Hall 1987; Marshall et al. 1988). This argument incorporates both the notion of structural change discussed above, and the deindustrialization (decline in manufacturing) argument evident in recent data. Service jobs also come and go, perhaps at different rates than manufacturing jobs, and for many of the same reasons that affect manufacturing, including technical change (investment in new processes which reduce labour input), intensification (reorganization of work processes to speed up work), and rationalization (reduction of overall capacity by closing the least profitable locations in an organization) (Buck 1988; Massey and Meegan 1982).

Service industries still depend on manufacturing, although perhaps not in the subordinate manner implied by the economic base model. The asymmetrical dependence of services on manufacturing was clearly found in a study of 26 countries by Park and Chan (1989). The linkages between manufacturing and services include the internal coordination of production and non-production activities taking place within firms as well as inter-firm linkages involving innovation and more routine activities such as transportation and distribution. Innovations originate primarily in manufacturing and flow largely to firms in the service sector (Robson, Townsend and Pavitt 1988; Scherer 1982). The most prominent example in recent years is the effect of the computer sector on virtually every service sector, from architecture to medicine, typing and retailing (Berndt and Malone 1995; Brynjolfsson and Hitt 1996).

However, the relationship between manufacturing and services is truly symbiotic in the case of producer services (Park and Chan 1989). The prominence of services as an employer has perhaps caused an ill-advised de-emphasis on manufacturing as the core of a prosperous economy. Spatial hierarchies and division of labour in services suggest that producer services are very different from routine, more footloose services (Coffey and Polèse 1989). It may be that producer services play a strategic role in increasing productivity in other sectors, through their sophisticated interactions with goods production (Hansen 1994). Further, innovation, whether in the form of new products and services or new production processes, can be seen as a producer service that takes advantage of, and may stimulate the development of, new products and infrastructures developed in other sectors and perhaps especially where information and expertise may not be available, such as in small manufacturing firms (MacPherson 1988a). Overall, services may be a reliable and high-income economic base only in large urban regions where head offices and other customers of services are concentrated.

The competitiveness of places: technological capability

The heightened economic competitiveness in the world has several dimensions, each of which has increased enormously since the mid-1980s. What comprises competitiveness? The most influential answer is found in the model of Porter (1990), whose framework was discussed earlier. Porter's approach, however, gives short shrift to several elements that have been central to research during the 1990s. The first of these continues to be technological change, which is perhaps the most important source of structural change in an economy, because it both enhances productivity and alters the mix of products, industries, firms and jobs which make up an economy. It causes these changes in a subtle manner, creating new jobs and firms, destroying old ones, and disturbing the equilibrium (Schumpeter 1934).

The second element, ignored in most post-war economic growth models, with their view of fixed capital, is human capital, which is formed or enhanced to utilize people's creativity, technological skills and entrepreneurship (Toye 1993). The third element, which builds upon human capability, is knowledge. A more accurate perspective on national and regional economic differences is not a focus on differences in resource endowment or differences in the rate of growth of capital or labour. 'It is the growth and accumulation of useful knowledge, and the transformation of knowledge into final output via technical innovation, upon which the performance of the world capitalist economy ultimately depends' (Griffin 1978: 14; Stewart 1978: 114–40). This is implicit in the new growth theories, and in the role of institutions, whether through explicit policy or through more subtle modes of social regulation.

Technological capability is at the heart of regional change. As outlined in Chapter 2, it applies at the level of the firm, of regions and of nations, and relates directly to notions of competitiveness and competition. The innovation gap is a primary source of development disparities, and it depends on not only the sectors, but also on the firms, their organizational structure, and the extent of their markets (Brugger and Stuckey 1987). More importantly, the need to shift to new products requires considerable learning on the part of any firm and set of firms that comprise an economy. This must be done by firms; the experience of state-owned enterprises (SOEs) outside the profit motive shatters virtually any possibility of SOEs performing at world-class levels. The acquisition of technological capability within firms is surveyed in Chapter 2, where the focus is on both conventional technical change and on the institutions that facilitate technical change. For firms that have learned sufficiently, the challenge is to remain competitive. This requires flexibility, an R&D capability, and the harnessing of capabilities outside the firm in the form of strategic alliances and 'virtual' organizations.

Much of the process of technical change is an outgrowth of the way in which technology is produced and exploited by capitalist firms (the topic of Chapter 3). Technology does not create itself, of course. Rather, it is a direct outcome of the choices and decisions of people and organizations (Bijker *et al.* 1987; Street 1992). Often, these choices are misguided, pouring resources into military expansion and trivial improvements of consumer goods. Awareness that technology is a mixed blessing has accompanied technical progress since the beginning. Both the development of new products in research laboratories and the transformation of production processes depend on firms' strategies, production relations, and their interrelationships with their competitors. Some of this topic is encompassed within the various 'cycle' models, ranging from product and profit cycles to the 'long waves' which seem to embody global technological change in a long-term manner.

Flexible forms of manufacturing appear to be supplanting mass production as a means of organizing production. They employ technology in new ways that combine product technology and process technology in a framework of global competition between firms. Chapter 4 deals with the various influences on firms' locations for production and non-production activities. The division of labour provides a succinct framework for the decisions locally and globally. It is important not to see this tendency as occurring only at the global scale. Firms, small and large alike, seek out locations where unions and labour power are weaker or less well developed as part of the society. The dynamics of capitalism differ significantly between small firms and large corporations. Chapter 5 focuses on entrepreneurs, networks of small firms, and Schumpeterian 'creative destruction'. Chapter 6 takes up the issue of large firms and their global production chains, which increasingly dominate economic activity at all spatial scales.

Keen competition takes place for technological competence and superiority, both on a local level and internationally. This is the latest arena where state intervention has interacted with private interests to generate policies that perceive and address the competitiveness of firms and of regions. The supply-side approach, which emphasizes the creation of firms, jobs and wealth based on internal resources, is a part – albeit an important part – of the development process (Eisinger 1988; Sweeney 1987). However, new firms and high technology involve critical synergies which determine the pattern of growth and development (D'Arcy and Guissani 1996; Stöhr 1986a). The challenge for all other nations, especially others in the Third World, is to imitate the success – the end, if not the means – of what has been called the 'East Asian miracle' (World Bank 1993). For the most part, this entails developing an industrial policy (often combined with a technology policy) in order to change a nation's position in the international division of labour (Evans 1995). Chapter 7 discusses policies and institutions for shaping economic change at the national as well as at the regional and local levels.

Global investment patterns and national, regional and local policies appear to determine much of what we see as the level of development in a particular place. However, learning about technology is necessary in developing countries and in post-socialist regimes facing capitalist competition. Chapter 8 takes up this topic, and assesses the prospects for 'catching up' in a competitive world. The transfer of technology is one of the few means available for nations to obtain technological capability which they lack, yet that is not an easy task, since effort and expertise are needed to absorb technology.

From a long-term perspective, economic structure connotes the endogenous characteristics of a region's economy which make up the capacity for economic growth. The presence of some characteristics, such as a relatively new stock of capital equipment, allow higher productivity and output for a given level of investment. Similarly, an excellent education system provides a pool of skilled workers who are better able to adapt to new methods of work. Regarding the need to make investments for the long term, Storper (1989: 236–7) notes that it is 'investments in new products and process development and in worker training and organizational skills that have long term payoffs in the form of increasing markets shares for firms and generation of high-skill high-wage employment for the society.' These issues are the focus of Chapter 9.

Industrial transformation in localities, regions and nations thus becomes the pivotal process to explain. The locally specific ways in which such transformations take place make the global view of this book useful by presenting an array of locally based empirical findings. The next chapter examines economic technological capability and technological change.

Chapter 2

Technological capability: the core of economic development

Economic change involves social, institutional and political elements – as well as economic factors – which come together distinctively in each place. Technology is one of the principal forces behind regional dynamics, but is dealt with unsatisfactorily by either neoclassical or Marxist approaches. Technology is behind the capability of multinational or transnational corporations to coordinate global operations; it is central to the competitive environment which firms and, increasingly, regions and nations must confront. Technology, along with capital and labour, is utilized differently by each firm or enterprise, as Chapter 3 will show. At the national and regional levels, where the aggregate impacts of firms' actions are felt, technology is more difficult for economic theory to capture and account for.

We begin the story with productivity, which is the fundamental way in which economic growth occurs. 'It can be said without exaggeration that in the long run probably nothing is as important for economic welfare as the rate of productivity growth' (Baumol, Blackman and Wolff 1989: 1). Productivity growth is considered to be the principal means by which a region or a nation can increase its level of income and the well-being of its population (Baumol 1989; Kendrick 1977). Only by increasing productivity can workers earn higher wages; conversely, low wages combined with low productivity results in high labour costs (Koretz 1995). Productivity growth is the only way for nations (and for firms) to pay for higher wages; indeed, this is why rising wages in NICs like Korea have led to Korean investment in other countries. Shoe production in Korea, the centre of athletic shoe production in 1981, had fallen dramatically by 1991, largely because of Korean firms producing (or contracting for production) in China, Indonesia and Thailand (Barff and Austin 1993; Lim 1994).

Technology is only one of several elements in productivity; the economic constructs of capital and labour represent such things as investment, education and skills. Other elements, less well understood, are strongly related to background or environmental factors that make some places more 'capable' than others. We actually know more about technology than neoclassical models have demonstrated, but we still know too little about technology and knowledge, about firms as organizations, and about institutions that comprise the environment within which firms – as well as people and organizations – operate (Nelson 1994a; OECD 1992). The translation of institutional and technological thinking to the scale of regions and places is not straightforward, and demands a fuller understanding of the locational behaviour and context of firms and of entrepreneurship, as later chapters will illustrate.

Production functions and equilibrium: the neoclassical model and alternatives

The production function approach to the study and measurement of economic growth is a direct outgrowth of its origins in neoclassical equilibrium economics. In this framework, all output (Q) is produced by two inputs, or *factors of production*, capital (K) and labour (L)

$$Q=f(K, L) \tag{2.1}$$

Typically, simple mathematical functions, particularly the Cobb–Douglas function, are utilized because of their ease of manipulation (Borts and Stein 1964); more complex formulations are reviewed by Andersson and Kuenne (1986).

In the Cobb–Douglas form,

$$Q= K^a\ L^b \tag{2.2}$$

Other conditions enter the world of the aggregate production function: identical products and production functions in all firms and locations, and a homogeneous capital stock, with the same technology and productivity assumed in all places.

The two-factor model can be used to measure productivity of capital (output per unit of capital) and of labour (output per unit of labour) in an economy. By adding technology to the model, the rate of growth of output (Q) over time can be attributed to the productivity of capital (K) and of labour (L):

$$q=ak+ bl+ ct \tag{2.3}$$

where q, k, l and t are growth rates of output, capital, labour and technology, c is the level of technical progress, and a and b are elasticities of substitution with respect to capital and labour, respectively. The sum of $a+ b$ (<0, $=0$ or >0) indicates whether there are decreasing, constant or increasing returns to scale. Hahn and Matthews (1964: 825–53) and Kennedy and Thirlwall (1972) review neoclassical views of technical progress, and Nelson (1994a) and Fagerberg (1994) review the relationship between technology and growth models.

The critical element is ct, a residual in Solow's (1957) original work in the 1950s, and later named total factor productivity (TFP) to represent the growth in output unexplained by growth in inputs, k and l. Productivity is the fundamental way in which economic growth takes place. Sometimes defined as 'making more out of less' (Chatterjee 1994), it is essential for an economy to produce more – not only by using more inputs, but by increasing the efficiency of those inputs. The easy way to raise output (i.e. to generate economic growth) is to increase the amount of capital and labour inputs. This can occur either by capital investment, using machinery to increase the amount that workers can produce, or by increasing the number of workers in the labour force. A great deal of output growth has taken place in many Western countries simply through the increase in the labour force participation rate of women. Krugman (1994c) sees the 'East Asian miracle' as something less than miraculous, having been the result largely of increases in labour skills (through education) and capital investment – increases which will not be able to be repeated and are not sustainable. More importantly, the gains in output are a result of these increases in capital and labour inputs, but not their productivity.

Productivity is measured most simply by labour productivity (output per worker or per unit of labour), or capital productivity (output per unit of capital). These simple fractions have been replaced by more sophisticated measures of total factor productivity (TFP), which take into account increases in both capital and labour and allow improvements in education and labour skills and improvements in the quality and efficiency of capital equipment. When the contributions from factor growth are deducted, what remains – so-called total factor productivity growth – is then further reduced by taking into account the contribution to growth from structural changes in the employment mix (from low-productivity to high-productivity activities), from better utilization of economies of scale, and other factors.

A great deal of research at the national level has attempted to understand the contributions of factors to variations in the rate of economic growth (Baumol, Blackman and Wolff 1989; Baumol, Nelson and Wolff 1994; Denison 1967, 1985; Jorgenson 1988; Odagiri 1985; Sato 1978). Overall, studies have found that capital investment growth accounts for less than half of the measured increase in output. The balance is attributable mainly to improvements in the quality of labour, from education, health, training and experience, all of which are considered investments in *human capital* (Becker 1964; MacKay 1993; McCrackin 1984; Nussbaum *et al.* 1988). In part because of differences in education and skills, national economies vary greatly in productivity growth. Among the industrial nations, productivity growth was highest during the 1960s and 1970s in Japan, and lowest in the UK and USA. Since 1979, Japan's rate of productivity growth has come down to below the OECD average of 2.7 per cent annually, and has been highest in Italy and the UK (Table 2.1). These differences also result from industry mix, since national productivity growth is a composite of the changes taking place across many sectors (McUsic 1987). But the principal cause of slow productivity growth is the failure of firms in some countries – notably the USA since 1960 – to take advantage of new technological ideas and to incorporate them into production (Baily and Chakrabarti

Table 2.1   Growth in manufacturing productivity in selected countries, 1960–1993 (per cent).

	USA	Canada	Japan	France	Germany	Italy	UK
1960–73	3.2	4.7	10.5	6.5	5.9	7.3	4.3
1973–80	1.2	1.6	7.0	4.6	3.8	3.7	1.0
1979–93	2.7	1.5	2.1	2.1	1.2	3.8	3.8

Source: based on McUsic (1987: 10, Table 9) and OECD (1995a: 43, Table 5.1).

1988). Broadberry (1994) attributes differing productivities to different technological systems, and demonstrates that the American, British and Japanese systems are distinct, making widespread adoption of one another's production systems unlikely.

From aggregate studies, then, a large residual continues to emerge beyond that which can be explained by increases in the quantity and quality of capital and labour. This residual, labelled 'technical progress' by Solow (1957), was disaggregated by Denison (1967) into three components: (1) resource shifts (from agriculture to industry) and economies of scale, (2) advances in technical, managerial and organizational knowledge, and (3) a further 'residual productivity'. Scott (1981) considers investment – both capital investment and investment in human capital – to account for nearly all of the 'technical progress' found in earlier growth accounting studies. This helps in measurement terms, but it fails to deal with the many ways in which productivity can improve without measurable investment, such as learning by doing and learning by using (Chatterjee 1994). Nelson (1981) sees technological advance as quite separate from capital growth and rising educational attainments, and all three sources as complementary 'ingredients' of productivity growth. Surveying the evidence historically, Maddison (1994: 53) concludes that 'technical progress is the most essential characteristic of economic growth.'

Elaboration of the neoclassical model permits sources of productivity growth to be distinguished. McCombie (1988a: 270), for example, includes three main types of productivity growth in addition to exogenous technical progress and capital deepening:

1. growth of productivity due to the improved inter-regional allocation of resources;
2. growth due to the improved allocation of resources between industries within a given region (i.e. the improved intraregional allocation of resources); and
3. the rate of technical progress in addition to ct (in equation (2.3)) due to the diffusion of innovations caused by differences in the level of technology to which the regions have access.

It is far more common for neoclassical analyses simply to assume that new techniques are freely available to all, and largely to disregard the actual mechanisms of technical change (Fagerberg 1994). The equilibrium solution is convergence of productivity and growth rates; in reality, what is occurring is countries 'catching up, forging ahead, and falling back' (Abramovitz 1986).

The neoclassical residual can be divided into two parts to reflect technological progress and catch-up, respectively (Fagerberg 1994: 1151). Convergence of productivity growth rates among countries – 'the convergence club' evident in Table 2.1 – is a result both of catch-up by the followers and reduced opportunity for learning on the part of the leaders (in this case, the USA and Japan) (Baumol, Blackman and Wolff 1989). Much of the research on this issue is historical, and draws parallels between the decline of British economic leadership and the more recent decline in American leadership. It is much easier today for 'followers' such as Korea and Taiwan to catch up, because much more knowledge is codified in books and more is taught in schools, compared with the hands-on experience necessary for technological learning up to the early twentieth century (Nelson and Wright 1994).

One realistic enhancement of the neoclassical model is the *vintage* approach, which acknowledges that not all machinery is alike. Technology is 'embodied' in capital equipment, and as progress is made, newer machines (newer vintages) make use of the most current knowledge and techniques of production, but these remain fixed at the level of productivity and labour intensity of their vintage (Salter 1966). The vintage concept appeared to allow for a portion of productivity growth that could not be accounted for by capital and labour inputs alone (Thirlwall 1972).

Vintage models measure cumulative capital investment, but capital which is fixed or invested in a particular year remains distinct from capital fixed in earlier and later years, for the duration of its productive life. The stock of productive capital, or the means of production, at any point in time, is the sum of invested capital of various different vintages. There are also rigidities which prevent the full impact of new vintages of machinery from taking effect for some time (Johansson and Strömquist 1981). Associated with each vintage are separate productivities and labour intensities and, thus, the aggregate productivity of total invested capital and the implied demand for labour are determined (Gertler 1988a).

The principal simplification imposed by vintage models – despite their apparent complexity – is that the diversity, across firms, establishments and regions, of production technologies is simply reduced to spatial variations in the mix of different vintages of capital. Varaiya and Wiseman (1981) and Rigby (1995) have shown that the regions of the USA vary significantly in the age of their manufacturing capacity. Complicating the picture is the fact that the technology of older machinery tends to be more labour-intensive, suggesting that plants with older capital stock will experience larger employment losses as the least competitive facilities are closed (Varaiya and Wiseman 1981: 441). This indeed has been the finding of research on plant closure (Chapter 4). Aggregate productivity data conceal a great deal of variation between individual plants (Carlsson 1981). Rigby's (1995) recent work on the USA also suggests that enormous sectoral and regional variation in capital investment has taken place, supports earlier work by Gertler (1986) and casts doubt on conclusions that there was a 'catastrophic' shift of capital to the sunbelt from the snowbelt (Casetti 1981).

Regional technologies differ in ways beyond varying regional rates of adoption of new vintages of technology (Blackley 1986; McCombie 1988a). Technologies are introduced and developed in many places, and even as they diffuse (unevenly) they are modified by each firm as they are adopted. For example, foreign-owned plants in Ireland exhibited twice the productivity of locally owned plants (Birnie and Hitchens 1994). Baily and Gersbach (1995) suggest that these productivity differences are a result of capital utilization decisions, manufacturing design and work organization, which vary from country to country within an industry, and that these nationally distinct characteristics move as firms set up operations in other countries.

Largely through the efforts of Webber (1987a,b; Webber and Foot 1988a,b), it is possible to analyse a Marxist model of production in a manner similar to that of neoclassical formulations. In a series of empirical studies, Webber and Tonkin (1987, 1988a,b) show that individual sectors in Canada differ markedly in the types of technical changes they underwent in response to declining rates of profit. The food industry was able to stave off profit decline largely by decreasing turnover times in production and by exploiting the technical advances of supplier industries. The clothing industry experienced little technical change, but was characterized by labour exploitation. Textiles firms, by contrast, generally incorporated increases in the technical composition of capital through capital investment. Knitting firms were somewhere in between these two extremes. In the wood, furniture and paper industries, the interaction between technical changes and market relations was more complex, and involved a combination of capital and labour adjustments. As these studies illustrate and as Chapter 3 will show, profit and growth are not constant or steady, but follow a pattern of 'long waves' of cyclical growth and decline. Technology is a key element of the resilience of capitalism that is not captured by a focus solely on labour.

Productivity in services

The growth of services, discussed in Chapter 1, poses a particular problem in the context of productivity growth. Services are typically thought to be less productive and less amenable to technological change than manufacturing industries (Baumol 1967). This is a result of the fact that productivity is typically measured as output per unit of labour, a criterion that works against many services, such as education, medical care and cultural activities, which are characteristically very labour-intensive. However, services are very diverse, ranging from very capital-intensive ones, such as banking, broadcasting and electric utilities, to the most labour-intensive, such as retail and wholesale trade (Kutscher and Mark 1983).

The intangible nature of services makes the measurement of productivity (output/worker) more difficult than in manufacturing, where products are standardized. Many services involve 'person-processing' in addition to information-processing, changing the state of people through educational, medical or social services (Gershuny and Miles 1983: 137–8). The output of services is hard to measure, as in, for example, an education or a surgical operation, because quality is an important dimension (Waite 1988: 13). Baumol, Blackman and Wolff (1989) suggest a new approach to measuring productivity in services, based on increased productive capacity. It remains true, however, that productivity measurement is problematic.

The service sector has been greatly affected by the rapid diffusion of information-based technology and computers (Barras 1990). Computer information services are particularly important to the service sector because many service industries (e.g. banking, finance, health, transportation, utilities, communications and business services) require substantial information handling (Quinn,

Baruch and Paquette 1987; Waite 1988). This trend is significant because it radically changes the skills necessary for such jobs (Cyert and Mowery 1987; Guile and Quinn 1988; Stanback 1987). The expected measurable rise in productivity from this capital investment, however, has not accompanied this increase in capital intensity.

Brynjolfsson (1993) clears up much of the confusion in the 'productivity paradox' surrounding investment in information technology (IT). Investment in computers has seemingly failed to spark increased productivity in the firms and industries adopting the new technology. Most of the explanation, it seems, is a result of poor measurement inherent in productivity accounting, especially in its inability to capture either changes in the quality of output or benefits from greater flexibility (but not greater quantity) of output (Brynjolfsson 1993). Indeed, Brynjolfsson and Hitt (1996) have found, using a detailed disaggregated data set, that investment in IT is significantly related to output growth. As one of the first studies to demonstrate this, it also attests to the need for reorganization of work in order for firms to benefit from computer technology (Gleckman et al. 1993). Brynjolfsson et al. (1994) suggest that IT leads to smaller firm sizes as firms are able to connect efficiently outside the organization, creating a 'connected corporation' (Lewis 1995). Kuttner (1993) identifies a second lingering productivity paradox in the USA: that of wages falling while productivity is rising. Given the standard connection made between productivity growth and rising standards of living, this is truly a paradox, but one which Bernstein (1995) explains by outsourcing and closures reducing job security.

In the absence of conventional relationships between productivity and investment, Port, King and Hampton (1988) suggest that the 'new math of productivity' uses time as the key variable, not return on investment, especially in investments to improve flexibility. Further, measuring knowledge within firms is now an objective in order to measure company intellectual capital (Stewart 1994a,b) and intangible assets such as knowledge and its contribution to company productivity and competitiveness (Merrifield 1994; Stewart 1995). The importance of knowledge is such that several firms have created the executive position of 'chief knowledge officer'. This is recognition of the belief that knowledge is *produced* and that its production can be managed (Gibbons et al. 1994).

Objections to the neoclassical model relating to technology are quite serious. Even respected economists such as Nelson (1981) have called it an 'art form' that ignores firm behaviour, including R&D, learning, and the nature of knowledge to not diffuse to all competitors. Recent views of productivity have focused on the dynamics of technical change at the level of the firm (Carlsson 1981; Cohen and Levinthal 1994; Dosi 1988; Gold 1979; Griliches 1984; Nelson 1981). Thomas (1986) discusses these ideas in a regional context. Rather than begin with the premise of an equilibrium of identical firms, companies are considered to vary – as they do in reality – in organization, and in their knowledge about and access to technology (Nelson 1981). Research and development (R&D) efforts persistently appear as important indicators of general progressiveness at the firm level in both neoclassical formulations and in 'evolutionary' theories of economic change (Dosi 1988; Nelson and Winter 1982). The model also neglects some essential characteristics of regional economies (Richardson 1973). In particular, regional production structures are assumed to be identical, despite substantial differences across regions in products, capital and labour inputs, and efficiency (Beeson and Hustad 1989; Clark, Gertler and Whiteman 1986; Gertler 1984; Lande 1978; Luger and Evans 1988).

New growth theories

Fagerberg (1994) identifies a number of interdependencies between technological progress and capital and labour, which make conventional methods of productivity growth accounting 'shaky' and, in effect, reliant on cumulative causation. Consequently, recent theoretical efforts have gone primarily into making technological advance endogenous, or internal, to models of economic growth. The 'new growth theories', reviewed by Nelson (1994a), Pack (1994), Petit (1995) and Romer (1994), include investments in R&D, in infrastructure and in human capital through education, which in turn generate spillovers and externalities, including economies of scale and cumulative causation. Representative works include Grossman and Helpman (1991), Jones (1995) and Romer (1990).

The conventional production function is expanded to include research, R, physical capital, K, and human capital, H. Thus, output is a function of all three inputs, or

$$Y = F(R, K, H) \qquad (2.4)$$

By aggregating R, K and H into a broad measure of capital, X, this becomes a linear function

$$Y = AX \qquad (2.5)$$

Externalities are invoked as offsetting diminishing returns. Another route to equation (2.5) may be taken by postulating that an increasing variety or quality of machinery offsets the tendency to diminishing returns, and that R&D is necessary to attain enhanced variety or quality (Grossman and Helpman 1991; Pack 1994; Romer 1990). Both the presence of externalities and monopoly power are 'important novelties' in the new growth theories (Verspagen 1992). In this formulation, A is a technological constant that represents a host of nationally (and regionally) distinct characteristics. However, as Pack (1994) stresses, testing such a model empirically leads to many difficulties. Verspagen (1992: 647), for example, notes that increasing returns to human capital leads to the conclusion that countries with the largest populations should experience the highest growth rates, which does not square with the facts. A second problem is the fact, acknowledged by Romer (1994: 20), that no data are available on local production of knowledge or inward flows of knowledge, leading researchers to use investment in physical capital as the principal empirical variable. Indeed, 'it is extremely difficult to identify anything approximating to a knowledge-producing sector in real economies' (Stern 1991: 127). Employing proxies,

Sengupta (1993) finds the new growth theory to account rather well for the process of growth in Korea. Moreover, significant problems remain over how human capital should be measured in empirical work; for example, whether stocks of, or increases in, education best reflect human capital (Gemmell 1996).

The basic notions – that technical change is largely endogenous, that technology is to some extent proprietary, and that growth from technical advance involves externalities and economies of scale – are not new, as Nelson (1994a: 291) emphasizes. The formal, mathematical modelling found in the new growth theories has simply captured much of what Nelson and others had been saying for some time (Nelson 1981; Nelson and Winter 1982). Nelson (1994a) asserts that the new formal growth theory is unlikely to change the basic understandings about economic growth, which had been largely known since the 1950s. The difference between 'appreciative' theory and formal, mathematical theory is not unlike the void seen in geography between Marxist theories and those derived from neoclassical origins (Bourne 1988). However, differences in labour skills, a consistent finding in empirical research (Ke and Bergman 1995; Kelley 1994), have not yet been incorporated realistically into models of growth and productivity.

A great deal of research on the topic of catch-up (Baumol, Nelson and Wolff 1994) also suggests that more is at work in economic growth than what can be captured by capital and labour, however broadly these are conceived. In particular, as Nelson (1981, 1994b, 1995) emphasizes, institutions matter greatly, and these vary from country to country. The national variation in not only technological capability, but also in economic and social values and ways of thinking, has taken on great importance, to some extent because of Porter's (1990) influential book, *The Competitive Advantage of Nations*. Porter emphasized the cross-national variation found in a multitude of political, social, legal and institutional elements of countries which affected profoundly their competitiveness in different industries. His framework suggests that these are variations that could be studied systematically, and national differences in policy regimes (Roobeek 1990) and in business cultures (Hampden-Turner and Trompenaars 1993) have been identified. A related flurry of research has focused on *national systems of innovation*, specifically those that influence the national variations in technological capability. Institutions and cultural and social norms also vary from place to place within countries, including differences in local technical culture that persist within nations (Chapter 7).

An important literature, developed separately from productivity and growth accounting, focuses on technology and more specifically on 'technology gaps' that have developed historically. The fundamental difference between the neoclassical model and technology-gap theories is the assumption in the former that technology is a public good, uniformly available. By contrast, technology-gap thinking takes technological differences as given, and as the prime cause of income differences across countries (Fagerberg 1994). The technology-gap theories, then, are also non-neoclassical, but are based primarily at the national scale and often relate to the less developed countries (Fagerberg 1988). Perez and Soete (1988) suggest that much of the knowledge needed to enter a technology in its early phase is publicly available through universities and other public sources, and only later becomes private or proprietary.

A fundamental flaw of both the neoclassical model and the new growth theory is a lack of attention to institutions and institutional change (Freeman 1994a). Indeed, Pack (1994) finds it ironic that the new growth theories focus on R&D and externalities rather than on organizations and institutions. As Nelson (1981: 1031) puts it, the neoclassical 'institutional environment is very simple – there is no place in the structure for labor unions, banking systems, schools, or regulatory regimes.' An equally restrictive aspect of the neoclassical model is the assumption that technological knowledge is a public good, freely available to all firms. Consequently, a major new area of research and modelling is in evolutionary or neo-Schumpeterian models and theories.

Evolutionary theories

An alternative approach for understanding productivity and growth comes from the Schumpeterian legacy. Schumpeter (1934) originally published his *Theory of Economic Development* in 1911, followed by work on business cycles in 1939. In particular, his concept of 'creative destruction' – of change taking place in capitalism primarily through radical innovations or other breakthroughs which make established competence and equipment obsolete – has become a metaphor for technological change (see Abernathy and Clark 1985). Largely because of the dominance of the neoclassical approach within economics, but also because of the difficulty of modelling Schumpeterian concepts, evolutionary theory has not yet had a major impact on economic growth theory, despite the endogeneity of technological progress (Brouwer 1991). In contrast to neoclassical models, evolutionary theories explicitly incorporate the variety of products, processes, economic agents and institutions that exist in the economy (Antonelli 1995: 93–5; Carlsson 1994; Dosi and Orsenigo 1994). However, because they tend to be more verbal (or 'appreciative') and because they are not tied to general equilibrium, evolutionary models have yet to find much favour among economic theorists (Clark and Juma 1988; Nelson 1994a,b). Examples of evolutionary approaches include Aghion and Howitt (1993), Arthur (1988), Brouwer (1991), Dosi *et al.* (1995), Nelson and Winter (1982), Nelson (1986a), Silverberg (1988, 1990), Silverberg and Lehnert (1994), and Silverberg and Verspagen (1994). The model of Dosi *et al.* (1995), for example, focuses on differences (or asymmetries) in firm performance (e.g. profits) and on life-cycle and sector-specific differences. The model's results are far from equilibrium, which, the authors assert, is as it should be.

The instability (or disequilibrium) and variety found in reality are the strengths of the evolutionary theories. In addition, realistic portrayals of the process of diffusion and the differential accumulation of technological capability in firms move beyond Schumpeter's own work (Freeman 1994b; Silverberg 1990). Boyer (1993) and Freeman (1994b) identify the advantages of neo-Schumpeterian models which 'try to formalize really existing economies' (Boyer 1993: 96).

Evolutionary modelling has been blended into Marxist accounts of technical change (Boyer 1988a; Webber, Sheppard and Rigby 1992). At the level of regions, Steiner (1990) is among the few who have attempted to address regions from an evolutionary perspective, stressing the adaptability or flexibility of regions (see also Killick 1995a). Antonelli (1995) has focused on 'localized' technological change, which builds from the concept of learning as constraining the range of possibilities within which technological change can occur, affecting the way in which diffusion takes place. 'Regional localization', however, is only a minor extension of his evolutionary approach.

Regional growth in equilibrium and disequilibrium

The analysis of regional growth, placed into the accepted neoclassical framework of competitive equilibrium by Borts and Stein (1964), has not moved much beyond it (Gertler 1984). Although this simplifies economic activity to an analytically manageable form, it neglects dynamic elements which do not easily collapse into capital and labour. As Gerking's (1994) review of research into regional productivity differences shows, regional research on this topic remains derivative of older attempts to dissect total factor productivity across regions (Hulten and Schwab 1984; Moomaw and Williams 1991). Thus far, the new growth theories, technology-gap concepts and evolutionary models have had little effect on formal modelling at the regional scale. In part, as well, regional research has been plagued by shortages and inconsistencies in data availability, especially for measuring capital stocks (Gerking 1994). The new estimates of Rigby (1995), therefore, are an important contribution.

The neoclassical model incorporates a theory of factor mobility as well as a theory of growth, and it has dominated research on capital and labour mobility. Given identical production functions in all regions, labour flows from low-wage to high-wage regions, and capital (or investment) flows in the opposite direction, since high wages imply low returns on capital, and low wages result in high returns. These flows continue until returns (wages) are equal in each region (Greenwood 1985). In this setting, a region can grow only if labour or capital flows there from other regions (Anderson 1976; Richardson 1971: 95). Factor mobility remains a key element in nearly all enhancements of the neoclassical model (Carlberg 1981; Clark, Gertler and Whiteman 1986; Ghali, Akiyama and Fujiwara 1981).

Neoclassical theory sees capital as malleable, able to assume new forms and incorporate new technologies as well as to change location without restriction (Gertler 1984). Since capital and labour are substitutes, labour-saving investment is a preferred means of increasing output. In the neoclassical model, labour is treated as a homogeneous input as well, with no recognition of varying skills or capabilities, and differences in the growth of output 'are due ultimately to variations between regions in the growth of their labour force' (Krugman 1994c; McCombie 1988a: 270). Labour-saving investment can result in 'de-skilling' of work, as tasks are simplified or relegated to machines, often then requiring labour with no particular skill (Braverman 1974; Hirschhorn 1984; Massey

1995; Shaiken 1984). The regional production function was adopted from the national scale to the regional scale with few if any modifications (Richardson 1973: 22–9). Thus, it is difficult for it to account for regional variations in labour skill and technology (Ke and Bergman 1995).

As at the international level, the neoclassical process of regional growth ultimately results in *convergence* in per capita incomes because, in the neoclassical model, growth is 'essentially a reallocative process' (Borts and Stein 1964: 106; McCombie 1988a). The evidence through the 1970s seemed to confirm such ideas in North America (Hewings 1977: 148–51; Newman 1984), the UK (Diamond and Spence 1983) and Spain (Cuadrado Roura 1982). The 1980s brought a return of widening differences in regional incomes in Japan (Abe and Alden 1988), the UK (Martin 1988, 1993), the USA (Carlino 1992; Hansen 1988), and throughout Europe (Dunford 1993; Suarez-Villa and Cuadrado-Roura 1993a). Thus, the convergence theory at the regional level seemed weaker than it did during the 1970s, given that divergence is attributed to an unexplained 'short-run adjustment to a new long-run equilibrium' (Carlino 1992: 12). In addition, Tam and Persky (1982) have documented increasing inequality *within* regions of the USA at the same time that interregional convergence was taking place.

The conflict between interregional equity and national efficiency has been a thorny issue in regional theory and policy for some time. In general, the most rapid rates of growth occur when economic activity has concentrated in large urban regions, maximizing national efficiency, a process which leads to inequality between regions. An inverted U-shaped curve, which describes this increasing divergence followed by convergence, is an expected pattern during the course of economic development (Adelman and Robinson 1989; Williamson 1965). During periods of rapid national growth, the gap between rich and poor areas can become quite large, as Lakshmanan and Hua (1987) show occurred in China from 1979 to 1984. A 'new Great Wall' between rural areas and rapidly growing urban areas has widened the gap between them in the Chinese push for growth (Aguinier 1988; Linge and Forbes 1990). Although there is serious reason to question the empirical inverted-U pattern as a general model or as a necessary evil (Gilbert and Goodman 1976; Hollier 1988), it continues to be part of the conventional wisdom in development studies (Alonso 1980a; Mera 1974; Renaud 1973).

A large amount of equilibrium-oriented regional economic research, especially in the USA, has attempted to account for migration (or interregional labour mobility) in terms of response to differentials in interregional rates of return to labour (wage levels) (Gober-Myers 1978; Greenwood 1975). Recent research has shifted from the neoclassical to a more pragmatic approach, primarily by adding amenities, climate, income growth and cost of living as further attractions – in addition to higher wages (Kahley 1991; Knapp and Graves 1989; Walters 1994).

The interplay between migration and regional growth is complex and includes a variety of issues, such as selectivity of migrants, whereby the most informed   and   most   productive   have   the   highest   propensity   to   move

(Greenwood and Hunt 1984). As discussed above, migration in the neoclassical paradigm is seen as an equilibrating process, but substantial evidence to the contrary has weakened appreciably its ties to the neoclassical paradigm (Clark and Ballard 1981; Knapp and Graves 1989). Migrants respond to much more than simply income levels; the possibility of an income gain is a necessary but by no means sufficient condition for migration. Mobility costs, spatial frictions, non-economic resistances to migration, occupation, job opportunities and family ties all enter into a migration decision (Gordon 1995; Greenwood 1985; Isserman *et al.* 1986). In addition to migration, other factors, such as fertility, are part of the picture of population and labour force change in a region (Alonso 1980b; Ettlinger 1988). The interrelationships between population, policy and well-being stand out most strongly in urban areas (Paris 1995). Causes and effects of international migration have also been topics of recent research (Beaverstock 1994; Greenwood 1994).

The study of capital movement, in contrast to the study of labour mobility, is more perplexing. Since capital flows are much more difficult to measure (Persky and Klein 1975; Richardson 1973: 103–13), capital investment flows are commonly measured by manufacturing location decisions, which represent only a subset of capital investment decisions. By virtually any measure used, however, capital is not available equally across space (Gertler 1984). The locational decisions of both people and of firms rely on information which is often far from perfect (thus violating one of the key assumptions of the neoclassical theory). Workers are not equally aware of wages in all places, and may migrate for non-economic reasons. Investors also have incomplete information about regional differentials in the return on capital, making such differentials a poor explanation of the inter-regional mobility of capital. Capital is not perfectly mobile for two other reasons. First, investments are often 'lumpy', whereby they must be made in given units that may be relatively large (e.g. a paper mill or an automobile assembly plant of minimum efficient size). Second, 'industrial inertia' suggests that once firms have made an investment at a location, the advantages of remaining there are greater than from moving elsewhere; this tendency may be far less pronounced than in the past (Clark and Wrigley 1995).

Disequilibrium models of regional growth

Alternatives to the equilibrium processes inherent in the neoclassical model are based explicitly or implicitly on the unbalanced growth in the circular–cumulative causation model. The process of circular and cumulative causation attempts to include a fuller set of the changes that take place within a region as growth takes place and reinforces prior growth, among them polarization and agglomeration economies. Attributable initially to Myrdal (1957), more complex conceptualizations have been developed by Thompson (1965), Kaldor (1970) and Pred (1977). Cumulative causation suggests that if a region gains some initial advantage, new growth and multiplier effects will tend to concentrate in this already expanding region, rather than in other regions. The effect goes beyond the multiplier effect. Differences in regional productivity growth are predominantly due to differences in output growth, which allow some regions to benefit more than others from economies of scale and agglomeration. Krugman (1995) criticizes simple cumulative causation models, but fails to acknowledge the more sophisticated variants developed in the last decade or so.

In these models, growth becomes self-reinforcing with strong endogenous forces tending to increase regional differences in productivity growth, which may persist for a long time (Dosi, Pavitt and Soete 1990; McCombie 1988b). In more formal presentations, this Verdoorn–Kaldor 'law' leads to cumulative causation: increased investment occurs in faster-growing regions, thereby reinforcing their higher growth (Dosi, Pavitt and Soete 1990; Swales 1983; Thirlwall 1983). Dosi (1984: 171) suggests that the Verdoorn–Kaldor relation captures the effect of technical change that is not embodied in capital equipment, as will be the case in more innovative sectors. Amable (1993) provides an application of such a model at the international scale. Antonelli (1995: 76–79) shows that the new growth theories implicitly capture the Kaldorian relationship between investment and productivity. The 'new growth theory' model of Englmann and Walz (1995) demonstrates that, with knowledge spillovers, agglomeration in one region is not necessarily a long-run situation.

To a large extent, cumulative causation is a natural corollary of agglomeration economies (Gore 1984: 49). 'Large urban regions are expected, ceteris paribus, to have higher rates of innovation, more rapid adoption of innovations, and higher proportions of skilled workers than smaller places' even if technological change is not endogenous to the process (Malecki and Varaiya 1986: 633; Meyer 1977). This process of cumulative causation as a result of economies of scale is the basis for Krugman's (1991, 1995) model of urban–rural differences. His model is, in effect, a simple core–periphery model with extremely simplifying assumptions.

Most formal models of disequilibrium regional growth largely keep to the rudimentary capital–labour constituents of economic activity, but structure them in a way that leads to outcomes other than regional equilibrium. Notable efforts at developing such a regional growth theory include Siebert (1969) and Richardson (1973). Virtually all such efforts strive to incorporate agglomeration economies and other trappings of cumulative causation. As with neoclassical flows of capital and labour, there is more than a grain of truth in models which account for cumulative processes favouring large regions. Indeed, Scott's (1988b,c) analyses of agglomeration economies suggest little decline in their influence. The advantages to both workers and firms from agglomeration are substantial. Proximity between employers and workers facilitates specialization and lowers training costs for firms. Employers have access to pools of labour in times of growth, and the costs and time of search for both parties is lower (Kim 1987; Pascal and McCall 1980). The process of agglomeration is returned to in Chapter 4.

In the sense that they are demand-oriented, the non-equilibrium approaches are 'post-Keynesian,' with growth responding to the rate of expansion of demand (McCombie 1988b). The Verdoorn–Kaldor 'law', for example, concerns the relationship between the growth rate of labour productivity and the rate of growth of output. A region's growth rate depends on several factors: the income elasticity and price elasticities of demand for its exports (as the economic base model posits), the rate of inflation, and the Verdoorn effect, which assumes rates of investment and productivity growth occur where output growth is greatest – a version of cumulative causation (Thirlwall 1974: 7). This particular disequilibrium model also concludes that manufacturing is the engine of growth, in concurrence with the 'manufacturing matters' school in the controversy over the role of the service sector discussed in Chapter 1 (Thirlwall 1983).

Among the strong arguments in favour of cumulative causation models was a need to allow for increasing returns due to scale and agglomeration economies in rich regions. Many researchers during the 1970s attempted to account for the observed ability of established regions to remain centres of production and economic capacity (Dixon and Thirlwall 1975; Pred 1977; Richardson 1973; Thirlwall 1974). Most accounts have relied on agglomeration economies, which are present to a greater degree in large cities and which have several functions in regional growth: to boost the rate of technical progress and productivity, to attract industry and capital into a region, to influence the migration decisions of households, and to improve the intra-regional spatial structure (Richardson 1973: 175–96). In operational terms, however, the effect of urban size in these models became primarily one of innovation diffusion down the urban hierarchy (Richardson 1973). Agglomeration economies, rather than technology, become the driving force behind regional growth in these models.

The decline of older industrial cities and the rise of industrial districts and peripheral areas during the 1980s complicated the picture, yet agglomeration remains central (Scott 1988b, 1995). Clark, Gertler and Whiteman (1986) cite investment flows out of large cities and into peripheral areas as evidence counter to agglomeration and cumulative causation. However, agglomeration and cumulative causation remain powerful concepts but, as at the level of the firm, lack of investment in new technology can lead to decline. For both firms and places, investment in technology is critical to future growth.

The process of technological change

We now turn to the capability and potential of places to control as well as to respond to economic change. By directing attention to local or indigenous capability, however, we see that microeconomic behaviour (i.e. the decisions and actions of individual people and firms) is more critical to the process of change than are larger, 'top-down' processes. As Dosi (1988: 1131) puts it, 'Innovative activities present – to different degrees – firm-specific, local, and cumulative features.' In particular, the ability of people and of organizations to experiment with, to learn and to become proficient in new technologies has a significance beyond that captured in past, or current, theoretical or policy milieux. Economists' use of the word 'local' is typically meant in the context of technological change, related to previous techniques in that the selection and adoption of new technology is influenced by the techniques already in use, and only as an afterthought to refer to a specific locality (Antonelli 1995; Stiglitz

1987). Rosenberg (1982: 8) describes the geographical variation in technological capabilities:

> One of the most compelling facts of history is that there have been enormous differences in the capacity of different societies to generate technical innovations that are suitable to their economic needs. Moreover, there has also been extreme variability in the willingness and ease with which societies have adopted and utilized technological innovations developed elsewhere. And, in addition, individual societies have themselves changed markedly over the course of their own separate histories in the extent and intensity of their technological dynamism. Clearly, the reasons for these differences, which are not well understood, are tied in numerous and complex ways to the functioning of the larger social systems, their institutions, values, and incentive structures.

The remainder of this chapter examines the manner in which technology is generated, acquired and utilized – all of which profoundly influence the process of economic development. The source of technology may be endogenous (or internal), generated primarily through research and development (R&D), a topic which Chapter 5 examines in greater detail. Alternatively, it can be obtained from exogenous (or external) sources – other people, other firms, other regions. If external sources are relied upon, the successful integration of new ideas and techniques demands an internal capability to assimilate external knowledge. This competence to discover, select, adopt, utilize, learn and improve new technology is a key determinant of the economic success of firms, of their employees, and consequently of the regions in which they are located.

The linear model

Technological change is a complex process – a black box – whose workings are only partially understood (Rosenberg 1982, 1994). The complexity lies partially in the diverse collection of phenomena which can be called 'innovation'. Bienaymé (1986: 139) distinguishes between (1) product innovations, (2) innovations destined to resolve, circumvent or eliminate a technical difficulty in manufacture or to improve services, (3) innovation for the purpose of saving inputs (e.g. energy conservation, automation, robotization), and (4) innovation to improve the conditions of work (security or safety measures). These very different entities have made generalization difficult. Most others refer to radically new innovations, minor innovations and incremental innovations (Ali 1994; Utterback 1994).

The 'linear model' of innovation (Figure 2.1) provides the conventional wisdom which underlies most policy thinking about technology and economic development. This 'pipeline' model (Brooks 1994), or 'ladder of science' (Gomory 1989), seemed to correspond to many of the visible successes of

Figure 2.1   The linear model of technological change.

science during and just after World War II, such as radar, the transistor, the computer, the laser, and biotechnology applications. The linear model suggests that the sequence from research through development to production and marketing is the standard or predominant path of innovation in both firms and national economies (Buswell 1983; Marquis 1988). In practice, the linear process is also described as a 'bucket brigade':

> Someone in the research lab comes up with an idea. Then it is passed on to the engineering department, which converts it into a design. Next, manufacturing gets specifications from engineering and figures out how to make the thing. At last, responsibility for the finished product is dumped on marketing (Mitchell 1989: 107).

The implications of the linear model for public policy are also straightforward. If the level of R&D is increased, for example, a corresponding increase in technological innovation should (eventually) follow. Carrying the argument one step further, since it is basic research from which innovation ultimately flows, government science and industrial policy must include measures aimed at achieving an appropriate balance between basic and applied research (Ronayne 1984: 64–5). The linear model is also an outcome of the neoclassical framework that finds 'market failure' in basic research (K. Smith 1995). The type of knowledge which flows from this effort is characterized by high risk, indivisibilities (and often large minimum scale), and difficulties in appropriating (monopolizing) the returns or benefits. Thus governments must engage in or subsidize basic research and create property rights in the 'intellectual property' that results via patents and other means.

Despite its appealing logic, most observers now stress the shortcomings of the linear model, especially the diversity of activities that make up the innovation process, the variation across industries, and the apparent disorderliness of the innovation process in reality (Autio and Laamanen 1995; Dosi 1988; Kline and Rosenberg 1986). Moreover, R&D activities represent only a portion of the entire set of activities and efforts in which firms engage in order to obtain and assimilate new technological knowledge (Leonard-Barton 1995; Nonaka and Takeuchi 1995; Thomson 1993). Patel and Pavitt (1994a) estimate the neglected portion of technical change at 40 per cent. Kline and Rosenberg (1986) maintain that technological change was never such a simple process in any firm, and have proposed an interacting, iterative model of the process of innovation as shown in Figure 2.2. Numerous feedbacks take place as solutions are sought to production problems, as new products are developed to meet a customer's needs, and as learning and process innovation take place during production (Casson 1987: 21–22; Shaw 1994; Teece 1988). Some learning involves generic knowledge, such as new scientific findings; other knowledge is firm-specific, usually related to technology platforms that can give rise to a variety of outputs (Myers and Rosenbloom 1996).

Market-driven innovation and rapidly changing technology suggest to corporate managers that the linear model is too slow and fraught with organizational barriers which contribute to failure (Frey 1989). More importantly, if

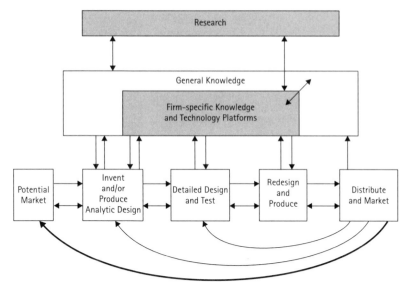

Figure 2.2   Feedbacks and interactions in the process of innovation. Source: based on Kline and Rosenberg (1986: 290, Figure 3) and Myers and Rosenbloom (1996: 216, Figure 9–3).

process R&D is not merely ignored until the end, it has the advantage of creating for a firm distinctive capabilities, in addition to reducing the time and lowering the costs of innovation (Pisano and Wheelwright 1995). In general, R&D by firms can be thought to serve two functions: learning as well as the pursuit of product and process innovation (Cohen and Levinthal 1989). These 'two faces of R&D' provide a firm with the awareness of and some degree of readiness to absorb new technologies – even those which originate from outside the firm and outside the industry (Cohen and Levinthal 1990, 1994).

New product innovations are the primary route of entry of new firms and new industries, and thus the greatest source of new jobs in an economy. Computers, electronics and biotechnology are prominent current examples of the job-creating effects of product innovation. Successive generations of innovations have permitted new firms to enter these industries and have created jobs in old firms. This process of 'creative destruction' occurs more in some settings than in others. Scherer (1982) found that in the USA, 74 per cent of firms' R&D efforts are aimed at new products, and only 26 per cent at internal processes. By 1992, the rate of product innovation had grown to 80 per cent (Caravatti 1992). In Italy, by contrast, 19.6 per cent of firms introduced only product innovations, 24.1 per cent only process innovations, and 56.3 per cent introduced both products and processes (Cesaratto and Sirilli 1992).

Despite its simplicity, elements of the linear model of technological change remain appropriate for understanding the dynamic nature of technology within economic activity. Particularly when viewed within the framework of market competition, product and process innovation and competition over time highlight flows of knowledge that originate in scientific research and manifest themselves in products, processes and new economic activity. The following section discusses in turn each of the components of the linear model, aiming to show the possible direct paths to regional growth and development. Clearly, the route will differ among firms and is often more circuitous and indirect, because of the feedback loops which are present (Figure 2.2). However, it is valuable none the less to assess the potential impact of each component.

Basic and applied research

The starting point of technological innovation in the linear model of technology is basic research. Basic, or scientific, research is primarily the purview of universities and government research institutes, although some is conducted at the central laboratories of large firms. For example, the French firm Thomson spends 3 per cent of its total R&D budget on basic research (Quéré 1994); 4.2 per cent of R&D projects of Norwegian firms had a time horizon of five or more years (Smith and Vidvei 1992). US firms, by contrast, invest an average of only 1.7 per cent in basic research (Whiteley, Bean and Russo 1996), indicative of a long decline in 'unfettered' research (Odlyzko 1996; Rosenbloom and Spencer 1996). Indeed, there are good reasons for firms to engage in basic research, despite its inherently high risks, long time horizon before profitability, and limited appropriability. The principal reason is what are called 'first-mover advantages' (Rosenberg 1990a), and this is considered by firms as by far the most effective means of capturing the profit from innovation – surpassing secrecy, patents and trademarks (Deiaco 1992).

The outcome of basic research is not a package of information or knowledge; rather, basic research, especially that conducted in universities and research institutes, constitutes the principal means of training new researchers. The skills and search processes embodied in these individuals go beyond the cumulative body of knowledge which also results (Pavitt 1993). Policies to support (subsidize) both institutions and the basic research activities that go on within them are justified since the results of basic research are published and otherwise public, and those trained can and do move elsewhere (Pavitt 1993: 38). For firms, their overall R&D effort, including basic research through product and process innovation, results in increased total factor productivity, as shown in Figure 2.3 (Bean 1995).

The feedbacks within the innovation process and the frequent and intermittent need for new scientific knowledge have led to a focus on the links between industry and academic institutions (Brooks 1994; Mogee 1980; Rosenberg 1991). These links are also used as a justification for increasing local or regional R&D funding: the expectation is that firms will form these links in the area, and that innovations and production will take place locally as well. Studies of university–industry links show that there is little real connection on which regional economic development could be based. The most important ties are often made across long distances, and with a fairly small number of prestigious institutions (Howells 1986; Massey, Quintas and Wield 1992). Although academics 'have a firm belief' in the linear model, industry repre-

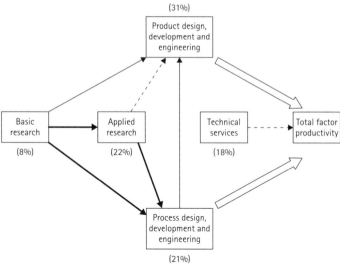

Figure 2.3 The impact of research and development activities on productivity. Source: adapted from Bean (1995: 29, Figure 11).

sentatives see academic research as contributing only indirectly to industrial innovation (as shown in Figure 2.3) through basic research and training activities (Rosenberg and Nelson 1994: 345). At the same time, firms typically organize their own R&D and downstream activities according to the linear model (Henry, Massey and Wield 1995). Overall, academic research is far from the only source of technology for firms. As Table 2.2 shows, users and competitors are major sources of innovative ideas (von Hippel 1988).

Applied research is the typical entry point of industrial firms into the innovation process, since they commonly undertake relatively little fundamental or basic research. At the stage of applied research, however, the capabilities of many firms match or exceed those of many universities and research institutes. Rosenberg and Nelson (1994) show that applied sciences and engineering in universities are considered more relevant to industrial technology than are basic sciences, such as physics or mathematics. Even the applied sciences provide relatively low percentages of the basis for new products and processes in all sectors except pharmaceuticals (Rosenberg and Nelson 1994: 343–4). In the applied research stage, potential products are already envisioned, although considerable effort – more focused in nature than in basic research – might still be necessary.

The biotechnology industry (considered a part of the pharmaceutical sector) illustrates well the place of applied research in the technological innovation process. Biotechnology has followed rather closely the linear sequence from university-based scientific research through to the marketing of innovative new products. The example of biotechnology also exemplifies the entry of large firms into the innovation process. Firms primarily from the pharmaceutical industry, but also from the agricultural products and chemicals sectors, have attempted both to influence the direction of research and to draw upon the

Table 2.2   Sources of innovative ideas in manufacturing.

Source of ideas	Percentage of firms ranking a source as 'important' or 'very important'
Users	86.0
Competitive situation	76.7
Internal R&D	70.3
Marketing department	61.0
Top management	60.3
Cooperation with other companies	40.6
Production department	32.2
Acquisition of equipment	29.5
Cooperation with universities	23.9
Public sector purchases	17.2
Consultants	15.1
Suppliers	13.1

Source: adapted from Deiaco (1992: 43, Table 5).

entrepreneurial energies of small firms and university scientists through equity investments, joint ventures, and contracts with university researchers (Kenney 1986). Indeed, networks linking research in firms, universities and research institutes are essential to this industry, and both the largest firms and new, small ones are important sources of innovation (Bower 1993; della Valle and Gambardella 1993; Grabowski and Vernon 1994). As commercial bio-technology products have emerged, small firms have joined with partners having manufacturing and marketing capabilities in order to compete in a global industry (Greis, Dibner and Bean 1995).

Product and process development

Product development is the last major stage in the linear model of innovation, and is that toward which the bulk of industrial R&D – outside Japan – is ori-ented (Caravatti 1992). Product development and refinement customarily occurs within product-line laboratories of large firms, rather than in central research facilities (Steele 1975). Interaction and 'coupling' with marketing and with manufacturing become critical as product design, production engineering and market acceptance all must be assessed and incorporated into decision-making. These tasks recur intermittently throughout a product's 'life', and perhaps more within firms which specialize and innovate as part of their routine activity (Sabel *et al.* 1987). Product development efforts face two critical needs: to shorten the 'cycle time' needed to produce a marketable product: and to maintain continual communication with customers and with other functions within and outside the firm that contribute to a successful new product (Calantone, Vickery and Droge 1995; Cooper and Kleinschmidt 1994, 1995; Cordero 1991; Millson, Raj and Wilemon 1992; Piore *et al.* 1994; Ulrich and

Eppinger 1995; Zangwill 1993). Many factors influence the speed and/or efficiency of innovation; Rothwell (1994a) lists 24 factors. There are disadvantages to accelerated product development, however, especially when it is focused on products that are quickly replaced by new products. Rapid innovation can become an end in itself, rather than a benefit for customers (Crawford 1992; Stalk and Webber 1993).

Process innovation is typically distinguished from product innovation, as if they are truly separate. In fact, the same technical advance typically is viewed as a product innovation by its producers and as a process innovation by those using it (Baldwin and Scott 1987: 144). A firm originating an innovation may be at either the producing or using level, and diffusion may occur upstream to producers, downstream to users, or horizontally to competitors of the innovator. The vast majority of process innovations in the service sector, in particular, are product innovations from the manufacturing sectors (Robson, Townsend and Pavitt 1988; Scherer 1982). As in product innovation, speed in process innovation confers a lead time ahead of competitors which provides appropriability outside the patent system (Harabi 1995).

Economic competitiveness is a product of the ability of firms to operate at the *best-practice* level in their industry. The traditional view of best practice focused almost solely on production technology (machinery, equipment, management practices, etc.), which ranges from the best currently known and available to the worst (often still used in poor countries). The spectrum from best-practice to worst-practice technology is largely a function of the age or vintage of capital equipment employed. Newer vintages will incorporate or embody newer concepts, techniques and knowledge which tend to give an advantage to firms – and regions – where newer technology is employed (Salter 1966; Varaiya and Wiseman 1981).

This traditional view has given way to a much broader understanding of best practice. This view extends beyond a firm to include its customers, suppliers, competitors and information sources (Leonard-Barton 1995; Trygg 1993). The development and nurturing of links to outside information networks goes well beyond what traditionally is encompassed by R&D (Håkansson 1989; Miller 1995; Rothwell 1992; Sweeney 1987). Yet, this concept of R&D as (among other functions) monitoring global sources of external information puts a firm in touch with the state of 'future best practice' (Mody, Suri and Tatikonda 1995; Ransley and Rogers 1994). Increasingly, best practice also includes issues of quality and customer satisfaction (Garvin 1987; Griffin *et al.* 1995). The need for networks and their links to outside knowledge becomes a key factor in all industries – not only in high-technology sectors. Custom products and meeting customers' requirements are common in semiconductors (Callahan and Diedrich 1992), machinery (Fransman 1984), and steel (Gold 1984).

Codified and tacit knowledge

Not all technological knowledge comes in the same form, just as it does not come from a single source. Technology is embodied in machinery and equipment, but this knowledge may be out of reach of customers or users without documentation and manuals that 'codify' it. These documents may be accessible or comprehensible only to repair technicians or others with adequate training. The fundamental knowledge is that which remains in the heads of the technical and research personnel of the manufacturer (Boisot 1995). The knowledge which they retain is tacit or 'fingertip' knowledge, as opposed to codified knowledge (David and Foray 1995; Kash 1989). Tacit knowledge flows primarily through informal networks, and these networks allow a firm to scan and to monitor both internal and external sources of knowledge (Faulkner, Senker and Velho 1995; Senker 1995).

Codified knowledge is that which is tangible in some way, usually in printed form, as in patent applications and scientific papers. Privately held knowledge and shared expertise, on the other hand, are tacit in nature, but they differ in the degree to which they are public or privately owned (Figure 2.4). Emergent technologies are likely to be uncodified, but information about them will diffuse to others outside the firm as they become key technologies for the firm or for the industry (Boisot 1995). Firms that do basic research can signal, through papers published by their researchers (a codified form), that they also possess other knowledge that cannot be (or has not yet been) published. This in turn raises their credibility for gathering information that can contribute to future research (Hicks 1995).

The organization of knowledge-based systems is far more complicated than the linear model, and has drawn considerably on understanding of Japanese approaches to learning and corporate management, which will be discussed in Chapter 3. A long line of research, both in advanced, high-tech environments, and from technology transfer, a topic which has a long and often isolated history, has focused on the need for technical competence in *both* the provider and the recipient (Chapter 8). If firms are 'learning organizations' then they must be able to learn – to gain knowledge – from many sources (Leonard-Barton 1995; Nevis, di Bella and Gould 1995). The simplest form of learning is 'learning by doing', suggested over 30 years ago by Arrow (1962) as a form of technology acquisition outside of formal R&D. The list of types of learning has expanded greatly over the years (Table 2.3). As a generalization, tacit knowledge is embodied in people, rather than in written form or in objects. Thus, it generally is acquired through recruitment (hiring), R&D and interpersonal networking (Faulkner, Senker and Velho 1995; Nonaka and Takeuchi 1995).

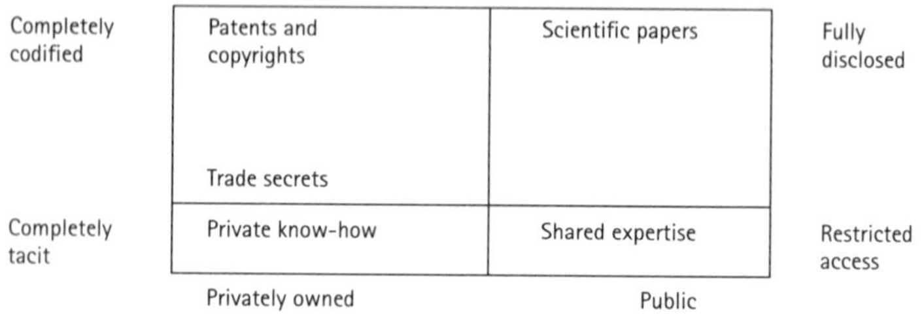

Completely codified	Patents and copyrights	Scientific papers	Fully disclosed
	Trade secrets		
Completely tacit	Private know-how	Shared expertise	Restricted access
	Privately owned	Public	

Figure 2.4   Relationships between types of knowledge and knowledge products. Source: based on David and Foray (1995: 33, Figure 1).

Table 2.3   Types or avenues of technological learning.

Learning by doing	(Arrow 1962)
Learning by using	(Rosenberg 1982)
Learning by operating; learning by changing; system performance feedback; learning by training; learning by hiring; learning by searching	(Bell 1984)
Learning by trying	(Fleck 1994; Rosenbloom and Cusumano 1987)
Learning by interacting	(Lundvall 1988)
Learning by selling	(Thomson 1989)
Learning from inter-industry spillover	(Malerba 1992a)
Learning to borrow	(David 1993)
Learning by failing	(Bahrami and Evans 1995)

An important element is the degree to which one can appropriate, or profit from, technical knowledge. Generally, as discussed earlier, patents confer property rights on the patent-holder, but it may well be that further know-how is needed in order to implement the technology efficiently. The 'regime of appropriability' – environmental factors other than firm and market structure – governs an innovator's ability to capture the profits generated by an innovation. The most important dimensions of such a regime are the nature of the technology and the strength of legal mechanisms of protection. Patents, copyrights and trade secrets (such as recipes and chemical formulas) are legal means of keeping a technology out of competitors' hands, but do not guarantee that imitation cannot take place (Teece 1986). Intellectual property law dilemmas related to legal copying *versus* piracy have exploded since digital technologies have emerged (*The Economist* 1996b; Lamberton 1994).

Most common is the evolutionary transformation of products and processes over time. In the early, 'preparadigmatic' stage of a technology's development, an innovation can become worthless quickly as new designs leapfrog it. As standardization of design takes place, an industry paradigm emerges, and the firm which gains most will tend to be the one which has a full array of *complementary assets* in order to exploit not only the innovative design but also to manufacture it competitively and bring it successfully to market (Dosi 1984; Teece 1986). Indeed, one kind of production may be physically impossible without another. Strength in electronic components, for instance, facilitates the development and production of robots and computers (Morgan and Sayer 1988: 21). Complementary assets include competitive manufacturing, distribution, service, a successful trade name, and complementary technologies (Cohen and Zysman 1987; Harabi 1995; Itami 1989; Porter 1987; Teece 1986: 289). A firm's technological capability, then, includes all of its complementary assets, and these allow a firm to profit from 'bunches' of related technologies when they appear (Delapierre 1988).

Neoclassical theory generally assumes regimes of 'tight' appropriability and zero transaction costs, where it does not matter whether an innovating firm has an in-house manufacturing capability, domestic or foreign. It can simply engage in arms-length contracting (such as licensing and co-production) for the sale of the output of the activity (R&D) in which it has a comparative advantage. In a regime of 'weak' appropriability, manufacturing may be necessary if an innovator is to appropriate the rents from an innovation. This is especially true where the requisite manufacturing assets are specialized to the innovation. If an innovator's manufacturing costs are higher than those of imitators, for example, the bulk of the profits will go to the imitators. Stobaugh (1985) illustrates with the example of petrochemical firms the importance of these activities beyond R&D.

Complementary assets are a persistent concern, where 'hollow' or 'virtual' corporations have lost capability in manufacturing and other functions (*Business Week* 1986; Cohen and Zysman 1987). Employees in foreign plants of transnational corporations acquire skills and know-how not maintained elsewhere in the firm. Malaysian experts from Intel's Penang factory had to be called in to help set up the chip assembly line of the firm's new factory in Arizona in 1983, because none of its US employees had that expertise any longer (Dreyfack and Port 1986). In essence, this situation is a result of separating R&D from the firm's complementary assets (Teece 1988: 277). Seen from another perspective, the critical knowledge in a situation such as setting up a production plant for a new product might be 'sticky' knowledge or information. It is 'sticky' because it can only be transferred as tacit knowledge or as learning by doing or by using, thereby requiring iterative consultation and travel (von Hippel 1994). In general, tacit information is hard to manage, suggesting that activities dependent on it should be kept inside the firms rather than trusted to outsiders (Chesbrough and Teece 1996).

The spectrum of complementary assets encompasses a range of capabilities which support and sustain the development and enhancement of technology. R&D capability is but one part of the range. The capabilities across the entire production process need not be present within a single firm. In fact, the strength of industrial districts lies in the inter-firm sharing of ideas and capabilities. The interconnectedness of sectors is a key aspect of the diffusion of product innovations from supplier sectors to user sectors (OECD 1995a; Pavitt 1984; Robson, Townsend and Pavitt 1988; Scherer 1982).

Production and the diffusion of process innovations

The diffusion of process innovation and the resulting distribution of best-practice technologies is a critical determinant of regional economic competitiveness. To a large extent, however, it remains somewhat a mystery as to why investment in new technologies varies from region to region. The simple and attractive finding, that the largest firms adopt new technologies earliest, has numerous proponents and supporters (Baldwin and Scott 1987; Ettlie and Rubenstein 1987; Mansfield 1993; Mansfield *et al.* 1977; Oakey, Thwaites and Nash 1980; Rees, Briggs and Oakey 1984; Stoneman and Kwon 1994). This finding is often used to justify the linear model of innovation, since large firms also do most of the R&D in any industry and some technologies require large investments in new plant (Ray 1989). In reality, there is no clear pattern of large-firm leadership, but a complementarity between large and small firms, as takes place in biotechnology (Rothwell and Dodgson 1994). Rather than size of firm, differences in 'the attitude of management' are likely to have the greatest impact on the application of new techniques (Ray 1969: 83).

For regions, the conclusion often drawn from the association between firm size and diffusion is that R&D leads to general economic competitiveness (Meyer-Krahmer 1985). For developing countries and peripheral regions, local or indigenous R&D is a major hurdle, since it demands managerial and technical skills often not found in local firms. The view of innovation as a continuous, nonlinear process thrusts complications into this argument. Innovations – especially process innovations – do not remain constant during their diffusion (Gold 1979; Rosenberg 1982). Rather, in large part because most process innovations are the product innovations developed by supplier firms, improvements and modifications alter the characteristics of the innovation over time. Thus, adoption may lag because of the expectation, based on past experience, that newer and better innovations will come along in the near future (Rosenberg 1982: 102–19).

A number of other factors contribute to delays in adoption, and again, regional variations are present. Adaptation and implementation within each adopting firm can greatly affect the rate of adoption of new technologies (Fawkes and Jacques 1987; Voss 1985). Perhaps even more important are access to information and channels of supply for the innovation (Ganz 1980) – factors which vary markedly from place to place (Brown 1981; Sweeney 1987). Information may be withheld or proprietary to an innovator, or it may slowly accumulate as firms adopt and gain experience with new technology. The availability of tacit 'expert information', often provided by third parties, such as consultants, government agents and early users, also affects the speed of diffusion (Mantel and Rosegger 1987). The slowness of diffusion is often noted as one of the reasons why equilibrium rarely characterizes economic change (Nelson 1981; Mowery 1988; Ray 1989; Soete and Turner 1984). There is also a need for 'unlearning' or discontinuing old practices associated with an older technology before implementation can take place (Abraham and Hayward 1984). Continual user–producer interaction is critical, which suggests that proximity (spatial proximity as well as proximity in terms of language, legal system and educational system) is important between producer and user (Fagerberg 1995; Gertler 1993).

One of the key aspects of the diffusion of innovations in industry is the organizational structure – the division of labour – of large firms. Process innovations are implemented earliest in branch plants of large, multilocational firms. If a process is still under development, it is likely to remain in the core region – the Southeast in Britain, the manufacturing belt in the USA – where most R&D in the firms takes place; once it is readied for standardized, large-volume production, adoption is found among smaller firms and peripheral locations (Oakey, Thwaites and Nash 1980; Rosenfeld 1992). All innovations are not alike, and the adoption of radical innovations is more likely to take place among larger firms, because they have the necessary technical specialists and knowledge to assimilate them, while incremental innovations are not as affected by firm size (Dewar and Dutton 1986).

The diffusion of product innovations

The diffusion of product innovations is somewhat different from that of processes. New products typically replace old ones but must be both manufactured and marketed. In British research, product innovations were 'adopted' earliest (i.e. produced) mainly in plants where R&D was done. In general, this can be thought of as typical of the pattern expected in the product/innovation cycle as the product moves from the innovation phase to the growth phase, where volume production is the priority. The combination of product and process innovation at this point relies on interaction between R&D and production within the firm (Utterback 1994). The implications of this geographical pattern for regional development are clear. Technological capability for new product R&D remains concentrated in those regions where early production and associated new employment also take place (Schmenner 1982; Thwaites 1983). Process innovations, which usually result in employment declines as new capital equipment reduces the demand for labour, are nevertheless related to product innovations. Product innovations, especially radical ones, usually require substantial process and organizational changes as well (Ettlie and Rubenstein 1987; Tidd 1993). It is large firms, although not the very largest, which tend to dominate in the introduction of radical product innovation.

The interaction between product and process innovation reinforces the organizing concept of best practice. In the process of diffusion, as goods and services flow between producers and users, a form of 'learning by interacting' occurs (Lundvall 1988). Firms which are active in product innovation tend to demand innovative components from their suppliers, thus reinforcing the concept of the 'user as innovator' (Foxall and Johnston 1987; von Hippel 1988). Firms which are abreast of the technical or machine dimension of technology tend to be competent in organizational, managerial and marketing technology as well. 'Knowledge technology' integrates these dimensions within a firm and provides the observed feedback, which weakens the linear model of innovation (Casson 1987; Shrivastana and Souder 1987). The various dimensions of technology provide the impetus for coupling or integration of different corporate functions, which is widely viewed as a critical element of the R&D strategy of firms (Chapter 3).

Knowledge as conceived here also enhances the ability of firms to utilize strategies for technology acquisition from outside the firm profitably, through licensing, joint ventures, equity participation in other firms, and outright acquisition of innovative firms (Friar and Horwitch 1986). Again, knowledge is multidimensional:

> Know-how depends in turn on 'know-that' and 'know-who', and upon being 'known-of'. Know-that is the factual knowledge that underpins all successful

problem-solving. Know-who is the knowledge of who is able to supply missing information and, more generally, of who is willing to buy or sell a resource that is not regularly traded on an organized market. Being known of means having a reputation that makes other people willing to offer information and, more generally, to become a trading partner (Casson 1987: 12).

For example, a reputation for product quality is invaluable in marketing a product, as a reputation for integrity and sound judgement is crucial in procuring finance for production (Casson 1987). The biotechnology industry discussed earlier illustrates how large firms, which must tend a broad portfolio of products and technologies, seek out new technological opportunities. Firms that acquire technology from outside must have substantial in-house R&D and it must be broad-based in order to integrate internal and external technology (Graham 1986). In essence, firms (and regions) follow technological trajectories which build on existing strengths (core competencies) and may have difficulty dealing with new paradigms (Dosi 1984; Nelson and Winter 1982).

The product cycle and economic development

Perhaps the dominant model for understanding the nature of technological change and regional economic development is the *product life-cycle* model and its corollaries, the profit cycle, the innovation cycle and the manufacturing process cycle (Hayes and Wheelwright 1988; Thomas 1975). These models describe the typical pattern of a product's development and production during its 'life': from R&D to market success to ultimate decline and replacement by new products (Figure 2.5). Product development peaks early in the commercial life of a product, when its ultimate design is still fluid; whereas process

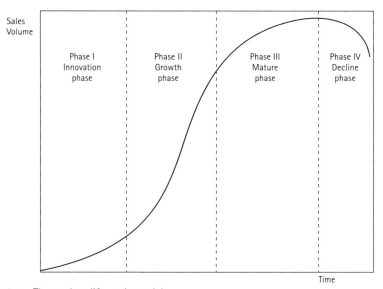

Figure 2.5   The product life-cycle model.

innovation begins to take precedence as the firm prepares for large-volume pro-duction (Utterback 1994). Other characteristics, especially those related to labour and management, also vary over time, in accordance with the innovativeness of the product and the technical expertise needed to produce it. In the innovation phase, as the marketing of a new product begins, firms require skilled labour, such as scientists and engineers, for refinements and improvements. The standardization or mature phase, by contrast, is character-ized by shifts of production to low-cost, and especially low-wage, locations (Abernathy and Utterback 1978). These changes are related to learning by doing, and to cost reductions associated with learning curves and experience curves, which illustrate declining unit costs as cumulative volume increases (Adler and Clark 1991; Ayres and Martinàs 1992; Henderson 1984).

The product life-cycle is a fundamental concept in marketing, where it is used to generalize about circumstances across stages for a product class or product brand (Baker 1983; Onkvisit and Shaw 1989). The product cycle was also used by Vernon (1966) to describe the investment behaviour of multinational firms in the 1950s and 1960s, when shifts to foreign markets generally coincided with a decline in a product's innovativeness. Beginning in the mid-1960s, when infra-structure and management innovations began to permit low wages, rather than markets, to draw multinational investment, the product life-cycle took on a more rigid interpretation, corresponding to the spatial division of labour. Some locations were preferred for R&D and new product manufacture; other sites (and entire countries) seemed to be chosen only for the routine manufacture of mature products (Fröbel, Heinrichs and Kreye 1980). Neither profit nor the search for lower costs adequately explains the shift to peripheral locations, for each industry is different (Storper and Walker 1989). In terms of regional technological capability, however, a bimodal core–periphery distinction seems to hold, with routine production regions typically operating far from global best practice. Examining the location of R&D activity, Cantwell (1995) concludes that Vernon's product cycle model remains largely valid, but must be extended to take into account the global networks of transnational corporations, which tap into expertise at several locations. Chapter 6 will return to the topic of global firms.

Markusen's (1985) *profit life-cycle* model is analogous to the product life-cycle and clarifies several of its points (Figure 2.6). Although Markusen presents her cycle model in the context of an industry (rather than a product) life-cycle, the mechanisms are similar. As Figure 2.6 shows, whereas profits are negative during the initial birth and design stage (I) of a product, the profit level of an innova-tion is greatest shortly after its introduction. This 'super profit' stage (II) derives from the monopoly position held by the innovator. Wheelwright and Clark (1992: 21–2) suggest that a six-month lead over competitors can triple the cumulative profit from a new product. Relatively soon after introduction, com-petitors enter the market (stage III), and the profit per unit drops sharply as output approaches saturation. If a product or industry follows the life-cycle from low to high volume, a 'shakeout' period ensues where competition shifts rather suddenly from product innovation to price, and from skilled labour-intensive to

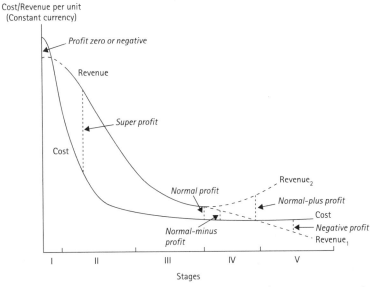

Figure 2.6   The profit life-cycle model. Source: after Markusen (1985: 28, Figure 3.1).

capital-intensive production, resulting in the demise of firms unable to make this transition (Olleros 1986; Utterback and Suárez 1993). The fourth stage is uncertain. In some industries firms will be able to earn profits, whereas in others competition eliminates all but the lowest-cost producers. Indeed, negative profits prevail in the final stage (V) of an industry, when large corporations disinvest and the sector becomes the domain mainly of small firms serving niche markets (Markusen 1985: 27–38).

Industry structure parallels these life-cycle changes (Dosi 1984; Onkvisit and Shaw 1989). A large number of competitors gives way to an oligopolistic market structure, a small group of firms which dominate production in an industrial sector. Industrial sectors differ significantly, but they can in general be classified according to their stage in the profit cycle. Generally, production-based industrial sectors follow an S-shaped pattern (Cooper and Schendel 1976; Utterback 1987), although other patterns are found (Storper and Walker 1989: 61). The life-cycle analogy is a convenience which fits many situations but to which few would expect strict adherence (Arnold 1985: 205–17; Dosi *et al.* 1995; van Duijn 1983).

The Abernathy–Utterback model of product and process innovation is complementary to the product life-cycle, but focuses on the types of innovation that take place at different points in the life of a product or firm (Abernathy and Utterback 1978; Utterback 1994). Product innovation is the focus of the firm's activities in the early stages, because products are more easily patented and thus secure monopoly profits. The need for product innovation wanes relatively quickly as the product is standardized for large-scale production, although it does not end, as Abernathy and Clark (1985) show in the case of the car industry, which remained innovative over many years. Process innovation, by contrast, is less critical early in a product's life but is critical over a fairly long period: first to attain some degree of standardization in production, which can be achieved with workers of lower skill than those in R&D who develop new products. Manufacturing strategies mirror these stages in the product life-cycle: innovators focus on new products and quick design changes; marketeers aim for a broad product line and flexibility in volume; and caretakers focus on price (Miller and Roth 1994).

The concept of 'technological paradigms' defines the ease of achievement of innovations and improvements – the technological opportunities – which vary from industry to industry (Dosi 1984, 1988; Klevorick *et al.* 1995; Nelson and Winter 1982). There are three principal sources of technological opportunities: advances in scientific understanding and technique, technical advances originating in other industries and institutions, and feedbacks from an industry's own technical advances. These suggest that it is critical for a firm to remain closely linked to these sources, particularly external ones (Cohen and Levinthal 1994; Klevorick *et al.* 1995). Opportunities also vary over the life-cycle: in maturity, technical changes are closely related to production, and technology is normally embodied into capital equipment, in contrast to the technology of new innovating firms, which is 'people-embodied' in a community or informal network (Dosi 1984: 193–4; Shearman and Burrell 1987). The relative lack of structure and standardization in new industries shifts dramatically toward a more limited and limiting technological environment as a sector's life-cycle progresses (Macdonald 1985). However, unanticipated changes occur in technology, as has taken place in optical lithography used to make semiconductors. These technological changes have permitted continued use of this technology as chip sizes have shrunk (Henderson 1995).

The technological opportunities present in an industry are often portrayed as an 'S-curve' that interprets technical performance, relative to the effort or expenditure on R&D, as increasing only slowly at first, but then exploding, followed by gradual maturation and ultimate decline (Foster 1986; Steele 1989). In this view, the upper limit or technological ceiling of technical performance is the natural limit of a given technology (Ray 1984). Only if there is discontinuity, usually a shift to a very different technological base – a new or more efficient raw material, a new product architecture, or a more reliable manufacturing process – can a new product (and its producer) supplant an old one (Abernathy and Clark 1985; Anderson and Tushman 1991). Such a change can occur quite suddenly, as happened when the share of electromechanical cash registers in the USA plunged from 90 per cent in 1972 to 10 per cent only four years later as electronic machines rapidly replaced the older technology (Foster 1986). A parallel transformation has taken place in the watch industry, which in 1974 was still dominated by 99 per cent production of mechanical watches. By 1986, this type of watch represented only 25 per cent of production, the rest accounted for by quartz electronic watches with either digital or analogue displays (Glasmeier 1991a; OECD 1988b).

Electronics and telecommunications technologies have provided numerous cases of radically new products as well as a proliferation of products. The life-cycles of successive products in the consumer electronic equipment industry embody the life-cycle concept and the need for constant innovation (Vickery 1989). The S-curve approach to understanding the maturation of technologies and of industries is readily meshed with management concerns, since companies must respond to these changes, which may well originate outside the firm (Steele 1989). Technological discontinuities are a major threat to firms and they can destroy the competence accumulated by firms and the dominance of a dominant design (Anderson and Tushman 1991). Firms must be prepared by continuously gathering both technical intelligence and market intelligence (Ashton and Stacey 1995; Barabaschi 1992; Cornish 1995). If a firm is unprepared for radical innovation, it is likely to under-invest and to display incompetence in regard to the new technology (R. Henderson 1993; Utterback 1994).

As a simplification, the product life-cycle cannot deal with complex products or product systems. In addition, more realistic in most industries is the notion of 'product families' (Uzumeri and Sanderson 1995). Most products are not unique, and it is common for innovators and imitators alike to develop offshoots from the original innovation. Especially significant are new combinations of components of assembled systems, often defining entirely new products or new product families (Amey 1995; Tidd 1995). In computers, the final product appears to have changed little, but the components have changed dramatically, and firms' capabilities have had to change along with them (Iansiti and Khanna 1995). Aerospace products, with their small production runs and inherent complexity, are typical of such complex systems (Miller *et al.* 1995). Moreover, technological knowledge and technological systems have regional and national characteristics, which means that firms must develop extensive cross-border networks that cross geographical as well as industrial, disciplinary and functional borders (Arcangeli 1993; Bowonder and Miyake 1993; Carlsson 1994; Imai and Baba 1991; Kodama 1995a; Nonaka and Takeuchi 1995). Although there are sequential aspects to a given product's development, internal (cross-functional) integration provides a firm with the ability to combine the knowledge and expertise of all participating units (Bowonder and Miyake 1993; Wheelwright and Clark 1992).

Despite its apparent linear nature, the advantages of the product cycle model are several: it emphasizes the labour as well as the capital needs of firms related to products at different phases; it emphasizes the ebb and flow of innovative activity observed in many industries; and it is directly related to potential locations of economic activity which vary with the type of activity undertaken. The volume of production largely defines the degree of innovativeness, non-routineness and flexibility: small-volume products embody these qualities; high-volume products concentrate on cost and economies of scale (Hayes and Wheelwright 1988: 433). In addition, a manufacturing process cycle (Suarez-Villa 1984), a skill-training life-cycle (Flynn 1993), an organizational life-cycle (Koberg, Uhlenbruck and Sarason 1996), a process cycle (Hayes and Wheelwright 1988), regional life-cycles (Norton and Rees 1979) and a tourist resort cycle (Agarwal 1994) extend the applicability of the temporal life-cycle concept. The technology cycle – incorporating technological discontinuities, the uncertainty they precipitate, the emergence of a dominant design, followed by incremental changes – addresses the evolution across individual products and their life-cycles (Tushman and Rosenkopf 1992). Major 'logistical revolutions' such as the Industrial Revolution were the result of several relatively sudden changes in the way that work was done (Andersson 1986; Freeman and Perez 1988).

The product cycle model, especially its regional variant, has undergone criticism in recent years (De Bresson and Lampel 1985; Steiner 1987; Taylor 1986). These criticisms basically address two elements. First, products are rarely constant and unchanging, even when in mass production and somewhat standardized. The Kline–Rosenberg portrayal of innovation embodies this dynamism. Improvements in products are made, often in back-and-forth competition between rival firms, and production techniques are enhanced. Second, as has been stressed, not all products fit the pattern of achieving mass production, where low cost and high volume are the norm. The standard typology of production systems, based on the work of Woodward (1965), includes batch, mass and continuous-process production. Custom, or one-of-a-kind, production is often added to this list. Reprogrammable machines now permit changes in products to be made readily and routinely, so that batch production is highly automated, rather than reliant on traditional craft skills (Hull and Collins 1987). Many products, especially custom and small-batch products, never attain large volumes (De Bresson and Lampel 1985; Hull and Collins 1987). Generally, product differentiation, a widespread corporate strategy, seems to contradict the homogenization of the mature stage of the product cycle (Porter 1980; Taylor 1987).

Industries differ in their adherence to the life-cycle primarily in their product volume. Boeing, for instance, produces very small runs of its (very large and complex) products: a total of 27 planes per month; only four of the 747 model are produced per month (Bannon 1996). The total production of Boeing's most popular model, the 737, has amounted to 2800 planes since 1968 (Rose 1996). Typically, the differences in production systems were drawn along dimensions of scale and complexity, resulting in four types: traditional batch, technical batch, mass production and continuous process (Hull and Collins 1987). Salais and Storper (1992) have proposed a more useful categorization of four 'worlds' of production, based on demand or market conditions (including uncertainty and expectations concerning product quality) and production technologies (Figure 2.7).

Generally, firms choose to compete *either* in new products, where innovativeness and newness are paramount for success, or in older, established products, for which low price and large volume predominate (Porter 1980). A distinct contrast in the basis for competitiveness is present. Low-volume products, whether truly new and innovative or serving a small market niche, require attention to flexibility and quality. Volume production, on the other hand, stresses dependability, uniformity and low cost. The Salais–Storper 'worlds' encompass these concerns as well as forms of flexibility (Chapter 4).

Finally, product life-cycles, when viewed in isolation, assume that products are independent of one another, although product improvements may prolong

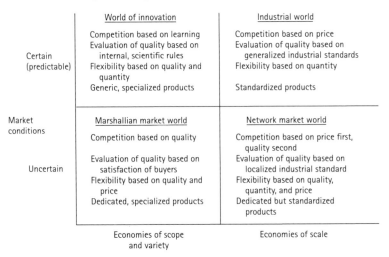

Figure 2.7   Four 'worlds' of production. Source: based on Salais and Storper (1992: 172, Figure 1).

a product's life. Other strategies by which declining industries can evade a decline in sales include producing variations on successful products, and adopting new technology, which can generate a new, higher level of sales (Hammermesh and Silk 1979; Porter 1980). The 'de-maturing' of products has been identified in the case of automobiles since the 1970s (Clark 1983), and televisions (Morgan and Sayer 1988; Rosenbloom and Abernathy 1982). The 'product family' is a variant of this idea, in which several models of a product (e.g. the Sony Walkman) aimed at specific market segments blend stability with rapid product change (Sanderson and Uzumeri 1995; Uzumeri and Sanderson 1995).

The pace of technological change has become more rapid in recent years, especially when viewed in terms of the life of products (Goldman 1982). Short product life-cycles are a direct consequence of product differentiation strategies, the purpose of which is to render older products obsolete (Baker 1983). As product life-cycles 'shorten' (illustrated in Figure 2.8), only an innovative firm is able to earn large profits, since there is too little time for imitators to attain large-scale production and profitability before the product is replaced by the next 'generation' of technology (von Braun, Fischer and Müller 1990). The short product cycle may be illusory, an artifact of product proliferation and product families. Consumers have more choices, and many of these are 'customized' (Pine 1993). Since technology is cumulative within firms and regions, the innovative firm or country today is, other things being equal, among the most likely to be innovative tomorrow (Dosi 1984: 223). However, R&D is needed to avoid surprise by radical innovations (Cohen and Levinthal 1989, 1994; R. Henderson 1993).

Product cycles in services take on a different dynamic than in manufacturing.

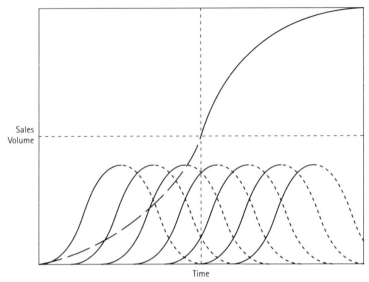

Figure 2.8   Short product life-cycles.

Barras (1986, 1990) has proposed a 'reverse product cycle' to describe the sequence typical in many service sectors. This begins with a first stage in which the delivery of existing services is made more efficient by the application of technology, especially computers and information technology. During a second stage, technology is applied to improve service quality. In the third stage, entirely new or customized services are generated. Financial services typify the sectors which have become more customized and knowledge-based over time (Alic 1994; Barras 1990). A related view suggests that manufacturing firms can add value as industries mature by adding to their products new applications, improved processes and system benefits not part of the original product (Fleming 1991; Goldhar, Jelinek and Schlie 1991; Lele 1986). In the mature elevator (or lift) industry, firms now gain 50–60 per cent and more of their revenues from servicing and modernization, rather than installation of new equipment (*The Economist* 1996c).

The product cycle and its counterparts, while they do not provide universal applicability, capture the skill and knowledge differences between economic activities and types of products. Not all products are manufactured in large volumes requiring mass production, a trait which characterizes entire industries such as aircraft and machinery (De Bresson and Lampel 1985; Sabel *et al.* 1987). The product cycle is less applicable to small niche markets, where the absence of scale and learning economies permits multiple designs and products (Teece 1986). Firms producing custom products in small volumes will not benefit from economies of scale, but rather from economies of scope (Chapter 4). Similarly, firms which concentrate on batch production are more likely to be specialized, flexible and continually innovative, thus describing a setting where technological capability must be among a firm's strengths.

The product cycle continues to be fundamental in business strategy, especially when seen as a succession of cycles as new products replace old (Macdonald 1985). Corporate strategies also take into account a 'portfolio' of products – at different stages of the life-cycle (Hax and Majluf 1984; Rink and Swan 1979). Thus, a measure of the innovativeness of a firm or industry is the proportion of its products which did not exist five years earlier. In one British study, this figure ranged from under 30 per cent in the metal, paper, stone, glass and clay industries to over 50 per cent in furniture, leather and clothing sectors (Baker 1983: 14). A survey of US firms in 1994 showed that on average 19.3 per cent of sales were derived from products new or improved within the past five years (Whiteley, Bean and Russo 1996). In many innovative firms, such as Hewlett-Packard, Merck, Bayer and Asahi Glass, that figure is 30 per cent or higher (Brenner 1994).

The context for technological change

Perpetual innovation and hypercompetition are two concepts used to describe the conditions of capitalism operating today (D'Aveni 1994; Kash 1989). To compete requires flexibility of several types and a capability in technology to respond to new opportunities and to unforeseen changes. Technological capability in firms or in regions is not fixed or permanent, since technology and the abilities of competitors are constantly changing. It relies on firms, on their activities, and how close they are to the state-of-the-art or best practice – itself a constantly moving target – at any point in time. Firms and countries which are not near the current 'technology frontier' both in science and in production find it increasingly difficult to keep up with changes in other places (Cohen and Zysman 1987; Katz 1982; Mody, Suri and Tatikonda 1995; Spence and Hazard 1988).

For a region, links to outside information networks and a high level of technical skill define a level of best practice. Most of all, technological capability relies on people in technological roles within organizations (Håkansson 1989). A concern for regional innovative capability became a focal point in regional research a few years ago, but it was concerned almost equally with large and small firms: the overall technological level of the region was the focus (CURDS 1979; Ewers and Wettmann 1980; Thwaites 1982). A great deal of the indigenous potential is reflected in the technological capability of a region, which determines whether innovation and entrepreneurship can take place. A rich environment enhances a firm's learning from workers, customers, suppliers and other sources (Harrington 1987; Sweeney 1987). Chapter 3 pursues the process of technological change from inside the firm, where choices and structures affect its ability to keep pace with competitors and to reap the profits from monopoly over innovations.

Conclusion

Economic change, including technological change, is an evolutionary process (Dosi 1988; Nelson and Winter 1982). In the course of this process, firms which have better routines for research, production, marketing and management generally 'will prosper and grow relative to those firms whose capabilities and behaviour are less well suited to the current situation' (Nelson 1987: 21). Much of technical change is cumulative within firms (Pavitt 1986) and within regions and nations, for several reasons. First, firms accustomed to organized R&D on old technologies may be more likely to learn how to attract and use scientists and engineers in the new technologies. Second, any new development often depends on upstream or downstream improvements in more conventional technologies. Third, there is evidence that effective assimilation of electronics-based technology depends on the more general competence in management (Cohen and Zysman 1987).

The extent to which innovation depends on people, their accumulated knowledge and capabilities gained through experience, and the information and contact networks on which they draw, is a characteristic often overlooked in prior research (Dosi 1988; Doz 1989; Malecki 1989). A regional setting or environment likewise has its fixed skills and capabilities; and its trajectories, like those of firms, are defined by the prevailing technological paradigm, as embodied in its population of people and of firms. Even in the absence of inter-firm linkages, a 'collective asset' of groups of firms and industries within countries or regions represents a set of technological externalities (Dosi 1988: 1146). Regional differences in company technological capability reflect the regional market environment and the product and process complexity demanded by customers, as well as the presence of suppliers and of firms' organizational structure (Alderman 1995). These are the synergies referred to less explicitly by Andersson (1985) and Stöhr (1986) in the context of creative regions and territorial innovation complexes, which will be returned to in Chapter 7. Economists have begun to realize that

> experiences and skills embodied in people and organizations, capabilities, and 'memories' overflowing from one economic activity to another tend to organize *context conditions* that are (a) country-specific, region-specific, or even company-specific and (b) as such, determine different incentives, stimuli, and constraints to innovation, for any set of strictly economic signals (Dosi 1988: 1146).

Thus, policy options will also differ from place to place, responding to the accumulated competences of firms and the specific clusters of interlinked firms and industries (Dosi, Pavitt and Soete 1990). The following chapter focuses on the internal organization of R&D within firms.

Chapter 3

Innovation in the firm: technology in the corporate context

As Chapter 2 has shown, technological capability is closely related to capability in R&D. This relationship ignores a number of ways in which new knowledge is acquired outside of formal R&D. The process of organized R&D remains a necessity for firms, regions and nations that aspire to have control over their technological destinies. It provides 'absorptive capacity' and the ability to make informed choices concerning technology and economic development. Moreover, for nations and regions indigenous R&D is essential if local values are to be incorporated in the products and processes undertaken there.

Innovation as an activity within organizations is the focal point of this chapter. We begin with an historical look at the 'technical enterprise' (Fusfeld 1986), which is propelled by industrial R&D and resultant innovations. High-technology industry and information technology receive special attention as prime movers in technological change at the end of the twentieth century. The importance of science and of uncertainty and unpredictability in the research and development process have made technology and its management key elements in the competitiveness of firms, regions and nations (Guile and Brooks 1987; Horwitch 1986). The technological strategies of firms and their place within the firm's core competences and capabilities, and the distinct methods employed by Japanese firms, illustrates the role of learning and communication. The chapter concludes with a discussion of strategic alliances and cooperation as ways by which firms obtain technology and other assets to enhance their competitiveness.

The growth of corporate innovation

Before 1900, there was relatively little organized research, and individual inventors dominated the course of technological progress (Hounshell 1996; Jewkes, Sawers and Stillerman 1969). Even in the nineteenth century, a research system had begun to evolve to exploit the work of inventors. Large American firms in a widespread manner had acquired patent and licensing rights to the work of independent inventors in machinery, eventually bringing them in-house (Nader 1994; Winder 1995). In addition, in many other countries learning and technology transfer took place by importing information and people and by systematic travel abroad (Myllyntaus 1990). Early work in metallurgy, construction and food-processing showed the application of science in production (Mowery and Rosenberg 1989).

The principal organized R&D activity was the in-house R&D of German chemical firms, and the early efforts by a few major US corporations (Hounshell 1996; Molina 1989: 183–95). Britain's early leadership in textile-related fields soon gave way to German applied research in chemicals, such as dyes and pharmaceuticals, and electric power (Keck 1993; Landau and Rosenberg 1992). By the 1930s, however, industrial research had become a major economic activity. In a 1928 survey of 600 American manufacturing firms summarized by Noble (1977: 111), 52 per cent of the companies engaged in research, 29 per cent supported cooperative research efforts, and 7 per cent had testing laboratories. The electrical and chemical industries (more than steel and textiles) depended on science from the outset of their development in the late 1800s (Chandler 1977; Hall and Preston 1988). In addition, even prior to 1940, those firms which had the greatest technological capability, represented by in-house R&D, were also among the major contractual users of independent research organizations, such as Battelle Memorial Institute and Arthur D. Little. 'Firms without in-house research facilities were handicapped in their ability to pursue R&D and innovation' (Mowery 1983a: 369). The lack of in-house R&D, as well as an inability to take advantage of integrating science and engineering – increasingly crucial as large systemic technologies evolved – characterized British R&D, in contrast to that in Germany and the USA (Mowery and Rosenberg 1989).

Corporate R&D in the beginning, as now, was dominated by a small number of very large firms. In 1938, just 13 companies employed one-third of all American research workers; 45 employed one-half (Noble 1977: 120). Even fewer engaged in basic or fundamental research (Chandler 1990: 604). In these firms, however, organized industrial research gave rise to a new field of expertise: research management. 'If science was to be effectively controlled, scientists had to be effectively controlled' (Noble 1977: 119). For research at General Motors in the 1930s, 'the morale of researchers was crucial', particularly for the long-range research the firm was cultivating at the time (Leslie 1980: 499). The professionalization of industrial R&D, and the distinct labour force on which innovation relied, demanded a different approach to management (Freeman 1982: 10–14). Universities, even sixty years ago, were considered 'knowledge factories' and were called upon to meet the science requirements of modern industry in two ways: as suppliers of trained research personnel, and as suppliers of applied research (Noble 1977: 158).

Military demands have played a large part in the transformation of R&D in many countries, but it has also created a division of and lack of coordination between industrial and military R&D (Dickson 1983; Horwitz 1979; Kaldor 1981; Tirman 1984). This occurred much less in Japan, where large conglomerates were able to transfer technology internally between military and commercial divisions (Samuels 1994). The post-war 'age of big science' (the 1950s and 1960s) saw a huge growth in corporate R&D, and the distinction and the division of labour between university and industrial research organization diminished as science and technology were seen as intertwined (Mowery and Rosenberg 1993). R&D became an 'institutionalized and integrated sector of corporate activity' by the 1960s (Kay 1979: 69). This was particularly the case in the electrical industry, where the importance of physics became clear as electronics technology emerged (Graham 1985). During and after World War II, government funding of research by industrial firms had become especially important in industries that served military priorities: aircraft, electrical goods and instruments (Graham 1985; Hall *et al.* 1987; Mowery and Rosenberg 1993). Large firms continue to dominate the performance of industrial R&D, and thereby control many of the causes and effects of technological change. The most research-intensive industries have remained fairly constant since the 1920s: chemicals (including pharmaceuticals), rubber (and plastics) and electrical machinery (Nelson and Rosenberg 1993). Since World War II, aerospace, computers and communication equipment have joined them in most countries (OECD 1995a). A convergence has also taken place in technology since the 1960s, as several nations have made big investments R&D and in education and training (Nelson and Wright 1992).

Technology: a long wave view

The rise of new industries and the successful integration of science and technology by firms does not occur in a steady, constant manner. Four alternating cycles of boom and bust have characterized capitalist development since the late 1700s, when the innovations that marked the onset of the Industrial Revolution were put into use. These 50-year cycles of growth and decline, first identified by Kondratieff in 1919 and later by Schumpeter and Kuznets, saw a resurgence in the late 1970s and 1980s. Entire industries, created or transformed as a result of key innovations, have allowed capitalism to maintain its vitality and 'creative destruction' as new sectors – and regions and nations – became the seedbeds of each upswing of innovation-based growth (Table 3.1). The resurgence of interest in these cycles or long waves focused on the swarms or bunches of innovations which have preceded each Kondratieff upswing (Ayres 1990a,b; Mensch 1979).

Especially important, according to Mensch, are *basic innovations,* which establish new branches of industry, and *radical improvement innovations,* which rejuvenate existing branches. Recent innovations identified as basic include xerography and satellite remote sensing (Steele 1989: 268). Within those new or renewed sectors, the basic or pioneering innovations are typically followed by a series of improvement innovations, corresponding to the life-cycles of industrial goods, such as successive generations of computers, as discussed in Chapter 2 (Mensch 1979: 52–4). Recalling the basis of the profit cycle (Chapter 2), 'a real technological revolution means, at least in its first phase, large differences in production costs between those firms that already apply the revolutionary technique and those that do not or do so only marginally' (Mandel 1980: 25).

From the point of view of impact on the economy, 'it is not the basic innovation but its *diffusion* across industry or the economy, and the *speed* of this diffusion, that matters. Only the widely-based rapid diffusion of some major innovations can be assumed to play any part in triggering off the Kondratiev – or any other – long-term upswing' (Ray 1980: 21, emphasis in original).

Table 3.1 The four Kondratieff waves.

	First 1787–1845	Second 1846–1895	Third 1896–1947	Fourth 1948–2000?
Key innovations	Power loom; steam power	Bessemer steel; steamship; railroads	Alternating current; electric light; internal combustion engine	Transistor; computer; ICT
Key industries	Cotton; iron	Steel; machine tools; ships	Cars; electrical engineering; chemicals	Electronics; computers; communications; aerospace; producer services
Industrial organization	Small factories; *laissez-faire*	Large factories; capital concentration; joint stock company	Giant factories; Fordism; cartels	Mixture of large and small factories; transnationals
Labour	Machine minders	Craft labour	Deskilling	Bipolar segmentation
International	Britain, workshop of the world	Germany, America in competition; capital export	USA, German leadership; colonization	American hegemony; Japanese challenge; rise of NICs; new international division of labour
Historical features	European wars; early railways	Opening of North America; global transport and communications	World wars; early mass consumption; Great Depression	Cold War; space race; 'global village'; mass consumption
Role of the state	Minimal army and police	Early imperialism	Advanced imperialism; science and education	Welfare state; warfare state; organized R&D

Source: Ayres (1990a,b); Hall and Preston (1988: 21, Table 2.2).

Innovation ceases to be a leading influence when improvement innovations are replaced with increasing frequency by *pseudo-innovations*, minor improvements and variations found particularly in consumer goods (Haustein and Maier 1980; Mensch 1979: 58). This syndrome is especially common in older sectors. 'New' food products which are merely variations of existing successful brands and 'new' annual models of automobiles with superficial exterior changes typically have fallen into this category. The new microwavable foods, which must be significantly different in composition and packaging from conventional products, are perhaps a step up from the pseudo-innovation category. Recent automotive innovations have also gone beyond their former tentative character, now going far beyond the annual cosmetic changes common during the 1960s (Amey 1995; K. Clark 1983).

Hall and Preston (1988: 25–6) summarize the role of technology in the context of Kondratieff long waves:

> Clusters of key interrelated technologies, developing through backward and forward linkages, are the real triggers of long waves. . . We believe that they tend to come forward when the returns from existing investments are declining. . . If the transition from one Kondratieff to the next requires not merely clusters of hardware innovations but transformations of the entire socio-economic framework, then in a sense the whole process is endogenous; the underlying mechanism is indeed the laws of motion of capital, represented by a falling rate of profit, which eventually must trigger not merely a set of technological innovations but also changes in the economic, social and political superstructure.

Radical innovations which constitute new technological revolutions or *techno-economic paradigms* are also disruptive for existing firms (Freeman and Perez 1988; Kleinknecht 1987: 202–3). This will show up in the competition among firms and industries over time. Firms respond to new technologies – or the anticipation of new technologies – in their allocations on R&D and among sectors and types of technologies (Kleinknecht 1987: 123). It is also possible that they cannot respond because of mismatches between the socio-institutional framework and the emerging techno-economic system (Tylecote 1995). Technological discontinuities (Tushman and Rosenkopf 1992) are similar in their competitive effects, but the new technologies may well affect only one industry; the response of established firms to some new technologies (e.g. ballpoint pens) may be less significant than others, such as transistors replacing vacuum tubes (Cooper and Schendel 1976; Soukup and Cooper 1983). The basic innovations of long waves and techno-economic paradigm shifts influence many sectors and tend to engender innovation and transformation across several sectors. Nearly a decade later, we can see that several aspects of the fourth Kondratieff as shown in Table 3.1 are breaking down, such as the Cold War and American hegemony. It remains to be seen just what the nature of the fifth Kondratieff will be (Ayres 1990b).

The clusters or swarms of innovations in each Kondratieff wave spawned the high-technology industries of their day, from the telegraph and telephone and the electrical innovations (batteries, generators, motors and electrical transmission) in the 1800s, to radio, television, radar, electronics and computers in the twentieth century. These are now merging into a 'convergent information tech-nology', integrating computers and telecommunications, which may be the carrier into the fifth Kondratieff. If the cycles adhere to their 50-year pattern, this wave should begin its upswing around the year 2000 (Hall and Preston 1988). Information technology is affecting both manufacturing, offering the potential to extend capital-intensive techniques to areas of industry notorious for their slow rates of technical change (Coombs, Saviotti and Walsh 1987; Hoffman and Rush 1988), and services, especially financial services, retailing and tourism (Bradley, Hausman and Nolan 1993; Freeman 1995a; Poon 1993). The blurring of industry boundaries affects both recipient sectors and those where innovations originate (Nichols-Nixon and Jasinski 1995).

Although the consensus view of long waves centres on the position of tech-nology, other causes may be related to them as well. Wars also follow up-and-down cycles and, when they do not come as needed for economic renewal, can be substituted by military spending to stimulate an economy (Berry 1991; Mager 1987). Wholesale prices and inflation also follow 50- to 60-year cycles, as do prices of key resources whose supply is strained. These resource constraints induce R&D on alternative resources (Volland 1987). What is especially appar-ent is that 'the dynamics of an upswing in cycles are the result of increased spend-ing induced by massive investment in new opportunities for profit' (Mager 1987: 208; see also Berry 1991; Mandel 1980: 60; Rosenberg 1982: 156). Social and institutional phenomena also appear to be related to long waves, such as managerial ideologies and labour activity (Barley and Kunda 1992). Technological revolutions demand changes in types of machine systems but, even more, changes in the organization of production and of the labour process (Boyer 1995; Kaplinsky 1984; Mandel 1980: 42–3; Marshall 1987).

Infrastructure investment both by the state and by the private sector has con-tinued to be significant, first in railways, telegraph and electrification, and cur-rently through investment in satellites, space technology and improved communications technology. Standardization and coordination are essential for infrastructure, however, and delays in this regard can thwart competitiveness. Such infrastructure systems have demanded very large-scale organizations. Several technological clusters or chains, such as the telephone and television, span across Kondratieff cycles, and these systems remain core technologies in the convergent information technology (Rosenberg 1994: 203–31).

These large-scale changes in technological regime, not in a single technology or industry, are the crux of the technological view of long waves (Perez 1983; Soete 1986). Radical innovations have important effects on neighbouring sectors and on the build-up of a supporting infrastructure. For instance, the rise of an automobile industry entailed not only the sale of cars, but also investments in road construction and traffic regulation, and in service and repair networks (Kleinknecht 1987). The development of clusters of innovations depends not only on a radical breakthrough in technology, but also on the nature of the link-ages between firms and industries (De Bresson 1989). Caracostas and Muldur (1995) believe that this has not yet occurred and, consequently, the fifth Kondratieff cycle is late in occurring. They see the variety of applications of ICT as unfocused and primarily job-destroying rather than job-creating. The issue of employment is an especially important one in advanced countries (Boyer 1995; Freeman 1995a; Tylecote 1995).

The location of success in new technologies can lead to a dramatic decline in national influence. British decline stemmed largely from an inability to compete with the giant business organizations that had emerged in Germany and in the USA by 1900. Innovation no longer depended on individual inventors but on systematic laboratory research, an educated workforce, and a knowledgeable management who could combine technology and markets in complex combinations. The German and American firms established licensing and patent channels as well as production facilities in Britain, marking the technological dependence of the UK in new technological developments. The largest part of Britain's failure may have stemmed from its inability to make the necessary organizational and sociopolitical adaptations to new technologies (Hall and Preston 1988; Jewkes, Sawers and Stillerman 1969; Mowery and Rosenberg 1989).

The geographical locus of the core technologies thus appears to shift from one wave to the next. Britain, the clear technological leader of the first and second Kondratieff cycles, was surpassed by Germany in the third. In the late 1800s, inventions by Edison and others were capitalized on by large US firms, leading to technological leadership for America. Since 1960, the success of Japan at production and marketing new technologies, although perhaps not at inventing them, is used to validate the role of broader organizational and socio-institutional innovations, and of coordination by the state, in national prosperity. The spread of information technology to Asia, especially the newly industrializing countries (NICs), raises questions about the geography of the fifth Kondratieff at the global scale. Freeman and Perez (1988) include as the technological leaders of the fifth Kondratieff Japan, the USA, Germany and Sweden.

Regional economies, like national economies and the world economy, may also go through long waves of economic activity (Booth 1987). New industries tend to emerge in regions not already dominated by major industries, or in regions which have been in decline for some time. Two dimensions of the regional long wave view are important. First, the idea that innovation is relatively more abundant in new regions owes its logic to the idea that old industries and large, established firms thwart the development of new ideas and the finance of new firms. Mature enterprises (and regions) lose their entrepreneurial energy, and new innovations and new sectors emerge in other places. Older regions, with infrastructure and a social and political structure geared to support the dominant employers, are less able to respond to entrepreneurs and to the needs of new industries (Norton and Rees 1979; Scott 1988c; Watkins 1980). This 'spatial succession' or 'regional rotation' has been a recurring observation (Boschma 1994; Goodman 1979; Markusen 1985: 42–50; Watkins 1980). Second, the growth of an industry in a region puts upward pressure on labour and land costs, driving economic activity to lower-cost regions. Particularly for mature products late in their product cycles, 'filtering down' the urban hierarchy is thought to take place, a dispersion from large urban regions where innovations unfold, based on an agglomeration of local skills and linked activities, to smaller regions where firms utilize unskilled labour as tasks are routinized (Markusen 1985; Moriarty 1991; Thompson 1965).

Not all are convinced that the long wave view is adequate to account for innovative activity, particularly in predictable 50-year intervals. Technology is a social outcome of the diverse decisions of large firms in their pursuit of profits, but it is not coordinated in such a way to predetermine cycles (Morgan and Sayer 1988). It also may not always be the case that new industries will not emerge in yesterday's regions (Marshall 1987), although the evidence from previous waves leads in that direction.

Science-push or market-pull?

The mechanisms apparent in long waves raise the question about the predominance of scientific discoveries or of market demand. Whether scientific discoveries 'push' innovation or, alternatively, market demand 'pulls' innovations from company laboratories, is a long-running controversy. It also remains relevant, and sheds additional light on the shift from adherence to the linear model to an interactive relationship between technology and its markets (Chidamber and Kon 1994). Mowery and Rosenberg (1979: 139) have disputed the market-pull conclusion: 'The uncritical appeal to market demand as the governing influence in the innovation process simply does not yield useful insights into the complexities of that process.'

By contrast, science-push (or technology-push) suggests that innovations must await technological progress. Von Hippel (1979) supports this view:

> 'Everyone knows' what the customer wants, but progress in technology is required before the desired product can be realized. In my work in the computer, plastics and semiconductor industries, I have often been told that new product needs were often not a problem: 'everyone knows' that the customer wants more calculations per second and per dollar in the computer business; 'everyone knows' that the customer wants plastics that degrade less quickly in sunlight; and 'everyone knows' that the semi-conductor customer wants more memory capacity on a single 'chip' of silicon. Under such circumstances a new customer request is not required to trigger a new product – only an advance in technology (von Hippel 1979: 106–7).

It is possible that links to science are more important in process R&D, whereas the appropriability of an innovation is more important for product innovations. For both types of innovation, the contributions of users (the market) are at least as important as the industry's own R&D (Nelson 1987: 65–71). In the extreme 'customer-active' case, the idea for a new product, and occasionally the product itself, is created by the customer, who then finds a manufacturer able to produce it. The more conventional approach, the manufacturer-active model, also demands input and feedback from users and customers, particularly in the early stages of a product's life (Baker 1983: 47–9; von Hippel 1988).

The traditional dichotomy of technology or market demand may instead be roundabout. Users who are familiar with technology stimulate technical advance, whereas suppliers tend to seek to broaden their set of customers or markets for their limited range of technologies. User-active innovations, then, are stimulated by technology-push (Voss 1984). A major technology-push, where basic science acts as a trigger for a cluster of basic innovations, has been a factor in the case of biotechnology as it was with electricity and chemicals and, more recently, with plastics and polymers. These arguments seem to imply an exogenous explanation of technology, by which the economy receives develop-ment impulses from erratic forward leaps in natural sciences. An additional role may be played by suppliers of research equipment and materials, who are major determinants of what can be done and how science can advance (Mowery and Rosenberg 1979). Thus, it is likely that both processes operate, and that tech-nology-push innovations are fewer in number, but 'fuel a larger number of incre-mental innovations' (Chidamber and Kon 1994: 108).

Part of science-push is related simply to the purposeful effort undertaken by industry to create new products and processes. The evolution and rapid growth of industrial R&D laboratories provided industry with experience in large-scale organized scientific research, both basic research and applied research (Noble 1977: 121). Finally, technological knowledge based on cumulative experience and learning often results from dissatisfaction with current technologies. The unreliability of the vacuum tube, and of the early transistors which replaced them, led to basic research programmes in solid-state physics, which in turn sparked microelectronics discoveries (Rosenberg 1982: 141–59). Market demand is then 'created' for products for which no need was previously felt (Shanklin and Ryans 1984).

It can be concluded, then, that both technological opportunity and market demand spark innovation (Mowery and Rosenberg 1979). 'If any generalisation can be made, technology-push tends to be relatively more important in the early stages in the development of the industry while demand-pull tends to increase in relative importance in the mature stages of the product cycle' (Coombs, Saviotti and Walsh 1987: 103). Even this conclusion varies across sub-sectors as well as across the life-cycles of industries (Walsh 1984).

High-technology industries: problems of definition and significance

The discussion of long waves of technological development indicates that the periodic rise in prominence of certain industrial sectors has been a characteristic of innovative technology. From textiles and iron to automobiles, aircraft and electronics, families of interrelated 'high-technology' industries have played sig-nificant roles in economic growth in their particular eras.

The common understanding of high technology unfortunately encompasses a range from state-of-the-art basic research through routine production activ-ities in the chemical and electronics sectors. In practice, available data prevent classification that can be meaningful both at the level of the establishment and for entire industries. Once industries are categorized as high technology, all establishments of all firms in such industries are *de facto* considered to be high technology (Markusen, Hall and Glasmeier 1986: 10–23; Thompson 1988b). Industries, however narrowly they are defined, exhibit a wide range of technologies and behaviours – a diversity ignored in virtually all classification schemes (Dosi 1988; Storper and Walker 1989). The aggregate data describe technological intensity (the phrase used by the OECD) of firms and industries, but these are rarely accurate for all the production and other facilities of a firm or sector.

Two indicators are most commonly used to define high-tech industries: (1) research and development (R&D) intensity, or the percentage of sales expended on R&D; and (2) technical workers (scientists, engineers and, often, technicians) as a percentage of the workforce. R&D intensity is intended to capture the rapid rate of change in products and technologies and the importance of technological effort within an industry or firm, indicated by the relative amount invested in the generation of new products and processes. Employing R&D or technical employment criteria separately results in different lists of sectors – sometimes broader, sometimes narrower. For example, using a criterion of an average expenditure on R&D exceeding 3 per cent of sales, Maidique and Hayes (1984) found only five US industries to be defined as high technology. These are chemicals and pharmaceuticals, machinery (especially computers and office machines), electrical equipment and communications, professional and scientific instruments, and aircraft and missiles. The OECD (1995a) classifies only six industries as high technology based on R&D intensity: aerospace, computers and office equipment, communications equipment and semiconductors, electrical machinery, pharmaceuticals, and scientific instruments (Table 3.2). It is still uncommon, however, to see services classified as high technology. Given the growth of services, it is advisable to include within the high-technology industries, service industries in which R&D intensity is also high: computer programming, data processing and other services; research and development laboratories; management consulting; and commercial testing laboratories (Browne 1983).

The second standard definition of high technology, technical (or technical and professional) occupations as a percentage of the labour force, is intended to measure the technical inputs into production in addition to R&D. Using the criterion that employment of scientists, engineers and technicians must exceed the national average for manufacturing industries, Markusen, Hall and Glasmeier (1986), for example, present a set of 29 three-digit sectors and 100 four-digit sectors. Using data at the aggregate sectoral level still has the effect of including labour-intensive assembly plants as high tech if the sector is so defined.

Using both R&D intensity and technical employment indicators, the US Department of Labor has standardized to some extent the definition of high-technology industry (Burgan 1985; Riche, Hecker and Burgan 1983). Despite the appeal of standardized definitions, they are often difficult to apply in places other than where they were developed. Hall *et al.* (1987), in a UK study parallel to that carried out in the USA by Markusen, Hall and Glasmeier (1986), were unable to replicate very closely the US definitions of high technology based on

Table 3.2   Industries classified according to R&D intensity (R&D expenditure/output).

Industries	Intensity, 1992
High intensity	8.1
Aerospace	12.4
Pharmaceuticals	11.9
Computers and office equipment	11.0
Communications equipment and semiconductors	9.0
Scientific instruments	6.4
Electrical machinery	2.7
Medium intensity	2.5
Motor vehicles	3.4
Chemicals excluding drugs	3.2
Other manufacturing industries	0.7
Non-electrical machinery	2.0
Rubber and plastic products	1.2
Non-ferrous metals	0.9
Other transport equipment	2.5
Low intensity	0.5
Non-metallic mineral products	1.0
Food, beverages, tobacco	0.3
Shipbuilding	—
Petroleum refining	1.0
Iron and steel	0.7
Metal products	0.7
Paper and printing	0.3
Wood products	0.2
Textiles, apparel and leather	0.3

Source: OECD (1995a: 114, 162).

occupations because of discrepancies in industry classifications and in available data.

The OECD standard employs R&D, strictly delineated according to its *Frascati manual,* to define high-technology industries (OECD 1994). This definition defines research and experimental development (R&D) to 'comprise creative work undertaken on a systematic basis in order to increase the stock of knowledge, including knowledge of man, culture and society, and the use of this stock of knowledge to devise new applications' (OECD 1994: 29). Explicitly excluded from R&D are education and training, scientific and technical information services, routine testing and analysis, specialized medical care, and production and related technical activities. A number of activities are recognized as at the boundaries of R&D, such as postgraduate studies, industrial design and trial production, some aspects of which are classified as R&D while others are excluded.

Any sectoral definition of high technology has a serious shortcoming for the study of economic activity geographically. If a definition of high tech is not disaggregated to the level of the individual plant, office, laboratory or other business establishment, then it will inaccurately reflect the firm (or, worse, the industry) average. Secondary data sources group establishments and firms into industrial sectors according to final product or service, and this aggregation combines the R&D, new product production, mass volume production, and other activities related to that output. The spatial division of labour is the principal complicating factor. A sector may be defined as high tech on the basis of aggregate indicators, despite the fact that most of its output is quite standardized, produced in large volume, and mainly employing low-wage workers for routine assembly. Electronics and computers, two 'core' sectors of high technology, largely follow this pattern. Moreover, large multi-sector corporations operate across a wide spectrum of industry and product types, although the standard practice worldwide is to allocate firms to a single sector. In part as a result of this diversity, the R&D activities within an industry group vary widely (Hughes 1988).

The Japanese concept of high technology includes both R&D intensity and system orientation, involving 'a package of technologies rather than individual technologies' (Imai 1988: 206). Excluded are R&D-intensive technologies that are isolated and independent; the focus on 'those high technologies that are strongly system-oriented as well as forming the basis of the new economic infrastructure', including microelectronics, biotechnology and new materials (Imai 1988). The Japanese definition, then, appears to be oriented toward core technologies associated with potential long-wave upswings. Somewhat similar is a diffusion-based definition, in which both *newly emerging* technologies (e.g. biotechnology, new materials and photovoltaic cells), and *widely diffusing* technologies (e.g. robotics, computers and telecommunications), are considered high tech (McArthur 1990). This perspective retains the importance of technological flows between sectors.

Innovation and technological change occur as well where no formal R&D is conducted (as Chapter 2 has stressed) through modifications, learning-by-doing and other informal means of technological learning. The technological intensity of an industry may be thought of as a composite of three distinct components: (1) the technological intensity of labour, relating to the amount of expertise and skill; (2) the technological intensity of capital, embodied in sophisticated machinery; and (3) the technological intensity of the product, indicated by the degree of industry investment in *new* products and processes (Bar-El and Felsenstein 1989). This multidimensional approach to defining high technology results in the dispersal of sophisticated capital equipment, but little decentralization of R&D and skilled labour inputs, to peripheral areas.

In addition to performing R&D, firms can purchase or acquire technology embodied in products sold by other industries. The OECD now routinely gathers data on goods-embodied diffusion to capture the R&D expenditures of upstream industries from which intermediate and capital goods are purchased.

The dominant 'user sectors' in 1990 were social and personal services in Italy, Japan, the UK and the USA. Although a few manufacturing sectors (e.g. aerospace, motor vehicles) appear as major technology users in OECD countries, most user industries are services, including construction, real estate and business services, and transport and storage (OECD 1995a). The synergies as well as the direct linkages between firms vary according to economic sector and the ways in which innovative activities proceed in various sectors. Pavitt (1984) categorizes industries into four types, according to their dominant source of technological innovation:

- supplier-dominated sectors
- specialized suppliers
- scale-intensive industries
- science-based sectors

These correspond to the ways in which, and where, knowledge is accumulated and utilized in innovation. The linkages between sectors inherent in Pavitt's approach suggest, in turn, the presence of an 'innovation multiplier' which benefits both user and supplier sectors (Bienaymé 1986). These inter-sectoral linkages are key to both sectoral and national accumulation of competitive advantage within an industry, its linked industries and national economies (Cohen and Zysman 1987; De Bresson 1989; Porter 1990; Robson, Townsend and Pavitt 1988; Scherer 1982). Pavitt (1994) has added a fifth sector, information-intensive industries, which comprises service sectors (Table 3.3). The OECD uses a five-industry classification, only slightly different from Pavitt's: resource-intensive, labour-intensive, specialized supplier, scale-intensive and science-based (OECD 1995a: 114).

The product life-cycle and its variants (Chapter 2) can help to clarify the meaning of high technology in a regional context. The non-routine work associated with R&D, prototype manufacturing and administrative functions of a firm are found in different locations – a spatial division of labour – from routine manufacturing, goods handling and back-office clerical activity. Non-routine and innovative activities common at the beginning of a product's 'life' require technical workers. Volume production largely entails the deskilling of work tasks and/or automation of production, and tends to seek out favourable local labour conditions.

In their strategy and behaviour, successful high-technology firms exhibit a paradoxical combination of continuity and chaos (Maidique and Hayes 1984). Continuity is revealed in firms' adherence to a relatively narrow spectrum of products and technologies, reinforcing the ideas discussed in Chapter 2 concerning technological trajectories and cumulative learning within firms. At the same time, successful firms are adaptable and able to change fairly rapidly as new technologies present themselves, but only within a cohesive organization that relies more on communication than on structure. Marketing or selling high-technology products is also different than for other products, whose demand is known or readily estimated. Products may need to be tailored to specific

Table 3.3 A technology-based classification of firms.

Characteristics	Category of firm				
	Supplier-dominated	Scale-intensive	Information-intensive	Science-based	Specialized supplier
Typical core sectors	Agriculture; housing; private services; traditional manufacturing	Steel; glass; automobiles; consumer durables	Finance; retailing; publishing; travel	Electronics; chemicals	Capital goods; instruments; software
Main sources of technological accumulation	Suppliers	Production engineering	Corporate software and systems engineering	Corporate R&D	Design and development; advanced users
Main channels of technology transfer	Purchase of equipment and related services	Purchase of equipment; know-how licensing	Purchase of equipment and software	Reverse engineering; R&D; hiring experienced scientists and engineers	Learning from advanced users

Source: based on Pavitt (1994: 360–1, Table 29.1).

customers, or markets may have to be created for new products whose character-istics and advantages are unfamiliar to customers (Shanklin and Ryans 1984; Zangwill 1993). This 'supply-side marketing' reinforces once again the science-push flow of technological innovation.

Other elements of company strategy and organization may be somewhat dis-tinct in high-technology firms from those in other industries. Coordination of marketing, research and engineering must be tighter for products whose window of opportunity is small and whose total market is uncertain but may well be small. In such a market niche, quality and dependability rate more highly than price (Riggs 1983). In actual practice, the concern with high technology exaggerates its significance. As Jean-Jacques Dudy, European director of science and technology for IBM, says: 'In modern industry there's no such thing as high-tech and low-tech. You need all-tech to be competitive' (Peterson and Maremont 1989: 34).

The military dimension of high technology

The attributes of high technology – high amounts of R&D spending and a sig-nificant proportion of scientists and engineers in the workforce – suggest that military expenditure is closely intertwined with high technology (Tirman 1984; Wells 1987). Modern military spending incorporates a heavy reliance on expen-sive and sophisticated weaponry (Gansler 1980). The driving force of military technology is one of technology-push and production for a market that tends to buy the newest technology available, regardless of price. This relative insulation from conventional market pressures has also led to 'the establishment of a class of technologically advanced firms which are organized in such a way that they are quite unlikely to produce commercially successful innovations' (Horwitz 1979: 284). The 'mummification' of defence manufacturers channels 'technical innovation along a dead end', with technologies for military purposes being dis-tinct from civil use (Harbor 1991; Kaldor 1981). Thus, commercial spin-offs from military production are infrequent in comparison with civilian produc-tion. This has posed particular problems for many military producers as govern-ments have reduced military expenditures in the wake of the Cold War. 'Defence conversion' to non-military products by these firms has proved difficult indeed (Alic et al. 1992; Gansler 1995; Markusen and Yudken 1992). (Policy issues concerning military technology are returned to in Chapter 7.)

A wide group of industrial sectors has depended on large defence budgets, especially aerospace shipbuilding and, increasingly, electronics and communica-tions (usually incorporated into aircraft and missiles) (Morton 1995). The growth of prominent high-tech regions, such as Silicon Valley, Los Angeles, and Boston in the USA, and the M4 corridor west of London in the UK, was to a large degree a result of ample budgets for research and procurement of elec-tronic, aerospace and other high-tech military devices (Barff and Knight 1988; Hall et al. 1987; Lovering 1988; Markusen et al. 1991). On the whole, much of what is considered 'high technology' is military in character, often masked by the nature of industrial and occupational categories.

Information technology

Information technology (IT) is a term commonly used to describe the combined utilization of electronics, telecommunications, software and decentralized computer workstations, and the integration of information media (voice, text, data and graphics) (Frisk 1988). As information technology has developed from several distinct technologies during the past few decades, it has had fundamental impacts on the way economic activity takes place. Manufacturing or production, once a very distinct operation from research, development or design, is now integrated into computer-integrated manufacturing and other configurations for flexible production (Chapter 4). More importantly, this integration has transformed the way in which companies are organized geographically. Computer networks can be organized in many different ways, corresponding to a company's overall structure, behaviour and strategy, and according to the demands of the industry. In a sense, four revolutions are occurring to confront companies simultaneously: globalization, computers, management and the information economy (Stewart 1993). Both facsimile (fax) technology, which allows images and text to be transmitted, and the development of networks of dedicated or private lines (often a portion of the channel capacity of satellites) that can be used as a secure intra-organizational network have dramatically increased international communications traffic (Daniels 1993).

Information technology as an infrastructure-related set of technologies has allowed firms in services, such as banking, tourism and consulting, to offer their services to their global customers in the locations where the latter do business (Moss 1987; Nusbaumer 1987b; Sassen 1995a). The new telecommunications infrastructure will favour large urban areas, especially those which serve as headquarters and financial capitals, and particularly the three major financial centres, London, New York and Tokyo (Moss 1986, Warf 1989), as well as a second tier of cities which are now also critical to corporate operations, including Hong Kong, Singapore and Seoul (Moss 1988).

Consequently, 'information-rich' and 'information-poor' regions are developing (Howells 1988). Indeed, although centres and peripheries are being redefined, with few exceptions one can expect cumulative causation forces and agglomeration economies to best account for the future pattern of regional comparative advantage (Gillespie and Williams 1988). New communications services are unlikely to be introduced uniformly across space, and 'are increasingly likely to favour investments in the existing concentrations of economic activity and areas of current economic advantage' (Goddard and Gillespie 1988: 144). The evidence thus far supports this conclusion. Innovations in telecommunications in the USA were introduced to connect the major metropolitan areas and, only years later, the networks became complete enough to serve many small places (Langdale 1983). The computer networks of several Canadian firms are structured to centralize control in Toronto (Hepworth 1989). The concentration of data flows in Europe shows that these are heavily over-represented in capital cities there as well (Gillespie *et al.* 1989).

On an international scale, certainly, the ability of a country to adopt new information technologies requires that it have an array of knowledge and skills and a number of prior technologies in place. Consequently, the nature of information technology, as an example of a complex technological system, is that it appears to be widening the gap between leaders and followers (Antonelli 1986a). To some degree, this appears to be a result of government regulation of information technologies, which has slowed their diffusion especially in developing countries (Katz 1988). As deregulation has proceeded during the 1990s, however, it has been possible for countries to leapfrog directly to new technologies, such as cellular telephones, which require no prior investment in cables and relatively low investment in antennas (Haynes 1993).

Control over space and over far-flung corporate networks has become a competitive objective. Telecommunications technology allows firms to overcome geographical restrictions, to take advantage of time–space compression, and to restructure business relationships by bypassing intermediaries while linking with desired organizations (Bakis 1987; Hammer and Mangurian 1987; Harvey 1988; Li 1995). Information is seen as a resource, to be managed or mismanaged (Bar *et al.* 1989). The 'network firm' takes advantage of information technology for procurement, manufacturing and marketing functions, in addition to control activities, such as accounting, forecasting and planning (Antonelli 1988a), and the ability to do this extends trends that began more than a century earlier (Beniger 1986; Headrick 1991). Information technology on a global, standardized network serves to reduce coordination costs both within and between firms (Antonelli 1988b). IT is a key ingredient in systems of flexible production, which may utilize facsimile (fax) machines to transmit instantly orders for the next shipment of parts or components to arrive in the next few hours. Service industries, however, are the biggest users of telecommunications technology, especially financial services (Daniels 1993; Warf 1989). Despite global communications, travel has not been replaced within global firms (Wooldridge 1995). Chapter 4 carries the implications of this technology, and its influence on location, further.

For developing countries, information technology was until recently seen more as a threat than as an opportunity. Communications cables were extended in the late 1800s throughout the world, including colonies in Africa and Asia, principally by British firms (Headrick 1991). The new technologies were seen by some to threaten to make developing countries more technically dependent on developed countries (King 1982; Su 1988). What has happened is that new wireless technologies have permitted links to the outside world at relatively low costs (Hanna 1991). Satellite technology means that global links are possible with only a small 'dish' as a ground station. Infrastructure investment and deregulation have prompted an 'explosion' throughout Asia (Jussawalla 1995).

Among the latest dimensions of information technology is the Internet, a loosely organized but highly efficient network of connections between computers throughout the world. It was initiated in the USA in the 1970s to link researchers, and use of the Internet has doubled each year since 1988, and now reaches five million 'host' computers (C. Anderson 1995). These are far from equally distributed throughout the world, being concentrated in two of the

Table 3.4   Internet use by country.

Country	Internet hosts per 1000 population, January 1995	Growth, 1994–1995 (%)
Finland	14	103
United States	12.2	100
Australia	9	50
New Zealand	9	441
Sweden	8.6	83
Switzerland	7.9	40
Norway	7.8	57
Canada	7	96
The Netherlands	6	98
Denmark	5	181
United Kingdom	4.2	112
Austria	3.9	92
Israel	2.9	96
Germany	2.8	77
Hong Kong	2.2	52
Belgium	2.0	125
France	1.8	68
Czech Republic	1.1	153
Japan	0.8	86
South Africa	0.7	147
Spain	0.6	141
Taiwan	0.6	83
Italy	0.4	80
South Korea	0.3	101
Poland	0.2	121

Source: calculated from C. Anderson (1995: 15).

Triad regions, North America and Western Europe (Table 3.4). Countries in northern Europe, as well as Australia and New Zealand, match or exceed Internet use in North America. Internet use closely parallels that for telephones (Anderson 1995: 15), since it relies largely on existing networks.

R&D as an economic activity

Breakthroughs and improvements in telecommunications and other technologies have come about primarily through the concerted effort of firms. The economic justification for industrial R&D is that firms want to produce technology, which is a form of knowledge, especially if they can exclude other firms from using it. Through ownership rights and intellectual property rights, companies carve out monopoly and first-mover advantages over new technologies (Wallerstein, Mogee and Schoen 1993). Especially in early stages, when knowledge is largely intangible or tacit, such technology is a nonrival good, unlike a piece of machinery, which can be used in only one place at a time. Technology is also partially non-excludable, because it can be used in more than one place at a time. The owners of technology may have difficulty preventing others from making use of it, especially unauthorized use (Grossman and Helpman 1991: 15–16). Through publications, patents and other means, much knowledge becomes generally available; other knowledge is specific to a particular task and may include large amounts of tacit (as opposed to codified) knowledge. Related to the non-excludability of knowledge is the point that *technological spillovers* may result from R&D. Other firms can obtain information or knowledge without paying for it (or at least without paying the original owner) and without recourse by the owner. Spillovers are a common means for economists to explain the benefits of agglomeration (Chapter 4), since a great deal of 'spillover' spread of knowledge occurs in local places, through communication and the mobility of workers.

The result is that innovating firms are more profitable than other firms. They also reap other, indirect effects from spillovers that create and enhance their competitiveness. Innovative firms 'are likely to be quicker, more flexible, more adaptable, and more capable of dealing with market pressures' than are non-innovators (Geroski, Machin and Van Reenen 1993). They are also more likely to be *active* with regard to both internal and external environments than are passive firms (Amendola and Bruno 1990).

Management of technology

As R&D assumed greater importance across a number of fields, research management itself became a growth business. Issues of staffing, structure and strategy are the principal dimensions believed to influence successful innovation (Betz 1987; Roberts 1987). Firms require of their technical and professional staff a set of 'critical behavioural roles', in addition to technical skills (Roberts and Fusfeld 1981). Many texts and evaluations are concerned with managing people in whom creativity and contact with outside information are the key to success (Allen 1977; Badawy 1988; Roberts 1987).

Corporate structure or organization is a constraint on the place of R&D both within the structure of the firm and in corporate strategy, and is regarded as a critical part of technology management (Adler 1989; Dumbleton 1986; Galbraith and Nathanson 1978; Roberts 1988; Souder 1983; Twiss and Goodridge 1989). A firm's structure reflects its management philosophy, especially with regard to its workers (Miles and Creed 1995). Structure also constrains strategy, forcing companies to adapt to changing competitive conditions with new organizational forms (Graham 1986; Kagono *et al.* 1985; Miles and Snow 1994). The formation of internal venture groups, to work on emerging technologies and to foster greater creativity and entrepreneurship in research, attempts to counter the highly structured company hierarchies which have evolved over several decades (Burgelman and Sayles 1986; Graham 1986; Mitchell 1989). An alternative mechanism is a 'skunk works', which brings together people from various parts of the firm, but for a single, dedicated purpose, rather than as an ongoing research laboratory (Single and Spurgeon 1996).

Strategy formulation, and attempts to anticipate technological developments and actions of competitors, incorporate R&D efforts as a long-term, as well as a short-term, investment (Ansoff 1987; Friar and Horwitch 1986; Maidique and Patch 1988). The reason for a concern with tight management procedures and links to corporate strategy stems in part from the fact that R&D expenditures, in general, are a drain on company profits (Morbey 1989). In the institutional framework of R&D, 'investment in R&D is an investment like any other, although it might include higher risks and higher potential pay-offs' (Kleinknecht 1987: 118). Mitchell and Hamilton (1988) suggest that standard corporate concern with return on investment is inappropriate in the case of R&D, which is directed toward building knowledge and reducing uncertainty. A short-term focus has led many companies to cut long-term basic research dramatically (Freundlich 1989). Short-termism and a lack of long-range planning are common in many companies in Europe and the USA (Hallsworth 1996; Szakonyi 1989; Tylecote and Demirag 1992). Instead of evaluating R&D expenditures in the same way as other investments, R&D programmes are best seen as similar to stock options, which provide an opportunity to make a profitable investment at a later date (Ellis 1988; Mitchell and Hamilton 1988; Steele 1988). Indeed, much of corporate innovative effort is 'learning by trying', guided by a consistent corporate strategy (Dodgson 1992; Fleck 1994; Rosenbloom and Cusumano 1987).

R&D contributes to corporate strategy because it is a central part of long-range thinking about potential changes and about the company's future. Through information from R&D activities, firms can assess the nature of their current technology portfolio and its life-cycles, and external forces such as partners and competitors (Sonneborn and Wilemon 1991; Sykes 1993). Innovations from outside a firm can alter radically the nature of the business (Jelinek 1984). Digital and electronics technologies are among those affecting many industries, from IT to toys and retailing. The capability for optical storage of digital information has given rise to new compact disc technology in audio, video and computers. Determining a focus in the midst of technological developments, especially those taking place in businesses seemingly unrelated to the firm, depends on organizational learning (Prahalad, Doz and Angelmar 1989). Technology strategy evolves based on a firm's capabilities and experiences, both of which evolve and change over time, as do the external forces of technology evolution and industry context (Burgelman and Rosenbloom 1989).

R&D management has evolved rapidly in recent years – so rapidly that 'third-generation R&D', described in 1991 (Roussel, Saad and Erickson 1991) was overtaken by 'fourth-generation R&D' (Miller 1995) and 'fifth-generation R&D' (Rogers 1996; Rothwell 1992) within a very short time. Third-generation management of R&D mainly seeks 'to organize R&D in a way that breaks the isolation of R&D from the rest of the company' (Roussel, Saad and Erickson 1991: 37). Fourth-generation R&D focuses more on customers, while fifth-generation R&D develops knowledge as the principal asset to be nurtured both within and outside the firm (Rogers 1996).

The essence of the shift is recognition of the feedback model of technological change (Chapter 2) and the necessity of overlapping and integrating several
distinct 'core business processes': customer communications, order fulfilment,
special orders (that allow mass customization), product development, capability
and architecture development, and strategy development (Miller 1995: 35).
Most important is the need to link firms, to create constant inter-firm (as well
as intra-firm) integration in order to avoid R&D isolation (Rothwell 1992;
Roussel, Saad and Erickson 1991; Steele 1991). The factors affecting corporate
R&D in the 1990s and beyond are largely exogenous, including the major
impact of new technologies, intense competition, high rates of technological
change, and rapid product cycles. Rothwell (1992: 232) lists the following as
dominant elements in corporate strategies at the present time:

- inter-firm integration (networking)
- technological accumulation
- integrated product and manufacturing strategies, such as design for
  manufacturability
- flexibility (organizational, product, manufacturing)
- product quality and performance
- the environment
- speed to market

Corporate strategy is the locus of this integration of R&D with other dimensions of corporate activity and of the consideration of its complex and interactive
nature (Table 3.5). The result of an effective strategy is a bundle of strategies that
encompass the entire organization (Rothwell 1992). Decisions concerning one
area or dimension have implications for other areas.

Table 3.5   Targets for corporate strategy.

Target area	Dimensions
Growth	Sales, profits, market share, organic, acquired
Integration	Vertical or horizontal
Finance	Equity, loans, internal, short/long-term investment ratio
Diversification or concentration	Product, market, product/market, geographical, technological
Aquisition/divestment	International, domestic
Evolution of corporate structure	Conglomerate, diversified, subsidiary, divisional
Production	Location, mass, batch, manual/automated
Skills	Management, marketing, technical, production
Technology	Existing/new, internal R&D, licensing, joint ventures corporate venturing, strategic alliances
Market positioning	Price, product differentiation, full range, segmentation, volume/niche
Distribution	Direct sales, agents

Source: based on Rothwell (1992, Figure 2).

Rothwell's (1992) five generations of the innovation process illustrate the growing complexity. First-generation innovation was based on *technology-push* and a simple linear model. The second generation was based on *need-pull*; this linear process emphasized marketing and markets as the source of ideas for R&D. Third-generation innovation was based on a *coupling or feedback model*, as represented in Figure 2.2; emphasis was on integration of R&D and marketing. The fourth-generation innovation process was an *integrated model*, concerned to create parallel development, integrated development teams, strong linkages with suppliers and with leading-edge customers, and horizontal collaboration. Fifth-generation innovation is based on a *systems integration and networking model*, comprising the features of the fourth-generation model, as well as flexibility, speed of development and quality. Key features of current best practice in R&D are a technology strategy and external awareness, as seen in constant global monitoring of external sources of information (Ransley and Rogers 1994).

Because of its institutionalized nature, R&D expenditure by firms tends strongly toward some stable target, such as a fixed percentage of sales or allocations by other 'comparable' firms, rather than to fluctuate annually (Kay 1979: 72–7). The importance of consistency is seen in the study by Hitt, Ireland and Goryunov (1988), in which R&D intensity was positively related to corporate performance only among firms which adhered to a single business or narrow spectrum of core businesses. Among small US firms, those with a full-time commitment to internal R&D consistently outperformed firms for which R&D was only a part-time activity (Parisi 1989). At the same time, it is not uncommon for small firms in both the USA and the UK to fail to account for, or to estimate accurately, either the cost of R&D or its contribution to firm performance (Oakey, Rothwell and Cooper 1988: 118–34).

Technological strategies of firms

Technology is a principal means by which firms compete. It can be 'created' given sufficient effort and expenditure, evidenced at the national scale in the 'big science' space and energy exploits of advanced economies, in contrast to persistent problems of housing, waste disposal, and cures for diseases such as cancer or AIDS. Technology begins, as Chapter 2 has shown, with basic research findings that might, or might not, result in marketable products. Such research is long-term and thus easily avoided by short-sighted management who do not see a near-term payoff (Rosenbloom and Abernathy 1982). The success of Japanese companies in capturing the VCR market over competitors in Europe and the USA is attributed to this short-sightedness. In addition, complementary assets, such as competitive manufacturing, suppliers, distribution, service, a proven trade name and complementary technologies, are of course involved, but a firm cannot survive – or will not grow – unless it undertakes periodic, if not constant, technological change.

Much of strategy involves competition and the ways in which strategy both generates competition and responds to it. Several characteristics of high-intensity competition, or hypercompetition, follow closely the characteristics of dynamic Schumpeterian competition rather than neoclassical type (D'Aveni 1994):

- firms aggressively position against one another by attempting to disadvantage opponents;
- firms create new competitive advantages which match or make obsolete opponents' advantages in four arenas of competition: (1) cost and quality; (2) timing and know-how; (3) geographic or product strengths; and (4) financial resources;
- firms attempt to stay ahead of their competitors in one or more of the four arenas of competition;
- firms create new competitive advantages that make the opponents' advantages irrelevant by moving to compete in another arena;
- temporary advantage and short periods of profit are achievable until competitors catch up with or outmanoeuvre the aggressor's last competitive move (D'Aveni 1994: 28).

A firm does not compete alone; especially as new industries evolve, industry 'ecosystems' develop to encompass customers and suppliers (Moore 1993). The ecosystem or 'industry social system' includes subsystems: an institutional subsystem, comprising governance structures, rules and standards; a resource procurement subsystem, where sources of basic research, finance and human resources are obtained; and an instrumental subsystem, including suppliers of R&D, manufacturing, marketing and distribution (Van de Ven and Garud 1989). Communication and information flow are essential with other parties in the ecosystem or social system, but perhaps especially with suppliers and users, as well as competitors (Håkansson 1987, 1989; Håkansson and Laage-Hellman 1984; von Hippel 1988).

Strategy implies a vision or intent concerning the firm's future direction. Strategy is achieved by accumulating resources – especially knowledge and complementary assets – and leading and converging them toward a goal. For example, Canon has assembled a set of competences in four areas. Its experience in cameras enabled it to develop skills in precision mechanics and fine optics. Adding to these, it developed skills in microelectronics (first deployed in auto-focus cameras and calculators) and electronic imaging; their combination has been blended in such products as laser printers, ink-jet printers, fax machines, copiers and cell analysers (Hamel and Prahalad 1994: 228). Similarly, Minnesota Mining and Manufacturing (3M) has used its core competences in adhesives, abrasives and coatings to enable it to develop new products at one of the highest rates in the world (Quinn 1992). Innovative companies derive 30 per cent or more of their sales from products new within the past five years; examples include Henkel, Hewlett-Packard, Merck, 3M, Bayer, and Asahi Glass (Brenner 1994). Firms like these actively pursue product diversification by exploiting technology-based extensions of existing businesses, a strategy that is associated with higher sales growth than more limited or focused strategies (Sjölander and Oskarsson 1995).

These *core competences* comprise an integration of skills that not only serve existing products and customers but are able to define new areas not currently being served (Hamel and Prahalad 1994; Quinn 1992). Unlike the smaller competitive steps of hypercompetition, core competences do not wear out, although their value declines over time if not sustained. In this way, firms can be ready to respond with products for demands that might well be unarticulated or unknown (Leonard-Barton 1995; Zangwill 1993). Stalk, Evans and Shulman (1992) insist that *capabilities* better capture the long-term strength of corporate strategy, since they encompass the entire value chain, whereas competences tend to emphasize expertise in technology or production. Technology is 'the most fundamental' of the core capabilities of a firm (Itami and Numagami 1992). Cumulative learning over time, based on core competences, is both profitable and difficult for competitors to imitate (Pavitt 1994). There is a risk of core competences becoming 'core rigidities' if customer or user needs are not kept prominent (Leonard-Barton and Doyle 1996).

The value chain is a central concept in management, encompassing the range of discrete activities a firm performs (or purchases) to design, produce, market, deliver and support its product (Porter 1985). A firm need not control or 'make' all of these activities itself. It can 'buy' or outsource those that are most distant from the firm's core competences (Quinn and Hilmer 1994). Another perspective insists that information-based resources, such as technological experience and feedback from customers, are *invisible assets* that are key to company adaptability (Itami 1987). Taken together, the *economic competence* of a firm, defined as the ability to identify, expand and exploit business opportunities, combines four types of capabilities: (1) selective or strategic, (2) organizational or coordinating, (3) technical, and (4) learning ability. Transnational firms are able to develop wider competence because of their interaction with a variety of markets, technologies, and competitors (Carlsson and Eliasson 1994). Even in low-tech industries, such as food, interaction with customers is common. Danish food producers test prototypes of products by flying them to overseas customers, who cook, taste and evaluate them in the context and language of the setting where they would be sold (Kristensen 1992). This is 'sticky' information that demands close interaction (von Hippel 1994).

R&D is an activity with uncertain outcomes, whether due to technical, market or policy matters (Freeman 1982: 148–55; Roussel, Saad and Erickson 1991). While *incremental* R&D has a high probability of success, *radical* R&D, with a payoff period of two to seven years, and *fundamental* R&D, with a payoff period of four to ten years, are highly uncertain (Roussel, Saad and Erickson 1991: 57). Among the preconditions for sustained corporate innovation is acceptance of the risk of innovation by top management (Rothwell 1992).

Some products end in failure on technical grounds; others are technical successes but fail to find a market; still others fail because of manufacturing problems. Overall, marketing factors, more than technical ones, have been found to differentiate between successful and unsuccessful new product innovation (Johne and Snelson 1988; Rothwell *et al.* 1974). Clearly, 'pseudo-innovations' and other minor changes involve the lowest uncertainty of any kind, and will tend to be preferred by managers (Kay 1979: 78–83). A firm can reduce uncertainty even in new markets and new technologies if new products are closely related to existing products and if the firm's existing R&D, engineering and production capabilities, and other complementary assets are drawn upon (Cooper 1984a,b; Cooper and Kleinschmidt 1987). In this way, both a producer and its customers learn about the new technologies (Maidique and Zirger 1985).

Markets are more difficult to predict in the case of truly innovative products (Shanklin and Ryans 1984). Technological discontinuities and the development of architectural or architectonic innovations severely disrupt stable industry patterns, destroying competences in entrenched firms (Anderson and Tushman 1991). Firms can respond to radical innovations and to architectural innovations – new combinations of components (Henderson and Clark 1990). These architectural innovations, such as the copier and the fax machine, can lead to entire 'product families' based on the capabilities which brought the components together in a new manner (Meyer and Utterback 1993; Uzumeri and Sanderson 1995). In other cases, seemingly similar products, such as computer hard disk drives, embodied new architectural characteristics as each new generation of drives was smaller and faster than previous products (Rosenbloom and Christensen 1994).

R&D as an ongoing company activity may be especially vital for firms in stagnant industries; those whose product life-cycles are longer and less numerous, such as household appliances and commodity chemicals (Clark, Freeman and Hanssens 1984; Linn 1984). In these sectors, R&D is often for product improvements to increase quality – again keeping the technological frontier in sight. The innovation process in these industries may be even more important than in rapidly growing industries, because innovations are less frequent and more pivotal (Hammermesh and Silk 1979; Tellis and Golder 1996).

There are a number of ways in which firms utilize technology as a basis of competition (D'Aveni 1994; Freeman 1982; Porter 1980, 1985; van der Meer and Calori 1989). The path or trajectory a firm chooses will be based to a large degree on its accumulated knowledge and its absorptive capacity (Chapter 2). Firms with an *offensive* strategy maintain a world-class research capability, usually in a central research laboratory, which is able to keep abreast of virtually any development that a competitor might unveil. This strategy obviously can be very costly, in terms of overhead on research laboratories and equipment as well as large staffs of researchers, but most firms that are leaders in their industries follow this strategy to some degree. If a company cannot keep a state-of-the-art R&D capability in all fields, research leadership in a few key technologies can carry over into other areas. R&D personnel prefer to work for employers who prize and reward research, thus making personnel recruitment and retention easier (Steele 1975). In smaller firms, such as those in the biotechnology sector, an offensive strategy entails continuous learning and training of its research employees. This has the effect of increasing professional motivation, from which both firm and employee benefit (Dodgson 1992).

Offensive R&D is aimed at being first to market with new innovations (Maidique and Patch 1988; Spital 1983). Especially in research-intensive sectors, such as pharmaceuticals and semiconductors, being first to innovate is a common strategy. Although it is usually a profitable and successful strategy, technological 'pioneers' also bear significant costs and can 'burn out' and be overtaken by later rivals (Olleros 1986; Porter 1985: 189–91). There are several causes of this burn-out, which differs from the usual shakeout of small firms that occurs somewhat later as a product or industry matures. First, 'pioneer externalities' benefit later entrants as technologies and markets turn, to some degree, into public goods which later entrants can access for a fraction of the pioneer's development cost. Second, market uncertainty, particularly a long payback period common to radical breakthroughs, can prompt a pioneer to leave the market to others. The market may develop slowly for other reasons, such as the initial lack of infrastructure or complementary technologies, for example software for robotics and airports for airplanes (Brown 1981; McIntyre 1988). Technological uncertainty may prevent rapid adoption of first-generation technology. Users' expectations that improved versions are just around the corner, as well as major incompatibilities as second-generation technologies emerge, can thwart the success of pioneers (Olleros 1986; Porter 1985; Rosenberg 1982; Rosenbloom and Cusumano 1987).

> At this fluid and uncertain stage, pioneers (somewhat like the early users on the other side of the market) will have to face up to a high probability not only of choosing the wrong initial technology, but also of being entirely leapfrogged by a later group of entrants riding a far superior and totally different technological approach (Olleros 1986: 15–16).

Because of these uncertainties, only a relatively small number of firms will be willing to follow an offensive strategy, and even those which do may well retreat somewhat to consolidate their former successes (Freeman 1982: 176). Solutions for a pioneer firm include subcontracting to keep investment costs low, and joint ventures with established marketers to speed up sales (and therefore returns on R&D investment) as have been common in the biotechnology industry. Licensing can also facilitate the commercialization of a firm's technology over that of rivals (Olleros 1986). In general, technology leadership is not enough; a firm must have (or obtain) leadership in other activities as well, and all functions must innovate (Abetti 1994).

Firms with a *defensive* strategy are able to react rapidly when a competitor firm unveils a new product, introduces a lower-cost version of a relatively new product, or may be known to be on the verge of new discoveries in some field. Firms that tend toward defensive R&D, or 'technological followership', must also maintain a sizable research and engineering presence, and may be pioneers in lowest-cost product design and manufacture (Porter 1985: 176–93). Such technological threats often emerge from other sectors, where it is more difficult to monitor them than from known competitors (Cooper and Schendel 1976; Foster 1986).

A third technological strategy is simply *imitation* of the technological moves of more innovative firms. Product imitations may be simple knockoffs or clones, utilizing low-cost manufacturing processes, rather than actual scientific research capability, at least in comparison with firms in either the offensive or defensive categories. Creative adaptations to other markets and technological leapfrogging are also forms of imitation that can be disruptive to an industry leader (D'Aveni 1994; Schnaars 1994). This strategy requires staying technologically current (Schnaars 1994).

Freeman also suggests that there are *dependent* firms, which are wholly reliant on others, such as suppliers, to initiate technical changes. A dependent firm will typically conduct no R&D at all and have no capability in product design. *Traditional* firms, which are usually suppliers to larger organizations, change only in response to specifications from the outside. They may be especially strong in craft skills. Finally, *opportunist* or *niche* firms may be quite innovative, but serve a market with few, if any, competitors, or settings where economies of scale or experience provide little advantage (Charles, Monk and Sciberras 1989: 157–8; Cooper, Willard and Woo 1986). By serving only small markets, niche producers can easily switch from product to product. Niche firms are often remarkably innovative and provide the foundation of many regional economies (Doeringer, Terkla and Topakian 1987: 82–96; Sabel *et al.* 1987).

A variant of the niche strategy that is used to enter new markets in order to perfect new technology is the 'thin markets' strategy. It makes use of 'learning by selling' and feedback from lead users (Thomson 1989; von Hippel 1988). Best applied in limited, specialized markets, this strategy involves convincing a small number of firms to purchase the new technology, even though its cost typically is higher than currently used products. Without these thin markets, some R&D would never even be attempted, and the essential experience of users would not be taken into account (Abernathy 1980; Lifton and Lifton 1989).

The technological capabilities of firms largely determine both their relationship with other firms and the strategies which are open to them (Bessant 1993; Taylor and Thrift 1982; Thorelli 1986). Arnold (1985: 119–24) has applied Freeman's strategy types to the technological strategies of firms in the television industry, and has found Japanese firms, and Sony in particular, to be the most consistently offensive. Finally, in addition to the technological aspects, strategies are influenced by the firm's complementary assets and the nature of its external linkages. A firm's size, core competences and accumulated learning may be more influential than a chosen strategy to be a technological leader or a follower (Pavitt 1994). Firms which rely primarily on suppliers are in a different position to firms which can maintain 'science-based' strategies (Pavitt 1984). National differences emerge regarding corporate strategies for new technologies. Swedish firms, for example, tend to maintain a narrow product range even where sales are broadly international, whereas Japanese firms routinely expand their technology base and their product range (Granstrand *et al.* 1990).

Corporate organization of R&D activities

In addition to the strategic importance of R&D, its place in the firm's organization has both management and geographic implications. Commonly, the principal organizational need is that R&D be near the firm's administrative headquarters to facilitate communication between the various functional sections of the firm, especially between R&D and marketing (Burgelman and Sayles 1986) and between R&D and manufacturing (Hughes Aircraft 1978). If an organization fails to keep its innovation-related functions together, 'intra-organizational dislocations' can create formidable barriers to innovation (More 1985). The interface between R&D and production becomes more significant as R&D is 'coupled' to a greater degree with manufacturing operations (Charles, Monk and Sciberras 1989: 139–42; Hull, Hage and Azumi 1985; Rubenstein 1989: 344–62).

The issue of centralization versus decentralization of R&D is one of the few issues that directly relates to regional technological capability, through its impact on R&D location. Because the corporate R&D function typically falls directly under top management, either at the corporate or the divisional level, it has often been remote from the other functions of the company. A central location allows economies of scale in facilities and equipment, minimal barriers to interaction, the potential for interdisciplinary efforts, and the ability to utilize large numbers of people on major projects (Gibbs *et al.* 1985; Graham 1986; Thomas 1983). A central laboratory with a broad charter is able to attract the best people because it closely resembles the academic environment with which the firm competes for researchers. R&D personnel prefer to work for employers who prize and reward research, and this makes recruitment easier for those firms and facilities (Graham 1985; Steele 1975; Thwaites and Alderman 1990).

The more common corporate administrative structure is a decentralized organization, organized on the basis of product line divisions or subsidiaries (Rubenstein 1989; Malecki 1980a). Long-range and basic research on relatively uncertain R&D tend to be centralized in one (or very few) central laboratories (Roussel, Saad and Erickson 1991). Product development, on the other hand, typically is decentralized to a number of manufacturing plants, where it can be more closely linked or 'coupled' with manufacturing and marketing (Maidique and Hayes 1984; Rubenstein 1989; Souder 1983; Tushman 1979; Westwood 1984). By interacting with R&D, product design and manufacturing can take on more 'upstream' roles, in addition to 'downstream' roles related to marketing and service (Gerwin and Guild 1994). Other advantages to dispersed R&D locations include escaping costs that may have become excessive in current locations (Saxenian 1983), and the ability to tap new sources of technical talent in new locations (Kanter 1984). Even in a seemingly decentralized structure, however, firms continue to concentrate their more innovative research at central laboratories and their less technical efforts, especially process R&D, at some – but not all – branch plants (Dalborg 1974; Howells 1984; Thwaites and Alderman 1990).

When R&D is decentralized in this manner, communication with other parts of a division is facilitated (Fuller 1983). However, geographically dispersed R&D tends to decrease the amount of communication possible between researchers, despite advances in electronic mail, unless they have the opportunity for face-to-face meetings as well (De Meyer 1993a). The use of IT remains more informal than formal even when widespread within the R&D networks of global firms (Howells 1995). There are other advantages to decentralization, such as encouraging entrepreneurship in large corporations, which can be facilitated by separate locations for R&D (Anderson 1969; Quinn 1979). This 'skunk works' strategy is also used to pull together teams with skills that otherwise might not interact (Single and Spurgeon 1996).

The issue of R&D organization reflects more fundamental strategic and philosophical foundations. Japanese firms tend to favour decentralized R&D in order to keep it close to the manufacturing process (Hull, Hage and Azumi 1985; Westney and Sakakibara 1986). At the same time, most Japanese firms also maintain large central research laboratories in which basic and applied research are concentrated (Kono 1984). In the USA, it is more common for a fairly large proportion of R&D to be centralized. Increasingly, however, firms outside Japan are upgrading engineering expertise, oriented toward both flexible and low-cost manufacturing processes, at production sites. As process engineering is decentralized, it is found at an increasing number of production sites (Ahlbrandt and Blair 1986; Dumbleton 1986). As with production plants and other parts of a corporation, R&D structures are largely the outcome of the historical development of the enterprise, including mergers and acquisitions (Thwaites and Alderman 1990). These distinct patterns have converged during the 1990s, as Japanese firms have begun to rely more on central R&D, and European and North American firms have decentralized (Roberts 1995).

Factors external to the firm and its organization are also important. These include the advantages of proximity to other firms, which can minimize the cost of, and maximize the opportunities for, acquiring information, whether from rivals, suppliers, customers, universities or other sources (Andersson 1985; Dalborg 1974; Oakey 1984; Rogers and Larsen 1984; von Hippel 1988). When a firm has decided on geographical dispersion of R&D, it tends to be constrained to areas where workers can be attracted and retained. Increasingly, location is seen as part of the 'creative climate' that companies are striving to create for their R&D operations (Martin 1984).

The contact networks of technical workers are a principal source of technical knowledge (Allen 1977; Håkansson 1987, 1989). In a study of 26 firms, the personal networks of researchers represented the third-largest source of new technologies (Bosomworth and Sage 1995: 37). Firms rely on the heterogeneous contacts and networks of individuals in order to acquire information from other organizations. The information 'gatekeeper' role is a well-known one, useful throughout the life-cycle of products (Badawy 1988; De Meyer 1985; Roberts and Fusfeld 1981). Increasingly, it is seen to be vital for firms to recruit personnel with certain contacts and personal networks in place, to encourage contacts to be formed and maintained, and to circulate people in order to develop their networks of contacts more fully, to the advantage of the firm (Ettlie 1980; Håkansson 1987; Shapero 1985). The common contact networks of rival firms even result in informal trading of know-how between competitors (von Hippel 1987). Large firms are best positioned to exploit information sources. The ability of large firms to gather and process information from external as well as internal sources does not guarantee that they will act competently. Fransman (1994a) details the decline of IBM in the face of knowledge that small computers were replacing mainframes. The accumulated knowledge contradicted the firm's managers' deep-seated belief in large computers. The way in which IBM has used knowledge contrasts with the approach common among firms in Japan.

Japanese firms: a distinctive approach to managing innovation

The description of corporate strategies and structures thus far fails to stress the Japanese firm and the very different forms found in Japanese firms. Japanese firms differ from Western firms in several respects (Aoki 1994). The firm functions as an *information system*, not simply as a decision-making organization. This information system operates both within the firm and across a 'family' of related firms in an enterprise group, in which cross-ownership is the norm. Affiliated companies add greatly to the technological capabilities of a firm, although 'it is not easy to understand how that network is managed' (Westney 1994: 172). Corporate structure is less important than in non-Japanese firms, and corporate culture accomplishes what organizational form tries to do in other firms in other countries (Song and Parry 1993).

The loosely structured Japanese organization is more evolutionary and adaptive to changes, because continual information permits learning to be ongoing throughout the organization (Imai 1992; Kagano *et al.* 1985). Horizontal coordination, rather than hierarchical coordination, is based on sharing knowledge and information (Aoki 1990). Horizontal integration within the firm has enabled firms such as Nissan and NEC to master new technologies and upgrade their capabilities in a dynamic manner (Iansiti and Clark 1994). Long-term, persistent learning has permitted Japanese firms, for example, to learn new technologies and build competence in optoelectronics (lasers) more effectively than European firms (Miyazaki 1994). A horizontal 'family' structure also has other advantages. It provides 'internal' customers to test the market for new products. It also provides a 'place' for interaction crucial to the innovation process (Imai 1994). Chapter 6 returns to this Japanese form of large enterprise.

The web of linkages internal as well as external to the firm provides an information redundancy that allows Japanese firms to take advantage of a larger number of sources of tacit and explicit knowledge sources (Nonaka and Takeuchi 1995). These overlapping sources are especially effective in the process of innovation, where a large number of potential ideas are reduced through the varied expertise and knowledge of team members (Nonaka 1990a, 1994). In effect, these and several other mechanisms provide integration of technologies with managerial functions (Bowonder and Miyake 1993). Table 3.6 illustrates the various mechanisms for functional integration in technology. These integrative mechanisms allow Japanese firms to lower transaction costs, achieve fusion of different technologies, reduce the cycle time between design and commercialization, achieve rapid introduction of new products, and develop multidimensional competences (Bowonder and Miyake 1993: 154). This permits Japanese firms in several sectors to be productive and competitive

Table 3.6 Mechanisms used by Japanese firms for functional integration in innovation.

Mechanism	Characteristics
Organizational intelligence	Technical, commercial and financial intelligence obtained through a variety of channels. This is processed and disseminated to various departments
Technology fusion	Fusing diverse technologies to obtain new, more innovative technologies
Concurrent engineering	Overlapping the phases of development to facilitate information exchange, performance feedback and technological improvements
Horizontal information flow structures	Job rotation, teams for new product development and technology assimilation, large trading houses
Corporate networking	Quick exchange of data, information, designs and other knowledge
Technology forecasting	An integrated, long-term vision of technologies, competencies and markets
Organizational learning	In-house, on-the-job training, new product subsidiaries, learning by doing, learning by using, learning by selling

Source: modified from Bowonder and Miyake (1993: 148, Table 1).

despite sometimes lower levels of R&D intensity. Papadakis (1995) attributes this to market-pull and emphasis on process innovation and manufacturing, in contrast to technology-push, which is dominant in most industries in the USA.

The Japanese system permits hybrid technologies and technology fusion in a *systemic* manner, which seems more difficult for non-Japanese firms to achieve. Three examples serve to illustrate this. The first is the 'tree' model used to represent companies and technologies. NEC portrays the firm as a tree, with technology as the roots, and several branches: communications, electronic devices, home electronics, computers and new opportunities (Branscomb and Kodama 1993: 27; Uenohara 1991). The tree model is more detailed in the case of Sharp Corporation, rooted in specific technologies such as digital recording, optical technologies and signal conversion, to propagate 'branches' such as electronic organs, satellite receivers, multi-channel recording and tapeless microcassettes (Tatsuno 1990: 83). An entire sector, the aircraft industry, has also been portrayed in the tree metaphor, rooted in basic technologies, with 'fruits' in new and enhanced products for several sectors, including cars, shipbuilding, energy and housing (Figure 3.1). A variation on the tree model is the 'bamboo innovation model' used by Sumitomo; bamboo begins as a single sprout, and other clumps of bamboo develop from the common roots over time to form clusters of related technologies (Branscomb and Kodama 1993: 26; Kodama 1995a: 47–8). The organic metaphor of a tree or bamboo plant embodies the connections between technologies and the relationship between various products and sectors. The

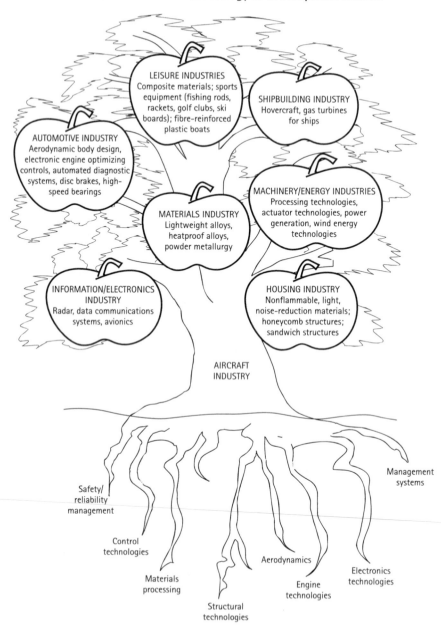

Figure 3.1   Japan's aerospace technology tree. Source: Samuels and Whipple (1989: 50).

linkages between technologies permit systemic products, such as robots, to be perfected by combining mechanics, electronics, sensors, new materials and software (Imai and Baba 1991).

A second example of Japanese systemic thinking is the global, rather than limited, search for new ideas and information (Tatsuno 1990: 76–80). This 'knowledge spiral' utilizes a global search of internal and external sources of tacit and explicit knowledge, permitting frequent feedback for improvements of existing products as well as development of new products (Nonaka and Takeuchi 1995: 70–3). The linkages and flows within intra- and inter-organizational networks, rather than science or the market, become the source of innovation. 'Cross-border networks' cross and transcend the boundaries of technologies, of departments within the firm, of firms, and of sectors (Imai and Baba 1991). Japanese firms have consistently relied on external sources of technology to a greater degree than European and North American firms (Roberts 1995).

The third example is the long-range 'vision' and 'day after tomorrow' R&D. The development of generic technologies (the 'roots' of the trees) is carried out in central or corporate R&D laboratories for use in manufacturing divisions. In effect, the 'day after tomorrow' R&D provides long-range capabilities for the firm (Uenohara 1991). In addition, long-range planning is common in large Japanese firms (Kono 1984), and these plans help to form the basis of 'visions of the future' coordinated by the Ministry of International Trade and Industry (MITI) (Tatsuno 1990).

The Japanese innovation management system assumes that workers and their information networks are critical to the success of the firm, as are small firms, ,with which subcontracting relationships are common. Internal labour markets and widespread rotation of R&D workers integrates the knowledge sets of workers in production, marketing and R&D (Fransman 1994b). Close relationships with subcontractors form another 'important channel of information interchange on market or technology matters between large and small firms' (Fruin 1992: 287). This 'micro–macro information loop' provides context-specific information more efficiently than could be done solely through market mechanisms (Imai 1992; Yangida 1992).

Global competition and strategic alliances

Despite the pace of technological effort expended by large firms, the diversity of technology and markets frequently confronts firms with a 'make or buy' decision concerning technology (Rubenstein 1989: 266–87). Uncertainty about the cost, performance and timing of internally developed innovations, and especially the narrow time frame within which innovations must be taken advantage of, has prompted *strategic alliances*. These partnerships, collaborations between competing corporations, combine the strengths of two (or more) competitors, often based in different countries. Strategic alliances have become a significant form of competition between transnational and other large companies (Chesnais 1988; Friar and Horwitch 1986; Mowery 1989; Niosi and Bergeron 1992; Yoshino and Rangan 1995). 'Global strategies' embodied in alliances are believed to be essential in order to compete (Hamel and Prahalad 1985; Hout, Porter and Rudden 1982; Littler and Wilemon 1991; Spence and Hazard 1988).

Such a *network strategy* in a corporation thrives on the basis of its linkages with other firms, whether as sources of technology or of other complementary assets. Indeed, in-house R&D may be less significant than production capabilities and other complementary assets (Pisano and Teece 1989; Pisano, Russo and Teece 1988). 'Strategic technology leveraging' and outsourcing of technology in a 'virtual R&D laboratory' fit the current era of 'downsized' firms which do less internal R&D, down to about 50 per cent from the 80 per cent typical in the 1970s (Jonash 1996).

Disadvantages of inter-firm cooperation in R&D include dependency on partners and high cost of negotiations and transactions. High transaction costs prevail most in the early and late stages of technological life-cycles (Brockhoff 1992). An external R&D strategy requires both constant monitoring of general technological trends and the capabilities of potential partners, and collaboration in fields where a firm's capabilities are not especially strong (Harris *et al.* 1996). The risk of outsourcing R&D is especially great in the case of systemic innovations, in which technology tends to be tacit and coordination throughout the product system is hard to manage, in contrast to autonomous, stand-alone innovations. Virtual firms are always dependent on their partners and suppliers, and the best examples of virtual firms (Nike, Toyota, Motorola) are those large enough to control the relationship (Chesbrough and Teece 1996). For these firms and for others, it is best to sustain internal investment to create capabilities in critical parts of the value chain, and to outsource only less critical technologies. A network firm can easily become a hollow corporation (*Business Week* 1986).

Linkages between competitors, as well as between dominant firms and suppliers, became during the 1980s probably the predominant form of corporate strategy (Chesnais 1988; Fusfeld 1994; Spekman 1988). The Triad – Europe, Japan and the United States – contains the dominant markets and producers in the international economy today, and firms in all three regions are central to the webs of alliances being formed in semiconductors and other high-technology sectors (Chesnais 1988; Ohmae 1985). There has been no slowdown in the formation of alliances, especially of R&D partnerships, and they are continuing to proliferate in IT (National Science Board 1996: 4-43–4-44). Developing countries appear to be 'locked out' of alliances in new core technologies (Freeman and Hagedoorn 1994).

Examples abound among the world's transnationals. General Electric has formed at least 29 alliances, most of them structured as joint ventures, with firms in France, Germany, Italy, Japan and the UK as well as competitors in the USA. Of General Motors' 16 alliances, most are with Japanese firms for the supply of parts or joint production (Yoshino and Rangan 1995: 171–2). Japanese semiconductor firms have allied extensively with competitors both within and outside Japan (Hobday 1989). The development of international collaborative ventures is common among firms in industries as diverse as steel, motor vehicles, robotics, biotechnology, computers and new materials (Hagedoorn 1995; Hagedoorn and Schankenraad 1990, 1992; Mowery 1989). In the case of an emerging technology such as biotechnology, such alliances permit three strategies to be exploited:

1. A *window strategy* allows a firms to identify and monitor leading-edge technologies developed elsewhere. Linkages will usually take the form of research grants and contracts to outside organizations, including universities and research institutes, or equity investments in new firms.
2. An *options strategy* is more selective, designating a small number of market or technical areas in which to participate. R&D contracts, licences, equity investments and joint ventures are common.
3. A *positioning strategy* reflects a commitment to a technology for commercial exploitation. R&D contracts, licences and joint ventures aimed at production are the types of alliance seen with this strategy (Hamilton 1986: 111–12; Olleros and Macdonald 1988; Pisano, Shan and Teece 1988).

Relationships between industry and universities in particular have grown dramatically, prompting critics to deride the pacts as making knowledge a commodity for sale (Peters 1989). These links often demand changes in policies on both sides of the relationship – to make university researchers more commercially oriented, and industry more patient (Geisler and Rubenstein 1989). A variety of types of links work best to make university/industry research succeed in the eyes of both parties (Bloedon and Stokes 1994).

Motives for cooperation vary across as well as within industrial sectors and by size of firm. An alliance can: (1) enhance a firm's competitiveness, (2) permit rationalization in a stable industry, (3) provide a transition to a new market, or (4) open up a new business. These motives and advantages differ between the partners (Table 3.7). Development of entirely new products based on complex systems is especially difficult, since it demands that the partners have complementary technologies and that they are able to achieve technology fusion across the organizations (Olleros and Macdonald 1988; Tidd 1995). Moreover, collaborations succeed only if both firms' in-house R&D gives them the ability to absorb new technologies (Mowery 1989). Consequently, it is more technologically competent firms, and R&D-intensive sectors, that are most extensively involved in strategic alliances (George 1995).

In biotechnology, large chemical and pharmaceutical firms ally with small firms in order to gain access to the latter's technology, whereas the biotech firms tap their larger partners' production and marketing capability. In aerospace, alliances have been concentrated in technology-oriented collaborations, including cooperative production, technology sharing and customer–supplier agreements, thereby creating quasi-vertical integration (M. Anderson 1995). In telecommunications, one of the sectors in which alliances have become most common, alliances range across the spectrum from market to hierarchy (Thorelli 1986). The forms include geographical commercial agreements, R&D consortia, complex ventures covering R&D, manufacturing and marketing, and self-contained joint ventures (Garrette and Quelin 1994). All these collaborations are difficult to manage and take considerable time, in order to develop trust both between the partners and between the personnel involved in the dual role (collaborating and competing) in the partnership (Häusler, Hohn and Lütz 1994). Personalities, personal relationships, cultural compatibility, trust and frequent

Table 3.7 Motives of partners in strategic alliances.

Motive of partner 1	Motive of partner 2			
	Enhance competitiveness	Rationalize production	Options for the future	Develop new business
Enhance competitiveness	Toshiba–Motorola (semiconductors)	GE–GEC (appliances)	Whirlpool–Philips (appliances)	Boeing–Mitsubushi Heavy Industries (aircraft)
Rationalize production	GEC–GE (turbines)	ASEA–Brown Boveri (power systems)	Dresser–Komatsu (earthmoving equipment)	Siemens–Corning (fibre optics)
Options for the future	GE–Bosch (motors)	Asahi Glass–Corning (television glass)	Ciba-Geigy–Corning (diagnostics)	Corning–Dow (silicone)
Develop new business	Kodak–Matsushita (batteries)	Fanuc–GE (factory automation)	PPG–Corning (construction glass)	Alliances in multimedia

Source: based on Yoshino and Rangan (1995: 176, Table 8.1).

communication are among the key factors affecting the outcome of collaborative product development (Bruce, Leverick and Littler 1995; Dodgson 1993) as well as of user–producer interaction generally (Gertler 1995). A real risk of formal collaboration, however, is the stifling of informal information flow (Macdonald 1992).

For other firms, the arms-length alliances are less attractive than are conventional means of acquiring technology, via merger and acquisition of other companies. Even here, successful mergers and acquisitions occur primarily when the technological environment of the acquired firm is known and understood; better yet is a 'patient partnership' instead of an expectation of a quick fix (Chakrabarti and Souder 1987). However, there is some evidence that corporate mergers decrease R&D funding, especially for basic research (National Science Foundation 1988).

Japanese firms have led the way in demonstrating the competitiveness provided by cooperation with suppliers and an emphasis on organization and manufacturing skills (Chesnais 1988: 69–78). Perhaps as a result of their preference for network structures, 'Japanese companies are the world's most aggressive participants in global alliances' (Okimoto and Nishi 1994: 204). The formation of a network of firms is a means of reducing risk and uncertainty. These networks may be formed between competitors, between manufacturers and suppliers, within channels of distribution, with spinoff enterprises, and within corporate groups (Kagono et al. 1985: 77–83). The flexibility afforded by external sources of R&D outweighs for many firms a loss of control (Riedle 1989: 219). However, network strategies are pursued differently by different types of firms, and illustrate that control is still possible. Japanese firms prefer joint ventures in which they are dominant, taking advantage of the technology or market presence of smaller firms (Tyebjee 1988).

Informal types of cooperative research are also prominent in Japan. Close ties are maintained between Japanese university professors and their former students, who may be working for a number of competing firms (Cutler 1989: 22). Professors are sought out as contacts for their networks of colleagues and former students more than for their technical knowledge, which often is greater inside the major companies (Westney 1993).

Cooperative industrial research is not new. In the form of Research Associations (RAs) it has been in existence in the UK since 1917. RAs account for a significant amount of R&D only in a few low-tech industries, however, such as clothing and timber and furniture (Johnson 1973; Johnson 1975: 190–208). Perhaps because of this low-tech bias, cooperative R&D may be perceived as a 'second-rate venture' or low priority for the companies involved, or for their researchers. In two large chemical firms, the best scientists were perceived to be kept for in-house research, rather than for joint venture research projects (Link and Bauer 1989: 95–6). It is not known whether this sort of bias afflicts R&D within strategic alliances. Finally, geography has been found to influence cooperative research among US firms. In 15 of 18 cases studied by Link and Bauer (1989: 96–7), 'when research partners were in a close proximity, the ease with which the projects were conducted and completed improved.'

Licensing strategies and technological capability

Licensing, or acquisition and sale of technology, provides an alternative to internal R&D for the purchasing firm, and provides a return on prior R&D investments and a source of revenue for further R&D by the firm selling its technology. From the point of view of a purchasing firm, licensing results in faster commercial development and market entry or enhanced market share than costly internal R&D would permit. It can also provide specialized knowledge and skills, and even stimulate a licensee's technological capability by making it more aware of the advantages of outside developments (McDonald and Leahey 1985). The advantages of licensed technology to the buyer depend heavily on how current the technology is, and whether the licensee is permitted to retain the rights to any improvements made and to export freely (Prasad 1981; Thomas 1988).

The firms most likely to have licensing-out as part of their strategic planning are large firms and those firms which have the highest R&D intensities (Adam, Ong and Pearson 1988; Bertin and Wyatt 1988; McDonald and Leahey 1985; Robinson 1988; Vickery 1988). The short life-cycles in R&D-intensive industries seem to be the motivation for firms in those sectors. The price which a technology licence can command depends on its competitiveness and its stage of development (Udell and Potter 1989). Patent protection or other strong means of appropriability, however, is costly to maintain, especially where product cycles are short.

For firms seeking to acquire technology, licensing may be a route to enhancing technological capabilities, but it appears that an existing capability is needed first. Firms that acquire a licence for a product or process tend to be younger, larger and, most importantly, have a greater overall technological capacity than firms without licences. Information on the availability of such licences is obtained most often from trade shows, followed by national and international contacts within the industry (Reid and Reid 1988). Travel abroad, internal R&D, and other indicators of awareness and absorptive capacity are essential to being aware of licensing possibilities (Allen *et al.* 1990; Atuahene-Gima 1993; Mowery 1989). In effect, the buyer, or user, of transferred technology needs technical expertise nearly equal to that of the supplier in order to absorb the technology. The necessary knowledge also includes contract administration and patent management, which are generally considered to be managerial, rather than technical, skills (Rubenstein 1980; Vakil and Brahmananda 1987).

Conclusion

Large-scale phenomena, such as long waves and the definition of high technology, affect the way technology is understood by those outside firms. Within firms, issues of strategy, organization and external relationships are the means of competing in a setting of rapid technological and political change. R&D is necessary for competitiveness but it is not sufficient to bring about mastery over all the facets of competition. Conventional strategies and structures to deal with technological change are changing to emulate the Japanese model of systems and networks. Contacts between people are in many ways the basis for success of firms in new technologies and in alliances and other cooperations. People – and their contacts and skills – also form the basis of what firms look for in locations.

The range of activities that affect and are influenced by technology have many geographical implications, which are the focus of the following chapter. The distinction between countries, regions and places with high levels of technological capability, and those with little such capability, is largely an outcome of the location decision of firms. Location as a competitive option has been transformed as technology has continued to advance. The location of specific labour skills, particularly their suitability for routine or non-routine activities, is a major element in the spatial transformation. No less important is the technology of production and its infrastructures, which allows a wide set of options to flexible firms.

Chapter 4

The location of economic activities: flexibility and agglomeration

The complex processes of innovation and economic activity do not take place in isolation of real places. It is these real places that generate the conditions that both enable and constrain companies as they pursue profitable activities. As it is for firms, it is difficult for regions and nations to retain accumulated advantages, and it may be necessary for other places to create conditions under which technological capability can take root and flourish. The actions of firms and their relationships with technology, with labour, and with other firms – large and small – set the conditions for national, regional and local prosperity and development.

The issue of flexibility is key to a discussion of how the location of economic activity takes place. Conventional industrial location theory has failed to be very useful in understanding or predicting the location of plant closures, of high-technology industry, or even of manufacturing plants, for which the theory was developed. Moreover, a fundamental transition seems to have been taking place since about 1970 to alter the 'rules of the game' both for corporations and for localities. The emergence of flexible production and inter-firm arrangements has vastly changed the way in which economic activity takes place as well as *where* it takes place. Flexibility is itself a flexible concept, encompassing several dimensions and strategies. Some economic activities continue to agglomerate in large urban regions, while other activities are able to operate even closely linked activities from widely dispersed locations. As firms increase their use of flexible methods of production, of work, and of inter-firm relationships, new interactions with governments also appear. Flexibility, its heterogeneity, and its implications for location theory, are the focus of this chapter.

Industrial location and the role of labour

The location of economic activity was once a relatively simple phenomenon to explain. Manufacturing was done by small, single-location companies, utilizing simple inputs to produce a single product. Unfortunately, the body of location theory developed to account for this type of firm is unable to illuminate or anticipate the actions of large companies or their networks of upstream and downstream linkages with firms of all sizes (Fredriksson and Lindmark 1979). Nor is it able to handle the various types of labour and technology that characterize the actual production of goods and services.

Location theory

Traditional, 'classical' location theory (Isard 1956; Smith 1981) had its origins in the work of Weber and the maturation of neoclassical economics. Weberian theory illustrates the idea that an optimal location for a firm can be derived, concentrating on minimization of transportation costs related to the distance from markets and from raw materials. Firms are assumed to be simple, producing a single product, and serving only nearby markets. Raw materials appear as the only critical inputs; labour, information and other inputs are ubiquitous, available everywhere. In this setting, the cost-minimizing (profit-maximizing) location is easily determined (Beckmann and Thisse 1986; Heijman 1990; Smith 1981). Linear programming models assist in the calculations for large problems, such as the location of a brewery which distributes its heavy product to a large number of distribution centres (Schmenner 1982). Nonlinear and integer programming models and multiple objective decision models extend the general idea that an optimal decision can be attained concerning a location or other objective (Nijkamp and Rietveld 1986). The characteristic of location theory which is prized by its admirers and derided by its critics is summed up in the description of Beckmann and Thisse (1986: 87): 'location theory has been developed through the incorporation of spatial variables – localized resources and distances – into microeconomic theory.' This framework neglects the requirements of contemporary firms for markets, skills and infrastructure, and for whom it is not costs that matter, but the quality of those inputs (MacCormack, Newman and Rosenfield 1994).

Weberian location, by focusing on the location decision, ignores the interplay between the decision to locate a company facility and the firm's larger and more intricate investment decisions, only one of which is to invest in a new production facility (Clark, Gertler and Whiteman 1986; Walker and Storper 1981). 'The primary issues for capitalists are *whether* to invest and *what* to invest in – what products, which processes, or which firms' (Walker and Storper 1981: 483). Seen in this context, a location decision cannot be separated from the larger competitive and profit-seeking context within which capitalist firms operate (Massey 1979; Walker 1988). Some of these decisions involve new investments (Schmenner 1982), whereas others largely revolve around disinvestments, or 'restructuring' (Bluestone and Harrison 1982; Massey and Meegan 1982).

Among the more valuable conclusions of classical location theory is the principle of agglomeration, i.e. that firms benefit through lower costs of production by operating in close proximity to other firms. Higher productivity results from the density of human and physical capital in an area (Ciccone and Hall 1996). These *agglomeration economies* are termed *localization economies* when they concern firms in the same or linked industries, or *urbanization economies* when they concern a general cost saving from location in an urban area.

The critical question is again whether to 'make or buy' the goods and services needed, i.e. to produce them internally or to purchase the inputs from firms through market linkages (Scott 1988c). Firms can attempt to internalize these linkages by being vertically integrated, which has been a primary mode of growth of large firms. Alternatively, firms can vertically disintegrate and purchase necessary inputs in external markets. Vertical disintegration is inherently more flexible than a system of internal transactions which must be monitored and managed (Casson 1987). Since the transmission of economic growth throughout an economy takes place mainly through inter-firm linkages, the location of linked firms is central to understanding the empirical outcome of development processes.

Vertical disintegration, or the fragmentation of production into a division of labour and production tasks undertaken by many different firms, is likely under certain circumstances (Scott 1988c: 25–7). First, as product differentiation increases and production runs become smaller, firms shift the uncertainties of volume onto subcontractors and input suppliers. Second, specialized subcontractors can achieve internal economies of scale by doing similar work for many different customers, to the advantage of all. Third, segmented labour markets, with clearly defined primary and secondary segments, tend to be characterized by disintegration of low-skill tasks to low-wage workers, most of which are in small firms, both in advanced countries and in Third World countries. International subcontracting has grown remarkably on a global scale, and is one of the major aspects of the international capitalist system (Germidis 1980). Fourth, geographical agglomeration can induce vertical disintegration, since transactions are easily found and conducted in metropolitan areas and industrial districts (Amin 1989a; Scott 1988c).

In sum, whether there are a few large firms or many small ones depends on the products and services produced and the nature of production, i.e. on industrial organization in the broadest sense (Sayer and Walker 1992). In turn, a setting in which there are many small firms producing unstandardized products will engender a markedly different regional economy from one in which standardized products are the output of large plants (Salais and Storper 1992). Innovative, knowledge-intensive production is increasingly likely to necessitate external sources of knowledge from a network of suppliers and other sources to enhance the competences managed internally. The complexity and diversity of economic activity means that there is simultaneously a tendency toward internalization and control, and a tendency toward vertical disintegration and links to other organizations (Sako 1994; Williger and Zuscovitch 1988).

In reality, production systems are much more complex than the above suggests. Network relations, including subcontracting, represents a middle ground between internalization (making) and open-market transactions (buying). Like joint ventures and other collaborative arrangements, subcontracting is 'neither purely firm-like nor purely market-like' (Casson 1987: 48). It also leaves the subcontractor free to form similar arrangements with other firms. The flexibility, if we may call it that, of subcontracting relations is why it is seen both in clustered settings and at great distances (Holmes 1986; Walker 1988: 389–91).

Depending greatly upon the industrial sector, production restructuring or reorganization may take the form of rationalization, intensification, or investment and technical change (Massey and Meegan 1982). The first two of these largely entail employment losses, whether through plant closure in the case of rationalization, or through capital intensification. 'Technical change' encompasses the array of shifts from one product line to another, typically involving opening new plants and closing old ones. It may involve a situation of 'jobless growth' as output rises while employment is stagnant or declining.

Plant closures must be seen within the broader context of corporate decisions (Watts and Stafford 1986). *Cessation closures* result from the decision to abandon a product or product line, a decision made where geography or specific locations are not really part of the analysis. *Default closures* are related to the decision to expand one (or more) existing plant in circumstances of slow growth and the less efficient plant(s) are closed by default. Finally, *selective closures*, which account for the majority of plant closures, involve the selection of, for example, the least profitable plant among several. Closure decisions are complex, as firms restructure and automate production but not in all locations at the same time (Peck and Townsend 1984, 1987). Most company closure decisions involve a combination of the elimination of old product lines and the retirement of old, inflexible technology (Schmenner 1982; Stafford 1991). A plant's 'life' may be relatively short in any location, particularly if it is tied to the production of a single product or product line. Only more 'flexible' plants can weather the turmoil of uncertainty. Those most likely to be considered flexible are plants affiliated with headquarters and R&D functions, and employment declines are less likely in those locations (Bassett 1986; Malmberg 1995; Schmenner 1982).

The spatial division of labour in large firms

In contrast to the simple, single-product firms of classical location theory, the internal complexity of firms, especially of the large organizations which dominate global, national and local economic activity, has spawned a massive literature on large, particularly transnational, corporations (Bade 1983; Bartlett and Ghoshal 1995; Dicken 1992; Dunning 1993b; Watts 1980). The global structure of these firms is the focus of Chapter 6, but the general behaviour of large firms is dealt with here.

One stream of this effort stresses the organization and growth of firms, their relationships with the external environment, and the ability of firms – especially large ones – 'to manipulate or modify their environmental context' (Hayter and Watts 1983: 161; McDermott and Taylor 1982). As Chandler (1962) suggested, organization and strategies for growth interact in the pursuit of profit and growth, with effects on location (Håkanson 1979). Large, especially transnational firms, have wide information networks and treat the location decision in a much more 'rational', informed manner than do small firms (Oster 1979; Schmenner 1982). Indeed, they are able to manipulate their environment – locations, labour, subcontractors, and even their competitors to some degree via alliances – in a highly effective manner. Small firms, competing against larger competitors in the segmented economy, typically must do so on several fronts simultaneously, but largely confined within the power networks of large firms (Fredriksson and Lindmark 1979; Harrison 1994; Taylor and Thrift 1982).

Labour and location

Labour, a fundamental factor of production in economic theory, is much more heterogeneous than conventional economic theory recognizes (Clark, Gertler and Whiteman 1986; Malecki and Varaiya 1986; Morrison 1990). Within advanced economies as well as between advanced and less developed societies, distinct (*dual* or *segmented*) labour markets are identifiable (Berger and Piore 1980; Peck 1996; Wilkinson 1981). These have been reinforced spatially by branch plant economies and the increasing concentration of control functions in large centres. In the spatial division of labour, rural and other previously unin-dustrialized regions tend to be home to manual workers (the secondary segment), in contrast to the primary segment of workers, which includes management, R&D workers and other white-collar occupations (Cooke 1983; Massey 1995). The diversity of worker functions and power results in a mosaic of labour costs, skills and characteristics from which firms can pick and choose those most suited to profitable activities (Cooke 1983; Harvey 1988; Peck 1989). Territorial clus-ters developed around a particular set of knowledge and skills, or around local customs regarding women's work, attract the portions of an industry suited to those locations (Gringeri 1994a; Hanson and Pratt 1992; Sayer and Walker 1992; Storper and Walker 1989: 144–7). Firms dependent on externalized skill formation, as opposed to internal training, benefit from agglomeration and the skills workers acquire from other local employers (Peck 1992: 340; Peck 1996).

Labour is far from homogeneous in quality or quantity among locations, and companies require different labour skills for different work tasks (Figure 4.1). As

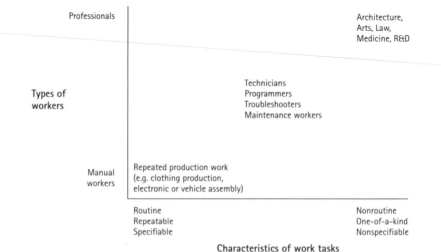

Figure 4.1   Labour skills required of workers for different kinds of work. Source: modified from Shapero (1985: xiii, Figure I–1).

one generalization, technical, engineering and scientific (*nonroutine*) skills are critical to R&D and new products. By contrast, especially for assembly and other *routine* production tasks, little skill is needed (Shapero 1985). This segmentation gives preference to *primary workers*, whose work is more often nonroutine and critical, and more difficult to control. Professional and craft workers have traditionally fallen into this segment, although many of their skills are being replaced by computer technology. Technological displacement is most common among craft workers, such as machinists, but also in the more routine work of architects and computer programmers.

Professional and technical workers are a small but important part of the spatial division of labour in each firm, and they constitute a significant segment of the labour market. Technical workers are important to – indeed, they serve to define the presence of – high-technology industries (Chapter 3). They are recognized as part of a rather separate labour market, made up of managerial, R&D and technical workers (Bailyn 1985). In the conventional segmentation of the labour market, these workers clearly hold independent primary jobs (Harrison and Sum 1979; Storper and Walker 1984). High-technology industry is prominent in its internal contrast between technical labour and less skilled labour (secondary jobs) utilized for standardized production (Batten 1985; Hall and Markusen 1985). The growth of these two ends of the skill spectrum has generated a 'vanishing middle' – the subordinate primary jobs, which have continued to shrink (Appelbaum 1984; Harrison 1984; Harrison and Bluestone 1988).

Not even technical jobs are secure, and the 1990s have made this abundantly clear. Firms have 'downsized' management functions, and technical tasks such as computer programming have been automated and deskilled to allow less skilled workers to perform them (Baldry 1988: 55–71; Kaplinsky 1984; Perrolle 1986). In the clothing industry, for example, computer-aided design (CAD) and manufacturing have eliminated the need for skilled graders (who produce patterns in various sizes), markers (who fit the patterns on fabric to minimize waste), and fabric cutters (whose accuracy and uniformity are essential) (Hoffman and Rush 1988).

Secondary workers face lower wages, less job security, fewer fringe benefits, limited upward mobility, overt control on the job, and seasonal work in some sectors (Storper and Walker 1984: 28; 1989). High turnover among unskilled workers results from dissatisfaction with jobs ('One job is as good or bad as the next') and from employers, who, having invested little in training unskilled workers, are able to replace them easily (Gulowsen 1988: 168). A three-tier society may be forming in many Western countries, as Hutton (1995) suggests concerning the UK: those with privileged, secure jobs; those with unattractive and insecure jobs; and the unemployed.

Primary and secondary labour markets overlap geographically, especially in urban regions. A mix of labour skills – including skilled and unskilled manual labour in addition to professional, technical and scientific workers – is interpreted as an economic advantage of urban regions and a source of urbanization economies (Doeringer, Terkla and Topakian 1987: 88–9; Oakey 1981; Scott

1993). Boddy and Lovering (1986: 226) explain the development of the Bristol region of the UK: 'A crucial factor behind the locality's retention and attraction of technologically advanced activity has been the ability of firms to combine highly qualified staff and more basic production workers, as a basis for both specialized R&D activity as well as production.' The tendency for R&D and managerial jobs to agglomerate in regions which are internally dualistic – having large numbers of primary workers as well as low-wage production and service workers – is perhaps the principal contradiction of contemporary high-tech industry (Saxenian 1983). California is another region which has profited from a diverse labour force (Scott 1993).

A key distinction among the labour markets described thus far is their geographical extent (Bouman and Verhoef 1986). The labour market is *local* for unskilled, semi-skilled and clerical personnel. It is *nationwide* for managerial and marketing talent, and increasingly *worldwide* for key technical specialists. The geographic market provides the comparisons for pay, fringe benefits and other conditions of employment (Riggs 1983; Storper and Walker 1984). Although the pay of professional workers tends to be nearly equal regardless of location, wages of blue-collar workers are very different across regions (Goldfarb and Yezer 1976, 1987).

Because different labour skills are found in different places, firms generally take advantage of, and thereby reinforce, the existing spatial distribution of labour types within their internal organization. Employment in rural areas, in particular, is associated with low wages, fewer fringe benefits and less attractive working conditions than in urban areas (Doeringer 1984; Smith 1981: 325–48). Firms characteristically avoid locating near one another in rural areas, in order not to 'bid up' wages of unskilled workers, but also to avoid competition for pools of skilled workers (Norcliffe and Zweerman Barschat 1994). In urban areas, the presence of a larger labour supply – of immigrants, for example – may drive down wage costs in some industries (Sassen-Koob 1989; Scott 1988b). Urban areas, especially larger ones, have the significant advantage for workers of providing a number of job opportunities without requiring a change of residence (Malecki and Bradbury 1992).

The *branch plant economy* is the prototypical outcome of the tendency toward corporate locations which discover, reinforce and create disparities in labour. The principal consequence for a region or locality of an economy which depends predominantly on branch plants is a limited labour force. Workers in branch plant regions tend to have few skills, since few are needed for the routine tasks of the factory or office. No innovation or decision-making takes place; these are performed elsewhere in the firm's network (Massey 1995; Watts 1981).

Using the core–periphery analogy to describe classes of firms, Danson (1982) suggests that labour market segmentation is a result of 'core' or 'centre' firms being responsible for most of the best jobs (Baron and Bielby 1980). Skilled jobs related to R&D, innovation, marketing and finance tend to be located in the dominant urban regions or in attractive, growing 'sunbelt' regions (Massey 1995). Clarke (1985: 234), in investigating this continuum, found that plants within the British chemical firm ICI are increasingly *either* central or peripheral; similar findings are reported by Malmberg (1995). Central plants are technologically advanced and have more highly skilled labour, whereas peripheral plants are likely to have only older, tried-and-tested technologies with very little on-site innovation. In between, semi-peripheral plants tend to have a mixture of old and new generations of equipment, but not the most recent forms. These plants are becoming either more central or more peripheral over time. The reason for the dichotomy is the 'coordination problem in industrial production', in which either routines are standardized or they are not – the counterpart of the distinction between routine and non-routine work (Malmberg 1995).

A key constituent of plant centrality is the mandate of the plant. A plant with a *world product mandate* will have the necessary R&D personnel, engineers and decision-makers to maintain a global state-of-the-art in products and processes (Etemad and Séguin Dulude 1986; Young, Hood and Dunlop 1988). The regional development outcomes will also vary. For instance, the degree to which input linkages are local or non-local directly determines the multiplier effect for the region. In both Florida and Limburg (Belgium), local purchases of inputs were higher among firms that had higher levels of R&D and higher employment of scientists and engineers, controlling for plant size and autonomy (Hagey and Malecki 1986; Kipnis and Swyngedouw 1988a). Like all firms, high-technology firms differ in the degree to which R&D is done at a given site; some operations are labour-intensive and do not need to be at central locations. Consequently, R&D employment intensity is greater in urban and suburban (in contrast to rural) locations – a pattern that applies to large and small firms alike (Felsenstein and Shachar 1988). This generalization does not preclude the presence of a small amount of R&D in peripheral areas (Kipnis and Swyngedouw 1988b; Malecki 1980a).

Labour costs vary markedly from place to place, both between and within nations. These costs, which include wages as well as non-wage benefits, are determined largely by the labour market institutions, rules and social 'safety nets', which vary from country to country (R. Freeman 1994). Consequently, because of both cost and skill variations, labour is the central factor among the possible influences on the location of economic activity. Labour tends to be place-bound, in contrast to the great geographical mobility of firms, and each place has its own distinctive industries, types of jobs, and communities which form around the local mix of jobs (*The Economist* 1996d; Massey 1995; Storper and Walker 1989: 155–7). Some, perhaps much, of the local variation in labour quality is a product of local modes of social regulation (MSRs), which are the state forms, social mores, laws and habits, which vary from place to place (Peck and Tickell 1995). These correspond to the conventions, the 'micro rules' concerning labour–management relations that generate differences in national and regional performance (Dosi and Kogut 1993; Salais and Storper 1992).

The evolution of regional and local economies involves, perhaps more than anything else, the development of localized labour skills and the agglomeration of linkages between local firms (Hekman and Strong 1981; Scott 1988b). The development of skills and the generation of economic activity which exploits those skills come about through the actions of large multilocational firms and of small local firms.

The location decision of the multilocational firm

The typical corporate location decision is a three-step process, in which a firm first selects a broad region which best serves its market, labour and resource needs. A dominant pattern in recent years has been an avoidance of unionism, even if this is associated with poorly educated or unskilled workers (Kenney and Florida 1993; Lloyd and Reeve 1982; Schmenner, Huber and Cook 1987). In the second step, a selection is made between levels of government, especially as a firm attempts to secure the best 'package' of incentives from various communities. Incentives from governments may include the provision of roads, tax abatements, subsidized loans and labour training, all of which have been typical packages offered to, and accepted by, Japanese car makers in recent years (Bachelor 1991; Newman and Rhee 1990). In general, American firms tend to be significantly more attracted by tax rates and incentives than do German or Japanese firms (Ulgado 1996). The third step is primarily a real estate decision regarding the actual site selection within a local area.

The focus in Weberian analysis on distance as the geographical variable on which location decisions are made greatly distorts the relative importance of manipulable inputs. In partial recognition that distance and transport costs have diminished in importance (to the point of irrelevance for many products and firms), the most frequent reaction has been the provision of lengthy lists of 'location factors', i.e. variables that 'influence the location decision'. Lists that include dozens of variables are common, serving to identify the possible items which a firm might consider (Blair and Premus 1987; Schmenner 1982). Despite lengthy lists and the growing importance of information technology and corporate communications, telecommunications is rarely included in studies of location factors for manufacturing (Hack 1992).

The length and complexity of some lists of location factors has led to a composite variable, *business climate*, which is 'a rough metric of a location's expected ability to maintain a productive environment over the foreseeable future' (Schmenner 1982: 53). Neoclassical price competition between firms 'seems less the crucial variable than how adaptive firms, workers and communities are in terms of the changing economic environment' (Clark 1986a: 418). Local economies can 'be differentiated along the basic dimension of economic uncertainty.' Local economies vary in the degree to which they 'absorb' within the workforce the fluctuations and uncertainties in the production process (Clark, Gertler and Whiteman 1986: 35). Unskilled workers, who tend to be local, less mobile, relatively abundant and found in many locations, are less able to create a labour relation in which the cost of uncertainty falls on the firm rather than on labour (in the form of unemployment). The avoidance of unions is commonplace (Thompson and Rehder 1995), despite research which shows that unionized plants have higher productivity (Freeman and Medoff 1984; Kelley 1994).

Labour is central to the notion of business climate. Annual rankings of state business climates in the USA have led to competition between states, and to a wide variety of incentives for industry, in an attempt to improve a state's ranking from year to year. A reduction in state-regulated labour costs, such as unemployment benefits and workers' compensation, or a halt in the growth of state expenditures, can markedly improve a state's ranking *vis-à-vis* its competitors, i.e. other states. Even with a broadening of the concern with variable costs to include more than taxation, it is still impossible to state that a favourable business climate leads to industrial growth (Erickson 1987). Skoro (1988: 151–2) is more blunt: business climate indexes are actually political statements and 'are useless as predictors' of economic growth. But it remains true, at least in the USA, that low levels of taxation are 'deemed essential to maintaining a good business climate' (Cobb 1993: 271).

When low costs and low wages are the basis for competition, then infrastructure, services and public facilities at the regional and local level are less able to meet the needs of a population and of industry (Power 1988; Tannenwald 1996). The trade-off between taxes and public services has been the focus of studies in the USA (Ameritrust and SRI Inc. 1986; Corporation for Enterprise Development *annual*). It is particularly difficult for localities and regions to maintain the level of public services if incentives and subsidies to relocating firms result in substantial revenue losses (Ihlanfeldt 1995; Lynch, Fishgold and Blackwood 1996; Wassmer 1994).

The relative unimportance of labour factors in many surveys is attributable to a lack of willingness on the part of business executives to admit openly that labour costs and pliability are critical. Business climate then serves as a code for the labour factors (Cobb 1993; Harrison 1984). Schmenner (1982: 150–1) presents similar findings: low wage rates and non-union sites are relatively unimportant, whereas 'favourable labour climate' is by a wide margin the most important factor in a location choice. In the widely cited growth of industry in the US South – the 'Sunbelt' – the mix of jobs new to the region are for the most part low-skill, low-wage routine production operations in both low-tech and high-tech sectors (Falk and Lyson 1988; Lyson 1989; Rosenfeld, Bergman and Rubin 1985; Rosenfeld and Bergman 1989). Business climate remains critical to the South's success. Sloan (1981: 12–13) described Greenville, South Carolina, as having 'the best business climate in the nation and, indeed, in the Western world':

> Greenville's climate is not simply a matter of its wages, its level of unionization, or its taxes. . . A captain of industry in Greenville is guaranteed that he won't have to put up with the headaches that make the life of an executive such an unending trial in other parts of the country – troublesome reporters, egghead intellectuals, antibusiness politicians.

Kanter (1995) includes Greenville – along with Boston and Miami – among 'world-class' localities, citing four elements in the community's success in attracting foreign firms such as BMW (Bavarian Motor Works): leadership, a hospitable business climate and work ethic, work-centred training and education, and an infrastructure for collaboration (Kanter 1995: 270). The 'leadership' may well be best represented by the 'rabid antiunionism of the South's political and economic leadership' (Cobb 1993: 271–2). Indeed, the Greenville area has one of the lowest levels of union membership in the USA.

Labour *skill* is a concept similar to business climate in the elasticity of its meaning. Skill more often means the behavioural characteristics of labour: such 'qualities as "good company employees", in terms of attendance, flexibility, responsibility, discipline, identification with the company and, crucially, work rate and quality' (Morgan and Sayer 1985: 390). The practice of choosing locations and workers on the basis of such behavioural traits is most frequently associated with Japanese firms (Henry 1987; Kenney and Florida 1993; Morgan and Sayer 1985), but it is by no means confined to them; Massey (1995: 55) gives similar description of IBM's selection of workers. Traits such as work ethic and worker attitude are subtle qualities which transcend the conventional concept of skill (Doeringer, Terkla and Topakian 1987: 90). Japanese firms seem to be more concerned with labour quality – defined in terms of adaptability, flexibility, loyalty, motivation and problem-solving capability – and screen many applicants (20 or more per vacancy) in order to find workers (Doeringer and Terkla 1992). In the end, business climate and its connotations about labour are contradictory: rankings of business climate and of 'worker climate' (measuring favourable working conditions) are inversely related in the US South (Cobb 1993: 272).

Rural areas and other 'greenfield' sites are preferred for new production because firms can hire people who do not think of themselves as belonging to an industrial workforce (Berger and Piore 1980; Clark, Gertler and Whiteman 1986). The establishment of non-union 'parallel production facilities' as a means of weakening the ability of unions to strike at main plants is another tactic (Bluestone, Jordan and Sullivan 1981). In the American apparel and shoe industries, almost all companies 'have located their US production plants in low-wage areas with a ready supply of female labour – isolated rural areas, many in mountain regions like the Appalachians and Ozarks; Mexican border communities; and large cities with substantial poor and/or immigrant populations' (Schmenner 1982: 121). Similar 'regional labour reserves' are common throughout the UK and Europe (Hudson 1983; Townsend 1986). The more successful German firms have remained competitive in Europe largely by establishing greenfield plants (Rommel *et al.* 1995). In both Europe and North America, some areas have attracted Japanese investment in car and electronic production, in large part, it is thought, because of workers' minimal factory experience and the absence of unionization (Hudson 1994; Kenney and Florida 1993; Morgan and Sayer 1988; Rubenstein 1992).

The primary activity of a company facility greatly affects its location. Browning (1980: 56–9) reports on one of the few surveys that systematically compares a set of location factors across various types of corporate facilities. The survey indicates that manufacturing plants consider a large set of factors to be important, led by availability of labour, availability of energy/fuel, and highway transportation. Distribution centres respond, not surprisingly, mainly to dimensions of market accessibility. Regional divisional offices, corporate headquarters and R&D facilities, on the other hand, have as their three chief location factors air transportation facilities, highway transportation and the availability of exec-utive/professional talent, which was distinguished from 'availability of labour'. Although problems of aggregation remain, in this case across sectors, this loca-tion survey addresses directly the spatial division of labour by demonstrating that different location factors influence the various functions of firms. Most importantly, it distinguishes between 'labour' and 'executive and professional talent' as distinct types of labour (Browning 1980; Time Inc. 1989: 19–21).

The location of non-production activities

When compared with the body of theory on the location of manufacturing, theory concerning non-production activities of firms is less well developed, despite the numerical significance of service and other non-manufacturing activities. A different categorization of labour – related to the mental division of labour – is significant. Reich (1991) classifies jobs into three categories: *routine production services, in-person services* and *symbolic–analytic services*. Routine 'back-office' jobs, which are mainly clerical and involve little customer contact, have shown the same dispersal tendencies as manufacturing plants. Thanks to information technology and telecommunications, back-office jobs now take place globally in many sectors (Glasmeier and Howland 1995; Grimes 1993). The second category, in-person service workers,

> . . . must have a pleasant demeanor. They must smile and exude confidence and good cheer, even when they feel morose. They must be courteous and helpful, even to the most obnoxious of patrons. Above all, they must make others feel happy and at ease. It should come as no surprise that, traditionally, most in-person servers have been women (Reich 1991: 176).

Symbolic analysts include problem-solving, problem-identifying and strate-gic brokering activities common in producer service and information-related jobs such as lawyers, software engineers and management consultants. Face-to-face contact and collaboration are essential for these activities, including R&D and other technological activities. The interactive nature of this non-routine work strongly influences the types of workers who will be employed, requiring a blend of collaborative and in-person skills (Reich 1991; Shapero 1985; Von Glinow 1988).

The prominence of information in modern economic activities obliges firms to attempt to minimize the cost of contacts and of acquiring information by locating in agglomerations of other, especially similar, firms (Felsenstein 1996; Johansson 1987; Oakey and Cooper 1989). In the context of non-routine activ-ities, an additional objective and advantage of agglomeration is to *maximize opportunities for acquiring information*, rather than only to minimize the costs of obtaining it (Oakey 1984; Rogers and Larsen 1984).

The location theory framework of cost minimization can be adapted to examine the location of non-routine activities, such as R&D, company headquarters and producer services. Many of the influences on location resemble traditional efforts at cost (especially transportation cost) minimization, despite arguments about the footloose nature of such activities. Czamanski (1981) usefully distinguishes between three components of 'friction of distance': (1) transport of goods; (2) movement of persons; and (3) transfer of ideas. For the similar case of producer services, Coffey and Polèse (1987b: 605) suggest that each producer service establishment is subjected to three locational pulls:

- towards the *market* (to minimize costs of communications, travel and courier services);
- towards *specialized labour pools* (to minimize recruitment and retention costs); and
- towards *large diversified service centres at the top of the urban hierarchy* (to minimize input costs).

All three factors concentrate a firm's attention on the top of the urban hierarchy. This is even more true for advanced producer services, which serve a global market and need access to the 'economies of overview' – the 'overview' of a variety of local niche markets in a global marketing strategy that is best accomplished in a large agglomeration well-linked in global networks (Moulaert and Djellal 1995; Moulaert and Gallouj 1993). Concerning transportation facilities, 'the *availability* and *convenience* of travel facilities appears to be rather more important than the cost of these facilities' (Dunning and Norman 1987: 625; emphasis in original).

Producer services, therefore, are far from an equalizing element in the space-economy. In both Europe and in North America, for example, producer services display a distinct bias toward concentration in a very small number of major cities (Daniels 1993; Howells 1988; Illeris 1989; Marshall *et al.* 1988; Moulaert and Tödtling 1995). This outcome is a product of the centralization of control possible – perhaps necessary – with modern computer networks (Hepworth 1989). In particular, it is evident that high-level control and decision-making activities are centralizing even while more routine data-processing activities are decentralizing (Howells 1988; Marshall *et al.* 1988). Much of the explanation of the 'North–South divide' in Britain can be attributed to regional inequality in producer services, since only the Southeast has above-average proportions of employment in banking, finance, insurance and business services (Martin 1988).

The economic advantages of location in large cities affect the behaviour both of firms and of individuals. From the firm's perspective, agglomeration economies revolve around the array of services and facilities available in large centres, which permit them to purchase services and material inputs from specialized suppliers (*The Economist* 1996d; O'hUallachain 1989; Scott 1988c). For individuals, the large labour markets found in major agglomerations increase their probability of suitable employment (Malecki and Bradbury 1992; Pascal and McCall 1980). A network of horizontal flows between cities, each specialized in certain services, is emerging in Europe, replacing the traditional hierarchy (Camagni and Salone 1992). This sort of urban network is less a size-based hierarchy of cities and more a function of the specific array of office activities and producer services found in various places.

Of all economic activities, producer services are perhaps most pulled toward urban agglomerations, at least toward those which meet 'certain urban size threshold requirements', which 'will in part be determined by the costs of recruiting (and keeping) specialized labour' (Coffey and Polèse 1987a: 609). These influences make agglomeration especially important in R&D (Lacroix and Martin 1988). The reduction of transaction costs possible in urban agglomerations, which accrues to all firms, as well as the *network economies* (reduction of costs as the number of users increases) important to service firms, result in further strengthening of agglomeration economies (Cappellin 1988; Scott 1988c). Access to global networks from discrete locations also focuses attention on large urban agglomerations (Moulaert and Gallouj 1993).

Location decisions for R&D are particularly infrequent for firms, compared with the more common decisions for offices, plants and other facilities. Most firms have relatively few R&D establishments – far fewer than their number of other types of facilities. Large US firms, for example, average around eight laboratories per firm (Malecki 1979: 311). But even for firms such as General Electric (US) with over 100 R&D facilities, and General Motors with dozens, one of the necessary characteristics of an R&D operation is stability – both for the firm's organizational structure and for the scientists and engineers who work in it. Despite some recent consolidation following mergers and acquisitions, the number of company sites where R&D is conducted is growing, as firms follow the Japanese model of locating R&D, especially product development, at factories (Hull, Hage and Azumi 1985; Kenney and Florida 1993: 63–70). The firm 3M (Minnesota Mining and Manufacturing) conducts R&D in 52 countries (Krogh and Nicholson 1990). In these 'technical branch plants' the attraction and retention of technical workers must enter the location decision, although generally it is not significant for plants where only production takes place (Glasmeier 1988a). Because of the need for both engineers and production workers, high-technology manufacturing in the USA has decentralized very little to rural and small-town locations (Barkley 1988; Glasmeier 1991b). In the semiconductor industry, R&D and sophisticated manufacturing operations remain strongly concentrated in the Silicon Valley area (Scott and Angel 1987).

Increasingly, firms are upgrading engineering expertise at production sites, oriented toward both flexible and low-cost manufacturing processes. This new geography of R&D is made possible by information technology, which has permitted increased specialization of R&D, along with its increased scale and intensity (Howells 1990a; Howells and Wood 1993; Thwaites and Alderman 1990). At peripheral production sites, however, even where some engineering work takes place, few linkages with local firms may develop (Gripaios *et al.* 1989; Turok 1993). Linkages are more likely to develop where R&D is conducted (Hagey and Malecki 1986; Lyons 1995).

The location decision for R&D thus incorporates both organizational and labour market demands (Casson 1991: 57–8). The organizational pull keeps a majority of R&D laboratories at or near the firm's headquarters (Lund 1986;

Malecki 1979). The joint location of R&D and headquarters is further demonstrated by the similarity of the location factors stressed by firms for the two facilities (Browning 1980: 58; Molle, Beumer and Boeckhout 1989). For both, availability of executive and professional talent and air accessibility are the most important factors; these are clearly among the typical advantages of large urban regions (Castells and Hall 1994; Harding 1989; Shove 1991). Similarly, a marked clustering of British pharmaceutical R&D appears to be largely attributable to the location of firms' headquarters; most outlier laboratories are associated with production plants (Howells 1984). The effect of the tie to headquarters is to constrain the location of most R&D to regions where firms' headquarters cluster, especially large urban regions.

The advantages of urban regions – quality of life, labour pools and transportation accessibility – are considerable in their attraction. The ready movement of technical workers to other sites (in order to visit other researchers and to interact with manufacturing facilities as production begins) requires rapid (and therefore usually air) transportation. Firms see a site with acceptable air service (frequent flights to many destinations) as a way of minimizing the time workers need to be away from their base of operation.

The attraction and retention of managerial and technical personnel necessitates attention to quality of life factors (Ady 1986; Malecki and Bradbury 1992). R&D workers, like other professionals in short supply, are mobile in the sense that their relative scarcity gives them labour market mobility, but they are in effect geographically somewhat immobile in that they are willing to live only in distinct types of places – those with an adequate quality of life (Buswell 1983). 'Quality of life' largely represents urban commercial amenities ('the potential for sophisticated leisure and consumption') and other correlates of city size sought by this well-paid, mobile segment of the population (Castells 1988: 60; Malecki and Bradbury 1992). This does not mean that worker preferences determine the location of R&D or of high technology, but it demonstrates that the common interests of mobile professionals and of their employers are satisfied best in urban agglomerations. Urban regions provide a large number of alternative employers, which attracts professional workers, whose skills are readily transferred to other employers (Angel 1989; Pascal and McCall 1980).

The reputation or image of a place also weighs heavily in job location decisions of such workers. A high quality of life and the reputation or perception that a place is 'high-tech' can weigh more heavily than other factors for scientists and engineers, outweighing the need to locate near major universities (Begg and Cameron 1988; Keeble and Kelly 1986; Macdonald 1986; Malecki and Bradbury 1992).

The opportunities for job mobility and entrepreneurship do not deter firms from locating in major urban agglomerations. Location of R&D in known entrepreneurial areas raises the risk of losing prized employees through job-hopping or spin-off, but it also increases the likelihood of finding workers who are leaving other firms, thus providing information and knowledge which are otherwise difficult to obtain (Angel 1989, 1991; Ettlie 1980; Oakey and Cooper 1989; Rogers and Larsen 1984). It benefits both employers and professionals to locate in the established agglomerations of an industry, where such information interchange is most likely (Oakey 1984; Saxenian 1994). The 'unconscious' clustering and 'involuntary' cooperation 'which quickly diffuses knowledge . . . throughout the industry' through the mobility of technical personnel is characteristic of high-tech regions (Noyce 1982: 14). The advantages of this dynamic have been the focus of research on the persistent dynamism of Silicon Valley (Bahrami and Evans 1995; Saxenian 1994), although it is not without its critics (Florida and Kenney 1990; Harrison 1994).

Universities, frequently cited as accounting for the location of R&D and high technology, must be considered an overstated ingredient. The two 'products' of universities – scientific and technical personnel and research findings – are equally available for purchase from a distance. The experience of Stanford University in Silicon Valley, of MIT in the Boston (Route 128) area, and of Oxford and the 'Cambridge phenomenon' in the UK all point to the fact that the growth of these areas as seedbeds of innovation and high technology owes more to the amenities of the urban or suburban regions in which they are located than to any close or direct relationship between firms and universities (Castells and Hall 1994; Gillespie *et al.* 1987; Howells 1986; Keeble 1989; Malecki 1986). If there is any effect, it appears to be related to the research activities of clusters of premier universities located near one another and where other R&D programmes are prominent (Antonelli 1986b; Lawton-Smith 1991; Malecki 1980b; Massey, Quintas and Wield 1992). In such settings, the external sources of knowledge – that obtained from universities, research institutes, and from other firms – is much higher (Davelaar and Nijkamp 1989; Lorenzoni and Ornati 1988). As a source of labour as well, local universities are a minor influence on firm location. Experienced workers are recruited in major agglomerations; firms recruit entry-level engineers quite widely outside any local area (Angel 1989: 109; Malecki and Bradbury 1992).

Urban agglomerations are particularly attractive to educated people with job mobility, and employers generally have difficulty attracting professional and technical workers to locations judged remote (Cooke 1985b). Suburban areas and prominent high-tech locations have the significant advantage of providing a number of job opportunities without requiring a change in residence. The attraction of large urban areas is stronger for dual-career couples, which have become an important component of the labour force (Gibbs *et al.* 1985; Malecki and Bradbury 1992). The success of corporate R&D programmes depends to an important degree on the ability of firms to attract and retain highly qualified technical and professional workers. The location of a firm's R&D facilities largely determines the degree to which workers will be initially attracted to, and be likely to remain with, the firm at that location.

The locational concentration of R&D in every country favours established regions (especially national capitals) and reinforces the regional economic growth of those areas where universities, industrial R&D, and national government R&D facilities and contracts are plentiful (Breheny and McQuaid 1987; Buswell, Easterbrook and Morphet 1985; Malecki 1980b). It is in the suburban zones of major urban regions, where the demands of professional workers for suburban locations and of firms for access to transportation and communication, reinforce the development of 'silicon valleys' (Antonelli 1987; Britton

1987: 174–8; Camagni and Rabellotti 1988; Howells and Charles 1988; Scott 1988b,c; Keeble 1988). An existing agglomeration of managerial, professional and technical staff already employed by other firms is a labour pool from which new employees can be recruited. In short, labour market and urban agglomeration advantages are by far the most important considerations for high-technology firms (Breheny and McQuaid 1987; Castells and Hall 1994; Macgregor *et al.* 1986; Oakey and Cooper 1989).

In the UK, the Southeast dominates in the location of high-technology manufacturing and services, with lesser concentrations in the Southwest and East Anglia – all south of the North–South 'divide' (Begg and Cameron 1988). In France, 'Paris's domination is in no way under challenge' (Pottier 1987: 220). However, the sunbelt region of France, Provence–Côte d'Azur on the Mediterranean coast, including the cities of Nice and Marseille, is a growing region of modern industry (Dyckman and Swyngedouw 1988). Likewise, production of high-technology products, such as aerospace and robotics, is distributed throughout France, but R&D remains concentrated in the Paris region, especially the suburban area south of the city, Paris-Sud (Castells and Hall 1994; Pottier 1987; Scott 1988c).

In Japan, both R&D and the production of high-technology products are concentrated in the Tokyo region, as is manufacturing of all types (Glasmeier and Sugiura 1991; Humphrys 1995; Nishioka and Takeuchi 1987). Although high-technology manufacturing plants with engineering groups are found throughout Japan, 'they are generally under the very strong influence of the Tokyo area because of their far weaker R&D functions and much lower level of technology' (Nishioka and Takeuchi 1987: 286). The geographical dualism of the Japanese industrial system has a distinct core–periphery pattern to it. Only Osaka competes in any way with Tokyo as a location for R&D (Kenney and Florida 1994a; Morita and Hiraoka 1988). Despite this spatial agglomeration, Japanese firms rarely utilize their competitors as an external labour market. It is ties to universities initially and, once hired, intra-firm transfers that are important to Japanese R&D and engineering (Kenney and Florida 1994a).

There is also evidence of a 'herd instinct' involved in the tendency toward agglomeration of high tech in the South of England, especially among US transnational firms in the Southeast (Hall *et al.* 1987: 177; Morgan and Sayer (1988: 236–8) and in Scotland's 'Silicon Glen' in the Glasgow region (Haug 1986). Even in the slow but steady rise in R&D activity by US transnationals in Scotland, it may well be that Scotland is primarily a 'hardware' rather than a 'software' or knowledge-based location for these firms (Hargrave 1985; J. Henderson 1989: 134–8). The R&D functions in Scotland tend to be of a product development nature, related to customer service, rather than embedded in the regional economy (Henderson and Scott 1987: 68; Turok 1993).

Post-Weberian location theory

To address corporate decisions only within the context of 'choosing locations' is to ignore the competitive and profit-seeking context which is behind location decisions (as well as product, technology and other) decisions. It is in the 'a-spatial – rather than in the simply spatial – sphere that the primary causal links exist between the wider economy and the individual company' (Massey 1979: 70). The spatial division of labour within large enterprises continues to be a very real phenomenon but, at the same time, a shift in empirical reality occurred during the 1980s, away from large firms and 'Fordist' mass production, and toward a more 'flexible' mode of accumulation which centred around networks of small firms (Best 1990; Lipietz 1986; Piore and Sabel 1984; Sabel 1982).

The behaviour of large, usually transnational, firms was the context for what has come to be known as 'Fordist' production or the Fordist regime of accumulation. Originating with the assembly line for automobile production pioneered by Henry Ford, Fordist factories were rational, with special-purpose machines, division of labour, and few authorized freedoms for workers (Biggs 1995). As a broader, economy-wide regime of accumulation, Fordism is characterized by a mass production culture, involving mass markets for standardized products, and a social contract between firms, workers and governments. The interplay between corporate strategy, government policy and labour generated an economic and social stability that began to crumble in the 1970s (Bluestone and Harrison 1982). The economic crisis of the 1970s had exposed the weaknesses of giant firms. Not only were the costs of vertical integration high, but producers in Japan and the NICs began to penetrate the American and European markets of the major TNCs. Consequently, 'flexible' production methods have been integrated into the organization of production in large firms as well as in networks of small firms. *Integration* is the key: aspects of Fordism have not entirely disappeared, nor are large firms vanishing to be replaced by networks of small, flexible competitors. Rather, capitalism has become more diverse, in large part by becoming more flexible in several different ways.

Flexibility

More flexible forms of *production*, of *work*, and of *inter-firm relations* have forced changes in the capitalist system and its components (firms, workers, governments and other institutions). Flexibility – 'the ability to change or react with little penalty in time, effort, cost or performance' – alters the orderly sequence suggested by the product cycle (Upton 1994: 73; see also Ayres and Steger 1985; Goldhar 1986). The principal push for flexibility is the speeding up of product cycles, which means that economies of scale and large production volumes no longer apply, and that much greater attention must be paid to product innovation in order to generate the required succession of new product cycles. The Ford Model T was available in 'any colour you like as long as it's black', a constraint generally unacceptable to consumers today (Bessant 1991). Instead of standardized, one-product-fits-all, high-volume production, firms aim toward market niches, 'mass customization' and the goals of product innovation and quality. These require, in turn, well-coordinated information and production (Goldhar 1986; Pine 1993). Finally, and most importantly, *dynamic flexibility* is 'the capacity of a production system to develop and/or assimilate new technologies' (Weinstein 1992: 33), incorporating new knowledge through continuous learning (Coriat 1992). This process of building capabilities for future competitiveness is centred in manufacturing and in no way negates mass production (Hayes and Pisano 1994).

Flexibility has become part of the prevailing perception about current economic change in the context of both firms and regions. Indeed, 'the use of the term "flexibility" has become so common that it cannot simply be dismissed as something not worth attention' (Boyer 1988b: 222). At the same time, the word has many connotations and dimensions, often resulting in confusion or overstatement (Kickert 1985; Raouf and Anjum 1995; Upton 1994). It is useful to distinguish between the three types of flexibility, for they represent truly different forms of organizing production. The organization of work and production is at the core of what we call flexibility, including:

1. the adoption of systemic computer-integrated manufacturing technologies;
2. the development of new systematic relationships between plants and firms; and
3. the adoption of a new flexible labour process in which the past tendencies towards the increasing division of tasks, the deskilling of work and the removal of control over production from the worker are reversed (Hoffman and Kaplinsky 1988: 331).

In addition to these internal, capital–capital and capital–labour changes, it is evident that there also is a search for new regulatory frameworks and for new geographies of production (Hudson 1994).

Flexible production

At the first level of analysis, production flexibility includes the spectrum of changes which result from automation. Automation based on computers and microelectronics has three qualities which push it beyond the concept of other labour-saving capital investment. First, flexibility is built into the machinery, which is general-purpose rather than product-specific. No set-up is required to switch to a different product. A new product can be built simply by programmed instructions on machines that can produce many different products (Shaiken 1984: 6–7). Second, this flexibility leads to a broader scope of application. The expense of new technology might be greater than that of previous generations of machines, but it provides a great deal more flexibility (to use the word in yet another sense) in product variety. This form of flexibility is especially important, because a firm with such a capability is able to handle both routine, volume production and more difficult (and profitable) non-standard orders, which allow it to accommodate small-volume new product introduction.

The smaller-volume production is vividly shown in the case of General Motors Corporation. The firm regularly sold one million of the Chevrolet Caprice, its best-selling car, in the early 1970s. By the late 1980s, the firm's best-sellers, the Corsica and Beretta, together managed annual sales of only about

350 000 (Taylor 1989). Consequently, GM and scores of other firms have been forced to alter their approach to production. The 'world car' strategy, in which a standardized product that could be made in large, efficient volumes from parts manufactured in giant specialized plants, and sold throughout the world, has not worked as variety has surpassed price (and product uniformity) as marketing virtues. Computer-aided manufacturing (CAM) technology is directed toward responding to diverse customer specifications (Gerwin 1989). Finally, an important goal in itself of programmable technology is improved quality and reliability, a factor more important than variety or price in many markets (Sciberras 1986; Starr and Biloski 1985). Quality is difficult to attain, however, because it demands even more modifications of workplace organization and of labour–management relations than does the production of diverse products (Cole 1995).

Economies of scope help to explain both the push toward flexible production within firms and the profusion of strategic alliances between firms (Charles, Monk and Sciberras 1989; Teece 1980). Internal economies of scope accrue to firms which can produce two or more different, related products together more cheaply than in isolation – ideal for situations of product differentiation. Scope economies also mean that there are no exit costs associated with any particular product design, and efforts to serve many small niche markets and even individual customization involve no cost penalty, so far as the factory is concerned (Goldhar, Jelinek and Schlie 1991). External economies of scope result when firms can use their know-how to integrate with the activities – particularly innovative activities – of other firms and other markets. These are obtained mainly through alliances between firms, providing advantages beyond the traditional, internal sorts (Cooke 1988; Molina 1989: 132–44), but they also arise from *untraded interdependencies* within a local area (Storper 1993, 1995a). Reve (1990) terms these economies of upstream integration and economies of downstream integration, and sees them as complementary to conventional scale and scope economies.

Within firms, the Fordist priority on mass production based on economies of scale has given way to economies of scope, cost savings based on producing a variety of products or services in small – even one-of-a-kind – batches. Ideally, such a factory 'can produce a continuous stream of different product designs at the same cost as an equal stream of identical products' (Goldhar 1986: 27; Goldhar and Jelinek 1983; Pine 1993). Pressures for both greater variety and reduced lead times are difficult to achieve, because quick delivery is typically based on standardization, whereas product variety requires a firm to be flexible and innovative. As competing firms aim for the same customers, price pressure also enters in, and both marketing and production systems need to be altered (Littler 1994; McCutcheon, Raturi and Meredith 1994; Stalk and Webber 1993). Marketing becomes the critical contact with the customer, not only for sales, but also for service opportunities and for gathering market intelligence (Cespedes 1994; Cornish 1995). Within the production system, *design for manufacture* simplifies product design to minimize the number of parts and to increase the number of common parts in different final products (Boorsma

1986; Charles, Monk and Sciberras 1989: 135–7). In general, close ties between engineering and manufacturing are essential to rapid response to customers' demands (Ulrich and Eppinger 1995; Winch 1994). The challenge is to maintain simplicity, rather than complexity, in design and organization, a competitive strength of German firms (Rommel *et al.* 1995).

The characteristics of multi-product, small-size production include:

- a variety of product items, produced in different volumes and with different due dates;
- a variety of production processes;
- complexity of production capacity;
- uncertainty of outside conditions;
- difficulty of production planning and scheduling; and
- a dynamic situation of implementation and control of production (Hitomi 1989).

These characteristics suggest several ways in which manufacturing is becoming more customer-responsive and 'service'-like (Table 4.1).

Economies of scope have not eliminated economies of scale. However, scale shifts from association with a specific product design and process configuration to association with the factory as a whole and its feasible range of product–process configurations (Goldhar, Jelinek and Schlie 1991: 248). This means that large firms will not be easily replaced by smaller, nimbler competitors (Harrison 1994). In the increasingly global food (or agribusiness) industry, product differentiation is commonplace, but within a Fordist system. Mass production of variety remains mass production, whether of shoe styles or electronic goods (Goldfrank 1994; Kim and Curry 1993).

Product variety is one measure of flexible production, but it is not simple to calibrate, especially in complex assembled products. In cars, for example, model mix complexity involves varying models, which means varying the mix of parts and options in the output produced. Variety and complexity are best absorbed with no loss in productivity in 'lean' production plants which incorporate a

Table 4.1   Service firm characteristics in flexible manufacturing firms.

High variety, with the goal of customization of product design for each customer
Rapid adoption of new technology and service concepts
Fast response time and short production cycles
Zero inventory and excess production capacity
Close linkage between producer and customer; very direct distribution channels
Flexible pricing and negotiated (contractual) relationships
High information content transactions between producer and customer
Long-term relationships in which both producer and customer learn and become more efficient
  in their transactions
Integrated physical and knowledge work activities
Customer participation in product design

Source: based on Goldhar and Lei (1994: 729, Table 1).

number of policies, including just-in-time inventory, work teams, job rotation, training of a multi-skilled workforce, continuous improvement efforts, and design for manufacturing (*The Economist* 1994b; MacDuffie, Sethuraman and Fisher 1996).

There are many types of flexibility and it is easier to simplify them into three categories of manufacturing flexibility: mix flexibility, new product flexibility and volume flexibility. The implementation of these, in turn, is affected by production technology, production management techniques, relationships with suppliers and subcontractors, human resource management, and the product development process. Perhaps most importantly, trade-offs must be made, especially regarding their market focus and regarding cutting costs versus maintaining or improving quality (Bertram and Schamp 1991; Suarez, Cusumano and Fine 1995). Flexibility is mostly about reducing time, not costs (Yamashina, Matsumoto and Inoue 1991).

Figure 4.2 illustrates that automation has different effects depending on where and how it is applied. Any production has three principal spheres of activity: design, information coordination and manufacture (Hoffman and Kaplinsky 1988: 56–61; Kaplinsky 1984). Automation may take place only within a given activity ('island automation'), such as an individual manufacturing step, like the sewing of buttonholes, or within computerized design, and not affect the other activities (Figure 4.2a). A higher level of automation involves the integration of activities within a given sphere of production (e.g. design or manufacture) but where each sphere is still unconnected to the others (Kaplinsky 1984). This level of automation, a *flexible manufacturing system* (FMS), may include up to several machining centres and/or robots, and permits the small-batch and custom production needed for economies of scope and product variety (Figure 4.2b). A British Aerospace FMS produces 2000 variants of small aircraft parts in batches of five to ten units each (Tchijov and Sheinin 1989).

The ultimate level of automation is the integration of design, manufacture and coordination into an integrated unit, labelled computer-integrated manufacturing (CIM) (Goldhar 1986; Goldhar, Jelinek and Schlie 1991) or 'systemofacture' (Figure 4.2c). Table 4.2 illustrates some of the contrasts between traditional technology and those in a CIM factory. CIM 'is fundamentally a strategy, a philosophy for improvement rather than a piece of equipment' (Bessant 1991: 16). Thus, most automation falls short of CIM and instead is largely confined to uncoordinated 'islands of automation' (Bessant and Haywood 1988; Kaplinsky 1984). CIM is still a goal toward which companies, especially the largest ones, are aiming (Edquist and Jacobsson 1988; Flynn and Cole 1988; Hoffman and Kaplinsky 1988: 146–52). As 'the benefits of flexible manufacturing are becoming available in different forms to suit different product/market characteristics', the beneficiaries may have begun to include smaller firms (Bessant and Haywood 1988: 354). However, automation technologies and their organizational counterparts are easily misunderstood and misused, and pose particular obstacles for small firms. 'Flexibility is much more an organisational property than a technical one' and is best managed by large

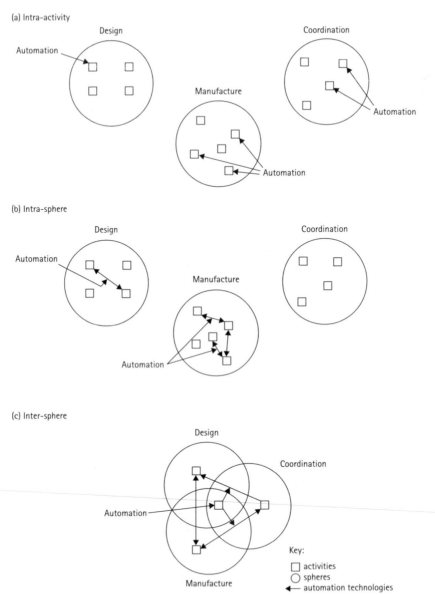

Figure 4.2   Different types or scales of automation. Source: Kaplinsky (1984: 27, Figure 2.4).

firms (Bessant and Haywood 1988: 359; Child 1987a). This is seen in the persistent patterns of adoption of flexible production techniques. However, even among big companies, implementation of new technology and integration of new systems into the production system remain difficult (Rush and Bessant 1992; Yamashina, Matsumoto and Inoue 1991). Japanese firms seem to have been the most successful at integrating the factors in CIM and its philosophy of continuous change (Sandoval 1994).

Table 4.2 Traditional technology contrasted with computer-integrated manufacturing (CIM) factory.

Traditional technology	Computer-integrated manufacturing
Management assumptions	
Economies of scale	Economies of scope
Flexibility and variety are costly	Flexibility increases profitability
Learning curves	Short product life-cycles
Specialized equipment	Multimission manufacturing
Work as a social activity	Unattended machining
Variable allocable costs	Aggregated costs mostly fixed and sunk
Standardization of product	Variety of product customization
Desired characteristics of operating system	
Centralization	Decentralization
Large plants, high volume	Small plants, close to the market
Job enrichment	Reward–responsibility systems
Focused factory	Frequent factory reorganizations
Smooth work flows	Inexpensive surge and turnaround capability
Low rates of change	Innovation encouraged
Inventory as a buffer for demand	Production closely linked to demand
Make to stock	Make to order

Source: based on Goldhar (1986: 29) and Goldhar, Jelinek and Schlie (1991: 249).

Robots and flexible production

Robots are the principal new technology of flexible production. They can be pro-grammed – and reprogrammed – and require dramatically less labour than do the production operations which they replace. The first robot was installed for indus-trial use by the Ford Motor Company in 1961, but robots diffused very slowly for several years. As the prices of robots have increased less rapidly than wages, the potential for robots to replace labour has increased. In addition, the per-formance and range of applications of robots have also improved, strengthening the position of robots *vis-à-vis* both labour and fixed automation (Dahlin 1993). While jobs are replaced by robotics, they tend to be unskilled, repetitious jobs; new jobs created by the adoption of robots demand a significant technical back-ground (Edquist and Jacobsson 1988; Hartmann *et al.* 1985). The scenario is similar outside the advanced economies. Transnational corporations, for their automated factories, 'will continue to seek cheap labour, the only difference is that the labour they now want has to be skilled' (Salih, Young and Rasiah 1988: 396).

Despite their advantages, the adoption of robots has been slow, except in Japan, which has led robot adoption from the mid-1970s, and in Sweden (Table 4.3). Although flexibility is commonly associated with small firms, rather than large firms, it is large firms which are overwhelmingly the early and persistent adopters of robots, FMS and other advanced manufacturing technologies (Acs, Audretsch and Carlsson 1991; Alderman and Fischer 1992; Cainarca, Colombo and Mariotti 1990; Gros-Pietro and Rolfo 1989; Jaakkola and Tenhunen 1993;

Table 4.3   International industrial robot stock.

Country		Number of robots			Robot density (number per 10 000 employed in manufacturing)
	1974	1981	1988	1993	1993
Australia		181	1 200	1 907	21.0
Austria		57	655	1 908	29.2
Benelux			1 171	3 000	18.2
Czech Republic[a]			5 691	6 700	—
Denmark		51	349	619	16.8
Finland		35	548	1 160	31.4
France	30		5 658	11 795	27.0
Germany	130	2 300	17 700	43 715	62.0
Hungary			61	247	2.5
Italy	90	450	8 300	19 568	69.7
Japan	1 000	21 000	176 000	368 054	324.2
Norway			473	604	22.8
Poland			471	648	2.1
Singapore		5	607	3 841	109.1
South Korea			—	6 000	19.4
Spain			1 382	3 974	20.1
Sweden	85	1 125	3 042	4 802	72.8
Switzerland			783	2 500	30.0
Taiwan		1	682	2 739	—
USSR/former USSR			59 218	65 000	22.7
United Kingdom	50	713	4 843	8 189	13.1
United States	1 200	6 000	32 600	50 000	29.9
Total		31 918	322 334	610 605	

Note: data missing for Czech Republic and Taiwan.
[a] 1988=total for Czechoslovakia; 652 robots were in Slovakia in 1993.
Source: data for 1974 from Tani (1989, Table 1); for other years from Karlsson (1994, Tables 1 and 6).

Mansfield 1993; Oakey and O'Farrell 1992). Small and medium-sized firms are more price-sensitive and have no accumulated experience with robots, so they are a more difficult market than are large firms (Dahlin 1993). Without concerted marketing, small firms are unlikely to acquire sufficient information to result in the adoption of advanced technologies (Dahlin 1993; Kelley and Brooks 1992).

Large firms are found in certain sectors, and these are where most robots have been adopted. Robotization has been greatest in the automotive industry, followed by the electrical/electronics industries; together, they account for over 50 per cent of applications in most countries (Tani 1989). Most Japanese robots are assembly robots, and these are mainly found in the electrical and electronics sector and in plastic moulding (Ishitani and Kaya 1989; Tani 1989; Yonemoto 1986). (Japan is the only country which classifies pick-and-place machines as robots, a fact which inflates its figures on robot penetration.) Japan's adoption of robots is also striking in its wider adoption within firms. Not only are there more Japanese robot users, but adopting firms also have many more of them (Mansfield 1989).

The adoption of robots and FMS by firms in Japan in several sectors is different from the situation in most other countries, where they are used predominantly in the automobile industry for welding tasks (Tani 1989). The diverse demand in Japan for new computerized equipment also stimulated development for specific small markets of machinery firms (Friedman 1988: 211–17). Small producers were able to utilize best-practice flexible machinery and to become internationally competitive. Two additional characteristics identify the Japanese market as unique. First, the large home market has permitted Japanese robot producers to reap economies of scale and to aim for a strategy of worldwide cost leadership. Second, many other firms, including those well-known in other sectors, such as Seiko Epson, Pentel, NEC, Yamaha, Fujitsu and Toshiba, have developed robots for their own use in small parts assembly. These firms compete fiercely on both technology leadership and price (Dahlin 1993). The widespread use of robots has permitted a great deal of learning – by doing, by using and by selling – among robot makers, which has enabled them to develop a wide base of knowledge about users' problems. The larger robot production base has also enabled a strong base of suppliers and subcontractors to develop (Bowonder and Miyake 1994).

Outside Japan, the adoption of robots and FMS has been slow both because of price and because flexible automation systems demand substantial human, organizational and managerial resources, which are in short supply in small firms (Mariotti and Mutinelli 1992). In the newly industrializing countries (NICs), numerically controlled machine tools have diffused rapidly, but this is less true of robots. Robots are most widely used in Singapore, a major centre of semiconductor production, almost entirely in semiconductor assembly operations of foreign-owned firms, and in South Korea and Taiwan. Second-tier NICs, such as Malaysia and Thailand, are far behind Korea and Singapore in the use of new technologies (Edquist and Jacobsson 1988).

Far less is known about the distribution of industrial robots within countries. The findings on the adoption of new production technologies in the UK and the USA suggest that traditional core-region locations with skilled labour and company R&D activities will be favoured (Gibbs and Edwards 1985; Rees, Briggs and Oakey 1986). Rural areas tend to lag, mainly as a result of small firms and their general lack of information and resources (Rosenfeld 1992).

Flexible manufacturing systems (FMS) – in effect, integrated clusters of robots – are far less prevalent. There are approximately 1000 such systems installed in the world, in the same principal sectors as robots: automotive parts, aerospace and non-electrical machinery (Mieskonen 1991; Warndorf and Merchant 1986). The highest levels of FMS implementation, measured by the ratio of the installed systems to employment, are found in Sweden and Finland, and may be largely a result of the strong institutional support that comprises the 'technological system' in those countries (Carlsson and Jacobsson 1994; Mieskonen 1991). The adoption of robots or FMS is no guarantee of competitiveness and profitability for firms. Much depends on how these are used within a production system (Krafcik 1988). For example, in a comparison of Japanese and US factories where FMS was utilized, Japanese firms used them to produce nearly ten times the number of different products. US and UK firms had opted for larger-scale, complex production in military-oriented industries (Jaikumar 1986; Tchijov 1992; Tchijov and Sheinin 1992).

Flexible manufacturing technologies are best integrated with other aspects of flexible production, including other systems and practices (Mieskonen 1991). CIM integrates both the hardware of robots and the software of CAD, computer-aided engineering, and computer-aided logistics (Tchijov 1992). The diffusion of CAD has taken place in a way much differently from that of robots. CAD is overwhelmingly found in the USA, where software capabilities are strongest (Table 4.4). Less than 2 per cent of all CAD 'seats' were in use in developing countries (Åstebro 1992).

As the most comprehensive technology incorporating robotics and other advanced machines, CIM has had several effects on workers and on management. More skilled workers are needed and more training is demanded. A team approach is seen as an extension of CIM implementation; communication is

Table 4.4 Distributon of computer-aided design (CAD), number of seats installed, 1986.

Country	CAD seats installed per 1000 employees
USA	6.33
Sweden	3.76
UK	3.17
France	2.89
Germany	2.62
Norway	2.59
Canada	2.30
Denmark	1.85
Finland	1.27
Singapore	0.99
Japan	0.72
Iceland	0.67
Taiwan	0.52
Italy	0.31
Argentina	0.22
Korea	0.13
India	0.06
Brazil	0.05

Source: modified from Åstebro (1992: 181).

better and faster; decision-making is decentralized; and job rotation is increased (Ayres and Raju 1992). In general, new technology is more than the addition of hardware or software. It involves a series of organizational changes that impact a firm externally, in its relations with other firms, and internally, in its organization of the work and production process (Rush and Bessant 1992).

The need for a new and different structure has led to the term *agile manufacturing*, which is meant to go beyond lean production or flexible production in its scope (Kidd 1994). Much of the emphasis of agility is on knowledge, networks, and the capabilities of people. Both CIM and agility represent major changes for firms. They stress learning, worker skills, and extensive communication within as well as outside the firm, especially with customers (Goldhar and Lei 1994; Goldman, Nagel and Preiss 1995; Kidd 1994; Nayyar and Bantel 1994). They also suggest new performance indicators that focus on non-financial measures (Table 4.5).

Flexible labour

Achieving productivity and efficiency in flexible production systems may rest largely on flexible labour. The presence of fewer routine tasks and few long production runs from flexible production leads to a demand for a 'highly skilled, flexible, coordinated, and committed work force' (Walton and Susman 1987). Generalizations about Japanese workers are indicative of these skills: 'The Japanese work hard'; they 'work cooperatively' (Dore 1987: 12); they are 'willing to do a variety of jobs' (Dore, Bounine-Cabalé and Tapiola 1989: 50). Both the technical demands and coordination suggest a need for education and training

Table 4.5 Examples of non-financial performance measures relevant to agile and flexible production.

Distance travelled by parts within factory
Number of material types used
Fraction of sales to repeat customers
Number of defects identified per employee
Amount of scrap
Energy consumption per unit process
Number and frequency of customer complaints
Part counts
Number of layers in organization
New product introduction time
Customer returns
Number of field repairs
Change-over times
Labour hours per unit process
Turnover of employees

Source: based on Kidd (1994: 253, Table 9.1).

programmes and more cooperative labour relations than was typical under Fordism (Boyer 1995).

This form of flexibility, identified above all with Japanese car makers, is closely related to and indeed evolved from Fordism (Gertler 1988b). 'The Japanese translation of the Fordist system . . . was simple. Toyota was the great innovator here, taking the minds+hands philosophy of the craftsmen era, merging it with the work standardization and assembly line of the Fordist system, and adding the glue of teamwork for good measure (Krafcik 1988: 43). The Toyota system evolved during the 1950s and 1960s, when the much smaller Japanese market stimulated a myriad of experiments in flexible production technology (Cusumano 1988). For automobile firms which flourished in the larger American and European markets under Fordist production, more immediate adjustments were needed as the basis of competition shifted from price to quality, and from standardization to variety. But production costs still matter. As the just-in-time (JIT) system keeps inventory levels at a minimum, a flexible work team minimizes the need for utility and repair workers, since other team members fulfil these tasks as well as substitute for absent co-workers (Krafcik 1988). The utilization of flexible labour seems to be much more significant to productivity (hours per vehicle) than the use of robotic technology. In 38 automobile plants located in Japan, North America and Europe, Krafcik (1988) found little correlation with the level of flexible technology. Data for 1995 continue to show Japanese firms performing best in average assembly times (Table 4.6).

Whether work changes comprise 'neo-Fordism' depends on the degree to which new forms of work organization are employed. Neo-Fordism within the workplace involves the integration of different productive subunits into a larger flexible manufacturing system for the production of a variety of products. This requires that workers themselves be flexible rather than rigid in the definition of the tasks for which they can be called upon (Blackburn, Coombs and Green 1985). Even if viewed solely within the framework of an individual firm, the implications are immense. For all employers, jobs and specific work tasks are more knowledge-based, interdependent and controlled by workers than under

Table 4.6 Average assembly times for a car or truck by North American car makers, 1995.

Firm	Average assembly time (labour hours per vehicle)
Nissan	27.4
Toyota	29.4
Honda	31.0
Ford	37.9
Chrysler	43.0
General Motors	46.0

Source: adapted from Suris (1996).

traditional Fordist rules (Boyer 1995). A concomitant change is the reduction in hierarchical bureaucracy, which means that workers can plan on lateral movement, rather than upward promotions, and multiple careers in a lifetime (Howard 1995). When combined with the potential of information technology and 'upskilling', the nature of work is changing greatly (Alic 1990; Osterman 1990).

Neo-Fordism also refers to production organization which replaces the task fragmentation, functional specialization, mechanization and assembly-line principles of Fordism with a social organization of production based on work teams, job rotation, learning by doing, flexible production and integrated production complexes (Kenney and Florida 1988). These are work practices for *functional flexibility* that have evolved largely in Japan within large firms, and involve both a willingness and an ability to be flexible (Dore, Bounine-Cabalé and Tapiola 1989). In a variety of respects, the 'Japanese model' of production stands in sharp contrast to the Fordist model, and may be incompatible with it (Ettlinger 1995). At the same time, all of these new forms of work organization are incremental developments of existing trends (Tomaney 1994). The Japanese model continues to involve large, powerful companies and use of tight relations with supplier firms (Hiraoka 1989; IILS 1993; Junkerman 1987).

Teamwork, usually embodied in 'quality circles', is among the most frequent aspects of the 'Japanization' of industry (Littler 1988). Teams are the central mechanism for achieving the functional integration of tasks, in response to continuous innovation, which is the heart of the Japanese model of work organization (Kenney and Florida 1993: 37). The term 'teams' has many meanings, and this accounts in part for the diversity found in implementing team-based work practices elsewhere (Cutcher-Gershenfeld *et al.* 1994). However, flexible production systems demand greater skills of labour, resulting in greater reliance on, and *less* flexible relationships with, labour (Gertler 1988b; Kawano 1993). Nor are decentralization and team-based work organization only found in Japanese firms or those trying to emulate them. They are also central to corporate efforts to improve product and service quality and to organizational responses to new technologies and competition (Cole 1995; Mohrman and Cohen 1995). The Japanese system, and its counterparts in Germany, Sweden and elsewhere, have advantages and disadvantages, illustrating the variety of responses to flexibility and adjustments to it (Boyer 1995).

These work environments are transplanted to countries which represent major markets for Japanese producers (Hiraoka 1989; Morgan and Sayer 1988; Thompson and Rehder 1995). Resistance from labour unions is often intense, and prevents the widespread adoption of Japanese labour–management relations (Hyman and Streeck 1988; Willman 1987). In fact, despite the global location of Japanese 'transplants' – especially in car production – work practices have not been transferred easily to North America, Europe or elsewhere (Babson 1995). There are deep and significant country differences, historical and cultural in nature, that contribute to persistent international variations (Buitendam 1987; Harber and Samson 1989; Holmes 1987; Kogut 1993; Wood 1988). These differences include the hiring of women workers and the presence of company slogans – both common in Nissan and Toyota plants in the USA but not in the UK (Emmott 1993: 72–3). Perhaps in part because the work environment cannot be duplicated exactly, productivity levels remain lower in Japanese plants abroad than in Japan (Emmott 1993: 153–60).

General Motors, the first US firm to work in a joint venture with Toyota in the USA, has learned a great deal about democratic Taylorism, the development of a learning bureaucracy, and the institution of a cooperative culture (Adler 1992), but these seem not to have spread within the firm sufficiently to affect overall efficiency (Table 4.6). The 'firm as community' may be the most difficult of Japanese work organization practices to transfer to other cultures and institutional settings (Dore 1987). By whatever name – flexible, agile or something else – new production organization relies heavily on people skills, including communication and cooperation (Kidd 1994: 362). In practice, even the people aspects have to take on hybrid forms (Sadler and Swain 1994; Thompson and Rehder 1995).

Neo-Fordism and post-Fordism are also used to describe the increased workload standardization that has accompanied information technology in office work. The proliferation of computer technology and word-processing capability has had several layers of effects. First, it has eliminated the prospect of employment for those whose entry-level skills do not include familiarity with computers, or sufficient literacy to solve non-routine problems. The computer skills needed for 'back-office' activities of banks, insurance companies, data-processing firms and others are not great, and many of these activities have gone to distant locations. Most back-office activities, which formerly were literally in a back office of the headquarters of such firms, have simply been suburbanized. In large part, suburban locations are where the demand for high-quality, 'cheap but educated' clerical labour is best met. Relatively high levels of education, language and communication skills, and middle-class manner and social values are sought in clerical workers (K. Nelson 1986). For these reasons, members of ethnic minority groups and others whose education-related skills do not meet the criteria are increasingly out of the running for such jobs (Baran 1985; Cyert and Mowery 1987; Stanback 1987).

A second effect has been to demand more flexibility on the part of workers. In addition to qualitative flexibility demanded by automated production, firms make use of numerical labour flexibility through the use of *contingent workers* or 'flexiworkers', terms used to designate workers hired at less the standard wage, for less than the standard workweek or workyear, or with less than standard fringe benefits (Belous 1989; Christopherson and Noyelle 1992; Dore, Bounine-Cabalé and Tapiola 1989; Standing 1992). This group is particularly common in the service sector, where part-time work is more common, among 'homeworkers' and, increasingly, in manufacturing among subcontractors (Christopherson 1989; Christopherson and Storper 1989; Harrison and Bluestone 1988; Hyman 1988; Morris 1988). Temporary help services, especially common in health care, business services, and finance and insurance, reduce workers' 'attachment' to, and expectations of, an employer. Although many such jobs are clerical, temporaries also include truck drivers, assemblers and, increasingly, professionals (Mangum, Mayall and Nelson 1985; Melcher 1996; Segal and Sullivan 1995). The percentage of workers who work neither full-time nor year-round is nearly 45 per cent in the USA, and 65 per cent in service industries, facts which are masked by statistics on 'employment' and 'unemployment' (Belous 1989; Christopherson 1989; Ettlinger 1988).

In addition to contingent work, many kinds of informal production in many countries are still common (Portes, Castells and Benton 1989). Part-time employees are overwhelmingly (over 60 per cent) female (Belous 1989: 50–2). This type of flexible labour force has been a major part of the success of the 'Third Italy' and other new 'flexible regions', where artisanal skills, to respond to new designs and new market signals, combine with self-exploitation, the use of family labour, evasion of tax and social security contributions, low overhead costs, and the use of cheap female and young workers, especially for unskilled work (Amin 1989b).

At the opposite extreme, labour skills and flexibility are demanded. Small-volume batch production systems require less labour than do massive mass-production facilities, but workers must be sufficiently educated and skilled to perform their jobs on an ever-changing mix of products. The performance of a range of tasks, or *polyvalence*, works best in a situation where worker discretion and judgement are also encouraged (Child 1987b). This is why technologically sophisticated plants can be found in rural areas as well as in urban agglomerations: skilled-labour pools can be protected from competition from other employers (Norcliffe and Zweerman Barschat 1994).

In the electronics industry, in many ways a prototype setting for the product cycle, chip design in R&D is now much more capital-intensive than previously, as expensive equipment is needed to create the intricate products, which are often of a semi-custom nature. This capital intensity would seem to render labour a less important consideration for the firm even at the production stage, where labour costs have been an important part of the strategy of US firms. By integrating technology development and production, US and Japanese firms have converged (Angel 1994: 190–2). The short life of many electronics products means that successive cost reductions through improvements in efficiency are less likely than in longer life-cycles, and equipment is usable over several product life-cycles, reducing average costs (Schoenberger 1986). As a result, non-routine, adaptive behaviour is demanded of firms, in contrast to the linear sequence seen in the various production-oriented life-cycle models (Beije 1987). This has parallels with the feedbacks in the innovation process discussed in Chapter 2.

Inter-firm relationships

Flexible production systems require, in turn, a tightly controlled stream of inputs tailored to the needs of production on both a short-term and a long-term basis. This requires different relationships between a firm and its suppliers, epitomized in Japanese vertical de-integration and innovative supplier relationships (Cusumano 1986). The distinction between Japanese supplier networks and those common in other firms is the rather strict hierarchical structure, in which a core firm utilizes a small number of large subcontractors which, in turn, are supplied by a larger set of sub-subcontractors, which are also served by an even larger lower tier of suppliers. The pyramidal structure means that a given firm has fewer direct suppliers than in the typical European or North American firm. For example, General Motors in 1988 had 2000 direct suppliers, and Volkswagen 1760. By contrast, Nissan had 160 direct suppliers, and Mazda 180. In an explicit attempt to imitate this structure, between 1988 and 1989, Ford of Europe reduced the number of its direct suppliers from 2100 to 1200 (Howells and Wood 1993: 110–21). An added benefit of such arrangements is that, with bigger orders, a firm can demand faster service from suppliers.

The smaller number of suppliers means that relationships with the suppliers can be more closely integrated with the needs – present and future – of the firm. A small number of *strategic suppliers* whose collaboration and technical skills are high are able to work with a company and solve design and production problems (Spekman 1988; Wood, Kaufman and Merenda 1996). Proximity usually is essential for problem-solving on new products and processes, because of the intensity and frequency of face-to-face and on-site communication needed (Gertler 1995; von Hippel 1994), although this is not always the case (Angel and Engstrom 1995; Appold 1995; Leus and Pellenbarg 1991).

Relationships with strategic suppliers take time and evolve over time and without specified life-cycles. 'They transform over time, merge, shift in focus and membership . . . The continuous interaction between firms offers, on the one hand, the opportunity for innovation and, on the other, the existence of a known and predictable environment in which it can be realised' (Easton 1992: 23–4; see also Håkansson 1992). However, for innovative firms, suppliers are among the most important sources of knowledge for innovation (Axelsson and Easton 1992; Håkansson 1989), as Chapter 2 has stressed. A propulsive firm can also spark competitiveness through its supplier network to a wider region (Ettlinger and Patton 1996). The notion of 'supplier' also includes seemingly routine service providers, especially those concerned with logistics and delivery aspects, which are critical to a customer-responsive strategy (Li 1995).

In the Japanese case, an additional consideration is significant: the corporate group or *keiretsu*. While there are several types of business groups, including those centred around banks and around trading companies, *keiretsu* is the term used commonly outside Japan to designate such corporate families (Ferguson 1990; Neff and Holstein 1990), although there are several types of enterprise groups (Imai 1994). The corporate family structure permits and facilitates very efficient technology transfer across industrial sectors based on high knowledge content, including tacit knowledge, by providing a 'place' for interaction to occur smoothly (Imai 1994: 122; Lakshmanan and Okumura 1995; Samuels 1994). Internal job transfers and other forms of learning create skills that are enterprise-specific or group-specific.

Cross-ownership links of firms in different sectors suggest that the core firm's control over the others is relatively strong in some cases, but by no means all. In the Toyota supplier association, for example, 36 of 171 members had 20 per cent or more of their shares owned by Toyota Motor in 1985. 'The relation between

Toyota Motor and its suppliers . . . appears to be basically not one of share-holding but of division of labour in the production process' (Odagiri 1992: 163).

Both production networks and *keiretsu* networks greatly blur the usual boundaries of the corporation. While payments by Nissan and Toyota to in-house suppliers represented only about 25 per cent of total sales (minus profits), within-group suppliers increase that total to over 70 per cent in both cases (Cusumano 1986: 159). Within some web-like networks, firms are not completely controlled by the core firm and may supply competitors as well (Odagiri 1992). Small subcontractors are the essence of the *keiretsu* system but their link to a core firm determines their circumstances (Sakai 1990). This is most likely in the more loosely structured horizontal *keiretsu*, which provides a quasi-internal source of technical knowledge as well as material supplies. In this structure, the pyramid is replaced by a cobweb in which cooperating small and medium-size firms interact (Furukawa, Teramoto and Kanda 1990; Groenewegen 1993; van Kooij 1991). Central coordination is present to a greater or lesser degree, depending on the network. Overall, subcontracting in Japan is 'a system of vertically disintegrated yet captive relationships' (Glasmeier and Sugiura 1991: 401).

These business groups seem to result in few measurable traditional benefits, such as profitability, but they provide other advantages that may be more important, including preferential financing, information exchange, fluid joint-venture arrangements, and trademarks. The ties permit close communication with, and job rotation in, the other firms, thereby broadening the experience and knowledge of engineers and managers in subcontracting firms (Miwa 1994; Odagiri 1992). These close relationships enable a high degree of trust to form (Ito 1994; Sako 1992). Finally, a firm's inter-organizational relationships may include not only suppliers but also research institutions, competitors, and customers or clients (Shaw 1994; van der Meer and Calori 1989).

Just-in-time production

One part of the Japanese system of inter-firm relations is the just-in-time (JIT) or *kanban* system of inventory management, developed by Toyota during the 1950s. It represents, along with lean production methods, what has been called Toyotism, the apparent successor to Fordism, as a model of networked production (Michalet 1991). 'In broad terms, the core of the JIT concept is the elimination of waste in all forms – production, materials, labour, time, energy, money and so on' (Arnold and Bernard 1989: 403). Instead of a producer of cars maintaining inventories of all the many hundreds of parts needed for the vehicles to be produced, parts suppliers are required to deliver these several times per week – or per day. This sort of system thus demands tight control over suppliers, who are also required to provide a higher level of quality: fewer defective parts per order with a goal of zero defects. In short, parts producers must operate at a higher frequency ('more often') and in smaller volumes ('less') than was true under traditional production organization (Arnold and Bernard 1989: 415; Fornengo 1988; Hoffman and Kaplinsky 1988; Lenz 1989).

A related aspect of Toyota's supplier network is its spatial concentration of suppliers around the firm's main assembly complex in Toyota City. This geographical pattern has been implemented in the USA, with greater distances, around the 'transplant corridor' along two interstate highways running south of Detroit, the traditional US car manufacturing hub (Kenney and Florida 1993; Klier 1994, 1995; Newman 1990; Rubenstein 1992). In both the USA and the UK, a large portion of Japanese auto parts and components are purchased from newly sited Japanese firms in those countries, rather than from existing firms (Pike 1996). This is a result of a lack of interest or a lack of confidence on the part of local companies (Foley *et al.* 1996).

A reduction in throughput time, or cycle time, becomes a source of profitability (Schmenner 1988). Focusing on a reduction of throughput time results in a reduction of inventories, set-up time and lot sizes. These changes, in turn, induce improved quality, revamped factory layout, stabilized production schedules and minimization of engineering changes. Impressive results have been reported as a consequence of implementing JIT into production systems, such as reduction of stocks by 50 per cent, reduction of transportation and stock-keeping costs by 20 per cent, and improvement of overall productivity by 25 per cent (Arnold and Bernard 1989). Mazda was able to reduce set-up time from 6.5 hours to 13 minutes after it incorporated new manufacturing systems between 1976 and 1980 (Hayes, Wheelwright and Clark 1988: 187). However, time savings such as these are not accounted for in conventional productivity measurements (Port, King and Hampton 1988: 104; Schmenner 1988; Stalk and Hout 1990).

JIT production affects many other activities of production and is impossible to separate from other aspects of Japanese production organization, especially labour relations and work organization (Hudson 1994; Kenney and Florida 1993; Linge 1991; Patchell and Hayter 1995). JIT necessitates in suppliers, for example, integrated data-processing for R&D, procurement, production planning, inventory control, and marketing (Arnold and Bernard 1989). Both Japanese and US car makers make significant use of electronic data interchange as well as engineering interaction, indicating both a high commitment to the relationship and a high degree of mutual trust. This is particularly common for critical and complex components such as power steering, wheels and shock absorbers. Trust is a means of overcoming uncertainty with regard to the product, its market and the design or engineering task, as well as the future behaviour of a partner (Bensaou and Venkatraman 1995).

Outside the vehicle sector, systems established by major retailers feed daily sales data to computers at several clothing manufacturers, itemizing the styles, colours and sizes that must be stocked. This demands implementation of bar codes, scanning equipment, electronic data interchange (EDI) and automated distribution systems (Abernathy *et al.* 1995; Braham 1986; Camagni and Rabellotti 1992; Caminiti 1989). Consequently, once again, flexible technologies appear to promote larger, rather than smaller, firm sizes. Finding customers for the more diverse array of new products also makes sales and marketing more important company capabilities (Sashittal and Wilemon 1994; Starr and Biloski 1985; Teece 1982).

The number of suppliers tends to drop substantially under JIT and other new inter-firm relationships. A proliferation of input producers is unwieldy to manage, and single-sourcing with strategic suppliers – those few that are reliable in terms of quality, delivery and response – becomes a solution (Bache *et al.* 1987; Quinn and Hilmer 1994). Suppliers may face increased costs – among them for computer systems and communication links – related to a push for high-quality, 'zero defects' production (Arnold and Bernard 1989). The communications needs of flexible production can be very large and costly, and the use of information technology (telematics) is a prominent aspect of supplier networks (Abernathy *et al.* 1995; Fornengo 1988; Rullani and Zanfei 1988).

The infrastructure demands of flexible production are great, both in communications and conventional transport infrastructure. Just-in-time supply systems, for example, require reliable, high-speed road networks (Janssen and van Hoogstraten 1989). However, reasons related to labour rather than infrastructure have kept JIT and its resultant agglomeration from becoming global phenomena. Especially in countries with a history of militant labour, the advantages of greenfield sites take precedence over the potential benefits of agglomeration. Clustered suppliers on the Toyota City model may 'depend on labor being weakly organized' (Sayer and Walker 1992: 185).

Networks of production

Subcontracting in the supply chain is a form of vertical collaboration, in contrast to horizontal collaboration, which occurs between partners at the same level in the production process. Both types of collaboration provide several sets of benefits: increased scale and scope of activities, shared costs and risks, and improved ability to deal with complexity (Dodgson 1994). Close, relational subcontracting also contrasts with traditional, arm's length relationships, and stresses one of the most 'non-economic' of variables: *trust*. Sako (1992: 37–47) details three types of trust. The first, *contractual trust*, is essentially the mutual expectation that promises made are kept. The second type, *competence trust*, concerns technical and managerial competence to carry out a task, and is demonstrated in accepting goods from a supplier without inspecting them. The third type, *goodwill trust*, refers to mutual expectations of open commitment to each other, seen in a willingness to do more than is formally expected, such as sharing of information. Sabel (1992) prefers the concept of 'negotiated loyalty'.

The legalistic nature of relations common among Anglo-Saxon firms (arm's length contractual relations) contrasts sharply with the relational or obligational contractual relations found among Japanese firms, and may thwart the development of cooperative relationships (Casson 1990; Granovetter 1985). Obligational relations represent not only an economic relationship, but also the social relation between trading partners based on mutual trust. Because of this strong foundation, transactions can take place without prior agreement or specification of all the terms and conditions of trade. Trust operates as the shortcut mechanism for communication and cooperation between firms (Hansen 1992). Trust and the embeddedness of economic relationships into 'the deeper social fabric' or the communal, non-economic institutions of some local areas, such as industrial districts, is what distinguishes them from other areas (B. Harrison 1992: 479).

Trust relationships can result in a supplier exceeding contractual requirements, whether by early delivery, higher quality or some other means of assuring goodwill (Sako 1992). The informal relationships on which inter-firm collaborations depend are fragile, and can be stifled by formal structures and contracts (Macdonald 1992). Trust is not created without effort. The investment made to build trust is a 'soft' investment, measured in people and their time, yet it represents a significant investment of resources (Easton 1992: 13–14). 'Through the combinations of economic and social relationships in the network, the information becomes rich, redundant and cheap' (Hertz 1992: 110). Trust is difficult to measure, but it forms the basis for the interactions that define a culture – national, regional or local – and allow values and norms to be passed on to succeeding generations (Fukuyama 1995).

Networks of suppliers on the Japanese model are also part of the restructured geography of production systems. In the vehicle industry, it is noteworthy that these retain a bias toward traditional auto manufacturing regions, because of the skill requirements needed to maintain quality in both components and in the final product. Japanese car assembly plants and their 'transplant' suppliers appear to have chosen locations in small towns to avoid as much as possible labour union organization, a strategy employed by General Motors as well (Clark 1986b; Kenney and Florida 1993; Mair, Florida and Kenney 1988). In other words, the dispersion of auto production which has been observed (Glasmeier and McCluskey 1987; Rubenstein 1992) retains proximity to the core region of North American auto production but on greenfield sites (Mair, Florida and Kenney 1988: 370; Schoenberger 1987). A subtle change has taken place in the proportion of components imported from Japan to car assembly plants. Formerly quite high (Morris 1988), these are now overwhelmingly supplied by 'transplant' suppliers operating from greenfield sites in the USA, the UK and Europe (Newman 1990; Newman and Rhee 1990).

The pattern used by US car makers is a 'rather odd hybrid called a JIT warehouse', which merely pushes the inventory costs away from the manufacturer and its suppliers and places them on the warehouse (Flynn and Cole 1988: 136). The same phenomenon of 'pseudo-JIT' is evident in Europe (Hudson 1994: 341). Even Japanese analysts portray their locations outside Japan as 'hybrid factories' in comparison with those at home (Abo 1994). It is auto parts plants, followed closely by auto assembly plants, that come closest to the ideal Japanese factory (in work organization, production control, procurement, group consciousness, labour relations and parent–subsidiary relations). Consumer electronics plants are least similar to plants in Japan (Kamiyama 1994). With only daily deliveries from a small number of mainly distant plants, the hybrid JIT system in the UK shows that flexible production and Japanese firms are not identical in all places (Morris 1988). JIT production is stretched further in Asia, where many of the linkages of Japanese car makers for parts and components are scattered throughout Asia (Hill 1989).

What has emerged in several contexts is a *network* model which affects both large and small firms (Antonelli 1988a; Cooke and Morgan 1993). 'We are not talking about independent small firms in the traditional sense, nor about sub-contractors for large firms, but about the development of an industrial system (almost a corporation) composed of interlinked but independently owned pro-duction units' (Amin 1989a: 118). The network form is 'neither market nor hierarchy', being distinct from both the hierarchical integrated firm and the arm's length relationship of market transactions (Larsson 1993; Nooteboom 1993; Powell 1990; Thorelli 1986; Yeung 1994a). As forms of governance – a term which refers to the rules and procedures that govern the behaviour of coor-dinating transactions – they are very different. Markets 'are a spontaneous coordination mechanism' that offers choice, flexibility and opportunity, but no trust is required, and agreements are enforced by legal sanction (Powell 1990: 301–3). Networks, on the other hand, 'are lighter on their feet' than hierarchies. 'Expectations are not frozen, but change as circumstances dictate' (Powell 1990: 303). Networks are not without problems and conflicts, largely because the par-ticipants remain in one way or another competitors. Networks also embody inflexibility in membership (outsiders may be excluded) and therefore adjust-ment to discontinuities can be difficult (Grabher 1993).

In short, networks are a flexible intermediate response ('make together') to the ever-present 'make or buy' decision (Camagni and Rabellotti 1992). Long-term relationships, rather than spot purchases from the lowest bidder, are espe-cially critical to industrial products where innovation is an important dimension (Håkansson 1987; Low 1996). In consumer products, long-term 'partnership' relationships are less common, and it is not unusual for lower-tier sub-contractors to be increasingly vulnerable (Crewe and Davenport 1992). The temptation of many firms is to turn over many, even most, company activities to partners and suppliers and become hollow. One solution is to retain control over core competences but to 'outsource' less critical activities (Chesbrough and Teece 1996). Another is to coordinate a web of partners from a 'strategic centre' (Lorenzoni and Baden-Fuller 1995).

The simple market–hierarchy dichotomy, however, also masks some impor-tant differences which were hinted at above concerning Japanese networks. This is seen in Figure 4.3, in which two dimensions are included: ownership integra-tion and coordination integration (Robertson and Langlois 1995). The classic 'Chandlerian' firm includes high degrees of both, and is the prototypical 'hier-archy' form. Several network forms contain varying degrees of integration of ownership and coordination. The Japanese network, with its combination of cross-ownership and inter-firm cooperation, is a truly intermediate case. Venture capital networks common in California's Silicon Valley have less own-ership control, but more than is found in either Marshallian districts or indus-trial districts of the type found in Italy. The presence of large or core firms, coordinating or controlling the production system, adds additional complexity to the two-dimensional portrayal in Figure 4.3 (Storper and Harrison 1991). Network forms also provide an important phenomenon unavailable to inte-grated firms: external intelligence from both direct and indirect network con-tacts, which provide external economies of learning (Nooteboom 1993).

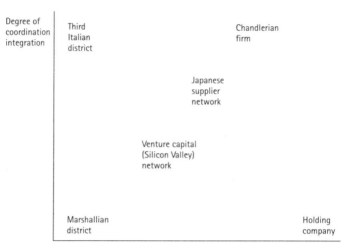

Figure 4.3   Two dimensions of integration. Source: modified from Robertson and Langlois (1995: 548, Figure 1).

The influence of informal social relationships, trust and cooperation makes prominent the role of people, or human agency, in economic activity. While business structures provide and enforce some coordination and power relations, they are unable to control completely the interactions of individuals. In knowledge-based businesses, companies attempt to take advantage of the relationships developed by individuals (Nonaka and Takeuchi 1995). Attempting to impose formal structures on the informal relationships can be counterproductive (Macdonald 1992). An explicit purpose of the Japanese corporate 'family' is to develop and retain informal relationships within the corporate group. The learning corporation acknowledges these relationships and, rather than merely exploiting them, works to facilitate the interactions on which people thrive and corporations profit (Leonard-Barton 1995).

Agglomeration revisited

Both network relations and flexible production suggest that spatial proximity is advantageous in order to maximize the frequency and intensity of interpersonal communication. It is unclear whether flexible systems have reduced the appeal of low-wage labour pools in favour of concentrations of higher-order, non-routine functions (Schoenberger 1987). One geographical impact of this form of technological and organizational change could be to induce industry to concentrate exclusively or mainly in areas where specialized firms and skilled labour are abundant, and where uncertainty and unforeseen changes could be easily accommodated.

A second scenario suggests that telecommunications technology will be able to replace the need for face-to-face contact, leading to dispersal of business activities. Even data-entry jobs, which are found in many locations around the world

as well as in rural regions of advanced economies, show a tendency to agglomerate in major urban centres and in some off-shore locations with pools of high-
skill, low-cost labour (Glasmeier and Howland 1995; Howland 1993).
Widespread dispersal of corporate functions is unlikely to happen, despite
experiments by transnational companies with 'cross-border teamwork' on
common projects (Howells and Wood 1993). Electronic communication in
R&D seems to be effective only if electronic contact is reinforced regularly by
face-to-face contact (De Meyer 1993a). The reagglomeration tendency of flexible production is not absolute in any case (Gertler 1988b, 1992; Holmes 1986;
Hudson 1994; Sayer and Walker 1992).

The advantages of agglomeration go beyond transaction cost linkages and
market and information access. Large firms try to maximize information-intensive contacts by centralizing in large urban centres. Around these cluster service
activities, for which large firms are the dominant market. Such linkages benefit
firms by stimulating innovation, especially product innovations (Davelaar and
Nijkamp 1989; MacPherson 1988b). Localized clusters or constellations permit
consultation, interaction and rapid response between firms, which is especially
important for niche producers outside of high-technology industries (De
Bresson 1989; Doeringer, Terkla and Topakian 1987; Lorenzoni and Ornati
1988). These synergistic effects comprise a cooperation effect that goes beyond
what can be accounted for by transaction costs and vertical disintegration
(Henry 1992). The cooperation effect is critical to the success of innovative
firms, whose environment must deal constantly with uncertainty (Foray 1991).
Thus, there are several ways in which agglomeration can be beneficial beyond
the traditional approach based on known inputs and transactions (McCann
1995). Together, these advantages are the source of Verdoorn effects (Chapter
2), or increasing returns to scale and scope (Scott 1995).

An array of other influences may be more important than urban size alone.
Regions dominated by large firms and by branch production plants are unlikely
to have the level of information, R&D and knowledge of the state-of-the-art
needed to spawn new firms, the second consequence (after linkages) of regional
economic development. This is summed up well by Sweeney (1985: 97):

> Areas dominated by large firms tend to have low entrepreneurial vitality. Such firms
> have internalised their information resources and networks . . . Areas dominated by
> branch plants of large firms also have low entrepreneurial vitality, their networks are
> with their distant parent company. Sub-contracting, an important source of start-up
> for new companies, is minimised by the large integrated firm and even more by
> branch plants. An important means of developing local networks for technology and
> information transfer is thus lost. Localities which are dominated by large firms are
> not centres of entrepreneurial vitality, partly because there is a lack of openness in the
> flow of information from the large to the small.

The development – or lack of development – of local linkages is the fundamental distinction between regions where development can be seen to have
taken place and where it has not (Amin 1989c; Miller and Coté 1987). Rural or
non-metropolitan regions may also be able to amass the vitality needed, provided

it encompasses inter-firm interaction, specialization, and availability of finance and labour (Camagni and Capello 1990).

There remains some controversy over whether only *new* industrial spaces are seedbeds of new technology (Scott 1988a,c). A decade ago, it seemed that the high-tech prosperity of the Boston area 'shows that an old, indeed very old, region can remain innovative' (Hall and Preston 1988: 261). Saxenian (1994) recently suggested that the cultural norms that govern individual and corporate behaviour in the Silicon Valley region are far more supportive of entrepreneurship and continual innovativeness than is the case in the Boston area. The presence of large firms, both locally grown and transnational, have not subverted the vitality of new firm formation (Bahrami and Evans 1995; Harrison 1994), although the combination of entrepreneurial fever and extreme focus on innovation may make the Silicon Valley production system best suited to innovation rather than to commercialization (Angel 1994; Florida and Kenney 1990; Hobday 1994a).

Clusters, milieus and districts

Industrial clusters are 'a variation on the theme of agglomeration economies' (Doeringer and Terkla 1995). Nothing new in the economic geography of industries, Porter's (1990) identification of regional clusters in several countries illuminated the phenomenon to many unaware of the concept. The identification of clusters starts with linkages and proximity, and becomes dynamic through face-to-face collaboration economies (Doeringer and Terkla 1995). The combination of sophisticated needs of customers and technical expertise in suppliers leads to mutually supportive interaction (DeBresson 1989; Marceau 1994). Proposals for policy initiatives to develop clusters, however, need to include actual interaction rather than single-sector clusters or linked sectors on the basis of national-scale input–output linkages (DeBresson 1989; Doeringer, Terkla and Topakian 1987; Held 1996; Rosenfeld 1995).

Not all spatial agglomerations of small firms in the same or related sectors necessarily comprise an industrial district or local industrial system. Of three textile regions examined in France, Italy and the UK, only the Italian case comprised a *filière* of specialized firms. Although the British district in Leicester has displayed an entrepreneurial culture in terms of new firm formation, it has failed to be either innovative or to seek and disseminate expertise among the firms in the area (Bull, Pitt and Szarka 1991). Thus, a functioning network of firms in a locale is an essential phenomenon for local development.

Dynamic local economies, like technically progressive firms, are open in giving as well as taking information and, like innovative firms, they continually search for information and maintain good internal communication flows (Sweeney 1987). The level of innovativeness in an area depends on the degree to which firms are linked to both *local* networks of suppliers and to *external*, especially global, markets. Firms in such dynamic, networked 'constellations' are more able and willing to seek information from outside sources (Lorenzoni and Ornati 1988). Regions with a technical culture (Sweeney 1991) are able to adjust to changing conditions, such as the dramatic shock which took place in the watch-making region of Switzerland when electronic technology replaced mechanical technology (Glasmeier 1991b; Maillat 1984). The Swiss district had to form both internal and external links in order to learn and incorporate the new technology and to add a fashion element on which they could capitalize in the Swatch (D'Aveni 1994: 302–10). Producers in Hong Kong, the second largest watch producer, have fewer worker skills to draw upon and focus on the low-price end of the market (Glasmeier 1994).

Generalized somewhat from the local technical culture is the concept of *innovative milieu* (Camagni 1991a; Hansen 1992). A milieu is a coherent whole in which a territorial production system, a technical culture, and firms and institutions are linked (Maillat and Lecoq 1992). In a milieu, trust and reciprocity are based on a system of implicit rules or cultural norms (or modes of social regulation) as well as on institutions that support innovation and flexibility. Accumulated managerial, technical and commercial competence is passed on to others (Brusco 1986). The role of regional and local institutions is a key aspect of a milieu, an example of which is the introduction of courses in microtechnical engineering in the Swiss Jura region's five technical colleges (Maillat *et al.* 1995). The links in a territorial network of this kind are structural, but they are above all cultural, and serve principally to reduce uncertainty (Camagni 1991b; Johannisson 1990a; Maillat 1990). The industrial milieu or district itself can be seen as a community or *collective entrepreneur*, with not only firms, but interfirm associations, worker organizations, financial institutions and governmental agencies also playing important roles (Best 1990; Courault and Romani 1992; Lorenz 1992; Maillat 1990; Pyke, Becattini and Sengenberger 1990).

The dynamic nature of learning shows close ties to the evolutionary approach to technological change (Chapter 2) as well as a view that the *territory* itself plays a role. The territory is a place of coordination and learning that goes beyond simple transaction cost-based agglomeration economies (Belussi 1996; Courlet and Pecqueur 1991; Courlet and Soulage 1995). Agglomeration facilitates interaction and sharing of *untraded interdependencies*, including labour force skills, sector-specific services, and information and tacit knowledge (Storper 1993, 1995a). These interdependencies are typically industry-specific sectoral clusters in which specialist firms interact intensively. Examples, in addition to the industrial districts and milieus discussed above, include the British motor sport industry (Henry, Pinch and Russell 1996), semiconductors in Silicon Valley (Angel 1994), and the image-producing (craft, fashion and cultural products) complex in southern California (Scott 1996a; Storper and Christopherson 1987). In other sectors in the same southern California region, such as household furniture, an absence of intra- and inter-sectoral links may be a principal cause of a lack of competitiveness in that industry (Scott 1996b). In part, the lack of a network in this sector is a widespread strategy of price competition which, as pointed out in Chapter 2, is unlikely to involve much innovativeness, knowledge or design inputs and, therefore, inter-firm dependencies are buried by inter-firm competition and an absence of trust.

Industrial districts are a particular type of agglomeration, characterized by 'a localized "thickening" of interindustrial relationships which is reasonably stable over time' (Becattini 1989: 132). The classic Marshallian district, so named because it was identified by Alfred Marshall (1920) at the turn of the century, is urban in location and usually located in the urban core. Jewellery-making remains a classic craft-based industry of this type (Scott 1994), and clothing and furniture-making are others (Scott 1984; Scott 1996b). Scott (1988b, 1993) has added to this list a number of industrial districts in southern California which centre on complex assembled products in which systems-house production by large firms is the norm. These are common in aerospace electronics. Using mutual interdependence via material linkages and subcontracting as well as untraded interdependencies, industrial districts are commonly associated with small firms in dispersed, rather than urban, settings.

The Italian industrial districts seem to be a distinct type of district, with a higher degree of cooperative coordination than is found in the Marshallian district (Robertson and Langlois 1995). Primarily comprised of small firms, like the Marshallian district, their markets are national or international, in contrast to traditional artisan firms and dependent subcontractors in Marshallian districts (Brusco 1986). Inter-firm relations – primarily between the small firms themselves and secondarily with outside customers, agents and competitors – stimulate innovations and best-practice technology. The Benetton group, which markets the products of small, mainly family-owned, knitwear firms in the Third Italy, is a prominent, oft-cited example (Belussi 1989; Rullani and Zanfei 1988; Scott 1988c).

In Japan, machinery districts in portions of Tokyo and in the Sakaki district illustrate that innovative, interconnected small firms are the core of such regions (Friedman 1988: 177–200; Takeuchi 1987; Takeuchi and Mori 1987). Webs of local linkages and subcontracting are the basis of the agglomeration advantages of such industrial districts. Family ties are also important and ease information flow between firms, and cooperation and sharing of new equipment is commonplace in 'Sakaki Inc.' (Friedman 1988: 196–8). Such production systems appear to be common in Japan and Europe, but less so in North America (Dimou 1994; Goodman, Bamford and Saynor 1989; Hansen 1991; Illeris 1992; Lewis and Williams 1987; E. Lorenz 1989; Maillat 1990; Pyke, Becattini and Sengenberger 1990; Pyke and Sengenberger 1992; Rosenfeld 1989–90; Sabel 1989; Sabel et al. 1987). In the USA, only Silicon Valley appears to have the characteristics of districts elsewhere (Perrow 1992).

The depiction of a tightly connected web of firms which mutually support one another is characteristic of the North–East–Central (NEC) region of Italy, also known as the Third Italy (along with the developed North and under-developed South) and characterized by small and medium-size firms. The emergence of this local production system in Emilia-Romagna, the centre of the Third Italy, has roots in sixteenth-century silk production in Bologna. For centuries, an informal economy in the surrounding region relied on work by women in their homes. In the 1950s, employment shifted out of agriculture into manufacturing, including shoes, textiles and machinery, produced by artisans and craftspeople. The specific skills required for each industry (metalworking, textiles, clothing, footwear, furniture) or a particular operation are often found only in quite limited areas (Capecchi 1989; Mazzonis 1989). The informal social and economic structure persists exclusively in the cottage industries in the Third Italy and is not found in urban areas (Courault and Romani 1992; Sabel 1982: 220). Artisan networks in Emilia-Romagna, Tuscany and other provinces of the Third Italy, in industries as diverse as knitwear, gloves, shoes and ceramic tiles, have also made impressive showings in world markets. The competitiveness of these industrial districts lies in their flexibility – first, in terms of labour, since they rely largely on family members rather than employees, and second, in terms of innovativeness and entrepreneurship based on artisanal skills (Brusco 1989; Piore and Sabel 1984: 213–29; Russo 1985). Another example is found in the Italian motorcycle industry, which has excelled in innovative designs by niche and specialist producers, aided by clusters of suppliers (Muffatto and Panizzolo 1996). Many new firms have emerged in the Third Italy in this sector, away from the industrial heartland around Turin and Milan (Cenzatti 1990).

The 'organized complexity' and networks of linkages have not diffused from Tuscany and Emilia-Romagna to the rest of Italy (Amin 1989b,c; Pezzini 1989; Sforzi 1989). The informal nature of the economy and society and local 'rules' keep most linkages local, between other small firms in the district. In both the Third Italy and the Sakaki district in Japan, local sharing of knowledge, machinery and trust among specialized innovative firms is the norm (Sabel 1982: 220–6). The cooperation and trust seen in industrial districts is considered part of the informal, 'preindustrial' character of such places (Sabel 1989: 47–52; B. Harrison 1992). Interdependence arises from the intense specialization of firms: 'The moment the firm begins to expand and move beyond its original specialty it finds itself dependent on the help of neighbours with complementary kinds of specialties; and because the neighbours can never exactly anticipate when they too will need assistance, the help is forthcoming' (Sabel 1982: 225). The industrial districts embody evolutionary economic processes, but with local and country-specific rules and conventions, that involve a collective efficiency (Belussi 1996; Schmitz 1992).

The most recent phase of development in the Italian industrial districts involves response to global competition. One reaction has been the incorporation of information technology. A telecommunications network permits contact between local firms, suppliers and buyers, in addition to conditions on the world market (Fornengo 1988; Rullani and Zanfei 1988). Price competition and reduced demand since the mid-1980s caused many Italian districts to fall on hard times and price competition eroded some of the trust and cooperation (Harrison 1994). This has forced the districts to adopt new strategies that, given their varied histories and cultures, differ between districts (Dei Ottati 1996; Varaldo and Ferrucci 1996). It is clear that firms, in Italy or elsewhere, cannot adapt to new or changing circumstances without local or regional institutions and a concerted policy effort (Cooke 1996a; Malecki and Tödtling 1995; Scott 1994; Triglia 1992).

Conclusion

Two things influence the innovativeness and competitiveness of places and countries. First and foremost, technical skills stand out as key to relating to the process of technological change and competition (Maggi and Haeni 1986; Patchell and Hayter 1995). Actual production systems are very complex and centre around organizational skills and information (Hepworth 1989: 146–9; Walker 1988). Yet, to quote Harvey (1988: 109): 'What is most interesting about the current situation is the way in which capitalism is becoming ever more tightly organized through dispersal, geographic mobility, and flexible responses in labour markets, labour processes, and consumer markets, all accompanied by hefty doses of institutional, product, and technological innovation.' Second, urban areas contain a complex mix or synergy of factors which smaller, more remote, places cannot attain (Bramanti and Senn 1990; Stöhr 1986). Especially in information and knowledge, urban areas sustain a level of creativity not easily found or generated in other settings (Andersson 1985). That is why producer services, which are strongly based on knowledge and symbolic analysis, are so clustered in cities – more so than is manufacturing.

'Post-Weberian location theory' attempts to explain the 'transition from Fordist to flexible accumulation' but well overstates the true situation (Harvey 1988; Harvey and Scott 1989). In seeking to develop a broadly applicable theory, it often fails to take fully into account the specificity of industries and of places (Sayer 1985; Walker 1985, 1988). More importantly, it imposes a structure of a systemic and overriding nature on what remains fundamentally a human process. New forms of production either work or do not work because of people and their actions, their abilities and skills, and their interpersonal contacts (Fadem 1984; Malecki 1989).

The stark dichotomy often presented between Fordist and flexible production is 'a caricature' (Amin 1994a: 15). There was never a single Fordism, but a 'series of interconnected and institutionally specific national Fordisms' (Peck and Tickell 1994: 285). However, it is clear that Fordism is declining as a production system, although what is replacing it is still subject to considerable debate (Amin 1994b; Amin and Robins 1990; Dunford and Benko 1991; Gertler 1988b, 1992; Jessop 1992a,b; Storper and Scott 1992). Moreover, beyond theoretical concerns, production cannot be decentralized without limit, because of very real limitations of technology, interpretation and coordination (Capello 1994; Malmberg 1995). There is considerable variety in the evolution toward more flexible, 'disorganized' work practices (Boyer 1988a,c; Lash and Bagguley 1988; Leborgne and Lipietz 1988). Whether there is a 'transition' to flexible accumulation deserves a sceptical eye, since it may be far from general or universal (Conti 1988; Thrift 1989). Large, global enterprises are far from eliminated, and they are often able to profit from their own size and organization as well as the flexibility present in other firms, organizations and structures (Amin and Robins 1991; Harrison 1994; Hoffman and Kaplinsky 1988).

The following chapter focuses on small firms and entrepreneurship, part of the flexibility seen in contemporary economies and a crucial part of a well-functioning regional economy. Industrial districts are re-examined in the light of the role played in them by small firms. Large firms, a complementary part of a capitalist economy, are returned to in Chapter 6.

Chapter 5

Entrepreneurs, small firms and economic development

Entrepreneurship, defined broadly, embraces small firms, innovation, and regional and local development policy. In many respects this broad combination is essential for grasping entrepreneurship both as a phenomenon and as a process that should be probed critically with regard to quality as well as quantity (Davidsson 1995). Casson (1982: 391), for example, believes that, in the long term, 'product innovation is the most important form of entrepreneurship', although other entrepreneurial roles have been suggested, such as the creation of intermarket linkages and coordination of production (Suarez-Villa 1991). It is not enough simply to grow; an economy must constantly improve in order to take advantage of technological change in the future. One phenomenon that generally signals a thriving economy is its rate of new firm formation. From Schumpeter's (1934) process of 'creative destruction' to a model of local development centred on entrepreneurship (Coffey and Polèse 1984, 1985), new firm formation is central to current thinking about regional and local well-being.

This chapter reviews some of the research on entrepreneurs, networks and economic development. It begins by discussing briefly our current understanding of the process of local development, and the role of entrepreneurship in that process (Malecki 1994). Then, attention turns to the 'entrepreneurial event' and the geographical environment within which that event takes place. The key aspect of favourable entrepreneurial environments, it turns out, is thriving networks of entrepreneurs, other firms and institutions, providing capital, information and other forms of support. The industrial district or *milieu* (Chapter 4) epitomizes these characteristics. Then, the chapter turns to policy issues, especially attempts to foster local development through the creation of innovative entrepreneurial environments and through the fostering of institutions, networks and a technical culture. The chapter concludes with some observations of entrepreneurship in developing countries.

The concept of entrepreneurship

The term 'entrepreneurship' has several levels of meaning, which makes it difficult to reach a consensus about an appropriate definition (Audretsch 1995; Cunningham and Lischeron 1991). At one level, entrepreneurship refers simply to small firms or enterprises, but 'intrapreneurship' within giant corporations has also become part of the vocabulary (Gibb 1990). A large part of the confusion stems from the fact that the entrepreneur as a key economic actor failed to be incorporated into the modern theory of the firm and disappeared from mainstream economic theory. 'The entrepreneur is shorthand for uncertainty, imperfect information, and the unknown. He operates in the shadowy world of intuition, ignorance, and disequilibrium' (Barreto 1989: 137).

In many settings, small businesses emerge as underground, 'black market' or otherwise informal economic activities outside the recognized and fully legal status of other firms. Bureaucratic barriers to formal and legal operation, including an array of permits and registrations, reduce the profit potential of a firm, and reinforce the decision by hard-working, competitive, and innovative people to remain apart from the formal economy (Bromley 1993; de Soto 1989). Most informal entrepreneurs are in activities that are easy to enter with relatively low costs and few entry barriers, such as food and drink vending and transportation (Fass 1995; Telscher 1994). In other settings, such as Kenya, informal activity is common in manufacturing (Juma, Torori and Kirima 1993). Informal enterprises are found in advanced economies as well, and are important to the individuals involved. Urban areas are common locations of an informal sector (Blair and Endres 1994; Knights 1996; Morales, Balkin and Persky 1995). However, rural areas in Europe and the USA also have informal economic activity (Gringeri 1994b; Stratigaki 1994; Williams and Windebank 1994).

At a second level, entrepreneurship refers to new firm formation, or the addition of new enterprises to the economy. The Coffey and Polèse (1984, 1985) model of local development argues that accumulated local knowledge, values, experiences and resources are significant influences on the formation of new firms. Entrepreneurship is the basis of local economic development because entrepreneurs respond to market opportunities left unfilled by large enterprises. Consequently, small business formation is an accepted component of national as well as local development (Blakely 1994; Luke *et al.* 1988; OECD 1989a).

A portion of small firm formation is a result of flexibility strategies by large firms to disintegrate their activities and to outsource production and services to outside vendors, some of which may be small firms. Such strategies have the effect of increasing the apparent importance of small firms in an economy and of downplaying the dominance of large firms (Harrison 1994; Semlinger 1993). One result has been lower levels of wages and fringe benefits common to small firms (Brown, Hamilton and Medoff 1990; Loveman and Sengenberger 1991; Zipp 1991). Nevertheless, a widespread trend toward small-scale production has occurred in many Western countries, and it has become standard thinking to place responsibility for job creation, at national as well as regional and local levels, on entrepreneurship (Fischer and Nijkamp 1988; Loveman and Sengenberger 1991).

At the highest level, entrepreneurship entails innovation (rather than imitation) and a system-wide coordination of complex production (Casson 1990). This view stems from Schumpeter's (1934: 66) suggestion that entrepreneurial innovation is the essence of capitalism and its process of 'creative destruction', embodied in new products, new production processes, new sources of raw materials and new forms of organization. Some technological developments, such as microelectronics, have presented numerous opportunities for innovation and for new firms and new industries to appear. Earlier, similar cases of technological change include the development of airplanes, motor vehicles and communications, all of which enabled entrepreneurs to create new enterprises to serve markets which at first were not well defined. The innovativeness of entrepreneurship lies in the ability of some new businesses to 'read' the market better than others do – not merely in the short term as arbitrageurs, but in the long term as fillers of innovative niches (Suarez-Villa 1989). Technological change and discontinuities make possible the economic opportunities that innovative and visionary entrepreneurs are able to exploit (Kyläheiko and Miettinen 1995).

Technological and entrepreneurial opportunities vary by sector, being highest in sectors where small-firm innovation is high relative to that of large firms (Acs and Audretsch 1989). Low entry barriers in other sectors attract imitative, rather than innovative, entrepreneurs. Much of what is called entrepreneurship falls into this category of imitation, especially in rural areas (Popovich and Buss 1989; Turok and Richardson 1991; Westhead 1990). New entrants have a greater likelihood of being innovative, and of surviving, in a market where economies of scale and routinized behaviours do not prevail. In this routinized regime, the metaphor of a revolving door captures the low probability of success. In an industry characterized by an entrepreneurial regime, new ideas and divergent behaviours can succeed, and small and new firms are better able to displace incumbents, as in the metaphor of a forest (Audretsch 1995).

The entrepreneurial event

The 'entrepreneurial event' (Shapero 1984) takes shape through the interaction of two sets of factors: personal and environmental. Sexton and Bowman (1985) believe that entrepreneurs exhibit more than merely the characteristics of capable executives, such as energy and a desire for risk-taking and autonomy. Roberts and Wainer (1971) found no motivational traits such as these, suggesting that home environment and educational level are most critical, especially whether one's father was an entrepreneur: 'entrepreneurial fathers are more likely to produce entrepreneurial sons' (Roberts and Wainer 1971: 108; de Wit and van Winden 1989; O'Farrell and Pickles 1989). Roberts (1991a) summarizes the personal factors as: family background; goal orientation, personality and motivation; 'growing up' (education and ageing); and work experience.

Personality is among the factors used by investors to evaluate new venture proposals (MacMillan, Siegel and Subba Narasimha 1985). A particularly intriguing finding related to personality is that of Cooper, Woo and Dunkelberg (1988), who found that most entrepreneurs are very optimistic about their ventures, including those who are poorly prepared to run a business. This may be related to the difference between entrepreneurial intentions and follow-through (Katz 1990). International research on personality finds that entrepreneurs exhibit greater individualism than do non-entrepreneurs (McGrath and MacMillan 1992; McGrath, MacMillan and Scheinberg 1992).

The pre-founding factors in successful new firms have been found to include more experience together, larger teams, more functional experience, and experience in rapid-growth firms in the same industry; a high-growth market, the presence of venture capitalists on the board, and equity being shared by the founders were not significant (Roure and Maidique 1986). Ray (1993) reviews a large number of entrepreneurial attributes, experiences and skills (personal and external) that affect entrepreneurship. In fact, the 'event' of founding a firm only begins a series of planned and unplanned events in the career or life of the entrepreneur (Harvey and Evans 1995).

Small versus large firms

In comparison with large enterprises, small firms have a number of advantages and disadvantages (Table 5.1). The advantages centre on an ability to react quickly to market opportunities, a willingness (if not an ability) to accept risk, and the power to communicate efficiently and informally. Flexibility to vary output volume in response to demand is a significant advantage of small firms in many industries (Feigenbaum and Karnani 1991). In short, small firms exhibit a flexibility and non-routineness of behaviour that is virtually impossible for large organizations to attain. On the other hand, small firms lack the resources, especially financial resources, available to large firms for expansion and diversification. By virtue of their size, large corporations can develop a wide, even global, network of information sources on markets, suppliers and technology. Large firms are also able to gain scale economies not possible in small enterprises (Rothwell 1989, 1994a; Rothwell and Zegveld 1982). Although models of growth and internationalization apply to few small firms, some grow to be major exporters and world-class enterprises and important

Table 5.1 Advantages and disadvantages of small firms relative to large firms.

Advantages	Disadvantages
Ability to react quickly to changing market demands	Inability to support formal R&D effort or to employ technical experts
Rapid decision-making owing to lack of bureaucracy	Lack of time and resources to identify and use external information sources
Willingness to accept risk	Difficulty acquiring capital for growth
Efficient, informal internal communication	Formal management skills often absent
'Fast learning' capability	Inability to attain economies of scale
Ability to dominate narrow market niches	Little bargaining power with suppliers and distributors
Flexibility to vary output volume	

Source: after Feigenbaum and Karnani (1991) and Rothwell and Dodgson (1991, 1994).

contributors to national economic competitiveness (Christensen 1991; Steed 1982).

The principal disadvantage faced by small firms is a shortage of resources, including capital, information and skills. Because they are small and often bound to local markets, few small firms are well informed about markets and suppliers elsewhere. 'The relative ability to meet the key criteria required by the market is the principal constraint on small firm growth, and the lack of skills and inadequate training at managerial, supervisory, and shopfloor levels is the proximate cause of the production problems' (O'Farrell and Hitchens 1989: 400).

Rothwell and Dodgson (1994: 310) maintain that 'innovatory advantage is unequivocally associated with neither large nor small firms.' The advantages of large firms are mainly material advantages related to their greater financial and technological resources. The greater resources in large firms permit a high level of external awareness and monitoring of external information sources on a global scale. Small firms are generally unable to match this degree of effort and, therefore, they are at a disadvantage *vis-à-vis* their larger competitors (Ransley and Rogers 1994). Small firms' advantages lie in their behavioural advantages, such as entrepreneurial dynamism, internal flexibility, and responsiveness to changing circumstances. Fast learning ability and widespread informal communication networks are also among the advantages of small firms (Julien 1995a; Rothwell 1989; Rothwell and Dodgson 1994).

These factors are not present in all small firms, however. Kelley and Brooks (1992) distinguish between firms with primarily active and social external linkages and those with passive and asocial linkages (Amendola and Bruno 1990; Estimé, Drilhon and Julien 1993). Passive/asocial firms rely on written media and routine machining products. Active/social firms, by contrast, utilize written sources as well as personal contacts with sales representatives, participation in trade shows, contact with vendors, and close relationships with special-order customers for sharing of technical information. The presence of active/social linkages more than triples the probability of adoption of production automation among the smallest firms (fewer than 20 employees) and more than doubles it among firms with 20–99 employees. Thus, if small firms seek out and obtain technical information from external resources, they are much more likely to compensate for their size limitation in the adoption of new technology (Julien 1995a; Rothwell 1992). The most likely firms to be active in seeking out external information are those with in-house R&D activity (Tsipouri 1991).

Modernization and keeping pace with technological change are generally difficult for small firms. The reasons for the slow pace of modernization among small firms include a lack of awareness of newer, proven manufacturing methods, and lack of opportunity to gain hands-on experience with new technologies (Kelley and Brooks 1989; Shapira 1990a,b). Julien (1995a) would seem to disagree with this pessimistic assessment, having found that small firms use varied sources for technological information. In this way, small firms can create value – social, cultural, political, economic, technical and technological – in a variety of ways through their network links, thus creating distinctive capabilities (Hardill, Fletcher and Montagné-Villette 1995).

Regional variation in entrepreneurship

Regional variation in entrepreneurship has been a recurring finding in research on new firm formation. Studies in the USA during the 1970s documented the fact that the pattern of firm births was the most significant determinant of regional fortunes (Birch 1987; Jusenius and Ledebur 1977). More recent, anecdotal accounts continue to reaffirm this fact (Ricklefs 1989). The 'regional factor' in entrepreneurship and innovation is among the most important issues for theory and policy (Thomas 1987), yet the specification and understanding of regional entrepreneurial environments remains a complex empirical issue (Dennis and Phillips 1990; Moyes and Westhead 1990). The issue of environments that influence business failure, on the other hand, has rarely been addressed (Westhead and Birley 1994).

Much of the conventional wisdom concerning regional economic environments grew out of research on branch plants and the spatial division of labour – characterized by the concentration of professional and technical workers in headquarters, offices, and research and development (R&D) facilities in some locations and of branch production plants in others (Chapter 4). This affects regional development potential in several ways. First, the skill level and education of branch plant employees tend to be relatively low, and their awareness of entrepreneurs, of business practices, and of sources of capital, information and other resources is also low. Second, these workers have little contact with innovative processes, the R&D being done elsewhere, so little innovation takes place. Third, communication in branch plants, moreover, tends to be vertical – with the firm's headquarters – rather than horizontal with other firms in the locality. As a result, places where branch establishments rather than local enterprises predominate tend to have low levels of entrepreneurship and of innovation (Cooper 1985; Sweeney 1987; Watts 1981). The spatial division of labour largely determines the possible paths for local development (Thompson and Thompson 1993).

The stifling effects of a branch plant economy on entrepreneurship are great, and cannot easily be overcome by policies to locate government research facilities in backward regions in the hope of generating spin-offs (Cooke 1985b). Supporting this is the work of Cooper (1973, 1985, 1986), who has persistently made the case that firms, not universities or government facilities, tend to be the incubator organizations of entrepreneurs. This is true even in high-technology sectors, in both Germany and the USA (Cooper 1985; Feeser and Willard 1988; Kulicke and Krupp 1987). However, if a corporate facility employs large numbers of technical workers, as in a 'technical branch plant' (Glasmeier 1988a), then entrepreneurship may occur. The type of incubator organization depends to some extent on the degree of novelty of the technology and of the market identified by the technology-based firm (Autio 1995). In a region with a vibrant university research environment, personal contacts between entrepreneurs and university researchers can provide a wealth of short-term specific collaborative projects and, over time, create an environment for entrepreneurship. This does not occur quickly, as the experiences of the Research Triangle in North Carolina in the USA and of Cambridge in the UK have shown. In both areas, many years elapsed before either could be termed a centre of entrepreneurial spin-offs.

Beyond the type of work found in various locations, what distinguishes successful entrepreneurial regions and locales from places where entrepreneurs are few and far between? Not all places can be generative of new businesses for two additional reasons. The first is the sectoral bias: new firms are not equally likely to arise in all industries. Entrepreneurs respond to the relative barriers to entry across sectors, and to the general level of opportunities presented in various technologies and markets (Nelson 1986b). Low entry barriers in retailing and services help to explain the abundance of firms in those sectors. However, the degree of innovativeness is particularly low in such sectors, where imitative and franchised establishments are standard, suggesting little long-term growth potential (Storey and Strange 1992; Wicker and King 1988). Sectoral selection, as well as product, market and export focus, are among the factors contributing to the successful growth of small firms in a study of eight European countries (Adams and Hall 1993). Generally, however, once an industry choice is made, industry dynamics and competitors are aspects of the environment largely beyond the control of individual entrepreneurs (Cooper and Gimeno Gascón 1992). The regional industrial mix thus influences the degree to which new firms are likely to be founded in any particular place. The sectoral variation is reinforced through the propensity for new firms to form in sectors already found in the area (Malecki 1990).

A second dimension of entrepreneurship that has geographical variation is the social mix of a place, especially regarding educational levels. This affects entrepreneurship because more educated people are more likely to have information that can be used in an enterprise. In technically based sectors, high levels of education and occupation in technical and professional occupations are far more common than in other industries. For a regional economy, 'a region's ability to attract and retain educated people is as important as its ability to attract firms' (Buss and Vaughan 1987: 445). The mix of jobs, and of people who fill them, is an outcome of corporate location decisions and industrial specialization. Social and occupational influences appear to be quite significant in reinforcing existing spatial contrasts, as research in the UK has repeatedly shown (Barkham 1992; Keeble 1990; Mason 1985). It is in such places that a sufficient number of potential entrepreneurs are present, as well as the other environmental factors that encourage entrepreneurship (Moyes and Westhead 1990). A further aspect of this reinforcement is that regions with small firms tend to generate new firms at higher rates (Garofoli 1992; Gerlach and Wagner 1994; Reynolds, Storey and Westhead 1994; Westhead and Moyes 1992). This statistical finding is an outcome of social characteristics and network links.

The elements of local/regional economic structure – labour, industrial and social characteristics – go part-way in explaining geographical variations in innovation and entrepreneurship. Some have generalized this ideal structure as *diversity*, representing an openness to new ideas – and, therefore, to new firms (Andersson 1985; Shapero 1984). Johannisson's (1993) analysis of 'local contexts' in Sweden found social diversity to be significant in explaining new firm formation, indicated by people employed in artistic professions and foreign citizens. The significance of economic diversity emerges as significant in empirical analysis (Friedman 1995; Reynolds, Miller and Maki 1993), but these variations remain difficult to explain with static variables and concepts (Donckels 1989; Reynolds 1994).

The role of the local environment in entrepreneurship and entrepreneurial success

Oddly absent from much of the standard research on entrepreneurship is the critical nature of the entrepreneur's local context, in which he/she operates on a daily basis. The fact that most contacts tend to be local – Sweeney (1987) postulates a radius of one-half hour travel time – is either unquestioned or ignored. Other research stresses the local area as essential and critical to the small firm's functioning and growth (Camagni 1991b, 1995a; Illeris 1992; Julien 1995b). Cooper (1985) has stressed *why* the local entrepreneurial environment is so important. Few entrepreneurs change location, and they start businesses related to what they did before. Thus, an individual accumulates *local knowledge* about his or her industry (such as customers and suppliers) in that particular region. Regions with high levels of entrepreneurship will tend to spawn further entrepreneurs. Because of both experience and information networks, the process of entrepreneurship 'is essentially geographically constrained' (Birley 1985: 112).

Thus, the 'environment for entrepreneurship' in a region or locale is a critical part of the entrepreneurial process itself, as well as of the chances for local economic development. This meaning of 'environment' goes well beyond that typical in organization theory (e.g. Tsai, MacMillan and Low 1991), but reflects the broader view of the social, economic, political, infrastructure and market dimensions of environmental munificence (Specht 1993). Roberts (1991a) presents the success of the Boston area within the context of attempts to understand and to create similar 'technopolis' growth elsewhere. He emphasizes aspects of local culture and attitude as critical to building a local environment that fosters entrepreneurship.

A critical, but somewhat complicating factor, is urban size. Technical and other information is more readily available in larger urban areas, as are larger pools of skilled workers, capital sources and amenities (Coffey 1990). Firms in urban regions are able to rely more upon the external R&D environment, whereas firms in rural or peripheral areas must depend to a greater extent on their own internal efforts (Bar-El and Felsenstein 1990; Lorenzoni and Ornati 1988). Indeed, large firms also try to maximize their information contacts by locating in large urban areas populated by innovative small firms (Pottier 1988). Likewise, small firms in high-technology sectors cluster where R&D and skilled labour are present, and where the local infrastructure and the 'environment for entrepreneurship' are found. Many, if not always all, of the factors cited as supporting an innovative environment and the 'environment for entrepreneurship' are generally those common to most, if not all, large urban regions (Bruno and Tyebjee 1982; Malecki and Nijkamp 1988; Moyes and Westhead 1990; Senker 1985).

A number of lists of critical factors have been proposed to characterize the entrepreneurial environment. Bruno and Tyebjee (1982) listed 12 factors which comprise such an environment:

1. venture capital availability;
2. presence of experienced entrepreneurs;
3. technically skilled labour force;
4. accessibility of suppliers;
5. accessibility of customers or new markets;
6. favourable governmental policies;
7. proximity of universities;
8. availability of land or facilities;
9. accessibility to transportation;
10. receptive population;
11. availability of supporting services; and
12. attractive living conditions.

While these will not be found in all large urban regions, most of the factors are what would be considered among the advantages of large urban economies.

Birch (1987: 140–65), describing job creation in the USA, lists five factors – essentially a subset of the factors identified by Bruno and Tyebjee – that enhance entrepreneurship, which are high-quality in some places and not in others: (1) educational resources, particularly higher education; (2) quality of labour; (3) quality of government; (4) telecommunications; and (5) quality of life. Birch's designation of educational resources is actually much more specific than it appears; he insists that research-based universities, at the leading edge of change, such as MIT and Oxford, are the necessary ingredient. His 'quality of labour' factor is perhaps less specific, referring not to scientists and engineers, but to skilled and adaptable workers, for whom training and adjustments are less costly, regardless of the wage level. Education at the primary and secondary levels (through age 18) is often a key dimension of this adaptable workforce. Bartik (1989) found that market demand in a state and education level (proportion of high-school graduates) were among the most significant influences on small business starts. Quality of government refers to the balance between public services and their cost – 'tax-efficiency' in Birch's terms. Although it conflicts with current minimalist views toward government, Bartik's study of small business start-ups in the USA suggests that 'some public services may encourage small business starts' (Bartik 1989: 1015).

Variables related to the lists above are useful in that they point to the fact that previous entrepreneurs (perhaps measured as number or density of, or employment in, small firms) may serve as role models or examples for new entrepreneurs. Empirical research 'has tended to focus upon variables which are relatively easy to measure' (Cooper and Gimeno Gascón 1992: 317). More detailed research into network processes, for example, tends to find that the relationships between location and new firm formation and success are much more complex, requiring qualitative methodologies with their own potential pitfalls (Borch and Arthur 1995).

Bearse (1981) proposed eight dynamic, if less easily measured, factors which contribute to the community climate for entrepreneurial activity: (1) the level of change/instability in the local economy resulting in gaps, imperfections and market failures; (2) the level of uncertainty created by unexpected events and inter-firm competitive rivalry; (3) the degree of fluidity in the social structure and the degree of institutional resources to provide linkage of entrepreneurs with needed resources, especially information; (4) the level of diversification in the industrial, occupational and social structure of the community; (5) the level of resources available such as information, capital, specialized services, space and number of attractive non-entrepreneurial opportunities; (6) the presence of a critical mass of entrepreneurs and institutions involved in the gestation of new hard and soft technologies and an active, supportive venture capital community; (7) the cultural traditions of the relevant groups effecting the atmosphere for entrepreneurship; and (8) government policy, including taxes, regulation and economic management. Bearse's factors are more dynamic, suggesting social, institutional and cultural processes at work, beyond the simple aggregation of resources.

Shapero (1984), in attempting to account for 'the entrepreneurial event', similarly focused on dynamic urban characteristics in an environment for entrepreneurship. Previously (Shapero et al. 1969), he had suggested that a technical labour pool and a good financial community were the most important local characteristics. As Shapero developed these ideas, he suggested a dynamic process in which local investment propensities and an industrial base of small businesses together lead to a local economic environment that exhibits a readiness to lend or invest in new and different companies. Four qualities distinguish dynamic cities from all the rest: (1) resilience, (2) creativity, (3) initiative taking, and (4) diversity (Shapero 1984). It is evident that he was identifying the same, difficult-to-create characteristics of a 'creative region' specified by Andersson (1985).

The relationship between entrepreneurship and technological innovation is thought to be particularly important to high technology. The conclusions of the report of the US Office of Technology Assessment (OTA 1984: 7) suggest the links which are present: 'The most important conditions for "home grown" [high-technology development] are the technological infrastructure and entrepreneurial network that encourage the creation of indigenous high-technology firms and support their survival.' The elements of this regional technological infrastructure cited include the following:

1. applied research and product development activities at nearby universities, federal laboratories and existing firms;
2. informal communication networks that provide access to information and technology transfer from those R&D activities;

3. a scientific and technical labour force, including skilled craftsmen, newly trained engineers and experienced professionals (who also represent a pool of potential entrepreneurs);
4. a network of experts and advisors (often augmented by university faculties) specializing in hardware, software, business development and venture capital;
5. a network of job shoppers and other suppliers of specialized components, subassemblies and accessories; and
6. proximity to complementary and competitive enterprises, as well as distributors and customers (Office of Technology Assessment 1984: 7).

Abetti (1992) has added the need for an executive champion and community support.

Dubini (1989) studied six cities in Italy to determine their environments for entrepreneurship, distinguishing between *munificent environments* and *sparse environments* (Table 5.2). Put briefly, access to other entrepreneurs, to consultants and to sources of information is far more readily available in munificent settings than in sparse environments (Dubini 1989). The various conditions discussed thus far can also be classified into regional infrastructure, spatial concentration and quality of life (Thomas 1987). Regional infrastructure includes capital, the economic–industrial base of technologically adept firms whose inputs and skills are transferable to new firms, a quality labour supply, technology networks, transportation and communication systems, and a sociopolitical structure of supporting institutions. Spatial concentration refers to the availability of input–output linkages and the synergy present in agglomerations. Quality of life is a less precise element that appears to operate through labour market choices of professional and technical workers. These comprise the elusive 'regional factor', which has proved difficult to define exactly (Thomas 1987). However, skills and entrepreneurship, unlike scientific knowledge, are more local phenomena, not readily transferable from place to place, and they depend

Table 5.2   Characteristcs of 'munificent' and 'sparse' environments for entrepreneurs.

Characteristics of munificent environments
Strong presence of family businesses and role models
A diversified economy in terms of size of companies and industries represented
A rich infrastructure and the availability of skilled resources
A solid financial community
Presence of government incentives to start a new business

Characteristics of sparse environments
Lack of an entrepreneurial culture and values, networks, special organizations or activities aimed at new companies
Lack of a tradition of entrepreneurship and family businesses in the area
Absence of innovative industries
Weak infrastructures, capital markets, few effective government incentives to start a new business

Source: after Dubini (1989).

on local economic structure as well as on the attitudes and culture of the region (Kristensen 1994; Spilling 1991). Recent empirical work has shown that the specification of entrepreneurial environments is complex, not reducing to a few simple variables manipulable by policy (Moyes and Westhead 1990).

More recent attempts to understand what comprises an entrepreneurial environment focus on regional and local institutions. Researchers of European regions have focused on such concepts as *institutional thickness* (Amin and Thrift 1993, 1994) and *social capital* (Putnam 1993) to characterize the mesh of public and private sector interactions that foster economic and social activity. The presence or absence of these institutions, in turn, may well be behind what entrepreneurship researchers had been struggling to depict in characterizing the environment for entrepreneurship. Building on this thinking, Flora and Flora (1993) have proposed elements of an 'entrepreneurial social infrastructure' which represents the presence of social capital in a region. Three dimensions are critical: symbolic diversity (signifying openness), resource mobilization (indicating equality and a willingness to invest collectively and locally), and quality of networks (which should be diverse, horizontally and vertically).

Entrepreneurial vitality, once initiated, becomes self-reinforcing and sustaining. A 'nutrient-rich' environment for entrepreneurship provides capital and (more importantly) information to prospective entrepreneurs (Krueger 1995). An 'information-rich environment' (Andersson 1985) and 'technical effervescence' (Miller and Coté 1987) are the principal characteristics of 'creative regions' or 'innovation know-how concentrations' (Perrin 1988a). The 'environmental texture' of such places – suppliers and infrastructures particular to the production requirements of a group of firms – is especially supportive for new firms (Lorenzoni and Ornati 1988). Similarly, a lead firm may play the role of coordinator within a constellation of firms, providing a link to sources of information, innovation and technology (Shaw 1991; Shepherd 1991).

The technological capability of a region is concerned both with the stock of knowledge in a region and with factors which encourage or inhibit the formation and development of technological capability within a region or nation. Capturing the same aspects of regional vitality, Sweeney (1987) has called this *innovation potential*. The factors which make up the innovation potential of a region are a complex mix of the following:

1. the sectoral and technological mix of the industry in a region;
2. the strength of the engineering sector;
3. the autonomy of decision-making in the industries and infrastructure of a region; or the dominance of branch plant employment;
4. the dominance of employment in one or two sectors, especially where these are of low use of best technical practice or are declining industries;
5. the strength or weakness of the quaternary information sector; and
6. the technological orientation of the educational system or lack of it (Sweeney 1987: 131).

A number of recent contributions have addressed the entrepreneurial environment. Smilor and Feeser (1991) have proposed a 'chaos model' for entrepreneurship, which takes into account the uncertainty and unpredictabil-

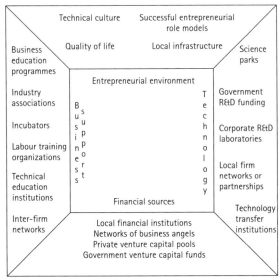

Figure 5.1 The complex institutional infrastructure of an entrepreneurial environment. Source: based on Smilor and Feeser (1991), Smilor, Gibson and Kozmetsky (1989) and Scott (1996b).

ity of the entrepreneurial process (Figure 5.1). Firms that are able to assemble four critical sets of factors – mainly from within the local environment – are most likely to succeed. These factors are talent, technology, capital and know-how, all of which must be present and acting in synergy for entrepreneurial success. Van de Ven (1993) develops the idea of an 'infrastructure for entrepreneurship', which encompasses environment in an industrial, technological and economic sense and as a set of public resource endowments that are largely local in nature. The endowments include some of the usual factors, such as basic scientific knowledge, financing mechanisms and a pool of competent labour. His infrastructure, however, is discussed 'at the macro-industry level' and, thus, neglects local or regional dynamics in the processes surrounding these factors. Cooke and Morgan (1993), on the other hand, take the opposite position, and suggest that we can characterize the five key elements of a 'networked region':

1. a thick layering of public and private industrial support institutions;
2. high-grade labour-market intelligence and associated vocational training;
3. rapid diffusion of technology transfer;
4. a high degree of inter-firm networking; and, above all,
5. receptive firms well disposed towards innovation.

It is clear from the research reviewed thus far that the ideal entrepreneurial environment is a setting where firms take advantage of agglomeration and proximity to utilize nearby sources of information, skilled labour, technology and capital. Standing in sharp contrast, the predominant empirical finding about small firms in peripheral areas is their relatively low level of innovativeness (Malecki and Nijkamp 1988; Sweeney 1987). In these places, more typical of rural areas, networks have not developed, innovation and technology are not native to the local culture and economy, and firms struggle to remain competitive. These include the Buffalo region (MacPherson 1991, 1992), north Florida (Malecki and Veldhoen 1993), Norway (Vatne 1995), Portugal (Fontes and Coombs 1995), and the UK (White *et al.* 1988). In general, firms in circumstances that fail to provide a diverse array of local information and other resources turn to external sources (Birley and Westhead 1990). In effect, they substitute non-local resources for the sparse set of (or non-existent) local resources (Brown and Butler 1993; Vaessen and Keeble 1995). In the absence of either local or external networks, small firms can become dependent on a single large customer (Young, Francis and Young 1994a). Such locales are among Dubini's (1989) sparse regions, where little networking or innovative entrepreneurship takes place (Davidsson 1995). In places where a supportive local milieu has not formed, fewer firms will be formed, and those that do form must be outward-looking, seek knowledge from outside the local region, and develop geographically widespread markets.

Part of the rural disadvantage derives from the obvious handicap, relative to urban areas, in access to suppliers and customers, information and labour (Keeble and Tyler 1995; Vaessen and Wever 1993). However, to merely distinguish urban from rural firms does not necessarily capture differences in survival rates of new firms (Stearns *et al.* 1995). When *networks* of firms are studied, it is found that the networks of the successful firms are non-local rather than (or more than they are) local. At times, these non-local networks rely on contacts made by an owner-manager in previous employment (Malecki and Veldhoen 1993; Vaessen and Wever 1993). Fewer nearby competitors, customers, suppliers and similar firms make such networking difficult (Pettit and Thompstone 1990), but they do not determine network behaviour. The level of innovativeness and competitiveness of firms in rural areas – or any area – depends not only on the degree to which firms are tied to *local* networks of suppliers but also to *external* markets (Camagni and Capello 1990; Marchesnay and Julien 1990; Turok and Richardson 1991).

Perhaps the ultimate sparse region is the one-company town. Hjalager (1989) detailed a number of stifling types of local economies, such as those dependent on mining and shipbuilding. Such places have few examples of entrepreneurship and little or no opportunity for entrepreneurial experience. Davidsson (1995) found that such towns in Sweden had the low birth rates of firms in both manufacturing and non-manufacturing industries. In rural locales, the motivation for starting a firm is more often personal than inspired by the local environment (Westhead 1995). The craft orientation of home-based businesses in the rural USA may be thought of as utilizing local resources, but they are very different resources from those found in urban areas (Carter, van Auken and Harms 1992).

The importance of networks

Empirical research consistently finds that learning about technologies occurs primarily via informal channels of communication – through interpersonal contacts (Allen, Hyman and Pinckney 1983; Håkansson 1987, 1989; MacPherson 1991; Meyers and Wilemon 1989; Pavia 1991; Thorngren 1970). This research has been fundamental to several threads of investigation which have identified the central role of geographical proximity, which facilitates face-to-face contact, and the critical nature of networks to firms' activities and competitiveness (Sabel 1989). Birley (1985) found that the main source of information about raw materials, supplies, equipment, space, employees and orders was the informal contacts of family, friends and colleagues, and Bryson, Wood and Keeble (1993) show that small service firms also rely heavily on informal personal networks.

Business networks begin as a set of interpersonal contacts (Aldrich and Zimmer 1986; Dubini and Aldrich 1991). They provide social support and self-confidence, a supply of resources needed by the business, and strategic capacity to learn and organize for new activities (Johannisson 1995). Research in Scandinavia on industrial networks shows the intricate nature of personal and firm networks (Håkansson 1989; Illeris and Jakobsen 1990). We may distinguish between a firm's *trade network*, involving linkages between producers and users of traded goods and services, and its *knowledge network*, where the focus is on the flow of information and exchange of knowledge irrespective of its connection to the flow of goods (Gelsing 1992).

Small firms have extensive contact networks, comprising mainly business contacts associated with commercial organizations, such as customers, consultants and other managers (Falemo 1989). However, because of the lack of resources associated with small size, and the inexperience of many new entrepreneurs, small firms are often disadvantaged in their ability to access and direct the flow of information into their organizations. Unable to maintain an R&D effort and 'a systematic technology watch', small firms use networks as 'antennae' and 'filters' of information (Estimé, Drilhon and Julien 1993: 56).

Small firms can benefit from gatekeepers to technology and information sources (Macdonald and Williams 1994). Small firms are more likely to rely on 'community entrepreneurs', who have the development of the local community and its firms as a goal (Cromie, Birley and Callaghan 1993; Johannisson 1990b; Johannisson and Nilsson 1989). These 'key individuals' use their extensive personal contacts to communicate across sectors (Cromie, Birley and Callaghan 1993; Stöhr 1990). They provide the necessary sorting and evaluating that others – and especially small-firm owners and managers – are less able to do (Rosenfeld 1992).

Technical services, in addition to information, are important to small firms. These services are likely to be available locally in suitable metropolitan environments, such as Toronto (MacPherson 1988b). In nearby Buffalo, New York, MacPherson found a much sparser environment for technical services. As discussed previously, the most competitive firms in this setting seek out technical services and information from outside the local area (MacPherson 1991, 1992). The firms which provide such technical services are often small but specialized in particular technologies and industrial settings. In a rare study of the other side of this relationship, Jones-Evans and Kirby (1995) describe in detail the relationships of 91 such consultancies and their customers in the Northeast of

England. The range of technical areas served by these consulting firms is large: 40 technological services, ranging from software applications, software development, and mechanical engineering (each offered by over 30 of the firms) to ceramic/glass technologies and aerospace engineering (each offered by only a single firm). Most of the firms had begun via work with their previous employer or contacts gained while working for their previous employer.

Interpersonal contacts provide the sorted and evaluated information firms need to apply to the context of the business, not simply raw information (Rosenfeld 1992). Information and social networks clearly are critical to business success – to firm formation as well as to survival and growth (Aldrich and Zimmer 1986; Birley 1985; Christensen *et al.* 1990; Johannisson 1990b; Sweeney 1987). At one level, information and contact with other firms are simply examples of the use of *external resources* critical to the success of flexible firms (Jarillo 1989). Initial contacts from social networks evolve into business-focused networks, and then into strategic networks, which allow firms to innovate and to thrive by their links to other organizations (Butler and Hansen 1991; Courlet and Pecqueur 1991; Dubini and Aldrich 1991; Falemo 1989). Indeed, the necessary progression from technological matters to markets (Roberts 1990) coincides with a shift in linkages from local to national and international markets (Autio 1994; Christensen 1991; Christensen and Lindmark 1993). Similarly, the personal networks of owner-managers vary according to the strategy chosen for the firm (Ostgaard and Birley 1994).

For small firms and new firms, contacts are especially likely to be local. Small firms are especially likely to become involved in informal arrangements with other small firms, as a natural consequence of familiarity between individuals (Julien 1995a). Indeed, it is the frequent face-to-face interaction that means most to small firms (Sweeney 1987). For young biotechnology firms, not only were most technology sources local (within 60 miles), but the most important technology sources were local (Delaney 1993).

Information networks are perhaps the most critical element in the development of a technical culture and technological capability (Sweeney 1987). As the preceding chapters have shown, producer–user interactions are especially fruitful, because they provide the necessary feedback to producers, and they allow users to successfully implement new technologies (Lundvall 1988; Meyers and Athaide 1991; von Hippel 1988). Proximity facilitates interaction between producers of machinery and new users in order to implement and assimilate the new technology embodied in complex machinery effectively (Gertler 1993, 1995). The inter-firm interaction he describes is found in numerous other settings, including technology districts (Storper 1992).

Personal contacts can be critical, as acquaintances become suppliers, customers or key agents of new technology. By far, the most common means of small technical consulting firms for identifying new clients is through personal contacts, rather than print advertising or cold calling (Jones-Evans and Kirby 1995). This occurs as contacts accumulated over long periods of time provide the 'lists' of information needed for an entrepreneur or organization to succeed. The lack of a network or networking can severely impair the competitiveness of firms, although there is disagreement about the role of gender (Aldrich, Reese and Dubini 1989; Cromie and Birley 1992). A prominent example is the need to have a global market – to export. For small firms, which typically lack resources and management capacity, networks developed for other purposes are the principal means of entering export markets (Christensen 1991). Perhaps because of their sparser networks, the very smallest firms (micro-enterprises) find it most difficult to export (Donckels and Hoebeke 1992). However, for firms in less-than-munificent environments, early orientation toward international markets is a means of success (MacPherson 1995).

The increased intensity of technological change means that, in contrast to the linear innovation model (which underlies product cycle theory), there is no longer a clear-cut differentiation and no clear sequence from research to development and to production and distribution. Firms are able to enhance their technological capabilities by learning from customers and from suppliers, by interacting with other firms, by searching for new technologies, and by taking advantage of spillovers from other industries (Lundvall 1988). Taken together, these sources provide the *know-why, know-how, know-who, know-when* and *know-what* necessary for entrepreneurial success (Johannisson 1991; Lipparini and Sobrero 1994). Firms that make greater use of external resources tend to grow faster than other firms (Jarillo 1989). Network arrangements – vertical and horizontal – provide a firm with its 'distinctive capabilities' that help it to create and add value (Hardill, Fletcher and Montagné-Villette 1995).

But a major difference remains between regions where networks are found and those where they are not: strong *local* government and nongovernmental institutions and the provision of a wide range of social services (Perrow 1992). The ideal institutional environment perhaps is found in industrial districts and innovative milieux. Much of our understanding of firms' networks comes from research into industrial districts, prominent in Denmark, Italy and elsewhere in Europe (Chapter 4). The identification of industrial districts in the Third Italy prompted a groundswell of interest in inter-firm relationships that go beyond material flows and include in fact unmeasurable connections related to family ties, cultural closeness and specialized knowledge.

Industrial districts and innovative milieus embody the interaction and dense network of linkages that comprise a local production system, usually around a single or highly related industries. Because of these linkages, the territory itself functions as a *collective entrepreneur*, with firms, as well as inter-firm associations, worker organizations, financial institutions and governmental agencies playing supporting roles (Best 1990). Not all spatial agglomerations of small firms in the same or related sectors necessarily comprise an industrial district or local industrial system. A functioning network of firms is an essential phenomenon for local development. Where such interaction is not present, small firm competitiveness as well as local development suffer (Bull, Pitt and Szarka 1991; Hardill, Fletcher and Montagné-Villette 1995).

A *milieu* embodies the necessary interactions in a particular way. Such a locality is comprised of a set of relations which unite a local production system, a set of actors and their representations, and an industrial culture (Camagni 1995a:

195). In an innovative milieu, two sets of effects operate simultaneously: proximity effects, such as reductions in costs because of quicker circulation of information, face-to-face contacts, and lower costs of collecting information; and socialization effects, related to collective learning, cooperation, and socialization of risks. These two processes are collective rather than explicitly cooperative and thus spread beyond any single bilateral inter-firm linkage. Dynamic processes of interaction and of learning characterize such milieus (Becattini 1991; Maillat 1995).

At the same time, a key characteristic of a milieu is its links to other networks in other regions. These global, or trans-territorial (or extra-territorial), networks provide access to a diversity of ideas and bases for comparison with local practices that are not internally generated (Amin and Thrift 1993; Camagni 1995a; Conti 1993; Maillat 1995; Tödtling 1995). In places where a milieu is not present, such as the UK, these external links in fact may weaken existing local ties (Bull, Pitt and Szarka 1991; Curran and Blackburn 1994; Hardill, Fletcher and Montagné-Villette 1995).

Several research findings point to the unique character of Silicon Valley as an environment for entrepreneurship. For example, Ohe *et al.* (1991), comparing entrepreneurs there and in Japan, found that significantly Japanese entrepreneurs had parents who were entrepreneurs. That is, the Silicon Valley environment provides a large number of entrepreneurial role models and examples outside the family context. This environment comprises a unique 'ecosystem' within which firms form and re-form through continual entrepreneurship. Networks of interpersonal relationships support both entrepreneurship and links between enterprises, large and small alike (Bahrami and Evans 1995). According to Perrow (1992), only Silicon Valley in the USA displays the characteristics found in European industrial districts (Cooke and Morgan 1993; Saxenian 1994). Others are sceptical about the entrepreneurial success in Silicon Valley. Harrison (1994) believes that it is less an entrepreneurial industrial district than a hub of global networks of large corporations. Hobday (1994a) suggests that the region's networks function solely for innovation but lack the complementary assets (such as marketing and distribution) needed for later stages of the product life-cycle.

Venture capital networks in the entrepreneurial environment

Venture capital appears in virtually every inventory of 'necessary' conditions for entrepreneurship. Venture capital holds a prominent place in the ideal environment within which new firms emerge. Initially a US phenomenon, venture capital investment has grown tremendously, especially in Europe (Bygrave and Timmons 1992). Since the 1970s, it has been clear that venture capital investments tend to concentrate in some firms, in some industries and in some technologies more than in others (Bean, Schiffel and Mogee 1975). To a large extent, whether a firm attracts venture capital is a result of whether it has planned strategically in four functional areas scrutinized by investors: marketing, the management team, technology and finances (Roberts 1991b). Depending on the firm's age, it should be oriented toward engineering to some extent in the early years, and progressively more toward product and marketing issues later on (Roberts 1990). In addition to these areas of project viability, Sargent and Young (1991) add past and current contexts and individual characteristics as determinants of the search for, and acquisition of, capital.

The appearance of the first, 'almost random' company formations in an area are the most difficult to account for, and may not always stimulate any follow-up of further entrepreneurship. However, there are substantial differences between localities in the degree to which local banks are willing to lend for new, untried ventures (Shapero *et al.* 1969; Hoffman 1972). If an area attains a level of sustained entrepreneurship, it is typically associated with the growth of a financial, legal and service community to support it. Reid and Jacobsen (1988) confirm the central role banks play in business information networks in Scotland.

The source of initial capital and of the 'almost random' appearance of the first entrepreneurs is perhaps related simply to the availability of start-up financing. Financing for start-up firms can come from many sources, including personal funds, family and friends, local bankers, and outside lenders, but it tends to come from informal (non-institutional) sources that operate almost entirely via a network of personal and *local* contacts (Bean, Schiffel and Mogee 1975; Wetzel 1983, 1986). In addition to their role in financing new firms, previous entrepreneurs share a variety of routine business knowledge that is necessary to operate a business, such as regulations, taxes, accounting, suppliers, customers, and marketing and distribution. Prior to 1958, individuals were the primary source of small business financing (Y. Henderson 1989). The prospective entrepreneur is likely to go to a lender with a reputation for backing new, unproven entrepreneurs and their start-up firms. Local bankers are unlikely to lend in such a risky situation – unless they have previously had successful experiences with firms of this type. In any event, banks are unlikely to make more than a small portion of their loans to new ventures, preferring to lend to firms which have already survived the start-up phase. However, once an area becomes known for its spin-off activity – in part a result of the willingness of local lenders – venture capital firms from other places may set up shop in order to profit from entrepreneurs in the area. This is certainly the experience of the Silicon Valley area, the premier technology-oriented venture capital complex (Florida and Kenney 1988a; Hambrecht 1984).

A critical theme from the point of view of entrepreneurial environments is the *local* nature of venture capital. The informal networks on which successful venture capital investments depend are the reason for the constrained geography (Doherty 1980). Since the greatest value added by venture capitalists comes from frequent contact and communication, and this contact decreases with distance, proximity is a critical issue in new firm formation and financing (Sapienza 1992). From another perspective, finance has long been local, based largely on the detailed knowledge and expertise of lenders and investors, which determines low- from high-risk investments (Hoffman 1972). This poses a problem for firms in rural areas, where information on venture capital is rare among bankers;

only those with extensive and widespread information networks are able to be gatekeepers for small rural firms (Pulver and Hustedde 1988).

Informal venture capital, from informal (non-institutional) sources, operates almost entirely via a network of personal, local contacts (Wetzel 1986). Although there is little solid data on informal investors, there are a large number of them in the USA, providing small investments for new ventures (Haar, Starr and MacMillan 1988). Collectively, they may provide more venture capital than that made available through the formal market, invest earlier in the life of new firms, and have longer 'exit horizons' than professional venture capital firms (Freear and Wetzel 1990; Wetzel 1987). In addition to their role as 'angels' in financing new firms, previous entrepreneurs act as role models and share a variety of routine business knowledge that is necessary to operate a business, such as regulations, taxes, accounting, suppliers, customers and distribution. Some of the advice from previous entrepreneurs – hardly available from any other source – concerns mistakes made and lessons learned (Egge and Simer 1988). However, 'angels' tend to consult each other significantly less than formal venture capitalists, who seek out information from colleagues in other firms (Fiet 1995).

Informal venture capital, provided by 'angels', is perhaps the greatest source of early-stage financing of new firms in several countries (Harrison and Mason 1992). Freear and Wetzel (1990) found that over 40 per cent of high-tech entrepreneurs in New England received funding from private individuals. This took place at earlier stages than when venture capital became prominent. Informal investment is widespread, to judge from studies of Canada, Sweden, the USA and the UK, but it is difficult to estimate its size precisely, because of the very nature of informal investing (Gaston 1989; Harrison and Mason 1991; Landström 1993; Wetzel 1986). The informal nature of informal venture capital also contributes to its inefficiency. Too little information about informal venture capital is available to those firms who seek it out; on the other hand, even angels have difficulty identifying firms which need finance (Mason and Harrison 1995). Freear, Sohl and Wetzel (1995) suggest that the difficulty of finding private investors may be offset by lower-cost financing. In addition, many 'angels' provide valuable advice, skills and networking that only a mentor can (or is willing to) provide (Mason and Harrison 1996).

The few studies to address the geographical dimensions of informal venture capital have found that most investments are concentrated within a 50 mile (80 km) radius from sources of early-stage investment (Aram 1989; Mason and Harrison 1995; Wetzel 1983). Formal venture capital investments also are typically made within the same radius, as Gibbs (1991) found in Manchester, England. McNaughton and Green (1989) also found Canadian venture capital investments to be very local in nature. The willingness of investors to enlarge the geographic scope of their investments increases with the size and stage of the investment (Gupta and Sapienza 1992). That is, earlier-stage investments, such as those by 'angels', are the most local in nature (Short and Riding 1989).

Venture capital firms link with others in order to gain information based on their distinctive competence, knowledge and information, not really for sharing risk (Bygrave 1987). The top 61 firms (of 464 studied) participated in 75 per cent of investments made from 1966 to 1982. Reinforcing the importance of geographical concerns, most of these links for information include California-based venture capital firms (Bygrave 1988; Bygrave and Timmons 1992). Venture capitalists serve as gatekeepers within the information networks that bind the venture capital industry together (Florida and Smith 1990). The California base of high-tech venture capital, centred on Silicon Valley, is clearly a major contributor to the success of that region (Hambrecht 1984; Levine 1983).

At times, this body of specialized information is seen to be necessary within the ventures that are financed, through direct involvement in management and strategic decision-making (Flynn 1991, 1995). The management role has always complemented that of financing, interestingly blending from outside newly financed ventures the role of capitalist and entrepreneur (Gorman and Sahlman 1989), mentor or consultant (Landström 1990, 1992). The level of involvement in firms varies, depending on perceived need on the part of venture capitalists (MacMillan, Kulow and Khoylian 1989). Robinson (1987) sees distinct 'strategic groups' evolving within the venture capital industry, distinguished on the basis of their sources of funds, the degree of management assistance they provide, and the size and stage of the investments.

Florida and Kenney, who have contributed most to our knowledge of the geography of venture capital in the United States, have documented that there are three types of venture capital complexes: technology-oriented (such as the San Francisco Bay area), finance-oriented (such as New York), and hybrid complexes (such as Minneapolis–St Paul) (Florida and Kenney 1988b). Geographical clustering near financial centres, such as Chicago and New York, is prominent, as is the critical nature of information flows within and between centres (Florida and Kenney 1988a). Consequently, business formation tends to generate the development of complexes in specific places, which reinforces flows of information for subsequent investments (Florida and Kenney 1988a). Early-stage investments are most local, as are small late-stage investments, whereas large late-stage investments tend to operate within national, even international, markets (Elango et al. 1995). These complexes, most of which are centres of high-technology industry, take considerable time to develop (Florida and Smith 1990). Cumulative venture capital investments by state from 1969 to 1983 are significantly associated with university R&D and with the presence of R&D facilities of large firms, neither of which can be accumulated in an area quickly (Malecki 1990). The local nature of venture capital, and the networks in place, suggest that capital is mobile in the USA only within the network structure of the industry (Florida and Smith 1993). A greater degree of concentration is evident in the UK, focused on Greater London and the Southeast, where 60 per cent of all investments were made during the period 1984 to 1987 (Martin 1989).

State incentives appear to play no role in attracting venture capital, according to a survey of 905 venture capital firms (Ball and Marquardt 1991). Moreover, state venture capital funds became a popular weapon in state arsenals for economic development in the 1980s. Eisinger (1991) identified 30 state venture capital programmes in 23 states in 1990. Despite optimism about such funds during the 1980s, several programmes suffered from a lack of political support in the early 1990s, in part because of the divergent goals of venture capitalists (high returns) and politicians (job creation) (Eisinger 1993).

It is clear that capital availability is an institutional and social issue. Networks of people who communicate with each other about business opportunities, procedures and management are key elements of a positive regional entrepreneurial climate. These networks are important sources of key information. Capital is actually less critical to small business success than more simple, but less easily supplied, inputs, such as information, business knowledge and management expertise. Put differently, information networks are fundamental to learning about how, and where, to raise capital.

The *entrepreneurial climate* of a place is, like its technical culture, probably the greatest influence on entrepreneurship as an ongoing part of a region's everyday life. The climate 'includes the whole system of *values* in a society': attitudes toward science, toward economic and social change, toward private enterprise, and toward risk (Piatier 1984: 160). This climate as it affects entrepreneurs relies almost entirely on a well-connected network of investors, especially informal investors, previous entrepreneurs, and an aura of non-routine, innovative activity (Miller and Coté 1987; Shapero 1984; Sweeney 1987). In the absence of these – in a sparse environment – new firm formation rates are low (Ashcroft, Love and Malloy 1991). The attitudes of investors, especially venture capitalists, are influential. It is evident from research by Murray and Lott (1995) that UK venture capitalists impose stricter criteria on technology-based enterprises than on non-technology investments. This would seem to confirm suspicions of an anti-technology culture in the UK.

The attitudes in the community as a whole are as important as solving the capital and other managerial problems of small businesses. Schell (1983) attributes much of the geographical variation in entrepreneurial activity to the developmental climate promoted by the power elite in a community. Schell suggests that one can group favourable government policy, receptive population and attractive living conditions into a broader *sociopolitical* variable, which has a major influence on entrepreneurial activity in a community or urban area (see also Freedman 1983). This has obvious parallels with the influence of a 'technical culture' on entrepreneurship (Sweeney 1991). Abetti (1992) includes community support among his key elements for an infrastructure for technological entrepreneurship. Bull and Winter's (1991) discussion of community differences focuses on community culture, attitudes and local opportunities as critical variables in the decision to start a new business.

The influence of entrepreneurial 'role models' and attitudes in a region is especially important in its entrepreneurial climate. Danson (1995: 86) says that 'knowing an entrepreneur is an important "rocket" in the process of converting potential into actual business creators.' Prior entrepreneurs provide not only information and experience, but also capital which they are often willing to invest in the new firms of others. However, how to generate the first 'almost random' entrepreneur remains poorly understood, and randomness has been cited in the formation of the Seattle software complex (Haug 1991).

Policies for entrepreneurial environments

Many are sceptical about the chances for government policies to create creative regions (Roberts 1991a: 31).

> In munificent environments, government funding is likely to scarcely enhance the diffusion of entrepreneurship, as the environment itself is stimulating and offers a wide choice of opportunities. . . In sparse environments, the presence of money directly available to entrepreneurs – which is the typical form blanket policies assume – is likely to result in a fruitless effort, since there is no infrastructure to support entrepreneurial effort (Dubini 1989: 25).

Sweeney (1991) also notes that policies are rarely able to compensate for the absence of a 'technical culture' and the networks of firms found in such places. This culture fosters a 'self-reproductive effect' that may be more important than investment in other aspects of a region (Eto and Fujita 1989). Some places have local technological capability; others do not (Asheim 1994). The local cultural factors related to higher levels of entrepreneurship – capital, a supportive entrepreneurial climate, information networks and innovation – are difficult to 'create' in a place. Despite this, local communities, regions and nations continue to attempt to create 'thicker' institutions, better-linked networks and a 'technical culture' (Sweeney 1995).

It can be argued that new firm formation is not the most appropriate policy goal. The ability for businesses to grow and prosper may be more important: 'The much more significant long term challenge to government is to generate competitiveness and increasing globalization among its small manufacturing enterprises' (Storey 1993: 78). A policy framework to address the problem of competitiveness needs to deal with information about best-practice technology and products. Although many small firms are innovative, they typically undertake no R&D and are heavily reliant on their external networks for information. Innovativeness appears to require *both* internal and external technical know-how (Julien 1995a; MacPherson 1992; Rothwell and Dodgson 1991).

There are three ways in which policy can address the needs of small firms (Chabbal 1995). The first is to channel government resources in the right direction, to provide technology and demand forecasts, fiscal incentives, performance-oriented standards, and regulatory measures that stimulate rather than impede innovation. The second route is to subsidize intermediaries, who then provide services and information for small firms. The third set of policy measures directly funds ways to increase the absorption capacity of firms by sharing risk, employing technical staff and hiring consultants. These traditional sorts of programmes all involve in some way the transfer of information to small firms (Estimé, Drilhon and Julien 1993: 69–76). The weakness of most programmes is that they fail to fall within the existing information network of small firms and, therefore, they often are not tailored to the needs of those firms (Estimé, Drilhon and Julien 1993: 78).

Networks

Network creation is a growing policy prescription for regions where networks have failed to emerge (Malecki and Tödtling 1995). Throughout the USA, for example, initially inspired by Piore and Sabel (1984), several networks have emerged to create the sorts of inter-firm cooperation found (especially) in Italy and Denmark (Bosworth and Rosenfeld 1993; Hatch 1988; Rosenfeld 1989–90). The common element of networks currently in place in the USA is that each has a coordinator or broker identified – an individual who serves as the hub and gatekeeper for the network of firms. The network coordinator, who may be a private consultant, an employee of a local economic development agency, or a firm owner or manager, appears to be particularly critical to network success or failure (Bosworth and Rosenfeld 1993; Lipnack and Stamps 1993).

What is perhaps most striking is the diversity in the origins, histories, local contexts and purposes of the networks. Each network is distinct in the way in which it is 'embedded' in its local (and state) politics, society, culture and economy. In order to be successful, a network, like any institution, must be embedded within the local socioeconomic structures in which it is located (Granovetter 1985). Describing the workings of several networks in Pennsylvania, Sabel (1992: 234) concludes that what matters most is 'the social system by which packages of programmes were defined and administered, rather than the precise definition of any single programme or service.' This means programmes (such as industrial extension as well as networks) wherein actors define their own needs, based on cooperation between the actors in particular industries in particular locales.

In some locations, where policies have attempted to encourage networking activity between firms (especially small and medium-size firms), it is difficult to blend the proper mix of private- and public-sector involvement and interaction (Pyke 1992). Indeed, public–private interaction is seen as key to creating supportive local institutions (Bennett and McCoshan 1993; Flynn 1993). Gibb (1993: 11) asserts that it is important to place the entrepreneurial institutional network in a non-governmental organization, such as a flexible manufacturing network. In this way, the firms are able to see themselves as part of a network, rather than as individuals or as isolated firms. Networks make the entire process of information-gathering easier and less costly for firms, an issue most significant to the newest and smallest firms. Services for networks, which can enhance the likelihood of inter-firm collaboration, are one of the most important categories of public policies in this regard (Mazzonis 1989; Pyke 1994).

Mønsted (1993) distinguishes between three types of networks, each serving a different function for the entrepreneur:

1. networks for service and assistance, i.e. to solve a specific problem;
2. networks for information and structuring, especially for knowledge about whom to contact for a specific purpose; and
3. networks for entrepreneurship and product development.

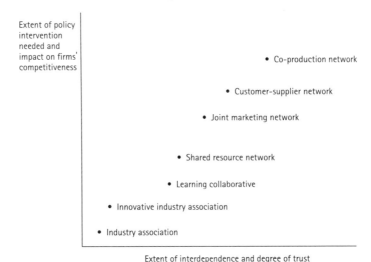

Figure 5.2   Levels of inter-firm collaboration. Source: modified from Bosworth (1995).

These networks are not needed in a simply sequential manner, as are models of network evolution suggested by Johannisson (1993) and Håkansson (1992). In each type of network, local trust-based relationships are critical (Mønsted 1993). In the absence of trust, communication is less frequent and full cooperation does not occur, as Lyons and Bailey (1993) found among small subcontractors in UK engineering. A progression of types of subcontracting and collaboration, incorporating degrees of coordination and of task complexity, as well as of inter-firm trust, has been proposed (Blenker and Christensen 1995; Bosworth 1995; Larson 1991). However, Furukawa, Teramoto and Kanda (1990) suggest that it is difficult even for Japanese firms to reach the last stage, that of joint production (Figure 5.2).

Networks allow small (and large) firms to expand the scope of their information-gathering activities with somewhat less effort and expense than either if all activities were internal to the firm's hierarchy, or if all interaction had to take place via market transactions (Thorelli 1986). Especially for marketing, firms use their networks as an alternative to vertical integration and diversification. However, a network involves more: technology transfer, information exchange, accounting and finance, as well as public and private interpersonal relations (Thorelli 1986: 46). By meeting these diverse requirements, networks provide 'thick' information not available from a single source (Imai and Baba 1991; Lorenzoni and Baden-Fuller 1995).

The social bonds formed with any network agent, like any other business contact, 'are often person-specific rather than firm-specific' (Thorelli 1986: 47). 'Personal contacts are the medium in which communication takes place' between organizations (Hamfelt and Lindberg 1987: 177). Trust is a key element in the social bonds formed (Casson 1990; Granovetter 1985; Sako 1992). Most indicative of trust are unstandardized or non-routine information exchange between firms (Gelsing 1992). Relationships between firms, like those between people (which they typically are), take time to develop. The first stage is a 'trial period' during which the prospective partners evaluate each other and learn about their respective businesses, their performance capabilities and, ultimately, their credibility. The second stage, partnership, involves more extensive and frequent communications, often in the context of changes, and reciprocated investments of time, people and equipment. Larsson (1993) suggests that the progression from arm's length, market exchanges to trust-based cooperation takes about two years, with increasing benefits over time in information and technical innovation. Once developed, trust-based relationships help firms to avoid legal and contractual problems (Jones-Evans and Kirby 1995). Moreover, 'the continuous interaction between firms offers, on the one hand, the opportunity for innovation and, on the other, the existence of a known and predictable environment in which it can be realised' (Easton 1992: 23–4). Benefits such as these are difficult to identify empirically, a fact that may inhibit the widespread creation of small-firm networks (Reese and Aldrich 1995; Rosenfeld 1996).

Although information networks are most dense in urban agglomerations, information can be enhanced in less munificent environments as well. In particular, the provision of intermediaries or liaisons who are technically proficient can greatly raise the level of knowledge in a region (Britton 1989; Kelley and Brooks 1989; Sweeney 1987: 239–62). This is the explicit goal of the technology, training and marketing networks established in one Austrian region (Grabher 1989). In most countries, the information needs of small firms have been neglected in favour of R&D and technology transfer policies which should (in theory) provide technological information that will eventually trickle down to all firms (Britton 1989). Indeed, Goodman, Meany and Pate (1992), in their review of government policies to create new ventures, cite few examples of policies that support new firms outside the area of R&D and high technology. High-technology firms in a sparse environment may well provide far fewer benefits than low-tech firms (Chandra and MacPherson 1994).

Small businesses vary enormously in terms of the types of activities in which they are engaged, their outlook in relation to the external world, and the resources at their disposal for networking. The latter will also depend in part on the character of the external environment itself, including the local environment (Blackburn, Curran and Jarvis 1993: 117). Bryson, Wood and Keeble (1993) show how resourceful consulting and market research firms can be, utilizing their network contacts both to identify clients and to cooperate with complementary firms on larger or more complex tasks. Rural and peripheral areas tend to be sparse environments for businesses. In general, 'small rural manufacturers face the problem of obtaining objective information, absorbing it, and evaluating the knowledge gained' (Rosenfeld 1992: 130). This lack of awareness is not ignorance, but an inability to obtain 'sorted' and evaluated information on which they can make modernization decisions (Rosenfeld 1992).

In the USA, neither the federal nor state governments have had any long-term policy interest in small firms or in their competitiveness. NASA's long-standing technology transfer programme had no emphasis on small firms. The list of programmes is longest in high technology, several of which support new technology-based businesses (Clarke 1990; Eisinger 1988). Clarke (1990: 164–5) describes the industrial extension services of several states, demonstrating that they are often geared toward improvement of business and management skills as well as upgrading technology. Industrial extension is a type of network, centred on a university or other technological source, with a mechanism for linking with firms, especially small firms. Simons' (1993) review confirms this characterization. Rees and Lewington (1990) include industrial extension services among a list of nine types of state technology development programmes, and as one of three in the area of technology upgrading.

Shapira (1990a) describes some common elements of success among state industrial extension programmes in the USA. Assistance should be tailored to the needs of individual firms and include information about upgrading beyond new machinery to include other technology needs, such as workforce training, quality control, shop-floor organization, management systems and inventory control. Efforts should extend beyond assisting individual manufacturers to form links with other firms and to include effective linkages with customers, training providers, research institutions, and state and local governments. A variety of 'new public infrastructures' for modernization of small firms have evolved in the USA since the late 1980s. These are intended to stimulate firms to pursue a technology and business upgrade path, but through pragmatic, rather than complex, technology. Integrated programmes, which make a range of services available in a way that is seamless to firms, are most effective (Shapira, Roessner and Barke 1995). Integrating programmes managed by different government agencies can be problematic (Cromie and Birley 1994), and to mesh with private-sector services may add an additional layer of complexity.

Extension services are especially valuable to small firms that lack the resources to conduct effective searches concerning new technology (Vaughan and Pollard 1986). Rosenfeld (1992: 143) provides evidence that few small rural firms are being served by existing state and federal technology extension services, a finding similar to that of Smallbone, North and Leigh (1993) concerning small UK firms, most of which drew on little or no external assistance of any kind. Other research outside the USA provides a number of hints about how industrial extension programmes could or should work. Autio (1994) shows convincingly that the technology transfer sources that firms use change significantly over the firm's life-cycle. This is the point made by Fosler (1990), who suggests that state programmes for business assistance should be appropriate to the variable life-cycle needs of the firm. One of the models of technology transfer to small firms comes from Japan, where a network of Kohsetsushi centres provides a locally specific base of knowledge and technology delivered to small firms by engineers (Cooke and Morgan 1994a; Shapira 1992).

Technical culture

Technical knowledge typically is considered especially important to high-technology firms, thus prompting the conclusion that proximity to universities should be an especially important locational factor. However, universities have not been prominent sources of spin-offs, despite the examples of MIT, Stanford and Cambridge so frequently cited (Cooper 1973; Garnsey and Cannon-Brookes 1993; Roberts 1991a). Smilor, Gibson and Dietrich (1990) add the University of Texas-Austin to this list. Instead, universities provide a necessary resource (i.e. technical knowledge) to an area, as well as a pool of well-educated people who are potential entrepreneurs. Thus, they contribute – often significantly – to the stock of knowledge which constitutes the technical culture of an area (Sweeney 1991). Even technical and scientific personnel generally lack entrepreneurial attitudes and management competence (Albert, Fournier and Marion 1991). An initial entrepreneurial role model can initiate a succession of spin-offs (Lawton Smith 1991).

Research universities are seen as the key institutions around which high-tech growth and spin-offs occur. Most accounts rely on three principal examples from the USA: Silicon Valley, Route 128 and Research Triangle (Rogers 1986). Rogers recognizes the importance of agglomeration: 'money goes to the academic haves, not the have-nots' (Rogers 1986: 177). The presence of an outstanding research university in a locale does not necessarily lead to the development of a high-technology centre. Evidence on this point is provided by such excellent universities as Berkeley, Cal Tech, Columbia, Chicago, Harvard and Johns Hopkins, none of which has played an incubator role (Feldman 1994; Roberts 1991a: 36). The presence of a local research university is simply not enough to offset shortcomings in entrepreneurial climate or venture capital.

The creation of science parks or research parks is an example of a policy that attempts (at least implicitly) to create complexes of inter-firm interaction through proximity and agglomeration or clustering. This policy is based on the observation of early examples in the USA, including Stanford Research Park as an element in the development of Silicon Valley. As Massey, Quintas and Wield (1992) and Johannisson et al. (1994) have shown, interaction does not necessarily take place despite geographical proximity; 'something else' is needed. This 'something else' is often described simply as 'synergy' (Castells and Hall 1994; Stöhr 1986), but presumably demands the presence of social structures of sociability and trust, and an industrial structure that demands interaction between firms (e.g. highly linked industries making flexibly changing products) (Amin 1994c). This synergy typically fails to develop in 'created' rather than spontaneous research parks (Goldstein and Luger 1990; Quintas, Wield and Massey 1992). Industry–academic links are typically not common, and may focus on large firms (as sources of faculty research funding) rather than on small firms (Bishop 1988; Howells 1986).

Policies based on the experience of successful places, then, are not likely to work in situations where networks and active firms are not part of the local culture. Some places are simply more open to new ideas; regions where imports are state-of-the-art and diverse are more likely to be innovative themselves (Malecki 1995). Regional culture is created and transmitted to future generations through education, training and acquired experience. Where institutions are present and well-functioning for passing on a technical culture, it is likely to endure. Essential industrial skills, however, frequently are not taught in schools. Tacit knowledge and skill are passed down by experience and through technical education. Successful regions will be those where workforce skills are associated with all stages of production – not simply research or high tech (Maillat and Vasserot 1988).

Policy in the context of small, flexible firms means that governments facilitate their existence by providing business/techno-institutional support and by playing an important role in terms of a social policy, cushioning the effects of flexibility (Helmsing 1993). The experience of industrial districts suggests that policies aimed at maintaining a high level of information flow and of worker skills can be very effective. (Mønsted (1991) discusses the worker skills needed in flexible small firms.) The benefit of policy has been illustrated by examples of the critical role of training and technology upgrading in Italy (Bigarelli and Crestanello 1994; Brusco 1992), Québec (Julien 1992), and Denmark (P. H. Kristensen 1992). The interaction between public and private sector in a locale appears to be of considerable importance in creating and maintaining contacts and generally in creating a supportive milieu for new firms (Donckels 1989; Miller and Coté 1987). This interaction must be localized, but may be similar in both new and restructuring regions, such as Austin, Texas (Smilor, Gibson and Kozmetsky 1989) and Pittsburgh (Ahlbrandt 1988).

Institutions

The emphasis of current local policy is to structure *local* growth 'from below' with minimal central direction (Albrechts *et al.* 1989; Malecki and Tödtling 1995; Stöhr 1990). Some of this takes place through the actions of 'community entrepreneurs' or gatekeepers. Lorenz (1992) refers to these as 'political entrepreneurs', policy-makers who encourage inter-firm communication and cooperation. Boyett and Finlay (1995) suggest that in a depressed region, where few entrepreneurs are present, a school headmaster can serve as a community entrepreneur, since his network of contacts outside the community may be greater than that of anyone else.

The presence of local 'community entrepreneurs', people with local knowledge and an ability to tap into local resources, contributes greatly to *institutional thickness* (Amin and Thrift 1993, 1994). The effort to foster networks is but one type of a large and diverse array of efforts to enhance or build local capacity (Bennett and McCoshan 1993; Stöhr 1990). Flynn (1993) has found that local 'sponsorship' of entrepreneurship significantly contributed to the rich infrastructure found in some American cities. Perhaps even more fundamentally, community leaders can provide moral leadership, signifying approval of entrepreneurial activity (Krueger 1995).

The 'Technopolis wheel' of Smilor, Gibson and Kozmetsky (1989) suggests that there is a critical need for many local actors and institutions in a region to interact. When this happens, they suggest, a place can successfully be seen as having an entrepreneurial culture. They identify seven 'segments' within the Austin, Texas, area: the university, large technology firms, small technology spin-off firms, the federal, state and local governments, and support groups, similar to Figure 5.1. 'Influencers' or leaders in one segment form networks by linking to other segments, acting as gatekeepers between organizational segments. Flynn's (1993) 'sponsors' and Abetti's (1992) executive champions perform a similar role. These institutions provide know-how to a region in the form of educational programmes, technical support programmes, capable local advisors and professional support organizations, as well as incubator organizations and business networks (Smilor and Feeser 1991). Scott (1996b) proposes a similar institutional infrastructure specific to the furniture sector. Institutions must be industry-specific as well as place-specific to be effective. Acting together, the various 'local players' can stimulate an innovative milieu by creating synergies of interaction and learning within an area, and linking with the technological and market environments outside the region (Maillat 1995).

These 'influencers' play the role of 'key individuals' common in Europe, serving a role in local or regional policy (Donckels and Courtmans 1990; Stöhr 1990). It takes more than a single individual, of course, to affect a region's development. The sorts of institutions that are able to evolve depend on the historical, cultural, social and political setting, as well as on the economic conditions present in the region. What is sometimes most difficult in backward regions is to form network links with the global market and its information networks, yet this is perhaps the most important task of all (Malecki and Tödtling 1995). Finally, Gibb (1993) and Johannisson (1993) suggest that the institutions that assist small businesses should be entrepreneurial in nature themselves, in order to respond flexibly to the differentiated needs of local environments.

Entrepreneurs and entrepreneurial environments in developing countries

The situation of entrepreneurs outside the advanced or developed economies is somewhat different. For example, the existence of small firms can be interpreted simply as a lack of employment opportunities in other firms or sectors (Tambunan 1994). In any event, Tambunan (1992a) has documented that very small cottage and household firms of 1–4 employees (a size category sometimes called microenterprises) – not larger firms – employ most people in Indonesia. These are found in a number of sectors, especially handicrafts, textile and leather, and wood, providing valuable linkages to agriculture for raw materials (Tambunan 1992b). However, for entrepreneurs in developing countries, as everywhere, 'profits are not everything, they are the only thing' (Fass 1995). Information sources are identical to those in advanced economies. Most start-up capital comes from family and friends, as opposed to the formal financial sector, but the latter is used to a greater extent by 'progressive' entrepreneurs in Pakistan (Altaf 1988).

A wide variety of informal and ingenious sources of capital is also used, often linked to supply, machinery or customers (Harper 1984). The Pakistani sports equipment industry, for example, involves the experience of players as users and testers of improvements in equipment (Altaf 1988: 210). As in advanced economies, networks of business people are central to success. In general, the more innovative and successful entrepreneurs in both China and India are those who utilize network links and synthesize knowledge thus obtained (Ramachandran and Ramnarayan 1993; Zhao and Aram 1995). Indeed, a tendency to rely on family and other 'conservative' non-business social networks can be a constraint on a firm's success (Özcan 1995). This is also true in developed countries (Donckels and Lambrecht 1995). However, differences in attitudes of entrepreneurs from those of non-entrepreneurs – a common theme of American research – prove not to be significant when examined in Asia (Korea, Thailand and China) (Stimpson *et al.* 1990).

Diversification and growth are difficult but possible. Small firms in Ghana in four sectors (carpentry, vehicle repair, blacksmithing and engineering) had conquered new markets and, to varying degrees, had succeeded in diversifying and upgrading production. However, in response to competition from new entrants, many firms tend to focus on price competition rather than product innovation (Dawson 1992). The choice is not easy for a small firm in a tough environment. Small firms that innovate are distinct from firms that compete mainly on price (Nadvi 1994). Price competition is a severe challenge for small firms in Peru; they are able to introduce new products but are less able to make process changes (Arellano, d'Amboise and Gasse 1991).

The success of industrial districts in Europe has led some to suggest similarities to the situation in developing countries:

1. a reliance on small and medium-size enterprises rather than large corporations;
2. strategic targeting of market niches appropriate for the small, flexible production runs in which small firms specialize;
3. a predominance of rural locations; and
4. a preponderance of informal interaction between the firms, rather than formal information sources (Späth 1992).

The experience of industrial districts emphasizes a high degree of collaborative activity, based on the fact that 'strength lies in clustering and cooperative competition which open up efficiency and flexibility gains which individual producers can rarely attain' (Schmitz and Musyck 1994: 890). Cooperative competition will be seen in inter-firm competition based on innovation rather than lowering wages, a socio-cultural identity which facilitates trust relations between firms and between employers and skilled workers, active self-help organizations, and active regional and municipal government which strengthens the innovative capacity of local industry (Schmitz and Musyck 1994).

However, Amin (1994c) suggests that the shift from an informal economy to an industrial district such as those in the Third Italy is not an 'automatic' process. The informality may or may not include the four features that are the essence of a district: inter-firm dependence, structures of sociability, a local industrial atmosphere and institutional thickness. Note that geographical agglomeration is not included among the key features. Rather, it is personal and business interaction, based on trust and the ability to develop institutional thickness. Informal economies are characterized by 'institutional thinness' and the absence of efficiently run, pro-active public institutions working together to provide support for the wider economic collectivity (Amin 1994c). The policy infrastructure at the local or regional level for assisting small firms is often completely absent.

Small firms in any context are dependent on their external environment (Julien 1995b; Uribe-Echevarría 1993), although the types of and reasons for dependence are rarely considered carefully (for an exception, see Oinas 1995). In the context of small firms in Latin America, Uribe-Echevarría (1993: 181) says:

> To be efficient, small-scale businesses need to externalize many functions which are internally performed in large firms. . . The smaller the firm the more likely that inter-firm collaboration would make a substantial contribution to efficiency. . . A high degree of openness is a major characteristic of the small-scale firm and this means that internal firm efficiency and competitiveness is dependent on an efficient inter-firm division of labour and on the efficiency of processes performed outside and beyond the control of the firm. For these reasons, small-scale firms must be conceived as a complex production system composed of various collaborating firms rather than exclusive independent firms.

The issue, then, 'is not *whether* small enterprises have growth and employment potential but *under what conditions*' (Schmitz 1982: 445, *emphasis in original*). Growth is extremely difficult in Africa, where innovation and technology have relied heavily on government research organizations, universities and foreign firms, and where links to commercialized innovation are neither strong nor necessarily the most appropriate. Juma, Torori and Kirima (1993) believe that the promotion of new technologies is best done by *technical entrepreneurs*, who combine business entrepreneurial activities with technical competence. However, they also see that African countries by and large lack an economic environment that is 'conducive to technological development. Such an environment must have adequate intellectual property protection, venture capital, supportive tax and tariff measures and basic research infrastructure' (Juma, Torori and Kirima 1993: 47).

Some technical entrepreneurs work in the informal sector, using labour-intensive (appropriate) technology which is geared to meet the needs of low-income groups. Technologists in these enterprises display creativity, innovativeness, flexibility and improvisation, working with limited tools, materials and other resources. 'In contrast to the usual picture of them making second-hand things in a second-rate way', these artisans add an innovative element even to products that are imitations, such as quality improvements and ways to lower the cost of production (Juma, Torori and Kirima 1993: 97).

In contrast to the Kenyan study by Juma, Torori and Kirima (1993), which portrays a generally positive picture of African small-scale artisans, Ndegwa (1994) paints a picture of failure. Few African businessmen succeed, in part because they have few interactions with Asian businesses, they over-diversify within an enterprise rather than specialize, and they choose sectors in which competition is too high. Himbara (1994) notes the tendency to hire members of the extended family rather than qualified personnel. Takyi-Asiedu (1993) suggests that entrepreneurial activity in Africa is 'retarded' by a tradition of low prestige of the private sector and because of poor education, which promotes poor record-keeping among business owners, leading to little understanding of the actual financial status of the business.

Government policy for the informal sector needs to create and maintain a supportive business environment and to improve access to customers. Although industrial estates have long been relegated to the edge of town or to undesirable locations, policies regarding them can improve the lot of entrepreneurs by allowing more convenient locations for interaction between firms as well as for access to customers (Fall 1989).

Dawson (1992) studied small firms in Kumasi, Ghana, where the city pursued a policy of clustering its small firms in a large industrial shanty town, Suame, north of the city. The clustering of firms in Suame has had two effects. First, inter-firm cooperation permitted small firms with limited staff or equipment to share work with, or to subcontract to, neighbouring enterprises. Second, engineering firms, which had maintained the highest level of competitiveness among the sectors studied, evolved into the manufacture and maintenance of equipment utilized by other small firms. These capital goods have improved the technological capability of user firms by allowing them to compete in niche markets that otherwise would not have been accessible (Dawson 1992). This suggests that the benefits of clustering are the same as those identified in Italy and elsewhere: greater innovativeness and success in market niches as a result of inter-firm interaction (Lundvall 1988). Schmitz (1992) is less optimistic about clustering *per se* to bring about other necessary effects, such as division of labour and specialization among manufacturers, the presence of specialized suppliers and producer services, and the emergence of agents and consortia to facilitate exporting and marketing.

The Kumasi firms studied by Dawson (1992) have begun to exhibit the necessary characteristics of collective efficiency. This is in marked contrast to his observations in Tanzania, where inter-firm linkages were much weaker (Dawson 1993). Within the industrial community of the Odawna Industrial Estate in Accra, Ghana's capital, certain positive characteristics are evident (McDade and Malecki 1997). Cooperation is commonplace, mainly because no firm has all the tools or equipment necessary for the range of work attempted; thus, borrowing from others is the norm. In addition, lending of employees to others is also common. This is evidence of cooperative competition as found in Europe. It is not clear whether *specialization* has taken place, along the lines of European industrial districts, outside of auto repair operations. However, it is clear that the use of 'community assets' in business creation and operation is common in Africa as well as in other settings (Diomande 1990).

African entrepreneurs have begun to export, filling large orders from Pier One, a large US retailer of imported products, although not without difficulties in quality, packaging, and obtaining an adequate supply of inputs (Biggs *et al.* 1994). Entrepreneurs everywhere face the same issues. They want to export, but lack knowledge of markets and export channels and procedures, whether in

Denmark or Mali (Christensen 1991; Kessous and Lessard 1993; Uribe-Echevarría 1993). Indeed, exports are a central element of successful firms. Through them, they learn the nuances of market demand and learn the importance of product quality and of new products. This is true among rattan furniture manufacturers in Indonesia (Davies 1991). Tambunan (1992c) stresses that, in order to export, small firms need the expertise and contacts provided by middlemen.

Conclusion

Recent research has demonstrated the intimate relation between entrepreneurship and regional and local development. Innovativeness developed within local inter-firm networks both supports existing firms and presents opportunities for entrepreneurs to start new businesses in order to serve newly identified markets. The importance of networks, of market information and of innovative niches sparks innovation in both high-technology industries and in traditional sectors (Ahlbrandt 1988; Doeringer, Terkla and Topakian 1987). In essence, networks of firms complement and, at times, substitute for a firm's own technological capability. More importantly, networks allow a firm to gain access to the links and assets necessary to succeed throughout the value chain.

The entire issue of territory, or local/regional environment, and its effects on enterprises within the territory remains largely undeveloped. Courlet and Soulage (1995) go some way toward a research agenda in this area. The types of relations which firms have with their local environments vary both because of characteristics of firms and because of characteristics of regions (Oinas 1995). As a result, policies – public as well as private – work best when they are tailored to local conditions (Bianchi and Giordani 1993). Thus, it is difficult for any 'recipe' from one place to work when transplanted into another place, with its unique culture, traditions, capabilities and networks.

Chapter 6

Corporations and networks of large firms

The growth of networks of small firms is merely one aspect of the network form of organization. Parallel to entrepreneurial small-firm networks is the emergence of large, often global, network companies. Some have developed almost exclusively through the use of relationships with other firms in the production system. Others are webs of relationships created by giant firms in many industries in an effort to develop transnational and trans-technological networks of capabilities. In both cases, large firms control large amalgams of resources across the globe, focusing on the major Triad markets and sources of technology. The result of this increasingly global presence is termed globalization.

Globalization affects places very differently, depending on the labour and other resources that might be tapped, the size of the market, or the prominence of the place as a 'world city'. The precise nature of global flows of investment and economic activity vary by sector, and this chapter examines briefly four very different sectors: aerospace, motor vehicles, footwear and clothing. The extent of the benefit of transnational involvement in any place is closely related to the degree to which a firm becomes 'embedded' in that place. This is a term that reflects the linkages and alliances, and capability for technological learning, that take place within a territory. This development potential is greatly influenced by global investment as well as by local competence.

Globalization of economic activity

Globalization can be defined as the widening and deepening of the operations of firms to produce and sell goods and services in more markets. These operations include traditional arm's length trade and direct investment, but also new forms of investment as well (Tanaka and Vickery 1993: 7). Globalization is more than *internationalization*, which refers simply to 'the increasing geographical spread of economic activities across national boundaries' (Dicken 1992: 1). Internationalization is not new, but globalization – signifying functional integration of internationally dispersed activities – is only recent. A consequence of globalization is that the 'nationality' of a product may be difficult to ascertain, being the outcome of a complex set of links in a production chain across several countries (Brainard 1993).

More is at issue than simply the spread of production to new locations. An array of other new forms of investment has evolved beyond foreign direct

191

investment (FDI) to include subcontracting, licensing, joint ventures, strategic alliances, franchising, management contracts, production-sharing and others (Helleiner 1989; Oman 1984; Tanaka and Vickery 1993). All of these involve the spread of advanced technologies, which are typically owned by transnational corporations, and which 'lock out' developing countries from the networks of alliances (Freeman and Hagedoorn 1994). The concentration of corporate research and development (R&D) in home countries and restrictive transfers of technology once seemed likely to perpetuate technological dependence (Germidis 1977). During the 1990s, however, two-thirds of all new R&D facilities within transnational firms have been located outside their home countries (UNCTAD 1994).

Most (if not all) of these new forms of production organization are the creation of large firms. Global corporations and their networks of production dominate world economic activity (Dicken 1992; Harrison 1994; Kozul-Wright 1995; Martinelli and Schoenberger 1991). The distinction between skill-intensive (and high-wage) activities and labour-intensive (and low-wage) activities creates and reinforces uneven development (Fröbel, Heinrichs and Kreye 1980). Globalization has also undercut the influence of labour unions in many countries (Jacoby 1995), but there is evidence of the development of a global solidarity network of unions (Herod 1995). Some believe that global labour standards are needed in order to avoid a 'race to the bottom' toward lower wages and less regulation of workplaces (Sengenberger and Wilkinson 1995).

Overall, globalization is best understood as a microeconomic phenomenon, one that is driven by the strategies and behaviours of firms (Oman 1994). Globalization also reflects several other phenomena beyond global inter-firm competition and cooperation, reflected in corporate alliances:

1. the decline in US economic hegemony and political leadership, connected to the end of the Cold War;
2. the rapid growth of the global financial market since the late 1970s, increasing the sensitivity and vulnerability of all countries to managing their economies and to controlling the value of their currencies; and
3. global concern about environmental threats (Oman 1994).

Multinational or transnational corporations (TNCs) have existed for many centuries, evolving through a sequence of three distinct stages. The earliest global firms were those organized to extract from other places natural resources and primary products not available at home, such as spices, silk, furs, gold and silver. The list expanded to include tropical fruits and other agricultural crops, petroleum, and other minerals. Foreign direct investment in natural resources represented 23 per cent of world FDI stock in 1970, but only 11 per cent by 1990 (UNCTAD 1995a: 10). Much of this took place as colonial ventures and the resultant development was highly concentrated, with few linkages and dual economies as the norm (Oman 1994: 39–41).

The second stage was the expansion of firms into foreign markets primarily for the sale of manufactured products, but it also included production as well, beginning in the second half of the nineteenth century. This market stage occurs among the wealthy countries (as well as the elites of Third World countries), where markets – consumers, industries and governments – can afford the products. Thus, trade between Europe, Japan and North America takes place largely between TNCs in these countries seeking markets for their manufactured products and services. Both the resource and the market objectives of TNCs maintain the traditional international division of labour embodied in Vernon's (1966) influential product cycle thesis. Only advanced economies could produce manufactured goods while they were profitable; underdeveloped countries had little role in the world economy other than as suppliers of primary inputs.

The third stage of transnational activity is very different. It relies on the 'new international division of labour', in which production tasks can be broken down into activities that can be done by unskilled workers in countries where labour costs are very low relative to the advanced countries (Figure 6.1). In most of Asia, workers earn a fraction of the wages and non-wage benefits enjoyed by workers in the USA or Europe. The emergence of manufacturing in Third World countries contrasts greatly with the previous role of those countries in the world economy. Indeed, direct investment in the form of factories and, probably even more important, the surge of subcontracting arrangements with Third World firms has altered the way in which economic development is viewed. Services had increased from 31 per cent to 50 per cent of total FDI stock between 1970 and 1990.

It was not until after World War II that the great surge in international production and the creation of 'global factories' occurred, although investment remained mainly market oriented and in developed economies. This growth in global (albeit mainly transatlantic) economic activity in the 1950s and 1960s was a result of several permissive or 'enabling technologies', which effectively compressed space and allowed large firms to become truly global. The international division of labour was, to a large degree, a result of three enabling changes in production:

1. developments in the technology and organization of production that subdivided and standardized complex production processes into simple units requiring minimal training or skills, thus allowing workers in virtually any location to perform required tasks;
2. improvements in telecommunications and transportation permit people, goods and information to travel efficiently and cheaply to any location on the globe, allowing industrial location and the management of production to be largely independent of geographical location;
3. the development of a worldwide reservoir of potential labour, not penetrated by unions, and therefore having little power to demand wages and fringe benefits (Bluestone and Harrison 1982: 115–8; Dicken 1992: 137–8; Fröbel, Heinrichs and Kreye 1980: 37–44).

To these, Doz (1987: 98–9) adds three other enabling conditions that led to true globalization:

4. the homogenization of markets, with the result that many products, such as watches, clothing and consumer electronics, can be sold as identical brands in many countries;

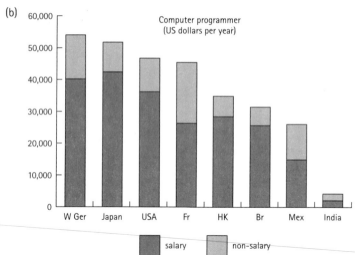

Figure 6.1   Labour costs for textile (a) and computer-sector workers (b, c) in selected countries. Source: based on *The Economist* (1994c: 63).

5. the removal or reduction of trade barriers, the success of export-promotion policies, and recognition that import substitution measures usually fail had the result that many more countries participate actively in the world economy; and
6. An organizational infrastructure for globalization in place within many firms or available from willing partners to facilitate market intelligence, foreign manufacturing, and distribution.

These conditions were necessary but not sufficient for industry globalization to take place. The final, essential factor is the intense competition between firms spurred by a combination of economies of scale and increased minimum

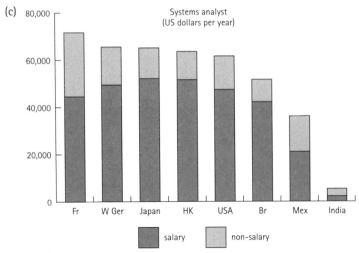

Figure 6.1   (cont.).

efficient scale of production, resulting in excess capacity. This would normally be expected to lead to price competition, but segmented markets, technological discontinuities (from energy and electronics), and fluctuating exchange rates have combined to insert the logic of shorter product life-cycles into the equation (Doz 1987).

The enabling technologies and conditions have allowed firms, particularly those already large, to develop a global strategy and control of product development, production and marketing. Internal forces also impinged on firms, including increasing scale economies, escalating R&D investments and shorter product life-cycles (Bartlett and Ghoshal 1995: 8). As a result, portfolio foreign investments 'gave way to strategically coordinated operations worldwide, exploiting comparative advantages of different countries for different types of activities' (Doz 1987: 97). During the 1960s and 1970s, these foreign operations were most often internal to large firms, reflected in large volumes of intra-firm international trade.

The 'enabling technologies' permitted managers to shift capital (as well as products) across long distances, and to operate far-reaching networks of production facilities. Deskilling, made possible by refinements in the technology and organization of production, alleviates firms' dependence on certain sets of skilled workers, with the result that some segments of production requiring low levels of skill are moved 'offshore' (i.e. overseas), while others remain near needed pools of specialized labour. The global semiconductor industry exemplified this tendency early on, taking advantage of export-oriented industrialization policies in Japan, Korea, Singapore and Taiwan (Angel 1994; Grunwald 1985; J. Henderson 1989; Molina 1989; Oman 1994; Scott 1987; Scott and Angel 1988; Schoenberger 1986). The trend continues in the software industry, which exploits low-cost Indian labour in Bangalore (*The Economist* 1996f).

Subtle changes in the division of labour reinforce regional clusters and core–periphery patterns. The first trend is the growing importance of knowledge-intensive industries and advanced production methods, which rely on highly skilled workers and an advanced technological and business infrastructure. Firms locate in places that provide access to these resources. The second trend is the increasing importance of the market and the need for firms to be close to final consumers, both producer and consumer, in order to adapt to customer needs, tastes and demands. Both trends are leading to a wider distribution of corporate activities, i.e. in more countries, but concentrated in regionally specialized industrial clusters (Tanaka and Vickery 1993).

From the simple or 'shallow' integration characterized by outsourcing and subcontracting only a portion of the value chain, an *integrated international production system* has developed. More complex integration strategies, enabled by information technology (IT), have turned geographically dispersed affiliates into regionally or globally integrated production and distribution networks. *Transnationalization* combines globalization (the spread of economic activity across national boundaries) and internationalization – (the establishment of links between national economies) (Radice 1995). Each element in the production chain is highly dependent on all other elements in the system, rendering coordination costs high. However, IT makes it possible for a firm to coordinate a web of spatially dispersed functions located in many different countries (UNCTAD 1994). The world's most transnational TNCs (ranked by percentage of foreign activity) are European, reflecting both small national markets and proximity of other markets within Europe (UNCTAD 1995a: 19–25) (Table 6.1).

There are many small and medium-sized TNCs as well, some of them nearly as transnational as the 100 largest firms on which Table 6.1 is based. The average transnationality index of 50 small and medium-sized TNCs is 33, compared with an average index of 41 for the world's largest firms (UNCTAD 1995a: 26). These small and medium-size TNCs are less likely than large TNCs to invest in developing countries (Fujita 1995a). A large proportion of SME TNCs have R&D facilities abroad: 36 per cent of those firms based in Europe and 31 per cent of US firms (Fujita 1995b). Many small TNCs have been transnational from their founding, plugging into an international network of contacts that provides resources and markets abroad (Christensen and Lindmark 1993; McDougall, Shane and Oviatt 1994). Other firms, especially in the clothing and shoe industries, are transnational through their linkages with subcontractors. These firms are vulnerable to the financial risk of dealing with small, undercapitalized firms, as well as to governance problems related to coordination with little power (Clark 1993).

TNCs based in developing countries, by contrast, have markedly lower indices of transnationality as well as generally lower levels of employment outside their home country (UNCTAD 1995a: 29–34). Developing country TNCs are based in Brazil, Mexico and the Asian NICs (Table 6.2). Much recent investment by firms in the Asian NICs has been directed toward China; nearly 75 per cent of all new FDI in China from 1990 to 1993 originated in Hong Kong, Singapore and Taiwan (UNCTAD 1995a: 34). These investments follow

Table 6.1 World's leading TNCs ranked by index of transnationality.

Rank	Company	Home country	Principal industry	Index of transnationality[a]
1	Nestlé	Switzerland	Food	92.0
2	Holderbank	Switzerland	Building materials	91.9
3	Thomson Corporation	Canada	Publishing	91.3
4	Electrolux	Sweden	Electronics	89.5
5	Asea Brown Boveri	Switzerland	Electrical equipment	89.1
6	Solvay	Belgium	Chemicals	88.3
7	Philips Electronics	Netherlands	Electronics	84.9
8	RTZ	UK	Mining	84.7
9	Ciba-Geigy	Switzerland	Chemicals	81.0
10	Michelin	France	Rubber and plastics	75.6
11	Grand Metropolitan	UK	Food	74.6
12	Seagram	Canada	Beverages	74.1
13	Glaxo Holdings	Switzerland	Pharmaceuticals	72.8
14	British Petroleum	UK	Petroleum	72.2
15	Alcan Aluminum	Canada	Metals	72.1
16	Roche Holdings	Switzerland	Pharmaceuticals	68.9
17	Stora	Sweden	Forestry products	68.1
18	Cable and Wireless	UK	Telecommunications	66.6
19	BAT Industries	UK	Tobacco	66.4
20	Total	France	Petroleum refining	66.2

Note: [a] The index of transnationality is the average of foreign assets to total assets, foreign sales to total sales, and foreign employment to total employment.
Source: extracted from UNCTAD (1995a: 20–3, Table I.7).

the network of Chinese family firms and business networks that invest in China as well as in centres of overseas Chinese businesses throughout the Pacific Rim (*The Economist* 1992; Leung 1993; Seagrave 1995; Yeung 1994b).

Global production systems

Foreign investment, like other strategic actions, requires time for learning and for network formation. Investment by Japanese firms in North America has taken place in two 'waves' that affect the prevalence of 'new' forms of work organization. Older Japanese plants, dating from the mid-1970s, did not attempt to incorporate teams or other Japanese work practices, but instead retained US work practices. These early overseas operations were also strongly dependent on inputs imported from Japan. Production in the NICs was – and remains – largely 'triangular', wherein the NICs import capital goods and technology from Japan and export consumer goods outside the region, mainly to Europe and North America (Aoki 1995: 338–9; Oman 1994: 49). Beginning in the mid-1980s, Japanese firms began to mesh their operations into networks

Table 6.2 World's leading TNCs based in developing countries, ranked by index of transnationality.

Rank	Company	Home country	Principal industry	Index of transnationality[a]
1	Creative Technology	Singapore	Electronics	58.3
2	Hyosung Corp.	Korea	Trading	46.7
3	Fraser & Neave Ltd	Singapore	Diversified	43.3
4	Dong Ah Construction	Korea	Construction	40.6
5	Acer	Taiwan	Electronics	40.2
6	Jardine Matheson Holdings Ltd	Hong Kong	Diversified	38.8
7	CDL Hotels International Ltd	Hong Kong	Hotels	35.8
8	Cemex SA	Mexico	Cement	35.3
9	Grupo Sidek	Mexico	Hotels	34.0
10	Hutchison Wampoa Ltd	Hong Kong	Diversified	32.8
11	Aracruz Cellulose SA	Brazil	Paper	31.5
12	Sime Darby Berhad	Malaysia	Food	30.3
13	Hong Kong and Shanghai Hotels Ltd	Hong Kong	Hotels	29.3
14	CITIC Pacific Ltd	Hong Kong	Diversified	28.7
15	Souza Cruz SA	Brazil	Tobacco	27.5
16	Grupo Televisa SA	Mexico	Media	27.5
17	Daewoo Group	Korea	Electronics	26.6
18	Sampo Corp.	Taiwan	Electronics	25.2
19	Tatung Co. Ltd	Taiwan	Electronics	25.2
20	Embraer	Brazil	Aerospace	24.8

Note: [a] The index of transnationality is the average of foreign assets to total assets, foreign sales to total sales, and foreign employment to total employment.
Source: extracted from UNCTAD (1995a: 20–3, Table I.7).

more similar to those in Japan, relying to a greater degree on local suppliers, many of them Japanese firms themselves (Edgington 1993). While Japanese work practices in North American 'transplants' have been known to vary considerably (Abo 1994), these later investments have more effectively blended Japanese and American work practices and management systems (Cutcher-Gershenfeld *et al.* 1994). A third wave has begun in several firms: that of full local globalization into a 'tetra-polar' – rather than a Triadic – 'strategic division of the world' that recognizes Europe, North America and Southeast Asia as major regions, in addition to headquarters operations, R&D and high-tech production in Japan (Edgington 1993). Fujitsu's operations exemplify this strategy in several different product lines, including semiconductors, telecommunications products and computers (Kondo 1995). Complex production networks, both internal within Japanese *keiretsu* and external (involving other firms as suppliers), are now typical within most Japanese corporations (Aoki 1995).

The integrated international production system has heightened the importance of a more 'eclectic' theory of multinational investment (Dunning 1979). This framework postulates that, at any point in time, the stock of foreign assets owned or controlled by a TNC is determined by (1) the extent and nature of ownership or firm-specific advantages of those firms; (2) the extent and nature of the location-bound endowments and markets of countries that create or add value to the firm's competitive advantages; and (3) the extent to which the market for these advantages, including those from transnationality itself, are best internalized by the firm, rather than marketed to foreign firms (Dunning 1993b: 81). The eclectic paradigm adds to Porter's 'diamond' of national competitive advantage (Chapter 1) by incorporating TNC strategies and activities, such as inward and outward investment and alliances (Dunning 1993a,b, 1995; Narula 1993; Rugman and D'Cruz 1993; Rugman and Verbeke 1993).

The stress on ownership or firm-specific factors, combined with location-specific factors, such as local institutions and local technological capability, produces a tension within transnationals. The essential characteristic of a TNC is the dynamism that comes from the tension between the 'integration logic' pursued by the parent corporation and the 'localization logic' of subsidiaries. 'Hybrid' factories and other units are the logical outcome of this tension (Abo 1994). These seem especially common in Japanese firms, which are 'reluctant multinationals' because their production system is so difficult to relocate to other countries and cultures (Hill and Lee 1994). Japanese overseas investment remained at very low levels until 1985, but has grown rapidly since then (Dicken 1992: 76–81). Service-sector FDI (especially banking and insurance) accounts for 74 per cent of all Japanese FDI in Europe (Thomsen 1993). In both services and manufacturing, Japanese firms have been attracted primarily by market access within the EU rather than in response to trade barriers or to seek resources in particular countries. As in the USA, Japanese manufacturing investments in Europe have been predominantly on greenfield sites in English-speaking countries (Thomsen 1993).

Transnational investment follows the Triad structure closely; the rest of the world, including Africa and South America, remains poorly served by the world's TNCs (Dunning 1993b). Foreign investment in Africa has been mainly in resources (oil and mining), rather than in manufacturing or services. Markets there remain too small, especially because of poverty, and unstable governments and burdensome bureaucracies make investments more risky than elsewhere (UNCTAD 1995b).

Beyond FDI, data shortcomings blur the true picture of globalization. Joint ventures and non-equity alliances typically are poorly accounted for, if tracked at all (Dunning 1993b: 285–310; Oman 1984). In some industries, however, international collaboration is a major mode of globalization. For example, because of national regulations, the pharmaceutical industry has very low levels of foreign trade. Firms in the industry are highly inclined to pursue R&D in the three Triad markets as well as to become involved in inter-firm collaborations and cooperative agreements (Howells 1990b; Howells and Wood 1993). Collaboration strategies have increased since the advent of biotechnology and

Table 6.3 Organizational characteristics of large firms.

Characteristics	Multinational firm	Global firm	International firm	Transnational firm
Assets and capabilities	Nationally self-sufficient and decentralized	Globally scaled and centralized	Sources of core competences centralized, other capabilities decentralized	Capabilities specialized, interdependent and dispersed
Role of overseas operations	Discerning and exploit local opportunities	Implementing parent firm's strategies	Adapting and leveraging parent firm's competences	Differentiated contributions by national units to integrated worldwide operations
R&D and knowledge transfer	Knowledge developed and retained within each national unit	Knowledge developed and retained at headquarters	Knowledge developed at headquarters and transferred to overseas units	Knowledge developed at national units; best features shared worldwide

Source: based on Bartlett and Ghoshal (1989: 65, Table 4.2).

its implications for new products, and concentration in the industry has increased through mergers and acquisitions, a trend that shows little sign of slowing in the 1990s (Tarabusi 1993). In most other sectors, networks of cooperative agreements, alliances, and strategic technology partnerships grew during the 1980s in many sectors (Hagedoorn 1995; Hagedoorn and Schakenraad 1990, 1992). In high-tech sectors, such as aircraft and computers, technology is the most important motive for alliances (Anderson 1995; Bartlett and Ghoshal 1995: 145). Alliances in IT have seen the greatest growth during the 1990s, surpassing those in biotechnology (National Science Board 1996: 4-43–4-44).

Corporate structure and strategy in global firms

The dilemma of centralization or decentralization, presented in Chapter 3 in the context of the multilocational firm, is always present and is particularly intense for the global enterprise. A traditional *multinational* firm decentralizes its various foreign subsidiaries in order to meet local needs and respond to diverse national interests. This structure is also referred to as 'multidomestic' (UNCTAD 1994: 137). *Global* firms attempt to standardize product design and manufacturing in centralized headquarters and R&D operations. An *international* strategy is somewhat decentralized but relies on transfers of knowledge and ideas to subsidiaries, which remain dependent on technological and market decisions. Finally, a *transnational* firm coordinates a number of national operations which serve as sources of ideas, skills, capabilities and knowledge for the entire corporation (Bartlett and Ghoshal 1989; Konsynski and Karimi 1993; see OTA (1994: 6) for a slightly different classification).

Three capabilities, then, are the keys to strategic management in a global business:

1. efficiency in maintaining control and coordination of subsidiaries;
2. an ability to change the nature of relationships between headquarters and subsidiaries, and between subsidiaries, when needed; and
3. flexibility to coordinate subsidiaries to take advantage of interdependencies and to deal with unusual markets and circumstances, such as government-controlled markets, e.g. in China (Doz, Prahalad and Hamel 1990: 119).

Coordination is particularly difficult for firms in business services based on partnerships, such as accounting, since there is no hierarchy or central control. In these firms, the 'corporate glue' is the web of formal and informal networks, reinforced by personnel transfers and meetings and seminars (Ferner, Edwards and Sisson 1995).

The Bartlett–Ghoshal scheme (Table 6.3) suggests an evolution from complete decentralization in the multinational firm to complete centralization in the global firm, and finally to a mix of the two in the international firm. The transnational structure emphasizes interdependence and horizontal flows, especially in learning, since knowledge can be developed in any of the firm's locations before being shared with other units. Philips, the Dutch electronics firm, is cited as a prototypical transnational (Bartlett and Ghoshal 1989; Howells and Wood 1993). The goal is to become a 'global network corporation', blending and taking advantage of the managerial systems of firms in other nations through network links, thereby being at the same time both global and a network, rather than a hierarchy. Asea Brown Boveri (ABB), created by a Swiss–Swedish merger in 1987, is reputed to be one of the first firms to take this form (Bartlett and Ghoshal 1995; Yoshino and Rangan 1995: 200–1).

The word 'glocalize' has been coined to combine global and local in a single concept. The goal of *glocalization* represents achieving a balance between being global, with the scale advantages associated with size and global scope, and being local within each regional or national market and network of resources. For many firms, information flow from the centre to the corporate units elsewhere is easier to achieve than information flow from various units to the centre and to other units (Cerny 1996; Gustavsson, Melin and Macdonald 1994). Rather than control and dependence, a firm must create a 'shared concern' for change among its subsidiaries (Prahalad and Doz 1981). In other words, a hierarchy has control advantages balanced against the fact that its standardization is not in tune with local needs, whereas a heterarchy, comprised of many different kinds of centres, has the principal disadvantage of being more local than meshed into the global enterprise (Håkanson 1990; Hedlund 1986). Because of the challenges to glocalize, it is difficult to construct and maintain a perfect network firm that balances control, learning and evolutionary change (De Meyer 1993a).

A network of facilities in different locations provides operating flexibility in the face of uncertainty, such as exchange rate fluctuations (Kogut 1990). Indeed, the utilization of a transnational network of facilities makes possible 'global switching' within the firm's network, which is a form of flexibility not available to small, non-global firms. Switching capability in production has been present for years, as in the parallel plant (Chapter 4). However, its value as an option, to coordinate and transfer resources within its international network, allows the firm to reduce uncertainty (Kogut and Kulatilaka 1994). The integration of operations provides both flexibility and corporation-wide economies of scale (McGrath and Hoole 1992). It also makes the manufacturing location decision much more complicated since not only do numerous internal functions need to be considered, but interactions with external suppliers and distribution links must also be taken into account. Short product life-cycles and the need for interaction with customers and suppliers make cost-based decisions to locate in low-wage locations short-sighted in comparison with a decision that will improve a firm's long-term 'network of capabilities' (Bartmess and Cerny 1993). Firms need to have access to markets, skills and infrastructure, but it is the quality of these (especially of skills), rather than their costs, which now matter most (MacCormack, Newman and Rosenfield 1994). Seen in the light of these factors, the location decisions in the semiconductor industry, as in most industries, reflects far more than the labour cost minimization emphasized in the new international division of labour (Geneau de Lamarlière 1991).

Switching is now occurring to a some extent in R&D and sales/marketing, where firms such as Hewlett-Packard are able to benefit from new product development in several locations, including Japan, Singapore and the UK (Howells and Wood 1993; Leonard-Barton 1995). R&D is becoming more locationally 'fluid' in both an organizational and an operational sense, becoming more like the pattern found in production and sales operations (Howells 1990a: 144). Multiple linkages, representing cross-functional communication, take place between headquarters and subsidiaries in firms such as Matsushita Electric and Philips (Bartlett and Ghoshal 1990).

Three types of subsidiaries, each with different levels of autonomy and integration, can be described: local implementer, specialized contributor and world mandate. A local implementer is a branch operation, modifying products developed elsewhere for local markets. A specialized contributor may be a global research centre with considerable expertise, but high dependence on the parent for new products. World mandate units exhibit strategic autonomy with respect to both new products and input linkages, with higher degrees of purchasing from outside the corporation (Birkinshaw and Morrison 1995). ABB fits the third model, conducting corporate R&D in six countries (Gwynne 1995).

Managing innovation and R&D in large firms is among the most difficult aspects of a TNC, and R&D remains the least globalized of all corporate activities (Doz 1987; Miller 1994; Patel and Pavitt 1991). The world's largest firms, which are also the largest holders of US patents, have not dispersed R&D as much as they have centralized it within their home countries. The large German chemical firms, Bayer, Hoechst and BASF, continue to invest nearly 60 per cent of their R&D expenditures in Germany (Bathelt 1995). Opportunities provided by acquisitions and alliances in the USA have prompted some shifts of R&D in these firms as well as in other high-tech sectors (Wortmann 1990).

'Listening posts' or surveillance units to follow competitors and to keep track of technological changes in various settings have grown rapidly (Håkanson 1990), as have international strategic alliances, but global firms continue to rely most on their domestic base, as Porter's (1990) model of competitive advantage suggests (Chapter 1). The corporate form is that of a 'polyp' firm, 'using its tentacles to acquire from each country its excellence in research rather than to decentralise its brain' (Archibugli and Michie 1995: 135). The objective of accumulating technical knowledge from many sources is the principal reason for firms to undertake internationalized R&D (De Meyer 1993b). Listening posts and intelligence scanning are productive, however, only if the 'best practices' and other new ideas identified are communicated to other corporate units (Bartlett and Ghoshal 1995: 672–3; Chiesa 1996).

Several factors reinforce the integrated transnational form. Centrally developed innovations face the risk of failing to be appropriate for markets in other countries; local R&D at several locations presents the risk of needless product differentiation when standardization would be preferable. The balance between differentiation and duplication in new products is always present (Kogut 1990). The integration between corporate R&D and other information and innovation-related functions typically has a geographical impact: R&D takes place at or near corporate headquarters, in order to communicate with corporate marketing, financial and strategy functions. Within TNCs, R&D and strategic activities are generally retained in the home country, where it is headquartered.

Subsidiaries elsewhere have been described as possessing only a *truncated* structure oriented toward routine production and marketing (Hayter 1982; Etemad and Séguin Dulude 1986). Consequently, the level of knowledge and information on the state-of-the-art in products, materials, markets and production processes is not available to these plants unless corporate headquarters decides to transfer them to other establishments. During the 1980s and 1990s, a greater number of R&D centres have been established, some of which, especially those in high-technology sectors, have been conducting basic research and autonomous research programmes. From these units, particularly if assigned a 'world product mandate', greater developmental effects on their region can result (Menzler-Hokkanen 1995; Young, Hood and Peters 1994). On the whole, however, R&D remains truncated, at least to the extent that basic research is the least likely activity to be found outside the central laboratory in the home country (Pearce and Singh 1991). The sort of R&D done in foreign locations, while amounting to 10 per cent of total R&D in a sample of firms in 1975, was overwhelmingly on development rather than research, and on improvements and modifications for foreign markets rather than entirely new products and processes (Mansfield, Teece and Romeo 1979).

Tight links between central research and national laboratories, reinforced by frequent job transfers, are a means of horizontal information flow typical of Japanese technology management (Chapter 3). However, Japanese firms, more than others, coordinate by decentralization. Matsushita has developed a hybrid structure ('decentralized centralization') in which, as assets and responsibilities passed on to subsidiaries increase, information and decision-making at the centre also increase (Bartlett and Ghoshal 1989). Stagnant conditions in Japan and a high yen have forced Japanese firms to decentralize operations more in order to take advantage of both capabilities and lower costs in other countries, creating a middle-up-down management structure, rather than purely top-down or bottom-up (Nonaka 1990b). Dunning (1993c) found that Japanese subsidiaries in the UK were much more controlled from corporate headquarters than were US-based firms, reflecting the desire by the Japanese firms to exploit firm-specific advantages. Japanese structures are Triad-based, and multiple independent 'international' headquarters in Europe, North America and Southeast Asia are intended to respond to specific local market needs (Hood, Young and Lal 1994; Nonaka 1990b). Hybrid policies are developed explicitly in order to balance and interrelate central and local conditions. High levels of personnel interchange and travel are needed in this system, with the benefit of enhancing tacit knowledge of diverse market conditions in a large number of people (Nonaka 1990b).

R&D historically has been the last aspect of corporate activity to take on a global dimension, since economies of scale and strategic control favour centralization. Several reasons motivate firms to move R&D abroad:

- to support local production;
- to acquire foreign technology;
- to customize products for local markets;
- to stay abreast of technological developments (the R&D unit as a 'listening post');

- to gain access to foreign scientists and engineers and R&D resources at universities, laboratories and institutes;
- to assist the parent company in meeting local regulations and product standards;
- to gain cost efficiencies (Dörrenbächer and Wortmann 1991; Håkanson and Nobel 1993a,b; OTA 1994: 76).

These represent two types of motives: those related to local markets in a more traditional sense, and those related to the generation of new technologies that can be used throughout the entire company. Beyond strategic motives, foreign R&D has also grown as a result of acquisitions of firms with established R&D capabilities that are preserved (Dörrenbächer and Wortmann 1991; Håkanson and Nobel 1993a). Japanese firms stand out as preferring 'greenfield' investment over acquisition in their investments in the USA (Caves 1993). The firms whose technological activities have grown the most outside their home base have done so more by mergers and acquisitions than by organic growth (Patel 1995).

From all of these sources, R&D by foreign affiliates in the USA increased substantially during the 1980s and 1990s, mainly through mergers and acquisitions rather than the establishment of 'greenfield' laboratories (OTA 1994; *Science* 1995). A recent assessment of R&D by foreign TNCs in the USA concluded that this was a positive-sum trend, i.e. that foreign technologies and methodologies imported from parent companies are greater than technologies transferred abroad (Reid and Schriesheim 1996). Recent large acquisitions in the pharmaceutical and biotechnology field have increased the amount of R&D done by foreign companies in the USA (Table 6.4). It is evident from the table that Japanese firms have taken the 'listening post' and global scanning strategy to heart: more firms have R&D facilities in the USA, but their laboratories, in average R&D employees per firm, are the smallest of the major investors. Japanese R&D spending remains 'almost entirely domestic' (Roberts 1995: 55). The Triad nature of global technology also continues to be the pattern, with firms based in Europe, the USA and Japan (in that order) investing in the other two regions at steadily increasing levels (OTA 1994). In the other direction, R&D units of European or US-based firms in Japan are less common, in part because of cultural and institutional conditions there (Westney 1990).

Technological capabilities outside the Triad economies have become important, and are likely to become more so as R&D activities are globalized and dispersed to more countries (Dunning 1994). In all contexts, competitive advantage is localized in some locations more than in others (Porter and Wayland 1995). These are agglomerations or localized production systems where several conditions come together to provide advantages that are not available everywhere, and perhaps nowhere else (Lipietz 1993). Some companies therefore utilize several 'home bases', including R&D and sophisticated production, rather than a single headquarters, for important markets.

In the transnational firm, location matters a great deal, for increasingly investment is not unidimensional, but involves a deep array of corporate functions (Porter and Wayland 1995). In this way, units of TNCs are embedded

Table 6.4 Largest foreign sources of R&D investment in the USA, 1993.

Country	Expenditures ($ billions)	R&D employees	Number of companies	Number of R&D facilities	Average number of R&D employees per company
Switzerland	2.524	14 700	16	45	919
Germany	2.321	19 200	32	95	600
United Kingdom	2.295	20 000	61	109	328
Canada	2.190				
Japan	1.781	11 800	107	219	110
France	1.204	9 300	22	52	423

Source: Science (1995), National Science Board (1996: 4-47–4-48), and calculations by author. Detailed data on Canada are not included in these sources.

simultaneously in two different networks: the internal corporate network and an external business and institutional network in each locality (Dicken, Forsgren and Malmberg 1994). However, the communication and coordination needs of large firms mean that large metropolitan regions are the major 'innovation poles' for R&D activities (Tödtling 1994). It is in these centres that telecommunications links are best, producer services are most available, and labour resources are most readily found (Lipietz 1993; Moulaert and Tödtling 1995).

Centralized control is still evident in the 'non-globalization' of technology, at least relative to the very global nature of production and sourcing (Patel and Pavitt 1991). R&D intensity levels are lower among foreign affiliates than in parent firms for all nationalities of firms. National and sectoral differences overshadow this generalization somewhat, but R&D generally 'moves overseas much more slowly than production, sourcing, and other business activities' (OTA 1994: 87).

In large measure, this is a result of the competitive advantages provided by a global firm's home economy, institutions and culture, on which a company's administrative heritage and firm-specific resources are based. Home country conditions and endowments, therefore, linger and affect all operations of a global firm in all its locations (Baily and Gersbach 1995; Dunning 1993b; Fladmoe-Lindquist and Tallman 1994; Porter 1990). As a result of the importance of home countries to global corporations, these firms overall contribute insufficiently to local technological accumulation in their other locations (Patel and Pavitt 1994c).

Based on data for 1981–1986, Dutch firms had the most globalized R&D, with 82 per cent of it outside the Netherlands, followed at some distance by Swiss firms with 28 per cent. At the opposite extreme, the R&D of Japanese firms was the least globalized: 0.6 per cent. US firms were also extremely low: 3.2 per cent of R&D (Patel and Pavitt 1991). Comparative figures for the USA in 1982 were 8.7 per cent, and in 1992 up to 12.7 per cent (OTA 1994: 86). Highly concentrated R&D activities appear to best serve the need for efficient and fast product variety. Miller (1994) has found that auto firms are uncertain about the degree to which their products (perhaps separated into under-body and upper-body portions) should be standardized globally or tailored for diverse markets. Consequently, the R&D of both US-based and Japanese car firms is highly concentrated in their home countries (Rubenstein 1994). Firms in the automobile industry continue to concentrate R&D and engineering activities near the home base; only firms pursuing distinct multi-regional strategies have partly dispersed these activities to major regional markets (Miller 1994).

Information technology in global firms

Computers and digital information networks function as the 'coordination technology' for multilocational firms by reducing the costs of coordination and stimulating the emergence of new, coordination-intensive business structures. These structures include networks of firms and virtual corporations for 'buying' inputs (discussed in Chapter 4), which are rendered preferable to internal ('making') by the newly lowered transaction costs (Malone and Rockart 1993). The firm's strategies for business and for information management can, and should, be aligned so that each function is served best by its telematics network (Konsynski and Karimi 1993). Information technology (IT) is the facilitating technology that permits the control and coordination essential to the functioning of transnational corporations, since networks can be structured to permit decentralized networks with central oversight (Li 1995).

IT has grown to have a strategic value of its own, growing in importance far beyond its simple infrastructural form. Its three impacts are (1) to compress time, (2) to overcome geography, and (3) to alter the structure of relationships, such as bypassing intermediaries. These permit a firm to be more efficient and effective, and also enable innovation, quality improvements and the penetration of new markets (Hammer and Mangurian 1987). The network of Volkswagen AG exemplifies this, with satellite connections linking its plants in the Czech Republic, China, Mexico, Spain and elsewhere with its headquarters in Wolfsburg, Germany. Satellite links enable the firm to bypass incompatible and costly national telecommunications networks (Keen and Cummins 1994: 95–6). Large flows of information within large firms such as ABB (Asea Brown Boveri) and Volvo are between their headquarters in Sweden and factories and other company locations in Europe (Lorentzon 1993). Private networks based on highly secure leased satellite capacity are the principal means of linking a multilocational firm (Hagström 1992; Langdale 1989; Mansell 1994).

IT has allowed firms to automate existing linkages as well as to create new ones and to integrate functions, such as budgeting and finance, with manufacturing and service provision in response to customers' orders in widespread local markets (Li 1995). Tourism has become an information-intensive industry, with tour operators linking travel agents, airlines and hotels. The technology has enabled an array of alliances and linkages that effect diagonal integration, linking services outside the traditional scope of tourism (such as banking and insurance) within flexibly defined packages for customers in many places with tourism opportunities in other places (Miller, Clemons and Row 1993; Poon 1993).

IT has been especially critical – and at the same time the critical constraint – to the globalization of R&D. R&D activities, like other non-routine activities, require frequent interaction, and for long-distance electronic communication to substitute effectively for face-to-face contact, the firm's network and its technology must work very smoothly. Despite IT's capabilities, firms continue to locate R&D physically near to headquarters, other R&D facilities or production sites. As firms and their own R&D – and even more so R&D conducted jointly with other firms in alliances and collaborations – become more international, dependence on computer communications networks grows (Howells 1990a, 1995).

Despite the capabilities of telematics technology in the 1990s, TNCs push those capabilities to the limit and demand innovation for faster, higher-capacity technology. For example, high-capacity T1 (1.544 mbps) circuits are unable to handle massive, high-resolution graphics files sent between Rockwell

International facilities in Europe and the USA (Keen and Cummins 1994: 228–9). Texas Instruments coordinates 195 sites in 30 countries, with eight million transactions over the network per day (Keen and Cummins 1994: 342–3). However, despite growing utilization of electronic communications, personal face-to-face contact remains essential for the confidence and trust needed between members of a research team (De Meyer 1993a,b).

The geographical concentration of R&D

In an international context, Vernon's 'product cycle' hypothesis suggested that new products will tend to be developed where multinational enterprises are able to centralize R&D, notably where scientists and engineers are found (Vernon 1966, 1974, 1979). This hypothesis has led to formal models which show that product development tends to remain concentrated in countries with large pools of skilled labour (Nelson and Norman 1977). As US firms lost their dominance to those based in Europe and Japan, the product cycle model effectively gave way to a Triad model where all three regions were essential bases of operation in integrated production. Also negating the product cycle model was the growth of the NICs and their rapid move away from only mature production toward high-skill and innovative products (Harris 1992).

Less attention has been paid to the R&D location decision within individual countries. For the similar case of regional headquarters, Dunning and Norman (1983) found that, in Western Europe, accessibility by air and availability of skilled labour are most important in the location decision of multinational firms. The concerns of firms favour large urban regions, since air connections as well as technologically advanced telecommunications are available earliest in large regions (Molle, Beumer and Boeckhout 1989). TNCs tend to cluster R&D activities in noted high-tech centres within foreign countries (Dunning 1994: 77–8). Japanese electronics firms have three-quarters of their R&D facilities in California alone, and Japanese automotive firms have over 80 per cent of their R&D facilities in just two states, California and Michigan (Serapio 1993). When other sectors are taken into account, California still contains 48 per cent of all Japanese R&D laboratories, far more than the 21 per cent of US manufacturing facilities of Japanese firms located there (Florida and Kenney 1994).

At the international level, the choices of large firms go beyond locations where scientific and engineering personnel can be found. Doz (1986) depicts the dilemma facing large multinational firms: they must, on the one hand, strive to coordinate and control their far-flung operations and, on the other hand, they face considerable pressure to decentralize activities – including R&D – to their various host countries. The dilemma is not an easy one. As a result, firms may perform R&D outside a handful of advanced countries, but the amounts tend to be small, the focus tends to be on minor adaptations, and it is often separated from local R&D or from commercial applications outside the local market (Mansfield, Teece and Romeo 1979; Prahalad and Doz 1981; Teece 1981). Nearly all R&D by major multinationals is kept within the advanced economies (in Europe, Japan and the USA), in each of which skilled professionals and 'pockets of innovation' in specific technologies are found (Etemad and Séguin Dulude 1987; Mansfield, Teece and Romeo 1979; Perrino and Tipping 1989; Ronstadt 1984). In the early 1970s, two-thirds of all US R&D abroad was in Canada, Germany and the UK (Lall 1979). Despite increased amounts of R&D overseas, R&D among Japanese firms 'is internationalized to a much lower degree than among US and Swedish' firms (Granstrand *et al.* 1990: 73). For custom production of some products, such as application-specific integrated circuits (ASICs), Japanese semiconductor firms have opened chip design centres in Europe and the USA (Hobday 1989). The scope of R&D activities of Japanese firms in the USA has increased markedly in recent years (Serapio 1993).

Countries with educated, English-speaking workforces, such as Israel and Malaysia, have become sites for significant amounts of R&D and engineering work (Rossant, Reed and Griffiths 1989; Salih, Young and Rasiah 1988). Israel has become an integral site for R&D for many of the world's motor vehicle firms, utilizing Israeli (and Russian emigré) scientific capability and technologies previously untapped by the car industry (Marcus, Stern and Mitchener 1996). India boasts a rare high-tech complex in the Bangalore area in the south of the country. A number of firms from the USA, Singapore and elsewhere subcontract work in electronics and software to Indian firms (*The Economist* 1996f).

Multinationals also reinforce the spatial division of labour within the countries in which they operate, developed and underdeveloped alike, by focusing investments and activities in existing regional clusters and in large metropolitan regions (de Vet 1993; Tödtling 1994). Among multinationals in the UK, for example, Hall *et al.* (1987) found that proximity to Heathrow Airport was a major consideration. Most of these firms also allocate their various functions to different locations in the UK; R&D and administration are kept within Berkshire in the Southeast, whereas production is found at peripheral Welsh or Scottish sites. For similar reasons, in Canada, US-based multinationals cluster in the Toronto region (Britton 1985). London ranks first among major European cities for both headquarters and R&D functions on the basis of a set of location factors. They further conclude that the relative attractiveness of regions for the location of such functions 'will not give way easily to deconcentration' (Molle, Beumer and Boeckhout 1989: 171).

Patents and national technological strength

Patent data provide a measure of levels of invention by firms and individuals and serve as a leading indicator of technological competitiveness (National Science Board 1993). Data are available over a long period of time and are broken down in detail by technical area and location. Drawbacks to patent data include incompleteness (because not all innovations are patented); variations across sectors in the propensity to patent – with notably low levels in software and biotechnology; and inconsistent quality and significance of inventions patented (Patel 1995). Most patents are granted to corporations, rather than to individuals, and this is even more true of foreign inventors (80 per cent versus 71 per

Table 6.5   US patents granted, by inventor residence.

Country	Total patents 1963–1993	Country	Patents 1993
USA	1 386 178	USA	53 236
Total non-US	812 012	Total non-US	45 107
Japan	269 116	Japan	22 292
Germany	175 494	Germany	6 890
UK	81 125	France	2 908
France	66 556	UK	2 294
Canada	38 948	Canada	1 943
Switzerland	36 327	Italy	1 286
Italy	24 627	Taiwan	1 189
Sweden	22 427	Switzerland	1 126
The Netherlands	20 956	The Netherlands	801
Australia	8 084	South Korea	779
Austria	8 026	Sweden	635
Belgium	7 878	Australia	378
USSR	6 898	Belgium	350
Taiwan	6 166	Israel	314
Denmark	4 620	Austria	313
Finland	4 173	Finland	293
Israel	4 132	Denmark	197
Norway	2 634	Spain	159
South Korea	2 539	Norway	117
Spain	2 509	South Africa	93

Source: adapted from National Science Board (1996: 274).

cent for patents to US inventors). Japan accounts for one-third of all US patents granted to non-US applicants over the period 1963–1993; Germany was granted over 21 per cent (Table 6.5).

More significant in Table 6.5 is to compare the two columns: that on the left reflects accumulated technological strength over the 31-year period, whereas that on the right designates current patent production for 1993, the latest year available. Here, Japanese inventors – giant firms among the world's leaders in R&D (Franko 1996) – accounted for 49.4 per cent of all foreign patents granted in 1993, while Germany obtained just over 15 per cent. More importantly, the current patent production data indicate that the NICs are taking their place among the world's technological leaders. Taiwan, ranked 14th in cumulative patents, is eighth in 1993 patents. South Korea, ranked 19th over the 1963–1993 period, is now in ninth place among non-US grantees of US patents in 1993. Israel and Spain have also improved their standing in the current patent list. Notably lower in current patents than in accumulated patents are the USSR (Russia), Australia and a number of small European countries, including Austria, Denmark and Sweden.

The list of top technological firms illustrates once again the strength of the

Table 6.6　Leading firms in patents granted by the US Patent Office, 1991 and 1992.

Firm	Country	Number of US patents, 1991 and 1992
Toshiba	Japan	2332
Hitachi	Japan	2304
Canon	Japan	1946
Mitsubishi Electric	Japan	1935
General Electric	USA	1918
Eastman Kodak	USA	1691
General Motors	USA	1653
IBM	USA	1522
Fuji Photo Film	Japan	1394
Philips	The Netherlands	1375
Du Pont	USA	1315
Motorola	USA	1302
Matsushita Electric	Japan	1293
Hoechst	Germany	1198
Siemens	Germany	1160

Source: adapted from Buderi *et al.* (1992: 68) and Coy, Carey and Gross (1993: 57–9).

Triad economies; all the leading firms are based in Japan, the USA, Germany or the Netherlands (Table 6.6). The same group of leading US and Japanese firms in Table 6.6 are also among the top ten in 1993 (National Science Board 1996: 6–20). European Patent Office data also show a Triad pattern. Over 78 per cent of all patents were granted in 1991 to inventors or firms in Europe, Japan or the USA. The NICs increased only slightly in their European patent totals, from 0.1 per cent of the total in 1982 to 0.4 per cent in 1991 (National Science Board 1996: 6–19).

Patents reflect the R&D priorities of firms as well as national technological strengths. Japanese patenting in 1993 emphasized technologies associated with IT, photography, photocopying, motor vehicles and consumer electronics. German patents were in printing, motor vehicles, and new chemicals and materials. Taiwan has shifted quickly from its patent focus in 1980 on toys and other amusement devices to areas related to electronics, semiconductors, visual display systems and advanced materials. South Korea, like Taiwan, has progressed into sophisticated technologies, including optics, superconductors and telecommunications (National Science Board 1996: 6-21–6-22).

Flexibility and agility in large firms

The advantages of large firms centre on their financial resources, which provide an ability to make large investments, and strong core capabilities or competences and other assets. These typically give a large firm both product diversity and global reach. Small firms, on the other hand, tend to be more focused and flexible, allowing them to be customer-oriented and to respond rapidly to demand signals. The market and technical linkage is often closer because of the personal aspect of the firm's founder. Large firms attempt to 'think small' by reorganizing R&D functions and make them report to the business or product group manager (Calvin 1995). This presumes that the 'right' person will be in the key post: one who is interdisciplinary and who functions easily as an interactive gatekeeper.

The operating flexibility permitted by a network of multiple operations within the organization is only one form of flexibility. Another is that afforded by strategic alliances and partnerships. These permit a firm to gain access to technologies, markets and capabilities it otherwise might not have and which would be costly to develop internally. The coordination of partnerships, especially international partnerships, is not easy, since it often involves deep cultural differences.

Nor are all network arrangements equally flexible. Belussi (1993) demonstrates that Benetton is a classic Fordist firm, with hierarchical relationships with its subcontractors, in a manner similar to Japanese *keiretsu*. In contrast, strategic alliances are flexible in a different way, since they need not be permanent, and past relationships can be re-formed if the situation calls for it (Bartlett and Ghoshal 1995: 382). Network links of this sort are *dynamic*, rather than static. More importantly, alliances – as a form of network link, rather than an internal structure – take on different forms and evolve to take on characteristics made necessary as the relationship evolves over time (Garrette and Quelin 1994; Håkansson 1992; Kanter 1994).

Patterns of transnational investment

The product cycle model suggests that the early overseas activities of most firms are predominantly mature technologies or resource-based investments. The largest overseas investments based in less-developed countries in the 1970s and early 1980s were from Brazil, Hong Kong, Singapore, South Korea, Taiwan, Argentina, Mexico, Venezuela and India. Many of the overseas investments were for resource-related purposes by state-owned oil firms, others for appropriate technology ('tropical technology') better suited to other developing countries, and others simply for first-mover advantages in a particular location (Lall 1983; Wells 1988). These 'third-world multinationals' tended, more than advanced-country TNCs, to form joint ventures with local firms and to gain access to high technology by taking equity shares in firms in developed countries (Lall 1983). Hong Kong investments still tend to be in finance, insurance, hotels and other property-related sectors (Mitchell 1995; Yeung 1994b).

As wages have risen and corporate capabilities have grown, firms based in the NICs found it necessary to expand abroad. Prior to the mid-1980s, Japan was the principal source of intra-regional investment in Asia, with the beginnings of Hong Kong investment in the special economic zones (SEZs) of Guangdong province in China and early Korean investment in Indonesia and Malaysia. The decade beginning in the mid-1980s produced an outpouring of investment throughout Asia, much of it directed toward China, but also to the ASEAN–4 and Vietnam (Alvstam 1995). Korean *chaebol*, or large conglomerates, have made widespread investments in manufacturing plants and R&D centres since the mid-1980s, in both developed and developing countries, through joint ventures as well as wholly owned operations (Jun 1995; Lee 1995). Korean firms' garment manufacturing plants in Bangladesh and Guatemala have brought modern production methods and technology with them (Petersen 1994; Rhee 1990). Little foreign investment by Korean firms, on the other hand, has gone to Australia, beyond those for traditional resource- and market-based purposes (Waitt 1994).

In China, foreign investment from 1981 to 1992, originating from 40 countries, surpassed that to any other country (UNCTAD 1994). Since 1993, FDI in China has accounted for over 50 per cent of the total invested in developing countries. China's 1993 FDI of US$33.8 billion overshadowed that in second-ranked Malaysia (US$4.3 billion) (World Bank 1996a). Most (66 per cent) of the investment into China came from Hong Kong, supplementing vast subcontracting networks in southern China. Japan, the second largest foreign investment source in Guangdong, accounts for an additional 16 per cent of the total. Foreign investors dominate the Shenzhen region of that province, nearest to Hong Kong; 53 per cent of industrial production is by firms from outside China (Leung 1996). A great deal of foreign investment is by overseas Chinese family firms through Hong Kong, Macau or Taiwan, utilizing pre-existing social ties and partnerships with state-owned enterprises (Eng and Lin 1996).

In Mexico, assembly plants called *maquiladoras* are the typical form of foreign investment. The earliest of these were part of 'twin plants' located on each side of the Mexico–USA border, with labour-intensive operations on the low-wage Mexican side of the border (Grunwald 1985). The border industrialization programme began in 1965, but was expanded in 1982 to become a mainstay of the country's export-oriented development strategy (Wilson 1992). By 1968, 79 plants were reported; in 1988, nearly 1400 manufacturers were assembling products, mainly for export markets outside Mexico (South 1990). In addition to those along the border, nearly 20 per cent of new plants are in interior locations (Wilson 1992: 47). *Maquiladoras* are also common throughout Central America and the Caribbean (Bonacich *et al.* 1994).

A great deal of offshore production has gravitated to export processing zones (EPZs), which are intended to attract TNC investment in labour-intensive operations. The first wave of EPZs was established during the 1970s and early 1980s mainly in the NICs, China, Mauritius and the Philippines, followed by a second wave in lower-cost countries, such as China, the Dominican Republic, Guatemala, Mexico, Sri Lanka and Tunisia. These second-wave zones have grown largely as a result of the relocation of manufacturing from the NICs by new TNCs based in them. The world total in 1990 was 173 EPZs (UNCTAD 1994: 190); Table 6.7 shows the leading EPZs in the early 1990s. The firms attracted to EPZs are, with the exception of large TNCs in electronics, more likely to be small and medium-sized firms (UNCTAD 1994: 191).

A division of labour is plainly evident in much investment, pioneered in Asia

Table 6.7 Employment in export processing zones or other special zones in developing countries, 1990 (or latest year).

Country	Number of employees in zones	Number of zones
China	2 200 000	7
Mexico	460 000	23
Puerto Rico	155 000	2
Dominican Republic	150 000	18
Brazil	137 000	1
Malaysia	98 900	10
Mauritius	90 000	7
Sri Lanka	71 358	2
Taiwan	70 700	3
Macao	60 000	4
Guatemala	55 000	1
Philippines	43 211	5
Haiti	43 000	2
India	30 000	6
Thailand	27 990	1
Egypt	25 000	1
Korea	21 910	2
Barbados	20 000	
Jamaica	18 000	4
Botswana	13 000	1

Source: adapted from UNCTAD (1994: 190, Table IV.11).

by Japanese outward investment beginning in the late 1960s, when mostly small firms relocated labour-intensive production to the NICs. Firms in the NICs later followed Japan's example. Hong Kong investors in large numbers moved labour-intensive activities into China's Guangdong province in order to exploit much lower labour costs (Lau and Chan 1994; Leung 1996). Similarly, Singapore firms have initiated a 'growth triangle' in order to move labour- and land-intensive operations to neighbouring Johor in Malaysia and the Riau Islands of Indonesia (Ho 1994; Thant, Tang and Kakazu 1994; Parsonage 1992). This growth triangle and others in Asia, including the Greater South China zone and the Yellow Sea zone, incorporate a division of labour and segmentation of production (Rimmer 1994; van Grunsven, Wong and Kim 1995). The product cycle logic is evident in the investments which have left Hong Kong (plastic goods and simple consumer electronics) compared with those which have remained in Hong Kong: products that require more skill in manufacturing or marketing, such as toys, fashion garments and watches (Lall 1983). By the 1990s, even these had moved northward into Chinese factories (Chiu and Levin 1995: 159).

Japanese firms, taking advantage of the lower labour costs in neighbouring Asian nations, had spread their production networks throughout much of Asia by the 1990s. Japanese electronics firms, for example, produce in all three zones of the Triad, but concentrate their investments in Asia. Of 840 companies producing in 41 countries throughout the world, 492 firms (58.6 per cent) are in the Pacific Rim, while 170 firms (20.2 per cent) are in North America and 136 firms (16.2 per cent) are in Europe. Japanese plants in Asia, both in the four NICs and in the ASEAN–4 (Indonesia, Malaysia, the Philippines and Thailand), produce more mature products than those produced in Japan, in line with the product cycle hypothesis and its 'flying geese' counterpart (Hill and Fujita 1996; Hill and Lee 1994). The time lag between production in Japan and the transfer of production to other countries in Asia has decreased, in response to both labour shortages and differences in relative wage levels (Hayashi 1994; Hiramoto 1995). Although set up initially as low-cost production locations, research and design activities are being transferred mainly to Singapore and Malaysia, but also to a lesser extent to South Korea and Thailand. Singapore has become an important information centre and regional headquarters location for Japanese electronics firms (Baba and Hatashima 1995). Recent Japanese investment in Asia (especially Indonesia, Malaysia, Singapore and Thailand) has involved large investments in automatic machines and robots in response to shortages of skilled labour. These are likely to prevent the transfer of higher levels of technology, including moulds and tools, design, and new product and equipment development (Yamashita 1995).

World cities

The location of economic activity in a global economy necessarily concentrates activities in major cities and, in effect, determines which cities are 'major'. The emergence of corporate networks in global production systems are coordinated from a relatively small set of *world cities* or *global cities*. Financial services, including banks and other financial institutions, have located, and added other services, in global cities in response to the needs of their major clients, the TNCs (Dicken 1992).

World cities or global cities are (1) command points in the organization of the world economy, where transnational firms place their management functions; (2) key locations and markets for leading industries, especially finance and advanced producer services; and (3) major sites of production for these sectors, including production of innovations (Sassen 1994: 4). The new hierarchy of cities, however, leaves most others – including most old industrial centres and port cities – largely without influence in the world economy (Friedmann 1986; Friedmann and Wolff 1982; Sassen 1994).

The world city phenomenon has been an object of research for only a decade, and changes in city status are already evident (J. Friedmann 1995). It is generally agreed that London, New York and Tokyo stand alone as the pre-eminent world cities, where the bulk of capital and control resides (Sassen 1991, 1994). Beneath them is a hierarchy of second-order financial and business centres, many of which have been financial centres for centuries, such as Amsterdam and Zurich, while others are gateways to major markets, as Hong Kong is to China. These centres link core economies to each other and to the leading three cities.

Table 6.8 The hierarchy of world cities.

Global financial centres	London	New York	Tokyo
Multinational centres	Frankfurt	Miami	Singapore
	Amsterdam	Los Angeles	
Important national centres	Paris	Mexico City	Seoul
	Zurich	São Paulo	Sydney
	Madrid		
Regional centres	Milan	Boston	Hong Kong
	Lyon	Chicago	Osaka–Kobe
	Barcelona	Houston	Shanghai
	Munich	Seattle	
	Düsseldorf–Cologne–Essen–	Toronto	
	Dortmund (Rhine–Ruhr	Montreal	
	region)	Vancouver	

Source: based on Friedmann (1995: 24–7 and Table 2.1).

The spatial arrangement of Friedmann's hierarchy of world cities contains the three distinct subsystems identifiable as the Triad structure (Table 6.8). Friedmann (1986) linked Africa into the European subsystem via Johannesburg, but has removed it in his recent hierarchy (J. Friedmann 1995). Simon (1995) suggests Cairo, Johannesburg and Nairobi as the nearest to world city status but not fully meeting that status owing to Africa's peripheral position in the world economy. Some core cities, such as Detroit, Honolulu, Miami and Mecca, are perhaps 'limited-service global cities' that are clearly important in one, but not all, dimensions of world city status (Nijman 1996; Thompson 1995). Cities can move up and down in the world city hierarchy, adding (or losing) essential global functions (Abbott 1996; J. Friedmann 1995; Warner 1994).

The global control functions which concentrate in world cities, supplemented by high technology and producer services and linked by telecommunications, are perhaps embedded not in a region or nation, but only in a 'space of flows' that makes it increasingly difficult for nation-states to regulate in any way (Castells 1989; Sassen 1995a,b). Physical infrastructure and amenities characterize world cities and their office-based functions, and air connections as well as IT link these cities at the highest levels of connectivity (Keeling 1995; Shachar 1995a). Flows of people, material and information form the economic, political and cultural links between world cities (Shachar 1995b; Smith and Timberlake 1995a,b). But financial activities and financial flows are perhaps the most difficult to regulate (Sassen 1995b; Warf 1995). The major international financial and business centres are also the major 'innovation poles' for R&D activities. It is in these centres that access to information networks is highest, telecommunications links are best, producer services are most available, and labour resources are most readily found (Casson 1991; Lipietz 1993;

Moulaert and Tödtling 1995; Tödtling 1994). In short, world cities provide access to global networks and, therefore, are preferred locations for global firms.

The significance of the world city concept is threefold. First, it captures the notion of an urban hierarchy, long a central concept in central place theory. Second, it includes the important flows within the network of global cities – not only up and down the hierarchy, but horizontally between functionally specialized cities (Camagni and Salone 1992). Third, it emphasizes the importance of large cities, whose essence comes from the need for face-to-face contact and their position as important nodes in global information networks (Moulaert and Djellal 1995; Parker 1995).

Production chains and global production

International production and sourcing reflects the integration of the value chain (Chapter 3) into a 'global factory' in manufacturing (Grunwald and Flamm 1985) and incorporating marketing, distribution and service (Dicken 1992). Since production steps can be separated, it is common for the sourcing of labour-intensive components and stages of production to be from low-wage countries, especially for products that are subject to intense price competition (Carillo Gamboa 1988; Levy and Dunning 1993: 21). Called *production chains* or *commodity chains*, the global structure of production incorporates elements of core–periphery relationships (Chapter 1) within the framework of TNCs and their networks of production relationships (Korzeniewicz and Martin 1994). FDI flows still take place largely between developed countries of the Triad. In 1993, inflows to Triad countries accounted for 62 per cent of all new FDI (UNCTAD 1995a: 3–12). These accumulated foreign investments have been mainly in high-technology sectors, where foreign enterprises account for a large share of production in several countries (Table 6.9). The Japanese economy is the least penetrated by foreign firms: only the chemical industry has a significant share (11 per cent) of production. In Canada and Europe, on the other hand, foreign firms account for over 50 per cent of production in motor vehicles, chemicals and computers.

Offshore manufacturing for European, Japanese and US markets takes place in three sets of locations:

1. Asian NICs, increasingly specialized in semi-skilled and skilled production of relatively sophisticated components;
2. a set of very low-wage countries, including China, Indonesia and Pakistan, which have taken over the role formerly played by the NICs as platforms for the most unskilled, labour-intensive assembly tasks, such as for apparel, shoes and toys; and
3. Mexico, which is unique in its low wages, high level of capabilities, and proximity to the large US market (Levy and Dunning 1993: 21–2).

Product differentiation, market orientation and flexible production favour industrial countries, to the detriment of low-wage locations (Schoenberger 1988). The agglomeration tendency is not complete, however, since markets largely drive the new strategies. Within the Third World, therefore, countries

Table 6.9 Leading sectors in share of production by foreign enterprises in selected countries.

Country	Leading production sectors by foreign enterprises	
Canada	Motor vehicles (85%)	Non-metallic products (55%)
France	Computers (71%)	Electronics (33%)
Germany	Computers (78%)	Food and beverages (21%)
Italy	Computers (63%)	Chemicals (30%)
Japan	Chemicals (11%)	Basic metals (1%)
UK	Computers (65%)	Chemicals (37%)
USA	Other manufacturing (30%)	Chemicals (27%)
	Chemicals (76%)	
	Chemicals (45%)	
	Chemicals (39%)	
	Electronics (55%)	
	Machinery and equipment (2%)	
	Motor vehicles (56%)	
	Non-metallic products (29%)	

Source: based on Papaconstantinou (1995: 219, Table 14).

which attract foreign investment are more often large markets, such as Mexico and Brazil, than sources of cheap labour (Hoffman and Kaplinsky 1988; Sayer and Morgan 1987).

Sectoral examples

It is useful to examine more closely a small number of individual industrial sectors. Each industry has its own inputs, customers, constraints and, indeed, its own culture. We look here at four sectors: aerospace, motor vehicles, footwear and clothing. These provide a diversity of characteristics which, together, illustrate that sectors are different and benefit from separate examination.

Aerospace

The aircraft or aerospace industry is 'the archetypical knowledge-intensive sector' (Samuels 1994: 278). It also has a potential for linkages and spillovers to other sectors which few other industries can match. As large systems comprising sophisticated components and subsystems, aircraft utilize several technologies, including safety and reliability, materials, aerodynamics, engines, electronics and, most importantly, systems integration to pull them all together. Military jet fighter aircraft embody even higher levels of technological sophistication (Samuels and Whipple 1989). Consequently, there are few firms worldwide in aerospace production, and these are located in the advanced economies: the USA, the UK, France, Germany, Australia, Belgium, Canada, Japan, Italy, the Netherlands, Sweden, Switzerland and Spain (Eriksson 1995; Todd and Simpson 1986).

The most significant feature of world aerospace production today is production-sharing and subcontracting. These are a result both of requirements to 'offset' costly purchases of aircraft and of pressures to find lower-cost sources of components to bring down costs (Todd 1992). By requiring that some portion of production take place within the country, technological capability can be acquired by local firms in the purchasing country (Fong and Hill 1992; Mowery and Rosenberg 1989: 194–7). Most of the world's aircraft designs and technologies derive from those of US or Soviet aircraft. China shifted during the 1970s from Soviet to Boeing designs. Outside the advanced countries, military aircraft capability was found in 18 NICs and developing countries. Of these, Argentina, Brazil (jointly with Italy), Israel, India and Taiwan had indigenous designs of either jet fighters or other military aircraft; all other countries produced under licence from other sources (Todd and Simpson 1986). On the whole, this short list of countries is a consequence of the critical dependence of the industry on access to plentiful supplies of both professional engineers and skilled production workers (Todd 1992).

Although military aircraft are assembled in many countries, usually as offset deals for purchases, very few countries have the capabilities to design, develop and produce entire commercial airliners; three firms (Boeing, Airbus and McDonnell Douglas) divide the world market. The largest and most profitable firm, Boeing, holds over half the world market. However, large portions – even

the majority – of an airframe are produced outside the country of final production. For example, for the 757 and 767 models, Boeing has major subcontracts
with 22 firms in 11 countries outside the USA, where it also has a large group
of suppliers and subcontractors (Eriksson 1995: 113–16).

The webs of collaborative agreements are to the advantage of the large producers. Subcontractors and alliance partners share in the cost of development of
new designs, reducing the very large costs of new airplane development.
Consequently, the aerospace sector has one of the most dense networks of strategic technology partnering (Hagedoorn 1995). Most collaborations in aerospace
during the 1980s (87 per cent) were within the Triad; only 13 per cent of the
production-sharing arrangements with developing countries were sufficiently
two-sided to be considered collaboration. Collaborations focus on technology
and cutting-edge research as much as market-driven partnerships (Anderson
1995). Technology transfer, while not often included within the strategy and
management of firms, is taking on an increasingly important role (Cusumano
and Elenkov 1994; Granstrand and Sjölander 1990).

For several reasons, including prestige and national pride, concern for
technological capability, and the leakage of large expenditures on imports,
European governments and their national or quasi-national aircraft makers have
cooperated quite strongly on aircraft design and construction at least since the
1960s. This culminated in a determined effort to challenge Boeing and its US
counterparts: the Airbus consortium, established in 1969 by Aerospatiale
(France), Deutsche Aerospace (Germany) and British Aerospace (UK), joined by
CASA (Spain) in 1972 (Eriksson 1995). This consortium, together with associ-
ates in Belgium and the Netherlands, has succeeded in producing several models
of commercial jet aircraft incorporating innovative design features, notably fly-
by-wire technology, which permitted a two-person (rather than the traditional
three-person) cockpit crew. Airbus is now the world's second-largest civil airframe
manufacturer, having surpassed McDonnell Douglas (Thornton 1995).

Increasingly, international subcontracting or production-sharing in aircraft is
taking place in Asia. Licensed manufacture typically involves older designs. Co-
production is a form of production on aircraft currently being sold and used. It
is considered an especially high form of technology transfer, wherein the recipient (usually also a firm in the customer nation) stands to gain access to advanced
aerospace technology (Todd and Simpson 1986). Japanese firms, beginning in
the 1950s, followed by firms from Taiwan in the late 1960s and South Korea in
the 1970s, have been heavily involved in the licensed production of US military
aircraft (Todd and Simpson 1986).

State involvement in national firms and in negotiations with foreign producers does much to shape the nature of aerospace competition and technological
learning within countries without full aerospace sectors. Infant-industry policies
and specialized knowledge have made some producers key players in the production of many models of aircraft (Eriksson 1995; Todd and Simpson 1986).
Korean producers Daewoo, Samsung and Korean Air have subcontracting
links with Boeing and several other aircraft firms. Only Chinese enterprises
encompass so large an array of subcontracting links. Chinese enterprises are

subcontractors to Boeing, McDonnell Douglas and several Airbus consortium partners for commercial jetliners, as well as to Canadair, Lockheed and Sikorsky for helicopters and turboprop aircraft. In India, Hindustan Aircraft Ltd (HAL) has also begun to engage in international subcontracting work in Bangalore, mainly as offset for purchase of British military aircraft in the mid-1980s and later as offset for purchases of Airbus planes. Indonesia has had a determined policy to develop technological capability in aerospace, negotiating for local production of 30–35 per cent of the cost of jet purchases (Fong and Hill 1992: 242). Indonesia has obtained technology from Spain, Germany and France and has ambitious plans to produce several commercial aircraft, including jets. Despite the accumulation of technological capabilities in aerospace in many parts of Asia, there is little intra-Asian cooperation and no intra-regional subcontracting links (Eriksson 1995: 209).

The potential of technology transfer in aerospace is large. Japanese firms since the 1950s have been able to absorb, master and modify a number of technologies central to military aerospace, but also with 'spin-on' capability to other sectors. Domestic content within Japan was as high as 75–80 per cent on some planes, which is much higher than in most countries. Cooperative interaction between competing firms allowed horizontal transfer of technology. Moreover, the fact that the subcontractors are parts of large corporations and *keiretsu*, including Misubishi, Fuji and Kawasaki, also provided opportunities for vertical transfer within these organizations (Samuels 1994). The tree metaphor – the aerospace industry as the trunk of a tree with roots in basic technologies and fruits in many industrial and consumer product lines (Chapter 3) – represents 'how the Japanese understand linkages across industries and the consequent strategic value of aerospace in particular' (Samuels 1994: 245). These Japanese firms are co-developing the Boeing 777, participating in the plane's design rather than 'simply bending metal to spec' (Samuels 1994: 255). Tremendous political controversy has surrounded Japanese–US co-development of the FS-X fighter, for which Mitsubishi Heavy Industries is the prime contractor. Opponents in the USA believed that it was giving away 'the keys to the kingdom' (e.g. software source codes, radar technologies). The Japanese firms, particularly Mitsubishi, are gaining experience in systems integration skills on a state-of-the-art project that are applicable in other aerospace areas (GAO 1995; Ó Tuathail 1992; Shear 1994).

Other Asian countries, notably Indonesia, have ambitious plans in aerospace, but have not accumulated the wide and deep capabilities found in Japan. The Brazilian firm Embraer has focused on small turboprop aircraft and has developed considerable indigenous design capability. However, on the whole, in contrast to the product cycle, aircraft production remains controlled from the innovative regions where it began, adding new locations of production that remain dependent on links to advanced-country producers (Todd 1992).

Motor vehicles

The motor vehicle industry, which now includes along with cars pick-up trucks, utility vehicles and minivans, was among the earliest to become transnational.

Before 1930, Ford had established subsidiaries to assemble vehicles from kits in 20 countries, a pattern imitated by other car manufacturers. Since 1970, product differentiation into hundreds of models and new production techniques originating mainly in Japan have raised the threshold of technical sophistication for entering the industry. Consequently, few new manufacturers have entered the industry, and nearly all of them, including the Korean firms Hyundai, Daewoo and Kia, are based on technology from established firms in Europe, Japan or the USA. Although the industry is not very high-tech, it has incorporated many new technologies (e.g. electronics) and new materials (e.g. plastics and ceramics) that remain beyond the capability of many economies (Oman 1989).

In 1976, nearly 88 per cent of all production of motor vehicles was found in developed market economies, especially the four leading countries: the USA (29.9 per cent), Japan (20.4 per cent), West Germany (10.1 per cent), and France (10.0 per cent). This location pattern had not changed greatly from that in 1967 (Lall 1980). By 1990, however, the industry was in 'permanent turbulence' (O'Brien 1992: 54). The three Triad regions had an even larger share of world production (93.9 per cent) than in 1970 (91.7 per cent). This production was dominated by 11 firms, each producing more than 1 million units, which together accounted for three-quarters of the world total of 45.7 million units. Only a few of these firms, however, had internationalized production to a significant degree. Toyota remained in 1990 'still astonishingly linked with its home base' in Japan, where 96.4 per cent of its output was manufactured (O'Brien 1992: 57). Ford, General Motors and Volkswagen were the most internationalized firms, with 57.4, 38.1 and 34.6 per cent of production in foreign countries (excluding licensed production and other non-equity links). Spain, for example, has attracted production facilities of Volkswagen, Renault and Peugeot, as well as more recently Ford and General Motors, both through acquisitions and on greenfield sites, resulting in a marked increase in the degree of external control of its auto industry (Lagendijk and van der Knaap 1995a; O'Brien 1992).

As in most industries, a central distinction exists between countries which are fully fledged producers of vehicles and those which assemble them using imported components, if not completely knocked-down kits (Dicken 1992: 271; Oman 1989). A car industry is a prestigious sector for many countries attempting to move upward on the development ladder, so some vehicle output is recorded in 44 developing countries (Oman 1989: 204–5). However, most remain virtually entirely dependent on foreign technology (Hill and Lee 1994). Recent investments by several car TNCs, such as Daewoo, Ford and Peugeot, in India have shifted from importing kits for assembly to developing complete manufacturing operations, including parts operations. However, experience has shown these firms that, even with the local partners which they all have, locally produced parts are unreliable, forcing car manufacturers to develop joint ventures between their global suppliers and Indian companies (Kripalani 1996).

Auto industry experts traditionally use an income level of US$2000–2500 as the threshold for local demand (O'Brien 1992: 59). Thus, production in China, which reached 370 000 cars in 1995, was mainly for government rather than household consumption (The Economist 1996g). Much of the production in developing countries, therefore, is intended for export. The growth of Mexico and of Eastern Europe as production locations combines local market demand with the attraction of low labour costs (O'Brien 1992).

Within East Asia, a stratified division of labour has evolved in the auto industry, maintaining dependence in the NICs and ASEAN countries on Japanese technology and components (Hill and Lee 1994). Korean firms, such as Hyundai and Daewoo, have been most successful in developing an export car industry beginning with assembly from knocked-down kits. These firms all use technology from US and Japanese firms (Kim and Lee 1994). Ties to US producers have been the route to exports in North America for Daewoo and Kia, but Hyundai persevered to develop its own marketing network. To a large degree, Korean automakers utilize Japanese technology, Korean capital, and North American markets (Lee and Cason 1994). They also have begun to make greater inroads into Europe. Thailand has become the third-largest Asian vehicle producer, after Japan and Korea, but as a branch-plant centre. Its market is attractive, and it is the second-largest market for pick-up trucks after the USA. Its 15 assembly plants are served by 350 parts suppliers, many of them Japanese transplants (*International Herald Tribune* 1996).

Mexico is another country whose role as an assembly site in the world motor vehicle industry grew rapidly during the 1980s. Ford has assembled cars in Mexico since 1925, followed by others serving the domestic market. Production for export began in earnest during the 1980s, following a series of government decrees and incentives for full production and local content. Plants were located in central locations as well as in *maquiladoras* along the Mexico–USA border. Production now includes engines and parts as well as complete cars and trucks, mainly in very modern facilities with robots and other highly automated equipment (Baker, Woodruff and Weiner 1992; Moreno Brid 1992; Truett and Truett 1994). Firms in Mexico now include Nissan, Renault and Volkswagen, in addition to Ford, General Motors and Chrysler (Moreno Brid 1992). As in most developing countries, much of the production involves assembly of imported parts because of the lack of competitive quality and cost among local suppliers (Truett and Truett 1994).

Footwear

The footwear (or shoe) industry has attracted a great deal of research interest as well as investment. Athletic shoes, or sport shoes, in particular, tripled in a decade to become a US$11.6 billion industry in 1992. Two firms, Nike and Reebok, alone accounted for 52 per cent of the US market in 1993. South Korea, and specifically the southern port of Pusan, became during the 1980s the 'sneaker capital of the world', in recognition of its place in the production of 11 major brands of shoes and 68.8 per cent of all US sport shoe imports in 1988. Just four years later, this percentage had dropped to 27.2 per cent, in response to rising labour costs (Lim 1994; Rosenzweig 1995). This was the result not of capricious decisions by US TNCs, but because of the development of some Korean and Taiwanese firms into first-tier 'developed partners' of Nike, the largest firm (Donaghu and Barff 1990). Nike, based in the USA, is a quintessential network firm, undertaking no manufacturing itself but subcontracting throughout Asia in a determined policy to retain control over design and marketing (Korzeniewicz 1994). Nearly all shoe production by Nike , Reebok and other firms for the US market now takes place in Asia (Barff and Austen 1993; Donaghu and Barff 1990; Rosenzweig 1995).

Production of simpler, low-value shoes shifted rapidly to Indonesia and to China from 1988 to 1992, with the benefit of guarantees by Nike if operations moved to lower-wage countries (Rosenzweig 1995). However, newer, higher-priced styles remain largely in Korea and Taiwan (Table 6.10). The Korean plants are able to respond within 45 days to orders for niche markets as small as 5000 pairs, compared with 90 days and minimum orders of 20000 pairs from China (Lim 1994: 574). As with the earlier footwear agglomeration in Pusan, the Chinese city of Putian, in Fujian province, has become the major site within China for production of athletic shoes. Investment there has come from 'developed production partners' in Hong Kong, South Korea and Taiwan; raw materials, equipment and management come from Taiwan, through Hong Kong, and South Korea. Orders from the USA from Nike and other producers are channelled to plants in Fujian (Chen 1994; Lim 1994).

While Taiwanese shoe production moved to China, the greatest amount of overseas investment in shoe production by Korean firms has gone to Indonesia (Rosenzweig 1995). In 1992, 67 of 121 overseas athletic shoe production lines by Korean firms were in Indonesia, followed by 31 in China and six in Thailand (Lim 1994: 577). Labour costs are the only significant cost difference between production in South Korea and in Indonesia, but it is a large difference: US$6.90 versus US$2.00, respectively, in 1991 (Lim 1994: 571).

Some US shoe producers subcontract only the labour-intensive stitched upper portion of the shoes to overseas plants in South Korea and Mexico in an attempt to avoid tariffs imposed on imports of full shoes (Barff and Austen 1993). Similar production chains operate in other types of footwear as well (Gereffi and Korzeniewicz 1990).

Clothing production
Clothing production was among the first sectors to take advantage of the new international division of labour (Fröbel, Heinrichs and Kreye 1980), and it

Table 6.10   Location of production of athletic shoes, in percentage of market share, 1988–92.

Country	Production		Price range of shoes produced 1992		
	1988	1992	Less than $8	$8–$16	More than $16
Korea	68.8	27.2	7.2	22.4	53.0
Taiwan	20.4	7.5	1.4	3.2	22.5
Indonesia	0.9	21.9	35.8	25.0	3.5
China	1.6	31.5	42.4	35.2	14.4
Thailand	4.3	8.9	10.9	10.6	3.3

Source: adapted from Lim (1994: 570, Tables 4 and 5).

continues to follow this pattern (van Geenhuizen and van der Knaap 1994). It has also been one of the most prolific users of new forms of investment, such as subcontracting and licensing arrangements. The low-skill and labour-intensive nature of clothing assembly, which is mainly sewing, has led to its almost ubiquitous spread throughout the world. In addition, the low cost of much clothing means that searching for lower wage levels drives a significant portion of the location of this industry. At the same time, branded clothing, fashion items and sportswear add price-inelastic goods to the picture (Oman 1989).

For many years, garment producers have relied on low-wage labour, primarily in Asia, to produce standard, low-cost clothing for industrialized markets in North America and Europe. As a set of standardized products which have large-volume sales through mass merchandisers and chain department stores, clothing manufacture (particularly assembly and sewing, often of pre-cut fabric components) was especially well-suited to low-wage locations, such as Asia and countries of the Caribbean. Thus, for many countries, including the NICs, clothing production was an early entry into production for export. As a low-skill sector, it was later dropped from domestic production in favour of higher-skill sectors, and firms used their accumulated knowledge to set up factories in other, lower-wage locations (Oman 1989; Rohwer 1995).

In addition to the importance of labour costs, the apparel or clothing industry also benefits greatly from faster turnaround in production. The clothing industry, like motor vehicles, has become more concerned with fashion, lead times, inventories, and linkages with retailers. The wholesale cost comparison between a domestically produced dress and an imported one leans in favour of imports, largely because of labour costs running 50 per cent or more below those in the USA, costs counterbalanced to some degree by shipping, duty and related charges. Increasingly, however, lead times (orders must be placed with sub-contractors months in advance) and speed of delivery are important, allowing retailers to charge prices that remain stable without markdowns or discounts for fashionable goods (Weiner, Foust and Yang 1988).

This trade-off between speed and low costs has long been present in clothing production (Steed 1981), but its significance has grown along with the importance of frequent style changes. The retailer Laura Ashley received only 65 per cent of its merchandise on time in 1991, resulting in substantial losses as out-of-season fashions arrived late at stores, no longer able to command full price. Manufacturers that have electronic data-processing links to major retailers can fill orders in as little as two days, and generally in less than a month for any item, compared with three to four months from plants in the Caribbean (for the US market) and longer from Asia, which is the major supply region for both the US and Western Europe. Thus, the return of clothing production to Britain and the USA is the industry's response to shorter product life-cycles, niche marketing, and demands for flexible relations with suppliers (Chapter 4) (Gibbs 1987, 1988; Weiner, Foust, and Yang 1988). To some extent, however, the ability of high-income countries to retain domestic clothing production has depended on the presence of underground activities in large cities that 'act as surrogate developing countries slowing down the shift' of labour-intensive production offshore

(Portes, Castells and Benton 1989; Spinanger 1992: 92). Emphasizing flexibility from inter-firm relations, Benetton has organized a pyramid of subcontractors and suppliers similar to the Japanese *keiretsu* but with strict control over prices and schedules (Belussi 1993; Fornengo Pent 1992).

'Lean retailing' strategies put great pressure on clothing manufacturers to adopt information systems, order fulfilment and distribution practices, and related services that enable them to fill retailers' orders rapidly, efficiently and flexibly. This ultimately shifts the burden of risk onto the manufacturers with regard to inventory (Abernathy *et al.* 1995). A five-day delay between order and domestic production can send retailers to another producer (Keen and Cummins 1994: 337). The process of creating samples in Asia for fashion clothing in North America previously meant several iterations of air freight shipments and one to two weeks lead time. Satellite communications to send and revise images of garments cuts this to one or two days, and CAD files transmit designs that detail individual stitches (Keen and Cummins 1994: 401–2). Firms in Hong Kong have been especially aggressive in enhancing their flexibility for the US, German and British markets (Chiu and Levin 1995). Outsourcing logistics operations to specialist firms can also better coordinate worldwide shipments of raw materials and manufactured goods (Keen and Cummins 1994: 634–5).

One result is a hierarchy of sources of global clothing production. Fashion-oriented and high-value 'designer' garments are still produced in France, Italy, Japan, the UK and the USA (Appelbaum, Smith and Christerson 1994). Quality brand clothing tends to come from the most established exporters, including Hong Kong, South Korea, Singapore and Taiwan. A third tier of producing nations provide lower-cost products for mass merchandise retailers: Brazil, China, Egypt, India, Indonesia, Mexico, the Philippines, Thailand and Turkey. Large-volume discount stores prefer the most inexpensive products, imported from a fourth tier of low-cost suppliers: Bangladesh, Central America, China, Mauritius, Oman, Sri Lanka and others. A fifth tier of producers is being developed as new, lower-cost sources of supply, including Cyprus, Lesotho, Madagascar, Burma (Myanmar) and Vietnam. Much of this production in the lower-tier locations is done through 'triangle manufacturing', in which an established exporter from Hong Kong or Taiwan shifts production to a lower-cost country, providing a retailer access to these locations through the NIC producers' social networks (Gereffi 1994). In addition to Asia, locations in Central America and the Caribbean also attract investment aimed at the US market (Bonacich and Waller 1994). By contrast, wealthy consuming countries are faced with declining employment in clothing production (Dicken 1992).

Technological change is more difficult to effect in clothing than in the related textiles industry, largely because of the complexity of sizes, fabrics and styles on ever-smaller production volumes (Dicken 1992; Hoffman and Rush 1988). Where it is being put into place, and even where it is not, low-wage countries are somewhat less appealing locations than previously. Pre-assembly tasks, such as marking and cutting, are those being automated most, shortening the time required from design to assembly. Being able to reduce the lead time provides the jump on competitors – and profitability – which innovation and fashion traditionally have provided. Innovations in sewing have been common primarily only among the largest firms, and along with the pressure to shorten lead times, promise to make even clothing production (long a low-tech entry point for low-wage countries) an industry increasingly found in developed countries and wealthy NICs (Hoffman and Rush 1988; Mody and Wheeler 1987). Clearly, trade restrictions have played a role in this predicament, and will continue to affect the competitiveness of poor countries in this and other industries (Dicken 1992: 254–7; Hoffman and Rush 1988: 192–205).

Linkages: subcontracting, partnerships and alliances

What is the developmental potential of a facility of a TNC? The conventional list of benefits includes capital, technology, managerial skills and access to export markets, as well as jobs, income and local linkages. For developing countries, the principal attraction of TNCs is their ability to provide jobs for rapidly growing populations. The entry of TNCs with higher-quality branded products may threaten local producers, but it also stimulates them to meet global standards (Jordan 1996b). Although critics maintain that TNCs bring only limited quantities of these benefits, neoconventional responses and analyses show that, with the exception of technology transfer, TNCs have beneficial effects (Biersteker 1978). 'FDI reshapes economies and societies far out of proportion to its nominal value' by bringing management and marketing knowledge as well as jobs (Rohwer 1995: 103). Because of the importance of technology and the tension in the power relationship between TNCs and nation-states, the bargaining relationship between them is complex and dynamic, shifting over time. As localities within nation-states increasingly attempt to attract FDI, it is the TNC that holds the power in an asymmetric relationship (Dicken 1994). Attraction of inward FDI and of linkages in production sourcing are considered counterbalances to the increasing level of outward investment by a country's firms in search of competitiveness (Papaconstantinou 1995).

Sklair (1994: 168–9) suggests that six criteria 'serve as a rough guide' to the positive development effects of TNCs:

1. linkages (backward and forward);
2. foreign currency earnings, reflecting higher added value retained in the host economy;
3. upgrading of personnel, including managers, technicians and skilled personnel;
4. technology transfer ('genuine' technology, as opposed to 'mere "technology relocation"');
5. conditions of work (relative to those in the rest of the host society); and
6. environmental impacts.

It is on technology, as the driver of development potential, that attention has tended to focus, in both advanced and developing countries (Dicken 1986; Farrell 1979; Germidis 1977; Young, Hood and Dunlop 1988). Most of the regional or local effect of any economic activity is a result of its larger effect beyond employment alone. Structural issues, such as technological (and, therefore, job and labour) sophistication and linkages with local suppliers, are more important long-term concerns than mere growth-related employment. As Dicken (1992: 409) puts it, 'the major need is to avoid *technological dependence*, because it is technology which is the seed corn of future economic development.'

In advanced countries, the impact of a TNC is scrutinized carefully. In Ireland, for example, branch plants of TNCs exhibit 'good' manufacturing features, such as exports, high-tech sectors and high levels of worker skills, in contrast to local firms, which tend to be small, low-tech, and to do minimal exporting (Foley and Griffith 1992). Similarly, Hughes (1993) finds that foreign firms in the UK are more efficient, more profitable, and pay their workers higher wages. Increasingly, developing countries also evaluate technological potential. China sees FDI and joint ventures as an opportunity to learn foreign technology and more subtle requirements such as product quality (Hamilton 1995).

Low levels of R&D on the part of TNCs have produced a long-standing interest in creating an indigenous technological capability in the Third World (Fuenzalida 1979), but it takes time for foreign technology to develop into local capability. A decade ago, Malaysians declared that the opportunities for technology transfer through 'learning by doing' had been substantially reduced because of the heavy dependence on parent companies, lack of linkages with local producers, limited R&D activities, and private business interests of the TNCs superseding national interests (Osman-Rani, Woon and Ali 1986: 58). These features, combined with a shortage of local skilled and technical personnel, kept technological capability weak in Malaysia as elsewhere in the Third World. Kunio (1988) described this 'technologyless' industrialization as dependent, 'ersatz' capitalism.

Time and policies can change the degree of local embeddedness and of technology transfer. Education and training, in particular, provide a labour force and local firms with greater technological capability (Kokko and Blomström 1995). By the mid-1990s, Malaysia had greatly enhanced its number of skilled personnel, through training and education and through the support of small firms which serve as suppliers to transnational firms (Rasiah 1994; M. Singh 1995). Recent studies have concluded that Malaysia is the Asian economy with a socio-economic infrastructure, technological infrastructure and production capacity highest among the 'near-NICs' and the most likely next Asian 'tiger', closely following South Korea, Singapore and Taiwan (Rausch 1995; Roessner *et al.* 1996).

The case of Singapore suggests that technological learning takes a long period of time. Singapore is cited as a regional centre for TNC headquarters and for knowledge-based activities, and has reached the fourth, and highest, level of technology transfer – design and *reverse transfer* to Hewlett-Packard units in Japan and the USA (Leonard-Barton 1995). Linkages to local electronics firms are more extensive than elsewhere in East Asia (Henderson 1994). Hobday (1994b) questions these optimistic assessments. He believes that local technological learning in Singapore – usually considered the most developed of the NICs – still lags behind that of advanced economies. Singaporean firms have mastered pre-electronic technologies, such as precision engineering, rather than software, which is the basis for technological advantage in microelectronics.

Cumulative learning occurred from a succession of TNC investments, such as that by Hewlett-Packard, but Singapore's capabilities focused on 'low-cost, high-quality production engineering, rather than information-based software skills or R&D' (Hobday 1994b: 854). The 'dependent production systems' in electronics prevent all but the Korean *chaebol* (Samsung, Daewoo, Hyundai and Goldstar [LG group]) from breaking out of their position within commodity chains (Henderson 1994).

With a similar goal in mind, investment in China largely takes the form of joint ventures between a TNC and a Chinese enterprise. For foreign firms, the attractions are the large Chinese market and low Chinese wages; for Chinese firms, acquisition of technology and of production and organization methods are primary objectives (de Bruijn and Jia 1993). Local input sourcing within China remains at low levels, both because of the capabilities of local suppliers and because of infrastructure problems within China, which prevent shipments being carried from very far from a plant (Leonard-Barton 1995).

It can be the case, however, that even local R&D activities of foreign firms can tap into unique local R&D resources yet produce little or no benefit to the host country (Granstrand, Håkanson and Sjölander 1993: 421). To a large extent, spillovers from FDI on local technological capability (of firms in the same sector) appear mainly to occur when the technology gap is small initially. That is, firms with few skills, far from the level of foreign firms, benefit relatively little from the presence of TNCs, but their more competitive counterparts are better able to learn from foreign investment (Kokko, Tansini and Zejan 1996).

How embedded in different national cultures or localities can a TNC be? The key issue is the extent to which a TNC participates in local economic and social networks, since it is these networks that characterize the local district or *milieu* and, ultimately, any locality (Dicken, Forsgren and Malmberg 1994). The degree of local embeddedness varies by function within firms as well as from firm to firm (Henderson 1994; Young, Hood and Peters 1994). Some of the degree of local involvement depends simply on the history of the firm in any locality. It takes time for links to form, whether a firm is small or large, local or non-local. But 'probably the most important single indicator of local embeddedness relates to supplier relationships' (Dicken, Forsgren and Malmberg 1994: 38).

For reasons related both to high quality standards not met by local suppliers and to the preference for developing close linkages with suppliers, Japanese firms have high levels of imported, as opposed to local, inputs (Hiramoto 1995; OTA 1994: 141). This may be partly explained by the FDI life-cycle theory, which suggests that new foreign affiliates tend to import intermediate inputs, but increase local sourcing over time as they develop supplier relations (Levy and Dunning 1993; OTA 1994: 144–50). Sony, a typical world-class Japanese firm, has a sequence for its manufacturing in Europe that involves the following steps:

1. export of knocked-down kits for local assembly;
2. moves to local manufacture with some procurement of electrical and mechanical components;
3. certain design facilities are localized, so that local components can be designed into products;

4. total design in Europe and manufacturing moves to a just-in-time philosophy, requiring an R&D centre; and
5. specialization by plant within Europe, controlled by Sony Europe headquarters (Hood, Young and Lal 1994: 102).

The fifth step represents fully integrated research and production facilities as a
strategic component of a firm's global R&D, sourcing and manufacturing operations (OTA 1994: 150). It is evident that few firms have attained the fifth level,
and those firms are mainly from small European countries, such as Sweden and
Switzerland, whose home markets and research resources are small. A similar
sequence is suggested by the European strategy of Nissan for car production
(Sadler 1992a: 153–7). This progression is followed by many TNCs for car production in Asia. FDI takes many forms, and contributes in varying degrees to
the technological and economic development of a region or nation (UNCTAD
1994: 166–73).

Are TNC purchase linkages like, or unlike, those of local firms? The answers
are mixed. Barkley and McNamara (1994) found no relationship between ownership and localness of linkages among foreign-owned and domestic manufacturers in two states in the USA. Few local linkages have emerged from the location
of Japanese plants in France (Guelle 1993) or from various foreign automobile
industry plants in Spain (Lagendijk and van der Knaap 1995b). By contrast, substantial local linkage is reported among Japanese plants in Wales (Munday, Morris
and Wilkinson 1995). Young, Hood and Peters (1994) propose a sequence of
emergence of regional clusters of local sourcing and innovation, based partly on
the experience in Scotland – a proposition refuted by Turok (1993).

Few local linkages arise from many TNC investments. In terms of the
sequence above, EPZs rarely move beyond the second stage, since their principal, and at times their only, purpose is to provide jobs at low wages. These 'dead-
end factory jobs', employing mostly women, have been standard for low-wage
employment by TNCs in many industries (Carillo 1994; Deyo 1989; Lim 1980;
Safa 1994). Linkages are minimal in many such cases, as in the Dominican
Republic (Kaplinsky 1993, 1995a; Willmore 1995) and in the cases of Mexico
(Grunwald 1985; Kenney and Florida 1994b; Sklair 1989) and China noted
earlier. The camera assembly operations of three Japanese firms throughout Asia
import all integrated circuits (chips), chip parts and focusing sensors from
Japan. The parts most commonly obtained locally or elsewhere in Asia are plastic
cores, sprockets, flash units and LCD panels. This allows the firms to avoid
becoming 'hollow' in high technology (Kodama 1995b).

In Mexico, a 1988 survey of 303 plants found only 4 per cent of them purchasing inputs within Mexico (South 1990). Although some inter-firm linkages
exist between foreign electronics *maquiladoras*, levels of local (Mexican) inputs
from domestic firms tend to be very low (Wilson 1992). This increase would
include purchases by Japanese firms from plants of their Japanese suppliers that
have also located in Mexico (Kenney and Florida 1994b). The few inputs purchased by TNCs from Mexican firms tend to come from major interior cities,
especially if the products are technical in nature, such as metal or plastic products (Brannon, James and Lucker 1994).

Both forward (downstream) and backward (upstream) linkages are possible, and the emergence of both depends on the capabilities of local firms to produce raw materials, parts, components and services (UNCTAD 1994: 192–5; Young, Hood and Peters 1994). As linkages are reduced to a smaller number of 'preferred' first-tier suppliers, it is less likely that every local economy will have producers who qualify. Instead, giant suppliers, themselves TNCs, locate in proximity to their globalized customers. This is especially noticeable in the auto industry, where the movement of Japanese 'transplant' suppliers has accompanied the location of assembly plants of the major car manufacturers to Europe and North America (Kenney and Florida 1993; Sadler 1992a). But it is not only Japanese firms that do this. Anderson and Holmes (1995) detail the growth of the Canadian firm Magna International, a preferred supplier to many auto TNCs.

The variability of local linkages is seen in the production of athletic shoes, which takes place largely in Asia, and has changed locations greatly in search of lower labour costs. In Malaysia and in Singapore, the determined development of labour skills in local firms has allowed them to become preferred suppliers of precision components to electronics TNCs. Much of this took place during the 1980s in response to increasingly flexible production and the need for local sources of supply. An increased use of automated machinery such as CNC by Malaysian firms took place only in response to demand by TNCs for high degrees of precision. However, the local firms' capabilities have allowed them to export through channels provided by their TNC partners throughout Southeast Asia as well as the USA (Rasiah 1994).

The more 'global' the market served by a firm, the more exclusive and limited is its choice of local suppliers, and especially few is its number of small subcontractors (De Toni, Nassimbeni and Tonchia 1995). As TNCs become more globally integrated, their local linkages in any location tend to shrink, as has occurred in the Spanish automobile parts industry (Lagendijk 1994). If this simply reflects the absence of appropriate firms with which they can interact, it also does not constitute *local* linkage and embeddedness (Dicken, Forsgren and Malmberg 1994). The tendency for TNCs to utilize a global set of linkages has been evident for some time (Fredriksson and Lindmark 1979). The US personal computer industry, despite its base in Silicon Valley, is characterized by a global web of supply linkages, rather than the presence of a 'PC district' (Angel and Engstrom 1995).

Conclusion

The globalization of economic activity is certain to continue, bolstered by new TNCs from regions such as Asia. Whether or not development can occur depends increasingly on the decisions of TNCs – not only whether or not to operate a facility or to subcontract production in a particular location, but also a number of choices regarding staff, skills, qualifications, input sources and technological sophistication. Taken together, these determine whether a region is being exploited for its relatively cheap labour or whether it is needed for its workers' skills that are not available elsewhere (Sklair 1994; UNCTAD 1994: 166–73).

Despite the apparent dispersion of economic activity, its concentration in relatively few places continues. These places, especially world cities, are those best-suited to optimize the dual needs of global firms, i.e. coordination and localization, or glocalization. Coordination demands access to global information networks, and localization dictates a significant degree of embeddedness into local information networks. All these factors have made the course of development in East Asia, at least, go beyond what explanations such as the product cycle or the new international division of labour can untangle. Strategic alliances permit firms in South Korea in particular to move toward technological independence (Hill and Lee 1994).

Given the imbalance between transnational firms, with their global sources of information, and countries, which compete with each other for investment, technology and other benefits of economic activity, it is difficult for real development to occur. For late-industrializing countries (all outside Europe and North America), acquiring technology is the most difficult challenge in a context of constant technological change. Amsden and Hikino (1994) suggest that the most successful response has been the organization of large business groups, including the *keiretsu* in Japan and the *chaebol* in Korea. These diversified industrial groups are able to marshal sufficient resources as well as to coordinate and execute complex projects in which learning opportunities are greater than from smaller, specialized activities (Henderson 1994). Exploiting multi-product externalities, *chaebol* and other business groups exemplify a conglomerate form early, rather than late, in the process of corporate growth (Amsden and Hikino 1994).

The following chapter addresses policy attempts at national, regional and local scales to influence the location of economic activity, through both attracting investment by TNCs and promoting endogenous development.

Chapter 7

Creating competitiveness in nations, regions and localities

The preceding chapters have shown that regional economic growth is a complex process which, despite similarities between places, is locally specific. The penchant to compete as well as to imitate successes observed in other times and places has been especially pronounced in the case of policies to *create* technological capability. At the national level, this is manifested in industrial policies and science and technology (S&T) policies that attempt to 'target' certain industries and technologies which are considered to have especially high potential for future growth and to protect traditional industries (OECD 1991). Industrial policy measures used to protect established sectors include subsidies, government procurement, tax preferences and national product standards. Increasingly, trade policies of both tariff and non-tariff varieties are being applied to mature sectors as well as to new, 'infant industries' (Boonekamp 1989). Macroeconomic policies are also critical since they influence the flow of finance to new industries and firms and create stable conditions in which entrepreneurs can operate (Porter 1990; Roobeek 1990).

Perhaps more important than specific types of policies is the combination of institutional and cultural forces that comprise the *national system of innovation* in each country. This system defines the goals as well as the means of economic progress. The entire system of innovation includes institutional structures, policy routines, forms of work organization, and political and market logics that differ between countries and, to a lesser degree, between regions (Zysman 1994). They also incorporate the specific national and regional mix of conventions common to a specific industry and those to which it is linked (Salais and Storper 1992). The linear model (Chapter 2) and its assumed link between overall R&D and employment growth in high-tech industry advocated a thrust for S&T policy that in many countries focused primarily, perhaps exclusively, on government R&D and failed to encompass the wider technological capabilities of firms (Mowery 1983b). Combined with the economic rationale of 'market failure' justifying a state role, government grants for R&D remain a popular policy (Tisdell 1981).

High technology is one dimension of national economic and industrial development efforts. The link between science and industry now stretches the usual meaning of S&T policy 'downstream' into industrial activity, and it pulls industrial policy 'upstream' into the source of competitiveness: technology (Arnold 1987; Brainard, Leedman and Lumbers 1988; Rothwell and Zegveld 1985: 108–57). This shift in the thrust of government S&T policy reflects both

234

a realization that a linear process of technological innovation no longer applies (if it ever did), and a concern with a larger set of 'barriers to innovation' which R&D effort alone cannot address. These include barriers related to government policy, such as regulation and standards, as well as those relating to communication and mobility of information and flows of capital (OECD 1980: 76–81; Piatier 1984).

This chapter begins the discussion of national systems of innovation, followed by some specific technology policies at the national scale, where they are most evident. Competition at the regional and local levels for economic and technological superiority is increasingly visible. An assessment of these policies concludes the chapter, including those aimed at high-technology development and others directed toward creating regional capabilities for learning and modernization.

National systems of innovation

National differences in the institutional and organizational structures supporting technological change have been called *national systems of innovation* (Nelson 1993). These structures go beyond a narrow view of innovation, and beyond earlier accounts of national research systems (Mowery and Rosenberg 1989) to encompass the range of state-societal arrangements and their influences on competitiveness (Freeman 1995b; Hart 1992). The existence of strong linkages between firms is characteristic of some sectors in some countries, but this alone cannot explain competitiveness well in sectors that have become transnational through alliances. Policies and practices relating to technical standards, human capital formation such as education and training programmes, information provision, and technology diffusion are among the areas in which public policies, institutions and networks of agencies have significant influence (Malerba 1992b). Lundvall (1992: 16) points out that Freeman (1987), referring to Japan, was the first explicit use of the concept of a national system of innovation. Institutions (informal as well as formal) themselves learn and evolve, generally to strengthen the national production system (Lundvall 1992). This may take the form of regulation as well as of explicit positive actions such as R&D funding. In general, national systems of innovation are an outgrowth of thinking on institutions and evolutionary economic change, but their proponents differ significantly (McKelvey 1991; Wijnberg 1994).

Perhaps because of the breadth of the concept, there is disagreement about the exact nature and influence of national systems of innovation. Chang and Kozul-Wright (1994), for example, believe that 'national systems of entrepreneurship' encompass a broader set of phenomena than do national systems of innovation. Their comparison of Sweden and South Korea suggests that institutional complexity and diversity are critical for development to take place. Some of what allows diversity is openness to outside ideas. Such openness has always been a means of learning about foreign technology, involving travel, attendance at trade shows and knowledge of foreign languages in addition to direct acquisition and purchase of technology (Myllyntaus 1990).

Technological systems (Carlsson and Jacobsson 1994; Carlsson and Stankiewicz 1991) and *innovation communities* (Lynn, Reddy and Aram 1996) also are similar to national systems of innovation. Interacting institutions, user–supplier linkages and other agents give rise to a critical mass of knowledge. This 'coevolution of technology and organization' takes place in the case of new technologies through the inputs of users, linked firms, government and 'spanning organizations' (Rankin 1995; Rosenkopf and Tushman 1994; Tushman and Rosenkopf 1992). This system, however, need not be national, and especially for small economies, can involve international linkages in a major way. Despite the differences in terminology, all of these approaches incorporate the role of institutions as integral to the accumulation of technological capability and to economic change (Metcalfe 1995; Zysman 1994). Fransman (1990) believes that technology-creating systems are both nationally specific and sector-specific. In the case of Italy, Malerba (1993) suggests that systems of innovation are distinct and locally specific for the small-firm networks, on the one hand, and national for the core R&D system of large firms, small high-tech firms and public research, on the other hand.

Niosi *et al.* (1993) suggest that four sets of flows or links are prominent in national systems of innovation: financial flows; legal and policy links; technological, scientific and informational flows; and social flows. Because these flows and linkages are dynamic, national systems of innovation, while historically and culturally rooted, are open systems that evolve as circumstances are altered (Niosi and Bellon 1994). Despite globalization through foreign investment and international R&D by transnational firms, national and local networks and information flows are modified but continue to function. To a large degree, these *filières* are the key element in national (and regional and local) systems of innovation, as well as in the process of economic growth (Dosi, Freeman and Fabiani 1994; Dosi, Pavitt and Soete 1990).

National systems of innovation, then, are a complex combination of institutions that support learning processes and technological accumulation. However, empirical work is difficult because it is difficult to identify which institutions, incentives and competences are important (Patel and Pavitt 1994b). Useful historical studies, such as those in Nelson (1993), have been unable to discern adequately such things as the role of large firms, the benefits of basic research, and the influence of workforce education and training. Perhaps more importantly, they have not been able to compare the institutional competences and ways in which they facilitate learning activities systematically (Patel and Pavitt 1994b). It is particularly difficult, unless a database exists from accumulated research, to know how firms are organized, how they operate, and how their actions are influenced by national variables and policies (Kenny 1995).

Differences across sectors and technologies, as well as differences related to interaction and cooperation within and between firms, result in varying competitiveness of national industries (Guerrieri and Tylecote 1994). There is growing evidence that global firms remain tied to their 'home base' and its national system. Research in Japanese firms, for example, takes places almost exclusively in Japan and is heavily dependent on both Japanese citations and collaborators (Hicks *et al.* 1994). The perspective of the Danish research team on national systems of innovation (Lundvall 1992) is both more process-oriented and more complex than that of many others, focusing on learning, social embeddedness, and the factors, linkages and public sector roles outlined by Porter (1990).

A related, but largely separate, literature has developed around the concept of *technology infrastructure*. This can be defined as the scientific, engineering and technical knowledge available to private industry, but must be considered to include generic technologies, 'infratechnologies' such as government laboratories whose research results are widely available, forums for collaboration, standards and intellectual property rights (Tassey 1991). The technology infrastructure is provided by a variety of institutions, public and private, with its principal objectives to create capabilities and build markets for new technologies (Justman and Teubal 1995). The benefits of technology infrastructure centre around the self-reinforcing interaction that results from external economies from strong domestic industries, a skilled labour pool and supplier base, and the knowledge base in an economy (Krugman 1992). The benefits, then, are relevance to industry and orientation to systemic needs which generally cannot be generated through the educational system or direct research support. More than in the case of research, technology infrastructure is a set of public goods and cooperation with users (Justman and Teubal 1995). Policies in both Japan and the USA have explicitly incorporated small and medium-sized firms into nationwide programmes, but with significant local variation and control (Shapira 1996).

Government policy and technology

Government activity in technology has been commonplace only since the Second World War. The major role played by technology in that conflict and the continuation of military priorities in the electronics and information technologies led to a convergence of three traditional foci of public involvement. Support of scientific and technical education and research, public procurement (largely for military purposes), and general modernization policies are three areas in which government policy has been customary (Nelson 1984: 13). As technological capability has grown to be the principal basis of national competitiveness – 'the new "holy grail" of international competition' – science policy has converged with industrial policy (Nau 1986: 9; Rothwell and Zegveld 1985). Consequently, a nation's firms and industries have become more significant than military might in the perceptions of leaders and citizens (Brandin and Harrison 1987; Kotler, Fahey and Jatusripitak 1985; Lewis and Allison 1982; Stopford and Strange 1991).

Continued national priorities concerning R&D and industrial policies are important arenas in which government policy is thought to affect a nation's status relative to other nations (Porter 1990: 617–82; Roobeek 1990). Table 7.1 compares the policy and social environments in seven countries as they affect technology. Some of these policies are directly aimed at technology, whereas

Table 7.1   Comparison of industrial policy characteristics in seven countries.

	USA	Japan	Germany	France	UK	Sweden	Netherlands
Strategies aimed at blurring boundaries between sectors	1	3	2	3	2	1	2
Integration of policy measures	1	3	2	3	2	2	2
Institutional continuity	2	3	2	3	1	2	2
Size of state sector	1	1	2	3	3	2	1
Intensity of generic policy	3	2	2	2	3	3	3
Intensity of sectoral policy	1	2	1	2	2	1	1
Intensity of demand policy	2	1	2	2	1	3	1
Role of defence in government demand	3	1	2	2	2	2	1
Stimulation of high-technology industries	3	3	3	3	2	2	3
Protection of older industries	2	1	2	2	2	1	2
Relative success of high-technology industries	3	3	2	2	1	2	1
Relative success of older industries	1	2	2	2	1	2	2
Competition policy/monopoly and fusion control policies	2	1	3	1	1	1	1
Regional dimension of industrial policy	2	1	3	2	2	2	1
Environmental/ecological dimension of industrial policy	2	2	2	1	1	3	2
Economic cooperation	1	3	3	2	1	3	2
Export stimulation policy	2	2	2	2	2	3	3
Import restriction as main target for national policies	3	2	1	2	2	2	1

Note: 1 = weak, 2 = moderate, 3 = strong.
Source: adapted from Kenworthy (1995) and Roobeek (1990).

others, such as institutional continuity and the size of the state sector, only implicitly address technologies or industries. The social environment refers prominently to the degree of social consensus and economic cooperation present in a country. The fact that some countries have some policies that can be considered strong while other policies are weak makes it difficult to compare them. A correlation analysis of policy orientations indicates that the most similar sets of national policies are those of France and Japan, the Netherlands and Japan, and France and the UK. The least similar are those of the USA and France (Malecki 1995). Freeman (1987) and Martin and Irvine (1989) also found similarities between Japan and Sweden in their long-term outlook in research foresight.

Two schools of thought exist concerning the ability of nations to capture, or even to influence significantly, technological activities within their borders. *Techno-nationalism* is the term used to describe national technology policies that attempt to promote national firms and national technological capabilities. High-technology policies related to research, industrial competitiveness and exports are common means of promoting high-tech industries in Europe, Japan and the USA and increasingly in other countries as well. *Techno-globalism*, on the other hand, sees these policies as futile in a world where high-tech industries have become transnational through alliances and other network links. This view believes that national policies are not very meaningful in a world where 'it has become less and less clear what it means to be a "Japanese" or an "American" or a "European" firm' (Eliasson 1991; Ostry and Nelson 1995: 61). The differences between nations consist less of the firms and their capabilities, which are effectively globalized and transnational, and more of the institutional differences found in the significant differences between national systems of innovation (Ostry and Nelson 1995).

Science policy and R&D priorities

One of the major established means that countries have to influence industrial competitiveness is in setting priorities for scientific and technical education and direct government funding of R&D. The level of government support varies widely, both in the amounts expended on R&D and in the purposes or objectives of those expenditures. Some countries with relatively low government involvement in R&D tend to have active transnational firms which are heavily involved in technology. Examples include Japan, Sweden and Switzerland. Direct government policies such as R&D may be less successful than they might, because other policies are more influential in creating the 'ecostructural dimensions' within which firms operate (Dunning 1994: 84).

A number of different goals are possible for government R&D. The OECD utilizes several categories of R&D: defence, economic development, health and environment, and space. In Table 7.2, it is the varying importance of military activity that stands out. Among the OECD countries, the USA, the UK, France and Sweden direct over 20 per cent of public R&D resources to defence purposes. In many countries the largest category of R&D funds goes to general

Table 7.2 Government R&D allocations in OECD countries.

Country	Government R&D as a percentage of total R&D	Objective as percentage of total government expenditure on R&D			
		Defence	Economic development	Health and environment	Space
USA	38.9	59.0	8.9	18.2	10.0
Canada	42.8	6.4	32.6	15.3	8.1
Japan	17.5	6.1	30.4	5.6	7.3
Australia	54.9	8.5	25.9	13.8	0
New Zealand	65.2	1.6	45.9	24.1	0.1
Austria	46.0	0	13.6	8.3	0.1
Belgium	31.3	0.2	19.5	7.5	13.5
Denmark	39.7	0.6	23.1	13.0	3.3
Finland	40.9	1.6	45.1	15.6	9.3
France	44.3	33.5	15.4	7.7	10.1
Germany	36.5	8.5	21.2	12.4	5.8
Greece	57.7	1.4	25.1	16.9	0.4
Iceland	69.8	0	51.4	7.2	0
Ireland	23.1	0	44.9	14.5	0.5
Italy	44.7	6.5	23.7	12.8	6.3
Netherlands	45.6	3.5	28.5	10.5	4.0
Norway	49.5	5.1	32.6	18.2	2.8
Portugal	59.8	0.3	37.6	18.9	0.3
Spain	50.2	12.5	28.7	12.1	7.1
Sweden	35.3	23.5	14.2	9.6	1.5
Switzerland	28.4	18.5	30.6	11.1	0
UK	33.5	45.1	15.8	12.4	2.7

Note: Data are for 1993 or latest year. Rows do not total to 100%; government support of general education is the largest category omitted from the table.
Source: Modified from OECD (1995a: 147, 149).

university support (OECD 1995a). Scientific research funding receives great scrutiny, with some science areas (such as biotechnology) designated as 'strategic' (Senker 1991). In the absence of major government research support for biotechnology firms, Canada, Britain and France have developed a variety of other public policy instruments to stimulate the growth of biotechnology firms (Walsh, Niosi and Mustar 1995). These illustrate the shift from research or science policy to innovation policy.

In addition to defence, 'big science' or megascience efforts are common in several countries, usually involving nuclear physics and space exploration. Such efforts are increasingly beyond the ability of a single country, and organizations such as CERN (Conseil Européan pour la Recherche Nucléaire) in Geneva and the Joint European Torus in Culham, UK, are examples of international cooperation in this area (Galison and Hevly 1992; Mowery and Rosenberg 1989; OECD 1995b). The cost of participation in these projects, affected by exchange rates, constrains budgets for other research activities (Williams 1996). Japan has added several big-science projects since the mid-1980s, adding to the country's importance for high-energy physics and other research (Normille 1996).

Defence technology as a priority area

Defence tends to have limited spillovers into commercial technology, often by design (Mowery and Langlois 1996). Chiang (1991) has suggested that, while a 'mission-oriented, trickle-down' strategy typical of military R&D has led to some new products and civilian applications, a 'diffusion-oriented, trickle-up' strategy is more fruitful. Experts are increasingly sceptical of the spin-off benefits of military spending – a 'myth' according to Alic *et al.* (1992: 54–81). For example, Samuels (1994: 21) suggests that despite the large amounts of advanced research done by private firms in the USA for defence purposes, US firms have 'failed to stay at the state of the commercial art in a range of technology-intensive sectors. . . Something happened to impede the "natural" inter-diffusion of military and civilian economies. I call it "spin-away".' Communication between the two sectors was thwarted by alienation, isolation and barriers, such as secrecy and procedures aimed at preventing (or at least impeding) technology diffusion. A further problem is that the criterion of success – the 'mission' or performance rather than cost – resulted in custom processes rather than processes geared toward volume production (Samuels 1994: 21–3).

Japan identified much earlier than US or European governments the concept of *dual use*: the emergence of a techno-military paradigm that depends on and reinforces technological advances in the civilian economy. The Japanese did not invent the alternative paradigm, but they coined a phrase to describe it: *spin-on* (Samuels 1994: 26). Spin-on involves the transfer of products and processes 'off the shelf' from civilian to military applications. It involves distinct informational infrastructures and different product and process R&D traditions (Cowan and Foray 1995). It is now seen as critical in the USA for several reasons: 1. Performance standards in commercial markets are equal to (or surpass) military specifications. In commercial markets, technology is used both to lower costs and to enhance performance. As a result, cost and performance each improved faster in the commercial than in the military sector, where only performance seemed to matter.

2. The large and increasing development costs for new technologies can now be supported as easily by the volume sales of consumer products as by the guaranteed markets of military procurement.

3. Product life-cycles in competitive markets are considerably shorter than are those for military systems, and the life-cycle gap is growing. Commercial producers have had to become significantly more responsive and flexible than military producers, whose product runs of smaller volumes are of longer duration. The civilian economy has proved itself an even more voracious consumer of technology-intensive products than the military (Samuels 1994: 28).

Samuels (1994: 31) believes that successful 'conversion' of military activity 'will require consolidation of a single technology industrial base, not simply the removal of barriers between two separate ones.' Two different cultures have evolved, divided by 'a wall of separation' between military and civilian markets. This wall seemed to inhibit horizontal learning as weapon systems were developed in isolation from other activities, both within firms and between firms. The 'technological divergence' that resulted has had long-term consequences for the firms whose technological capabilities were developed under the protective umbrella of stable or growing military budgets (Alic *et al.* 1992; Gansler 1980; Markusen and Yudken 1992).

Despite the apparent logic of dual-use technology, firms dependent on military spending are not moving very quickly in that direction. Instead, they are merging and taking over competitors, consolidating the industry to fewer firms (Forsberg, Peach and Reppy 1994). This is considered necessary both for efficiency and to end protection of national champion firms (*The Economist* 1995a). Aerospace producers have also expanded their international efforts as their home markets have shrunk. These efforts include increased marketing in export markets, offshore sourcing and offsets in order to win contracts, and strategic alliances with competitors (Chinworth and Mowery 1995; Forsberg 1994; Valéry 1994). In short, the military segment of the aerospace industry has become just as global as the civilian airframe industry discussed in Chapter 6.

As military budgets have shrunk, the firms have also 'downsized' their workforces, largely paid for by the Pentagon (Fialka 1996; Forsberg, Peach and Reppy 1994). Dual use remains in the USA very high-tech in orientation, largely avoiding both incremental infrastructural technologies and concerted commitment toward areas of national need, such as the environment, mass transportation and renewable energy resources (Markusen and Yudken 1992: 128). In addition, while spending on weapon systems has fallen, R&D has not, being shifted to 'information age' technologies (Berkowitz 1995; Clawson 1996; Morton 1995).

Because the USA has had no explicit industrial or technology policy (the implicit policy being military spending), 'there is no US government agency with a clearly defined responsibility for managing technology initiatives that span several agencies' (OTA 1993: 29; Markusen 1986; Mowery 1992). Adoption of a technology policy in the USA 'would require elevating commercially competitive technologies to a position of national priority equal to that previously held by national defense' (Rycroft and Kash 1992: 235). Indeed, new types of policies are needed to fit the new context of complex products developed in a framework of collaborative innovation (Rycroft and Kash 1994).

In summary, defence conversion has proven difficult for firms and for government institutions. The latter include Department of Energy weapons laboratories, which were largely devoted to nuclear arms technology and are finding it difficult to adapt to new public missions, such as electric cars and related energy technologies (Branscomb 1993a; OTA 1993). Overall, the USA has only recently encouraged inter-firm collaboration in pre-competitive technologies; traditionally, until the mid-1980s, such activities were considered to violate anti-trust laws (Branscomb 1993b). There remains little consensus about the best path for technology policy in the USA and in the UK, in large part because of ideological conflicts related to any form of industrial policy (Farrell *et al.* 1992; Hirst 1989). Indeed, opposition to such policies has increased as faith in the market has increased (De Bandt 1994).

Diffusion-oriented policies

In contrast to mission-oriented policies, diffusion-oriented policies 'seek to provide a broadly based capacity for adjusting to technological change throughout the industrial structure' (Ergas 1987: 205). The USA, the UK and France are regarded as having followed mission-oriented policies, whereas Germany, Japan, Switzerland and Sweden have been diffusion-oriented. Britain and France have developed political and industrial structures similar to those in the USA, and this similarly has inhibited the sharing of technologies within as well as between firms (Chesnais 1993; Walker 1993). Sweden, Germany and Japan, on the other hand, have institutional and industrial arrangements that encourage the transfer of know-how between military and civilian activities (Ziegler 1992). Japanese licencing and co-production of US military technologies helped firms greatly in other areas. According to a Hitachi executive: 'the defense-related business helps us see and touch high technology faster than any other business' (Samuels 1994: 183). Through military licencing and, later, co-production, technology diffused throughout the Japanese economy. It did so along three dimensions: *horizontally* (between prime contractors); *vertically* (between the primes, their subcontractors and suppliers); and *across* military and commercial applications (internally within the diversified prime contractors and within their flexible suppliers). The 'wall' separating military from commercial technologies was, in Japan's case, a 'glass wall' (Samuels 1994).

These categories, made principally on the basis of the share of total government R&D devoted to defence, show little sign of changing a decade later. A key part of a diffusion-oriented policy are strong institutions and mechanisms for technology transfer. The weapons laboratories have operated along the lines of the linear model (Chapter 2), rather than attempting to learn and serve the needs of the market. In addition, the nature of the laboratories' bureaucracies has inhibited the formation of trust relationships critical to fruitful technological relationships (Branscomb 1993a).

Alic *et al.* (1992) propose a new basis for technology policy, intended to replace the traditional objectives of basic research, technology development for public missions, and commercial development. Their categories are as follows:

1. path-breaking technology, with a time horizon of ten years or more and high risk, to be performed in universities, national laboratories and industrial R&D laboratories;
2. infrastructural technology, involving low risk and focusing on incremental improvements in quality or productivity, and providing continuous benefits; and
3. strategic technology, where the business risks exceed the technical risks and the time horizon is about five years, to be performed by business-centred consortia at the advice of business and technical experts (Alic *et al.* 1992: 382–3).

The selection of 'path-breaking', critical or strategic technologies is not without pitfalls, however. Some specific priority technologies that appear in nearly all reports include computer-integrated manufacturing, robotics, artificial intelligence, high-performance computing, computer displays, signal processing, human factors, networking, aerospace propulsion, materials processing, composites, optoelectronics and microelectronics. This leads to over-investment and excessive competition, resulting in price competition and shorter product lifecycles (Brahm 1995). In addition, many of these technologies are very broad (e.g. robotics and biotechnology), providing little guidance for R&D programme managers (Branscomb 1993c: 54). Most lists of critical or strategic technologies also fail to distinguish between generic technologies, which could be useful in a number of applications, and those which involve fairly well-defined and specific applications. Part of the confusion is that the term 'strategic' has several meanings: technological, trade, industrial and military (Soete 1994).

A more useful distinction is made by Rycroft and Kash (1992), who see excessive emphasis on the linear model and particularly on basic and applied research. They identify three sectors that have benefited from continuous policy support in the USA over several decades: agricultural products; defence-related aerospace, computing and instruments; and medical products, especially pharmaceuticals. These illustrate the benefits of three distinct government roles: (1) underwriting a substantial portion of high-risk R&D; (2) serving as a 'marriage broker' to link industry, government and universities to create an organizational system that can support continuous innovation; and (3) manipulating the market to create demand for new products and processes. This view sees innovation policy as 'aimed at helping companies innovate successfully, i.e. helping them get new products and processes onto the market' rather than focusing on advancing scientific knowledge (Chabbal 1995: 104–5; Rothwell 1994b; Rycroft and Kash 1992).

Industrial, innovation and technology policy _____

A distinct shift occurred during the 1980s to broaden the notion of science or R&D policies into policies that incorporated the mix of industrial, competition, technology and science policies into a dynamic policy set 'focused on the promotion and adoption of new technology (that is, the commercial development of the fruits of basic research)' (Ostry 1990: 53; Gibbons *et al.* 1994: 157–60; Graham 1995; Kaell, Ireland and Sadeque 1995). Regardless of how policies and direct expenditure on R&D differ across countries, the government–corporate interface is an essential aspect of what is now generally called *innovation policy.* Governments play a significant – and perhaps growing – role in protecting and aiding national firms and industries in global competition (Porter 1990). This 'reindustrialization' role of government marks the joining of industrial and science policies – a shift that has grown to encompass many efforts to promote competitiveness (Ostry 1990).

Although the lack of attention to innovation and technology has changed dramatically, specific policies for industrial innovation continue to 'represent only a small portion of overall government efforts' (Brown 1995: 16). Most efforts are more indirect, as Table 7.1 suggests, involving trade and competition policies as much as, or more than, S&T policies. Technological innovation, particularly in certain high-tech industries such as computers, electronics, aerospace and biotechnology, increasingly is seen as a major driving force behind national economic growth and competitiveness. This realization has led to both the expansion of traditional research and education programmes and the creation of a host of new, untested programmes intended to stimulate industrial innovation and technology transfer (Roessner 1989: 310; Roobeek 1990).

Among the needs for industrial policy is the decline of older industries in many developed countries as these sectors become dominated by enterprises in less developed countries. In 1978, Japan began to deal with the problems of 'specific depressed industries' – picking losers rather than winners (Peck, Levin and Goto 1988). The depressed industries include both energy-intensive mineral-processing and petroleum-based products, as well as shipbuilding and cotton and wool textiles. Similarly, France instituted in 1984 a set of 15 'conversion poles' to address problems of industrial decline in places where employment in the coal, steel and shipbuilding sectors has been in steady decline (Tuppen and Thompson 1994).

Most policies toward specific industries involve subsidies of various sorts (grants, tax concessions, soft loans, equity participation) in selected sectors (Brown 1995). These subsidies have been lowest in Japan and the United States (among the OECD countries), and highest in Sweden, Norway and Ireland (Ford and Suyker 1990). The reduction of subsidies has been a priority of the European Union as a condition for joining the European Monetary Union (EMU). Hidden subsidies, such as loans at below-market rates, rent-free premises, and procurement privileges, are also common and particularly difficult to detect (World Bank 1995b). The support by the French government of its 'national champion' firms is a common example (Hart 1992; Toy 1994).

These subsidies represent the 'sheltered culture' common in Europe, which contrasts with the outward-looking 'exposed culture' of Japan (Derian 1990).

Particularly in developed economics, a great deal of total national R&D is funded by business enterprises. This is especially true in Japan and Germany, which do not have the marked defence orientation found in the USA, the UK or France. The commercial inclination of R&D, which also reflects a tendency for businesses to invest heavily in R&D, is related to the success of Japanese and German businesses in world markets. In support of these observations, Teece (1991) suggests that sector-specific targeted policies are less effective than are national differences in industrial structures, the cost of capital, education systems and the macroeconomic environment, all of which represent broader institutions rather than policy alone. Innovation policy is an offensive strategy, similar to that of firms (Chapter 3), relying upon technological knowledge, flexibility and production efficiency. This requires macro-economic policies that encourage investment and competition rather than protection (Fröhlich 1989). Eliasson (1991) goes further, asserting that in a world of TNCs and mobile industrial knowledge, national industrial policies are inefficient and ineffective.

We next look at specific policy environments in Japan, Europe and the USA. Technology policy in the NICs and in developing countries is discussed in Chapter 8.

Japan

Of all developed nations, Japan is thought to have perhaps the most conscious, focused and articulated technology policy. While the roots of Japanese industrial policy date back to the nineteenth century, the Ministry of International Trade and Industry (MITI) was established in the late 1940s to direct the reconstruction of Japan's war-ravaged economy (Magaziner and Hout 1980; Prestowitz 1988: 122–44). 'Administrative guidance', the management of competition and the nurturing of technological development are seen in an elaborate system of 'protocols' and conventions – sometimes tacit, at other times explicit – to induce domestic firms, even as they compete, to negotiate constantly with their competitors and with bureaucrats, especially within MITI (Dore 1986; Samuels 1994; Tsuru 1993). Japanese policies 'have converged on a national commitment to indigenize technology, to diffuse it throughout the economy, and to nurture firms that could benefit' (Samuels 1994: 55). The contrasts with the US policy culture are striking. The Japanese sought to facilitate technology diffusion, whereas Americans worried about its 'proliferation' (Samuels 1994: 65).

MITI involvement was evident in the computer industry, an early strategic sector. Japanese firms were far behind their US competitors, and major cooperative projects were organized to raise Japanese competitiveness (Arnold 1987; Roobeek 1990; Shinjo 1988). Cooperative research, funded partially by the government, was the norm in Japan until the 1980s, with MITI funding accounting for 40–50 per cent of research budgets, and the rest divided between member firms (Flamm 1988: 140; Peck and Goto 1981). Government procurement policy also served to protect the computer industry when it was in its 'infant' stage, when an informal 'buy Japanese' policy prevailed (Flamm 1988). Whether through government policy or company strategy, by 1990 Japanese firms had become dominant in the fastest-growing portion of the computer market: laptop or portable computers, based on accumulated capabilities in technologies for batteries, LCDs and disk drives. Another deliberate attempt to develop technological capability in a technology and its linked industries is exemplified in the case of aerospace technology. Developing such skills helped the 'roots' and 'fruits' of aerospace to grow, through its linkages with other sectors (Chapter 3). Space and satellite technology and commercial jet aircraft have been Japanese beneficiaries of this effort (Valéry 1989).

The oil crisis of 1973 accelerated a process of strategic selection that had begun in 1970, when MITI's 'Vision for the 1970s' was published. The core of this 'vision', repeated and intensified in its successors, 'Long-Term Vision of the Industrial Structure' (1975) and 'MITI Policy Vision for the 1980s', was the shift from capital-intensive heavy industries (e.g. steel, shipbuilding and automobiles) and resource-dependent industries to knowledge-intensive machining and assembly industries, including general machinery, electronic and electrical equipment, transport equipment, and precision instruments (Uekusa 1988). The 'Vision for the 1980s' bluntly 'called for developing an industrial structure with high technology as its core', referred to as a 'creative, knowledge-intensive industrial structure' (Uekusa 1988: 97). Much of this 'Vision for the 1980s' was in response to a 1981 white paper that assessed Japanese technological strength along several dimensions relative to its national competitors – France, West Germany, the UK and the USA (Anderson 1984). Gaps identified at that time have clearly been closed, judging by the strength of Japanese firms in patenting activity, a key technological indicator (Chapter 6). The MITI 'Vision for the 1990s' emphasizes quality-of-life priorities and 'unstrategic sectors', such as resorts, interior decorating and fashion (Schlesinger 1990). Among the latest 'visions' is 'The New Earth 21–Action Program for the Twenty-First Century', which focuses on clean industrial technologies that will place Japan as 'a leader in global environmental technology' (Myers 1992).

The Japanese approach to technological forecasting from which the 'visions' have emerged is well-suited to identifying new technological paradigms early. Like many other processes in Japan, forecasts are developed by formal and informal consultations with thousands of experts, rather than relying on published statistics (Freeman 1987: 55–90; Kuwahara 1996). Inter-firm interaction also facilitates organizational learning within the large firms that are the hubs of the Japanese economy (Fruin 1994). Several OECD countries have experimented with a similar broad consultation approach to technology foresight (Elzinga 1987; Martin 1996). Given the nature of technological trajectories, there is often little difference between the resultant priorities (Grupp 1996; Kuwahara 1996; Quévreux 1996; Walshe 1996).

MITI's role in Japan's success may be overstated, since the ministry merely 'was responding to what business had already begun' (Fruin 1992: 168). The success of several Japanese export industries was unrelated to MITI (or any other) policy, and included cameras, bicycles, motorcycles, pianos, zip-fasteners and consumer electronics. From the mid-1960s onwards, a number of other industries developed without any reliance on industrial protection and promotion policies, including colour televisions, clocks, calculators, electric wire, machine tools, textile machinery, agricultural machinery and robots (Freeman 1987: 28; Komiya 1988: 7–8). To this list can be added compact disc players, facsimile (fax) machines, semiconductor lasers and VCRs (Freeman 1987: 28; Gover 1995: 30). Many of the products which Japan dominates are a result of foreign technology imported and then creatively adapted and improved (Mansfield 1988; Nelson 1984). As Rosenberg (1982: 273) notes, the Japanese elevated 'to a fine art what they call *improvement engineering*.' Although not responsible for any major or original inventions, this skill 'enabled them to draw upon a large inventory of foreign technologies and reshape them to their own requirements with a high degree of sophistication.'

The inclusion of machine tools in the preceding list is significant. Beginning with the Machinery Industry Law in 1957, MITI has attempted to coordinate the thousands of Japanese machine tool producers, without success (Friedman 1988: 84; Tsuruta 1988). It was firms, rather than MITI, which carried out the adjustment policy for declining industries (Peck, Levin and Goto 1988). In addition, some MITI projects, such as an electric car project, have been unsuccessful.

Overall, however, the coordinated priorities and R&D funding have had a significant effect on Japanese competitiveness, in part because of attention to markets and international competitiveness associated with Japanese R&D, in contrast to the military priorities found in some other advanced countries (Goto and Wakasugi 1988; Gross 1989). Japanese firms lost interest in cooperative research consortia in the 1980s, despite MITI's continued promotion of them. As the firms have become global competitors, they see less need for cooperation (often only a public show) with their competitors at home. 'MITI discovered that pushing out on the technology frontier was substantially more difficult than "catch-up" policies that targeted existing technologies.' The 'Fifth Generation' and supercomputer efforts of the 1980s fell apart for this reason (Callon 1995: 183). Fierce competition, not cooperation, is the central force in Japan's economy and, consequently, now in its industrial policy as well (Callon 1995). In most areas, 'while companies are the "motor", the Japanese government plays a major supportive role' (Fransman and Tanaka 1995: 47). Corporate strategies are oriented toward future possibilities, with 'roots' in basic technologies and branches and fruits in linked sectors (Valéry 1989: 9–12). Japanese firms do not blindly follow MITI directives, but compete strongly, with high levels of R&D, both in the domestic market in Japan and internationally (Majumdar 1988). Competition, and the mix and balance of central organization and market dynamism, are elements of strength in the Japanese system (Okimoto 1989).

MITI's role may have declined, but Japanese institutions – its national innovation system – remain robust. The interdependence of bureaucracy, firms and financial institutions provides information as well as financial capital, and reinforces the *keiretsu* and *keiretsu*-like linkages between firms (Bowonder, Miyake and Linstone 1994b; Fruin 1992). Evans (1995) suggests that Japan has the most well-developed *embedded autonomy* in its government bureaucracies. The public service is highly regarded in Japan (Dore 1987).

An interplay between government policy and the banking system in Japan also aids its technological competitiveness. In addition to participation in large, risky projects, the Industrial Bank of Japan has a research staff that monitors trends in industries and of individual clients. Through this 'technological intelligence' role, the IBJ helps its clients to diversify into more competitive, higher-technology product lines (Jéquier and Hu 1989: 119–20). In this active model of banking, also found in Germany, banks are among the 'technological institutions' that cannot be ignored when discussing technology policies (Jéquier and Hu 1989: 193). The Japanese trading companies, or *sogo shosha*, by coordinating investments and projects, serve a somewhat similar function (Kojima and Ozawa 1984).

Bowonder, Miyake and Linstone (1994a) suggest several elements – some governmental, some industrial – as instrumental in Japan's growth:

- the status of manufacturing facilities in firms
- the availability of human skills
- systems of information support
- organizational and management systems
- planning systems (government–firm linkages)
- technology diffusion systems (firm–market–government linkages)
- financial investment systems
- internationalization (international production and marketing networks).

The failings of Japanese science and research (in contrast to engineering and product development) are widely recognized. The universities are especially weak, certainly in comparison with corporate R&D laboratories (Anderson 1992; Hamilton 1992; Odagiri and Goto 1993; Tatsuno 1990: 218–60). Perhaps in response to this situation, many Japanese firms have established relationships with, and even entire research institutes in, universities in the USA (Flam 1992; Tatsuno 1990: 259–60). Fransman and Tanaka (1995) dispute the characterization of Japanese universities as weak, using evidence from biotechnology. None the less, the Japanese government has allocated a massive increase in basic research, in an attempt to raise the country's stature in pure science and inventiveness (*The Economist* 1996e). This reflects a growing awareness that the 'twenty-first-century system' will involve Japan not as a borrower catching up, but as an industrial leader of technologies based on research-based high technology, as well as on precision and high skill (Yamamura 1987: 187).

Europe

Partially as a reaction to the rapid rise in Japanese competitiveness, the science policies of European nations began in the 1970s to include investments in 'strategic' industries and in 'national champion' firms as policy priorities (Foray, Gibbons and Ferné 1989). Large national firms which might be seen as equal competitors to Japanese firms and to IBM, including International Computers Limited (ICL) in the UK, Compagnie International pour l'Informatique (CII) in France, and Siemens in West Germany, were 'placed on a high-powered diet of protection, procurement preferences, and subsidies' (Flamm 1988: 154). Government support for computer R&D rose steeply during the 1970s, but remained largely national in scope (Ballance 1987; Roobeek 1990).

Throughout Europe, individual national champion firms and strategic partnerships between those firms received massive funding for R&D ventures (Arnold 1987; Hobday 1989: 232). Critics of this approach contend that the top-down approach and the focus on large 'national champion' firms common in Europe is an anachronism in a time of global firms and entrepreneurship (Carliner 1987; Woods 1987). Others contend that the nationalistic thinking behind British and other European policies is misplaced and that global strategies are still too rare (de Woot 1990). Moreover, comparisons made with the USA and Japan alone neglect the growing role of the NICs in world trade (Oshima 1987).

European policy-makers reacted to the rapid Japanese technological ascent in the 1970s with alarm. A perceived 'technology gap' *vis-à-vis* Japan and the USA is an overgeneralization, according to Patel and Pavitt (1987), since a significant gap exists only in electronics and software, and overlooks leading European positions in chemicals and nuclear energy, a lead over the USA in automobiles and metals, and over Japan in aerospace and technologies exploiting raw materials. It also ignores the presence of top-quality research institutes and long-standing national traditions in several industries. In this view, Europe, the USA and Japan represent 'three worlds of technology' based on distinct traditions and strengths (Speiser 1988).

The European Union (EU) and its predecessor, the EC, has been instrumental in organizing and funding cooperative R&D programmes among firms located throughout Europe to increase European technological capability in the broad area of information technology (Nueño and Oosterveld 1986). Collaborative activity between firms and governments increased markedly, both in individual countries and under the umbrella of the EC and later the EU (Foray, Gibbons and Ferné 1989). The first such programme was ESPRIT (European Strategic Programme for Research and Development in Information Technologies), which began in 1982. It has been followed by several others, in addition to R&D programmes in other broad areas. EUREKA (the European Research Coordinating Agency), started outside the EC in July 1985 to promote cooperative, transnational R&D not only between firms, but also between firms and universities, government agencies and research organizations (Clery 1993; de Woot 1990; OECD 1989b: 180–8; Onida and Malerba 1989; Sharp and Shearman 1987: 72–3). ESPRIT, EUREKA, R&D in Advanced Communication Technologies for Europe (RACE), Basic Research in Industrial Technologies (BRITE) and others attempt to bring a competitiveness to Europe via European producers 'to allow European manufacturers to be part of the core rather than part of the periphery' (Davis 1988: 85; OTA 1991: 209–26). These generally embody greater coherence than US policy, influenced principally by the Japanese model (Ostry 1990: 70–5). However, a lack of coordination of national policies remains (Micossi and Viesti 1991).

Small firms see potential benefits from cooperative R&D, including risk-sharing and the ability to monitor technological frontiers, get advice on technological trajectories, and prepare for technological jumps and changes in the competitive environment (Onida and Malerba 1989: 162). However, large firms play a preponderant role in European programmes to date, which focus on technology-push, a fact that may well limit their success (Woods 1987). Recent assessments concur that the EC/EU programmes have benefited primarily large firms in core countries, which might not need the subsidy in any case. Small firms in peripheral parts of Europe, such as Spain, are distant from the state-of-the-art and therefore gain less from such programmes than core firms (Barañano 1995).

European governments have cooperated in high-technology ventures since the 1950s, when CERN was organized for high-energy physics research (Martin and Irvine 1984). The Airbus Consortium, now Airbus Industrie, is a major success for collaborative European technology. Its partners include Aerospatiale (France) and Deutsche Aerospace Airbus (Germany), both with 37.9 per cent shares, British Aerospace (20 per cent), and CASA (Spain) with 4.2 per cent. Associate members include Belgian Belairbus and the Dutch firm Fokker. High initial subsidies for development costs (Todd and Simpson 1986: 198) have declined but not disappeared as the consortium's various passenger jets have attracted significant market share, now second only to Boeing as a supplier to the world's airlines. The consortium has effectively coalesced national industrial policies and desires for a world-class aerospace industry into a commercially successful enterprise (Thornton 1995). Airbus is perhaps one of the best examples of national policies crafted and implemented with a knowledge of the international structure of an industry (Stopford and Strange 1992: 96). Analyses of the benefits of the European Space Agency (ESA) suggest that, within a large programme, learning spreads within the network of subcontractors and suppliers, benefiting a large number of firms (Zuscovitch and Cohen 1994).

Specific national programmes have also emerged, usually around a set of selected high-technology sectors (Rothwell and Zegveld 1988), and always evolving from the long-standing institutional culture of the country (Duchêne and Shepherd 1987). Among the largest programmes is the Alvey programme in the UK, which began in 1983 to improve the British position in microelectronics. It was the first British attempt to move beyond defence R&D and fundamental research conducted in universities and, more importantly, it involved collaboration between firms and between industry, government, and universities and polytechnics (Freeman 1987: 120–38; Hobday 1988). As a programme of long-term research, its benefits are also long-term: accelerating, broadening and deepening the R&D undertaken. What remains unaddressed by programmes such as Alvey are the organizational, social, economic and institutional issues that underpin the wider innovation process (Quintas and Guy 1995). In general, UK innovation policy has been too oriented toward high technology, and not toward the other elements of the national system of innovation (Ashcroft, Dunlop and Love 1995).

Implicit industrial policy is also evident in Europe. The linkages between industrial policy, the competitive environment and corporate strategy within a national system of innovation determine the ability of firms to prosper. Regulations regarding safety and pricing and close links with doctors through the National Health Service helped British pharmaceutical firms to meet evolving world standards of competition. More protectionist French policies regarding price-setting and a research climate focused in government laboratories resulted in a rapid decline of French firms (L. Thomas 1994).

Sector-specific policies have emerged as well, especially in biotechnology, where the flurry of new firms in the USA and the naming of biotechnology as a next-generation technology by MITI in Japan spurred the creation of European policies (Fransman and Tanaka 1995). The divergence between a market-led approach with no central direction in the USA and the coordination found in Japan has led to policies in Europe, such as the Dutch Biotechnology Programme, somewhere 'between dirigism and laissez-faire' (Cantley 1986; Rip and Nederhof 1986; Sharp 1987). Linkages among firms and between academic and industrial research on the Japanese model are the preferred approach in European policy. The US model of high-technology entrepreneurship has been difficult to emulate, given different traditions and the shortage of venture capital (Sharp 1987).

North America

In North America, US policy has been less explicitly interventionist – and less coordinated – than policies in Europe or Japan. For years, government procurement for military and space programmes was believed to be a superior method of reaping the benefits of high technology (Allen et al. 1978; Molina 1989; Nelson 1984; Roessner 1987). This policy has recently been called into question, both because of the reduced potential for commercialization of military technology, and because of diminished concerns about military threats in comparison with economic ones. 'The pattern of indirect commercial or economic benefits – spin-offs – is no longer providing the United States with enough technologies that are competitive in the international marketplace' (Kash 1989: 37). However, dependence on Defense Department funding has continued to characterize the US approach to S&T policy, for software development, advanced semiconductor manufacturing techniques, and other technologies that have a dual use (Borrus 1988; Ostry 1990). Beyond military demand, US S&T policy is only indirect and implicit, working through the regulatory and tax systems (Bean and Baker 1988; Carliner 1987; Rothwell 1980).

The result is an R&D-based model, with high levels of funding for basic research in telecommunications, biomedical applications, computers and aerospace (Teske and Johnson 1994). In addition to high-profile cooperative R&D projects, such as the Microelectronics and Computer Technology Corporation (MCC) and the Semiconductor Research Corporation (SEMATECH), the trend for American firms has been more toward one-to-one contractual joint ventures between firms, where the costs and benefits are allocated in advance. Most such collaboration – often organized as cooperative research and development alliances, or CRADAs – has been for basic research, supplemented by participation in university research centres, some of which are supported by the US National Science Foundation (Arnold 1987; Fusfeld and Haklisch 1987). Until recently, however, diffusion-oriented technology policies to a wider range of firms were more common at the state level than in federal policy (Teske and Johnson 1994).

In Canada, the negative effects of external control and technological dependence prevent it from maintaining an 'offensive strategy' across a wide spectrum of technologies. Foreign ownership strongly influences Canadian R&D, and inhibits the development of an indigenous innovative capability (McFetridge 1993; Palda and Pazderka 1982). The Canadian economy is characterized by truncation of R&D toward minimal fine-tuning and adaptation of products for the Canadian market, combined with minimal levels of R&D in Canada by subsidiaries of multinational corporations (Britton and Gilmour 1978; Etemad and Séguin Dulude 1986).

Overall, national innovation or technology policies have a significant effect on the competitiveness of firms, both through the distribution of subsidies and institutional support and the development of new institutions critical to the nurture and growth of new industries. Many policies, however, utilize alliances and collaboration, and these have a tendency to exclude some firms because of nationality, size and other reasons. This has the effect of reducing access to technology and investment, and of promoting techno-nationalism in a world of multi-domestic, if not global, firms (Florida 1995; Soete 1994).

Policies for regional and local competitiveness

Regional policy

Policies intended to alter geographically uneven development have emerged since the 1930s, mainly using subsidies for manufacturing to create jobs (Cobb 1993). Construction projects for infrastructure in lagging areas also became a common mechanism with which to provide jobs, if only temporarily (Leven 1985; Savoie 1986). The growth pole model and related 'scientific' approaches dominated regional policy during the 1960s and 1970s (Higgins and Savoie 1988, 1995). Subsidies and infrastructure investment again were common elements, focusing on a pole or city within a designated region, in the hope of generating growth based on cumulative causation and spread in that region. Although it was one of the most elaborately developed and widely used concepts in regional policy, growth centre policy failed to counteract market forces, which continued to favour attractive regions, world cities and 'sunbelt' areas.

The failure of such policies to deter market forces provides a central message: economic activity refuses to become anything but 'uneven'. Despite some degree of 'counterurbanization' (net migration away from established urban areas) during the 1970s, Richardson's (1973) observation of the spatial pattern of recent economic change as 'decentralized concentrated dispersion' remains accurate. Population and economic activity have dispersed to only a fairly small number of concentrations – urban areas – where growth has occurred primarily in a decentralized fashion in the suburban and ex-urban periphery.

In the absence of market forces, under central planning, the USSR and the countries of Eastern Europe experienced polarization as pronounced as in capitalist economies, if not more so. The concern for efficiency over regional equity in investment location, embodied in large industrial complexes in a small number of locations and industrial investment in established centres, reinforced this tendency (Fuchs and Demko 1979; Kowalski 1986).

A prominent dilemma in regional policy has been the question of 'people prosperity or place prosperity' (Agnew 1984). A concern for people led to proposals that people in backward regions could best be helped by subsidizing their outmigration to other regions (Hansen 1973). The 'people versus place' choice arises repeatedly as policies attempt at considerable cost to create jobs in backward regions (Chisholm 1987). Regional 'triage', favouring investment in some places at the expense of others, is fairly pervasive in regional policies, including growth pole and growth centre policies (Agnew 1984). It may well be that policies aimed at specific groups of disadvantaged people may be more effective than policies targeting lagging regions (Hansen 1995). Bolton (1992) suggests that the issue is both an ethical one and one that involves the 'sense of place' perceived by people in a region.

Growth poles and growth centres

The influential *growth pole* concept (Perroux 1955) was based on input–output data that identified not only the upstream sectors on which other sectors relied for inputs, but also forward (downstream) linkages (Boudeville 1966). A distinction was made between *growth poles*, set in the economic space of input–output relations, and *growth centres*, propulsive industries set in a regional context (Moseley 1974; Polenske 1988). Growth pole policies were applied in literally dozens of countries during the 1960s and 1970s (Kuklinski 1972, 1975, 1978, 1981; Kuklinski and Petrella 1972; Lo and Salih 1978).

Growth centres were tied to optimism concerning the process of 'trickle-down' or 'spread' effects, based on Hirschman (1958) and Myrdal (1957). Higher incomes and economic growth were envisioned to emanate outward from a growth centre over time, gradually affecting the entire hinterland of the centre. Agglomeration economies were a key element of growth centre policies, in both an industrial and a spatial sense (Moseley 1974). The creation of planned industrial complexes, clustering linked industries together in a particular location, was especially prominent in Canada and in the Soviet Union (Czamanski and Czamanski 1977; Karaska and Linge 1978; Luttrell 1972; Norcliffe and Kotseff 1980). Similar complexes emerged from industrial policies to create heavy and chemical industries in several developing countries (Auty 1994; Todd and Hsueh 1992). As Higgins (1983: 8) describes it:

The greatest attraction of all was that application of the growth pole doctrine seemed to require so little in the way of intervention. All we needed to do was lure some propulsive industries (and in the euphoria of the time, all lurable industries seemed more propulsive than repulsive) into urban centres of retarded regions. Then . . . we would sit back and let the market generate spread effects to the peripheral region.

In general, growth centre policies often resulted in 'cathedrals in the desert', i.e. 'industrial complexes whose developmental impulses are real enough, but which are channelled to linked firms and industries hundreds of miles away' (Moseley 1974: 5). The conclusion of Spanish regional policy can be generalized to other developed countries: 'the ineffectiveness of regional policies that are contrary to the market forces promoting economic growth and structural change' (Suarez-Villa and Cuadrado Roura 1993b: 150).

The Italian case provides a clear situation where regional policy, specifically growth poles, failed to have any discernible beneficial effect at all. The southern portion of Italy, the *Mezzogiorno*, has long been less industrial, and has much lower incomes and higher rates of unemployment than northern Italy, where industrial agglomerations such as Milan and Turin are found. Through both subsidies to private firms and investments made by the Italian government through its large state holding companies and semi-public firms in oil, petrochemicals and steel, 80 per cent of all new investment was required to be located in the south (Sundquist 1975: 179–87). The large, capital-intensive plants had relatively little subsequent effect on employment or income in the region (Amin 1985; Dunford 1988: 169). Moreover, local linkages were minimal and multiplier effects in the *Mezzogiorno* were small (Dunford 1986; Martinelli 1985). 'The entrepreneurs who had been relied on to establish satellite plants, it turned out, did not exist' (Sundquist 1975: 181). More recent assessments reach an identical conclusion (Florio 1996).

The shift away from regional policy

France presented an early experiment of Perroux's growth pole concept, through a set of *métropoles d'équilibre* that were intended to decentralize growth away from the Paris region (Dunford 1988: 231–95; Moseley 1974: 41–50). Marseille, the second largest French city, would seem to have been a likely candidate for a successful growth centre, one of several internationally competitive industrial complexes envisioned (Dunford 1988: 249). However, the plan to create in nearby Fos-sur-Mer an integrated port and industrial zone to rival Rotterdam did not quite succeed. Instead, what emerged was a dualistic economy, with multi-plant organizations importing their requirements and exporting their output from the region (Kinsey 1978). Lessons learned from the French experience with regional policy presaged issues for later policies. Efforts were focused on large firms, rather than on small and medium-size enterprises, and were centred on the number of jobs, not on the type of jobs, created, which were frequently unskilled and poorly paid (Dunford 1988).

Hansen (1987: 11–12) has summarized the top-down French regional development of the 1960s:

It was based on large-scale, spatially-concentrated industrial and infrastructure investments, with decision-making largely in the hands of large industrial oligopolies and financial institutions. . . Although a considerable amount of industrial decentralization took place in this context, the quality of the decentralized jobs left much to be desired. In retrospect, it is apparent that externally-induced growth typically did not provide a solid basis for sustained regional or local development.

Consequently, French regional theory and policy have shifted 'away from top-down models in favour of endogenous development at the regional and local levels' (Hansen 1987: 5; Tuppen and Thompson 1994). In addition, French policies, national as well as local, began during the 1980s actively to attract foreign investors (Tuppen and Thompson 1994).

The 1990s brought an eclecticism that contrasts sharply with attempts at scientific and general theories, methods and models. However, they have also brought a return to growth pole ideas, seen in the 'growth triangles' of Asia (Thant, Tang and Kakazu 1994).

Only one thing emerges from this survey of recent literature in the field of regional development: we are in an era of extreme fluidity and flexibility regarding location of industry, agglomeration and deglomeration, integration and disintegration, polarization and 'polarization-reversal'. The only principles that seem to prevail are 'it depends' and 'anything goes' (Higgins and Savoie 1995: 178–9).

The period of active regional policy evident in most Western countries during the 1960s and 1970s is now much reduced in favour of *laissez-faire* and reliance on the market. The impact of regional development programmes was 'overshadowed by sectoral development programmes, many of which have regional economic implications' in West Germany and the USA (Romsa, Blenman and Nipper 1989: 51). The *implicit* or *indirect* regional effects of other, sectoral policies, on the other hand, have been enormous. Policies include tax structure and macroeconomic policy, which favour some sectors and regions, social security, which stimulated migration to the sunbelt, and defence spending, which is highly biased geographically. In fact, the largest implicit industrial and regional policy in the USA has been defence spending (Markusen 1986). Regional policy in the USA can be characterized as 'informal industrial policy', increasingly decentralized to state and local governments (Markusen 1995).

In large part because of the absence of regional policy at the national (or federal) level in Canada and the USA, the individual provinces, states and localities began to take uncoordinated initiatives to promote economic development (Haider 1986; Osborne 1988). The decentralization of policy, perhaps a spontaneous move toward bottom-up policy, became widespread among the developed countries by the 1980s (Albrechts *et al.* 1989; Fox Przeworski 1986).

Regional policy in Europe in the 1990s

Many assessments of British regional policy, centred around the subsidization of industrial location in designated 'assisted areas' located primarily in the North of England, Scotland, and Wales, have been positive (Ashcroft 1982). However, measurement problems plague such evaluations, and Buck and Atkins (1983), for example, conclude that the benefits of such policies are usually overstated. However, in part because of policy bias toward investment (i.e. subsidies for capital investment), the policy cost per job generated was quite high (Diamond and Spence 1983). Martin (1988: 408) is less sure of positive effects, concluding that 'regional policy did little to reduce or eliminate the unemployment differential between the "industrial periphery" and the prosperous "south and east".' Whether it was regional policy that attracted firms and investment to assisted areas, for example, rather than simply the availability of low-wage labour, is not easily sorted out.

In part because of the EU structural funds, regional policy in European countries (or member states) has been in steady decline, especially in northern Europe. In addition, the European Commission has intervened to control the extent of designated assisted areas and incentives within them, again mainly in northern Europe. Thus, EU policy has focused primarily on the most backward areas (Bachtler and Michie 1993; Sadler 1992b). In the UK, regional assistance is now dwarfed by EU structural funds and 'by other, ostensibly "non-regional" forms of government spending . . . that have far-reaching and uneven effects on the different areas of the country' (Martin 1993: 804). In addition, a series of local development initiatives have emerged but these lack coordination or a national framework (Bovaird 1992).

The European Union (formerly the European Community) has taken an important role in regional policy throughout Europe. Through the European Regional Development Fund (ERDF), which since 1975 and more significantly since 1988 has provided regional subsidies throughout the EU, the supranational unit approves nationally designated regions for assistance. Several development objectives are given priority for 1994–1999: regions lagging behind in development (Objective 1); areas in industrial decline (Objective 2); fight against long-term unemployment, youth unemployment, and exclusion from the labour market (Objective 3); preventive adaptation of the workforce to industrial and production system changes (Objective 4); adjustment of agricultural structures and modernization of the fishing industry (Objective 5a); vulnerable rural zones (Objective 5b); and regions with very low population density (Objective 6). Although all have spatial variations, Objectives 1, 2, 5b and 6 are considered to represent EU regional policy at present (Alden 1996).

The Single European Act obliges the EU to reduce the differences between regions in an effort to realize the objective of social cohesion. The largest beneficiaries of the EU's structural funds (including the Fund for Regional Development, the Social Fund and the Guarantee Fund for Agriculture) from 1988 to 1993 were Ireland, Greece and Portugal, Europe's traditional periphery, whereas Italy and Spain received the largest per capita expenditure (Sengenberger 1993). However, the Merseyside (Liverpool) region of the UK was granted Objective 1 status in 1993, placing it among those 'regions whose development is lagging behind' (Boland 1996). EU research and technology development (RTD) funds also are directed to some extent toward less favoured regions, particularly those outside France, Germany and the UK, Europe's largest R&D-performing countries (Higgins 1991). However, the levels of support remain too low to turn around the prospects of backward regions (Amin and Malmberg 1992).

The addition of new member states to the EU and the impending addition of countries in Eastern Europe suggests that there will not be much stability to regional policy in the coming years (Hardy *et al.* 1995). Nor will the presence of the supranational authority of the EU prevent the growing competition between localities and regions within Europe, both for mobile investment and for status regarding EU programmes (Lloyd and Meegan 1996; Nordström 1996). The regional disparities that emerged under socialism are giving rise to a new set of disparities, related to infrastructure, the pattern of foreign investment, and West–East contrasts that favour regions nearest to EU boundaries (Downes 1996; Smith 1996).

European regional policy thinking also revolves around regions that do not follow national boundaries. One proposal has eight European 'super regions' (Gripaios and Mangles 1993). More linked to urban nodes are the various maps of the new 'Europe of the regions', based on the presence of strong economies in Europe's world cities and sunbelt regions, and in the 'banana' stretching from southern England through northern Italy (Nijkamp 1993). These new regions have prompted new thinking about regional cooperation and integrating institutions that go beyond traditional regional development concerns (Cappellin 1993).

The local policy dimension

During the 1980s, development policies emerged to embrace a much greater orientation on local and informal mechanisms and on stimulating private investment and entrepreneurship (Marelli 1985). In general, 'local economic development activities have assumed the importance once attached to regional policy in both Europe and North America' (D'Arcy and Guissani 1996). To some extent, this reflects a 'hollowing out' of the national state, which has resulted in a post-Fordist replacement of the Keynesian welfare state: the Schumpeterian workfare state and a focus on labour market flexibility in a context of international competition (Jessop 1994; Peck 1996).

As Chapter 5 has demonstrated, not all areas are equally prone to success in entrepreneurship. New firm formation remains a process heavily biased toward areas where entrepreneurship has occurred previously, and tends to reinforce the growth of places and regions where education and opportunity are greatest. It is not difficult to conclude that regional growth based on entrepreneurship could have the same concentrated pattern as that based on large-scale enterprises. The success of some localities, including industrial districts, has led to a proliferation of (often duplicative) local development efforts (Amin and Malmberg 1992; Sengenberger 1993). Local authorities or governments were previously relatively passive or reactive with respect to technological and economic change. They often learned of new technologies late in their development or after their diffusion was well under way. Since competition between places is fierce, local efforts are constrained by the existing situation, and favour cumulative strengths found only in agglomerated regional economies. 'There is no obvious first best approach to local economic development' and each locality will depend on local institutions, priorities and relationships (D'Arcy and Guissani 1996: 171). Thus, there are strategic as well as economic determinants of local competitiveness (Kresl 1995).

Competition for economic development in the USA is a big business. All 50 states and thousands of cities, counties, suburbs and smaller communities take part in what has been called a 'second civil war' (Ryans and Shanklin 1986). These governmental units are complemented by a group of private sector interests, especially property owners and land developers, local chambers of commerce, utility firms, and banks (Levy 1990). Similar 'city-marketing' takes place in the Netherlands and elsewhere (Borchert 1994), but the USA has more individual entities competing for jobs and industry than any other country. The larger, better-funded industrial development groups, which tend to be those in large cities, are better able to create and maintain connections to other groups and individuals. These external connections and the knowledge they provide yield a better – even a state-of-the-art – mix of incentives, promotional advertising and ultimately, greater job creation (Humphrey, Erickson and McCluskey 1989).

Industrial policy traditionally was the responsibility of national governments, but increasingly regions and cities are crafting their own responses to economic competition. Although evident in the USA in the 1970s, well before the Reagan era (Cobb 1993; Goodman 1979), the trend toward a greater local *entrepreneurial* role grew greatly in the 1980s (Clarke and Gaile 1992; Eisinger 1988; Fox Przeworski 1986; Haider 1986; Harvey 1989). This involves new forms of inter-local competition, based on knowledge of the process of entrepreneurship rather than on zero-sum smokestack chasing (Blakely 1994; Fosler 1992; Isserman 1994; Leicht and Jenkins 1994). Specific national and local forms of local development and local policy are formed and sustained by local cultural norms and bonds (Ettlinger 1994).

The entrepreneurial city is observed in many countries but about it perhaps too little theory exists (Clarke 1993; Hall and Hubbard 1996). The market orientation poses a different set of expectations on local government – more focused on growth and less on social needs (Bellone 1988; Clarke 1993). Increasingly, local policies involve *partnerships* between public and private sector actors (Bennett and McCoshan 1993). The 'participatory, partnership nature' of local self-improvement programmes made people from state agencies, firms, universities and consultancies learn about each other's capabilities and needs (Isserman 1994: 89). However, the business view tends to dominate partnerships in the USA, usually because of greater uncertainty on the part of public sector actors (Rubin 1988: 250), compared with their greater professionalism in the UK (Wolman and Stoker 1992). This tends to reinforce the characterization of local development policies since the 1980s as 'neoliberal' (Benington and Geddes 1992). Perhaps because of the priorities of local business elites, industrial recruitment ('smokestack chasing') continues to be very popular (Loveridge

1996; Wood 1993). More than at larger geographic scales, it is easier to identify those who lose and those who benefit from policies within individual localities (Leitner 1990).

Places – including cities, regions and nations – have turned to marketing themselves in the same manner as consumer products. This is not a completely new phenomenon, but it has taken on a much larger importance in the last ten years. In response to rapid technological change, global competition and inter-governmental power shifts, places see a need to advertise their attractions to target markets. These target markets include four fairly distinct groups: visitors, residents and workers, business and industry, and export markets. For each of these, a marketing programme can include creation of a positive image, developing attractions, and improving local infrastructure and quality of life (Gold and Ward 1994; Kotler, Haider and Rein 1993; Ryans and Shanklin 1986).

Two aspects of place marketing are important: first, the explicit alteration of a long-held image through a 'make-over' and, second, amassing local political support and priority toward investments needed to effect a change. The make-over is a common feature of local development policy, involving the creation of a new image and new 'positioning' of a place in the minds of investors and decision-makers (Haider 1992; Holcomb 1994; Loftman and Nevin 1996; Short *et al.* 1993). Older forms of 'place promotion', focused on the intrinsic attributes of a place, have evolved into marketing to match the demands of targeted customers (Ashworth and Voogd 1994; Kotler, Haider and Rein 1993).

Typically, marshalling local political support is done by a coalition of those who have a vested interest in infrastructure improvements and the growth of the local market, such as banks, newspapers and landowners, although their activities are often behind the scenes (Axford and Pinch 1994; Cox and Mair 1988). Competition takes various forms. Cities compete fiercely for conventions, fairs and exhibitions in Europe and in North America (Rubalcaba-Bermejo and Cuadrado-Roura 1995; Zelinsky 1994). However, competition between places can distract local leaders from focusing on their strengths in order to compete with other places in new areas. Perhaps even more difficult is institutionalizing collective learning processes locally (Knight 1995). Cox (1995) suggests a reason for the inability to focus: that 'communities' or 'cities' consist of highly diverse interests which have to be coordinated on behalf of local economic development.

Seldom are local policies and promotions evaluated, and these tend to avoid key questions, such as 'What is a job?' and 'How long does it last?' (Foley 1992). When evaluations are done frequently, they find that few jobs – and even fewer good jobs – result from promotional and make-over efforts (Fenich 1994; Loftman and Nevin 1996). The tendency remains to 'shoot anything that flies; claim anything that falls' (Rubin 1988). The major conclusion of this short-term job-counting is that local economic development is in practice much more concerned with growth than with development (Chapter 1) (Wolman and Spitzley 1996).

Of major concern in many of the more neoliberal policies is a focus on the labour market and training, with the objective of making workers more flexible for the needs of local employers (Benington and Geddes 1992). The failure of the Training and Enterprise Councils (TECs) to improve the skills of the British workforce is a result of the many contradictions in this major ideological project, which has gone further in Britain than in the USA (Jones 1996; Peck 1996).

National differences exist, as might be expected, reflecting the power and resources of local authorities. In the USA, for example, business groups are relatively influential and active, in contrast to a greater role by local politicians in the UK (Hall and Hubbard 1996). Local modes of social regulation are a product of the local state and culture as well as those at the national level. These create a local institutionalization of labour markets that determines the degree to which labour can be made flexible (Peck 1996).

An example of local industrial development effort is in southern California, centred on Los Angeles, to replace its dependence on a declining military sector with an electric vehicle industry. The centre of car production in the USA is the Detroit area, but environmental concerns and the lingering promise of electric vehicles has taken root largely elsewhere, notably in southern California. The development of such an industry relies on technologies markedly different from those in the internal combustion engine, and hinges on the technology of rechargeable batteries. Battery technology is evolving only slowly, and in the 1990s most experimental vehicles are still seen loaded with banks of batteries in order to be capable of a trip of a few hundred kilometres. Based on local technological capabilities in southern California, efforts have emerged to attempt to develop not only the necessary technologies but also the markets and institutions necessary for commercial success (Slifko and Rigby 1995).

Regional systems of innovation: creating a 'learning region'

The external economies generated by strong firms, a labour and supplier base, and a knowledge base are more often local or regional than national (Krugman 1992; Porter 1990). The vitality of industrial districts revolves around the learning efficiency of these areas, and they are based on cultural norms that are not the same everywhere or easily transplanted or created (Saxenian 1994; Sweeney 1996). It takes decades for a regional technological infrastructure to develop; a fact that regional and local governments, like national governments, find difficult to accept (Castells and Hall 1994; Haug and Ness 1992). When it does exist, in combination with a technical culture and strong institutions, learning proceeds efficiently based both on local knowledge and assets and on links to networks elsewhere (Maillat 1995; Storper 1995b). The strength of the system depends greatly on competent governments and firms working to understand and support one another for the benefit of the region and its population.

The allure of high technology sparked many local and regional policies to create or generate innovativeness in peripheral areas or regions and to upgrade the technological capability of local firms through regional innovation centres (Brainard, Leedman and Lumbers 1988: 25–30; Malecki and Nijkamp 1988). This is taking place despite a belief by some that 'it is difficult to escape the conclusion that high technology policy is best left to nations rather than to regions or urban areas.' Much of the policy infrastructure, including capital markets, tax policy, and government procurement, operate only at the national level (Macdonald 1987: 368–9; Power 1988: 174–8). On the other hand, much of what supports the competitiveness of firms is local in character (Porter 1990: 154–9; Senker 1985).

Policies, mostly in a local, decentralized manner, are attempting to create milieus and regional and local systems of innovation (Camagni 1995b). This is much the same as the discussion in Chapter 5 concerning policies to create local institutions to support entrepreneurship. The local systems in Baden-Württemberg and Italy provide models for other regions. The challenges are multi-faceted, involving technical education and services for small firms (Bianchi and Bellini 1991; Bianchi and Giordani 1993; Brusco 1992). Policies are particularly challenging in the case of lagging regions, such as parts of peripheral Europe. It is most useful in that situation to integrate policies addressing different aspects of the local environment (e.g. entrepreneurship, infrastructure and training), targeting existing local knowledge, and being selective in the number of sites in order to focus resources sufficiently (Camagni 1995b).

In fact, the local institutions that support learning in firms and in workers comprise what can be called a *regional system of innovation*, similar in nature to a national system of innovation (Arcangeli 1993; Cooke and Morgan 1994b). The regional system links global knowledge of generic technologies to specific applications produced by local firms (Arcangeli 1993). The importance of links to global networks is a recurrent finding in recent research on industrial districts and technology districts (Amin and Thrift 1992; Maillat 1995; Mueller and Loveridge 1995; Storper 1993). But the greater risk is that the interactive networks of small and medium-size firms will break down or become competitive rather than collaborative (Harrison 1994). It is the firms in an area on which the innovation system relies, and public structures play only a supportive role (Cooke and Morgan 1994b). Many of the greatest challenges are people-related: the key network people must have networking skills, be psychologically open, combine technology, business, management and marketing skills, be able to convince firms to join networking activities, themselves be innovative and initiative-taking, and be well-networked within their own country as well as with innovation centres in Europe, Japan and North America (Cooke 1996b: 170).

The *local technological infrastructure* – the counterpart to the same concept at the national level discussed earlier – is more difficult for local policies to influence. Feldman and Florida (1994), for example, include in the concept university R&D, industrial R&D, agglomerations of related industry, and specialized business services. None of these is typically an object of local development, and they can be influenced only indirectly by investment and promotion of quality-of-life areas or amenities such as arts and culture to attract the elite workers in knowledge-based activities (Gottlieb 1994; Knight 1995). In line with targeting local policies, however, places keen to promote the biotechnology industry have successfully used incubators as a means to promote new firms in this sector (Blakely and Nishikawa 1992).

Policies for regional high-tech development _____

Tremendous competition has ensued regarding the competition for high technology. Competition based on offering incentives to research-based organisations 'can widen rather than narrow regional disparities' (Brainard, Leedman and Lumbers (1988: 30). Competition for high technology was a major fashion throughout the 1970s and 1980s (Eisinger 1988: 266–89; OTA 1984). Research parks or science parks were created as potential cores of new Silicon Valleys, in an effort to emulate the early successful experience of Stanford Research Park in Palo Alto, California, or of Route 128 surrounding Boston. Many regions and communities failed to differentiate within high-tech industry and attracted only branch plants, and then wondered why spin-offs did not take place (Malecki 1984; Miller and Coté 1987; Ryans and Shanklin 1986). Overall, the tendency has been for regions already strong in high tech to grow stronger as new firms are formed and corporations locate new facilities.

The designation with a catchy label of 'high-tech highways' is a particularly popular way to add high tech to conventional industrial recruitment (Table 7.3). These designated regions or corridors are intended to inspire perceptions similar to those elicited by Silicon Valley, Route 128 and the Research Triangle (Farrell 1983; Rogers and Larsen 1984). Many of them are imprecise or optimistic; others are so large in area that any uniqueness of location is lost. Some are also fleeting, vanishing after a short-term boom.

More importantly, not all policies are intended to spawn or support new firms, and instead only foster technological innovation in large corporations. However, the models created by Silicon Valley and Route 128, with their successions of spin-off firms, have inspired an assortment of policies to boost regional

Table 7.3 Popular names for high-tech regions.

Name	Location
Bionic Valley; Biomed Mountains	Salt Lake City
Ceramics Corridor	Corning, New York
Laser Lane	Orlando, Florida
Medical Mile	West of Philadelphia
Optics Valley	Tucson, Arizona
Satellite Alley	Montgomery County, Maryland (northwest of Washington, DC)
Silicon Bavaria	Munich, Germany
Silicon Bayou	Lafayette, Louisiana
Silicon Desert	Phoenix area
Silicon Forest	Portland, Oregon
Silicon Gulch	Austin, Texas
Silicon Mountain	Colorado Springs

Source: after Farrell (1983); Herbig (1994); Kelly *et al.* (1992) and Rogers and Larsen (1984: 242–51).

innovative capacity and entrepreneurial activity. Sternberg's (1996a) compre-hensive assessment concludes that the implicit effects of technology policies that lack explicitly spatial goals dominate and result in spatial unevenness, rein-forcing a few core regions. This generalization holds both in mission-oriented countries (France, the UK and the USA) and in diffusion-oriented countries (Germany and Japan).

'Targeting' industrial recruitment toward high-tech industries is another common approach, aimed at state-developed lists of 'next-generation' high-technology industries (C. Thompson 1987). Of the 35 state programmes for advanced technology that were in place in the USA by 1985 (compared with only four in 1979), most were primarily concerned with focused industrial recruitment (Allen and Levine 1986; OTA 1984). State advertising emphasizes a combination of the area's 'high-tech traditions', skilled labour and state uni-versities, together with established local advantages such as low taxes, low wage levels and other elements of a good business climate. Less typical is for indus-trial recruitment to attract firms establishing R&D facilities rather than merely branch manufacturing plants.

The experience of Silicon Glen in Scotland for other regions highlights the necessity of several conditions, most of which were noted in Chapter 6: large urban region, air connections, local university sources of workers, and patience. The long-term character of Scotland's high-tech development is striking; US firms set up their first branch plants there in the 1940s. R&D was not common until the 1970s, long after the first plants opened (Haug 1986). The Scottish semiconductor complex remains dependent on R&D and designs imported from the USA, and cannot yet be called a self-sustaining complex (J. Henderson 1989: 153).

In each case, success has seemed to elude peripheral regions for reasons that are somewhat easily identified. A prominent shortcoming of peripheral regions seems to be their low innovation potential, an outcome of the relative scarcity of R&D, especially industrial R&D, carried out there (Ewers and Wettmann 1980). R&D facilities alone, however, are no guarantee of spin-offs, even in the long run. Some places with considerable R&D have not been able to generate new firms in significant numbers, lacking synergy and local networks and com-petitive clusters of firms (Castells and Hall 1994).

Sternberg (1996a) generalizes from an analysis of seven high-tech areas (Silicon Valley, Greater Boston, Research Triangle, Western Crescent, Cambridgeshire, Munich and Kyushu) that government R&D expenditures, agglomeration (city size), the research and education infrastructure, and the age of the region are the most significant factors behind the success of a high-tech region. He concludes that the growth and development of high-tech regions is determined by a number of factors similar to those proposed by Porter's (1990) model (Chapter 1): interrelated production networks of large and small enter-prises, endowments of production factors such as skilled labour and risk capital, the demand for new knowledge-intensive products, and entrepreneurial strate-gies and competition. To these he adds a factor more significant at the regional level: 'both implicit and explicit technology policy' (Sternberg 1996b: 80).

The Japanese technopolis plan

The most ambitious example of deliberate high-technology development is the technopolis concept in Japan, a plan to reduce regional disparities and to transform all of Japan into a high-tech archipelago by building a network of regional high-tech cities (Tatsuno 1986; Toda 1987). Tsukuba Science City, the top tier of current Japanese policy, was planned during the 1960s and is now the home of two universities and 50 national research institutes. It serves as a prototype for 26 technopolises and research cores (Kawashima and Stöhr 1988; Onda 1988). The criteria used by MITI to select the locations include a typical set of urban attributes: proximity to a 'mother city' of at least 150 000 population to provide urban services, proximity to an airport or bullet train station, an integrated complex of industrial, academic and residential areas, and a pleasant living environment. These criteria generally correspond to the location factors proposed as favouring R&D and technological activities.

The purpose of the technopolis policy is to foster two types of R&D: transfer type or manufacturing-oriented R&D, and frontier or knowledge-oriented R&D (Imai 1986; Toda 1987). Manufacturing-based R&D and technology transfer between firms in specific industries in each local area have proceeded to some degree (Brainard, Leedman and Lumbers 1988: 77–8). However, it is less certain that 'frontier' R&D will take place. The centre of frontier R&D, Tsukuba, itself suffers from the typical problem of a government R&D centre: little non-government R&D is found there, largely because as it was planned manufacturing operations were restricted. Although Tsukuba is modelled on Silicon Valley, Japanese culture has been slow to spawn commercial spin-off firms (Castells and Hall 1994; Glasmeier 1988b: 275). It is too early to know if a set of government research institutes deriving from the New Earth 21 'vision' in environmental technology in the new Kansai Science City near Osaka will have the same experience. These institutes include the Research Institute of Innovative Technology for the Earth (RITE), the International Centre for Environmental Technology Transfer (ICETT), and the United Nations Environment Programme International Environmental Technology Centre (UNEP/ITEC) to add to those in telecommunications and other technologies (Castells and Hall 1994: 76–81; Myers 1992).

The technopolises have been unable to reduce significantly the allure and advantages of Tokyo within Japan for important R&D and other key corporate activities. As occurred in the implementation of growth centre policies in virtually all countries, the intense competition between candidate regions has diluted the potential for diminishing the Tokyo region's dominance in Japanese technology (Glasmeier 1988b). The allure of the Tokyo agglomeration has not been diminished by the technopolis plan, if only because of the concentration in Tokyo of residential amenities, top universities, and existing corporate headquarters and R&D (Sternberg 1995). Indeed, the success of a technopolis is highly dependent on its proximity to Tokyo (Sternberg 1995; Stöhr and Pönighaus 1992). The presence of the Kansai Science City in the Osaka agglomeration perhaps shows a realization that attempting to attract innovative activities to peripheral areas will not work. In addition, university–industry research cooperation is weak, further hindering the development potential from technopolises, regional science parks and other local efforts at high-tech development (Normille 1994).

Other national high-tech policies for regional development

The agglomeration of high-tech industry, much of it based on military production, characterizes the situation in many countries. For example, Canadian aerospace firms, which depend upon US military contracts, are geographically concentrated in Toronto and Montreal (Todd and Simpson 1985). To these can be added other clusters, such as an IT cluster in the Ottawa area (Britton 1996). German military production has its core area in Bavaria, especially in the electronics-related sectors, despite the presence of significant production centres in northern Germany (Kunzmann 1988). French aerospace production, much of which is military, has decentralized somewhat outside Paris, to Toulouse, Marseille and Bordeaux, although the highest skilled activities such as R&D in nearly all sectors remain largely in the Paris region (Beckouche 1991; Pottier 1987). These examples demonstrate the geographical concentration, rather than the dispersion, of technology, even in the face of strong government influence.

In the context of government research facilities, where profitability is not an explicit concern, scientific work undertaken in a location that requires subsidies becomes more costly, and perhaps also somewhat less effective. The extra costs of a subsidy are likely to be long-term, associated with attracting and retaining a labour force of mobile professionals, as well as costs connected with travel from a remote site to other research centres. When such considerations are taken into account, the decentralization of R&D is difficult to justify (Lacroix and Martin 1988). It is difficult to attract R&D activities to remote locations because many technical people will not locate there (Cooke 1985b; Malecki and Bradbury 1992).

Government research facilities generate few wider regional economic benefits, those being mainly associated with a concentration of high-income jobs. In addition, these facilities tend to have a low spin-off rate in both the UK and the USA (Cooper 1986; Lawton-Smith 1996). Basic research facilities are especially likely to have a low incidence of entrepreneurship, because entrepreneurial opportunities are less likely to present themselves from basic research than from other types of R&D that are spurred by market opportunities. Government research facilities may attract other research through their contribution to an area's technical labour pool. However, many government facilities are simply too large and isolated, dominating their regions in the manner of company towns, generally stifling the potential for entrepreneurship and diversified economic growth.

Industrial modernization

It became clear during the 1980s that high-technology industry was not the answer for every region. Excessive competition and a tendency for firms to gravitate towards places with the best resources left many countries and localities behind. Instead, the needs of firms in low-technology industry, if met, could assist these firms – large and small alike – to be competitive on a world-class basis. The best summary of industrial modernization is made by Shapira, Roessner and Barke (1995: 69):

> Industrial modernization is thus a complex problem, involving technology, information, management, training and financing, and raising questions of structures, private and public–private relationships, attitudes, policies and practices. It is a problem with multiple dimensions. Addressing the problem at the 'micro' level of the firm and its managers is critical; but the problem also involves 'macro' economic, technological and social policies, as well as 'meso' issues of business relationships and practices, institutional linkages and inter-firm networks, and public–private cooperation.

Regional technology transfer has become a major goal, following the lead of Japan's excellent Kohsetsushi centres (Shapira 1992, 1996). Technology transfer is not guaranteed to work, even if it is ostensibly part of a regional innovation policy, especially if it is targeted toward mainly large firms. National differences in technology transfer programmes emerge, reflecting large-scale differences in national systems of innovation and mission or diffusion orientation (Hassink 1992). Even policies that are aimed at small firms may fail, unless they include a pro-active process of seeking out small-firm clients (rather than waiting for active firms to seek out information) and long-term financing to provide continuity (Hassink 1996).

The system in Baden-Württemberg is considered the best system of institutions, providing training, information and R&D that support innovation. Small firms do not have to bear the burden of flexible production; 'many of the costs . . . are shared by or embedded in a deep network of organizations and practices in the political economy' of the region (Herrigel 1993: 17). Indeed, the institutional thickness is so great and redundant that Baden-Württemberg is a model of a networked region, in contrast to the dirigisme represented by French or Japanese technopoles or the grassroots Kohsetsushi centres (Cooke and Morgan 1994a). The institutional thickness has also in some ways encouraged firms not to collaborate, since it has allowed them to draw upon local institutions, and upon large firms such as Robert Bosch, rather than upon other small firms (Grotz and Braun 1993; Mueller and Loveridge 1995). The increasing globalization and necessity for the skill-intensive R&D of flexible production has caused a serious need for collaboration so that the regional system of innovation does not break down (Cooke and Morgan 1994a).

Because it has concentrated on complex and sophisticated new technologies, traditional technology policy has affected perhaps 5–10 per cent of firms, and typically the larger ones. Some local and regional technology strategies have evolved in the USA to address the needs of the other 90–95 per cent of firms. One of the best in the USA is the Ben Franklin Partnership, which is decentralized to four regions of Pennsylvania, each with a different industrial focus (Rahm and Luce 1992). These are coordinated in a national network of Manufacturing

Technology Centers, of which there are now 35, each focused on a different technology, as well as several other pilot programmes, outreach centres and state industrial extension programmes (Shapira, Roessner and Barke 1995).

The creation of inter-firm networks on the model of European industrial districts is growing as a regional as well as an urban strategy. This is not an easy task because, unlike growth centres, we now know that more than money is needed; institutions and a collective culture must be fostered within the local culture (Indgaard 1996; Malecki and Tootle 1996). The Danish model has been a top-down effort to create local networks, succeeded by a Technology Partnership programme (Huggins 1996). The provision of advice and technical support for small firms is an increasingly common aspect of policy, but remains unco-ordinated and largely a matter of experimentation (Britton 1991). State policies in the USA and local initiatives in the UK have evolved to respond to local conditions, but there is a risk that each locality will be unlinked to national databases and remain relatively unaware of expertise and experiences in other places that would be valuable (Gittell and Kaufman 1996; Haughton 1993).

The Austin experience illustrates the significance of cooperative institutional arrangements, especially among governments, firms, universities and other groups (Smilor, Gibson and Kozmetsky 1989). Scott (1994, 1996b) has shown the shortcomings of the weak institutional environment of southern California. However, few areas are willing to take the time to develop local industries, especially those based on small firms. In part, this is because a single large employer employs so many more people than a cluster of small firms. Added to this is the dependence of most small firms on the work provided by large companies (Young, Francis and Young 1994a,b). Creating a networked, learning region is one of the greatest regional policy challenges as we move into the twenty-first century (Cooke 1996b).

University funding

Three principal results are desired from the enhancement of universities. First, research findings lead to scientific and technological innovations, in accordance with the linear model, but also as a part of technological advance more generally. Second, development of a centre of excellence in a certain field can create or enhance a favourable 'high-tech' public image and reputation. Third, training and education provide a pool of labour, which can be important for regional recruiting (Angel 1989; Peters 1989; Shapero 1985). Boosting funding levels at government-supported universities is a relatively easy way to do something that visibly improves the high-tech status of the region. Consequently, universities are found on most checklists of high-tech location factors, but their actual effect is far from clear-cut.

A fourth effect of universities is probably the most desired, yet the least common: spin-offs of new technology-based firms. Segal (1986), drawing from British experience, makes the germane point that high-tech spin-offs take place in some locales – around the *best* institutions – without any direct university–industry connections being present. The Oxford example is a recent case in point (Lawton-Smith 1990). The Stanford and MIT examples in the

USA have probably distorted the perceived role of universities, but they do serve as (perhaps unrealistic) models for other regions (Castells and Hall 1994; Howells 1986). Research – especially the best research – can be procured from a distance, as university-industry partnerships and research support agreements in biotechnology by large drug and chemical firms have shown. To assume that universities function as 'knowledge centres' around which innovative firms will cluster is unrealistic (Howells and Charles 1988; Massey, Quintas and Wield 1992; Nijkamp and Mouwen 1987).

Despite this, many universities have instituted focused programmes, concentrating research funding on selected high-tech fields. This widespread targeting in a decentralized system runs the risk that all regions will pick the same small set of sectors, as happens in national strategic sectors. This has the additional disadvantage that a specialization in one or another research field may decrease the flexibility of universities to move into other fields or to promote interdisciplinary collaboration when the related specializations are located elsewhere (OECD 1981: 56).

The success of some areas and not others emphasizes once again the role of agglomeration, especially the combination of both government R&D funds and industrial R&D at disproportionate levels (Feldman and Florida 1994). The three most-cited high-tech regions (Silicon Valley, Route 128 and Research Triangle) have both an urban setting and a cluster of at least three universities in close proximity. However, a technological region needs more than university research and corporate R&D. It requires the dynamism of linked firms which produce best-practice goods and services.

Science parks

Science parks, with the clean office and research atmosphere of R&D facilities, have settled into suburban locales throughout the world. Whether called science parks, research parks or technology parks, these more specialized developments cater to the preference for a campus-like setting with low-density, often dispersed, building sites. Onida and Malerba (1989: 163–4) suggest that for large firms in particular, science parks allow collaborative links to be established with a recognized 'centre of excellence' in a field, and to take advantage of an agglomeration of researchers and new graduates. The 'prestige factor' weighs heavily in the decisions of large firms, but does not necessarily indicate any linkage or interaction with the local universities – or with one another (Johannisson et al. 1994; Joseph 1988).

Most experience shows that an urban environment is necessary for success. Britain's Cambridge Science Park – set up after the 'Cambridge Phenomenon' was well along – had nothing to do with the attraction of the Cambridge area for high-tech firms, although it now probably enhances the area's attraction. Proximity to London is one of Cambridge's principal attributes. Germany has also embraced science parks or 'technopolises' as a policy goal throughout the country, usually as local development efforts (Boucke, Cantner and Hanusch 1994). In general, the parks preserve the regional imbalance, which favours the prosperous German south (Schamp 1987).

Science parks are now common throughout Europe, North America and else-where (Gibb 1985). However, of the more than 100 science parks across the USA, occupancy tends to be significant only in places where high tech has been successful for other reasons, such as Stanford Research Park, Princeton Forrestal Center, and New Haven Science Park near Yale University. Each of these is located within a major urban region and is affiliated with a world-class research university. Whether the parks are oriented toward new technology-based firms or R&D facilities of TNCs depends on the innovation policy of each country (Komninos 1992).

In France, science parks take the form of Technology Centres and Regional Centres for Innovation and Technology Transfer (CRITT), which have the added objective of decentralization of economic activity from Paris (Perrin 1988b). French high-tech policy combines traditional top-down strategies with local initiatives, especially in the Grenoble and Lyon areas in southeastern France (Dyckman and Swyngedouw 1988). Sophia-Antipolis, outside Nice, is perhaps the most successful of the French *technopoles* (Perrin 1988b), but it has failed to develop a true innovative milieu (Castells and Hall 1994: 88–93). The similarity between the *technopoles* and the *métropoles d'équilibre*, the French growth poles of the 1950s, is perhaps not a coincidence.

Science parks or research parks, therefore, are an attractive but highly uncer-tain policy, often presenting little more than a theme for real estate or property sales. This may attract some firms, but parks themselves do not increase the pro-pensity for new firms to form (Britton and Gertler 1986; Felsenstein 1994). Only metropolitan regions and their bundle of amenities and infrastructure are even potential locations for new firm formation (Goddard, Thwaites and Gibbs 1986). The complex and dynamic advantages associated with urban size – face-to-face communication, pools of workers or the potential to attract and keep them – outweigh the largely aesthetic attributes of a science park. Policies have been unable to create the critical mass necessary to attract and keep professional workers, except in large urban areas. The synergy of amenities, accessibility and agglomeration factors found in large urban regions cannot really be found in smaller regions (Andersson 1985; Castells and Hall 1994; Miller and Coté 1987).

It is not surprising, then, that so few science parks in the USA and elsewhere have been successful, or that the most successful are in large urban areas (Cox 1985). The advantages present in existing concentrations of high technology make it very difficult for new areas to supplant the established high-tech regions (Malecki and Nijkamp 1988). Given the 'right' conditions, however, science parks can add measurably to regional economic development (Luger and Goldstein 1991).

Simple solutions, such as building a science park, do not create the synergy necessary for a self-sustaining area. An alternative view is that of a local or regional ecosystem, a 'constellation of specialized enterprises' with which large firms can link (Bahrami and Evans 1995). A similar idea is expressed in the Austin 'technopolis wheel', which includes venture capital, a service infra-structure, a talent pool and an entrepreneurial culture (Chapter 5). None of these synergistic developments has yet ensued from the various high-tech centres developed in the UK, Germany, Japan or Korea. Even where symbolic value has been attained, few spin-offs or local linkages have emerged (Oh and Masser 1995).

Directing technology: encouraging the development of learning regions

The strength of industrial and innovation policies is that they are based on a long-term vision of what the future will comprise, both in technological trajectories and in industrial specialization. The greatest risk of such policies is not that they will fail, but that too many other regions and nations will compete for the same goal by means of subsidies and incentives – a form of 'race to the bottom' and one of several competitive races evident in contemporary policy (Marceau 1994). It does not take high technology or frontier industries to sustain an economy. The true benefits of economic development – local linkages and continuing entrepreneurship – do not require high technology. Firms need a web of interactions and information flows within and into the region. Flows and linkages to the outside drain a region of its ideas, talent and control, unless they are balanced by a receptivity to new ideas coming from the outside. Some places – nations and regions – are simply more open to new ideas just as they are to a diversity of imports. Regions where imports are diverse and state-of-the-art are most likely to be innovative themselves. Imports, in turn, are likely to be innovative if learning by searching is taking place in the region in an active R&D environment, by a creative and knowledge-oriented labour force (Johansson and Westin 1987).

The easy answer to the failure to generate indigenous growth is the relative scarcity of R&D carried out in some regions and countries. Industrial R&D is important because it represents an 'active' outlook on the part of the firm and a level of technological progressiveness and an 'open mind', reaching out for new information and being receptive to it (Sweeney 1987: 130). Technically progressive firms take part openly in information exchange, they continually search for information, and they maintain internal communication (Carter and Williams 1959; Sweeney 1985: 95–6). In sum, regions and 'localities having high entrepreneurial vitality have characteristics similar to those of technically progressive firms, openness in giving as well as taking information, continuing effort in their own search for information and good internal communication flows. The vitality, once initiated, becomes self-reinforcing and sustaining' (Sweeney 1985: 95–6).

Coordination of the many aspects of the policy system will not work unless the private sector is part of the regional technological infrastructure and part of the networks operating there. An 'infrastructure for collaboration' between public and private sectors will resolve some of the ignorance and antagonism that frequently exists between the two sectors. In addition, worker skills and attitudes to producing quality work are among the 'invisible' factors in a local economy (Doeringer and Terkla 1990; Kanter 1995). To these we can add the 'institutional thickness' that defines the collective order of a local economy, providing the coordination necessary for a productive local economy (Amin and Thrift 1993, 1994; Scott and Paul 1990). When these local systems are in place, a locality may be able to withstand the closure of a large employer (Hammonds and Sager 1995).

Conclusion

Technological competition has had some positive effects on national and local policy. It has prompted a more long-term perspective about economic development, and it has shown the significant advantages to be gained from investments in human capital, especially through education. Interregional competition based on quality of universities, educational attainment and quality of life is an improvement over that centred on low wages, low taxes and undervaluing of education (Cobb 1993). Over the long run, regions will be better off for having devoted money to education at all levels, to investments in public infrastructure (whether justified under the rubric of quality of life or not), and to thinking in terms of economic diversity and competitiveness. The creation of new high-technology complexes will not be an everyday, or everyplace, occurrence.

At the same time, technology is not fixed in either time or space, and competitiveness today does not ensure competitiveness tomorrow. Scientific advances made in one location, whether a university or corporate laboratory, shift to other locations where further development takes place, and to yet other locations as commercial products enter into production. The aggregate economic impacts are thus dispersed to, and divided among, several locations. With large corporations, this internal process of technology transfer may have few benefits for any region or country. The same is true of most inter-firm technology transfer via licensing and other arrangements. In the end, corporate strategies and decisions regarding the location of activities determine where the benefits of science and technology end up. Only active learning regions comprised of active, innovative firms will be able to take advantage of external sources of knowledge.

It is the entrepreneurial spin-off process which is the principal mechanism of technology transfer. Indeed, new ideas enter an economy primarily through the identification of opportunities by entrepreneurs. The local nature of entrepreneurship poses great challenges, but just such a process is the basis of the successes which national and regional science and technology policies are trying to imitate. The process of entrepreneurship may be more important to regional and local economies than the process of technological change. People – skilled people – are the key element in the networks that tie a place to other places and keep innovativeness alive.

Chapter 8

The technological and competitive challenge for developing countries

The unrelenting pace of technological advance and fierce capitalist competition in products and services poses great dilemmas for those who aspire to enter global markets. While some industries and products are somewhat sheltered from the 'continuous product innovation' (Storper 1992) and 'perpetual innovation' of high-technology sectors (Kash 1989), no sector is immune from the technologically derived standards of quality and price that are set by world-class firms. Although competition was (in the recent past) predominantly price-driven, 'it has now become technology-driven' (Stevens and Andrieu 1991: 116). The 'international rules of the game' encompass not only product trade, but also trade in services, the creation and diffusion of technology, foreign direct investment and strategic corporate alliances, all of which are becoming key determinants of international competitiveness (dos Reis Velloso 1994; Stevens and Andrieu 1991; Stopford and Strange 1992).

This chapter assesses the economic progress and prospects of countries that do not fall into the club of 'advanced' economies, including both the world's population giants – China, India, Indonesia, Brazil and Russia – and the smaller economies that have been remarkably successful during the past three decades. The NICs of Asia (Hong Kong, South Korea, Singapore and Taiwan) identified technological development as a means by which to create jobs and to develop indigenous elements for future growth. Particularly critical to understanding their success is the complex interaction of different institutions and policies – implicit as well as explicit – which were the focus of the preceding chapter. As Figure 8.1 illustrates, there are aspects of growth which governments can affect directly, such as macroeconomic stability. There are also aspects which they are unable to deal with directly but which they can influence indirectly, such as the competitive behaviour of firms. Having said that, policies for innovation and entrepreneurship and for the functioning of the economy are essential, and require *flexibility* in order to respond to changing conditions in the world economy, in specific product markets and in technology (Killick 1995a; Chang and Kozul-Wright 1994; Lundvall 1992; Nelson 1993).

After a brief section on S&T and competitiveness, this chapter assesses the East Asian 'miracle' and its policy conditions for other Asian countries as well as those undergoing transition from central planning. The necessity and mechanisms of learning technology are followed by a look at the challenge of learning and competition in the context of production flexibility. Technology

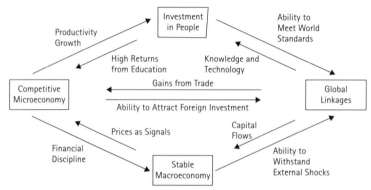

Figure 8.1   The complex interaction of firm and government policies in economic development.
Source: modified from World Bank (1991: 6, Figure 4).

transfer, a traditional route of technology acquisition, and appropriate technology are discussed briefly. The final section deals with the institutions that support upgrading of technological capability – acquiring the ability to compete in the coming century.

The necessity for science and technology

Research and development (R&D) is generally seen as a luxury affordable only by wealthy nations. The product cycle conjecture (Vernon 1966) underscored the assumption that innovation begins in rich countries with markets for new products and services, highlighting both the contrast between rich and poor nations and the direction of technological dependence. In fact, a significant portion of R&D can be performed only by people who have attained a relatively high level of education, typically at least a post-secondary technical education. At higher levels of state-of-the-art research, a graduate degree (and usually a doctorate) is the entry credential to research laboratories where such work is done.

It is well known that considerable disparity in educational opportunities is found among the nations of the world. Tertiary education (post-secondary schools and universities) is the level required for research and development and other technological activities. This level of education remains limited to elites in many, if not most, developing countries. The percentage of the 20–24 age group enrolled in post-secondary schools averaged 51 per cent in high-income countries in 1992, but only 19 per cent in the upper-middle-income category and only 5 per cent among low-income countries (World Bank 1995a: 216–17).

R&D is necessary, and has benefits beyond innovation alone. It also creates a supply of scientists and engineers with problem-solving skills, familiarity with research methodology and instrumentation, and membership in informal networks of professional peers (Bell and Pavitt 1993a: 273). However, more than education and R&D are needed. To create modern industries and businesses, entrepreneurs also need information not available from the educational system – information about foreign machines, technical processes and business practices (Headrick 1988: 352). Equally important are close links with international scientific communities, especially for monitoring research and keeping abreast of new developments (Shahidullah 1991). This form of R&D – 'international technology intelligence' – is essential for identifying alternative sources of technology (Radnor and Kaufman 1988).

In most developing countries, there is a wide separation of R&D from production, and this gap reinforces the preference of firms for foreign technology (Fransman and King 1984; Silveira 1985; Wionczek 1979). The gap is enlarged further by a lack of functioning networks of communication between government and university scientists on the one hand, and industrialists and other technology users on the other (Reddy 1979; Stewart 1978). Perhaps the greatest weakness in S&T in developing countries is the fact that little industrial R&D takes place. Government R&D institutes, rather than firms, perform most of the R&D in developing countries (Crane 1977). Companies that do their own R&D are able to benefit more from technology imports. They are better informed about the technology market before becoming buyers, and they import only those components they are unable to produce or purchase economically or fast enough. However, the more technically progressive firms also tend to be the largest ones. Small firms are generally not involved in either importing technology or conducting R&D (Desai 1980, 1985). Government research laboratories, which are expected to provide technology to small firms, tend to have few, if any, links to small firms. These institutes are generally removed from manufacturing and marketing, and thus do little to assist the competitiveness of small firms (Desai 1980). Moreover, government monitors of foreign technical collaborations attempt to prevent 'over imports' of imported technology, and can often serve to reduce rather than increase national technical capability (Deolalikar and Evenson 1990: 251).

Measured by R&D and other input measures, the technological gap between advanced countries and developing countries generally appears to be growing, not shrinking, with few exceptions (Roessner *et al.* 1996). Moreover, an inadequate base of skills and the absence of both a socioeconomic infrastructure and a technological infrastructure prevent necessary learning activities from taking place. Learning is essential to both enhancing production capacity and accumulating technological capabilities. This takes place most often through informal technological activities, rather than in formal R&D. Informal technological activities are closely associated with formal R&D, in the sense that skilled and technically competent personnel are central to both sets of activities. But in most developing countries, S&T policy needs to focus on implementation and absorption, rather than on state-of-the-art technology as viewed in advanced countries (Shahidullah 1991). Different methods of technology acquisition and diversified sources may be a better means to reduce technological dependence (Ernst and O'Connor 1989). In addition, networks of communication and information flow – from firm to firm, from government R&D facility to firms, and with foreigners – are critical to knowing about and learning technology. The NICs, especially South Korea and Taiwan, provide one model for development in a technology-based world.

Global competitiveness

The key standard of competitiveness is *best-practice technology:* the best products, the most efficient production methods, the most innovative markets. The continual transformation of products and processes makes it imperative that information acquisition, concerning new techniques and the actions of other producers, be a routine part of business activity. As new technology and products are learned, acquired, evaluated and improved upon, a firm or region comes to know about best-practice technology and to be prepared for new and substitute products in order to be 'world competitive' (Dore 1989). Moreover, products must meet international standards of quality, materials, workmanship, after-sale service and delivery schedules (Rhee 1990).

The critical nature of acquiring knowledge refers to two levels of knowledge: global best practice and niche market opportunities. Global best practice is the most difficult to learn, since it demands that firms compete in – or be linked directly to – the global scale of competition. Unless they learn the norms and standards of global competition, firms generally fail to be competitive (Baily and Gersbach 1995). Knowledge of market niches also requires a high degree of contact with markets. This means that exports are required for competitiveness (Roessner and Porter 1990). Export-oriented manufacture has to meet international quality and price competition standards, and this stimulates firms to seek out information on new technology and ways to adapt and blend new with old technology (Ichimura 1990). Knowledge is not only of the high-tech variety. It also derives from tailoring goods to specific niche markets that can and will pay a premium price. Firms that supply global firms also need to know best practice. TNCs are keenly aware of the standards to which they are held, and they must hold their suppliers to a similar level of quality and delivery (Levy and Dunning 1993).

Accumulating technological capability over time is an essential, but not a simple, task. Bell and Pavitt (1993a,b) list the major features of technology accumulation:

1. resource inputs (research, design, prototype products, process and production engineering);
2. the central role of firms: 'By concentrating on other institutions, science and technology policy in most developing countries has been misplaced; the objective should be to encourage the development of technological capabilities within firms because market mechanisms alone may be insufficient' (p. 262);
3. tacit knowledge – the rules of thumb embodied in people and institutions and acquired only with experience;
4. learning by doing and by other methods;
5. cumulative change;
6. externalities, appropriability and uncertainty;
7. sectoral differences;
8. inter-firm linkages and networks; and
9. the complementarity of technology imports and local technological accumulation.

Bell and Pavitt (1993a: 270–2) also characterize best-practice national systems for the accumulation of technology as similar to Porter's (1990) 'diamond' model of the determinants of national advantage (Chapter 1). The process of technological accumulation is exemplified best in the experience of the NICs, but their experience also raises critical questions concerning the role of government policy in facilitating that accumulation.

Business strategies within firms (related to price, quality and features) must be integrated with technology strategies (survival, catching up, leadership orientation). This is common within companies in advanced countries (Chapter 3), but is far from standard in many developing countries (Sharif 1994a,b). However, transformation of business practices at the micro level, i.e. within the firm – is necessary but is not sufficient to bring about competitiveness. 'Competitiveness is created at the firm level', but it requires a 'systemic competitiveness' based on 'complex patterns of interaction between government, enterprises, and other actors . . . in order to shape a supportive environment' specific to each place (Meyer-Stamer 1995: 148). *Systemic competitiveness* refers to the interaction of the components of the national economy, including the financial, production, innovation and governance systems (Bradford 1994). As a framework for thinking about policy and the role of government, the systemic paradigm is 'consistent with a redefined state capable of supporting initiative, innovation and investment in the private sector by providing a strategic framework for investment decisions, channels for interaction between the public and private sectors, and supportive policies for economic growth' (Bradford 1994: 58; Lim and Song 1996: 76).

Nowhere is the interaction between firm behaviour and public and private institutions more controversial than in East Asia, where the success of the NICs is attributed by some to neoliberal *laissez-faire* policies, and by others to a powerful mix of public involvement in technological accumulation and economic success (Brohman 1996).

An East Asian 'miracle'? Industrial and technology policy in the development process

The World Bank's (1993) study, *The East Asian Miracle*, is a highly visible and controversial effort to explain the success of eight high-performing Asian economies (HPAEs) – Japan, the 'four tigers' (Hong Kong, South Korea, Singapore and Taiwan), and three others: Indonesia, Malaysia and Thailand. It also takes pains to denounce the usefulness of government intervention and industrial policies. The World Bank's answers to what was responsible for the 'miracle' were first proposed in the bank's 1991 report (World Bank 1991), which recommended a 'market-friendly' strategy as the crux of government policy. The market-friendly approach includes policy choices related to economic 'fundamentals' as well as selective interventions and the performance of national institutions (Figure 8.2). To these the bank adds two forms of competition as essential: market-based competition, both in export and domestic markets, and contest-based competition, where firms compete for information, credit and

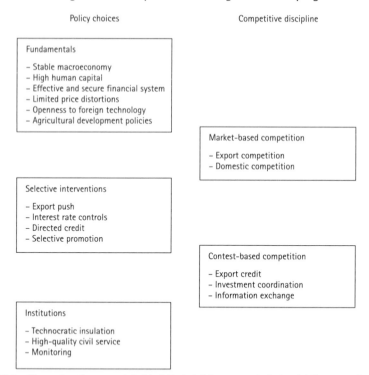

Figure 8.2   The policy framework behind East Asia's economic 'miracle'. Source: after World Bank (1993: 88, Figure 2.1).

other preferences according to clear and well-defined rules that have no favourites. Together, the policy choices and competitive discipline imposed lead to accumulation, effective allocation of capital investment and of labour (human capital), and productivity growth. The outcomes are desirable ones: rapid and sustained growth and an equal income distribution (World Bank 1993: 88).

The market-friendly, neoliberal policy regime has become standard for the World Bank and its sister institution, the International Monetary Fund (IMF), in structural adjustment programmes that are conditions for World Bank and IMF financing. 'The essence of such adjustment, in its "ideal" form, consists of removing all selective government interventions from the economy' (Lall 1994a: 78). This standard, 'ideological' policy prescription results in a 'stable macro-economy' but also in lower wages, and no assurance of growing competitiveness of local firms (Amsden 1994; Amsden and van der Hoeven 1996; Lall 1994a).

To a large extent, the debate over the 'miracle' is a debate about industrial policy. 'The clear message of the study is that if industrial policies could not succeed in the East Asian countries with their highly efficient bureaucracies, *ipso facto* these would be inappropriate for the rest of the developing world, which is not blessed with such high quality administrative assets' (A. Singh 1995: 99). Industrial policy differs greatly throughout the world, and the USA is widely considered to have no industrial policy, as Chapter 7 has shown. There are many variations of policy regimes among the advanced countries and it is difficult to judge the effectiveness of the combinations of policies found in any country (A. Singh 1995). The World Bank concludes, based on a narrow view of industrial policy, that such intervention does not work, or does not work as well as sound economic fundamentals. When the evidence is clear that the interventions of some countries contributed to their extraordinary growth, 'this was only possible because of highly unusual historical and institutional circumstances' (World Bank 1993: 366).

The neoliberal policy of minimal intervention has good intentions when it concerns macroeconomic issues – 'No one proposes bad macro policies' (Lall 1994b: 646). But the fact is that governments and other institutions may be crucial if economies and economic actors are going to be able to deal with the uncertainty and rapid change that is part of technological change. The neo-classical tradition that holds sway at the World Bank provides little or no support for industrial policy (Pack and Westphal 1986). This line of thinking allows for policy to counter market failure, but it is failures in skills, in information and in technology that stand out as critical areas for policy (Lall 1994a,b). In part, the issue is one of which metaphor best describes the process of economic growth and the role of government: that of the *engine* of capital or human capital accumulation, the *chemical* metaphor of the catalyst, the *biological* metaphor of government adaptive to the changing needs of the economy, or the *physics* metaphor of equilibrium that sees no role for government (Stiglitz 1996).

The espousal of 'market-friendly' policies also contradicts the experience of the eight countries on which it is based, and the importance of selective interventions (Pack and Westphal 1986). Perhaps in Japan, with the dominant role of business, government intervention 'is unlikely to have played the decisive role' (Crook 1993: 14). In the rest of East Asia, the story is different. In addition to policies that were able to shift as firms learned about technology and markets, all four NICs emphasized development of human resources through education. Infrastructure provision and human resource development are considered benign, market-friendly policies that have undoubtedly contributed to East Asian development (Brohman 1996; Kim 1993a).

It is clear, however, even from the 'miracle' report, that governments in East Asia had a heavy involvement in the economic progress of their economies. This took different forms in different countries, but Perkins (1994) identifies three distinct groups: the manufactured export-led state interventionist model of Japan, South Korea and Taiwan; the free-port service, commerce-dominated model of Hong Kong and Singapore; and a model of economies rich in natural resources but not in human resources (Indonesia, Malaysia and Thailand). The distinctions between these are glossed over in the World Bank study but have been the subject of a great deal of other research which suggests that in South Korea, Singapore and Taiwan, intervention has included but has gone beyond macroeconomic policies to involve an array of policies targeted at economic decisions in particular firms and sectors (Amsden 1989; Deyo 1987; Lall 1994a; Wade 1990).

Others are not convinced that a miracle ever took place. Krugman (1994c) believes that only large increases in the quantity – but not in the quality – of capital and labour inputs stimulated productivity increases, which can be neither repeated nor sustained. The surge of new labour force entrants, especially of young women, has been noted by others (Lim 1980; Salaff 1992).

What is clear is that the HPAEs were outward-looking rather than inward-looking and autarchic, and this orientation seems critical for all economic development. Import substitution was used only as a means of infant-industry promotion, and producers were pushed to face market pressures with regard to prices and product quality in a fairly short time (Evans 1995; Perkins 1994). But most importantly, all of the HPAEs have taken a view which the 'miracle' report and standard neoclassical economics downplay: that 'technological change is at the heart of industrialization' and economic development (Pack and Westphal 1986: 87). It is the *combination* of a market orientation that is aware of world standards and the locally based technological basis for attaining them that is the development challenge. 'The learning process faces a number of market failures that conventional trade theory ignores or assumes away. Once they are taken into account, however, the scope for industrial policy in creating and sustaining comparative advantage becomes more apparent' (Lall 1994a: 74). Chang (1994: 89) puts it more strongly: 'Industrial policy is a superior way to promote technical change.' For late industrializers, learning is the key process, to be superseded by innovating (Amsden 1989, 1994). The learning processes depend critically on local conventions, institutions, and the development of inter-firm interdependence, but these have the desired developmental results only where global and local market needs are also met. 'The constant and uncertain process of learning differs radically from the standard neoclassical model of firm development, and leads to different policy implications' (Lall 1994b: 648; Storper 1995a).

Weiss (1990) suggests that there are two alternative pathways of scientific and technological development: a competitive, market-oriented path and a protected, non-market path. South Korea and Taiwan have gone furthest down the former, and India and Mexico were (with the exception of the USSR) furthest down the protected path. Contact in the NICs with global best practice was continual, through alliances with TNCs rather than through licences for obsolete technology, a persistent flaw of many Indian firms (Evans 1995). 'Enforced competition' and lack of protection of 'national champion' firms stand out in East Asian growth (Stopford and Strange 1992: 219–20). These comprise part of the market-friendly policy of East Asia espoused by the World Bank. Capitalism, by some definitions, is characterized by the risks of loss by individuals who stand to make personal gains; a policy regime that protects individuals and groups from risks is counter to economic growth (Engerman 1994; Evans 1995; Rosenberg and Birdzell 1986).

Perhaps most important, human capital investment in East Asia enhanced the skills of workers, and it was combined with the growth of entrepreneurial organizations that could put technological skills to productive use (Evans 1995: 216). The World Bank stresses the need for primary education, but tends to ignore the need for tertiary education of scientists and engineers for R&D and technological learning, which were an important dimension of the path taken by both Taiwan and South Korea (Ranis 1995).

Each country's policy experience was distinct, as were other elements of growth. Despite being lumped together by most observers, 'certain policies were given high priority in some places and scarcely existed in others' (Woronoff 1992: 169). Among the most stark contrasts is the dominance of large firms in South Korea – the *chaebol* – and their almost complete absence in Taiwan (*The Economist* 1990; Koo 1987; McKay and Missen 1995). Although they compete in most sectors, the *chaebol* have not followed identical paths (Chen and Sewell 1996). However, while government intervention in economic activity was standard practice throughout East Asia, this was not done in a statist, dirigiste manner, but with a respect for the market and the needs of firms entering the market in each sector (Evans 1995). *Developmental states*, with their enlightened and autonomous bureaucracies, were best able to do this, utilizing *midwifery* to assist new enterprises to emerge or existing groups to try new ventures, and *husbandry* to encourage firms to meet the challenges of the market. Douglass (1994: 560) suggests that 'only a strongly interventionist state can steer a course through the socially and politically arduous processes of late industrialisation in a highly competitive world economy.' In all four NICs, the developmental state structures were in place by 1965, and had already shifted from import substitution to outward-looking policies (Castells 1992; Rimmer 1995).

It is this flexibility in government policy, made possible by bureaucracies competent to identify the need for change and to carry it out, that distinguish East Asia from other places (Evans 1995; Ranis 1995). These might be called 'flexible rigidities' in institutional structures and actions (Chang 1995b; Dore 1986). The uncertain, evolutionary, disequilibrium process of learning requires 'a complex network of economic and social relations' and 'institutional diversity' rather than rigidity (Chang and Kozul-Wright 1994: 884). National entrepreneurial states are able to foster disequilibrium learning by encouraging firms themselves to *learn by monitoring* (Sabel 1994). Flexibility in this sense includes both short-term and long-term actions by individuals, firms and institutions (Table 8.1).

We next look briefly at stages of technological development in the East Asian model of technology upgrading. This is followed by brief descriptions of several economies and their development paths, focusing in particular on their attention to technological development and the creation of creative 'learning' economies.

The challenge of technology upgrading

Among the most systematic approaches to developing a technological capability is the *followers' strategy for technological development*, which emphasizes the need for indigenous human resources to allow a nation or region to 'shift' to the skilled labour-intensive activities found in the early stage of the product life-cycle and at higher levels in the international division of labour (Cumings 1987; Evans 1995; Sen 1979). Japan was the first country to follow this sequence, and has been emulated (more or less explicitly) by South Korea and Taiwan. In the initial stage, *implementation* of imported foreign technology and dependence on

Table 8.1   Dimensions of flexibility in an economy.

	Type of flexibility	
	Responsive (short-term)	Innovative (long-term)
Agents		
Individuals	Elasticity of demand Elasticity of labour supply	Investment in skills Entrepreneurship

Firms and other
    organizations
	Elasticity of supply
	Imitation and adaptation of
	  products and processes
		Investment, R&D and
		  innovation

Institutions	Transaction costs
	Policy management
		Public investment in
		  education, research and
		  infrastructure
		Sociopolitical innovation

Determinants of flexibility	Information Market efficiency Openness Political autonomy Population age structure	Education Technological capability Industrialization Historical and social influences

Source: Modified from Killick (1995b: 8, Figure 1.2).

foreign experts prevail. The second stage, *assimilation* of the technology, permits product diversification based on indigenous capabilities. A local parts industry to serve the expanded production may also emerge. Finally, the third stage comprises *improvement* of technology to enhance competitiveness of both products and processes in international markets (Kim 1980). A key element in this model is the development of local scientific and engineering talent. A fourth stage would be the development of an independent innovative capability.

Instead of systems of production, countries and their industries must develop *systems of learning* and *systems of searching* for future technology (Andersen and Lundvall 1988; Bell 1984). Hobday (1995) has generalized the experience of the NICs into a model of export-led technological learning from behind the technology frontier. It involves a progression from simple to complex learning and R&D. External sources of information can initially be purchased, but they will only be absorbed, and therefore effective in the long run, if there is sufficient local technical capability (Ernst and O'Connor 1989: 23; Lall 1995). Taking an optimistic view, Ernst and O'Connor (1989: 24) believe that the range of opportunities opened up by new technologies is so wide that no country and no firm can close off all options or monopolize all the potential innovations. Thresholds for R&D and investment are relatively low in some areas, such as software, instrumentation and machinery. Some of these require skills that can be acquired through formal education and training, rather than through extensive learning by doing. Perhaps most importantly, competition between technology suppliers gives new entrants opportunities to bargain for access to technology. Thus, Ernst and O'Connor (1989: 91–2) see a real possibility of 'catching up' by being early entrants into new technology systems.

However, 'a real catching-up process can only be achieved through acquiring the capacity for participating in the generation and improvement of technologies as .opposed to the simple "use" of them' (Perez and Soete 1988: 459). Catching up and overtaking established technological leaders poses formidable problems for imitators and aspirants for leadership, since they must aim at a moving target. It is no use simply importing today's technology from the leading countries, for by the time it has been introduced and assimilated the leaders have moved on (Freeman 1988: 73). It is 'a hard slog rather than a leapfrog' to learn what is needed to move from one vintage of technology to another (Hobday 1994b, 1995: 1188).

Another part of catching up involves the entire spectrum of information technologies or informatics. Hanna (1991) suggests that investment in communications infrastructure – together with developing the human resources to exploit it – has permitted the Asian NICs to be linked to international economic activity via satellite television, digital telephone systems and facsimile (fax) machines, among others. With such technology, however, comes the expectation that industry and services will advance to the same, best-practice level found in advanced countries, such as integration of design, supply of inputs, production and marketing and the development of information networks for financial and other services.

Much of what we know about economic competitiveness from the advanced countries, many (or most) of them in Europe, is that the original specialization of small countries was influenced by resource endowment, but was more affected by cumulative technology and skill accumulation over long periods (Freeman 1988: 79–80). For small countries, in particular, complete self-reliance is virtually impossible, and therefore both an R&D capability and links to knowledge in the world at large – such as learning by searching – are essential (Bagchi 1988; Freeman and Lundvall 1988; Walsh 1987). Specialization, cooperation and internationalization are the best choices for small countries in the global context (Simai 1990: 115–16).

For all technological late-comers, innovating is more difficult than learning. Even though there is no model to follow and emulate at the technological frontier, it is easier for learners such as the NICs to become innovators than for the USA and Europe, accustomed to being innovators, to become learners (Amsden 1989). However, a paradox emerges: 'the quicker a country learns and the closer it approaches the world technological frontier, the sooner it exhausts the opportunities to grow further by borrowing.' Innovating remains the only growth mechanism that can be sustained indefinitely (Chapter 2) (Amsden and Hikino 1993: 259).

The separation of production from R&D and other forms of technological learning confronts many countries without established conventions to support links between sectors. The separation in developing countries between R&D and production highlights the fact that neither fully accounts for technological capability (Bhalla and Fluitman 1985; Segal 1987; Sharif 1986). R&D is essential to the improvement and innovativeness of technologies over the longer run, and it makes it possible to obtain or adopt technologies which are nearer to the international state-of-the-art. Production skills allow for continual innovation and significant inputs to the design of new products and processes.

No set of policies will produce instant – or even quick – results. However, policies that create a competitive environment are essential (Pack 1993: 299–300). In addition, the policy context implicit in both Figures 8.1 and 8.2, concerning an environment of competitive firms, links to outside knowledge sources and investment in human capital, seems particularly valuable.

Stages of technological development

Stages in industrial development that generally correspond to the notion of technological learning are found in the sequences of industrial development in several Asian countries. Four tiers of industries correspond to successively higher capital–labour ratios and higher levels of technological sophistication (Ozawa 1995; UNCTAD 1995a: 239–44):

- Tier 1: labour-intensive light industries (e.g. toys, clothing, footwear, sporting goods);
- Tier 2: scale-intensive heavy and chemical industries (e.g. steel, metals, fertilizers, synthetic resins, basic chemicals);
- Tier 3: assembly-based industries where product differentiation and both scale and scope economies dominate (e.g. motor vehicles, televisions, other consumer durables); and
- Tier 4: innovation-intensive 'Schumpeterian' industries in which R&D and close customer interaction are key inputs (e.g. aircraft, computers, pharmaceuticals).

This sequence (or one very similar to it) has been followed more or less explicitly by the NICs both in the sectoral progression above and within industries, such as textiles and electronics, where the division of labour allows entry in labour-intensive production followed by moves 'upstream' as learning takes places in firms and linkages develop with other firms. The search for cheaper labour is another motivation, pushing those activities offshore (i.e. overseas) and forcing firms to learn more skill-intensive activities (UNCTAD 1995a).

A second sort of 'stages' model is seen in the 'flying geese' paradigm (Chapter 6) (Cumings 1987; UNCTAD 1995a: 258–60). As a product-cycle-based model, it suggests that technological upgrading takes place mainly through FDI from advanced countries, such as Japan. Hobday (1994c) suggests that the diversity of experience among the NICs, but particularly the strength of their local firms as exporters, does not support the flying geese model. Adopting Japanese manufacturing techniques, if not fully emulating Japan, leads to a different 'follower' model based on the extent of adoption of these techniques (Kaplinsky 1995b).

A sequence of technological development is clearly reflected in policies for 'infant industries' and export promotion, a model that South Korea has followed in its industrial development, through both the selection of strategic industries and the evolution of policy mechanisms to promote learning and competitiveness on the part of firms (Enos and Park 1988; Kim, Lee and Lee 1987; C. H. Lee 1995; Linge and Hamilton 1981: 32–5; Yu 1995). From the standpoint of learning, production capability must precede investment capability and innovation capability (Kim 1980, 1993a; Kim and Lee 1987). The aerospace industry is now, as it has been in Japan, a sector designated as embodying technological expertise (Eriksson 1995: 203–4; Nakarmi, Shao and Griffiths 1989). Korean firms, especially Daewoo, Samsung and Korean Air, are heavily involved in subcontracting for Airbus, Boeing and McDonnell Douglas. 'Strong government support' is characteristic of the development of aircraft industries in all countries, despite the conclusion that 'there is no connection between the time of introduction of aircraft manufacturing . . . and the subsequent development in capability' (Eriksson 1995: 204).

This technological upgrading, even more than previous inroads in older industries, has threatened the developed countries, whose comparative advantage has rested on technology-intensive exports (Cumings 1987). Protectionist curbs on imports, which earlier affected steel, textiles and clothing, have spread to automobiles and electronics products, two sectors which appear to be priority sectors for NIC industrial policies. Partly to head off such protectionism, some major firms from NICs such as Taiwan and South Korea began in the 1980s to make direct investments in Europe and North America (OECD 1988a: 71–2) and, more recently, elsewhere in Asia, as well as in South America and Africa (*The Economist* 1996h; Jun 1995). Overall, it is not yet clear that the NICs have upgraded sufficiently to move from cost-based to product-based competitiveness and the added value which that will provide (Henderson 1994).

National experiences with technological development

South Korea

The Korean policy regime, perhaps the most studied after that of Japan, changed over time in anticipation of, and in response to, the changing competitive environment and the abilities of its firms (Kim and Dahlman 1992). Like Japan, it has used incentives to private industry, rather than government subsidies and R&D (Rosenberg 1990b: 153). Some of this was through Korea's Heavy and Chemical Industry (HCI) Plan, which was similar to that in Taiwan (Auty 1994; Haggard and Cheng 1987). The 'hard state and efficient administration' worked in cooperation with the *chaebol* to promote rapid industrialization (C. H. Lee 1995). There is evidence of a mix of neoclassical and anti-neoclassical elements in the evolution of, and variation in, comparative advantage and productivity in Korean industries (J. Lee 1995; Sokoloff 1995). Overall, Sokoloff (1995) concludes that the industries receiving government policy assistance realized lower, rather than higher, rates of productivity growth from 1963 to 1979.

The successful technology-exporting firms in the NICs have combined local technological capabilities with foreign technological elements. 'Successful technological development requires access to foreign technology' (Dahlman and Sercovich 1984: 42). After obtaining foreign technology, conscious effort is needed to assimilate, adapt and make effective use of it. Technology exports facilitate technological development by permitting economies of scale and accumulation of experience, including access to additional foreign technology from foreign collaborators. South Korea, perhaps more than any other country, has pursued an export-led development for these very reasons (Dahlman and Sercovich 1984). 'Exporting has been viewed as something of a life or death struggle in Korea', and it has ensured that Korean-made products meet global best-practice specifications (Kim 1993a: 178). In contrast to Taiwan, Korea's exports are dominated by four giant conglomerate firms, or *chaebol*, which control electronics and computers, as well as automobiles, shipbuilding and steel. The four largest *chaebol* (Daewoo, Hyundai, LG Group and Samsung) account for 84 per cent of all Korean production (*The Economist* 1996i). Thus, small firms and entrepreneurs play only a minor role in the Korean economy. All small firms are part of the supplier networks of the *chaebol*, and this relationship rather than the size of the firm defines eligibility for government programmes to upgrade technology (McKay and Missen 1995).

South Korea was among the most open economies to foreign technology. Both imports and exports of technology have allowed South Korea to accelerate its technological development and industrialization. Buyers of outputs and suppliers of equipment and materials together comprise the most important sources of technology for Korean firms (Enos and Park 1988; Kim and Dahlman 1992; Westphal, Rhee and Pursell 1984). However, diversification of technology sources away from licensing and toward R&D, mergers and acquisitions, and joint ventures and alliances with foreign firms have become common strategies (Chen and Sewell 1996; Jun 1995). Samsung, has followed a calculated globalization strategy, with 167 foreign branches in 56 countries in 1991, including 38 production subsidiaries and numerous alliances and acquisitions (C. Lee 1995; UNCTAD 1995a: 253). The Korea Institute of Electronics Technology and all four large *chaebol* maintain R&D operations in Silicon Valley to keep up with developments in the industry. These facilities also facilitate the hiring of US-trained Korean engineers and computer scientists (Chung 1986).

Despite the World Bank's (1993) assessment, it has been clear for some time that 'Korea's industrial development has been characterised by a high degree of state intervention' (OECD 1988a: 34). This 'state capitalism' (Woronoff 1992) has included both diffusion-oriented and mission-oriented policies (Yu 1995). The diffusion-oriented policies include a number of ways in which national capacity to absorb and institutionalize external science and technology is enhanced, such as building R&D institutions, developing a supply of scientists and engineers, and channelling financial resources to research and other risky ventures (Roessner, Porter and Xu 1992; Yu 1995). The mission-oriented policies include targeted technology development projects for next-generation technologies in seven industries (e.g. 1 gigabyte DRAM chips in electronics, an artificial-intelligence-based computer capable of two translations). These are part of the Science and Technology Development Plan to Join the Rank of the Seven Most Advanced Countries, commonly called the G–7 Project or the HAN (highly advanced nation) project. Announced in 1991, the HAN project also includes a plan to develop expertise in seven base generic technologies in new materials, machinery, bioengineering, energy and atomic power (Yu 1995: 93–4). As in Japan, this research activity is promoted and coordinated by the government but is performed by the firms. The plan is partially an attempt to wean South Korea from the 'technology chains' that tie it to Japan. 'The more Korea exports in "high-tech" products, the more it has to import from Japan' (Yu 1995: 97).

South Korea has other weaknesses in its potential for sustained growth, based on shortcomings in basic research, primarily because of weaknesses in its universities (Lim and Song 1996). In contrast, the *chaebol* have aggressive in-house capabilities, as well as networks in Silicon Valley and elsewhere to tap information and US-trained personnel (Kim 1993b). Although small firms are encouraged as a counterbalance to the giant *chaebol*, there are few signs of networking among the small firms. Even the eligibility of a small firm for government preferences requires that it be in a subcontracting relationship with, and be recommended by, a *chaebol* (McKay and Missen 1995: 76). Science parks and high-technology 'valleys' are in place, but with the large-firm culture in Korea, it is unclear whether this can lead to industrial district-type networking (*The Economist* 1990; McKay and Missen 1995; Park and Markusen 1995).

Hong Kong

Only in Hong Kong is the image of a *laissez-faire* policy accurate, but it was combined with unparalleled access to labour and other connections within nearby China (Haggard and Cheng 1987; Lall 1994a). Government policy was mainly to ensure an adequate supply of industrial land, transport and communications, water and other infrastructure. The development of new products, processes, design and management was left to individual companies. In the 1990s, the government began to exert a 'minimum intervention with maximum support' industrial policy and to play a more active role in technological upgrading away from labour-intensive activities. A new University of Science and Technology aims to become the 'the MIT of Asia' by attracting and keeping talented researchers (Farley 1993; Lindorff and Engardio 1992). Several technology-oriented institutions have been created, and support for R&D and several science parks are planned in a TECHNET scheme (Yeh and Ng 1994). The fact that little upgrading has occurred, and yet Hong Kong continues to succeed by flexibly coordinating labour-intensive production networks in southern China, suggests that upgrading might not be a necessary part of the development process (Lui and Chiu 1994).

Hong Kong is a world trading and financial centre, familiar with advanced technology and world market demands and, thus, able to be an effective hub for information. It is a 'capitalist paradise' that avoided targeting industries, preferring to let entrepreneurs make decisions in a flexible manner (Woronoff 1992). Hong Kong's incorporation into China in 1997 will likely see China take advantage of Hong Kong's global scanning, technological efforts and capitalist traditions (Liang and Denny 1995).

Taiwan

Taiwan, a country with a significant presence of small firms, has seen considerable success in sectors favouring a high-tech industrial structure. The Taiwanese computer industry appears to have followed the followers' model. In the mid-1980s, it was known primarily for its manufacture of low-cost 'clones' of personal computers. Several firms were very successful, learning from and making adaptations for world markets (Gerstenfeld and Wortzel 1977). By the end of the 1980s, Taiwanese producers had moved into newer technology not far behind the industry state-of-the-art (Yang 1989). The country's industrial strategy for the 1980s selected three strategic industries: information, electronics and machinery, and biotechnology (OECD 1988a: 39). However, Taiwan has major bottlenecks of personnel in key engineering and management jobs, to some extent reinforced by its role in satellite production for Japanese firms (Chiang 1989). Thus, reverse engineering is still the most common means of acquiring technology; invention remains a more distant goal (Hou and Gee 1993). Despite the lack of capability, Taiwan has designated ten newly emerging industries and eight key technologies for the 1990s in order to move away from low-end production (Andrews 1992). A number of policies encourage Taiwan's small firms to undertake R&D, especially in designated strategic areas (Hou and Gee 1993).

Because Taiwan's industrial structure is based in small enterprises, it has been somewhat handicapped in its development of high-technology sectors (OECD 1988a: 39). To counteract this, in 1969 the Hsinchu Science-Based Industrial Park in Taiwan was conceived. By the end of 1984, 56 firms were operating in the park, including many leading international firms. By 1994, there were nearly 150 firms and 13 000 researchers. Many of them are part of a 'reverse brain drain' of skilled Taiwanese who were educated abroad (Barnathan, Einhorn and Nakarmi 1992; *The Economist* 1994d; Simon and Schive 1986). The overwhelming emphasis of the Hsinchu complex is electronics, including computers, semiconductors and telecommunications. Perhaps because of the agglomeration economies, Hsinchu, unlike Japan's Tsukuba, with which it is compared, is a source of many entrepreneurial spin-offs, and demand for space is so great that a new park in southern Taiwan is planned (*The Economist* 1994d). Location in the science park is dependent upon potential investors satisfying park administrators that they will make a significant contribution to Taiwan's technological development, and the fulfilment of technology transfer criteria are evaluated annually (Chen and Sewell 1996).

Taiwanese firms have responded to global competition with five types of strategies: overseas mergers, outward investment, joint efforts to upgrade the level of technology, technology alliances, and a mixture of economy of scale and economy of scope approaches (San 1991: 63–9). Its product mix in the electrical and electronics industry has plainly shifted from low-tech items in the 1960s, such as electric fans, to computer systems and integrated circuits in the late

1980s (UNCTAD 1995a: 255). Largely because of its small, flexible firms, Taiwan's electronics sector is more involved in design and Korea's more in volume production. The capabilities of the two may well converge as each moves in the other direction (Chen and Sewell 1996). Taiwan has an institutional structure well suited to the development of small firms (Hou and Gee 1993).

Singapore

Singapore, more than most countries, has followed the Japanese lead in formulating S&T-oriented industrial policies. For example, Singapore has pursued a 'fast follower' strategy focused on a set of industries which will lead it to become 'developed into a modern industrial economy based on science, technology, skills and knowledge' (Rodan 1989: 147–8). Its industries earmarked for the 1980s were to produce for markets in the advanced countries, and 'increasingly in much higher value-added areas' (Rodan 1989: 147–8). The industries included are on the lists of other countries as well, such as machine tools, computers, optical instruments and advanced electronic components (Rodan 1989: 147–8; Wong 1995). Considerable government investment is behind such an effort, including a Software Technology Centre in Singapore Science Park, the incorporation of Singapore Aircraft Industries in 1982, and the Singapore Technology Corporation, formed to develop and market Singapore-made high-technology products. Collaborative ventures with French, German, Japanese and US partners are also aimed in the direction of high technology (Rodan 1989: 149–53).

However, Singapore's policies in S&T seem to have been secondary to the push to attract TNC investment, for which providing skilled workers is the greatest need as investment becomes more high-tech (Hakam and Chang 1988; Tan and Tan 1990). The dominant form of industrial upgrading has tended to involve 'either the introduction of greater automation or higher value-added products rather than a shift away from the assembly process as such. The more conceptual stages of production still tended to elude Singapore' (Rodan 1989: 179). Singapore's strategy has been based increasingly on 'strategic partnership and networking with high-tech TNCs and other international innovation sources' and it is unclear whether this is a path toward technological dependence or toward the intended technological upgrading and development (Wong 1995). Japanese firms, in particular, seem unwilling to invest in Singapore's upgrading strategy (Rodan 1989: 180). Consequently, Singapore seems to remain behind in the software elements of high-tech industries, such as design (Hobday 1994b). None the less, Singapore announced in mid-1996 a massive package of incentives, not for chip design, but to lure additional foreign investment in semiconductor manufacturing (Clifford and Port 1996). In order to deal with the problem of labour costs without losing investment to its Asian competitors, Singapore announced what would be the first of several 'growth triangle' plans, locating labour- and land-intensive operations to neighbouring Johor in Malaysia and the Riau Islands of Indonesia, especially Batam (Ho 1994; Thant, Tang and Kakazu 1994; Parsonage 1992; van Grunsven, Wong and Kim 1995).

Like Hong Kong and competing with it, Singapore also prizes its place as a world city. The 1991 Strategic Economic Plan includes positioning Singapore as a global city or total business hub in the Asia Pacific region on a level equal to other leading global cities (Wong 1995). Its telecommunications infrastructure is a high priority, based on Singapore as 'the intelligent island' (K. Singh 1995; Sisodia 1992). It ranked among the top ten best cities for business in the world in a 1994 compilation, based on cost of living, non-stop air connections, office rents and cultural openness (Saporito 1994).

Malaysia

Neighbouring Malaysia has noted the same lack of R&D on the part of both Japanese and American companies (Fong 1986: 75–6). Fong's (1986) findings concerning the inability of Malaysian firms to seek out export opportunities are pertinent. Firms in the plastics, textile, and veneer and plywood industries, for example, are not major players in international markets. Fong suggests that, 'besides the upgrading of technology, Malaysian planners ought to seriously consider means of "broadening the horizon" of Malaysian firms' (Fong 1986: 191). Taiwan has served as a model for Malaysian electronics firms, which serve as original equipment manufacturers (OEMs) for foreign TNCs in order to learn and to gain expertise and knowledge about foreign market demand (Kassim 1995).

Best practice or competitiveness can be assessed at the scale of national industries, as in the case of Malaysia, where manufacturing is considered the principal sector that could enable the nation 'to attain the status of an advanced newly industrialized country (NIC) by the end of this decade' (Fong 1986: vii). Fong (1986) found that a large technology and productivity gap exists between the industrial technology of Malaysian firms compared with Japanese firms in five sectors (Fong 1986: 184–7). In nearly all industries, this was attributable to the much higher capital intensity of technology employed by Japanese firms. There is considerable competition from neighbouring Singapore, where R&D in the electronics and computer sectors is increasingly concentrated, while labour-intensive operations have been shifted to Malaysia, where R&D is uncommon (Fong 1986: 74–6; Hakam and Chang 1986).

The 'major industrial strategy' continues to be 'to transform Malaysian manufacturing industries into high-value-added and high-technology industries', involving 'technological upgrading, human resource development, and industrial linkages' (Kassim 1995: 173). Singh (1988: 84) is less optimistic about this strategy, because 'the "know-how" and "know-why" of modern technology remain beyond the reach of Singapore and Malaysia; much of the more advanced activities are supervised by foreign technologists without greatly enhancing local capabilities.' Despite the slow progress, there is considerable cross-national evidence that human capital is a key feature of the growth of Malaysia, where TNCs have deepened their operations as they have expanded them. Recent research shows that Malaysia stands out as the country whose human capital has improved dramatically in a relatively short time, rivalling that of the NICs (Rausch 1995; Roessner et al. 1996; Tan 1993). This success story masks the large social and political divisions within Malaysia that may threaten long-term development (Lubeck 1992).

Thailand

Thailand has been labelled as a 'tiger' economy and an HPAE more because of its attraction to TNC investment than because of well-conceived technological strategies (Westphal *et al.* 1990). It is weaker than either Malaysia or India in technological infrastructure (Roessner *et al.* 1996). Its firms do little R&D, thus remaining 'remarkably incapable of "innovating" and creating new technology' (Sripaipan 1995: 158). Thailand's Seventh Plan for 1992–1996 was the first to target specific sectors, which are a much lower-tech group than in the countries discussed thus far: metalworking and machinery, electronics, textiles, food, plastic, gems and jewellery, and iron and steel. Acquisition of technology takes place mainly by imports of goods, turnkey plants or FDI, not by R&D or even by licensing or consultants' advice. Thai observers see technological capability as a long-term prospect, requiring enhanced development of education (Sherer 1996; Sripaipan 1995).

Indonesia

Indonesia is less prominent in many of the accounts of East Asian success. Its huge population (184 million), the fourth largest in the world, means that it must create jobs for labour-force entrants; most of these so far have been low-wage jobs in textile and shoe production. A series of market-friendly policies, including deregulation, 'debureaucratization' and privatization, have included Indonesia among the World Bank's HPAEs, despite a preponderance of state-owned firms. Aircraft and telecommunications are among the Eight Vehicles for Industrial Transformation (EVIT), to achieve competitiveness in eight state-owned high-tech industries, including defence, energy, electronics and communication, and aerospace, selected as priority industries because of the dispersed nature of the Indonesian archipelago. An area of relative success has been in aircraft, where a determined effort has gone on since production under licence began in 1976, progressing through locally designed aircraft (Alam 1995).

More than any of the HPAEs except perhaps South Korea, Indonesia has a top-down political structure; it is also characterized by widespread corruption, and few strong private firms. It remains to be seen if the S&T system will survive President Suharto and lead to widespread technological upgrading (Rachman 1993). Indonesia's production capacity, which measures supply and quality of skilled labour, capability of indigenous management and the existence of local suppliers, is the lowest among a set of Asian countries studied, and lower than either China or India (Rausch 1995: 72; Roessner *et al.* 1996).

India

Indian self-reliance has resulted in little attention being given, for decades, to world technology reconnaissance and learning, but also a bias toward big-science projects (Dore 1984; Lall 1985). This focus has succeeded in military production and electric power generation, but has not generated widespread economic development (Morehouse and Gupta 1987). The inward focus and inattention to export markets has hindered entrepreneurs. Recent attention to exports has permitted clusters of garment producers, by contrast, to develop industrial-district structures to support high-volume production (Cawthorne 1995).

Indian state-owned firms faced a set of 'hierarchies linking ministries, high-tech SOEs, and principal customers [that] more or less replaced markets' (Ramamurti 1987: 273). Although this can have some positive effects, India's technological lag is particularly great in

> electronics and semiconductors, for which the country has relied largely on locally developed technology. As a result, there has been an adverse impact on production and technological developments in electronics equipment and products and on electronics applications in various other branches, especially capital goods manufacture, where, with its large pool of cheap skilled and semiskilled labour, India could have built up major export capability (Marton 1986: 238).

Indeed, the focus on the internal, rather than external, market has harmed India's potential in computers, since labour-intensive methods in offices and industries are the norm (Gupta 1986). India has been much more restrictive than the HPAEs toward imports of technology and has not used exports to broaden its technological capability. 'India's bias toward technological self-reliance has condemned large sectors of industry to technological obsolescence – there are limits to what developing countries can do on their own without periodic injections of new elements of foreign technology' (Dahlman and Sercovich 1984: 45). Licensing of foreign technology is the preferred mode of technology acquisition in India, rather than FDI (Subrahmanian 1993), but the problem is that licensed technology is typically farther removed from best-practice technology than any other mode (Mowery and Oxley 1995). However, firms that have entered export markets show a marked tendency to set up in-house R&D units and to have higher R&D intensities (Kumar and Saqib 1996).

India, like Brazil, has failed to match the developmental nature of South Korea, in part because of becoming 'bogged down in restrictive rule-making' and heavy investment in state-owned enterprises (Evans 1995: 15). The Indian bureaucracy has social and caste-based elements that place India somewhere between a predatory and a developmental state (Evans 1995). At the same time, it has pockets of social capital ('development without growth'), as in the state of Kerala, which few other countries have achieved (Franke and Chasin 1990; Heller 1996).

Restrictions on technology imports and a preference for licensing rather than foreign investment have been the norm. These policies, along with 'no serious attempts at upgrading technology or developing domestic design capacity', meant that there was little concern for product quality or improving processes to lower costs (Subrahmanian 1993: 103). The poor quality of Indian goods has permitted a surge of foreign brand-name consumer products to overwhelm the market (Jordan 1996b). The removal of the 'license raj' has led to a higher degree of foreign investment; for example, in software, where the growth of Bangalore is a result of liberalization combined with sector-specific policies. State-owned firms, long a staple in India, remain a priority in many sectors (McDowell

1995). Part of Bangalore's base as a high-tech centre is a result of Bharat Electronics Limited, a government defence firm, which serves as the 'mother hen' for the electronics sector in the area (Singhal and Rogers 1989).

Latin America

Outside Asia, the experience with development, especially technological development, and with a positive role of government, is mixed. In Latin America, for example, financial debt has forced some countries to retain an import-substitution policy orientation, especially with regard to payments for foreign technology. In both Brazil and Mexico, import substitution and exports rely largely on the activities of foreign firms (Marton 1986; OECD 1988a). Mexico's efforts to increase 'local content' jeopardizes its ability to develop an export capability, because it 'is dependent not only on a continuing stream of investment into the country, but also on conditions in potential export markets' (Miller 1986: 195). Similarly, Mexico has been much more interventionist than South Korea, especially through long traditions of subsidies, state ownership and protection. Liberalization policies have also had mixed success (Lall 1994a). It may be that, in addition to people at the top committed to reform and bureaucrats qualified to implement it, a national trauma such as hyperinflation is needed to spark change in Latin America (Grimond 1993).

R&D throughout Latin America also suffered during the 1980s. The percentage of GDP invested in R&D averaged 0.45 per cent (well behind the 2.0 per cent in the EU and 2.9 per cent in the USA) but this is mainly in university research, not in industrial R&D. Thus, Latin America's patent data are less than 0.2 per cent of the totals for the EU or the USA, despite a larger population base (Ayala 1995). In general, the institutions to support research are weak, and political considerations often dominate over scientific criteria (da Costa 1995). With no long-term S&T strategy and little involvement with the private sector, little private R&D takes place, except in a few resource-based sectors (Wionczek 1993).

In Brazil, R&D has been emphasized only in sectors with export potential, such as military goods, but not in other industries, such as computers (Frischtak 1986). For Brazil, after a miracle period from the mid-1960s to the mid-1970s, the 1980s was 'a lost decade.' Its inward-looking approach to development presented a stark contrast to the outward-orientation of the Asian NICs (Ferraz, Rush and Miles 1992). A form of 'associated capitalism' developed, characterized by state-owned firms alongside large national firms and TNCs. Entrenched social inequality has kept the educational and scientific infrastructure of the country quite poor and funded almost exclusively by the government. The remaining investment is by Brazilian firms; TNCs do no R&D in Brazil (Dahlman and Frischtak 1993). Since most production is aimed at the domestic market, rather than the world market, quality is poor compared with world standards. Although institutions are in place to modernize industry, little has happened. 'Flexible industrialisation is reliant upon a flexible state' (Ferraz, Rush and Miles 1992: 233). Private industry has learned 'to be nimble to escape the dread hand of government' in such a 'predatory state' (Evans 1995; Grimond 1993: 21).

Perhaps the best example of ill-considered government policy is Brazil's nationalistic Informatics Law of 1984, which was intended to encourage a home-grown computer industry. Instead, according to a former science minister, the result is that Brazil is probably a generation behind in computer technology, and computers are so costly that they are far less common than elsewhere in the world. 'Everything comes down to two critical variables in the end: fiscal reform and responsible government leadership' (MacDonald, Hughes and Crum 1995: 168).

In only two areas have government R&D efforts been effective: aerospace and agro-technology (Dahlman and Frischtak 1993: 437). Embraer was able to progress from a heavily protected and subsidized public enterprise to a world-class competitor, combining cost competitiveness and technological proficiency. Licensing and learning technology from Italian and US companies enabled Embraer to design, produce and service a line of commuter aircraft. With their longer production runs, the aircraft sector allows for more learning effects than is the case in computers and other short product cycle industries (Frischtak 1994). Similarly, Engesa simultaneously acquired and internally developed technologies for its military vehicle products, with which it has had marked success (Graham 1990; Lock 1986). As Brazilian export arms development proceeded, the policy remained, in Catrina's (1988: 113) words: 'keep it simple, keep it cheap' for both externally purchased and internally developed technology. This defined the product niche to which Engesa aspired – one that arms producers in Asia (such as Indonesia and Malaysia) have also emphasized (Ohlson 1986). For producers in other sectors, conforming to the demands of flexible production is a formidable task (Ferraz, Rush and Miles 1992; Fleury 1995).

Brazil is attempting to define an industrial policy that utilizes elements of the Japanese and East Asian example as well as the 'Scandinavian model', which shows the opportunities for industrial specialization and international linkages through technological progress in natural-resource industries. The technology policy proposed for Brazil is 'creative catching up' – 'accompanying the international technological frontier closely and creatively' (dos Reis Velloso 1994: 112). This has barely begun in a concerted way, and its success remains to be seen.

In Argentina, protectionist policies also promoted 'industries of national interest' and the creation of a 'second best' industrial sector (Katz and Bercovich 1993: 454). In a number of industries, local capabilities grew through learning activities until the 1970s, when several previously important sectors (e.g. machine tools, cars and tractors) contracted significantly and manufacturing facilities of TNC car makers were closed. New potential now seems to be found mainly in a few manufacturing sectors such as steel and cars, and in resource-based products such as agriculture and petrochemicals (Katz and Bercovich 1993).

The transition from central planning

The former communist nations of Eastern Europe have faced a difficult transition to full participation in the global capitalist system. Central planning dominated Soviet, Chinese and Eastern European governments after the Second World War; it lingers in Cuba, North Korea and, in modified form, in China and India. One way of understanding such a system is that they 'sought to correct market failures by replacing the market' rather than by working within a market framework (Stiglitz 1996: 156).

Russia and Eastern Europe

Central planning was relatively ineffective in promoting innovation. Central priorities governed items and quantities to be produced, and determined sources of supply. Consumer demand, input prices and competitors' inroads (the motivations for automated, flexible production) played no role in the socialist system. Thus, the impetus toward productivity – and, even more, toward product innovation – was not as compelling as in competitive market economies. This is certainly the case at the factory level, where there was little incentive for managers to improve product designs, quality or efficiency beyond that demanded by central planning authorities (Chiang 1990; Shmelev and Popov 1989). Although the introduction of the basic oxygen process in steel production began in the USSR and in Japan at the same time in the 1950s, it is nearly at saturation in Japan, but affecting only 30 per cent of production in Russia (Perminov 1992).

Two principal shortcomings noted by Soviet observers were ponderous bureaucratic structures to manage science and marked immobility of scientists (Sagdeev 1988). To a large extent, a dual system evolved, one for military and space technology and the other for civilian technology (Chiang 1990). None the less, several areas of technology had been competitive with Western technology. Notable among Soviet technological accomplishments were space and defence equipment, welding equipment, cooling technologies for blast furnaces, electromagnetic casting of copper, and surgical instruments. Many of these were best-practice technologies licensed to Western companies (Bornstein 1985; Kiser 1989). Similarly, Polish and Czechoslovakian technology was sold to both Western firms and other Eastern European enterprises (Monkiewicz and Maciejewicz 1986: 74–115). At the opposite end of the spectrum of priorities, especially in services, the technological level was poor. Most significantly, the Soviet Union largely missed out on the revolutions in biotechnology and computers, the latter a result of a 1962 decision to eliminate the computer division of the Academy of Sciences (Chiang 1990; Galuszka *et al.* 1988). The greatest question is to what extent Russian science – much of it world-class – will survive in an era without funding. Its scientists have largely dispersed throughout the world, and those who remain live a precarious existence with little support for their research (Aldhous 1994).

The traditional stumbling block for Soviet innovation was not a lack of R&D or scientific capability, which was rather strong (Kontorovich 1994). Its greatest weakness was weak links between research and production, seen in factories without engineering facilities and in R&D organizations that lacked production engineering capability or pilot production plants (Amann 1986; Kassel 1989).

The interaction with suppliers and repeated incremental changes common in market economies, and embodied in the interactive feedback model of innovation (Chapter 2), therefore, was scarcely evident under central planning (Bornstein 1985). Awareness of global markets, alternative suppliers and inputs, and energetic interaction between users and innovators is rare but not impossible in Russia. The Ivanovo Machine Tool Amalgamation, which manufactures flexible manufacturing systems, had customers around the world in the late 1980s, paying attention to world standards of product quality and providing service to its customers in Switzerland and West Germany from a service department in Switzerland (Kiser 1989: 151–61).

Skowronski (1987) generalized the problem as one of too few small enterprises, since it is these which are most effective in technology transfer, as the Ivanovo example illustrates. The scarcity of competitive enterprises, and of a mix of small, medium-size and large firms, suggests that it may be best to support a core of highly efficient enterprises, rather than inadequate support for all enterprises (Perminov 1992: 374). Despite the image in the West of giant enterprises, many firms are too small to compete against TNCs in world markets (Amsden, Kochanowicz and Taylor 1994).

Institutional structures are in need of reform, but these change at different rates and demand informal as well as formal changes (Murrell 1996). Commercial culture and entrepreneurship 'move at a snail's pace' in contrast to prices, which move rapidly. The pace of reform is taking place at different rates, and the World Bank (1996b) has identified four groups of countries, according to the degree to which economic liberalization toward a market economy has taken place:

Group 1: Poland, Slovenia, Hungary, Croatia, FYR of Macedonia, Czech Republic, Slovak Republic
Group 2: Estonia, Lithuania, Bulgaria, Latvia, Albania, Romania, Mongolia
Group 3: Kyrgyz Republic, Russia, Moldova, Armenia, Georgia, Kazakhstan
Group 4: Uzbekistan, Ukraine, Belarus, Azerbaijan, Tajikistan, Turkmenistan

Although Vietnam and China are considered separately and are not assigned to a group, their liberalization index would place them in Group 2, as countries with the second-highest degree of liberalization (World Bank 1996b: 14).

Transportation, storage, distribution and information flow infrastructures are not yet in place to support a market in either Russia or China (Tsang 1996). Horizontal flow of information between enterprises is especially lacking (Staudt 1994). Finally, the importance of 'sophisticated and demanding buyers', also a key element in national and regional competitiveness (Porter 1990), played no role in the absence of market demand. Bureaucracies in large enterprises continue to prevail in many places, and suggest that enterprises in Eastern Europe will not become competitive quickly. The tendency under central planning was to focus on routine rather than non-routine activities, and therefore 'to upgrade traditional technologies, rather than develop and produce new ones' (Kassel 1989: 65; Staudt 1994). This makes it even more difficult to work on problems of quality (Amsden, Kochanowicz and Taylor 1994: 66–9).

'For most transition economies, the risks of government failure probably out-weigh those of market failure' and institutional reforms are at least as important as macroeconomic reforms (C. H. Lee 1995: 41). Some state role is needed during the transition, but the East Asian model has not had influence in Eastern Europe (Amsden, Kochanowicz and Taylor 1994; Chang 1995a; C. H. Lee 1995). Pseudo-socialism has been replaced by pseudo-capitalism, in part through pseudo-privatization (Amsden, Kochanowicz and Taylor 1994: 11–13). 'What Eastern Europe needs most urgently is a strategy to overhaul the now-decrepit state system' (Chang 1995a: 396). This includes a number of areas. Industrial research is unlikely to develop the links required to other organizations, such as universities, research institutes and manufacturing enter-prises, unless explicit policies are put in place (Mowery 1994). Industrial policy also seems advised in several areas: infrastructure investment, training, R&D activity, technology dissemination, setting up financing agencies, export pro-motion, and the development of market structures (Landesmann and Abel 1995).

Rapid 'big bang' transition policies based on neoclassical economics ignore or, at best, downplay the existence of the pervasive nature of the state. Breaking it down piecemeal or without this understanding means that the connection between state ownership and the social obligations of the enterprise (e.g. provi-sion of low-rent housing) is lost. People are hurt far more by the shift to market rents, when wages do not rise accordingly, than by the advantages of private ownership (Tsang 1996). Privatization has taken a number of forms, including voucher systems, collectives and other types of organization.

Moreover, the *laissez-faire* policies associated with 'big bang' transition in Eastern Europe ignore East Asian experience in favour of Western models:

> East Asia has demonstrated that unlike developed countries, which compete interna-tionally on the basis of research and development, or undeveloped countries, which do so on the exclusive basis of low labour costs, semi-industrialized countries compete on the basis of total costs, borrowing foreign technology and then sub-stantially improving such technology incrementally. Making borrowed technology work optimally takes time, however, and in this interval, depending on the industry, some form of government involvement has usually been indispensable (Amsden, Kochanowicz and Taylor 1994: 111).

China

China's reforms began after the death of Mao Zedong in 1976, but incre-mentally – 'touching stones to cross the river' (Nolan 1995: 400). As a socialist market economy, China's institutional arrangements and policies are a 'kind of interventionist halfway house that most economists would predict would perform very badly.' But it has achieved fast growth, with low inflation and little foreign debt (Nolan 1995: 408–9). Beginning at the same time, a distinct shift in China's regional development took place – from the spatial balance and dom-inance of interior industrial cities to new coastal locations along the 'golden coastline', where all special economic zones (SEZs) and open coastal cities were located. The new regional policy envisions growth diffusing from the coast to the interior much like descending steps on a ladder (Fan 1995).

Chinese industry, like that in the Soviet Union, maintains a distinct separation between research and manufacturing, even in high-technology industries such as semiconductors (Simon and Rehn 1987: 269; 1988). The transfer of technology from defence to civilian sectors is, along with that from research to production and from coastal regions to the interior, among the recent reforms of the Chinese research system (Jin and Porter 1988).

Centrally planned economies such as China have had explicit policies to promote certain industries. China's National Science Plan of 1956 included the electronics industry, greatly expanded in importance, along with computers and telecommunications, in later national plans (Simon and Rehn 1988: 59–65). Electronics technology was seen in 1978 as the hallmark of modernization, and one of the 'four modernizations' (industry, agriculture, national defence, and science and technology) proclaimed in that year (Simon and Rehn 1988: 14–15). More recently, a series of big-science projects have been proposed as part of the economic plan for 1996–2000 (Mervis 1995). Alongside these national efforts at technological upgrading, China uses foreign investment not only for access to world markets but also to learn about foreign technologies that are part of direct investment (Ding 1995). In addition, 'new technology enterprises' in computers and other technology-intensive sectors have spun off from state R&D institutes, some in joint ventures with foreign firms, especially in 52 development zones. Technological learning and development of a new core technology, i.e. that of computerizing Chinese characters, partially supported by the government, has resulted in competitiveness based on the local specificity of demand for hardware and software which not even Japanese or Taiwanese firms could fill (Gu 1996).

Privatization of state-owned enterprises exhibits striking national differences. China has two prominent types of non-state – but also non-private – enterprises: 240 000 urban collectives affiliated with municipalities, counties or districts, accounting for 12 per cent of total industrial output in 1993; and 1.8 million township and village enterprises, accounting for 26 per cent of total industrial output. Individual and family businesses, foreign firms and joint ventures – the typical definition of private-sector organizations – accounted for 18 per cent of 1993 industrial production (World Bank 1995b: 66). The decline in state-owned enterprises evident recently is due mainly to the better-managed state-owned businesses joining foreign partners in joint ventures (Ding 1995). Several of these new combinations have merged into large competitive firms on the lines of those in Europe or South Korea, but with Chinese characteristics, such as enterprise groups that resemble Japanese *keiretsu* or Korean *chaebol*. The same is taking place as township and village enterprises form enterprise groups (Nolan 1996).

China's infrastructure is widely cited as inferior. Among the few plans for upgrading is a highway network proposal for the eastern half of the country, especially the Beijing, Shanghai and Hong Kong triangle. One of several economic cooperation zones is the 'new golden triangle' of Hong Kong–Taiwan–

Shanghai (Rimmer 1994; van Grunsven, Wong and Kim 1995). These suggest that a 'Greater China' could be the fifth, and largest, 'tiger' (Engardio, Borrus and Gross 1992). In several respects, Shanghai appears as a major world city of the future, both through recreating its traditional role as scientific centre of China and as a centre of new science-based entrepreneurial ventures (Plafker 1994).

China is a 'late-late developer' and, like the NICs before it, 'imbued with an impatient catch-up mentality in much the same way Japan' and the NICs were (Chan 1995: 450). As such, it has attempted to borrow from foreigners principles and models to use in its own development. As the state sector is reformed, it is pulled in two directions: toward the Japanese organization system and the Western market system. Chan (1995) believes that Chinese enterprises are leaning in the direction of the Japanese system, which is more community-oriented and egalitarian in its worker–management relations than is the Western model. This exists and is developing side-by-side with the market-oriented model of the non-state sector, including most foreign enterprises and joint ventures. China's catching-up development policy is embodied in the 'twenty words principle', referring to 20 Chinese characters that signify grasping opportunities, deepening reforms, expanding openness, promoting development and maintaining stability (Ding 1995: 64). In many ways, however, China was able to learn through its 'Hong Kong connection' just as Hong Kong benefited from access to Chinese labour supplies. More than one-half of Chinese exports pass through Hong Kong merchants. Hong Kong continues to provide knowledge and intermediary services with the capitalist world, and is expected to do so in the future (Panagariya 1995).

Africa

Nowhere has less growth and development taken place than in Africa. Indeed, incomes shrank rather than grew during the 1980s (Thorbecke and Koné 1995). The poor performance of African countries can be attributed to three principal factors: a lack of openness to trade, a lack of market incentives, and a lack of national saving (Sachs 1996). Whether explicitly or implicitly, African economies resemble those of the centrally planned economies. Nowhere else is there such economic inflexibility (Killick 1995c).

The World Bank's structural adjustment programmes (SAPs) have attempted to create the macroeconomic environment for sustained growth. The elements are the same as those espoused in other World Bank pronouncements discussed earlier in this chapter: get macroeconomic policies right, encourage competition, and use scarce institutional capacity wisely (World Bank 1994a: 9). Particularly in state-owned enterprises (parastatals), little change has taken place in most countries, including those in SAP reforms. Dozens, and in some cases, hundreds of public enterprises dominate most African economies, with negative effects on competition and access to financial resources (World Bank 1994a: 99–111).

Ghana has reduced its public-sector personnel most, and as the size of the government sector is reduced, a surge of small firms has been seen (Logan and Mengisteab 1993; Osei *et al.* 1993). A number of institutions have been put in place since 1970 to assist and promote small firms in Ghana, one of the most successful examples of structural adjustment. SAPs have favoured small firms that are able to modernize and upgrade their products and services to compete locally with imports and, in some cases, in export markets as well, such as niches where innovation and flexibility favour small firms over large ones. Linkages with other, less innovative, small firms have the effect of upgrading the technological capabilities of the latter (Dawson 1993).

Thus far, SAP reforms have not led to successful exports of manufactured goods or, even less, of technological capabilities. Most countries are still dependent on agricultural or mineral commodities in export markets. Industrial policies seem necessary in all countries that are entering world markets for industrialized goods, as opposed to primary products (Lall and Stewart 1996). Export markets for African businesses, as elsewhere, are a means to learn about expectations regarding quality, packaging and planning for large orders (Biggs *et al.* 1994).

The fact that the most successful entrepreneurs are the most-educated suggests the links between policy – in this case toward education and training – and economic development. Education and training increase awareness of new and alternative technologies of the production, products and training methods needed (Birks *et al.* 1994). While basic education is essential, Africa cannot neglect secondary and tertiary education, especially technical and vocational education, in order to attain and keep national institutional capacities, rather than be the victims of consultants (Chung 1996; Fabayo 1996). The human capital factor is perhaps the major explanation for the sorry state of African economies, especially if that factor is stretched to encompass the people in political leadership and institutions (Bell 1991; Berthélemy and Lecaillon 1995).

Technological dependence in Africa is severe and pervasive, primarily because of colonialism and continued poverty. Production suffers from the resultant lack of skills and lack of interest in manufacturing. With a shortage of technical and managerial skills, turnkey technology transfer promotes dependence on unmodified imported technologies, which are rarely mastered through learning by doing (Fabayo 1996; Wangwe 1993). Even Zimbabwe, relatively developed industrially, 'is severely underdeveloped technologically' (Fayez 1993). Attention to human capital at the national level and to learning mechanisms at the firm level is the imperative for technological development in Africa (Biggs, Shah and Srivastava 1995).

Learning and the costs of not learning

Technological innovation requires technological capability, which comes about only as a result of effort. To appreciate technological capability,

> an important distinction must be made regarding the depth of understanding involved in the transformation of inputs into outputs. . . While it might be possible

for a firm to make an exact replica of another firm's product without an understanding of the fundamental principles underlying the product's working, to change the product will require a greater degree of understanding; the bigger the change, the greater the amount of knowledge that will be required (Fransman 1984: 33–4).

The ultimate goal for firms and nations is *technological mastery*, in the direction of international best practice. This target affects, in turn, all the important decisions involved in technology development (Mytelka 1985; Pack 1993; Roessner and Porter 1990). This sequence can also be simplified into *simple or process learning* and *product learning* (Teubal 1987: 124). Bell and Pavitt (1993b) draw a distinction between production capacity, which primarily encompasses traditional knowledge for operating or technology-using capability; and technological capability, which represents technology-changing skills. The gap between the two is large and growing, such that it requires a great deal of gradual, incremental and cumulative learning, as well as supportive educational and infrastructural policies (Hobday 1994b).

There are many ways by which new technology is learned (Chapter 2), and these apply to firms in developing countries just as much as to those in the Triad economies. The learning mechanisms form a hierarchy that indicates technological capacity itself as well as, indirectly, the degree of dependence on external sources of technology (Bell 1984; Malerba 1992a). Doing-based learning occurs passively, virtually automatically and costlessly as production ('doing') takes place (Bell 1984: 189). Experience-based learning (which Bell calls *learning by using*) involves not just steady improvements in productivity but also incremental *increases in understanding* of the design and performance of a product and the machinery with which it is produced.

Systematic learning involves explicit effort and investment in the acquisition of technological capacity, largely outside the scope of conventional R&D (Bell 1984; Pack 1993). The most elementary form of learning is *learning by operating*, a variant of learning by doing or by using, which can progress into *learning by changing*: improving upon equipment and techniques as experience with them is gained. Monitoring and recording the performance of a technology, or *system performance feedback*, can generate understanding about why certain things work and others do not. This information is neither automatic nor costless, depending on both time and production volume, and on the allocation of resources to generate the flow of data. Bell's fourth type, *learning through training*, retains an explicit element of dependence on external sources of technology. Personnel can be trained to operate machinery and to produce items (the *how* of technology) clearly without necessarily learning *why*, what is behind the technology (Bell 1984: 196–7; Enos and Park 1988: 125–30).

Greater control over the knowledge carried about in people is represented by the fifth and sixth forms of learning. *Learning by hiring* permits firms to create technological capacity, not simply to accumulate it. Hiring of nationals educated abroad has been a high priority recently for both South Korea and Taiwan (Pack 1993). Finally, *learning by searching* assumes that an organization has the capability to investigate various sources of information, to absorb 'disembodied' knowledge and information about several types of technology, and to choose the most suitable one. This form of learning requires an explicit allocation of resources for non-production tasks, and is usually considered as R&D (Bell 1984). All of these costly means of learning serve to alter the capacity for technological change within a firm directly and, Cohen and Levinthal (1989) argue, an R&D capability encompasses most, if not all, of these means. Knowledge of the competent firms from which to acquire the newest techniques embodies a set of competencies that David (1993) calls *learning to borrow*.

The experience associated with repeated production leads to a diverse array of information sources and knowledge which lead, in turn, to ideas for further innovation. Equipment suppliers, input suppliers and customers are among the best sources of new ideas. To sum up, Lall (1990: 61) stresses that 'no amount of national provision of physical or human resources or policy support will lead to competitiveness and dynamic growth if the firms concerned cannot bring the package together in the form of viable capabilities.' Tremendous variations are present in the response of firms to national endowments and to government interventions. 'Research, learning, and investment are required by firms before endowments become capabilities' (Lall 1990: 61). However, as an 'economy's technological capabilities increase, the technological challenges to the economy also change in ways that demand increasing organizational flexibility inside the economy, including the development of technological networks among cooperating firms' (Vernon 1989: 34).

Flexibility and the new rules of competition

The increasing pace of technological change, short product life-cycles, and product differentiation benefit innovative firms over imitators. Fewer products fit the classic life-cycle pattern of long production runs and large volumes. In this setting, technology does not flow down or diffuse to less innovative countries; rather, relative advantages and disadvantages remain more or less constant in a cumulative *technology gap*. The concentration of technical change in a few rich countries further reinforces disparities between rich and poor countries. By far the largest fraction of global R&D expenditure is located in developed countries, as is the greatest employment of scientists and engineers. Consequently, 'a fundamental distinction between rich and poor countries is that poor countries are for the most part *recipients* of technology developed in rich countries, while rich countries, as a block, generate their own technology' (Stewart 1978: 274).

Scale economies continue to matter for small countries. For them, the problems of learning technology and other 'rules of the game' centre around both inadequate market size – (relative to minimum efficient scale, i.e. the scale of production needed to make efficient use of capital equipment) and an insufficient base of related or linked firms. The latter shortcoming results in reduced opportunities for user–producer interactions from which to learn about, and to learn from experience with, new techniques or products (Andersen and Lundvall 1988). Small developing countries are too small to permit agglomeration economies, adequate pools of skilled labour, managers, and other 'critical-mass' advantages common to the theories and experiences of advanced countries. Perhaps more importantly, a lack of technical expertise makes them especially unable to keep up with a constantly changing best practice (Sagasti 1988). The inability to identify technology which satisfies their own commercial and technical requirements as well as an inability to bargain effectively for it with overseas suppliers are especially difficult for government policies to address (Forsyth 1990: 157).

Large-scale production, typified in many respects by Fordism, led to the conclusion that many economies are simply too small to support large-scale production and they are therefore doomed to, at best, a second-rate status in the world economy. This view, related to the familiar paradigm of firm growth, ignores the coexistence of large- and small-scale firms in many industries in both developed and underdeveloped countries. Indeed, small firms are seen as the agile producers of flexible specialization, rather than the backward, marginal sector of a dualistic economy. An additional shortcoming, one that has historically impinged on small countries, seems less severe than in the past: the need for large-volume production in order to be considered worthwhile as a source of supply for export markets (Forsyth 1990: 111–20). In small developing countries, it may no longer be the case that, in well-chosen market niches, 'industrial sectors are too small to provide the opportunity for widespread interlocking of firms into an industrial complex' (Forsyth 1990: 74).

Mass-production development strategies did not lead automatically to technological capacity, especially as the logic and organization of propulsive economic activity changed from that of the 1960s. The new logic, founded on economies of scope and the advantage of time and of scarce knowledge, means that 'technological-knowledge mastery is central to the economic destiny of nations and regions, and there is no way to short-circuit it via the mere implantation of hardware or even large segments of input–output systems in the way that appeared possible in the 1950s' (Storper 1995a: 401). Therefore, the smaller production runs of post-Fordist production suggest enhanced possibilities for serving niche (regional and local) markets in developed countries (Oman 1994: 93).

At the same time, three elements of 'bad news' accompany the shift to flexible production (Oman 1994). While minimum efficient production levels have dropped, these levels remain high relative to many developing countries, making export-oriented policies still important. Second, flexible production is 'quite demanding in terms of its human-resources and infrastructure requirements' (Oman 1994: 94). Third, even though production levels and plant sizes have become smaller, there is no trend toward smaller organizations, because fixed costs remain high for R&D, design and marketing. That is, one scale factor has increased: the indirect costs of production, especially R&D – a fact that works against small firms, even those in a network, as they try to keep up with technologies and competitors from other locations. The greater range of skills imperative in flexible production is also overlooked in much of what has been written about it (Kaplinsky 1989).

'It is open to question whether small firms have the information about new products, markets and other conditions to which they are supposed to react with such promptness and flexibility, especially when compared to large firms', which have received the primary benefit of policy attention (Lyberaki and Smyth 1990: 135). No individual firm, even the largest, is able to master or to dominate; all competitors are operating in alliance with other firms – large and small. While there is some evidence of networking behaviour outside the advanced economies, it is not a common phenomenon (McDade and Malecki 1997).

Technology transfer: no easy route to competitiveness

Without high levels of competence, technology transfer is a means of acquiring technology from elsewhere. International technology transfer is the most common means of narrowing the gap between global best practice and local technology. Technology is transferred internationally usually by global corporations to local enterprises in Third World countries, either *bundled* or *unbundled*. The latter refers to the separation of various elements of a technology, such as R&D, construction, manufacturing, marketing, training and co-production (Robinson 1988: 5–6). In essence, management skill is needed 'to weld these various elements of knowledge into a viable productive effort' (Clark 1985: 183). It is the supplier's ability to provide a complete bundle or package that keeps the supplier in a strong bargaining position. The supplier has an incentive to keep technical knowledge relatively secret in order to differentiate from that of competitors and to appropriate the benefits of that knowledge by selling it as a commodity (Clark 1985).

Without technology transfer, the difficulties that confront economies in attempting to create competitive local industries are enormous. Firms must be able to recognize certain technologies as outdated and inadequate, and be able to identify technologies that need to be acquired from foreign sources rather than be developed (with greater delay) domestically (Katz 1982). Only with this knowledge can an importer be in a strong bargaining position *vis-à-vis* suppliers of technology (Forsyth 1990; Simai 1990). For firms from any country, 'staying in the loop' requires alliances with innovative leaders (Mody 1989).

> Nowadays most of the know-how needed is the proprietary knowledge of large corporations in the advanced countries – not just, or not so much, that licensable knowledge which they have tied up in patents, as the know-how which makes the production process viably cheap and efficient – and which they keep secret. And in many fields there really is no sensible substitute for transferring production technology other than buying it from – or getting it through often costly collaboration with – foreign firms. The world is unlikely ever again, for example, to see a national automobile industry founded except as a result of technical collaboration with a major foreign producer. Fortunate the country which can get fairly quickly from maintenance mastery to reproduction mastery to improvement mastery (Japan, for instance, with General Motors and Ford – but then with much simpler 1920s/1930s technology). Less fortunate the countries – India, Russia – which fail to make it to improvement mastery levels and require new transplants from Fiat or Suzuki every decade or so (Dore 1989: 105).

There are two motivations for recipients of technology transfers. One is to increase the production of newer, innovative products in order to increase the added value or profitability of economic activity. Low-risk activities, such as production and marketing of established products, yield dependable but relatively small returns. Direct import 'is the lowest level of technology acquisition. The product is imported as a "package" with the only substantial "local" content coming, perhaps, from the assembly process. The importing country will acquire some knowledge of the technology, particularly its operation and maintenance, but will only acquire a limited capability in design and manufacture' (Thomas 1988: 327). Preliminary production and marketing of unproven products are riskier ventures, but potentially able to reap 'super profits.' Information gathering and R&D (or learning by searching) are the most risky, but possess the highest potential return (Robinson 1988: 48–9). As one moves from production to design, a corresponding increase in the need for management and technical skills arises. The ability of Taiwan's small semiconductor firms to master chip design contrasts with the capability of the Korean *chaebol* in production (Chen and Sewell 1996). This suggests that Taiwan's firms will be relatively more successful in the flexible production regime, while Korean firms will continue to do well in the Fordist, large-firm forms of flexibility seen in strategic alliances and other strategies (Henderson 1994: 283). It remains to be seen which scenario will dominate in the future.

This reflects the second motivation for technology transfer: to increase indigenous technological capability (Felker and Weiss 1995). Technology transfers become partial as transferees acquire greater technological capability and require less complete packages of technology (Robinson 1988). Adoption and diffusion of new technology seem preferable to trying to create it, since they demand less traditional R&D, but they still require a high level of technical skills (Vickery and Blair 1989). The international diffusion of technology 'has been selective and unequally distributed' due to a 'lack of finance, limited capacities of host countries to monitor, unpackage and absorb foreign technologies, and to the tremendous economic and social follow-on costs involved in the transfer of "inappropriate" technologies' (Ernst and O'Connor 1989: 29). Because the purchase of foreign technology is offered as the path of least resistance, developing countries tend to under-invest in R&D (Moore 1983: 49). However, in the end, 'creating an inventive capacity' is a central goal of the development process (Amin 1986: 169). A niche market is the most successful initial route to this capability, since it can start with low levels of output (Bae and Lee 1986; Kim, Lee and Lee 1987). Taiwan's experience in chip design, noted earlier, is an example.

For many industries in developing countries, technology is seen mainly as the acquisition of machinery in a branch plant or a turnkey operation; thus, it originates entirely in another place and culture. The capital-goods industry – machines which produce other products – is a key element in the diffusion of technology among firms and among sectors (Enos and Park 1988; Fransman 1986).

The success of technology transfer depends less on the support of the exporter than on the ability and willingness of the importing society to accept and absorb the technology. Over the past century, technology has increased dramatically and technology transfer has become more difficult for recipients. Where craftsmen could formerly understand, copy and improve technologies, this now requires knowledge of science and engineering, as well as literacy. As a consequence, developing countries now must virtually always turn to the advanced countries for their capital equipment (Headrick 1988: 11). Local or domestic technological capability is indispensable in order to alter, modify and adapt transferred technology to local conditions (Chantramonklasri 1990). The technological capability or know-how embodied in a technical labour force, especially when employed in private enterprises, provides a firm and a nation with the skills necessary to evaluate new technologies as they emerge in other places. Local learning (by doing and by other means) and informal skills may be more important than R&D in mastering imported technology. This learning contributes to knowledge that can be used to change designs, production processes, and the way in which a technology is used (Barker *et al.* 1986). R&D can contribute only to transformations of designs. Experience in production suggests other changes in production methods and design alterations, but cannot address ways in which a product may be used (Thomas 1988).

The cultural gap between foreign and local experts can delay rapid transfer (Scott-Stevens 1987). Consultants are an important part of the technology transfer process. They are central experts in the global network of S&T information (Ashton and Stacey 1995), and they serve to bridge the managerial gap common to firms in developing countries (Bessant and Rush 1995). Their success in developing countries, however, is related directly to the capacity of the local staff to absorb the technology. Human capital is most critical, and where it is in short supply, as in Africa, technology transfers may be unsuccessful (Niosi, Hanel and Fiset 1995).

Appropriate technology

The question of whether transferred technology is 'inappropriate' for less developed countries arises frequently (Bhalla 1979; Clark 1985; Stewart 1978, 1981, 1987). To a large extent, concern over appropriate technology stems from the interest in basic needs and bottom-up planning and, therefore, is especially relevant in the context of rural and agricultural technology, where skills and resources are far fewer than in urban areas, where the needs for technology nearer to the present technology may be greater (Roy 1994).

For developing economies, technology transfer affirms their technological dependence on other nations and firms from which they obtain technology. Control over the pace and form of technology remains where R&D and improvements in production process technology are ongoing. The 'image of modernity' and the conditions placed by international sources of finance have also influenced the adoption of inappropriate technologies over indigenous ones. Indeed, it is state-owned enterprises in Africa that are particularly attracted to large-scale, capital-intensive technologies, i.e. inappropriate technologies (James 1995).

The adoption of imported modern technology can destroy knowledge of traditional technologies and, because of their complexity, prevent learning by doing by semi-skilled and skilled artisans without sufficient formal engineering-related education (Bhalla 1979). In addition, modern technologies demand modern or imported managers and managerial techniques. And spare parts for repairs must come almost exclusively from the country – and firm – from which the equipment was purchased, thus extending technological dependence well beyond the initial decision (Stewart 1978).

A great deal of effort has been made during the past two decades to 'blend' new technologies to the situation of small-scale and traditional activities in the Third World (Bhalla and James 1988). Many of these utilize microelectronic technology applied to education, health care and social services; applications in production have thus far been limited to NICs such as Brazil, Hong Kong and Singapore, where organizational flexibility and skill in management are present (Bhalla 1988). Older technologies, especially those adapted for the conditions of poor countries, can be an alternative to 'new' technologies. However, this comes with a price, as the new technologies, although requiring skills and infra-structure, add greatly to productivity (Stewart 1990: 322).

The shortage of managerial capacity, distinct from technical knowledge, is a critical constraint on industrial growth in underdeveloped countries (Clark 1985: 183; Sharif 1994a,b). Managerial dependence is interdependent with technological dependence (Stewart 1978: 65), and can prevent both entrepren-eurship and expansion of technological capability (Chantramonklasri 1990; Vakil and Brahmananda 1987). As Stewart and Nihei (1987: 151) put it in dis-cussing Indonesia, 'the top three priorities for expanding absorptive capacity are management, management, and management.' As a result, the development effects of transferred technology are minimal: too few firms are formed, too little information is exchanged.

The role of institutions

It is evident that the process of development is complex, with a variety of actors playing major roles. In the case of the 'developmental states' of East Asia, pro-viding conditions to facilitate and encourage private-sector activity, thereby reducing both direct state involvement and subsidies, has been a key feature of their recent history. Bureaucracies with 'embedded autonomy' perform best, maintaining an insulation from political and social influences while at the same time remaining closely connected with, and understanding the workings of, private firms. Brazil and India are frequently cited examples of countries whose bureaucracies have been unable to find the public–private symbiosis that emerged in South Korea and, earlier, in Japan (Evans 1995).

The technological environment of a nation depends on a stable macro-economic environment or 'market-friendly' policies. It also depends in large part on the legal and institutional structure within which firms must operate. Perhaps the most important role for government is the provision of a legal system that defines property rights (including intellectual property), contracts and bankruptcy (World Bank 1996b). Among the effects of such a legal system are rules by which companies know with some certainty the degree to which they can appropriate, or profit from, an innovation. However, beyond the general, economy-wide level, policies can 'overcome weaknesses in the entrepreneurial fabric', and the strategies and actions of firms themselves are critical for exploiting and learning from market opportunities (Hobday 1995: 1188–9). Increasingly, these strategies must include finding partners to minimize costs and risks, to specialize according to capabilities and to share tasks (Evans 1995; Frischtak 1994: 611).

Perhaps more important than formal structures and institutions are the conventions that support learning and movement along a technological trajectory – creating and sustaining a technical culture within an economy (Storper 1995a; Sweeney 1991). This culture is needed to keep pace with innovations and international technical knowledge. To do so, human resources must be skilled and able to switch to new, frontier technologies. 'The ability to keep pace with ongoing innovations is a much more powerful determinant of competitiveness than cost advantages due to low wages' (Mody, Suri, and Tatikonda 1995: 583).

More is at work, however, than property law and R&D capability. As standardization of design takes place and an industry paradigm emerges, the firms which gain most will tend to be those which have a full array of complementary assets in order not only to exploit the innovative design but also to manufacture it competitively and bring it successfully to market. A firm's technological capability includes all of its complementary assets, and these allow a firm to profit from 'bunches' of related technologies when they appear (Delapierre 1988). The diverse nature of technology means that informal technology transfer, as well as that through normal commercial channels, is necessary. Informal methods include visits abroad, attendance at seminars and conferences, participation in fairs and exhibitions, and utilization of the published literature (Simai 1990: 132–3).

Conclusions and suggestions for policy

In summary, science and technology can no longer be narrowly focused on basic research or scientists working in isolation. Indeed, it is necessary to think about innovation in a broad sense, 'not focussed on the high-technology fringe' (Bradford 1994: 60). Networks of many types are needed, with many links, in many locations. Correspondingly, policies for science and technology must be aware of much more than science and technology. The entire world economy is not only relevant, but provides models other than the East Asian variety (dos Reis Velloso 1994). At the level of competition, only competitive firms are able to be aware of what is needed to compete. The needs of firms suggest that some policies are helpful, even essential: telecommunications and transportation infrastructures and education are two prominent examples.

More specifically, both the array of factors that explicitly affect science and technology and those which only indirectly influence the accumulation of technological capability must be addressed. These include, first, a concern for market structure, so that firms are subject to competitive pressures at home as they will be in global markets (Bell and Pavitt 1993b; Porter 1990). Second, market failure still applies in the areas of education, training and research, so these must be done and coordinated by government, but not so that firms' actions in these areas are excluded or inhibited. Third, university research, which is usually basic or fundamental in nature, provides important skills, background knowledge, familiarity with research methodologies and instrumentation, and membership in informal and international networks of professional peers. Fourth, governments need to support the institutions that comprise the technology infrastructure of an economy, institutions that complement and sustain the actions of private firms (Bell and Pavitt 1993b: 173–7). The fact that so many countries target the same strategic industries and strategic technologies suggests that there will be overcrowding and competition, and perhaps a failure to be prepared for unexpected technologies. Creating an environment conducive to innovative activity and risk-taking – in whatever sectors – is perhaps a better policy (O'Connor 1995).

A free flow of information and feedback must take place, and social structures cannot inhibit this flow. A policy commitment to support R&D for monitoring 'international technology intelligence' for alternative sources of technology is an important allocation of government funds (Radnor and Kaufman 1988). Broad economic policies (those affecting credit, trade, investment and labour) and human resource policies, especially regarding education and training, are also needed to support scientific and technological activities (Dahlman 1989; UN Office for Science and Technology 1980). Finally, policies must be flexible enough to change over time in response to the capabilities of local firms and of the labour force.

Chapter 9

Development in a competitive world: challenges for the twenty–first century

The imperatives of technological change constantly affect business enterprises and determine the conditions of work for people. Whether a firm keeps up with, or falls behind, the technological frontier largely defines its fortunes, the prospects for its employees and, in turn, the economic development outcomes for places – localities, regions and nations. Technology, along with globalization, is the principal source of structural change and employment growth and decline (Pianta, Evangelista and Perani 1996; Wolff 1996). These are issues that affect us all, but some places are more in control of their destiny than others, by virtue of the fact that their workers and firms are more prepared for the future.

This chapter surveys some of the central themes that face society at the end of the 1990s. Although it is not claimed that technology is the answer to all of our present and future dilemmas (it has not solved all of the problems of the past; indeed, it has created many of them), it is among the most useful frameworks for addressing them. Technology, as this book has shown, is not simply machines, software or engineering knowledge. It is all those, together with the set of structures or arrangements – the institutions and conventions – which enable it to operate within a society. Seen in this light, technology is far from autonomous. It is a human and social creation, and technological change is a result of choices, most of them explicit but some of them implicit as well. Technology can promote regress as well as progress; the increasingly privatized entertainment permitted by personal electronic technology, for example, has greatly reduced social interaction (Street 1992).

In this final chapter we will look at several future issues for technology and economic development, including basic needs for human development, environmental issues, employment and human capital, and infrastructures for future technologies.

Technology and the future

Although many lists of future dilemmas could be devised, Whiston (1994) has suggested four challenges related to innovation that will overshadow policy for the future. These focus the discussion in this chapter:
1. to provide basic necessities of life for all;
2. to search for and develop further socially and environmentally sustainable

methods of organization, production, manufacture, and usage of materials and resources;

3. to develop organizational and political structures for full, and meaningful, employment; and

4. to develop effective and efficient methods of human resource development, including education and training, accessible to all.

Basic needs

The first of these recalls the discussion of Chapter 1 regarding development, as opposed to growth. Development includes basic human needs for adequate food, shelter and medical care, as well as choices and the freedom to make those choices (Sen 1988). From the individual's point of view, a job (not to mention a choice of employment options) to provide for and improve the lot of one's family is a key priority not always met in many of the world's economies. Aggregate measures of human development capture many of these basic needs, and they highlight the sharp contrasts between the 'have' nations and the 'have-nots'. Structural change remains more important than economic growth *per se*, and requires attention to both humanitarian and human resource development needs (Aturupane, Glewwe and Isenman 1994).

Environmentally sustainable development

Environmental considerations and apprehension over global sustainability have grown in recent decades, as consumption of resources has outstripped population growth (Steer and Lutz 1993). Many firms have embraced 'green' technologies, whether through actual environmental responsibility or primarily to create a good public image. More broadly, reduction (of materials used), re-manufacturing, recycling and reuse are growing components of an environmentally conscious corporate strategy for competitive advantage. These four processes have demands and implications that differ across the product life-cycle, including the early design stage, where 'design for disassembly' is seeing increased use. Such environmental practices have also become part of best practice or excellence for firms to attain, with standards (ISO 14000) that supplement the ISO 9000 standards for quality (Hitomi 1996; Sarkis and Rasheed 1995; Shrivastava 1995). Whether industrial production can be 'sustainable' remains an open question (Hudson 1995).

Outside the boundaries of the firm, at the regional and local level, *industrial ecology* (or industrial metabolism or symbiosis) represents the interrelationship of various technologies. By-products of production become not merely waste or trash, but inputs to linked industries that can use them. A variety of technical and legal issues are involved, especially regarding hazardous materials. Major research initiatives are under way, notably at the Zero Emissions Research Initiative (ZERI) in Japan, where identifying the 'missing links' in an inter-industry cluster bears similarity to earlier industrial complexes and growth centres (Frosch 1994; Gertler and Ehrenfeld 1996; Socolow *et al.* 1994; Weaver 1995).

At the local and regional level, new initiatives are difficult to put into practice side-by-side with existing priorities (Anderson, Kanaroglou and Miller 1996; Hardy and Lloyd 1994; Roberts 1994). It is clear, however, that local authorities, particularly in the UK, are taking a more active role in environmental management than was the case previously (Gibbs 1996; Gibbs and Healey 1995). Some environmental issues centre around energy use. The 'energy crisis' of the 1970s provided a sudden trauma to which most firms and institutions have responded in order to reduce consumption (J. Martin 1990). Least change has taken place in transport, where public transport must compete with the convenience of cars (Carson 1996). Research initiatives for an electric vehicle are under way in several countries, including Japan, Germany, France, Italy, the UK and the USA (Quandt 1995), where this technological opportunity is incorporated into national and local economic development plans (Slifko and Rigby 1995). Another energy crisis appears to be in the world's future as demand by developing countries increases rapidly (Carr 1994).

Despite occasional policy and media awareness of global environmental issues, international linkages remain poorly understood and difficult to analyse (Stevens 1993). Examples of environmentally conscious actions, such as Canon's global centre in Dalian, China, for recycling and refurbishing of cartridges for laser printers (Shrivastava 1995: 197), ignore the fact that 'dirty' jobs such as this continue the spatial division of labour by locating such work not in rich countries, but in poor ones. Activities closest to environmental best practice tend to be found in 'core' locations (Taylor 1996). Innovation-driven environmental policies are not yet common, since innovation is often ignored when policy and regulation (both economic and environmental) are discussed (Banks and Heaton 1995; McMorran and Wallace 1995).

Human capital and economic development

Economic development includes – indeed, economic growth is often measured solely by – employment. Regional and national fortunes depend on the activities of the firms operating within them, and also on the strength of institutions, including educational and research institutions and informal networks. For firms, the imperatives include a strong commitment to R&D and being prepared for the eventuality of technological change and discontinuities (Chapter 2). The challenge for the modern firm, according to Romer (1993), is simultaneously to replicate designs, products and processes that work, and to search constantly for new and different specifications. All of these non-routine activities need skilled workers for the tasks involved.

At the national level, investment must be made in education, in infrastructure for new technologies, and in diffusing knowledge, all with the aim of enhancing national capabilities (Freeman 1995a). These influences, while difficult to measure precisely, continue to determine economic growth (Guellec 1996; Scholing and Timmermann 1988). Public investment in education and training is one of the few variables (of 21 studied) that significantly affected growth in GDP in the USA from 1955 to 1992 (Cullison 1993). At the same time, much also depends on the investments made by firms in people, for these accumulate into a body of know-how, resources, strategies and habits that represent assets complementary to innovation embodied in equipment and machines (R. Thomas 1994). Moreover, competitiveness is embodied not only in the capacities of individual firms but in the 'web of interconnections' that establishes the opportunities for all firms (Cohen and Zysman 1987: 102). This view of interconnectedness between producing firms, their suppliers and their customers (within *filières*) depends on production systems acting as carriers of knowledge, skills and organizational techniques for an economy – and as a system of innovation or technological system (Carlsson 1994; Lundvall 1992; Nelson 1993).

Policy for employment is not strictly the province of government, therefore, since other institutions – private as well as public–private in nature – significantly influence knowledge accumulation and distribution. These include (at least) training and education, finance, and a 'diffusion-oriented' or 'distribution-oriented' system of innovation (David and Foray 1995: 55–9). Policies depend greatly upon the 'technical culture' of places, and this culture varies between nations, between regions and between localities. Skills and entrepreneurship, unlike scientific knowledge and technology, are very local phenomena, and they are especially critical to economic change and Schumpeterian creative destruction (Chapter 5). High-skill workers both determine, and are determined by, the local training and education system, reflecting and sustaining the local technical culture (Bradley and Taylor 1996).

National competitiveness, then, depends on economic and industrial performance, as it once did on military strength. Whether a nation's firms and industries are internationally competitive depends heavily on the technical capabilities present. These capabilities are represented, first, by skilled, technical workers and, second, by the general educational level of the labour force. Indeed, Boyer (1995) places skill acquisition as one of the central areas where policies either enhance or inhibit the development of a learning economy. Increasingly, it is recognized that public effort must be complemented by private-sector efforts to develop human resources (Ramos 1994).

Significant national differences persist in training practices and in educational institutions and practices. In the UK, for example, despite greater demands for technical and engineering skills, significantly fewer workers with such skills are available than in Germany or Japan, presenting a persistent source of concern (Prais 1988; Shackleton 1995; Walker 1980; Warner 1994). Countries where public expenditure on training and other labour market policies represents more than 1 per cent of GDP include (in order): Sweden, Finland, Germany, Denmark, Ireland, Norway, the Netherlands and Belgium. Japan and the USA rank lowest among the OECD countries, but far more training is provided by employers in Japan (Shackleton 1995). At the same time, Shackleton (1995: 238) warns against governments trying to 'pick 'n mix from different training cultures' not suited to a nation's institutions, history, and economic and political environment. We next look briefly at culture as it affects human resource development.

Culture

National culture affects attitudes about economic development and about training and education. At the most general level, national cultures differ along dimensions related to family values, roles of individuals, a tendency to analyse or to integrate, individualism versus communitarianism, a sense of time as sequence versus time as synchronization, and social equality versus hierarchy (Hampden-Turner and Trompenaars 1993; Hofstede 1980). Such cultural values, especially regarding inclusion and exclusion, directly affect access to information and education in a society. These affect legal systems and industrial organization which, in turn, significantly influence the appropriability of technology, the principal incentive for innovation. Cultural or societal values, then, directly influence the transmission of skills, industrial relations, and the perceived role of government in such matters.

But far more than culture accounts for the development of institutional systems that define work, employer–worker relations, and the ability of these to adapt to changing conditions. For example, the firm is seen as a welfare institution in Sweden, with roles that include training and education (Eliasson 1988). Not only in Sweden, but in the German and Japanese models as well, extensive intra-firm or enterprise-based training has been the norm, albeit with variations (Belussi and Garibaldo 1996; Jürgens 1993; Marsden 1993; Shackleton 1995). All three models, while different, have contributed to a strong structural competitiveness in their economies (Boyer 1995). The German system of lengthy apprenticeships is looked to by many as a model for producing highly skilled workers. Comparative studies of the systems of training in Britain, Germany and the USA reinforce impressions of the US system being the most oriented toward general education rather than job-specific skills (Dolton 1993; Lynch 1993; Steedman 1993). In the USA, 'private firms underinvest in training because such investments can relatively easily be lost. In contrast to investments in capital goods, which can be bolted down, a worker can take his or her expensive training to another firm' (Spring 1989: v).

Culture affects what individual firms do as well. Rigid social hierarchies thwart innovativeness, whereas cultural values that reinforce individualism are more innovative (Shane 1992). Culture affects the degree of scanning for information outside the firm and the amount of long-range planning among top managers in the USA and nine European countries (Hegarty and Hoffman 1990). 'Germanic' managers scanned social trends significantly more than those in other cultural groups, and also engaged to a greater degree in long-range planning; 'Anglo' managers, on the other hand, scanned technical trends more than any other group. Ganitsky and Watzke (1990) suggest that different time horizons are often central to such cross-cultural differences, and this was one of seven dimensions included by Hampden-Turner and Trompenaars (1993) to account for major cultural variations in capitalism. African culture, especially views of equality and distribution, is blamed for at least part of that continent's problems in capitalist economic growth (Kennedy 1988: 4–5).

One could also question whether the East Asian 'miracle' was the result of cultural attributes, such as diligence, hard work and educational attainment. A cultural explanation ('the Korean character') is used by Enos and Park (1988) in the context of South Korea's rapid rate of absorption of petrochemical technology:

> Valuable national traits are evident in Korea's engineers – the desire to acquire modern knowledge, combined with mechanical aptitude; the courage to undertake unfamiliar activities; the lack of resentment at working intensely and regularly for long hours; a spirit of cooperation; a willingness to subordinate private interests to collective goals; a rough, combative energy; and an urgent pragmatism – all tend to enable them to absorb foreign ideas, foreign techniques (Enos and Park 1988: 108).

Perhaps this 'character' and its traits are simply a result of culture, but it seems more likely that they are values embedded in institutions and conventions. Culturally, the free exchange of information in Japan has led to more informal learning, such as learning by doing, than has occurred where people are over-protective and secretive about the transmission of knowledge. Thus, some of the international variation in skills may be cultural in nature. In Japan and South Korea, the preoccupation of middle-class parents with their children's school performance is thought to reflect the cultural value placed on schooling (Lee and Yamazawa 1990). It also indicates, however, the functioning of a system in which corporations hire, at each status level, from the graduates of particular institutions according to their prestige.

A Confucian work ethic appears to account for some of the East Asian 'miracle' (L. Harrison 1992), but Confucianism, like market-friendly policies alone, is probably not the answer to East Asian success (Kim 1994). 'Once education is accounted for, there is usually very little variation across racial or ethnic boundaries in economic achievement' (Riedel 1988: 26–7). What can be concluded is that countries with more elitist educational systems and more restricted entry to technical education are at a disadvantage. Global networks based on ethnic ties and trust provide a related cultural rationale for economic vitality (Kotkin 1992; Seagrave 1995).

Skills and capabilities: education and training

In a time of global or transnational firms as a principal source of employment, the fortunes of countries – and, even more, of regions and localities – depend on industry mix and product mix and how well local industries and firms fare relative to their competitors. Intelligent enterprises and agile corporations need, more than anything else, people who will bring knowledge into the organization. Corporate (and regional) technological capability is enhanced by interaction: inter-firm linkages within networks. Inter-firm linkages facilitate collective learning and represent an indicator of development far more advanced than employment alone. Local linkages support other firms, with impacts on local economic development, seen most vividly in innovative milieus and industrial districts (Chapters 4 and 5).

The advantages of flexible production over mass production, and of economies of scope (product variety) over economies of scale (production

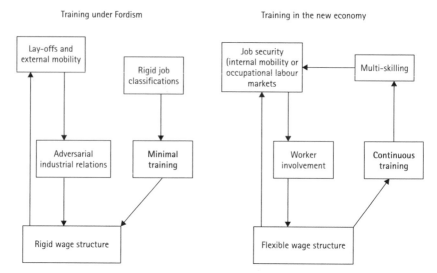

Figure 9.1   Training systems of Fordism and in the new economy. Source: modified from Boyer (1995: 125, Figure 9).

volume) are powerful, but only if highly skilled workers and adequate networks for telecommunications are available. Flexible production leads to new priorities regarding worker skills, requiring multi-skilling, or polyvalent skills, and continuous, rather than minimal and narrow training. Figure 9.1 suggests that, through worker involvement, the new economy training model results in a virtuous circle of continuous training. The Fordist training system, by contrast, becomes trapped in adversarial industrial relations.

Because of cultural differences and because conditions are rarely optimal (implementation of flexible technology is very difficult and the needs for worker skills are constantly changing), many firms have been unable to shift to post-Fordist systems (Chapter 4). Belussi and Garibaldo (1996) suggest that there are four geographical blocs: the Anglo-American flexibilization of the Fordist system; the Euro-corporation skill-based model, based on collective labour regulation and co-determination; the Asiatic-corporatist model, based on individual models of work transactions; and the paleo-Manchesterian development of the former socialist economies. Nowhere have there evolved true non-Fordist, skill-based economies. The Anglo-American system is considered the 'low road' approach that relies on a dual labour market, with serious weaknesses compared with systems elsewhere (Doeringer 1994; Howell 1994; Peck and Jones 1995; Warner 1994). Beneath the dual economy, and in some ways as a result of the inadequacy of secondary jobs, inner cities contain those discouraged and excluded from the labour force. Solutions for urban poverty in advanced countries, for example, may depend greatly on local training initiatives within a broad framework of 'economic reintegration' for those excluded from opportunities (McGregor and McConnachie 1995).

Skills and the learning of new skills is an even greater challenge for developing countries (Storper 1995a). At a time of reduced budgets in response to structural adjustment programmes, countries must address human resource development at all three levels of education: primary, secondary and tertiary (Riddell 1996). Access to education varies tremendously from country to country. Differential access within countries, but especially poor countries, means that education beyond the secondary level is likely to be available only in major cities, such as national capitals. In order to address the massive shortages of skilled labour for their operations in Asia, many TNCs have taken to training workers (*The Economist* 1995b).

Formal education is one important element contributing to national labour skills. At the same time, higher levels of education have negative impacts on those with less education, who are passed over by employers (Goux and Maurin 1996; Wood 1994). The existence of schools alone make very little difference 'to a society that does not provide appropriate channels in which school-learning can be put to use' (Peattie 1981: 152). Both investment in education and a labour market and enterprises that needed educated and skilled workers are part of the East Asian 'miracle' (World Bank 1993). None the less, schooling is 'the basic mode of technical training . . . the means for generating the technical skills needed for economic growth' (Peattie 1981: 143). The level of these skills 'is normally a pre-condition for and often a determinant of economic performance and international competitiveness' (Warner 1994: 348).

General education also provides important skills, especially literacy and numeracy, and awareness about phenomena outside of daily existence. A further, long-term effect of education is that if one receives more education, then one's peer group and interpersonal relationships comprise a larger proportion of informed and skilled people from whom to obtain useful knowledge. Finally, a higher level of educational attainment transfers into ability to deal with non-routine activities.

Flexible production and the prominent place of small firms forces labour training to the forefront of local policy (Lloyd 1989). Flexible firms need skilled and flexible workers. High-technology industries, in particular, demand understanding of complex capital equipment, technical documentation, and integration of complex technologies (Bartel and Lichtenberg 1987). While large-scale projections of increased skill requirements are easily made, regional and local variations are prominent, suggesting that training and education policies must be locally based (Foley, Watts and Wilson 1992; Spenner 1988).

Skills: ever rising

The basic skills required in the new economy include 'deep' technical skills, in addition to skills for learning, communication, adaptability, personal management, group effectiveness and influencing others (Carnevale 1995: 241). Carnevale (1995: 244–5) suggests eight categories of worker training that address these skill needs:

1. organizational training (e.g. management and supervisory training and team training);

2. technical training to develop, install and maintain new technologies as they arise;
3. skill training to learn new technology and new software;
4. customer interface training for employees who work with customers;
5. strategic training for specific goals, such as quality;
6. professional training to help non-technical professionals (e.g. accountants, architects, doctors) keep up with new technology;
7. basic skills training in reading, writing and computation; and
8. regulated training to respond to environmental, safety and other regulations as they arise.

Many of the basic skills resemble personal traits, but they also vary according to the demands of local employers. The fullest range of skills will be found in non-routine jobs, but a number of these basic skills are required by routine work, especially in the service sector. Walt Disney Corporation, for example, selects workers 'who are enthusiastic, who have pride in their work, who can take charge of a situation without supervision' (Henkoff 1994: 118). Generally, service firms do not need workers with high levels of education, technical expertise or experience. They need 'people who are resilient and resourceful, empathetic and enterprising, competent and creative – a set of skills, in short, that they once demanded only of managers' (Henkoff 1994: 110).

In the financial service sector, a slightly different set of categories of skills is proposed:
1. *social*, for effective interpersonal communication;
2. *product-knowledge*, for effective marketing and selling of services;
3. *keyboard and diagnostic*, for interface with systems and resolution of problems that arise; and
4. *entrepreneurial*, for ensuring the viability of individual cost or profit centres in an organization (Rajan 1987: 225).

In such a setting, gatekeepers and people with extensive contacts are valuable in ways that the concept of 'skills' is unable to measure. Finding, retaining and rewarding 'knowledge workers' involves far different criteria than have been common for other forms of work (Despres and Hiltrop 1996).

In a setting where custom products and short product life-cycles are the norm, many work tasks are non-routine, and thus the largely personal and interpersonal skills and adaptability are essential. Howell and Wolff (1992) propose a simple, three-category system of labour skills:
1. *cognitive skills*, typical of symbolic analysts (Chapter 4);
2. *interactive skills*, or 'people skills' , common to professionals whose jobs deal with the public, such as physicians and lawyers; and
3. *motor skills*, common in blue-collar jobs, and which have been showing an absolute decline since 1950.

Despite these trends, technology is not a job-destroyer; industries with high levels of new investment stimulate demand for more educated workers (Bartel and Lichtenberg 1987; Wolff 1996).

The most skilled sets of jobs, which embody a composite of language, mathematical and reasoning skills, on the other hand, are expected to double as a percentage of the total. Emphasizing the continuing increase in entry-level skills, Johnston and Packer (1987: 100) state that 'jobs that are currently in the middle of the skill distribution will be the least-skilled occupations of the future, and there will be very few net new jobs for the unskilled.' For those who do not have basic skills, the growing demand for multiple, or polyvalent, skills is even more difficult.

The decline in the demand for unskilled, usually manual, workers has been seen as a result of technological change in all countries (Johnston and Packer 1987; Brainard, Leedman and Lumbers 1988). In essence, entry-level skills are rising most rapidly, a fact which hits hardest those who are disadvantaged or are members of minority populations, who often find it difficult to acquire the necessary entry-level skills (Cyert and Mowery 1987). Recent experience and projections illustrate the changing skill mix found in the labour market. Low-skill jobs, such as labourers, are expected to decrease by more than 50 per cent.

As their skill needs have increased, the hiring criteria of firms have gone beyond a set of technical skills. In interviews, attitude is also evaluated. Demonstrations of politeness and motivation were considered more important than English/verbal skills and physical appearance in a study of 3000 employers in four large US urban areas. Most jobs available to workers with low levels of education require the daily performance of one or more cognitive/social tasks, including dealing with customers, reading and writing, arithmetic calculations, and the use of computers (Holzer 1996).

Education and training programmes are the primary systems by which the human capital of a nation is preserved and increased (Johnston and Packer 1987: 116; Porter 1990; Tallman and Wang 1992). Post-secondary, non-university training is especially weak in *laissez-faire* nations, such as the USA. The pace of technological change means, however, that 'schools cannot hope to prepare workers for emerging skill needs as they initially arise.' As training needs become known over the skill-training life-cycle, however, 'skills become more generalized and transferable among employers.' At that point, schools can provide such training (Flynn 1993: 149–50). Despite the fragmented training in the United States, many small firms are involved in training, often in conjunction with local community colleges (Baker and Armstrong 1996; Mangelsdorf 1993). Small firms, which 'need people with a specific skill in twos and threes', are unable to justify fully fledged training programmes (O'Farrell and Hitchens 1988: 414). In general, it is the growth-oriented SMEs that take advantage of external training programmes in the UK (Vaessen and Keeble 1995).

The need for worker skills varies over the life-cycle of a product (Carnevale, Gainer and Meltzer 1988; Flynn 1993). In the *skill-training life-cycle*, 'products, production processes, and technologies are seen as dynamic phenomena whose skill and training requirements change as they evolve' (Flynn 1993: 7). The size of the labour pool needed for a particular skill varies across the life-cycle, and thus the difficulty of finding workers to fill positions (which are at first ill-defined) is a predicament seldom explored in regional analysis. For example, if new skills are needed and are unavailable in the external labour market, firms commonly rely on training by equipment manufacturers. This skill-transfer process requires close collaboration between employers and educational and

training institutions for identifying skill needs and standardizing training programmes in those skills. These skill needs are local because labour markets are
locally unique, comprising local workers, workplaces and local histories (Flynn
1993). The effects of innovation on labour and employment are many and
varied (Fischer 1990; Osterman 1988). Technological change affects not only
the number of jobs but also work tasks, skill requirements, occupations and
work environments.

People are critical throughout the process of technological change. In all settings, the skills of people – for accepting and interpreting information, for
improving and enhancing technology, and for generating new knowledge – ultimately determine economic outcomes. Whether in low technology or high technology circumstances, people define what organizations and nations can
accomplish. An educated, skilled population has far more opportunities for
change, innovation and new endeavours than one where lives are trapped in a
routine of poverty. While education and its advantages in the wider economy are
typically considered national investments, regional systems of innovation and
learning continue to furnish examples that differ from national patterns.

Infrastructure for development

Even in an era of downsized governments and hollow states, some functions
remain important for governments to perform. Among these is ensuring an adequate infrastructure for new technologies, particularly telecommunications
(Freeman 1995a). Infrastructure, or social overhead capital, has always been a
part of development (Hirschman 1958). Infrastructures and shifts to new transport infrastructures are central to each of the Kondratieff long waves (Grübler
1990).

In a national context, physical infrastructures are critical, because standards
of international commerce demand movements of goods and information in
certain forms and formats. Plain old telephone service (POTS) is no longer adequate for the wide range of information and telecommunications technologies.
The transition to digital networks will require massive, usually national, investments in telecommunications infrastructure (Arnold and Guy 1989). The telephone network ('the messenger') is one of the seven wonders of the modern
world, continually changing and expanding since its creation over a century ago
to incorporate microwave, satellite and fibre-optic technologies (*The Economist*
1993). The network is able to deliver not only voices, but also data, images and
video. POTS is a basic infrastructure, but one (along with electricity, water and
transportation) unavailable to many parts of the world (World Bank 1994b). At
the same time, the universal, standard nature of the POTS network is breaking
down as deregulation and competition favour new services and network
enhancements first (or only) in major markets, such as world cities (Mansell
1993).

Other infrastructures allow nations to participate in global economic activity. Air and sea transportation demand modern airports and seaports.
Investments must be made in air traffic control, security and facilities in order

to attract international investment. Innovations in port technology have insisted on containerized cargo, able to be shipped by sea, rail or highway, and large vessels (Brookfield 1984). The decisions of ship operators about port selection for new services depend largely on state-of-the-art or best-practice facilities and operations being available (Willingale 1984). Once again, some places can be linked into the global network of world cities while others are largely left out.

Places compete for port traffic, especially for that based on new technology, such as container cargo. Asian ports have embraced containerization as the region's importance in exports has grown. Hong Kong and Singapore are the world's busiest container ports, superseding Rotterdam and New York, which led in 1975 (Hayuth 1990). Newer ports in Malaysia and China, such as Klang and Tianjin, are being added to the list of major shipping ports (*The Economist* 1994e; Todd 1994). In addition to containerization, three other technologies are transforming ocean shipping: larger ships, larger trains serving ports, and computerized freight tracking and billing systems. These technologies, and concentration on fewer ports as shipping firms provide round-the-world service, are altering the geography of ports (Kuby and Reid 1992; Machalaba 1996; Slack 1993). While all major ports are not world cities, there are similarities in the spatial structure of transport networks and other aspects of the world-city system (Dogan 1988).

Air transport infrastructure also grows in response to the increase in air traffic. Air service is essential to producer services and knowledge-based work (Chapter 4). In addition to its importance in moving people, the air transport system is increasingly important to air cargo for just-in-time delivery. Industrial complexes centred on airports are a new element of the global production system (Kasarda 1991).

Time clocks and the pace of change

All development is about change, but all changes do not take place at the same rate; different time clocks seem to apply to different phenomena. Energy and environment are related to the slower transition processes, including construction and infrastructure investment, and are related more to technological breakthroughs and long waves (Chapter 3) than to rapid economic, social and institutional response (Starr, Searl and Alpert 1992). Other processes are medium-speed or fast processes, responsive to choices of workers and firms, for example, or to the steady ageing of a population (Wegener 1986). Killick (1995b) suggests similar adjustment periods to describe economic flexibility (Figure 8.1). Investment in infrastructure, innovation and education are among the responses that require long periods of adjustment; information and supply–demand transactions are among the short-adjustment responses.

Storper (1988) provides a related perspective, distinguishing between events, structures and processes. Events, which are typically 'small', are the outcomes of structured, but not fully determined, situations. They are the results of choices and strategies by individuals and actors (human agents) undertaken within structured circumstances. Sequences and collections of these small events produce large processes, and large (global) outcomes of small events may not be fully predictable from the specific events themselves. The large processes thus generated may prompt reproduction or change in big structures. An example may be found in long-term structural change, which, based on disequilibrium, results from two types of smaller changes which take place within firms: productivity increases from new processes and the growth of new industries through the creation of new products. Technology and innovation within an industry involve three 'clocks' related to demand, technology and rivalry. Taken together, they define the uncertainty to which new and existing firms respond as new innovations and industries emerge (Macdonald and Wang 1994).

Conclusion

We can usefully translate a recent summary of international competitiveness into the regional context:

> The . . . competitiveness of a [regional] economy is built on the competitiveness of the firms which operate within, and export from, its boundaries, and is, to a large extent, an expression of the will to compete and the dynamism of firms, their capacity to invest, to innovate both as a consequence of their own R&D and of successful appropriation of external technologies; but
>
> The competitiveness of a [regional] economy is also more than the simple outcome of the collective or 'average' competitiveness of its firms; there are many ways in which the features and performance of a [regional] economy viewed as an *entity* with characteristics of its own, will affect, in turn, the competitiveness of firms (Chesnais 1986: 91).

Despite numerous policy efforts to disperse new technology and innovative economic activities, they display a persistent tendency toward agglomeration and concentration. Given the nature of non-routine economic activities, there are sound reasons for this agglomeration tendency (Chapter 4). The places that offer conditions for 'regional creativity' and learning have intensified levels of personal contacts, linked internally to both the region and global networks (Amin and Thrift 1992; Andersson 1985; Storper 1993).

The innovation process is lengthy and complex and all the necessary pieces may neither originate in a place nor always benefit the economy of that place. No linear model or simple one-way causality leads from science and technology to regional economic development. Instead, there are strong, mutually supportive relationships that work best when science and technology are part of the local culture, economy and society.

Technology cannot be planned for, in the manner of selecting industries and jobs. Technologies change and new industries or market opportunities may arise which are best accommodated by combinations of large and small firms, in conjunction with local, regional and national institutions. From a human standpoint, a well-educated and skilled population will be best able to capitalize on new opportunities and to take them into the future. Localities, regions and nations are constrained by the imperatives of the marketplace, but they learn, adopt and adapt knowledge and technology only through the skills of their people.

References

Abbott C. (1996) The internationalization of Washington, DC. *Urban Affairs Review* **31**: 571–94

Abe H., Alden J. D. (1988) Regional development planning in Japan. *Regional Studies* **22**: 429–38

Abernathy F. H., Dunlop J. T., Hammond J. H., Weil D. (1995) The information-integrated channel: a study of the US apparel industry in transition. *Brookings Papers on Economic Activity: Microeconomics*: 175–246

Abernathy W. J. (1980) Innovation and the regulatory paradox: toward a theory of thin markets. In Ginsburg D. H., Abernathy W. J. (eds) *Government, Technology, and the Future of the Automobile.* New York, McGraw-Hill: 38–61

Abernathy W. J., Clark K. B. (1985) Innovation: mapping the winds of creative destruction. *Research Policy* **14**: 3–22

Abernathy W. J., Utterback J. M. (1978) Patterns of industrial innovation. *Technology Review* **80** (5): 40–7

Abetti P. A. (1992) Planning and building the infrastructure for technological entrepreneurship. *International Journal of Technology Management* **7**: 129–39

Abetti P. A. (1994) Impact of technology on functional roles and strategies: illustrative cases in the USA, Japan and France, and lessons learned. *International Journal of Technology Management* **9**: 529–46

Abo T. (ed.) (1994) *Hybrid Factory: The Japanese Production System in the United States.* New York, Oxford University Press

Abraham S. C. S., Hayward G. (1984) Understanding discontinuance: towards a more realistic model of technological innovation and industrial adoption in Britain. *Technovation* **2**: 209–31

Abramovitz M. (1986) Catching up, forging ahead, and falling behind. *Journal of Economic History* **46**: 385–406

Acs Z. J., Audretsch D. B. (1989) Small-firm entry in US manufacturing. *Economica* **56**: 255–65

Acs Z. J., Audretsch D. B., Carlsson B. (1991) Flexible technology and firm size. *Small Business Economics* **3**: 307–19

Adam Y., Ong C. H., Pearson A. W. (1988) Licensing as an alternative to foreign direct investment: an empirical investigation. *Journal of Product Innovation Management* **5**: 32–49

Adams G., Hall G. (1993) Influences on the growth of SMEs: an international comparison. *Entrepreneurship and Regional Development* **5**: 73–84

Adelman I., Robinson S. (1989) Income distribution and development. In Chenery H., Srinivasan T. (eds) *Handbook of Development Economics*, volume II. Amsterdam, North-Holland: 949–1003

Adler P. S. (1989) Technology strategy: a guide to the literatures. In Rosenbloom R. S., Burgelman R. A. (eds) *Research in Technological Innovation, Management and Policy*, volume 4. Greenwich, CT, JAI Press: 25–151

Adler P. S. (1992) The 'learning bureaucracy': New United Motor Manufacturing, Inc. In Cummings L. L., Staw B. M. (eds) *Research in Organizational Behavior*, volume 15. Greenwich, CT, JAI Press: 111–94

Adler P. S., Clark K. B. (1991) Behind the learning curve: a sketch of the learning process. *Management Science* 37: 267–81

Adriaansen W. L. M., Storm S. T. H., Waardenburg J. G. (1992) Forty years of experience in development theory and practice: an introduction. In Adriaansen W. L. M., Waardenburg J. G. (eds) *A Dual World Economy: Forty Years of Development Experience*. Oxford, Oxford University Press: 1–52

Ady R. M. (1986) Criteria used for facility location selection. In Walzer N., Chicoine D. (eds) *Financing Economic Development in the 1980s*. New York, Praeger: 72–84

Agarwal S. (1994) The resort cycle revisited: implications for resorts. In Cooper C. P., Lockwood A. (eds) *Progress in Tourism, Recreation and Hospitality Management*, volume 5. Chichester, John Wiley: 194–208

Aghion P., Howitt P. (1993) A model of growth through creative destruction. In Foray D., Freeman C. (eds) *Technology and the Wealth of Nations: The Dynamics of Constructed Advantage*. London, Pinter: 145–72

Agnew J. A. (1984) Devaluing place: 'people prosperity versus place prosperity' and regional planning. *Environment and Planning D: Society and Space* 1: 35–45

Aguinier P. (1988) Regional disparities since 1978. In Feuchtwang S., Hussain A., Pairault T. (eds) *Transforming China's Economy in the Eighties*, volume II: *Management, Industry and the Urban Economy*. Boulder, CO, Westview Press: 93–106

Ahlbrandt R. S. (1988) Adjusting to changes in traditional markets: the problems of small manufacturers in older industrial regions. *Economic Development Quarterly* 2: 252–64

Ahlbrandt R. S., Blair A. F. (1986) What it takes for large organizations to be innovative. *Research Management* 29 (2): 34–7

Alam D. (1995) Building a strong S&T system in Indonesia: policies in a transitional economy. In Simon D. F. (ed.) *The Emerging Technological Trajectory of the Pacific Rim*. New York, M. E. Sharpe: 186–210

Albert P., Fournier R., Marion S. (1991) Developing entrepreneurial attitudes and management competence among scientists: the Groupe ESC Lyon's experience. *Entrepreneurship and Regional Development* 3: 349–62

Albrechts L., Moulaert F., Roberts P., Swyngedouw E. (eds) (1989) *Regional Policy at the Crossroads: European Perspectives*. London, Jessica Kingsley

Alden J. (1996) Regional development strategies in the European Union: Europe 2000+. In Alden J., Boland P. (eds) *Regional Development Strategies: A European Perspective*. London, Jessica Kingsley: 1–13

Alderman N. (1995) Company classification and technological change: a new perspective on regional innovation. In Bertuglia C. S., Fischer M. M., Preto G. (eds) *Technological Change, Economic Development and Space*. Berlin, Springer-Verlag: 160–83

Alderman N., Fischer M. M. (1992) Innovation and technological change: an Austrian–British comparison. *Environment and Planning A* 24: 273–88

Aldhous P. (1994) A scientific community on the edge. *Science* 264: 1262–4

Aldrich H., Reese P. R., Dubini P. (1989) Women on the verge of a breakthrough: networking among entrepreneurs in the United States and Italy. *Entrepreneurship and*

Regional Development 1: 339–56

Aldrich H., Zimmer C. (1986) Entrepreneurship through social networks. In Sexton D. L., Smilor R. W. (eds) *The Art and Science of Entrepreneurship.* Cambridge, MA, Ballinger: 3–23

Ali A. (1994) Pioneering versus incremental innovation: review and research propositions. *Journal of Product Innovation Management* 11: 46–61

Alic J. A. (1990) Who designs work? Organizing production in an age of high technology. *Technology in Society* 12: 301–17

Alic J. A. (1994) Technology in the service industries. *International Journal of Technology Management* 9: 1–14

Alic J., Branscomb L. M., Brooks H., Carter A. B., Epstein G. L. (1992) *Beyond Spinoff: Military and Commercial Technologies in a Changing World.* Boston, Harvard Business School Press

Allen D. N., Levine V. (1986) *Nurturing Advanced Technology Enterprises.* New York, Praeger

Allen J. (1988) Service industries: uneven development and uneven knowledge. *Area* 20: 15–22

Allen T. J. (1977) *Managing the Flow of Technology.* Cambridge, MA, MIT Press

Allen T. J., Cogan D. J., O'Doherty D., O'Sullivan B. A. (1990) Direct acquisition of technology by Irish industry: results of a survey of Irish-owned companies licensing patented technology. In O'Doherty D. (ed.) *The Cooperation Phenomenon: Prospects for Small Firms and the Small Economies.* London, Graham and Trotman: 78–99

Allen T. J., Hyman D. B., Pinckney D. L. (1983) Transferring technology to the small manufacturing firm: a study of technology transfer in three countries. *Research Policy* 12: 199–211

Allen T. J., Utterback J. M., Sirbu M. A., Ashford N. A., Hollomon J. H., (1978) Government influence on the innovation process. *Research Policy* 7: 124–49

Alonso W. (1980a) Five bell shapes in development. *Papers of the Regional Science Association* 45: 5–16

Alonso W. (1980b) Population as a system in regional development. *American Economic Review* 70: 405–9

Altaf Z. (1988) *Entrepreneurship in the Third World: Risk and Uncertainty in Industry in Pakistan.* London, Croom Helm

Alvstam C. (1995) Integration through trade and direct investment: Asian Pacific patterns. In Le Heron R., Park S. O. (eds) *The Asian Pacific Rim and Globalization.* Aldershot, Avebury: 107–28

Amable B. (1993) National effects of learning, international specialization and growth paths. In Foray D., Freeman C. (eds) *Technology and the Wealth of Nations: The Dynamics of Constructed Advantage.* London, Pinter: 173–88

Amann R. (1986) Technical progress and Soviet economic development: setting the scene. In Amann R., Cooper J. M. (eds) *Technical Progress and Soviet Economic Development.* Oxford, Basil Blackwell: 5–30

Amendola M., Bruno S. (1990) The behaviour of the innovative firm: relations to the environment. *Research Policy* 19: 419–33

Ameritrust, SRI Inc. (1986) *Indicators of Economic Capacity.* Cleveland, Ameritrust Corporation

Amey R. G. (1995) Automotive component innovation: development and diffusion of engine management technologies. *Technovation* 15: 211–23

Amin A. (1985) Restructuring in Fiat and the decentralization of production into southern Italy. In Hudson R., Lewis J. (eds) *Uneven Development in Southern Europe.*

London, Methuen: 155–91

Amin A. (1989a) A model of the small firm in Italy. In Goodman E., Bamford J., Saynor P. (eds) *Small Firms and Industrial Districts in Italy.* London, Routledge: 111–22

Amin A. (1989b) Flexible specialisation and small firms in Italy: myths and realities. *Antipode* 21 (1): 13–34

Amin A. (1989c) Specialization without growth: small footwear firms in Naples. In Goodman E., Bamford J., Saynor P. (eds) *Small Firms and Industrial Districts in Italy.* London, Routledge: 239–58

Amin A. (1994a) Post-Fordism: models, fantasies and phantoms of transition. In Amin A. (ed.) *Post-Fordism: A Reader.* Oxford, Blackwell: 1–39

Amin A. (ed.) (1994b) *Post-Fordism: A Reader.* Oxford, Blackwell

Amin A. (1994c) The difficult transition from informal economy to Marshallian industrial district. *Area* 26: 13–24

Amin A., Malmberg A. (1992) Competing structural and institutional influences on the geography of production in Europe. *Environment and Planning A* 24: 401–16

Amin A., Robins K. (1990) The re-emergence of regional economies? The mythical geography of flexible production. *Environment and Planning D: Society and Space* 8: 7–34

Amin A., Robins K. (1991) These are not Marshallian times. In Camagni R. (ed.) *Innovation Networks: Spatial Perspectives.* London, Pinter: 105–18

Amin A., Thrift N. (1992) Neo-Marshallian nodes in global networks. *International Journal of Urban and Regional Research* 16: 571–87

Amin A., Thrift N. (1993) Globalization, institutional thickness and local prospects. *Revue d'Économie Régionale et Urbaine* 3: 405–27

Amin A., Thrift N. (1994) Living in the global. In Amin A., Thrift N. (eds) *Globalization, Institutions and Regional Development in Europe.* Oxford, Oxford University Press: 1–22

Amin S. (1986) Is an endogenous development strategy possible for Africa? In Ahooja-Patel K., Drabek A. G., Nerfin M. (eds) *World Economy in Transition.* Oxford, Pergamon: 159–72

Amsden A. H. (1989) *Asia's Next Giant: South Korea and Late Industrialization.* New York, Oxford University Press

Amsden A. H. (1994) Why isn't the whole world experimenting with the East Asian model to develop?: Review of *The East Asian Miracle. World Development* 22: 627–33

Amsden A. H., Hikino T. (1993) Borrowing technology or innovating: an exploration of the two paths to industrial development. In Thomson R. (ed.) *Learning and Technological Change.* New York, St Martin's Press: 243–66

Amsden A. H., Hikino T. (1994) Project execution capability, organizational know-how and conglomerate corporate growth in late industrialization. *Industrial and Corporate Change* 3: 111–47

Amsden A. H., Kochanowicz J., Taylor L. (1994) *The Market Meets its Match: Restructuring the Economies of Eastern Europe.* Cambridge, MA, Harvard University Press

Amsden A. H., van der Hoeven R. (1996) Manufacturing output, employment and real wages in the 1980s: labour's loss until the century's end. *Journal of Development Studies* 32: 506–30

Andersen E. S., Lundvall B.-A. (1988) Small national systems of innovation facing technological revolutions: an analytical framework. In Freeman C., Lundvall B.-A. (eds) *Small Countries Facing the Technological Revolution.* London, Pinter: 9–36

Anderson A. G. (1969) The role of outlying laboratories. *Research Management* 12:

141–8

Anderson A. M. (1984) *Science and Technology in Japan.* London, Longman

Anderson A. M. (1992) Japanese academics bemoan the cost of years of neglect. *Science* **258**: 564–9

Anderson C. (1995) The accidental superhighway: a survey of the Internet. *The Economist* 1 July

Anderson F. J. (1976) Demand conditions and supply constraints in regional economic growth. *Journal of Regional Science* **16**: 213–24

Anderson M. (1995) The role of collaborative integration in industrial organization: observations from the Canadian aerospace industry. *Economic Geography* **71**: 55–78

Anderson M., Holmes J. (1995) High-skill, low-wage manufacturing in North America: a case study from the auto parts industry. *Regional Studies* **29**: 655–71

Anderson P., Tushman M. L. (1991) Managing through cycles of technological change. *Research-Technology Management* **34** (3): 26–31

Anderson W. P., Kanaroglou P. S., Miller E. J. (1996) Urban form, energy and the environment: a review of issues, evidence and policy. *Urban Studies* **33**: 7–35

Andersson A. E. (1985) Creativity and regional development. *Papers of the Regional Science Association* **56**: 5–20

Andersson A. E. (1986) The four logistical revolutions. *Papers of the Regional Science Association* **59**: 1–12

Andersson A. E., Kuenne R. E. (1986) Regional economic dynamics. In Nijkamp P. (ed.) *Handbook of Regional and Urban Economics*, volume 1: *Regional Economics.* Amsterdam, North-Holland: 201–53

Andrews J. (1992) A change of face: a survey of Taiwan. *The Economist* 10 October

Angel D. P. (1989) The labor market for engineers in the US semiconductor industry. *Economic Geography* **65**: 99–112

Angel D. P. (1991) High technology agglomeration and the labor market: the case of Silicon Valley. *Environment and Planning A* **23**: 1501–16

Angel D. P. (1994) *Restructuring for Innovation: The Remaking of the US Semiconductor Industry.* New York, Guilford

Angel D. P., Engstrom J. (1995) Manufacturing systems and technological change: the US personal computer industry. *Economic Geography* **71**: 79–102

Ansoff H. I. (1987) Strategic management of technology. *Journal of Business Strategy* **7** (3): 28–39

Antonelli C. (1986a) The international diffusion of new information technologies. *Research Policy* **15**: 139–47

Antonelli C. (1986b) Technological districts and regional innovation capacity. *Revue d'Économie Régionale et Urbaine* **5**: 695–705

Antonelli C. (1987) The determinants of the distribution of innovative activity in a metropolitan area: the case of Turin. *Regional Studies* **21**: 85–93

Antonelli C. (1988a) The emergence of the network firm. In Antonelli C. (ed.) *New Information Technology and Industrial Change: The Italian Case.* Dordrecht, Kluwer: 13–32

Antonelli C. (ed.) (1988b) *New Information Technology and Industrial Change: The Italian Case.* Dordrecht, Kluwer

Antonelli C. (1995) *The Economics of Localized Technological Change and Industrial Dynamics.* Dordrecht, Kluwer Academic

Aoki M. (1990) Toward an economic model of the Japanese firm. *Journal of Economic Literature* **28**: 1–27

Aoki M. (1994) The Japanese firm as a system of attributes: a survey and research agenda. In Aoki M., Dore R. (eds) *The Japanese Firm: The Sources of Competitive Strength.* Oxford, Oxford University Press: 11–40

Aoki T. (1995) Integration in the Asian Pacific Rim. In Simon D. F. (ed.) *Corporate Strategies in the Pacific Rim: Global versus Regional Trends.* London, Routledge: 334–80

Appelbaum E. (1984) High tech and the structural employment problems of the 1980s. In Collins E. L., Tanner L. D. (eds) *American Jobs and the Changing Industrial Base.* Cambridge, MA, Ballinger: 23–48

Appelbaum R. P., Smith D., Christerson B. (1994) Commodity chains and industrial restructuring in the Pacific Rim: garment trade and manufacturing. In Gereffi G., Korzeniewicz M. (eds) *Commodity Chains and Global Capitalism.* Westport, CT, Praeger: 187–204

Appold S. J. (1995) Agglomeration, interorganizational networks, and competitive performance in the US metalworking sector. *Economic Geography* 71: 27–54

Aram J. D. (1989) Attitudes and behaviors of informal investors toward early-stage investments, technology-based ventures, and coinvestors. *Journal of Business Venturing* 4: 333–47

Arcangeli F. (1993) Local and global features of the learning process. In Humbert M. (ed.) *The Impact of Globalisation on Europe's Firms and Industries.* London, Pinter: 34–41

Archer B. H. (1976) The anatomy of a multiplier. *Regional Studies* 10: 71–7

Archibugli D., Michie J. (1995) The globalisation of technology: a new taxonomy. *Cambridge Journal of Economics* 19: 121–40

Arellano R., d'Amboise G., Gasse Y. (1991) Administrative characteristics and performance of small and medium-sized businesses in a developing country. *Entrepreneurship and Regional Development* 3: 317–34

Arndt H. W. (1987) *Economic Development: The History of an Idea.* Chicago, University of Chicago Press

Arnold E. (1985) *Competition and Technological Change in the Television Industry: An Empirical Evaluation of Theories of the Firm.* London, Macmillan

Arnold E. (1987) Some lessons from government information technology policies. *Technovation* 5: 247–68

Arnold E., Guy K. (1989) Policy options for promoting growth through information technology. In OECD *Information Technology and New Growth Opportunities.* Paris, Organisation for Economic Co-operation and Development: 133–201

Arnold U., Bernard K. N. (1989) Just-in-time: some marketing issues raised by a popular concept in production and distribution. *Technovation* 9: 401–31

Arrighi G. (ed.) (1985) *Semiperipheral Development: The Politics of Southern Europe in the Twentieth Century.* Beverly Hills, CA, Sage

Arrow K. J. (1962) The economic implications of learning by doing. *Review of Economic Studies* 29: 155–73

Arthur W. B. (1988) Competing technologies: an overview. In Dosi G., Freeman C., Nelson R., Silverberg G., Soete L. (eds) *Technical Change and Economic Theory.* London, Pinter: 590–607

Ashcroft B. (1982) The measurement of the impact of regional policies in Europe: a survey and critique. *Regional Studies* 16: 287–305

Ashcroft B., Dunlop S., Love J. H. (1995) UK innovation policy: a critique. *Regional Studies* 29: 307–11

Ashcroft B., Love J. H., Malloy E. (1991) New firm formation in the British counties with special reference to Scotland. *Regional Studies* 25: 395–409

Ashcroft B., Swales J. K. (1982) The importance of the first round of the multiplier process: the impact of civil service dispersal. *Environment and Planning A* 14: 429–44

Asheim B. T. (1994) Industrial districts, inter-firm cooperation and endogenous technological development: the experience of developed countries. In *Technological Dynamism in Industrial Districts: An Alternative Approach to Industrialization in Developing Countries?* New York, United Nations: 91–142

Ashton W. B., Stacey G. S. (1995) Technical intelligence in business: understanding technology threats and opportunities. *International Journal of Technology Management* 10: 79–104

Ashworth G., Goodall B. (eds) (1990) *Marketing Tourism Places.* London, Routledge

Ashworth G. J., Voogd H. (1994) Marketing and place promotion. In Gold J. R., Ward S. V. (eds) *Place Promotion: The Use of Publicity and Marketing to Sell Towns and Regions.* Chichester, John Wiley: 39–52

Åstebro T. (1992) The international diffusion of computer aided design. In Ayres R. U., Haywood W., Tchijov I. (eds) *Computer Integrated Manufacturing*, volume III: *Models, Case Studies, and Forecasts of Diffusion.* London, Chapman and Hall: 171–96

Atuahene-Gima K. (1993) Determinants of inward technology licensing intentions: an empirical analysis of Australian engineering firms. *Journal of Product Innovation Management* 10: 230–40

Aturupane H., Glewwe P., Isenman P. (1994) Poverty, human development, and growth: an emerging consensus? *American Economic Review* 84 (2): 244–9

Audretsch D. B. (1995) *Innovation and Industry Evolution.* Cambridge, MA, MIT Press

Autio E. (1994) New, technology-based firms as agents of R&D and innovation: an empirical study. *Technovation* 14: 259–73

Autio E. (1995) Four types of innovators: a conceptual and empirical study of new, technology-based companies as innovators. *Entrepreneurship and Regional Development* 7: 233–48

Autio E., Laamanen T. (1995) Measurement and evaluation of technology transfer: review of technology transfer mechanisms and indicators. *International Journal of Technology Management* 10: 643–64

Auty R. M. (1991) Creating competitive advantage: South Korean steel and petrochemicals. *Tijdschrift voor Economische en Sociale Geografie* 82: 15–29

Auty R. M. (1993) *Sustaining Development in Mineral Economies: The Resource Curse Thesis.* London, Routledge

Auty R. M. (1994) *Economic Development and Industrial Policy: Korea, Brazil, Mexico, India and China.* London, Mansell

Axelsson B., Easton G. (eds) (1992) *Industrial Networks: A New View of Reality.* London, Routledge

Axford N., Pinch S. (1994) Growth coalitions and local economic development strategy in southern England: a case study of the Hampshire Development Association. *Political Geography* 13: 344–60

Ayala F. J. (1995) Science in Latin America. *Science* 270: 826–7

Ayres R. U. (1988) Technology: the wealth of nations. *Technological Forecasting and Social Change* 33: 189–201

Ayres R. U. (1990a) Technological transformations and long waves. Part I. *Technological Forecasting and Social Change* 36: 1–37

Ayres R. U. (1990b) Technological transformations and long waves. Part II. *Technological Forecasting and Social Change* 36: 111–37

Ayres R. U., Martinàs K. (1992) Experience and the life cycle: some analytic implications. *Technovation* 12: 465–86

Ayres R. U., Raju V. (1992) Diffusion of CIM technologies. In Ayres R. U., Haywood W., Tchijov I. (eds) *Computer Integrated Manufacturing*, volume III: *Models, Case Studies, and Forecasts of Diffusion*. London, Chapman and Hall: 263–86

Ayres R. U., Steger W. A. (1985) Rejuvenating the life cycle concept. *Journal of Business Strategy* **6** (1): 66–76

Baba Y., Hatashima H. (1995) Capability transfer in the Pacific Rim nations: the case of Japanese electrical and electronics firms. *International Journal of Technology Management* **10**: 732–46

Babson S. (1995) Restructuring the workplace: Post-Fordism or return of the foreman? In Asher R., Edsforth R. (eds) *Autowork*. Albany, State University of New York Press: 227–56

Bache J., Carr R., Parnaby J., Tobias A. M. (1987) Supplier development systems. *International Journal of Technology Management* **2**: 219–28

Bachelor L. W. (1991) Michigan, Mazda, and the factory of the future: evaluating economic development incentives. *Economic Development Quarterly* **5**: 114–25

Bachtler J., Michie R. (1993) The restructuring of regional policy in the European Community. *Regional Studies* **27**: 719–25

Badawy M. K. (1988) What we've learned: managing human resources. *Research-Technology Management* **31** (5): 19–35

Bade F.-J. (1983) Large corporations and regional development. *Regional Studies* **17**: 315–25

Bae Z., Lee J. (1986) Technology development patterns of small and medium sized companies in the Korean machinery industry. *Technovation* **4**: 279–96

Bagchi A. K. (1988) Technological self-reliance, dependence and underdevelopment. In Wad A. (ed.) *Science, Technology, and Development*. Boulder, Westview Press: 69–91

Bahrami H., Evans S. (1995) Flexible re-cycling and high-technology entrepreneurship. *California Management Review* **37** (3): 62–89

Bailly A., Boulianne L., Maillat D., Rey M., Thevoz L. (1987) Services and production: for a reassessment of economic sectors. *Annals of Regional Science* **21** (2): 45–59

Bailly A., Maillat D., Coffey W. J. (1987) Service activities and regional development: some European examples. *Environment and Planning A* **19**: 653–68

Baily M. N., Chakrabarti A. K. (1988) *Innovation and the Productivity Crisis*. Washington, Brookings Institution

Baily M. N., Gersbach H. (1995) Efficiency in manufacturing and the need for global competition. *Brookings Papers in Economic Activity: Microeconomics*: 307–58

Bailyn L. (1985) Autonomy in the industrial R&D lab. *Human Resource Management* **24**: 129–46

Baker M. J. (1983) *Market Development: A Comprehensive Survey*. Harmondsworth, Penguin

Baker S., Armstrong L. (1996) The new factory worker. *Business Week* 30 September: 59–68

Baker S., Woodruff D., Weiner E. (1992) Detroit south. *Business Week* 16 March: 98–103

Bakis H. (1987) Telecommunications and the global firm. In Hamilton F. E. I. (ed.) *Industrial Change in Advanced Economies*. London, Croom Helm: 130–60

Baldry C. (1988) *Computers, Jobs, and Skills: The Industrial Relations of Technological Change*. New York, Plenum

Baldwin W. L., Scott J. T. (1987) *Market Structure and Technological Change*. Chur, Harwood Academic

Ball A. D., Marquardt R. A. (1991) How do venture capitalists rank potential investments? The role of government incentives. *Regional Science Perspectives* **21** (1): 50–66

Ball R. M. (1989) Some aspects of tourism, seasonality and local labour markets. *Area* **21**: 35–45

Ballance R. (1987) *International Industry and Business: Structural Change, Individual Policy and Industry Strategies.* London: Allen and Unwin

Banks R. D., Heaton G. R. (1995) An innovation-driven environmental policy. *Issues in Science and Technology* **12** (1): 43–51

Bannon L. (1996) Boeing will increase production further on three jetliner models. *Wall Street Journal* 19 March: B8

Bar F., Borrus M., Cohen S., Zysman J. (1989) The evolution and growth potential of electronics-based technologies. *STI Review* **5**: 7–58

Barabaschi S. (1992) Managing the growth of technical information. In Rosenberg N., Landau R., Mowery D. C. (eds) *Technology and the Wealth of Nations.* Stanford, Stanford University Press: 247–78

Baran B. (1985) Office automation and women's work: the technological transformation of the insurance industry. In Castells M. (ed.) *High Technology, Space, and Society.* Beverly Hills, CA, Sage: 143–71

Barañano A. M. (1995) The Spanish innovative firm and the ESPRIT, RACE and EUREKA programmes: an organizational approach. *Technovation* **15**: 339–50

Bar-El R., Felsenstein D. (1989) Technological profile and industrial structure: implications for the development of sophisticated industry in peripheral areas. *Regional Studies* **23**: 253–66

Bar-El R., Felsenstein D. (1990) Entrepreneurship and rural industrialization: comparing urban and rural patterns of locational choice in Israel. *World Development* **18**: 257–67

Barff R., Austin J. (1993) 'It's gotta be da shoes': Domestic manufacturing, international subcontracting, and the production of athletic footwear. *Environment and Planning A* **25**: 1103–14

Barff R. A., Knight P. L. (1988) The role of federal military spending in the timing of the New England employment turnaround. *Papers of the Regional Science Association* **65**: 151–66

Barker C. E., Bhagavan M. R., Mitschke-Collande P. V., Wild D. V. (1986) *African Industrialisation: Technology and Change in Tanzania.* Aldershot, Gower

Barkham R. (1992) Regional variations in entrepreneurship: some evidence from the United Kingdom. *Entrepreneurship and Regional Development* **4**: 225–44

Barkley D. L. (1988) The decentralization of high-technology manufacturing to non-metropolitan areas. *Growth and Change* **19** (1): 13–30

Barkley D. L., McNamara K. T. (1994) Local input linkages: a comparison of foreign-owned and domestic manufacturers in Georgia and South Carolina. *Regional Studies* **28**: 725–37

Barley S. R., Kunda G. (1992) Design and devotion: surges of rational and normative ideologies of control in managerial discourse. *Administrative Science Quarterly* **37**: 363–99

Barnathan J., Einhorn B., Nakarmi L. (1992) Bringing it all back home. *Business week* 7 December: 133–5

Baron J. N., Bielby W. T. (1980) Bringing the firms back in: stratification, segmentation, and the organization of work. *American Sociological Review* **45**: 737–65

Barras R. (1986) Towards a theory of innovation in services. *Research Policy* **15**: 161–73

Barras R. (1990) Interactive innovation in financial and business services: the vanguard of the service revolution. *Research Policy* **19**: 215–37

Barreto H. (1989) *The Entrepreneur in Microeconomic Theory: Disappearance and Explanation.* London, Routledge

Bartel A. P., Lichtenberg F. R. (1987) The comparative advantage of educated workers in implementing new technology. *Review of Economics and Statistics* 69: 1–11

Bartik T. J. (1989) Small business start-ups in the United States: estimates of the effects of characteristics of states. *Southern Economic Journal* 55: 1004–18

Bartlett C. A., Ghoshal S. (1989) *Managing across Borders: The Transnational Solution.* Boston, Harvard Business School Press

Bartlett C. A., Ghoshal S. (1990) Managing innovation in the transnational corporation. In Bartlett C. A., Doz Y., Hedlund G. (eds) *Managing the Global Firm.* London, Routledge: 215–55

Bartlett C. A., Ghoshal S. (1995) *Transnational Management,* second edition. Chicago, Irwin

Bartmess A., Cerny K. (1993) Building competitive advantage through a global network of capabilities. *California Management Review* 35 (2): 78–103

Bassett K. (1986) Economic crisis and corporate restructuring: multinational corporations and the paper, printing and packaging sector in Bristol. In Taylor M., Thrift N. (eds) *Multinationals and the Restructuring of the World Economy.* London, Croom Helm: 311–43

Batey P. J. W. (1985) Input–output models for demographic–economic analysis: some structural comparisons. *Environment and Planning A* 17: 73–99

Batey P. W. J., Rose A. Z. (1990) Extended input–output models: progress and potential. *International Regional Science Review* 13: 27–49

Bathelt H. (1995) Global competition, international trade, and regional concentration: the case of the German chemical industry during the 1980s. *Environment and Planning C: Government and Policy* 13: 395–424

Batten D. (1985) The new division of labor: the mobility of new technology and its impact on work. *Computers and the Social Sciences* 1: 133–9

Baumol W. J. (1967) Macroeconomics of unbalanced growth: the anatomy of urban crisis. *American Economic Review* 57: 415–26

Baumol W. J. (1989) Is there a U. S. productivity crisis? *Science* 243: 611–15

Baumol W. J., Blackman S. A. B., Wolff E. N. (1989) *Productivity and American Leadership: The Long View.* Cambridge, MA, MIT Press

Baumol W. J., Nelson R. R., Wolff E. N. (eds) (1994) *Convergence of Productivity: Cross-national Studies and Historical Evidence.* New York, Oxford University Press

Bean A. S. (1995) Why some R&D organizations are more productive than others. *Research-Technology Management* 38 (1): 25–9

Bean A. S., Baker N. R. (1988) Implementing national innovation policies through private decisionmaking. In Roessner J. D. (ed.) *Government Innovation Policy: Design, Implementation, Evaluation.* New York, St Martin's Press: 75–89

Bean A. S., Schiffel D. D., Mogee M. E. (1975) The venture capital market and technological innovation. *Research Policy* 4: 380–408

Bearse P. J. (1981) *A Study of Entrepreneurship by Region and SMSA Size.* Philadelphia, Public/Private Ventures

Beaverstock J. V. (1994) Re-thinking skilled international labour migration: world cities and banking organisations. *Geoforum* 25: 323–38

Becattini G. (1989) Sectors and/or districts: some remarks on the conceptual foundations of industrial economics. In Goodman E., Bamford J., Saynor P. (eds) *Small Firms and Industrial Districts in Italy.* London, Routledge: 123–35

Becattini G. (1991) The industrial district as a creative milieu. In Benko G., Dunford

M. (eds) *Industrial Change and Regional Development.* London, Belhaven: 102–14

Becker G. S. (1964) *Human Capital.* New York, Columbia University Press

Beckmann M. J., Thisse J.-F. (1986) The location of production activities. In Nijkamp P. (ed.) *Handbook of Regional and Urban Economics*, volume 1: *Regional Economics.* Amsterdam, North-Holland: 21–95

Beckouche P. (1991) French high-tech and space: a double cleavage. In Benko G., Dunford M. (eds) *Industrial Change and Regional Development.* London, Belhaven: 205–25

Beeson P. E., Hustad S. (1989) Patterns and determinants of productive efficiency in state manufacturing. *Journal of Regional Science* 29: 15–28

Begg I. (1993) The service sector in regional development. *Regional Studies* 27: 817–25

Begg I. G., Cameron G. C. (1988) High technology location and the urban areas of Great Britain. *Urban Studies* 25: 361–79

Beije P. R. (1987) Innovation and production: two types of firm behaviour. In Rothwell R., Bessant J. (eds) *Innovation: Adaptation and Growth.* Amsterdam, Elsevier: 227–36

Bell D. (1973) *The Coming of the Post-industrial Society.* New York, Basic Books

Bell D. N. F. (1993) Regional econometric modelling in the UK: a review. *Regional Studies* 27: 777–82

Bell M. (1984) 'Learning' and the accumulation of industrial technological capacity in developing countries. In Fransman M., King K. (eds) *Technological Capability in the Third World.* New York, St Martin's Press: 187–209

Bell M., Pavitt K. (1993a) Accumulating technological capability in developing countries. In Summers L., Shah S. (eds) *Proceedings of the World Bank Annual Conference on Development Economics 1992.* Washington, World Bank: 257–81

Bell M., Pavitt K. (1993b) Technological accumulation and industrial growth: contrasts between developed and developing countries. *Industrial and Corporate Change* 2: 157–210

Bell R. M. (1991) The development of scientific and technological institutions in Africa: some past patterns and future needs. In *The New Challenge of Science and Technology for Development in Africa.* Nairobi, ICIPE Science Press: 61–86

Bellak C. J., Weiss A. (1993) A note on the Austrian 'diamond'. *Management International Review* 33 (special issue 2): 109–18

Bellone C. J. (1988) Public entrepreneurship: new role expectations for local government. *Urban Analysis* 9: 71–86

Belous R. S. (1989) *The Contingent Economy: The Growth of the Temporary, Part-Time and Subcontracted Workforce.* Washington, National Planning Association

Belussi F. (1989) Benetton: a case-study of corporate strategy for innovation in traditional sectors. In Dodgson M. (ed.) *Technology Strategy and the Firm: Management and Public Policy.* London, Longman: 116–33

Belussi F. (1993) The transformation of the 1980s: growth of network companies, or the return of flexibility in large businesses? In Dodgson M., Rothwell R. (eds) *Small Firms and Innovation* (Special Publication of the *International Journal of Technology Management*). Geneva, Inderscience: 188–99

Belussi F. (1996) Local systems, industrial districts and institutional networks: towards a new evolutionary paradigm of industrial economics? *European Planning Studies* 4: 5–26

Belussi F., Garibaldo F. (1996) Variety of pattern of the post-Fordist economy: why are the 'old times' still with us and the 'new times' yet to come? *Futures* 28: 153–71

Bender L. D. (1975) *Predicting Employment in Four Regions of the Western United States.* Technical Bulletin 1529. Washington, US Department of Agriculture, Economic

Research Service

Beniger J. R. (1986) *The Control Revolution: Technological and Economic Origins of the Information Society.* Cambridge, MA, Harvard University Press

Benington J., Geddes M. (1992) Local economic development in the 1980s and 1990s: retrospect and prospect. *Economic Development Quarterly* **6**: 454–63

Bennett R. J., McCoshan A. (1993) *Enterprise and Human Resource Development: Local Capacity Building.* London, Paul Chapman

Bensaou M., Venkatraman N. (1995) Configurations of interorganizational relationships: a comparison between US and Japanese automakers. *Management Science* **41**: 1471–92

Berger S., Piore M. J. (1980) *Dualism and Discontinuity in Industrial Societies.* Cambridge, Cambridge University Press

Berkowitz B. D. (1995) Warfare in the information age. *Issues in Science and Technology* **12** (1): 59–66

Berndt E. R., Malone T. W. (eds) (1995) Special issue on information technology and the productivity paradox. *Economics of Innovation and New Technology* **3**: 177–322

Bernstein A. (1995) The wage squeeze. *Business Week* 17 July: 54–62

Berry B. J. L. (1991) *Long-Wave Rhythms in Economic Development and Political Behavior.* Baltimore, Johns Hopkins University Press

Berthélemy J.-C., Lecaillon J. (1995) Synthesis. In Berthélemy J.-C. (ed.) *Whither African Economies?* Paris, Organisation for Economic Co-operation and Development: 149–60

Bertin G. Y., Wyatt S. (1988) *Multinationals and Industrial Property: The Control of the World's Technology.* Hemel Hempstead, Harvester Wheatsheaf

Bertram H., Schamp E. W. (1991) Flexible production and linkages in the German machine tool industry. In de Smidt M., Wever E. (eds) *Complexes, Formations and Networks.* Utrecht, Royal Dutch Geographical Society: 69–80

Bessant J. (1991) Trends and perspectives in the development and diffusion of CIM. In *Computer-Integrated Manufacturing: Perspectives for International Economic Development and Competitiveness.* Geneva, United Nations Economic Commission for Europe and Industrial Development Organization: 3–22

Bessant J. (1993) The lessons of failure: learning to manage new manufacturing technology. *International Journal of Technology Management* **8**: 197–215

Bessant J., Haywood B. (1988) Islands, archipelagoes and continents: progress on the road to computer-integrated manufacturing. *Research Policy* **17**: 349–62

Bessant J., Rush H. (1995) Building bridges for innovation: the role of consultants in technology transfer. *Research Policy* **24**: 97–114

Best M. H. (1990) *The New Competition: Institutions of Industrial Restructuring.* Oxford, Polity Press

Betz F. (1987) *Managing Technology.* Englewood Cliffs, NJ, Prentice-Hall

Beyers W. B. (1976) Empirical identification of key sectors: some further evidence. *Environment and Planning A* **8**: 231–6

Beyers W. B. (1979) Contemporary trends in the regional economic development of the United States. *Professional Geographer* **31**: 34–44

Beyers W. B. (1983) The interregional structure of the US economy. *International Regional Science Review* **8**: 213–31

Beyers W. B., Alvine M. J. (1985) Export services in postindustrial society. *Papers of the Regional Science Association* **57**: 33–45

Bhalla A. S. (ed.) (1979) *Towards Global Action for Appropriate Technology.* Oxford, Pergamon

Bhalla A. S. (1988) Microelectronics use for small-scale production in developing countries. In Bhalla A. S., James J. (eds) *New Technologies and Development Experiences in 'Technology Blending'*. Boulder, CO, Lynne Reiner: 53–64

Bhalla A. S., Fluitman A. G. (1985) Science and technology indicators and socio-economic development. *World Development* 13: 117–90

Bhalla A. S., James J. (eds) (1988) *New Technologies and Development Experiences in 'Technology Blending'*. Boulder, CO, Lynne Reiner

Bhattacharya P. C. (1993) Rural-urban migration in economic development. *Journal of Economic Surveys* 7: 243–81

Bianchi P., Bellini N. (1991) Public policies for local networks of innovators. *Research Policy* 20: 487–97

Bianchi P., Giordani M. G. (1993) Innovation policy at the local and national levels: the case of Emilia-Romagna. *European Planning Studies* 1: 25–41

Bienaymé A. (1986) The dynamics of innovation. *International Journal of Technology Management* 1: 133–59

Biersteker T. J. (1978) *Distortion or Development? Contending Perspectives on the Multinational Corporation*. Cambridge, MA, MIT Press

Bigarelli D., Crestanello P. (1994) An analysis of the changes in the knitwear/clothing district of Carpi during the 1980s. *Entrepreneurship and Regional Development* 6: 127–44

Biggs L. (1995) Building for mass production: factory design and work process at the Ford Motor Company. In Asher R., Edsforth R. (eds) *Autowork*. Albany, State University of New York Press: 39–63

Biggs T., Moody G. R., van Leeuwen J.-H., White E. D. (1994) *Africa Can Compete! Export Opportunities and Challenges for Garments and Home Products in the U.S. Market*. Discussion paper 242. Washington, World Bank

Biggs T., Shah M., Srivastava P. (1995) *Technological Capabilities and Learning in African Enterprises*. Technical paper 288. Washington, World Bank

Bijker W. E., Hughes T. P., Pinch T. J. (eds) (1987) *The Social Construction of Technological Systems: New Directions in the Sociology and History of Technology*. Cambridge, MA, MIT Press

Birch D. L. (1987) *Job Creation in America*. New York, Free Press

Birkinshaw J. M., Morrison A. J. (1995) Configurations of strategy and structure in subsidiaries of multinational corporations. *Journal of International Business Studies* 26: 729–53

Birks S., Fluitman F., Oudin X., Sinclair C. (1994) *Skills Acquisition in Micro-Enterprises: Evidence from West Africa*. Paris, Organisation for Economic Co-operation and Development

Birley S. (1985) The role of networks in the entrepreneurial process. *Journal of Business Venturing* 1: 107–17

Birley S., Westhead P. (1990) 'North–south' contrasts in the characteristics and performance of small firms. *Entrepreneurship and Regional Development* 2: 27–48

Birnie J. E., Hitchens D. M. W. N. (1994) Comparative manufacturing productivity in the Republic of Ireland. *Regional Studies* 28: 747–53

Bishop P. (1988) Academic–industry links and firm size in South West England. *Regional Studies* 22: 160–2

Bivand R. (1981) Regional policy and asymmetry in geographical interaction relationships. In Kuklinski A. (ed.) *Polarized Development and Regional Policies: Tribute to Jacques Boudeville*. The Hague, Mouton: 219–29

Blackburn P., Coombs R., Green K. (1985) *Technology, Economic Growth and the*

Labour Process. London, Macmillan

Blackburn R. A., Curran J., Jarvis R. (1993) Small firms and local networks: some theoretical and conceptual explorations. In Robertson M., Chell E., Mason C. (eds) *Towards the Twenty-First Century: The Challenge for Small Business.* Macclesfield, Nadamal Books: 105–23

Blackley P. R. (1986) Urban-rural differences in the structure of manufacturing production. *Urban Studies* 23: 471–83

Blair J. P., Endres C. R. (1994) Hidden economic development assets. *Economic Development Quarterly* 8: 286–91

Blair J. P., Premus R. (1987) Major factors in industrial location: a review. *Economic Development Quarterly* 1: 72–85

Blakely E. J. (1994) *Planning Local Economic Development: Theory and Practice,* second edition. Thousand Oaks, CA, Sage

Blakely E. J., Nishikawa N. (1992) State economic development strategies for biotechnology. *Economic Development Quarterly* 6: 241–54

Blenker P., Christensen P. R. (1995) Interactive strategies in supply chains – a double-edged portfolio approach to small- and medium-sized subcontractors' position analyses. *Entrepreneurship and Regional Development* 7: 249–64

Bloedon R. V., Stokes D. R. (1994) Making university/industry collaborative research succeed. *Research-Technology Management* 37 (2): 44–8

Bluestone B., Harrison B. (1982) *The Deindustrialization of America.* New York, Basic Books

Bluestone B., Jordan P., Sullivan M. (1981) *Aircraft Industry Dynamics.* Boston, Auburn House

Blumenfeld H. (1955) The economic base of the metropolis: critical remarks on the 'basic-nonbasic' concept. *Journal of the American Institute of Planners* 21: 114–32

Boddy M., Lovering J. (1986) High technology industry in the Bristol sub-region: the aerospace/defence nexus. *Regional Studies* 20: 217–31

Boisot M. H. (1995) Is your firm a creative destroyer? Competitive learning and knowledge flows in the technological strategies of firms. *Research Policy* 24: 489–506

Boland P. (1996) Regional economic development and institutional mechanisms in Merseyside: Objective 1 status. In Alden J., Boland P. (eds) *Regional Development Strategies: A European Perspective.* London, Jessica Kingsley: 107–28

Bolton R. (1982) Industrial and regional policy in multiregional modeling. In Bell M. E., Lande P. S. (eds) *Regional Dimensions of Industrial Policy.* Lexington, MA, Lexington Books: 169–94

Bolton R. (1985) Regional econometric models. *Journal of Regional Science* 25: 495–520

Bolton R. (1992) 'Place prosperity vs people prosperity' revisited: an old issue with a new angle. *Urban Studies* 29: 185–203

Bonacich E., Cheng L., Chinchilla N., Hamilton N., Ong P. (eds) (1994) *Global Production: The Apparel Industry in the Pacific Rim.* Philadelphia, Temple University Press

Bonacich E., Waller D. V. (1994) The role of U.S. apparel manufacturers in the globalization of the industry in the Pacific Rim. In Bonacich E., Cheng L., Chinchilla N., Hamilton N., Ong P. (eds) *Global Production: The Apparel Industry in the Pacific Rim.* Philadelphia, Temple University Press: 80–102

Boonekamp C. (1989) Industrial policies of industrial countries. *Finance and Development* 26 (1): 14–17

Boorsma J. (1986) Design for assembly. In Bolwijn P. T., Boorsma J., van Breulkelen Q.

H., Brinkman S., Kumpe T. (eds) *Flexible Manufacturing: Integrating Technological and Social Innovation.* Amsterdam, North-Holland: 101–29

Booth D. E. (1987) Regional long waves and urban policy. *Urban Studies* 24: 447–59

Borch O. J., Arthur M. B. (1995) Strategic networks among small firms: implications for strategy research methodology. *Journal of Management Studies* 32: 419–41

Borchert J. G. (1994) Urban marketing: a review. In Braun G. O. (ed.) *Managing and Marketing of Urban Development and Urban Life.* Berlin, Dietrich Reimer: 415–27

Borchert J. R. (1978) Major control points in American economic geography. *Annals of the Association of American Geographers* 68: 214–32

Bornstein M. (1985) *East–West Technology Transfer: The Transfer of Western Technology to the USSR.* Paris, Organisation for Economic Co-operation and Development

Borrus M. G. (1988) *Competing for Control: America's Stake in Microelectronics.* Cambridge, MA, Ballinger

Borrus A., Maremont M. (1988) The Japanese go globe-trotting, but the yen stays home. *Business Week* 17 October: 45–8

Borts G. H., Stein J. L. (1964) *Economic Growth in a Free Market.* New York, Columbia University Press

Boschma R. (1994) *Looking through a Window of Locational Opportunity: A Long-Term Analysis of Technological Upheavals in Great Britain and Belgium.* Amsterdam, Thesis

Bosomworth C. E., Sage B. H. (1995) How 26 companies manage their central research. *Research-Technology Management* 38 (3): 32–40

Bosworth B. (1995) Interfirm cooperation: the points of intervention. *Firm Connections* 3 (1): 2–5

Bosworth B., Rosenfeld S. (1993) *Significant Others: Exploring the Potential of Manufacturing Networks.* Chapel Hill, NC, Regional Technology Strategies

Bottrill C. G., Pearce D. G. (1995) Ecotourism: towards a key elements approach to operationalising the concept. *Journal of Sustainable Tourism* 3: 45–54

Boucke C., Cantner U., Hanusch H. (1994) 'Technopolises' as a policy goal: a morphological study of the Wissenschaftstadt Ulm. *Technovation* 14: 407–18

Boudeville J.-R. (1966) *Problems of Regional Economic Planning.* Edinburgh, Edinburgh University Press

Bouman H., Verhoef B. (1986) High-technology and employment: some information of the Netherlands. In Nijkamp P. (ed.) *Technological Change, Employment and Spatial Dynamics.* Berlin, Springer-Verlag: 289–98

Bourne L. S. (1988) Different solitudes and the restructuring of academic publishing: on barriers to communication in research. *Environment and Planning A* 20: 1423–5

Bovaird T. (1992) Local economic development and the city. *Urban Studies* 29: 343–68

Bower D. J. (1993) New product development in the pharmaceutical industry: pooling network resources. *Journal of Product Innovation Management* 10: 367–75

Bowonder B., Miyake T. (1993) Japanese innovations in advanced technologies: an analysis of functional integration. *International Journal of Technology Management* 8: 135–56

Bowonder B., Miyake T. (1994) Creating and sustaining competitiveness: an analysis of the Japanese robotics industry. *International Journal of Technology Management* 9: 575–611

Bowonder B., Miyake T., Linstone H. (1994a) The Japanese institutional mechanisms for industrial growth: a systems perspective – Part I. *Technological Forecasting and Social Change* 47: 229–54

Bowonder B., Miyake T., Linstone H. (1994b) The Japanese institutional mechanisms for industrial growth: a systems perspective – Part II. *Technological Forecasting and*

Social Change 47: 309–44

Boyer R. (1988a) Technical change and the theory of 'Régulation'. In Dosi G., Freeman C., Nelson R., Silverberg G., Soete L. (eds) *Technical Change and Economic Theory*. London, Pinter: 67–94

Boyer R. (1988b) Defensive or offensive flexibility? In Boyer R. (ed.) *The Search for Labour Market Flexibility: The European Economies in Transition*. Oxford, Oxford University Press: 222–51

Boyer R. (ed.) (1988c) *The Search for Labour Market Flexibility: The European Economies in Transition*. Oxford, Oxford University Press

Boyer R. (1993) Introduction to part II. In Foray D., Freeman C. (eds) *Technology and the Wealth of Nations: The Dynamics of Constructed Advantage*. London, Pinter: 95–106

Boyer R. (1995) Training and employment in the new production models. *STI Review* 15: 105–31

Boyett I., Finlay D. (1995) The pillar of the community: back to entrepreneurial basics? *Entrepreneurship and Regional Development* 7: 105–18

Bradford C. I. (1994) The new paradigm of systemic competitiveness: why it matters, what it means and implications for policy. In Bradford C. I. (ed.) *The New Paradigm of Systemic Competitiveness: Toward More Integrated Policies in Latin America*. Paris, Organisation for Economic Co-operation and Development: 41–65

Bradley S. P., Hausman J. A., Nolan R. L. (eds) (1993) *Globalization, Technology, and Competition: The Fusion of Computers and Telecommunications in the 1990s*. Boston, Harvard Business School Press

Bradley S., Taylor J. (1996) Human capital formation and local economic performance. *Regional Studies* 30: 1–14

Braham P. (1986) Marks and Spencer: a technological approach to retailing. In Rhodes E., Wield D. (eds) *Implementing New Technologies*. Oxford, Basil Blackwell: 123–41

Brahm R. (1995) National targeting policies, high-technology industries, and excessive competition. *Strategic Management Journal* 16: 71–91

Brainard R. (1993) Globalisation and corporate nationality. *STI Review* 13: 163–90

Brainard R., Leedman C., Lumbers J. (1988) *Science and Technology Policy Outlook 1988*. Paris, Organisation for Economic Co-operation and Development

Bramanti A., Senn L. (1990) Product innovation and strategic patterns of firms in a diversified local economy: the case of Bergamo. *Entrepreneurship and Regional Development* 2: 153–80

Brandin D. H., Harrison M. A. (1987) *The Technology War: A Case for Competitiveness*. New York, John Wiley

Brannon J. T., James D. D., Lucker G. W. (1994) Generating and sustaining backward linkages between *maquiladoras* and local suppliers in northern Mexico. *World Development* 22: 1933–45

Branscomb L. M. (1993a) National laboratories: the search for new missions and new structures. In Branscomb L. M. (ed.) *Empowering Technology: Implementing a US Strategy*. Cambridge, MA, MIT Press: 103–34

Branscomb L. M. (1993b) The national technology policy debate. In Branscomb L. M. (ed.) *Empowering Technology: Implementing a US Strategy*. Cambridge, MA, MIT Press: 1–35

Branscomb L. M. (1993c) Targeting critical technologies. In Branscomb L. M. (ed.) *Empowering Technology: Implementing a US Strategy*. Cambridge, MA, MIT Press: 36–63

Branscomb L. M., Kodama F. (1993) Technology strategies of Japanese high-tech companies. In Cutler R. S. (ed.) *Technology Management in Japan*. Boulder, CO, Westview Press: 11–29

Braudel F. (1982) *The Wheels of Commerce: Civilization and Capitalism 15th–18th Century*, volume 2. New York, Harper and Row

Braverman H. (1974) *Labor and Monopoly Capital*. New York, Monthly Review Press

Breheny M. J., McQuaid R. W. (eds) (1987) *The Development of High Technology Industries: An International Survey*. London, Croom Helm

Brenner M. S. (1994) Tracking new products: a practitioner's guide. *Research-Technology Management* **37** (6): 36–40

Britton J. N. H. (1985) Research and development in the Canadian economy: sectoral, ownership, locational, and policy issues. In Thwaites A. T., Oakey R. P. (eds) *The Regional Impact of Technological Change*. London, Frances Pinter: 67–114

Britton J. N. H. (1987) High technology industry in Canada: locational and policy issues of the technology gap. In Breheny M. J., McQuaid R. W. (eds) *The Development of High Technology Industries: An International Survey*. London, Croom Helm: 143–91

Britton J. N. H. (1989) A policy perspective on incremental innovation in small and medium sized enterprises. *Entrepreneurship and Regional Development* **1**: 179–90

Britton J. N. H. (1991) Reconsidering innovation policy for small and medium sized enterprises: the Canadian case. *Environment and Planning C: Government and Policy* **9**: 189–206

Britton J. N. H. (1996) Specialization versus diversity in Canadian technological development. *Small Business Economics* **8**: 121–38

Britton J., Gertler M. (1986) Locational perspectives on policies for innovation. In Dermer J. (ed.) *Competitiveness through Technology*. Lexington, MA, Lexington Books: 159–75

Britton J. N. H., Gilmour J. M. (1978) *The Weakest Link: A Technological Perspective on Canadian Industrial Underdevelopment*. Ottawa, Science Council of Canada

Britton S. (1991) Tourism, capital, and place: towards a critical geography of tourism. *Environment and Planning D: Society and Space* **9**: 451–78

Broadberry S. N. (1994) Technological leadership and productivity leadership in manufacturing since the industrial revolution: implications for the convergence debate. *Economic Journal* **104**: 291–302

Brockhoff K. (1992) R&D cooperation between firms – a perceived transaction cost perspective. *Management Science* **38**: 514–24

Brodsky H., Sarfaty D. E. (1977) Measuring the urban economic base in a developing country. *Land Economics* **53**: 445–54

Brohman J. (1996) Postwar development in the Asian NICs: Does the neoliberal model fit reality? *Economic Geography* **72**: 107–30

Bromley R. (1993) Small-enterprise promotion as an urban development strategy. In Kasarda J. D., Parnell A. M. (eds) *Third World Cities: Problems, Policies, and Prospects*. Newbury Park, CA, Sage: 120–33

Brookfield H. (1975) *Interdependent Development*. London, Methuen

Brookfield H. C. (1984) Boxes, ports, and places without ports. In Hoyle B. S., Hilling D. (eds) *Seaport Systems and Spatial Change*. Chichester, John Wiley: 61–79

Brooks H. (1994) The relationship between science and technology. *Research Policy* **23**: 477–86

Brouwer M. (1991) *Schumpeterian Puzzles: Technological Competition and Economic Evolution*. London, Harvester Wheatsheaf

Brown B., Butler J. E. (1993) Networks and entrepreneurial development: the shadow of borders. *Entrepreneurship and Regional Development* 5: 101–16

Brown C., Hamilton J., Medoff J. (1990) *Employers Large and Small.* Cambridge, MA, Harvard University Press

Brown L. A. (1981) *Innovation Diffusion: A New Perspective.* New York, Methuen

Brown M. (1995) *Impacts of National Technology Programmes.* Paris, Organisation for Economic Co-operation and Development

Browne L. E. (1978) Regional industry mix and the business cycle. *New England Economic Review* November/December: 35–53

Browne L. E. (1983) High technology and business services. *New England Economic Review* July/August: 5–17

Browning J. (1980) *How To Select a Business Site.* New York, McGraw-Hill

Bruce M., Leverick F., Littler D. (1995) Complexities of collaborative product development. *Technovation* 15: 535–52

Brucker S. M., Hastings S. E., Latham W. R. (1990) The variation of estimated impacts from five regional input–output models. *International Regional Science Review* 13: 119–39

Brugger E. A., Stuckey B. (1987) Regional economic structure and innovative behaviour in Switzerland. *Regional Studies* 21: 241–51

Bruno A. V., Tyebjee T. T. (1982) The environment for entrepreneurship. In Kent C. A., Sexton D. L., Vesper K. H. (eds) *Encyclopedia of Entrepreneurship.* Englewood Cliffs, NJ, Prentice-Hall: 288–307

Brusco S. (1986) Small firms and industrial districts: the experience of Italy. In Keeble D., Wever E. (eds) *New Firms and Regional Development in Europe.* London, Croom Helm: 184–202

Brusco S. (1989) A policy for industrial districts. In Goodman E., Bamford J., Saynor P. (eds) *Small Firms and Industrial Districts in Italy.* London, Routledge: 259–69

Brusco S. (1992) Small firms and the provision of real services. In Pyke F., Sengenberger W. (eds) *Industrial Districts and Local Economic Regeneration.* Geneva, International Institute for Labour Studies: 177–96

Bryan D. (1995) *The Chase across the Globe: International Accumulation and the Contradictions for Nation States.* Boulder, CO, Westview Press

Brynjolfsson E. (1993) The productivity paradox of information technology. *Communications of the ACM* 36 (12): 67–77

Brynjolfsson E., Hitt L. (1996) Paradox lost? Firm-level evidence on the returns to information systems spending. *Management Science* 42: 541–58

Brynjolfsson E., Malone T. W., Gurbaxani V., Kambil A. (1994) Does information technology lead to smaller firms? *Management Science* 40: 1628–44

Bryson J., Wood P., Keeble D. (1993) Business networks, small firm flexibility and regional development in UK business services. *Entrepreneurship and Regional Development* 5: 265–77

Buck N. (1988) Service industries and local labour markets: towards 'an anatomy of service job loss.' *Urban Studies* 25: 319–32

Buck T., Atkins M. (1983) Regional policies in retrospect: an application of analysis of variance. *Regional Studies* 17: 181–9

Buderi R., Carey J., Gross N., Miller K. L. (1992) Global innovation: Who's in the lead? *Business Week* 3 August: 68–73

Buitendam A. (1987) The horizontal perspective of organization design and new technology. In Pennings J. M., Buitendam A. (eds) *New Technology as Organizational Innovation.* Cambridge, MA, Ballinger: 59–86

Bull A. C., Pitt M., Szarka J. (1991) Small firms and industrial districts: structural explanations of small firm viability in three countries. *Entrepreneurship and Regional Development* 3: 83–99

Bull I., Winter F. (1991) Community differences in business births and business growths. *Journal of Business Venturing* 6: 29–43

Burgan J. U. (1985) Cyclical behavior of high tech industries. *Monthly Labor Review* 108 (May): 9–15

Burgelman R. A., Rosenbloom R. S. (1989) Technology strategy: an evolutionary process perspective. In Rosenbloom R. S., Burgelman R. A. (eds) *Research in Technological Innovation, Management and Policy*, volume 4. Greenwich, CT, JAI Press: 1–23

Burgelman R. A., Sayles L. R. (1986) *Inside Corporate Innovation.* New York, Free Press

Business Week (1986) The hollow corporation. 3 March: 57–85

Buss T. F., Vaughan R. (1987) Revitalizing the Mahoning Valley. *Environment and Planning C: Government and Policy* 5: 433–47

Buswell R. J. (1983) Research and development and regional development. In Gillespie A. (ed.) *Technological Change and Regional Development.* London, Pion: 9–22

Buswell R. J., Easterbrook R. P., Morphet C. S. (1985) Geography, regions and research and development activity: the case of the United Kingdom. In Thwaites A. T., Oakey R. P. (eds) *The Regional Impact of Technological Change.* London, Frances Pinter: 36–66

Butler J. E., Hansen G. S. (1991) Network evolution, entrepreneurial success, and regional development. *Entrepreneurship and Regional Development* 3: 1–16

Bygrave W. D. (1987) Syndicated investments by venture capital firms: a networking perspective. *Journal of Business Venturing* 2: 139–54

Bygrave W. D. (1988) The structure of the investment networks of venture capital firms. *Journal of Business Venturing* 3: 137–57

Bygrave W. D., Timmons J. A. (1992) *Venture Capital at the Crossroads.* Boston, Harvard Business School Press

Cainarca G. C., Colombo M. G., Mariotti S. (1990) Firm size and the adoption of flexible automation. *Small Business Economics* 2: 129–40

Calantone, R. J., Vickery S. K., Droge C. (1995) Business performance and strategic new product development activities: an empirical investigation. *Journal of Product Innovation Management* 12: 214–23

Callahan J., Diedrich P. (1992) Organizational learning across critical linkages: the case of captive ASIC design and manufacturing. *Technovation* 12: 433–46

Callon S. (1995) *Divided Sun: MITI and the Breakdown of Japanese High-Tech Industrial Policy, 1975–1993.* Stanford, Stanford University Press

Calvin D. W. (1995) Thinking small in a large company. *Research-Technology Management* 38 (5): 18–21

Camagni R. (ed.) (1991a) *Innovation Networks: Spatial Perspectives.* London, Pinter

Camagni R. (1991b) Local 'milieu', uncertainty and innovation networks: towards a new dynamic theory of economic space. In Camagni R. (ed.) *Innovation Networks: Spatial Perspectives.* London, Pinter: 121–44

Camagni R. (1995a) Global network and local milieu: towards a theory of economic space. In Conti S., Malecki E. J., Oinas P. (eds) *The Industrial Enterprise and Its Environment: Spatial Perspectives.* Aldershot, Avebury: 195–214

Camagni R. (1995b) The concept of *innovative milieu* and its relevance for public policies in European lagging regions. *Papers in Regional Science* 74: 317–40

Camagni R., Capello R. (1990) Towards a definition of the manoeuvering space of local development initiatives: Italian success stories of local development – theoretical conditions and practical experiences. In Stöhr W. B. (ed.) *Global Challenge and Local Response*. London, Mansell: 328–53

Camagni R., Rabellotti R. (1988) Innovation and territory: the Milan information technology field. In Giaoutzi M., Nijkamp P. (eds) *Informatics and Regional Development*. Aldershot, Avebury: 215–34

Camagni R., Rabellotti R. (1992) Technology and organization in the Italian textile-clothing industry. *Entrepreneurship and Regional Development* 4: 271–85

Camagni R., Salone C. (1992) Network urban structure in Northern Italy: elements for a theoretical framework. *Urban Studies* 30: 1053–61

Caminiti S. (1989) A quiet superstar rises in retailing. *Fortune* 120 (9): 167–74

Cantley M. F. (1986) Long-term prospects and implications of biotechnology for Europe: strategic challenge and response. *International Journal of Technology Management* 1: 209–29

Cantwell J. (1995) The globalisation of technology: what remains of the product cycle model? *Cambridge Journal of Economics* 19: 155–74

Capecchi V. (1989) The informal economy and the development of flexible specialization in Emilia-Romagna. In Portes A., Castells M., Benton L. A. (eds) *The Informal Economy: Studies in Advanced and Less Developed Countries*. Baltimore, Johns Hopkins University Press: 189–215

Capello R. (1994) Towards new industrial and spatial systems: the role of new technologies. *Papers in Regional Science* 73: 189–208

Cappellin R. (1988) Transaction costs and urban agglomeration. *Revue d'Économie Régionale et Urbaine*: 261–78

Cappellin R. (1993) Interregional cooperation in Europe: an introduction. In Cappellin R., Batey P. W. J. (eds) *Regional Networks, Border Regions and European Integration*. London, Pion: 1–20

Caracostas P., Muldur U. (1995) Long cycles, technology and employment: current obstacles and outlook. *STI Review* 15: 75–104

Caravatti M.-L. (1992) Why the United States must do more process R&D. *Research-Technology Management* 35 (5): 8–9

Carillo J. (1994) The apparel maquiladora industry at the Mexican border. In Bonacich E., Cheng L., Chinchilla N., Hamilton N., Ong P. (eds) *Global Production: The Apparel Industry in the Pacific Rim*. Philadelphia, Temple University Press: 217–29

Carillo Gamboa J. (1988) Globalization of industry through production sharing. In Muroyama J. H., Stever H. G. (eds) *Globalization of Technology: International Perspectives*. Washington, National Academy Press: 86–105

Carlberg M. (1981) A neoclassical model of interregional economic growth. *Regional Science and Urban Economics* 11: 191–203

Carliner G. (1987) Industrial policies for emerging industries. In Krugman P. R. (ed.) *Strategic Trade Policy and the New International Economics*. Cambridge, MA, MIT Press: 147–168

Carlino G. A. (1992) Are regional per capita earnings diverging? *Business Review, Federal Reserve Bank of Philadelphia* March/April: 3–12

Carlsson B. (1981) The content of productivity growth in Swedish manufacturing. *Research Policy* 10: 336–54

Carlsson B. (1994) Technological systems and economic performance. In Dodgson M., Rothwell R. (eds) *The Handbook of Industrial Innovation*. Aldershot, Edward Elgar: 13–24

Carlsson B., Eliasson G. (1994) The nature and importance of economic competence. *Industrial and Corporate Change* 3: 687–711

Carlsson B., Jacobsson S. (1994) Technological systems and economic policy: the diffusion of factory automation in Sweden. *Research Policy* 23: 235–48

Carlsson B., Stankiewicz R. (1991) On the nature, function and composition of technological systems. *Journal of Evolutionary Economics* 1: 93–118

Carnevale A. P. (1995) Enhancing skills in the new economy. In Howard A. (ed.) *The Changing Nature of Work.* San Francisco, Jossey-Bass: 238–51

Carnevale A. P., Gainer L. J., Meltzer A. S. (1988) *Workplace Basics: The Skills Employers Want.* Washington, US Department of Labor

Carr E. (1994) Power to the people: a survey of energy. *The Economist* 18 June

Carson I. (1996) Taming the beast: a survey on living with the car. *The Economist* 22 June

Carter C., Williams B. (1959) The characteristics of progressive firms. *Journal of Industrial Economics* 7: 87–104

Carter R. B., van Auken H. E., Harms M. B. (1992) Home-based businesses in the rural United States economy: differences in gender and financing. *Entrepreneurship and Regional Development* 4: 245–57

Cartwright W. R. (1993) Multiple linked 'diamonds' and the international competitiveness of export-dependent industries: the New Zealand experience. *Management International Review* 33 (special issue 2): 55–70

Casetti E. (1981) A catastrophe model of regional dynamics. *Annals of the Association of American Geographers* 71: 572–9

Casetti E., Pandit K. (1987) The non linear dynamics of sectoral shifts. *Economic Geography* 63: 241–58

Casson M. (1982) *The Entrepreneur: An Economic Theory.* Oxford, Martin Robertson

Casson M. (1987) *The Firm and the Market.* Cambridge, MA, MIT Press

Casson M. (1990) *Enterprise and Competitiveness.* Oxford, Clarendon Press

Casson M. (1991) A systems view of R&D. In Casson M. (ed.) *Global Research Strategy and International Competitiveness.* Oxford, Basil Blackwell: 39–67

Castells M. (1988) The new industrial space: information-technology manufacturing and spatial structure in the United States. In Sternlieb G., Hughes J. W. (eds) *America's New Market Geography.* New Brunswick, NJ, Center for Urban Policy Research: 43–99

Castells M. (1989) *The Informational City.* Oxford, Blackwell

Castells M. (1992) Four Asian tigers with a dragon head: a comparative analysis of the state, economy, and society in the Asian Pacific Rim. In Appelbaum R. P., Henderson J. (eds) *States and Development in the Asia Pacific Rim.* Newbury Park, Sage: 33–70

Castells M., Hall P. (1994) *Technopoles of the World: The Making of 21st Century Industrial Complexes.* London, Routledge

Cater E. (1988) The development of tourism in the least developed countries. In Goodall B., Ashworth G. (eds) *Marketing in the Tourism Industry: The Promotion of Destination Regions.* London, Croom Helm: 39–66

Catrina C. (1988) *Arms Transfers and Dependence.* Philadelphia, Taylor and Francis

Caves R. E. (1993) Japanese investment in the United States: lessons for the economic analysis of foreign investment. *The World Economy* 16: 279–300

Cawthorne P. M. (1995) Of networks and markets: the rise and rise of a South Indian town, the example of Tiruppur's cotton knitwear industry. *World Development* 23: 43–56

Cenzatti M. (1990) Restructuring in the motorcycle industry in Great Britain and Italy until 1980. *Environment and Planning D: Society and Space* 8: 339–55

Cerny K. (1996) Making local knowledge global. *Harvard Business Review* 74 (3):

22–38

Cesaratto S., Sirilli G. (1992) Some results of the Italian survey on technological innovation. *STI Review* **11**: 79–96

Cespedes F. V. (1994) Industrial marketing: managing new requirements. *Sloan Management Review* **35** (3): 45–60

Chabbal R. (1995) Characteristics of innovation policies, namely for SMEs. *STI Review* **16**: 103–40

Chakrabarti A. K., Souder W. E. (1987) Technology, innovation and performance in corporate mergers: a managerial evaluation. *Technovation* **6**: 103–14

Chan A. (1995) Chinese enterprise reforms: convergence with the Japanese model? *Industrial and Corporate Change* **4**: 449–70

Chandler A. D. (1962) *Strategy and Structure*. Cambridge, MA, MIT Press

Chandler A. D. (1977) *The Visible Hand: The Managerial Revolution in American Business*. Cambridge, MA, Belknap Press of Harvard University Press

Chandler A. D. (1990) *Scale and Scope: The Dynamics of Industrial Capitalism*. Cambridge, MA, Belknap Press of Harvard University Press

Chandra B., MacPherson A. D. (1994) The characteristics of high-technology manufacturing firms in a declining industrial region: an empirical analysis from western New York. *Entrepreneurship and Regional Development* **6**: 145–60

Chang H.-J. (1994) *The Political Economy of Industrial Policy*. New York, St Martin's Press

Chang H.-J. (1995a) Return to Europe?: Is there anything for eastern Europe to learn from East Asia? In Chang H.-J., Nolan P. (eds) *The Transformation of the Communist Economies*. New York, St Martin's Press: 382–99

Chang H.-J. (1995b) Explaining 'flexible rigidities' in East Asia. In Killick T. (ed.) *The Flexible Economy: Causes and Consequences of the Adaptability of National Economies*. London, Routledge: 257–96

Chang H.-J., Kozul-Wright R. (1994) Organising development: comparing the national systems of entrepreneurship in Sweden and South Korea. *Journal of Development Studies* **30**: 859–91

Chantramonklasri N. (1990) The development of technological and managerial capability in the developing countries. In Chatterji M. (ed.) *Technology Transfer in the Developing Countries*. London, Macmillan: 36–50

Charles D., Monk P., Sciberras E. (1989) *Technology and Competition in the International Telecommunications Industry*. London, Pinter

Charney A. H., Taylor C. A. (1983) Consistent region-subregion econometric models: a comparison of multiarea methods. *International Regional Science Review* **8**: 59–74

Charney A. H., Taylor C. A. (1986) Integrated state-substate econometric modeling: design and utilization for long-run economic analysis. In Perryman M. R., Schmidt J. R. (eds) *Regional Econometric Modeling*. Boston, Kluwer-Nijhoff: 43–92

Chatterjee S. (1994) Making more out of less: the recipe for long-term economic growth. *Business Review, Federal Reserve Bank of Philadelphia* May/June: 3–15

Chen C.-F., Sewell G. (1996) Strategies for technological development in South Korea and Taiwan: the case of semiconductors. *Research Policy* **25**: 759–83

Chen X. (1994) The new spatial division of labor and commodity chains in the Greater South China Economic Region. In Gereffi G., Korzeniewicz M. (eds) *Commodity Chains and Global Capitalism*. Westport, CT, Praeger: 165–86

Chesbrough H. W., Teece D. J. (1996) When is virtual virtuous? Organizing for innovation. *Harvard Business Review* **74** (1): 65–73

Chesnais F. (1986) Science, technology and competitiveness. *STI Review* **1**: 85–129

Chesnais F. (1988) Technical co-operation agreements between firms. *STI Review* 4: 51–119

Chesnais F. (1993) The French national system of innovation. In Nelson R. R. (ed.) *National Innovation Systems: A Comparative Analysis*. New York, Oxford University Press: 192–229

Chiang J.-T. (1989) Technology and alliance strategies for follower countries. *Technological Forecasting and Social Change* 35: 339–49

Chiang J.-T. (1990) Management of technology in centrally planned economies. *Technology in Society* 12: 397–426

Chiang J.-T. (1991) From 'mission-oriented' to 'diffusion-oriented' paradigm: the new trend of US industrial technology policy. *Technovation* 11: 339–56

Chidamber S. R., Kon H. B. (1994) A research retrospective of innovation inception and success: the technology-push, demand-pull question. *International Journal of Technology Management* 9: 94–112

Chiesa V. (1996) Strategies for global R&D. *Research-Technology Management* 39 (5): 19–25

Child J. (1987a) Organizational design for advanced manufacturing technology. In Wall T. D., Clegg C. W., Kemp N. J. (eds) *The Human Side of Advanced Manufacturing Technology*. New York, John Wiley: 101–33

Child J. (1987b) Managerial strategies, new technology, and the labor process. In J. M. Pennings, A. Buitendam (eds) *New Technology as Organizational Innovation*. Cambridge, MA, Ballinger: 141–77

Chinworth M. W., Mowery D. C. (1995) Cross-border linkages and the US defense industry: outlook and policy challenges. *Technovation* 15: 133–52

Chisholm M. (1987) Regional development: the Reagan–Thatcher legacy. *Environment and Planning C: Government and Policy* 5: 197–218

Chiu S., Levin D. A. (1995) The world economy, state, and sectors in industrial change: labor relations in Hong Kong's textile and garment-making industries. In Frenkel S., Harrod J. (eds) *Industrialization and Labor Relations*. Ithaca, NY, ILR Press: 143–75

Christensen P. R. (1991) The small and medium-sized exporters' squeeze: empirical evidence and model reflections. *Entrepreneurship and Regional Development* 3: 49–65

Christensen P. R., Lindmark L. (1993) Location and internationalization of small firms. In Lundqvist L., Persson L. O. (eds) *Visions and Strategies in European Integration*. Berlin, Springer-Verlag: 131–51

Christensen P. R., Eskelinen H., Forsström B., Lindmark L., Vatne E. (1990) Firms in network: concepts, spatial impacts and policy implications. In Illeris S., Jakobsen L. (eds) *Networks and Regional Development*. Copenhagen, NordREFO: 11–58

Christopherson S. (1989) Flexibility in the US service economy and the emerging spatial division of labour. *Transactions of the Institute of British Geographers* NS 14: 131–43

Christopherson S., Noyelle T. (1992) The US path toward flexibility and productivity: the re-making of the US labour market in the 1980s. In Ernste H., Maier V. (eds) *Regional Development and Contemporary Industrial Response: Extending Flexible Specialisation*. London, Belhaven: 163–78

Christopherson S., Storper M. (1989) The effects of flexible specialization on industrial politics and the labor market: the motion picture industry. *Industrial and Labor Relations Review* 42: 331–47

Chung F. (1996) Education for Africa's development. *Development* June: 41–5

Chung J. C. (1986) Korea. In Rushing F. W., Brown C. G. (eds) *National Policies for Developing High Technology Industries: International Comparisons*. Boulder, CO,

Westview Press: 143–72

Ciccone A., Hall R. E. (1996) Productivity and the density of economic activity. *American Economic Review* 86: 54–70

Clark C. (1957) *The Conditions of Economic Progress*. London, Macmillan

Clark G. L. (1986a) Regional development and policy: the geography of employment. *Progress in Human Geography* 10: 416–26

Clark G. L. (1986b) Restructuring the US economy: the NLRB, the Saturn project, and economic justice. *Economic Geography* 62: 289–306

Clark G. L. (1993) Global interdependence and regional development: business linkages and corporate governance in a world of financial risk. *Transactions, Institute of British Geographers* NS 18: 309–325

Clark G. L., Ballard K. P. (1981) The demand and supply of labor and interstate relative wages: an empirical analysis. *Economic Geography* 57: 95–112

Clark G. L., Gertler M. S., Whiteman J. (1986) *Regional Dynamics: Studies in Adjustment Theory*. Boston, Allen and Unwin

Clark G. L., Wrigley N. (1995) Sunk costs: a framework for economic geography. *Transactions, Institute of British Geographers* NS 20: 204–23

Clark K. B. (1983) Competition, technical diversity, and radical innovation in the US auto industry. In Rosenbloom R. S. (ed.) *Research on Technological Innovation, Management and Policy*, volume 1. Greenwich, CT, JAI Press: 103–49

Clark N. (1985) *The Political Economy of Science and Technology*. Oxford, Basil Blackwell

Clark N., Juma C. (1988) Evolutionary theories in economic thought. In Dosi G., Freeman C., Nelson R., Silverberg G., Soete L. (eds) *Technical Change and Economic Theory*. London, Pinter: 197–218

Clark W. A. V., Freeman H. E., Hanssens D. M. (1984) Opportunities for revitalizing stagnant markets: an analysis of household appliances. *Journal of Product Innovation Management* 1: 242–54

Clarke I. M. (1985) *The Spatial Organisation of Multinational Corporations*. New York, St Martin's Press

Clarke M. K. (1990) Recent state initiatives: an overview of state science and technology policies and programs. In Schmandt J., Wilson R. (eds) *Growth Policy in the Age of High Technology: The Role of Regions and States*. Boston, Unwin Hyman: 149–70

Clarke S. E. (1993) The profound and the mundane: analyzing local economic development activities. *Urban Geography* 14: 78–94

Clarke S. E., Gaile G. L. (1992) The next wave: postfederal local economic development strategies. *Economic Development Quarterly* 6: 187–98

Clawson P. (ed.) (1996) *Strategic Assessment 1996: Instruments of US Power*. Washington, National Defense University, Institute for National Strategic Studies

Clery D. (1993) A mixed report card for critical technology projects. *Science* 260: 1736–8

Clifford M. L., Port O. (1996) This island is crazy for chips. *Business Week* 16 September: 58–9

Cobb C., Halstead T., Rowe J. (1995) If the GDP is up, why is America down? *The Atlantic Monthly* 276 (4) October: 59–78

Cobb J. C. (1993) *The Selling of the South: The Southern Crusade for Industrial Development, 1936–1990*, second edition. Urbana, University of Illinois Press

Coffey W. J. (1990) Panacea or problem? The role of services and high technology in regional development. *Revue d'Économie Régionale et Urbaine* 5: 715–34

Coffey W. J., Polèse M. (1984) The concept of local development: a stages model of endogenous regional growth. *Papers of the Regional Science Association* 54: 1–12

Coffey W. J., Polèse M. (1985) Local development: conceptual bases and policy implications. *Regional Studies* 19: 85–93

Coffey W. J., Polèse M. (1987a) Trade and location of producer services: a Canadian perspective. *Environment and Planning A* 19: 597–611

Coffey W. J., Polèse M. (1987b) Intrafirm trade in business services: implications for the location of office-based activities. *Papers of the Regional Science Association* 62: 71–80

Coffey W. J., Polèse M. (1989) Service activities and regional development: a policy-oriented perspective. *Papers of the Regional Science Association* 67: 13–27

Cohen W. M., Levinthal D. A. (1989) Innovation and learning: the two faces of R&D. *Economic Journal* 99: 569–96

Cohen W. M., Levinthal D. A. (1990) Absorptive capacity: a new perspective on learning and innovation. *Administrative Science Quarterly* 35: 128–52

Cohen W. M., Levinthal D. A. (1994) Fortune favors the prepared firm. *Management Science* 40: 227–51

Cohen S. S., Zysman J. (1987) *Manufacturing Matters: The Myth of the Post-Industrial Economy.* New York, Basic Books

Cole R. E. (ed.) (1995) *The Death and Life of the American Quality Movement.* New York, Oxford University Press

Colombo U. (1988) The technology revolution and the restructuring of the global economy. In Muroyama J. H., Stever H. G. (eds) *Globalization of Technology: International Perspectives.* Washington, National Academy Press: 23–31

Conroy M. E. (1975) *The Challenge of Urban Economic Development.* Lexington, MA, Lexington Books

Conti S. (1988) The Italian model and the problems of the industrial periphery. In Linge G. J. R. (ed.) *Peripheralisation and Industrial Change.* London, Croom Helm: 37–52

Conti S. (1993) The network perspective in industrial geography: towards a model. *Geografiska Annaler* 75B: 115–30

Cooke P. (1983) Labour market discontinuity and spatial development. *Progress in Human Geography* 7: 543–65

Cooke P. (1985a) Class practices as regional markers: a contribution to labour geography. In Gregory D., Urry J. (eds) *Social Relations and Spatial Structures.* London, Macmillan: 213–41

Cooke P. (1985b) Regional innovation policy: problems and strategies in Britain and France. *Environment and Planning C: Government and Policy* 3: 253–67

Cooke P. (1988) Flexible integration, scope economies, and strategic alliances: social and spatial mediations. *Environment and Planning D: Society and Space* 6: 281–300

Cooke P. (1996a) Building a twenty-first century regional economy in Emilia-Romagna. *European Planning Studies* 4: 53–62

Cooke P. (1996b) The new wave of regional innovation networks: analysis, characteristics and strategy. *Small Business Economics* 8: 159–71

Cooke P., Morgan K. (1993) The network paradigm: new departures in corporate and regional development. *Environment and Planning D: Society and Space* 11: 543–64

Cooke P., Morgan K. (1994a) The creative milieu: a regional perspective on innovation. In Dodgson M., Rothwell R. (eds) *The Handbook of Industrial Innovation.* Aldershot, Edward Elgar: 25–32

Cooke P., Morgan K. (1994b) The regional innovation system in Baden-Württemberg. *International Journal of Technology Management* 9: 394–429

Coombs R., Saviotti P., Walsh V. (1987) *Economics and Technological Change.* London,

Macmillan

Cooper A. C. (1973) Technical entrepreneurship: What do we know? *R&D Management* **3** (1): 59–64

Cooper A. C. (1985) The role of incubator organizations in the founding of growth-oriented firms. *Journal of Business Venturing* **1**: 75–86

Cooper A. C. (1986) Entrepreneurship and high technology. In Sexton D. L., Smilor R. W. (eds) *The Art and Science of Entrepreneurship*. Cambridge, MA, Ballinger: 153–68

Cooper A. C., Gimeno Gascón F. J. (1992) Entrepreneurs, processes of founding and new-firm performance. In Sexton D. L., Kasarda J. D. (eds) *The State of the Art of Entrepreneurship*. Boston, PWS-Kent: 301–40

Cooper A. C., Schendel D. (1976) Strategic responses to technological threats. *Business Horizons* **19** (1): 61–9

Cooper A. C., Willard G. E., Woo C. Y. (1986) Strategies of high-performing new and small firms: a re-examination of the niche concept. *Journal of Business Venturing* **1**: 247–60

Cooper A. C., Woo C. Y., Dunkelberg W. C. (1988) Entrepreneurs' perceived chances for success. *Journal of Business Venturing* **3**: 97–108

Cooper R. G. (1984a) How new product strategies impact on performance. *Journal of Product Innovation Management* **1**: 5–18

Cooper R. G. (1984b) New product strategies: what distinguishes top performers? *Journal of Product Innovation Management* **1**: 151–64

Cooper R. G., Kleinschmidt E. J. (1987) New products: what separates winners from losers? *Journal of Product Innovation Management* **4**: 169–84

Cooper R. G., Kleinschmidt E. J. (1994) Determinants of timeliness in product development. *Journal of Product Innovation Management* **11**: 381–96

Cooper R. G., Kleinschmidt E. J. (1995) Benchmarking the firm's critical success factors in new product development. *Journal of Product Innovation Management* **12**: 374–91

Corbridge S. (1990) Development studies. *Progress in Human Geography* **14**: 391–403

Corbridge S. (1994) Bretton Woods revisited: hegemony, stability, and territory. *Environment and Planning A* **26**: 1829–59

Corbridge S., Martin R., Thrift N. (eds) (1994) *Money, Power and Space*. Oxford, Blackwell

Cordero R. (1991) Managing for speed to avoid product obsolescence: a survey of techniques. *Journal of Product Innovation Management* **8**: 283–94

Coriat B. (1992) The revitalization of mass production in the computer age. In Storper M., Scott A. J. (eds) *Pathways to Industrialization and Regional Development*. London, Routledge: 137–56

Cornish S. L. (1995) 'Marketing matters': the function of markets and marketing in the growth of firms and industries. *Progress in Human Geography* **19**: 317–37

Corporation for Enterprise Development (annual) *The Development Report Card for the States*. Washington, Corporation for Enterprise Development

Courault B. A., Romani C. (1992) A reexamination of the Italian model of flexible production from a comparative point of view. In Storper M., Scott A. J. (eds) *Pathways to Industrialization and Regional Development*. London, Routledge: 205–15

Courlet C., Pecqueur B. (1991) Local industrial systems and externalities: an essay in typology. *Entrepreneurship and Regional Development* **3**: 305–15

Courlet C., Soulage B. (1995) Industrial dynamics and territorial space. *Entrepreneurship and Regional Development* **7**: 287–307

Cowan R., Foray D. (1995) Quandaries in the economics of dual technologies and spill-overs from military to civilian research and development. *Research Policy* 24: 851–68

Cox K. R. (1995) Globalisation, competition and the politics of local economic development. *Urban Studies* 32: 213–24

Cox K. R., Mair A. (1988) Locality and community in the politics of local economic development. *Annals of the Association of American Geographers* 78: 307–25

Cox R. N. (1985) Lessons from 30 years of science parks in the USA. In Gibb J. M. (ed.) *Science Parks and Innovation Centres: Their Economic and Social Impact.* Amsterdam, Elsevier: 17–24

Coy P., Carey J., Gross N. (1993) The global patent race picks up speed. *Business Week* 9 August: 57–62

Crane D. (1977) Technological innovation in developing countries: a review of the literature. *Research Policy* 6: 374–95

Crawford C. M. (1992) The hidden costs of accelerated product development. *Journal of Product Innovation Management* 9: 188–99

Crewe L., Davenport E. (1992) The puppet show: changing buyer–supplier relationships within clothing retailing. *Transactions, Institute of British Geographers* NS 17: 183–97

Crook C. (1989) Poor man's burden: a survey of the Third World. *The Economist* 23 September

Crook C. (1993) Turning point: a survey of the Japanese economy. *The Economist* 6 March

Cromie S., Birley S. (1992) Networking by female business owners in Northern Ireland. *Journal of Business Venturing* 7: 237–51

Cromie S., Birley S. (1994) Relationships among small business support agencies. *Entrepreneurship and Regional Development* 6: 301–314

Cromie S., Birley S., Callaghan I. (1993) Community brokers: their role in the formation and development of new ventures. *Entrepreneurship and Regional Development* 5: 247–64

Cuadrado Roura J. R. (1982) Regional economic disparities: an approach and some reflections on the Spanish case. *Papers of the Regional Science Association* 49: 113–30

Cullison W. E. (1993) Public investment and economic growth. *Federal Reserve Bank of Richmond Economic Quarterly* 79 (4): 19–33

Cumings B. (1987) The origins and development of the Northeast Asian political economy: industrial sectors, product cycles, and political consequences. In Deyo F. C. (ed.) *The Political Economy of the New Asian Industrialism.* Ithaca, NY, Cornell University Press: 44–83

Cunningham J. B., Lischeron J. (1991) Defining entrepreneurship. *Journal of Small Business Management* 29: 45–61

CURDS (1979) *The Mobilisation of Indigenous Potential in the U.K.* Report to the Regional Policy Directorate of the European Community. Newcastle-upon-Tyne, University of Newcastle-upon-Tyne, Centre for Urban and Regional Development Studies

Curran P., Blackburn R. (1994) *Small Firms and Local Economic Networks: The Death of the Local Economy?* London, Paul Chapman

Cusumano M. A. (1986) Diversity and innovation in Japanese technology management. In Rosenbloom R. S. (ed.) *Research on Technological Innovation, Management and Policy*, volume 3. Greenwich, CT, JAI Press: 137–67

Cusumano M. A. (1988) Manufacturing innovation: lessons from the Japanese auto industry. *Sloan Management Review* 30 (1): 29–39

Cusumano M. A., Elenkov D. (1994) Linking international technology transfer with strategy and management: a literature commentary. *Research Policy* 23: 195–215

Cutcher-Gershenfeld J., Nitta M., Barrett B., Belhedi N., Bullard J., Coutchie C., Inaba T., Ishino I., Lee S., Lin W.-J., Mothersell W., Rabine S., Ramanand S., Strolle M., Wheaton A. (1994) Japanese team-based work systems in North America: explaining the diversity. *California Management Review* 37 (1): 42–64

Cutler R. S. (1989) A comparison of Japanese and US high-technology transfer practices. *IEEE Transactions on Engineering Management* 36: 17–24

Cyert R. M., Mowery D. C. (1987) *Technology and Employment: Innovation and Growth in the US Economy*. Washington, National Academy Press

Czamanski D. Z. (1981) A contribution to industrial location theory. *Environment and Planning A* 13: 29–42

Czamanski D. Z., Czamanski S. (1977) Industrial complexes: their typology, structure and relation to economic development. *Papers of the Regional Science Association* 38: 93–111

Czamanski S. (1974) *Study of Clustering of Industries*. Halifax, Dalhousie University, Institute of Public Affairs

Czamanski S., Czamanski D. Z. (1976) *Study of Spatial Industrial Complexes*. Halifax, Dalhousie University, Institute of Public Affairs

Da Costa L. N. (1995) Future of science in Latin America. *Science* 270: 827–8

Dahlin K. (1993) Diffusion and industrial dynamics in the robot industry. *International Journal of Technology Management* 8: 259–81

Dahlman C. J. (1989) Technological change in industry in developing countries. *Finance and Development* 26 (2): 13–15

Dahlman C. J., Frischtak C. R. (1993) National systems supporting technical advance in industry: the Brazilian experience. In Nelson R. R. (ed.) *National Innovation Systems: A Comparative Analysis*. New York, Oxford University Press: 414–50

Dahlman C. J., Sercovich F. C. (1984) *Local Development and Exports of Technology: The Comparative Advantage of Argentina, Brazil, India, the Republic of Korea, and Mexico*. Staff working paper 667. Washington, World Bank

Dalborg H. (1974) *Research and Development – Organization and Location*. Stockholm, Stockholm School of Economics, Economic Research Institute

Daniels P. W. (1982) *Service Industries: Growth and Location*. Cambridge, Cambridge University Press

Daniels P. W. (1993) *Service Industries in the World Economy*. Oxford, Blackwell

Daniels P. W. (1995a) Services in a shrinking world. *Geography* 80 (2): 97–110

Daniels P. W. (1995b) The internationalisation of advertising services in a changing regulatory environment. *Service Industries Journal* 15: 276–94

Danson M. W. (1982) The industrial structure and labour market segmentation: urban and regional implications. *Regional Studies* 16: 255–65

Danson M. W. (1995) New firm formation and regional economic development: an introduction and review of the Scottish experience. *Small Business Economics* 7: 81–7

D'Arcy É., Guissani B. (1996) Local economic development: changing the parameters? *Entrepreneurship and Regional Development* 8: 159–78

Davelaar E. J., Nijkamp P. (1989) The role of the metropolitan milieu as an incubation centre for technological innovations: a Dutch case study. *Urban Studies* 26: 517–25

D'Aveni R. A. (1994) *Hypercompetition: Managing the Dynamics of Strategic Maneuvering*. New York, Free Press

David P. A. (1993) Knowledge, property, and the system dynamics of technological change. In Summers L. H., Shah S. (eds) *Proceedings of the Annual World Bank*

Conference on Development Economics 1992. Washington, World Bank: 215–48

David P. A., Foray D. (1995) Accessing and expanding the science and technology base. *STI Review* 16: 13–68

Davidsson P. (1995) Culture, structure and regional levels of entrepreneurship. *Entrepreneurship and Regional Development* 7: 41–62

Davies S. P. (1991) The entrepreneurial capabilities of rural furniture manufacturers in central Java, Indonesia: a framework and case study. *Entrepreneurship and Regional Development* 3: 253–67

Davis G. A. (1995) Learning to love the Dutch disease: evidence from the mineral economies. *World Development* 23: 1765–99

Davis W. E. (1988) The dynamics of competition in information technology. In Schütte H. (ed.) *Strategic Issues in Information Technology*. Maidenhead, Pergamon Infotech: 75–87

Dawson J. (1992) The relevance of the flexible specialisation paradigm for small-scale industrial restructuring in Ghana. *IDS Bulletin* 23 (3): 34–8

Dawson J. (1993) Impact of structural adjustment on the small enterprise sector: a comparison of the Ghanaian and Tanzanian experiences. In Helmsing A. H. J., Kolstee T. (eds) *Small Enterprises and Changing Policies*. London, Intermediate Technology Publications: 71–90

De Bandt J. (1994) Policy mix and industrial strategies. In Bianchi P., Cowling K., Sugden R. (eds) *Europe's Economic Challenge: Analyses of Industrial Strategy and Agenda for the 1990s*. London, Routledge: 1–15

Debbage K. (1990) Oligopoly and the resort cycle in the Bahamas. *Annals of Tourism Research* 17: 513–27

Debbage K. (1992) Tourism oligopoly is at work. *Annals of Tourism Research* 19: 355–9

De Bresson C. (1989) Breeding innovation clusters: a source of dynamic development. *World Development* 17: 1–16

De Bresson C., Lampel J. (1985) Beyond the life cycle: organizational and technological design. I: an alternative perspective. *Journal of Product Innovation Management* 2: 170–87

De Bruijn E. J., Jia X. (1993) Transferring technology to China by means of joint ventures. *Research-Technology Management* 36 (1): 17–22

Deiaco E. (1992) New views on innovative activity and technological performance: the Swedish innovation survey. *STI Review* 11: 35–62

Dei Ottati G. (1996) Economic changes in the district of Prato in the 1980s: towards a more conscious and organized industrial district. *European Planning Studies* 4: 35–52

Delaney E. J. (1993) Technology search and firm bounds in biotechnology: new firms as agents of change. *Growth and Change* 24: 206–28

Delapierre M. (1988) Technology bunching and industrial strategies. In Urabe K., Child J., Kagano T. (eds) *Innovation and Management: International Comparisons*. Berlin, Walter de Gruyter: 145–63

Della Valle F., Gambardella A. (1993) 'Biological' revolution and strategies for innovation in pharmaceutical companies. *R&D Management* 23: 287–302

De Meyer A. C. L. (1985) The flow of technological information in an R&D department. *Research Policy* 14: 315–28

De Meyer A. (1993a) Management of an international network of industrial R&D laboratories. *R&D Management* 23: 109–20

De Meyer A. (1993b) Internationalizing R&D improves a firm's technical learning. *Research-Technology Management* 36 (4): 42–9

Denison E. F. (1967) *Why Growth Rates Differ: Postwar Experience in Nine Western Countries.* Washington, Brookings Institution

Denison E. F. (1985) *Trends in American Economic Growth, 1929–1982.* Washington, Brookings Institution

Dennis W. J., Phillips B. D. (1990) The synergism of independent high-technology business starts. *Entrepreneurship and Regional Development* 2: 1–14

Deolalikar A. B., Evenson R. E. (1990) Private inventive activity in Indian manufacturing: its extent and determinants. In Evenson R. E., Ranis G. (eds) *Science and Technology: Lessons for Development Policy.* Boulder, CO, Westview Press: 233–53

De Oliveira Campos R. (1982) Take-off and breakdown: vicissitudes of the developing countries. In Kindleberger C. P., di Tella G. (eds) *Economics in the Long View: Essays in Honour of W. W. Rostow,* volume 1. New York, New York University Press: 116–40

Derian J.-C. (1990) *America's Struggle for Leadership in Technology.* Cambridge, MA, MIT Press

Desai A. V. (1980) The origin and direction of industrial R&D in India. *Research Policy* 9: 74–96

Desai A. V. (1985) Market structure and technology: their interdependence in Indian industry. *Research Policy* 14: 161–70

De Soto H. (1989) *The Other Path: The Invisible Revolution in the Third World.* New York, Harper and Row

Despres C., Hiltrop J.-M. (1996) Compensation for technical professionals in the knowledge age. *Research-Technology Management* 39 (5): 48–56

De Toni A., Nassimbeni G., Tonchia S. (1995) Small local firms inside the supply chain: challenges and perspectives. *Small Business Economics* 7: 241–9

De Vet J. M. (1993) Globalisation and local and regional competitiveness. *STI Review* 13: 89–122

Dewar R. D., Dutton J. E. (1986) The adoption of radical and incremental innovations: an empirical analysis. *Management Science* 32: 1422–33

De Wit G., van Winden F. A. A. M. (1989) An empirical analysis of self-employment in the Netherlands. *Small Business Economics* 1: 263–72

De Woot P. (1990) *High Technology Europe: Strategic Issues for Global Competitiveness.* Oxford, Basil Blackwell

Deyo F. C. (1987) Coalitions, institutions, and linkage sequencing – toward a strategic capacity model of East Asian development. In Deyo F. C. (ed.) *The Political Economy of the New Asian Industrialism.* Ithaca, NY, Cornell University Press: 227–47

Deyo F. C. (1989) *Beneath the Miracle: Labor Subordination in the New Asian Industrialism.* Berkeley, University of California Press

Diamond D., Spence N. (1983) *Regional Policy Evaluation: A Methodological Review and the Scottish Example.* Aldershot, Gower

Dicken P. (1986) Multinational enterprises and the local economy: some further observations. *Area* 18: 215–21

Dicken P. (1992) *Global Shift: The Internationalization of Economic Activity,* second edition. New York, Guilford

Dicken P. (1994) Global–local tensions: firms and states in the global space economy. *Economic Geography* 70: 101–28

Dicken P., Forsgren M., Malmberg A. (1994) The local embeddedness of transnational corporations. In Amin A., Thrift N. (eds) *Globalization, Institutions, and Regional Development in Europe.* Oxford, Oxford University Press: 23–45

Dickson K. (1983) The influence of Ministry of Defence funding on semiconductor research and development in the United Kingdom. *Research Policy* 12: 113–20

Dimou M. (1994) The industrial district: a stage of a diffuse industrialization process – the case of Roanne. *European Planning Studies* 2: 23–38

Ding J. (1995) *China's Domestic Economy in Regional Context.* Washington, Center for Strategic and International Studies

Diomande M. (1990) Business creation with minimal resources: some lessons from the African experience. *Journal of Business Venturing* 5: 191–200

Dixon R., Thirlwall A. P. (1975) A model of regional growth-rate differences on Kaldorian lines. *Oxford Economic Papers* 27: 201–14

Dodgson M. (1992) Strategy and technological learning: an interdisciplinary micro-study. In Coombs R., Saviotti P., Walsh V. (eds) *Technological Change and Company Strategies.* London, Academic Press: 136–63

Dodgson M. (1993) Learning, trust and technological collaboration. *Human Relations* 46: 77–95

Dodgson M. (1994) Technological collaboration and innovation. In Dodgson M., Rothwell R. (eds) *The Handbook of Industrial Innovation.* Aldershot, Edward Elgar: 285–92

Doeringer P. B. (1984) Internal labor markets and paternalism in rural areas. In Osterman P. (ed.) *Internal Labor Markets.* Cambridge, MA, MIT Press: 271–89

Doeringer P. B. (1994) Can the US system of workplace training survive global competition? In Asefa S., Huang W.-C. (eds) *Human Capital and Economic Development.* Kalamazoo, MI, W. E. Upjohn Institute for Employment Research: 91–107

Doeringer P. B., Streeten P. P. (1990) How economic institutions affect economic performance in industrialized countries: lessons for development. *World Development* 18: 1249–53

Doeringer P. B., Terkla D. G. (1990) How intangible factors contribute to economic development: lessons from a mature local economy. *World Development* 18: 1295–308

Doeringer P. B., Terkla D. G. (1992) Japanese direct investment and economic development policy. *Economic Development Quarterly* 6: 255–72

Doeringer P. B., Terkla D. G. (1995) Business strategies and cross-industry clusters. *Economic Development Quarterly* 9: 225–37

Doeringer P. B., Terkla D. G., Topakian G. C. (1987) *Invisible Factors in Local Economic Development.* Oxford, Oxford University Press

Dogan M. (1988) Giant cities as maritime gateways. In Dogan M., Kasarda J. D. (eds) *The Metropolis Era*, volume 1: A *World of Giant Cities.* Newbury Park, CA, Sage: 30–55

Dogan M., Kasarda J. D. (eds) (1988) *The Metropolis Era*, volume 1: *A World of Giant Cities.* Newbury Park, CA, Sage

Doherty E. (1980) How venture capital networks work. *Venture* 2 (7): 44–6

Dolton P. J. (1993) The economics of youth training in Britain. *Economic Journal* 103: 1261–78

Donaghu M. T., Barff R. (1990) Nike just did it: international subcontracting and flexibility in athletic footwear production. *Regional Studies* 24: 537–52

Donckels R. (1989) New entrepreneurship: lessons from the past, perspectives for the future. *Entrepreneurship and Regional Development* 1: 75–84

Donckels R., Courtmans A. (1990) Big brother is watching over you: the counselling of growing SMEs in Belgium. *Entrepreneurship and Regional Development* 2: 211–23

Donckels R., Hoebeke K. (1992) SME-led growth in the Belgian economy: fact or fiction? *Entrepreneurship and Regional Development* 4: 155–64

Donckels R., Lambrecht J. (1995) Networks and small business growth: an explanatory model. *Small Business Economics* 7: 273–89

Dore R. (1984) Technological self-reliance: sturdy ideal or self-serving rhetoric? In Fransman M., King K. (eds) *Technological Capability in the Third World.* London, Macmillan: 65–80

Dore R. (1986) *Flexible Rigidities: Industrial Policy and Structural Adjustment in the Japanese Economy 1970–80.* Stanford, Stanford University Press

Dore R. (1987) *Taking Japan Seriously: A Confucian Perspective on Leading Economic Issues.* London: Athlone

Dore R. (1989) Latecomers' problems. In Cooper C., Kaplinsky R. (eds) *Technology and Development in the Third Industrial Revolution.* London, Frank Cass: 100–7

Dore R., Bounine-Cabalé J., Tapiola K. (1989) *Japan at Work: Markets, Management and Flexibility.* Paris: Organisation for Economic Co-operation and Development

Dörrenbächer C., Wortmann M. (1991) The internationalization of corporate research and development. *Intereconomics* 26 (3): 139–44

Dosi G. (1984) *Technical Change and Industrial Transformation.* London: Macmillan

Dosi G. (1988) Sources, procedures, and microeconomic effects of innovation. *Journal of Economic Literature* 26: 1120–71

Dosi G., Freeman C., Fabiani S. (1994) The process of economic development: introducing some stylized facts and theories on technologies, firms and institutions. *Industrial and Corporate Change* 3: 1–47

Dosi G., Kogut B. (1993) National specificities and the context of change: the coevolution of organization and technology. In Kogut B. (ed.) *Country Competitiveness: Technology and the Organizing of Work.* New York, Oxford University Press: 249–62

Dosi G., Marsili O., Orsenigo L., Salvatore R. (1995) Learning, market selection and the evolution of industrial structures. *Small Business Economics* 7: 411–36

Dosi G., Orsenigo L. (1994) Macrodynamics and microfoundations: an evolutionary perspective. In Granstrand O. (ed.) *Economics of Technology.* Amsterdam, Elsevier: 91–123

Dosi G., Pavitt K., Soete L. (1990) *The Economics of Technical Change and International Trade.* Hemel Hempstead, Harvester Wheatsheaf

Dos Reis Velloso J. P. (1994) Innovation and society: the modern bases for development with equity. In Bradford C. I. (ed.) *The New Paradigm of Systemic Competitiveness: Toward More Integrated Policies in Latin America.* Paris, Organisation for Economic Co-operation and Development: 97–119

Douglass M. (1994) The 'developmental state' and the newly industrialised economies of Asia. *Environment and Planning A* 26: 543–66

Downes R. (1996) Regional policy development in Central and Eastern Europe. In Alden J., Boland P. (eds) *Regional Development Strategies: A European Perspective.* London, Jessica Kingsley: 256–72

Doz Y. (1986) *Strategic Management in Multinational Companies.* Oxford, Pergamon

Doz Y. (1987) International industries: fragmentation versus globalization. In Guile B. R., Brooks H. (eds) *Technology and Global Industry: Companies and Nations in the World Economy.* Washington, National Academy Press: 96–118

Doz Y. (1989) Competence and strategy. In Punset E., Sweeney G. (eds) *Information Resources and Corporate Growth.* London, Pinter: 47–55

Doz Y., Prahalad C. K., Hamel G. (1990) Control, change, and flexibility: the dilemma of transnational collaboration. In Bartlett, C. A., Doz Y., Hedlund G. (eds) *Managing the Global Firm.* London, Routledge: 117–43

Dreyfack K., Port O. (1986) Even American knowhow is headed abroad. *Business Week*

3 March: 60–3

Drucker P. F. (1989) *The New Realities.* New York, Harper and Row

Du F., Mergenhagen P., Lee M. (1995) The future of services. *American Demographics* 17 (11): 30–47

Dubini P. (1989) The influence of motivations and environment on business start-ups: some hints for public policies. *Journal of Business Venturing* 4: 11–26

Dubini P., Aldrich H. (1991) Personal and extended networks are central to the entrepreneurial process. *Journal of Business Venturing* 6: 305–13

Duchêne F., Shepherd G. (eds) (1987) *Managing Industrial Change in Western Europe.* London, Frances Pinter

Dumbleton J. H. (1986) *Management of High-Technology Research and Development.* Amsterdam, Elsevier

Dunford M. (1986) Integration and unequal development: the case of southern Italy. In Scott A. J., Storper M. (eds) *Production, Work, Territory.* Boston, Allen and Unwin: 225–45

Dunford M. F. (1988) *Capital, the State, and Regional Development.* London, Pion

Dunford M. (1993) Regional disparities in the European Community: evidence from the REGIO databank. *Regional Studies* 27: 727–43

Dunford M., Benko G. (1991) Neo-Fordism or post-Fordism?: Some conclusions and further remarks. In Benko G., Dunford M. (eds) *Industrial Change and Regional Development.* London, Belhaven: 286–305

Dunn M. H. (1994) Do nations compete economically? A critical comment on Prof Krugman's essay 'Competitiveness: a dangerous obsession'. *Intereconomics* 29: 303–8

Dunning J. H. (1979) Explaining changing patterns of international production: in defence of the eclectic theory. *Oxford Bulletin of Economics and Statistics* 41: 269–95

Dunning J. H. (1993a) Internationalizing Porter's diamond. *Management International Review* 33 (special issue 2): 7–15

Dunning J. H. (1993b) *The Globalization of Business.* London, Routledge

Dunning J. H. (1993c) The governance of Japanese and U.S. manufacturing affiliates in the UK: some country-specific differences. In Kogut B. (ed.) *Country Competitiveness: Technology and the Organizing of Work.* New York, Oxford University Press: 203–224

Dunning J. H. (1994) Multinational enterprises and the globalization of innovatory capacity. *Research Policy* 23: 67–88

Dunning J. H. (1995) Reappraising the eclectic paradigm in an age of alliance capitalism. *Journal of International Business Studies* 26: 461–91

Dunning J. H., Norman G. (1983) The theory of the multinational enterprise: an application to multinational office location. *Environment and Planning A* 15: 675–92

Dunning J. H., Norman G. (1987) The location choice of offices of international companies. *Environment and Planning A* 19: 613–31

Dyckman J. W., Swyngedouw E. A. (1988) Public and private technological innovation strategies in a spatial context: the case of France. *Environment and Planning C: Government and Policy* 6: 401–13

Easton G. (1992) Industrial networks: a review. In Axelsson B., Easton G. (eds) *Industrial Networks: A New View of Reality.* London, Routledge: 3–27

Edgington D. W. (1993) The globalization of Japanese manufacturing corporations. *Growth and Change* 24: 87–106

Edquist C., Jacobsson S. (1988) *Flexible Automation: The Global Diffusion of New Technology in the Engineering Industry.* Oxford, Basil Blackwell

Egge K. A., Simer F. J. (1988) An analysis of the advice given by recent entrepreneurs to prospective entrepreneurs. In Kirchhoff B. A., Long W. A., McMullan W. E., Vesper K. H., Wetzel W. E. (eds) *Frontiers of Entrepreneurship Research 1988.* Wellesley, MA: Babson College, Center for Entrepreneurial Studies: 119–33

Eisinger P. K. (1988) *The Rise of the Entrepreneurial State: State and Local Economic Development Policy in the United States.* Madison, University of Wisconsin Press

Eisinger P. (1991) The state of state venture capitalism. *Economic Development Quarterly* 5: 64–76

Eisinger P. K. (1993) State venture capitalism, state politics, and the world of high-risk investment. *Economic Development Quarterly* 7: 131–9

Elango B., Fried V. H., Hisrich R. D., Polonchek A. (1995) How venture capital firms differ. *Journal of Business Venturing* 10: 157–79

Eliasson G. (1988) *The Knowledge Base of an Industrial Economy.* Stockholm, Industrial Institute for Economic and Social Research

Eliasson G. (1991) The international firm: a vehicle for overcoming barriers to trade and a global intelligence organization diffusing the notion of a nation. In Mattsson L.-G., Stymne B. (eds) *Corporate and Industry Strategies for Europe.* Amsterdam, Elsevier: 139–70

Ellis L. W. (1988) What we've learned: managing financial resources. *Research-Technology Management* 31 (4): 21–38

Elzinga A. (1987) Foresighting Canada's emerging science and technologies. In Brotchie J. F., Hall P., Newton P. W. (eds) *The Spatial Impact of Technological Change.* London, Croom Helm: 343–56

Emmott B. (1993) *Japanophobia: The Myth of the Invincible Japanese.* New York, Times Books

Eng I., Lin Y. (1996) Seeking competitive advantage in an emergent open economy: foreign direct investment in Chinese industry. *Environment and Planning A* 28: 1113–38

Engardio P., Borrus A., Gross N. (1992) 'Greater China' could be the biggest tiger of all. *Business Week* 28 September: 58

Engerman S. L. (1994) The big picture: how (and when and why) the West grew rich. *Research Policy* 23: 547–59

Englmann F. C., Walz U. (1995) Industrial centers and regional growth in the presence of local inputs. *Journal of Regional Science* 35: 3–27

Enos J. L., Park W.-H. (1988) *The Adoption and Diffusion of Imported Technology: The Case of Korea.* London, Croom Helm

Ergas H. (1987) Does technology policy matter? In Guile B. R., Brooks H. (eds) *Technology and Global Industry: Companies and Nations in the World Economy.* Washington, National Academy Press: 191–245

Erickson R. A. (1987) Business climate studies: a critical evaluation. *Economic Development Quarterly* 1: 62–71

Erickson R. A., Gavin N. I., Cordes S. M. (1986) Service industries in interregional trade: the economic impacts of the hospital sector. *Growth and Change* 17 (1): 17–27

Eriksson S. (1995) *Global Shift in the Aircraft Industry: A Study of Airframe Manufacturing with Special Reference to the Asian NIEs.* Gothenburg, University of Gothenburg, School of Economics and Commercial Law, Department of Human and Economic Geography

Ernst D., O'Connor D. (1989) *Technology and Global Competition: The Challenge for Newly Industrializing Economies.* Paris, Organisation for Economic Co-operation and Development

Estimé M.-F., Drilhon G., Julien P.-A. (1993) *Small and Medium-sized Enterprises:*

Technology and Competitiveness. Paris: Organisation for Economic Co-operation and Development

Etemad H., Séguin Dulude L. (1986) Inventive activity in MNEs and their world product mandated subsidiaries. In Etemad H., Séguin Dulude L. (eds) *Managing the Multinational Subsidiary: Response to Environmental Changes and to Host Nation R&D Policies*. New York, St Martin's Press: 177–206

Etemad H., Séguin Dulude L. (1987) Patenting patterns in 25 large multinational enterprises. *Technovation* 7: 1–15

Eto H., Fujita M. (1989) Regularities in the growth of high technology regions. *Research Policy* 18: 135–53

Ettlie J. E. (1980) Manpower flows and the innovation process. *Management Science* 26: 1086–95

Ettlie J. E., Rubenstein A. H. (1987) Firm size and product innovation. *Journal of Product Innovation Management* 4: 89–108

Ettlinger N. (1988) American fertility and industrial restructuring: a possible link? *Growth and Change* 19 (3): 75–93

Ettlinger N. (1991) The roots of competitive advantage in California and Japan. *Annals of the Association of American Geographers* 81: 391–407

Ettlinger N. (1994) The localization of development in comparative perspective. *Economic Geography* 70: 144–66

Ettlinger N. (1995) Modes of corporate organization and the geography of development. *Papers in Regional Science* 71: 107–26

Ettlinger N., Patton W. (1996) Shared performance: the proactive diffusion of competitiveness and industrial and local development. *Annals of the Association of American Geographers* 86: 286–305

Evans P. B. (1995) *Embedded Autonomy: States and Industrial Transformation*. Princeton, Princeton University Press

Ewers H.-J., Wettmann R. W. (1980) Innovation-oriented regional policy. *Regional Studies* 14: 161–79

Fabayo J. A. (1996) Technological dependence in Africa: its nature, causes, consequences and policy derivatives. *Technovation* 16: 357–70

Fadem J. A. (1984) Automation and work design in the US: case studies of quality of working life impacts. In Warner M. (ed.) *Microprocessors, Manpower and Society*. New York, St Martin's Press: 294–310

Fagerberg J. (1988) International competitiveness. *Economic Journal* 98: 355–74

Fagerberg J. (1994) Technology and international differences in growth rates. *Journal of Economic Literature* 32: 1147–75

Fagerberg J. (1995) User-producer interaction, learning and comparative advantage. *Cambridge Journal of Economics* 19: 243–56

Falemo B. (1989) The firm's external persons: entrepreneurs or network actors? *Entrepreneurship and Regional Development* 1: 167–77

Falk W. W., Lyson T. A. (1988) *High Tech, Low Tech, No Tech*. Albany, State University of New York Press

Fall P. N. (1989) The informal sector in developing countries: understanding the organization and mechanisms for workable government policy encouragement. *Journal of Business Venturing* 4: 291–7

Fallows J. (1995) *Looking at the Sun: The Rise of the New East Asian Economic and Political System*. New York, Vintage

Fan C. C. (1995) Of belts and ladders: state policy and uneven regional development in Post-Mao China. *Annals of the Association of American Geographers* 85: 421–49

Farley M. (1993) Jockeying for position in the world after 1997. *Science* **262**: 360–1

Farness D. H. (1989) Detecting the economic base: new challenges. *International Regional Science Review* **12**: 319–28

Farrell C., Mandel M. J., Pennar K., Carey J., Hof R., Schiller Z. (1992) Industrial policy: call it what you will, the nation needs a plan to nurture growth. *Business Week* 6 April: 70–5

Farrell K. (1983) High tech highways. *Venture* **5** (9): 38–50

Farrell T. M. A. (1979) Do multinational corporations really transfer technology? In Thomas D. B., Wionczek M. S. (eds) *Integration of Science and Technology with Development*. New York, Pergamon: 69–78

Fass S. M. (1995) Fast food in development. *World Development* **23**: 1555–73

Faulkner W., Senker J., Velho L. (1995) *Knowledge Frontiers: Public Sector Research and Industrial Innovation in Biotechnology, Engineering Ceramics, and Parallel Computing*. Oxford, Clarendon Press

Fawkes S. D., Jacques J. K. (1987) Problems of adoption and adaptation of energy-conserving innovations in UK beverage and dairy industries. *Research Policy* **16**: 1–15

Fayez M. B. E. (1993) Zimbabwe. In Patel S. J. (ed.) *Technological Transformation in the Third World*, volume II: *Africa*. Aldershot, Avebury: 143–316

Feeser H. R., Willard G. E. (1988) Incubators and performance: a comparison of high and low growth high tech firms. In Kirchhoff B. A., Long W. A., McMullan W. E., Vesper K. H., Wetzel W. E. (eds) *Frontiers of Entrepreneurship Research 1988*. Wellesley, MA, Babson College, Center for Entrepreneurial Studies: 549–63

Feigenbaum A., Karnani A. (1991) Output flexibility – a competitive advantage for small firms. *Strategic Management Journal* **12**: 101–14

Feldman M. P. (1994) The university and economic development: the case of Johns Hopkins University and Baltimore. *Economic Development Quarterly* **8**: 67–76

Feldman M. P., Florida R. (1994) The geographic sources of innovation: technological infrastructure and product innovation in the United States. *Annals of the Association of American Geographers* **84**: 210–29

Felker G. B., Weiss C. (1995) An analytic framework for measuring technological development. In Simon D. F. (ed.) *The Emerging Technological Trajectory of the Pacific Rim*. New York, M. E. Sharpe: 385–400

Felsenstein D. (1994) University-related science parks: 'seedbeds' or 'enclaves' of innovation? *Technovation* **14**: 93–110

Felsenstein D. (1996) High technology firms and metropolitan locational choice in Israel: a look at the determinants. *Geografiska Annaler* **78B**: 43–58

Felsenstein D., Shachar A. (1988) Locational and organizational determinants of R&D employment in high technology firms. *Regional Studies* **22**: 477–86

Fenich G. G. (1994) An assessment of whether the convention center in New York is successful as a tool for economic development. *Economic Development Quarterly* **8**: 245–55

Ferguson C. H. (1990) Computers and the coming of the U.S. keiretsu. *Harvard Business Review* **68** (4): 55–70

Ferner A., Edwards P., Sisson K. (1995) Coming unstuck? In search of the 'corporate glue' in an international professional services firm. *Human Resource Management* **34**: 343–61

Ferraz J. C., Rush H., Miles I. (1992) *Development, Technology and Flexibility: Brazil Faces the Industrial Divide*. London, Routledge

Fialka J. J. (1996) Pentagon helps contractors pay merger costs with a plan opponents call 'payoffs for layoffs'. *Wall Street Journal* 22 July: A16

Fiet J. O. (1995) Reliance upon informants in the venture capital industry. *Journal of Business Venturing* 10: 195–223

Fischer M. M. (1990) The micro-electronic revolution and its impact on labour and employment. In Cappellin R., Nijkamp P. (eds) *The Spatial Impact of Technological Change.* Aldershot, Avebury: 43–74

Fischer M. M., Nijkamp P. (1988) The role of small firms for regional revitalization. *Annals of Regional Science* 22 (1): 28–42

Fisher A. G. B. (1933) Capital and the growth of knowledge. *Economic Journal* 43: 379–89

Fjellman S. M. (1992) *Vinyl Leaves: Walt Disney World and America.* Boulder, CO, Westview Press

Fladmoe-Lindquist K., Tallman S. (1994) Resource-based strategy and competitive advantage among multinationals. In Shrivastava P., Huff A. S., Dutton J. E. (eds) *Advances in Strategic Management,* volume 10A: *Resource-Based View of the Firm.* Greenwich, CT, JAI Press: 45–72

Flam F. (1992) Japan bids for US basic research. *Science* 258: 1428–30

Flamm K. (1988) *Targeting the Computer: Government Support and International Competition.* Washington, Brookings Institution

Flammang R. A. (1979) Economic growth and economic development: counterparts or competitors? *Economic Development and Cultural Change* 28: 47–61

Flammang R. A. (1990) Development and growth revisited. *Review of Regional Studies* 20 (1): 49–55

Fleck J. (1994) Learning by trying: the implementation of configurational technology. *Research Policy* 23: 637–52

Fleming S. C. (1991) Using technology for competitive advantage. *Research-Technology Management* 34 (5): 38–41

Fleury A. (1995) Quality and productivity in the competitive strategies of Brazilian industrial enterprises. *World Development* 23: 73–85

Flora C. B., Flora J. L. (1993) Entrepreneurial social infrastructure: a necessary ingredient. *Annals of the American Academy of Political and Social Science* 529: 48–58

Florida R. (1995) Technology policy for a global economy. *Issues in Science and Technology* 11 (3): 49–56

Florida R., Kenney M. (1988a) Venture capital-financed innovation and technological change in the USA. *Research Policy* 17: 119–37

Florida R., Kenney M. (1988b) Venture capital and high technology entrepreneurship. *Journal of Business Venturing* 3: 301–19

Florida R., Kenney M. (1988c) Venture capital, high technology and regional development. *Regional Studies* 22: 33–48

Florida R., Kenney M. (1990) *The Breakthrough Illusion: Corporate America's Failure to Move from Innovation to Mass Production.* New York, Basic Books

Florida R., Kenney M. (1994) The globalization of Japanese R&D: the economic geography of Japanese R&D investments in the United States. *Economic Geography* 70: 344–69

Florida R., Smith D. F. (1990) Venture capital, innovation, and economic development. *Economic Development Quarterly* 4: 345–60

Florida R., Smith D. F. (1993) Venture capital formation, investment, and regional industrialization. *Annals of the Association of American Geographers* 83: 434–51

Florio M. (1996) Large firms, entrepreneurship and regional development policy: 'growth poles' in the Mezzogiorno over 40 years. *Entrepreneurship and Regional Development* 8: 263–95

Flynn D. M. (1991) The critical relationship between venture capitalists and entrepreneurs: planning, decision-making, and control. *Small Business Economics* 3: 185–96

Flynn D. M. (1993) A critical exploration of sponsorship, infrastructure, and new organizations. *Small Business Economics* 5: 129–56

Flynn D. M. (1995) A preliminary examination of organizational and other factors affecting performance in new ventures: the view of venture capitalists. *Entrepreneurship and Regional Development* 7: 1–20

Flynn M. S., Cole D. E. (1988) The US automobile industry: technology and competitiveness. In Hicks D. A. (ed.) *Is New Technology Enough? Making and Remaking US Basic Industries.* Washington, American Enterprise Institute: 86–161

Flynn P. M. (1993) *Technology Life Cycles and Human Resources.* Lanham, MD, University Press of America

Foley A., Griffith B. (1992) Indigenous manufacturing enterprises in a peripheral economy and the single market: the case of the Republic of Ireland. *Regional Studies* 26: 375–86

Foley P. (1992) Local economic policy and job creation: a review of evaluation studies. *Urban Studies* 29: 557–98

Foley P., Hutchinson J., Herbane B., Tate G. (1996) The impact of Toyota on Derbyshire's local economy and labour market. *Tijdschrift voor Economische en Sociale Geografie* 87: 19–31

Foley P. D., Watts H. D., Wilson B. (1992) Introducing new process technology: implications for local employment policies. *Geoforum* 23: 61–72

Fong C. O. (1986) *Technological Leap: Malaysian Industry in Transition.* Oxford, Oxford University Press

Fong P. E., Hill H. (1992) Government policy, industrial development and the aircraft industry in Indonesia and Singapore. In van Liemt G. (ed.) *Industry on the Move: Causes and Consequences of International Relocation in the Manufacturing Industry.* Geneva, International Labour Office: 235–57

Fontes M., Coombs R. (1995) New technology-based firms and technology acquisition in Portugal: firms' adaptive responses to a less favourable environment. *Technovation* 15: 497–510

Foray D. (1991) The secrets of industry are in the air: industrial cooperation and the organizational dynamics of the innovative firm. *Research Policy* 20: 393–405

Foray D., Freeman C. (eds) (1993) *Technology and the Wealth of Nations: The Dynamics of Constructed Advantage.* London, Pinter

Foray D., Gibbons M., Ferné G. (1989) *Major R&D Programmes for Information Technology.* Paris, Organisation for Economic Co-operation and Development

Ford R., Suyker W. (1990) Industrial subsidies in the OECD countries. *OECD Economic Studies* 15: 37–81

Fornengo G. (1988) Manufacturing networks: telematics in the automotive industry. In Antonelli C. (ed.) *New Information Technology and Industrial Change: The Italian Case.* Dordrecht, Kluwer Academic: 33–56

Fornengo Pent G. (1992) Product differentiation and process innovation in the Italian clothing industry. In van Liemt G. (ed.) *Industry on the Move: Causes and Consequences of International Relocation in the Manufacturing Industry.* Geneva, International Labour Office: 209–33

Forsberg R. (ed.) (1994) *The Arms Production Dilemma: Contraction and Restraint in the World Combat Aircraft Industry.* Cambridge, MA, MIT Press

Forsberg R., Peach A., Reppy J. (1994) US airpower and aerospace industries in transition. In Forsberg R. (ed.) *The Arms Production Dilemma: Contraction and Restraint in the World Combat Aircraft Industry.* Cambridge, MA, MIT Press: 111–38

Forsyth D. J. C. (1990) *Technology Policy for Small Developing Countries.* New York, St Martin's Press

Fosler F. S. (1990) State strategies for business assistance. In Schmandt J., Wilson R. (eds) *Growth Policy in the Age of High Technology: The Role of Regions and States.* Boston, Unwin Hyman: 171–94

Fosler F. S. (1992) State economic policy: the emerging paradigm. *Economic Development Quarterly* 6: 3–13

Foster R. (1986) *Innovation: The Attacker's Advantage.* New York, Simon and Schuster

Foxall G., Johnston B. (1987) Strategies of user-initiated innovation. *Technovation* 6: 77–102

Fox Przeworski J. (1986) Changing intergovernmental relations and urban economic development. *Environment and Planning C: Government and Policy* 4: 423–38

Franke R., Chasin B. (1990) The Kerala experiment: development without growth. *Technology Review* 93 (3): 43–51

Franko L. G. (1996) The Japanese juggernaut rolls on. *Sloan Management Review* 37 (2): 103–9

Fransman M. (1984) Promoting technological capability in the capital goods sector: the case of Singapore. *Research Policy* 13: 33–54

Fransman M. (ed.) (1986) *Machinery and Economic Development.* New York, St Martin's Press

Fransman M. (1990) *The Market and Beyond: Cooperation and Competition in Information Technology Development in the Japanese System.* Cambridge, Cambridge University Press

Fransman M. (1994a) Information, knowledge, vision and theories of the firm. *Industrial and Corporate Change* 3: 713–57

Fransman M. (1994b) Knowledge segmentation – integration in theory and in Japanese companies. In Granstrand O. (ed.) *Economics of Technology.* Amsterdam, Elsevier: 165–87

Fransman M., King K. (eds) (1984) *Technological Capability in the Third World.* New York, St Martin's Press

Fransman M., Tanaka S. (1995) Government, globalisation, and universities in Japanese biotechnology. *Research Policy* 24: 13–49

Fredriksson C. G., Lindmark L. G. (1979) From firms to systems of firms: a study of interregional dependence in a dynamic society. In Hamilton F. E. I., Linge G. J. R. (eds) *Spatial Analysis, Industry and the Industrial Environment,* volume 1: *Industrial Systems.* London, John Wiley: 155–86

Freear J., Sohl J. E., Wetzel W. E. (1995) Angels: personal investors in the venture capital market. *Entrepreneurship and Regional Development* 7: 85–94

Freear J., Wetzel W. E. (1990) Who bankrolls high-tech entrepreneurs? *Journal of Business Venturing* 5: 77–89

Freedman A. (1983) New technology-based firms: critical location factors. In Hornaday J. A., Timmons J. A., Vesper K. H. (eds) *Frontiers of Entrepreneurship Research 1983.* Wellesley, MA: Babson College, Center for Entrepreneurial Studies: 478–94

Freeman C. (1982) *The Economics of Innovation,* second edition. Cambridge, MA, MIT Press

Freeman C. (1987) *Technology Policy and Economic Performance: Lessons from Japan.* London, Pinter

Freeman C. (1988) Technology gaps, international trade and the problems of smaller and less-developed economies. In Freeman C., Lundvall B.-A. (eds) *Small Countries*

Facing the Technological Revolution. London, Pinter: 67–84

Freeman C. (1994a) The economics of technical change. *Cambridge Journal of Economics* 18: 463–514

Freeman C. (1994b) Innovation and growth. In Dodgson M., Rothwell R. (eds) *The Handbook of Industrial Innovation.* Aldershot, Edward Elgar: 78–93

Freeman C. (1995a) Innovation in a new context. *STI Review* 15: 49–74

Freeman C. (1995b) The 'national system of innovation' in historical perspective. *Cambridge Journal of Economics* 19: 5–24

Freeman C., Hagedoorn J. (1994) Catching up or falling behind: patterns in international interfirm technology partnering. *World Development* 22: 771–80

Freeman C., Lundvall B.-A. (eds) (1988) *Small Countries Facing the Technological Revolution.* London, Pinter

Freeman C., Perez C. (1988) Structural crises of adjustment, business cycles and investment behaviour. In Dosi G., Freeman C., Nelson R., Silverberg G., Soete L. (eds) *Technical Change and Economic Theory.* London, Pinter: 38–66

Freeman R. B. (ed.) (1994) *Working under Different Rules.* New York, Russell Sage Foundation

Freeman R. B., Medoff J. L. (1984) *What Do Unions Do?* New York, Basic Books

Freundlich N. (1989) Spreading the risks of R&D. *Business Week* 16 June: 60–4

Frey D. N. (1989) Junk your 'linear' R&D! *Research-Technology Management* 32 (3): 7–8

Friar J., Horwitch M. (1986) The emergence of technology strategy: a new dimension of strategic management. In Horwitch M. (ed.) *Technology in the Modern Corporation: A Strategic Perspective.* Oxford, Pergamon: 50–85

Friedman D. (1988) *The Misunderstood Miracle: Industrial Development and Political Change in Japan.* Ithaca, NY, Cornell University Press

Friedmann J. (1966) *Regional Development Policy: A Case Study of Venezuela.* Cambridge, MA, MIT Press

Friedmann J. (1986) The world city hypothesis. *Development and Change* 17: 69–83

Friedmann J. (1995) Where we stand: a decade of world city research. In Knox P., Taylor P. J. (eds) *World Cities in a World-System.* New York, Oxford University Press: 21–47

Friedmann J., Wolff G. (1982) World city formation: an agenda for research and action. *International Journal of Urban and Regional Research* 6: 309–43

Friedmann J. J. (1995) The effects of industrial structure and resources upon the distribution of fast-growing small firms among US urbanised areas. *Urban Studies* 32: 863–83

Frischtak C. R. (1986) Brazil. In Rushing F. W., Brown C. G. (eds) *National Policies for Developing High Technology Industries: International Comparisons.* Boulder, CO, Westview Press: 31–69

Frischtak C. R. (1994) Learning and technical progress in the commuter aircraft industry: an analysis of Embraer's experience. *Research Policy* 23: 601–12

Frisk T. (1988) The future state of information technology: a technological assessment. In Schütte H. (ed.) *Strategic Issues in Information Technology.* Maidenhead, Pergamon Infotech: 15–26

Fröbel F., Heinrichs J., Kreye O. (1980) *The New International Division of Labour.* Cambridge, Cambridge University Press

Fröhlich H.-P. (1989) International competitiveness: alternative macroeconomic strategies and changing perceptions in recent years. In Francis A., Tharakan P. K. M. (eds) *The Competitiveness of European Industry.* London, Routledge: 21–40

Frosch R. A. (1994) Industrial ecology: minimizing the impact of industrial waste.

Physics Today November: 63–8

Fruin M. (1994) *The Japanese Enterprise System: Competitive Strategies and Cooperative Structures.* Oxford, Clarendon Press

Fruin W. M. (1992) *The Japanese Enterprise System: Competitive Strategies and Cooperative Structures.* Oxford, Clarendon Press

Fuchs R. J., Demko G. J. (1979) Geographic inequality under socialism. *Annals of the Association of American Geographers* **69**: 304–18

Fuenzalida E. E. (1979) The problem of technological innovation in Latin America. In Villamil J. J. (ed.) *Transnational Capitalism and National Development.* Atlantic Highlands, NJ, Humanities Press: 115–27

Fujita M. (1995a) Small and medium-sized transnational corporations: trends and patterns of foreign direct investment. *Small Business Economics* 7: 183–204

Fujita M. (1995b) Small and medium-sized transnational corporations: salient features. *Small Business Economics* 7: 251–71

Fukuyama F. (1995) *Trust: The Social Virtues and the Creation of Prosperity.* New York, Free Press

Fuller R. A. (1983) Decentralized R&D organization. In Brown J. K., Elvers L. M. (eds) *Research and Development: Key Issues for Management.* Report 842. New York, The Conference Board: 34–7

Furukawa K., Teramoto Y., Kanda M. (1990) Network organization for inter-firm R&D activities: experiences of Japanese small businesses. *International Journal of Technology Management* **5**: 27–41

Fusfeld H. I. (1986) *The Technical Enterprise: Present and Future Patterns.* Cambridge, MA, Ballinger

Fusfeld H. I. (1994) *Industry's Future: Changing Patterns of Industrial Research.* Washington, American Chemical Society

Fusfeld H. I., Haklisch C. S. (1987) Collaborative industrial research in the US. *Technovation* **5**: 305–15

Galbraith J. R., Nathanson D. A. (1978) *Strategy Implementation: The Role of Structure and Process.* St Paul, MN, West

Galison P., Hevly B. (eds) (1992) *Big Science: The Growth of Large-Scale Research.* Stanford, Stanford University Press

Galuszka P., Marbach W. D., Brady R., Javetski B., Schares G. (1988) Soviet technology. *Business Week* 7 November: 68–78

Ganitsky J., Watzke G. E. (1990) Implications of different time perspectives for human resource management in international joint ventures. *Management International Review* **30** (special issue): 37–51

Gansler J. S. (1980) *The Defense Industry.* Cambridge, MA, MIT Press

Gansler J. S. (1995) *Defense Conversion: Transforming the Arsenal of Democracy.* Cambridge, MA, MIT Press

Ganz C. (1980) Linkages between knowledge, diffusion, and utilization. *Knowledge: Creation, Diffusion, Utilization* 1: 591–612

GAO (General Accounting Office) (1995) *US–Japan Cooperative Development: Progress on the FS-X Enhances Japanese Aerospace Capabilities.* Gaithersburg, MD, US General Accounting Office

Garnsey E., Cannon-Brookes A. (1993) The 'Cambridge Phenomenon' revisited: aggregate change among Cambridge high-technology companies since 1985. *Entrepreneurship and Regional Development* **5**: 179–207

Garofoli G. (1992) New firm formation and local development: the Italian experience. *Entrepreneurship and Regional Development* 4: 101–25

Garrette B., Quelin B. (1994) An empirical study of hybrid forms of governance structure: the case of the telecommunications equipment industry. *Research Policy* 23: 395–412

Garvin D. A. (1987) Competing on the eight dimensions of quality. *Harvard Business Review* 65 (6): 101–9

Gaston R. J. (1989) The scale of informal capital markets. *Small Business Economics* 1: 223–30

Geisler E., Rubenstein A. H. (1989) University-industry relations: a review of major issues. In Link A. N., Tassey G. (eds) *Cooperative Research and Development: The Industry–University–Government Relationship*. Boston, Kluwer Academic: 43–62

Gelsing L. (1992) Innovation and the development of industrial networks. In Lundvall B.-A. (ed.) *National Systems of Innovation*. London, Pinter: 116–28

Gemmell N. (1996) Evaluating the impacts of human capital stocks and accumulation on economic growth: some new evidence. *Oxford Bulletin of Economics and Statistics* 58: 9–28

Geneau de Lamarlière I. (1991) The determinants of the location of the semiconductor industry. In Benko G., Dunford M. (eds) *Industrial Change and Regional Development*. London, Belhaven: 171–89

George V. P. (1995) Globalization through interfirm cooperation: technological anchors and temporal nature of alliances across geographical boundaries. *International Journal of Technology Management* 10: 131–45

Gereffi G. (1994) The organization of buyer-driven global commodity chains: how US retailers shape overseas production networks. In Gereffi G., Korzeniewicz M. (eds) *Commodity Chains and Global Capitalism*. Westport, CT, Praeger: 95–122

Gereffi G., Korzeniewicz M. (1990) Commodity chains and footwear exports in the semiperiphery. In Martin W. G. (ed.) *Semiperipheral States in the World-Economy*. Westport, CT, Greenwood Press: 45–68

Gereffi G., Korzeniewicz M. (eds) (1994) *Commodity Chains and Global Capitalism*. Westport, CT, Praeger

Gerking S. (1994) Measuring productivity growth in US regions: a survey. *International Regional Science Review* 16: 155–85

Gerking S. D., Isserman A. M. (1981) Bifurcation and the time pattern of impacts in the economic base model. *Journal of Regional Science* 21: 451–67

Gerlach K., Wagner J. (1994) Regional differences in small firm entry in manufacturing industries: Lower Saxony, 1979–1991. *Entrepreneurship and Regional Development* 6: 63–80

Germidis D. (ed.) (1977) *Transfer of Technology by Multinational Corporations*. Paris: Organisation for Economic Co-operation and Development

Germidis D. (ed.) (1980) *International Subcontracting: A New Form of Investment*. Paris, Organisation for Economic Co-operation and Development

Geroski P., Machin S., Van Reenen J. (1993) The profitability of innovating firms. *Rand Journal of Economics* 24: 198–211

Gershuny J. I., Miles I. D. (1983) *The New Service Economy*. London, Frances Pinter

Gerstenfeld A., Wortzel L. H. (1977) Strategies for innovation in developing countries. *Sloan Management Review* 19 (1): 57–68

Gertler M. S. (1984) Regional capital theory. *Progress in Human Geography* 8: 50–81

Gertler M. S. (1986) Regional dynamics of manufacturing and non-manufacturing investment in Canada. *Regional Studies* 20: 523–34

Gertler M. S. (1988a) Some problems of time in economic geography. *Environment and Planning A* 20: 151–64

Gertler M. S. (1988b) The limits to flexibility: comments on the post-Fordist vision of production and its geography. *Transactions, Institute of British Geographers* NS **13**: 419–32

Gertler M. S. (1992) Flexibility revisited: districts, nation-states, and the forces of production. *Transactions, Institute of British Geographers* NS **17**: 259–78

Gertler M. S. (1993) Implementing advanced manufacturing technologies in mature industrial regions: towards a social model of technology production. *Regional Studies* **27**: 665–80

Gertler M. S. (1995) 'Being there': proximity, organization, and culture in the development and adoption of advanced manufacturing technologies. *Economic Geography* **71**: 1–26

Gertler N., Ehrenfeld J. R. (1996) A down-to-earth approach to clean production. *Technology Review* **99** (2): 48–54

Gerwin D. (1989) Manufacturing flexibility in the CAM era. *Business Horizons* **32** (1): 78–84

Gerwin D., Guild P. (1994) Redefining the new product introduction process. *International Journal of Technology Management* **9**: 678–90

Ghali M., Akiyama M., Fujiwara J. (1981) Models of regional growth: an empirical evaluation. *Regional Science and Urban Economics* **11**: 175–90

Gibb A. A. (1990) Entrepreneurship and intrapreneurship – exploring the differences. In Donckels R., Miettinen A. (eds) *New Findings and Perspectives in Entrepreneurship.* Aldershot, Avebury: 33–67

Gibb A. A. (1993) Key factors in the design of policy support for the small and medium enterprise (SME) development process: an overview. *Entrepreneurship and Regional Development* **5**: 1–24

Gibb J. M. (ed.) (1985) *Science Parks and Innovation Centres: Their Economic and Social Impact.* Amsterdam, Elsevier

Gibbons M., Limoges C., Nowotny H., Schwartzman S., Scott P., Troiw M. (1994) *The New Production of Knowledge.* London, Sage

Gibbs D. (1991) Venture capital and regional development: the operation of the venture capital industry in Manchester. *Tijdschrift voor Economische en Sociale Geografie* **82**: 242–53

Gibbs D. C. (1987) Technology and the clothing industry. *Area* **19**: 313–20

Gibbs D. C. (1988) Restructuring in the Manchester clothing industry: technical change and interrelationships between manufacturers and retailers. *Environment and Planning A* **20**: 1219–33

Gibbs D. C. (1996) European environmental policy: the implications for local economic development. *Regional Studies* **30**: 90–2

Gibbs D. C., Alderman N., Oakey R. P., Thwaites A. T. (1985) *The Location of Research and Development in Great Britain.* Newcastle-upon-Tyne, University of Newcastle, Center for Urban and Regional Development Studies

Gibbs D. C., Edwards A. (1985) The diffusion of new production innovations in British industry. In Thwaites A. T., Oakey R. P. (eds) *The Regional Impact of Technological Change.* London, Frances Pinter: 132–63

Gibbs D. C., Healey M. (1995) Local government, environmental policy and economic development. In Taylor M. J. (ed.) *Environmental Change: Industry, Power and Policy.* Aldershot, Avebury: 151–67

Gibson L. J. (1993) The potential for tourism development in nonmetropolitan areas. In Barkley D. L. (ed.) *Economic Adaptation: Alternatives for Nonmetropolitan Areas.* Boulder, CO, Westview Press: 145–64

Gibson L. J., Worden M. A. (1981) Estimating the economic base multiplier: a test of alternative procedures. *Economic Geography* 57: 146–59

Gilbert A. (1988) The new regional geography in English and French-speaking countries. *Progress in Human Geography* 12: 208–28

Gilbert A. G., Goodman D. E. (1976) Regional income disparities and economic development: a critique. In Gilbert A. G. (ed.) *Development Planning and Spatial Structure*. New York, John Wiley: 113–41

Gillespie A. E., Goddard J. B., Hepworth M. E., Williams H. (1989) Information and communications technology and regional development: an information economy perspective. *STI Review* 5: 85–111

Gillespie A., Howells J., Williams H., Thwaites A. (1987) Competition, internationalisation and the regions: the example of information technology production industries in Europe. In Breheny M. J., McQuaid R. W. (eds) *The Development of High Technology Industries: An International Survey*. London, Croom Helm: 113–42

Gillespie A., Williams H. (1988) Telecommunications and the reconstruction of regional comparative advantage. *Environment and Planning A* 20: 1311–21

Gillis W. R. (1987) Can service-producing industries provide a catalyst for regional economic growth? *Economic Development Quarterly* 1: 249–56

Gilmour J. M. (1975) The dynamics of spatial change in the export region. In Collins L., Walker D. F. (eds) *Locational Dynamics of Manufacturing Activity*. New York, John Wiley: 59–82

Gittell R. J., Flynn P. M. (1995) The Lowell high-tech success story: what went wrong? *New England Economic Review* March/April: 57–70

Gittell R. J., Kaufman A. (1996) State government efforts in industrial modernization: using theory to guide practice. *Regional Studies* 30: 477–92

Glasmeier A. K. (1988a) Factors governing the development of high tech industry agglomerations: a tale of three cities. *Regional Studies* 22: 287–301

Glasmeier A. K. (1988b) The Japanese Technopolis programme: high tech development strategy or industrial policy in disguise? *International Journal of Urban and Regional Research* 12: 268–84

Glasmeier A. (1991a) Technological discontinuities and flexible production networks: the case of Switzerland and the world watch industry. *Research Policy* 20: 469–85

Glasmeier A. K. (1991b) *The High-Tech Potential: Economic Development in Rural America*. Piscataway, NJ, Center for Urban Policy Research

Glasmeier A. (1994) Flexibility and adjustment: the Hong Kong watch industry and global change. *Growth and Change* 25: 223–46

Glasmeier A., Howland M. (1994) Service-led rural development: definitions, theories, and empirical evidence. *International Regional Science Review* 16: 197–229

Glasmeier A. K., Howland M. (1995) *From Combines to Computers: Rural Services and Development in the Age of Information Technology*. Albany, State University of New York Press

Glasmeier A. K., McCluskey R. E. (1987) US auto parts production: an analysis of the organization and location of a changing industry. *Economic Geography* 63: 142–59

Glasmeier A., Sugiura N. (1991) Japan's manufacturing system: small business, subcontracting and regional complex formation. *International Journal of Urban and Regional Research* 15: 395–414

Glasson J., van der Wee D., Barrett B. (1988) A local income and employment multiplier analysis of a proposed nuclear power station development at Hinkley Point in Somerset. *Urban Studies* 25: 248–61

Gleckman H., Carey J., Mitchell R., Smart T., Roush C. (1993) The technology payoff. *Business Week* 14 June: 57–79

Glickman N. J. (1971) An econometric model of the Philadelphia region. *Journal of Regional Science* 11: 15–32

Glickman N. J. (1977) *Econometric Analysis of Regional Systems*. New York, Academic Press

Gober-Myers P. (1978) Employment-motivated migration and economic growth in post-industrial market economies. *Progress in Human Geography* 2: 207–29

Goddard J., Gillespie A. (1988) Advanced telecommunications development and regional economic development. In Giaoutzi M., Nijkamp P. (eds) *Informatics and Regional Development*. Aldershot, Avebury: 121–46

Goddard J., Thwaites A., Gibbs D. (1986) The regional dimension to technological change in Great Britain. In Amin A., Goddard J. B. (eds) *Technological Change, Industrial Restructuring and Regional Development*. London, Allen and Unwin: 140–56

Gold B. (1979) *Productivity, Technology, and Capital*. Lexington MA, Lexington Books

Gold B. (1984) Integrating product innovation and market development to strengthen long-term planning. *Journal of Product Innovation Management* 1: 173–81

Gold J. R., Ward S. V. (eds) (1994) *Place Promotion: The Use of Publicity and Marketing to Sell Towns and Regions*. Chichester, John Wiley

Goldfarb R. S., Yezer A. M. J. (1976) Evaluating alternative theories of intercity and interregional wage differentials. *Journal of Regional Science* 16: 345–63

Goldfarb R. S., Yezer A. M. J. (1987) Interregional wage differential dynamics. *Papers of the Regional Science Association* 62: 45–56

Goldfrank W. L. (1994) Fresh demand: the consumption of Chilean produce in the United States. In Gereffi G., Korzeniewicz M. (eds) *Commodity Chains and Global Capitalism*. Westport, CT, Praeger: 267–79

Goldhar J. (1986) In the factory of the future, innovation *is* productivity. *Research Management* 29 (2): 26–33

Goldhar J. D., Jelinek A. (1983) Plan for economies of *scope*. *Harvard Business Review* 61 (6): 141–8

Goldhar J. D., Jelinek M., Schlie T. W. (1991) Flexibility and competitive advantage – manufacturing becomes a service business. *International Journal of Technology Management* 6: 243–59

Goldhar J. D., Lei D. (1994) Organizing and managing the CIM/FMS firm for maximum competitive advantage. *International Journal of Technology Management* 9: 709–32

Goldman A. (1982) Short product life cycles: implications for the marketing activities of small high-technology companies. *R&D Management* 12 (2): 81–9

Goldman A. (1993) Agricultural innovation in three areas of Kenya: neo-Boserupian theories and regional characterization. *Economic Geography* 69: 44–71

Goldman S. L., Nagel R. N., Preiss K. (1995) *Agile Competitors and Virtual Organizations*. New York, Van Nostrand Reinhold

Goldstein H. A., Luger M. I. (1990) Science/research parks and regional development theory. *Economic Development Quarterly* 4: 64–78

Gomory R. E. (1989) From the 'ladder of science' to the product development cycle. *Harvard Business Review* 67 (6): 99–105

Goodman E., Bamford J., Saynor P. (eds) (1989) *Small Firms and Industrial Districts in Italy*. London, Routledge

Goodman J. P., Meany J. W., Pate L. E. (1992) The government as entrepreneur: industrial development and the creation of new ventures. In Sexton D. L., Kasarda J. D.

(eds) *The State of the Art of Entrepreneurship*. Boston, PWS-Kent: 68–85

Goodman R. (1979) *The Last Entrepreneurs*. New York, Simon and Schuster

Gordon I. (1995) Migration in a segmented labour market. *Transactions, Institute of British Geographers* NS **20**: 139–55

Gore C. (1984) *Regions in Question: Space, Development Theory and Regional Policy*. London, Methuen

Gorman M., Sahlman W. A. (1989) What do venture capitalists do? *Journal of Business Venturing* **4**: 231–48

Goto A., Wakasugi R. (1988) Technology policy. In Komiya R., Okuno M., Suzumura K. (eds) *Industrial Policy of Japan*. Tokyo, Academic Press: 183–204

Gottlieb P. D. (1994) Amenities as an economic development tool: Is there enough evidence? *Economic Development Quarterly* **8**: 270–85

Goux D., Maurin E. (1996) Changes in the demand for skilled labour in France, 1970–93. *STI Review* **18**: 125–61

Gover J. (1995) Corporate management of R&D – lessons for the US government. *Research-Technology Management* **38** (2): 27–36

Grabher G. (1989) Regional innovation by networking: the case of southern Lower Austria. *Entrepreneurship and Regional Development* **1**: 141–6

Grabher G. (1993) The weakness of strong ties: the lock-in of regional development in the Ruhr area. In Grabher G. (ed.) *The Embedded Firm: On the Socioeconomics of Industrial Networks*. London, Routledge: 255–77

Grabowski H., Vernon J. (1994) Innovation and structural change in pharmaceuticals and biotechnology. *Industrial and Corporate Change* **3**: 451–89

Graham C. P. (1990) Technology and Third World defense manufacturing: the Brazilian firm Engesa. *Defense Analysis* **6**: 367–83

Graham E. M. (1995) Competition policy and the new trade agenda. In OECD. *New Dimensions of Market Access in a Globalising World*. Paris, Organisation for Economic Co-operation and Development: 105–18

Graham J., Gibson K., Horvath R., Shakow D. M. (1988) Restructuring in US manufacturing: the decline of monopoly capitalism. *Annals of the Association of American Geographers* **78**: 473–90

Graham M. B. W. (1985) Industrial research in the age of big science. In Rosenbloom R. S. (ed.) *Research on Technological Innovation, Management, and Policy*, volume 2. Greenwich, CT, JAI Press: 47–79

Graham M. B. W. (1986) Corporate research and development: the latest transformation. In Horwitch M. (ed.) *Technology in the Modern Corporation: A Strategic Perspective*. Oxford, Pergamon: 86–102

Granovetter M. (1985) Economic action and social structure: the problem of embeddedness. *American Journal of Sociology* **91**: 481–510

Granstrand O., Håkanson L., Sjölander S. (1993) Internationalization of R&D – a survey of some recent research. *Research Policy* **22**: 413–30

Granstrand O., Oskarsson C., Sjöberg N., Sjölander S. (1990) Business strategies for new technologies. In Deiaco E., Hörnell E., Vickery G. (eds) *Technology and Investment: Critical Issues for the 1990s*. London, Pinter: 64–92

Granstrand O., Sjölander S. (1990) Managing innovation in multi-technology corporations. *Research Policy* **19**: 35–60

Grant R., Lyons D. (1990) The Republic of Ireland in the world-economy: an exploration of dynamics in the semiperiphery. In Martin W. G. (ed.) *Semiperipheral States in the World-Economy*. Westport, CT, Greenwood Press: 125–39

Greenwood M. J. (1975) Research on internal migration in the United States: a survey.

Journal of Economic Literature 13: 397–433

Greenwood M. J. (1985) Human migration: theory, models, and empirical studies. *Journal of Regional Science* 25: 521–44

Greenwood M. J. (1994) Potential channels of immigrant influence on the economy of the receiving country. *Papers in Regional Science* 73: 211–40

Greenwood M. J., Hunt G. L. (1984) Econometrically accounting for identities and restrictions in models of interregional migration. *Regional Science and Urban Economics* 14: 113–28

Greis N. P., Dibner M. D., Bean A. S. (1995) External partnering as a response to innovation barriers and global competition in biotechnology. *Research Policy* 24: 609–30

Griffin A., Gleason G., Preiss R., Shevenaugh D. (1995) Best practice for customer satisfaction in manufacturing firms. *Sloan Management Review* 36 (2): 87–98

Griffin K. (1978) *International Inequality and National Poverty*. London, Macmillan

Griliches Z. (ed.) (1984) *R&D, Patents, and Productivity*. Chicago, University of Chicago Press

Grimes S. (1993) Exploring the potential of telecommunications: perspectives from the European periphery. In Bakis H., Abler R., Roche E. M. (eds) *Corporate Networks, Telecommunications and Interdependence*. London, Belhaven: 31–47

Grimond J. (1993) Under construction: a survey of Latin America. *The Economist* 13 November

Gringeri C. E. (1994a) Assembling 'genuine GM parts': rural homeworkers and economic development. *Economic Development Quarterly* 8: 147–57

Gringeri C. E. (1994b) *Getting By: Women Homeworkers and Rural Economic Development*. Lawrence, University Press of Kansas

Gripaios P., Bishop P., Gripaios R., Herbert C. (1989) High technology industry in a peripheral area: the case of Plymouth. *Regional Studies* 23: 151–7

Gripaios P., Mangles T. (1993) An analysis of European super regions. *Regional Studies* 27: 745–50

Groenewegen J. (1993) The Japanese group. In Groenewegen J. (ed.) *Dynamics of the Firm: Strategies of Pricing and Organisation*. Aldershot, Edward Elgar: 96–113

Gros-Pietro G. M., Rolfo S. (1989) Flexible automation and firm size: some empirical evidence on the Italian case. *Technovation* 9: 493–503

Gross N. (1989) MITI: the sugar daddy to end all sugar daddies. *Business Week* 23 October: 112

Grossberg A. J. (1982) Metropolitan industrial mix and cyclical employment stability. *Regional Science Perspectives* 12 (2): 13–25

Grossman G. M., Helpman E. (1991) *Innovation and Growth in the Global Economy*. Cambridge, MA, MIT Press

Grotz R., Braun B. (1993) Networks, milieux and individual firm strategies: empirical evidence of an innovative SME environment. *Geografiska Annaler* 75B: 149–62

Grubel H. G. (1987) All traded services are embodied in materials or people. *The World Economy* 10: 319–330

Grübler A. (1990) *The Rise and Fall of Infrastructures: Dynamics of Evolution and Technological Change in Transport*. Heidelberg, Physica-Verlag

Grunwald J. (1985) The assembly industry in Mexico. In Grunwald J., Flamm K. (eds) *The Global Factory*. Washington, Brookings Institution: 137–79

Grunwald J., Flamm K. (eds) (1985) *The Global Factory: Foreign Assembly and International Trade*. Washington, Brookings Institution

Grupp H. (1996) Foresight in science and technology: selected methodologies and recent activities in Germany. *STI Review* **17**: 71–99

Gu S. (1996) The emergence of new technology enterprises in China: a study of endogenous capability building via restructuring. *Journal of Development Studies* **32**: 475–505

Guéhenno J.-M. (Elliott V., trans.) (1995) *The End of the Nation-State.* Minneapolis, University of Minnesota Press

Guelle F. (1993) Risks and opportunities from Japanese direct investments: the French case. In Humbert M. (ed.) *The Impact of Globalisation on Europe's Firms and Industries.* London, Pinter: 135–40

Guellec D. (1996) Knowledge, skills and growth: some economic issues. *STI Review* **18**: 17–38

Guerrieri P., Tylecote A. (1994) National competitive advantages and microeconomic behaviour. *Economics of Innovation and New Technology* **3**: 49–76

Guile B. R., Brooks H. (eds) (1987) *Technology and Global Industry: Companies and Nations in the World Economy.* Washington, National Academy Press

Guile B. R., Quinn J. B. (eds) (1988) *Technology in Services.* Washington, National Academy Press

Gulowsen J. (1988) Skills, options and unions: united and strong or divided and weak? In Hyman R., Streeck W. (eds) *New Technology and Industrial Relations.* Oxford, Basil Blackwell: 160–73

Gupta A. (1986) India. In Rushing F. W., Brown C. G. (eds) *National Policies for Developing High Technology Industries: International Comparisons.* Boulder, CO, Westview Press: 89–110

Gupta A. K., Sapienza H. J. (1992) Determinants of venture capital firms' preferences regarding the industry diversity and geographic scope of their investments. *Journal of Business Venturing* 7: 347–62

Gustavsson P., Melin L., Macdonald S. (1994) Learning to glocalize. In Shrivastana P., Huff A. S., Dutton J. E. (eds) *Advances in Strategic Management*, volume 10B: *Interorganizational Relations and International Strategies.* Greenwich, CT, JAI Press: 255–88

Gwynne P. (1995) Managing 'multidomestic' R&D at ABB. *Research-Technology Management* **38** (1): 30–3

Haar N. E., Starr J., MacMillan I. C. (1988) Informal risk capital investors: investment patterns on the east coast of the USA. *Journal of Business Venturing* **3**: 11–29

Hack G. D. (1992) Telecommunications: making the site selection connection. *Area Development* **27** (4): 69–71

Hagedoorn J. (1995) Strategic technology partnering in the 1980s: trends, networks and corporate patterns in non-core technologies. *Research Policy* 24: 207–31

Hagedoorn J., Schankenraad J. (1990) Inter-firm partnerships and co-operative strategies in core technologies. In Freeman C., Soete L. (eds) *New Explorations in the Economics of Technical Change.* London, Pinter: 3–37

Hagedoorn J., Schankenraad J. (1992) Leading companies and networks of strategic alliances in information technologies. *Research Policy* 21: 163–90

Hagey M. J., Malecki E. J. (1986) Linkages in high technology industries: a Florida case study. *Environment and Planning A* 18: 1477–98

Haggard S., Cheng T.-J. (1987) State and foreign capital in East Asian NICs. In Deyo F. C. (ed.) *The Political Economy of the New Asian Industrialism.* Ithaca, NY, Cornell University Press: 84–135

Hagström P. (1992) Inside the 'wired' MNC. In Antonelli C. (ed.) *The Economics of Information Networks.* Amsterdam, North-Holland: 325–45

Hahn F. H., Matthews R. C. O. (1964) The theory of economic growth: a survey. *Economic Journal* 74: 779–902

Haider D. (1986) Economic development: changing practices in a changing US economy. *Environment and Planning C: Government and Policy* 4: 451–69

Haider D. (1992) Place wars: new realities of the 1990s. *Economic Development Quarterly* 6: 127–34

Hakam A. N., Chang Z.-Y. (1988) Patterns of technology transfer in Singapore: the case of the electronics and computer industry. *International Journal of Technology Management* 3: 181–8

Håkanson L. (1979) Towards a theory of location and corporate growth. In Hamilton F. E. I., Linge G. J. R. (eds) *Spatial Analysis, Industry and the Industrial Environment*, volume 1: *Industrial Systems*. London, John Wiley: 115–38

Håkanson L. (1990) International decentralization of R&D – the organizational challenges. In Bartlett C. A., Doz Y., Hedlund G. (eds) *Managing the Global Firm*. London, Routledge: 256–78

Håkanson L., Nobel R. (1993a) Foreign research and development in Swedish multinationals. *Research Policy* 22: 373–96

Håkanson L., Nobel R. (1993b) Determinants of foreign R&D in Swedish multinationals. *Research Policy* 22: 397–411

Håkansson H. (ed.) (1987) *Industrial Technological Development: A Network Approach*. London, Croom Helm

Håkansson H. (1989) *Corporate Technological Behaviour: Co-operation and Networks*. London, Routledge

Håkansson H. (1992) Evolution processes in industrial networks. In Axelsson B., Easton G. (eds) *Industrial Networks: A New View of Reality*. London, Routledge: 129–43

Håkansson H., Laage-Hellman J. (1984) Developing a network R&D strategy. *Journal of Product Innovation Management* 1: 224–37

Hall C. M. (1989) The definition and analysis of hallmark tourist events. *GeoJournal* 19: 263–8

Hall P. (1987) The anatomy of job creation: nations, regions and cities in the 1960s and 1970s. *Regional Studies* 21: 95–106

Hall P., Breheny M., McQuaid R., Hart D. (1987) *Western Sunrise: The Genesis and Growth of Britain's Major High Tech Corridor*. London, Allen and Unwin

Hall P., Markusen A. (eds) (1985) *Silicon Landscapes*. Boston, Allen and Unwin

Hall P., Preston P. (1988) *The Carrier Wave: New Information Technology and the Geography of Innovation 1846–2003*. London, Unwin Hyman

Hall T., Hubbard P. (1996) The entrepreneurial city: new urban politics, new urban geographies? *Progress in Human Geography* 20: 153–74

Hallsworth A. G. (1996) Short-termism and economic restructuring in Britain. *Economic Geography* 72: 23–37

Hallwood C. P. (1988) Host regions and the globalization of the offshore oil supply industry: the case of Aberdeen. *International Regional Science Review* 11: 155–66

Hambrecht W. R. (1984) Venture capital and the growth of Silicon Valley. *California Management Review* 26 (2): 74–82

Hamel G., Prahalad C. K. (1985) Do you really have a global strategy? *Harvard Business Review* 61 (4): 139–48

Hamel G., Prahalad C. K. (1994) *Competing for the Future*. Boston, Harvard Business School Press

Hamfelt C., Lindberg A. K. (1987) Technological development and the individual's contact network. In Håkansson H. (ed.) *Industrial Technological Development: A Network Approach.* London, Croom Helm: 177–209

Hamilton D. P. (1992) Industry steps in to fill the gap in basic research. *Science* **258**: 570–1

Hamilton D. P. (1995) China, with foreign partners' help, becomes a budding technology giant. *Wall Street Journal* 7 December: A11

Hamilton F. E. I., Linge G. J. R. (1983) Regional economies and industrial systems. In Hamilton F. E. I., Linge G. J. R. (eds) *Spatial Analysis, Industry and the Industrial Environment,* volume 3: *Regional Economies and Industrial Systems.* London, John Wiley: 1–39

Hamilton W. F. (1986) Corporate strategies for managing emerging technologies. In Horwitch M. (ed.) *Technology in the Modern Corporation: A Strategic Perspective.* Oxford, Pergamon: 103–18

Hammack D. C., Young D. R. (eds) (1993) *Nonprofit Organizations in a Market Economy: Understanding New Roles, Issues, and Trends.* San Francisco, Jossey-Bass

Hammer M., Mangurian G. E. (1987) The changing value of communications technology. *Sloan Management Review* **28** (2): 65–71

Hammermesh R. G., Silk S. B. (1979) How to compete in stagnant industries. *Harvard Business Review* **57** (5): 161–8

Hammonds K. H., Sager I. (1995) The town IBM left behind. *Business Week* 11 September: 104–13

Hampden-Turner C., Trompenaars A. (1993) *The Seven Cultures of Capitalism.* New York, Currency Doubleday

Hanna N. (1991) Informatics and the developing world. *Finance and Development* **28** (4): 45–7

Hansen N. M. (1973) *Location Preferences, Migration, and Regional Growth.* New York, Praeger

Hansen N. (1987) The evolution of the French regional economy and French regional theory. *Review of Regional Studies* **17** (3): 5–13

Hansen N. M. (1988) Economic development and regional heterogeneity: a reconsideration of regional policy for the United States. *Economic Development Quarterly* **2**: 107–18

Hansen N. (1990) Innovative regional milieux, small firms, and regional development in Mediterranean France. *Annals of Regional Science* **24**: 107–23

Hansen N. (1991) Factories in Danish fields: How high-wage, flexible production has succeeded in peripheral Jutland. *International Regional Science Review* **14**: 109–32 ·

Hansen N. (1992) Competition, trust, and reciprocity in the development of innovative regional milieux. *Papers in Regional Science* **71**: 95–105

Hansen N. (1993) Producer services, productivity, and metropolitan income. *Review of Regional Studies* **23** (3): 255–64

Hansen N. (1994) The strategic role of producer services in regional development. *International Regional Science Review* **16**: 187–96

Hansen N. (1995) Addressing regional disparity and equity objectives through regional policies: a sceptical perspective. *Papers in Regional Science* **74**: 89–104

Hanson S., Pratt G. (1992) Dynamic dependencies: a geographic investigation of local labor markets. *Economic Geography* **68**: 373–405

Harabi N. (1995) Appropriability of technical innovations: an empirical analysis. *Research Policy* **24**: 981–92

Harber A. D., Samson D. A. (1989) Japanese management practices: an integrative framework. *International Journal of Technology Management* **4**: 283–303

Harbor B. (1991) Technological divergence in the development of military and civil communications systems: the case of Ptarmigan and System X. *Defense Analysis* 7 (4): 81–96

Hardill I., Fletcher D., Montagné-Villette S. (1995) Small firms' 'distinctive capabilities' and the socioeconomic milieu: findings from case studies in Le Choletais (France) and the East Midlands (UK). *Entrepreneurship and Regional Development* 7: 167–86

Harding C. F. (1989) Location choices for research labs: a case study approach. *Economic Development Quarterly* 3: 223–34

Hardy S., Hart M., Albrechts L., Katos A. (eds) (1995) *An Enlarged Europe: Regions in Competition?* London, Jessica Kingsley

Hardy S., Lloyd G. (1994) An impossible dream? Sustainable regional economic and environmental development. *Regional Studies* 28: 773–80

Hargrave A. (1985) *Silicon Glen: Reality or Illusion?* Edinburgh, Mainstream Publishing

Harper M. (1984) *Small Business in the Third World.* Chichester, John Wiley

Harper R. A. (1982) Metropolitan areas as transactional centers. In Christian C., Harper R. A. (eds) *Modern Metropolitan Systems.* Columbus, OH, Merrill: 87–109

Harrington J. W. (1987) Strategy formulation, organisational learning, and location. In van der Knaap B., Wever E. (eds) *New Technology and Regional Development.* London, Croom Helm: 63–74

Harris R. C., Insinga R. C., Morone J., Werle M. J. (1996) The virtual R&D laboratory. *Research-Technology Management* 39 (2): 32–6

Harris R. I. D. (1987) The role of manufacturing in regional growth. *Regional Studies* 21: 301–12

Harris R. G. (1992) New theories of international trade and the pattern of global specialisation. In van Liemt G. (ed.) *Industry on the Move: Causes and Consequences of International Relocation in the Manufacturing Industry.* Geneva, International Labour Office: 25–50

Harrison B. (1984) Regional restructuring and 'good business climates': the economic transformation of New England since World War II. In Sawers L., Tabb W. K. (eds) *Sunbelt/Snowbelt: Urban Development and Regional Restructuring.* New York, Oxford University Press: 48–96

Harrison B. (1992) Industrial districts: old wine in new bottles? *Regional Studies* 26: 469–83

Harrison B. (1994) *Lean and Mean: The Changing Landscape of Corporate Power in the Age of Flexibility.* New York, Basic Books

Harrison B., Bluestone B. (1988) *The Great U-Turn: Corporate Restructuring and the Polarizing of America.* New York, Basic Books

Harrison B., Sum A. (1979) The theory of 'dual' or segmented labor markets. *Journal of Economic Issues* 13: 687–706

Harrison D. (ed.) (1992) *Tourism and the Less Developed Countries.* London, Belhaven

Harrison L. (1992) *Who Prospers? How Cultural Values Shape Economic and Political Success.* New York, Basic Books

Harrison R. T., Mason C. M. (1991) Informal investment networks: a case study from the United Kingdom. *Entrepreneurship and Regional Development* 3: 269–79

Harrison R. T., Mason C. M. (1992) International perspectives on the supply of informal venture capital. *Journal of Business Venturing* 7: 459–75

Hart J. A. (1992) *Rival Capitalists: International Competitiveness in the United States, Japan, and Western Europe.* Ithaca, NY, Cornell University Press

Hartmann G., Nicholas I., Sorge A., Warner M. (1985) Computerized machine tools, manpower consequences and skill utilization: a study of British and West German manufacturing firms. In Rhodes E., Wield D. (eds) *Implementing New Technologies*. Oxford, Basil Blackwell: 352–60

Harvey D. (1988) The geographical and geopolitical consequences of the transition from Fordist to flexible accumulation. In Sternlieb G., Hughes J. W. (eds) *America's New Market Geography*. New Brunswick, NJ, Center for Urban Policy Research: 101–34

Harvey D. (1989) From managerialism to entrepreneurialism: the transformation in urban governance in late capitalism. *Geografiska Annaler* 71B: 3–17

Harvey D., Scott A. (1989) The practice of human geography: theory and empirical specificity in the transition from Fordism to flexible accumulation. In Macmillan B. (ed.) *Remodelling Geography*. Oxford, Basil Blackwell: 217–29

Harvey M., Evans R. (1995) Strategic windows in the entrepreneurial process. *Journal of Business Venturing* 10: 331–48

Hassink R. (1992) *Regional innovation policy: case-studies from the Ruhr area, Baden-Württemberg and the North East of England*. Utrecht, Netherlands Geographical Studies

Hassink R. (1996) Technology transfer agencies and regional economic development. *European Planning Studies* 4: 167–84

Hatch C. R. (1988) *Flexible Manufacturing Networks: Cooperation for Competitiveness in a Global Economy*. Washington, Corporation for Enterprise Development

Haug P. (1986) US high technology multinationals and Silicon Glen. *Regional Studies* 20: 103–16

Haug P. (1991) Regional formation of high-technology service industries: the software industry in Washington State. *Environment and Planning A* 23: 869–84

Haug P., Ness P. (1992) Technological infrastructure and regional economic development of biotechnology firms. *Technovation* 12: 423–32

Haughton G. (1993) The local provision of small and medium enterprise advice services. *Regional Studies* 27: 835–42

Häusler J., Hohn H.-W., Lütz S. (1994) Contingencies of innovative networks: a case study of successful interfirm R&D collaboration. *Research Policy* 23: 47–67

Haustein H.-D., Maier H. (1980) Basic improvement and pseudo-innovations and their impact on efficiency. *Technological Forecasting and Social Change* 16: 243–65

Hax A. C., Majluf N. S. (1984) *Strategic Management: An Interpretive Assessment*. Englewood Cliffs, NJ, Prentice-Hall

Hayashi T. (1994) Restructuring of items within a product line: a case study of Japanese multinational enterprises in the electric machinery industry. *Environment and Planning A* 26: 509–26

Hayes R. H., Pisano G. P. (1994) Beyond world-class: the new manufacturing strategy. *Harvard Business Review* 72 (1): 77–86

Hayes R. H., Wheelwright S. C. (1988) Matching process technology with product/market requirements. In Tushman M. L., Moore W. L. (eds) *Readings in the Management of Innovation*, second edition. Cambridge, MA, Ballinger: 417–43

Hayes R. H., Wheelwright S. C., Clark K. B. (1988) *Dynamic Manufacturing*. New York, Free Press

Haynes P. (1993) End of the line: a survey of telecommunications. *The Economist* 23 October

Hayter R. (1982) Truncation, the international firm and regional policy. *Area* 14: 277–82

Hayter R. (1986) Export performance and export potentials: western Canadian exports of manufactured end products. *Canadian Geographer* **30**: 26–39

Hayter R., Watts H. D. (1983) The geography of enterprise: an appraisal. *Progress in Human Geography* 7: 157–81

Hayuth Y. (1990) Globalization of the world economy: the transportation viewpoint. In Shachar A., Öberg S. (eds) *The World Economy and the Spatial Organization of Power.* Aldershot, Avebury: 90–9

Headrick D. R. (1988) *The Tentacles of Progress: Technology Transfer in the Age of Imperialism, 1850–1940.* Oxford, Oxford University Press

Headrick D. R. (1991) *The Invisible Weapon: Telecommunications and International Politics 1851–1945.* New York, Oxford University Press

Healey M. J., Dunham P. J. (1994) Changing competitive advantage in a local economy: the case of Coventry, 1971–90. *Urban Studies* **31**: 1279–301

Heath E., Wall G. (1992) *Marketing Tourism Destinations: A Strategic Planning Approach.* New York, John Wiley

Hedlund G. (1986) The hypermodern MNC – a heterarchy? *Human Resource Management* **25** (1): 9–35

Hegarty W. H., Hoffman R. C. (1990) Product/market innovations: a study of top management involvement among four cultures. *Journal of Product Innovation Management* 7: 186–99

Heijman W. J. M. (1990) The neoclassical location model of firms: a solution procedure. In Dietz F., Heijman W., Shefer D. (eds) *Location and Labor Considerations for Regional Development.* Aldershot, Avebury: 5–15

Heilbroner R. L. (1963) *The Great Ascent: The Struggle for Economic Development in Our Time.* New York, Harper and Row

Hekman J. S., Strong J. S. (1981) The evolution of New England industry. *New England Economic Review* March/April: 35–46

Held J. R. (1996) Clusters as an economic development tool. *Economic Development Quarterly* **10**: 249–61

Helleiner G. K. (1989) Transnational corporations and foreign direct investment. In Chenery H., Srinivasan T. N. (eds) *Handbook of Development Economics,* volume II. Amsterdam, North-Holland: 1441–80

Heller P. (1996) Social capital as a product of class mobilization and state intervention: industrial workers in Kerala, India. *World Development* **24**: 1055–71

Helmsing A. H. J. (1993) Small enterprise and industrialization policies in Africa: some notes. In Helmsing A. H. J., Kolstee T. (eds) *Small Enterprises and Changing Policies.* London, Intermediate Technology Publications: 24–38

Henderson B. D. (1984) *The Logic of Business Strategy.* Cambridge, MA, Ballinger

Henderson D. (1993) The EC, the US and others in a changing world economy. *The World Economy* **16**: 537–52

Henderson J. (1989) *The Globalisation of High Technology Production.* London, Routledge

Henderson J. (1994) Electronics industries and the developing world: uneven contributions and uncertain prospects. In Sklair L. (ed.) *Capitalism and Development.* London, Routledge: 258–88

Henderson J., Scott A. J. (1987) The growth and internationalisation of the American semiconductor industry: labour processes and the spatial organisation of production. In Breheny M. J., McQuaid R. W. (eds) *The Development of High Technology Industries: An International Survey.* London, Croom Helm: 37–79

Henderson R. (1993) Underinvestment and incompetence as responses to radical innovation: evidence from the photolithographic alignment equipment industry.

Rand Journal of Economics 24: 248–70

Henderson R. (1995) Of life cycles real and imaginary: the unexpectedly long old age of optical lithography. *Research Policy* 24: 631–43

Henderson R. M., Clark K. B. (1990) Architectural innovation: the reconfiguration of existing product technologies and the failure of established firms. *Administrative Science Quarterly* 35: 9–30

Henderson Y. K. (1989) The emergence of the venture capital industry. *New England Economic Review* July/August: 64–79

Henkoff R. (1994) Finding, training and keeping the best service workers. *Fortune* 130 (7) 3 October: 110–22

Henry D. L. (1987) How Japanese executives select US sites. *Area Development* 22 (8): 24–8, 120–46

Henry N. (1992) The new industrial spaces: locational logic of a new production era? *International Journal of Urban and Regional Research* 16: 375–96

Henry N., Massey D., Wield D. (1995) Along the road: R&D, society and space. *Research Policy* 24: 707–27

Henry N., Pinch S., Russell S. (1996) In pole position? Untraded interdependencies, new industrial spaces and the British motor sport industry. *Area* 28: 25–36

Hepworth M. (1989) *Geography of the Information Economy.* London, Belhaven Press

Herbig P. A. (1994) *The Innovation Matrix: Culture and Structure Prerequisites to Innovation.* Westport, CT, Quorum

Herod A. (1995) The practice of international labor solidarity and the geography of the global economy. *Economic Geography* 71: 341–63

Herrigel G. (1993) Large firms, small firms, and the governance of flexible specialization: the case of Baden-Württemberg and socialized risk. In Kogot B. (ed.) *Country Competitiveness: Technology and the Organizing of Work.* New York, Oxford University Press, 15–35

Hertz S. (1992) Towards more integrated industrial systems. In Axelsson B., Easton G. (eds) *Industrial Networks: A New View of Reality.* London, Routledge: 105–28

Hessels M. (1994) Business services in the Randstad Holland: decentralization and policy implications. *Tijdschrift voor Economische en Sociale Geografie* 85: 371–8

Hettne B. (1990) *Development Theory and the Three Worlds.* London, Longman

Hewings G. J. D. (1977) *Regional Industrial Analysis and Development.* London, Methuen

Hewings G. J. D. (1985) *Regional Input–Output Analysis.* Beverly Hills, CA, Sage

Hewings G. J. D., Jensen R. J. (1986) Regional, interregional and multiregional input-output analysis. In Nijkamp P. (ed.) *Handbook of Regional and Urban Economics,* volume 1: *Regional Economics.* Amsterdam, North-Holland: 295–355

Hewings G. J. D., Sonis M., Jensen R. C. (1988) Fields of influence of technological change in input–output models. *Papers of the Regional Science Association* 64: 25–36

Hicks D. (1995) Published papers, tacit competencies and corporate management of the public/private character of knowledge. *Industrial and Corporate Change* 4: 401–24

Hicks D., Ishizuka T., Keen P., Sweet S. (1994) Japanese corporations, scientific research and globalization. *Research Policy* 23: 375–84

Higgins B. (1983) From growth poles to systems of interactions in space. *Growth and Change* 14 (4): 3–13

Higgins B., Savoie D. J. (eds) (1988) *Regional Economic Development: Essays in Honour of François Perroux.* Boston, Unwin Hyman

Higgins B., Savoie D. J. (1995) *Regional Development Theories and Their Application.* New Brunswick, NJ, Transaction Publishers

Higgins T. (1991) The geopolitics of research funding in Europe and the USA: some policy aspects. *International Journal of Technology Management* **6**: 507–25

Hill R. C. (1989) Comparing transnational production systems: the automobile industry in the USA and Japan. *International Journal of Urban and Regional Research* **13**: 462–80

Hill R. C., Fujita K. (1996) Flying geese, swarming sparrows or preying hawks? Perspectives on East Asian industrialization. *Competition and Change* **1**: 285–97

Hill R. C., Lee J. (1994) Japanese multinationals and East Asian development: the case of the automobile industry. In Sklair L. (ed.) *Capitalism and Development*. London, Routledge: 289–315

Himbara D. (1994) *Kenyan Capitalists, the State, and Development*. Boulder, CO, Lynne Reinner

Hiramoto A. (1995) Overseas Japanese plants under global strategies: TV transplants in Asia. In Frenkel S., Harrod J. (eds) *Industrialization and Labor Relations*. Ithaca, NY, ILR Press: 236–62

Hiraoka L. S. (1989) Japanese automobile manufacturing in an American setting. *Technological Forecasting and Social Change* **35**: 29–49

Hirschhorn L. (1984) *Beyond Mechanization*. Cambridge, MA, MIT Press

Hirschman A. (1958) *The Strategy of Economic Development*. New Haven, CT, Yale University Press

Hirst P. (1989) The politics of industrial policy. In Hirst P., Zeitlin J. (eds) *Reversing Industrial Decline? Industrial Structure and Policy in Britain and Her Competitors*. Oxford, Berg: 269–87

Hitomi K. (1989) Non-mass, multi-product, small-sized production: the state of the art. *Technovation* **9**: 357–69

Hitomi K. (1996) Manufacturing excellence for 21st century production. *Technovation* **16**: 33–41

Hitt M. A., Ireland R. D., Goryunov I. Y. (1988) The context of innovation: investment in R&D and firm performance. In Gattiker U. E., Larwood L. (eds) *Managing Technological Development: Strategic and Human Resources Issues*. Berlin: Walter de Gruyter: 73–91

Hjalager A.-M. (1989) Why no entrepreneurs? Life modes, everyday life and unemployment strategies in an underdeveloped region. *Entrepreneurship and Regional Development* **1**: 85–97

Hjalager A.-M. (1994) Dynamic innovation in the tourism industry. In Cooper C. P., Lockwood A. (eds) *Progress in Tourism, Recreation and Hospitality Management*, volume 6. Chichester, John Wiley: 197–224

Ho K. C. (1994) Industrial restructuring, the Singapore city-state, and the regional division of labour. *Environment and Planning A* **26**: 33–51

Hobday M. (1988) Evaluating collaborative R&D programmes in information technology: the case of the UK Alvey programme. *Technovation* **8**: 271–98

Hobday M. (1989) Corporate strategies in the international semiconductor industry. *Research Policy* **18**: 225–38

Hobday M. (1994a) Innovation in semiconductor technology: the limits of the Silicon Valley model. In Dodgson M., Rothwell R. (eds) *The Handbook of Industrial Innovation*. Aldershot, Edward Elgar: 154–68

Hobday M. (1994b) Technological learning in Singapore: a test case of leapfrogging. *Journal of Development Studies* **30**: 831–58

Hobday M. (1994c) Innovation in East Asia: diversity and development. In Dodgson M., Rothwell R. (eds) *The Handbook of Industrial Innovation*. Aldershot, Edward

Elgar: 94–105

Hobday M. (1995) East Asian latecomer firms: learning the technology of electronics. *World Development* 23: 1171–93

Hoffman C. (1972) The role of the commercial loan officer in the formation and growth of new and young technical companies. In Cooper A. C., Komives J. L. (eds) *Technical Entrepreneurship: A Symposium.* Milwaukee, Center for Venture Management: 165–88

Hoffman K., Kaplinsky R. (1988) *Driving Force: The Global Restructuring of Technology, Labor, and Investment in the Automobile and Components Industries.* Boulder, CO, Westview Press

Hoffman K., Rush H. (1988) *Micro-electronics and Clothing: The Impact of Technical Change on a Global Industry.* New York, Praeger

Hofstede G. (1980) *Culture's Consequences: International Differences in Work-Related Values.* Beverly Hills, Sage

Holcomb B. (1994) City make-overs: marketing the post-industrial city. In Gold J. R., Ward S. V. (eds) *Place Promotion: The Use of Publicity and Marketing to Sell Towns and Regions.* Chichester, John Wiley: 115–31

Hollier G. P. (1988) Regional development. In Pacione M. (ed.) *The Geography of the Third World: Progress and Prospects.* London, Routledge: 232–70

Holmes J. (1986) The organization and locational structure of production subcontracting. In Scott A. J., Storper M. (eds) *Production, Work, Territory.* Boston, Allen and Unwin: 80–106

Holmes J. (1987) Technical change and the restructuring of the North American automobile industry. In Chapman K., Humphrys G. (eds) *Technical Change and Industrial Policy.* Oxford, Basil Blackwell: 121–56

Holzer H. J. (1996) *What Employers Want: Job Prospects for Less-Educated Workers.* New York, Russell Sage Foundation

Hood N., Young S., Lal D. (1994) Strategic evolution within Japanese manufacturing plants in Europe: UK evidence. *International Business Review* 3: 97–122

Horvath R. J. (1994) National development paths 1965–1987: measuring a metaphor. *Environment and Planning A* 26: 285–305

Horwitch M. (ed.) (1986) *Technology in the Modern Corporation: A Strategic Perspective.* Oxford, Pergamon

Horwitz P. (1979) Direct government funding of research and development: intended and unintended consequences. In Hill C. T., Utterback J. M. (eds) *Technological Innovation for a Dynamic Economy.* Oxford, Pergamon: 255–91

Hou C.-M., Gee S. (1993) National systems supporting technical advance in industry: the case of Taiwan. In Nelson R. R. (ed.) *National Innovation Systems: A Comparative Analysis.* New York, Oxford University Press: 384–413

Hounshell D. A. (1996) The evolution of industrial research in the United States. In Rosenbloom R. S., Spencer W. J. (eds) *Engines of Innovation: US Industrial Research at the End of an Era.* Boston, Harvard Business School Press: 13–85

Hout T., Porter M. E., Rudden E. (1982) How global companies win out. *Harvard Business Review* 60 (5): 98–108

Howard A. (1995) A framework for work change. In Howard A. (ed.) *The Changing Nature of Work.* San Francisco, Jossey-Bass: 3–44

Howell D. R. (1994) The skills myth. *The American Prospect* 18: 81–90

Howell D. R., Wolff E. N. (1992) Technical change and the demand for skills by US industries. *Cambridge Journal of Economics* 16: 127–46

Howells J. R. L. (1984) The location of research and development: some observations and evidence from Britain. *Regional Studies* 18: 13–29

Howells J. (1986) Industry–academic links in research and innovation: a national and regional development perspective. *Regional Studies* 20: 472–6

Howells J. (1988) *Economic, Technological and Locational Trends in European Services.* Aldershot, Avebury

Howells J. (1990a) The location and organisation of research and development: new horizons. *Research Policy* 19: 133–46

Howells J. (1990b) The internationalization of R&D and the development of global research networks. *Regional Studies* 24: 495–512

Howells J. R. (1995) Going global: the use of ICT networks in research and development. *Research Policy* 24: 169–84

Howells J., Charles D. (1988) Research and technological development in the 'less-favoured' regions of the European Community: a UK dimension. In Dyson K. (ed.) *Local Authorities and New Technologies: The European Dimension.* London, Croom Helm: 24–48

Howells J., Wood M. (1993) *The Globalisation of Production and Technology.* London, Belhaven

Howland M. I. (1984) Regional variations in cyclical employment. *Environment and Planning A* 16: 863–77

Howland M. (1993) Technological change and the spatial restructuring of data entry and processing services. *Technological Forecasting and Social Change* 43: 185–96

Hudson R. (1983) Regional labour reserves and industrialisation in the EEC. *Area* 15: 223–30

Hudson R. (1994) New production concepts, new production geographies? Reflections on changes in the automobile industry. *Transactions, Institute of British Geographers* NS 19: 331–45

Hudson R. (1995) Towards sustainable industrial production: but in what sense sustainable? In Taylor M. J. (ed.) *Environmental Change: Industry, Power and Policy.* Aldershot, Avebury: 37–55

Hudson R., Lewis J. (eds) (1985) *Uneven Development in Southern Europe.* London, Methuen

Huggins R. (1996) Technology policy, networks and small firms in Denmark. *Regional Studies* 30: 523–6

Hughes Aircraft (1978) *R&D Productivity*, second edition. Culver City, CA, Hughes Aircraft Company

Hughes K. (1988) The interpretation and measurement of R&D intensity – a note. *Research Policy* 17: 301–7

Hughes K. S. (1993) Foreign multinationals and economic competitiveness: the UK experience. In Humbert M. (ed.) *Impact of Globalisation on Europe's Firms and Industries.* London, Pinter: 127–40

Hull F. M., Collins P. D. (1987) High-technology batch production systems: Woodward's missing type. *Academy of Management Journal* 30: 786–97

Hull F., Hage J., Azumi K. (1985) R&D management strategies: America versus Japan. *IEEE Transactions on Engineering Management* 32: 78–83

Hulten C. R., Schwab R. M. (1984) Regional productivity growth in US manufacturing: 1951–78. *American Economic Review* 74: 152–62

Humphrey C. R., Erickson R. A., McCluskey R. E. (1989) Industrial development groups, external connections, and job generation in local communities. *Economic Development Quarterly* 3: 32–45

Humphrys G. (1995) Japanese industry at home. *Geography* 80 (1): 15–22

Hutton W. (1995) The 30–30–40 society. *Regional Studies* **29**: 719–21

Hyman R. (1988) Flexible specialization: miracle or myth? In Hyman R., Streeck W. (eds) *New Technology and Industrial Relations*. Oxford, Basil Blackwell: 48–60

Hyman R., Streeck W. (eds) (1988) *New Technology and Industrial Relations*. Oxford, Basil Blackwell

Iansiti M., Clark K. B. (1994) Integration and dynamic capability: evidence from product development in automobiles and mainframe computers. *Industrial and Corporate Change* **3**: 557–605

Iansiti M., Khanna T. (1995) Technological innovation, system architecture and the obsolescence of firm capabilities. *Industrial and Corporate Change* **4**: 333–61

Ichimura S. (1990) Institutional factors and government policies for appropriate technologies in South-east Asia. In Chatterji M. (ed.) *Technology Transfer in the Developing Countries*. London, Macmillan: 307–19

Ihlanfeldt K. R. (1995) Ten principles for state tax incentives. *Economic Development Quarterly* **9**: 339–55

IILS (International Institute for Labour Studies) (1993) *Lean Production and Beyond: Labour Aspects of a New Production Concept*. Geneva, International Institute for Labour Studies

Illeris S. (1989) *Services and Regions in Europe*. Aldershot, Avebury

Illeris S. (1992) The Herning-Ikast textile industry: an industrial district in West Jutland. *Entrepreneurship and Regional Development* **4**: 73–84

Illeris S., Jakobsen L. (eds) (1990) *Networks and Regional Development*. Copenhagen, NordREFO

Imai K. (1986) Japan's industrial policy for high technology industry. In Patrick H. (ed.) *Japan's High Technology Industries: Lessons and Limitations of Industrial Policy*. Seattle, University of Washington Press: 137–69

Imai K. (1988) Industrial policy and technological innovation. In Komiya R., Okuno M., Suzumura K. (eds) *Industrial Policy of Japan*. Tokyo, Academic Press: 205–29

Imai K. (1992) The Japanese pattern of innovation and its evolution. In Rosenberg N., Landau R., Mowery D. C. (eds) *Technology and the Wealth of Nations*. Stanford, Stanford University Press: 225–46

Imai K. (1994) Enterprise groups. In Imai K., Komiya R. (eds) *Business Enterprise in Japan: Views of Leading Japanese Economists*. Cambridge, MA, MIT Press: 117–40

Imai K., Baba Y. (1991) Systemic innovation and cross-border networks: transcending markets and hierarchies to create a new techno-economic system. In *Technology and Productivity: The Challenge for Economic Policy*. Paris, Organisation for Economic Co-operation and Development: 389–405

Indgaard M. (1996) Making networks, remaking the city. *Economic Development Quarterly* **10**: 172–87

Ingalls G. L., Martin W. E. (1988) Defining and identifying NICs. In Norwine J., Gonzales A. (eds) *The Third World: States of Mind and Being*. Boston, Unwin Hyman: 82–98

Ingham B. (1993) The meaning of development: interactions between 'new' and 'old' ideas. *World Development* **21**: 1803–21

International Herald Tribune (1996) Auto jobs make Thailand region's biggest wheel. 9 May: 15

Ioannides D. (1995) Strengthening the ties between tourism and economic geography: a theoretical agenda. *Professional Geographer* **47**: 49–60

Isard W. (1956) *Location and Space-Economy*. Cambridge, MA, MIT Press

Ishitani H., Kaya Y. (1989) Robotization in Japanese manufacturing industries.

Technological Forecasting and Social Change 35: 97–131

Isserman A. M. (1977) The location quotient approach to measuring regional economic impacts. *Journal of the American Institute of Planners* 43: 33–41

Isserman A. M. (1980) Estimating export activity in a regional economy: a theoretical and empirical analysis of alternative methods. *International Regional Science Review* 5: 155–84

Isserman A. M. (1985) Economic-demographic modeling with endogenously determined birth and migration rates: theory and prospects. *Environment and Planning A* 17: 25–45

Isserman A. M. (1994) State economic development policy and practice in the United States: a survey article. *International Regional Science Review* 16: 49–100

Isserman A., Taylor C., Gerking S., Schubert U. (1986) Regional labor market analysis. In Nijkamp P. (ed.) *Handbook of Regional and Urban Economics*, volume 1: *Regional Economics*. Amsterdam, North-Holland: 543–80

Itami H. (1987) *Mobilizing Invisible Assets*. Cambridge, MA, Harvard University Press

Itami H. (1989) Mobilising invisible assets: a key for successful corporate strategy. In Punset E., Sweeney G. (eds) *Information Resources and Corporate Growth*. London, Pinter: 36–46

Itami H., Numagami T. (1992) Dynamic interaction between strategy and technology. *Strategic Management Journal* 13: 119–35

Ito M. (1994) Interfirm relations and long-term continuous trading. In Imai K., Komiya R. (eds) *Business Enterprise in Japan*. Cambridge, MA, MIT Press: 105–15

Jaakkola H., Tenhunen H. (1993) The impact of information technology on Finnish industry: a review of two surveys. *STI Review* 12: 53–80

Jacobs J. (1984) *Cities and the Wealth of Nations*. Random House, New York

Jacoby S. M. (1995) Social dimensions of global economic integration. In Jacoby S. M. (ed.) *The Workers of Nations*. New York, Oxford University Press: 3–29

Jaikumar R. (1986) Post-industrial manufacturing. *Harvard Business Review* 64 (6): 69–76

James J. (1995) *The State, Technology and Industrialization in Africa*. London, Macmillan

Janssen B., van Hoogstraten P. (1989) The 'new infrastructure' and regional development. In Albrechts L., Moolaert F., Roberts P., Swyngedouw E. (eds) *Regional Policy at the Crossroads*. London, Jessica Kingsley: 52–66

Jarillo J. C. (1989) Entrepreneurship and growth: the strategic use of external resources. *Journal of Business Venturing* 4: 133–47

Jelinek M. (1984) Rethink strategy or perish: technology lessons from telecommunications. *Journal of Product Innovation Management* 1: 36–42

Jensen C., Leijon S. (1996) Theorizing and conceptualizing regions: the West Sweden region – an idea searching for a (re)form. In Alden J., Boland P. (eds) *Regional Development Strategies: A European Perspective*. London, Jessica Kingsley: 14–37

Jéquier N., Hu Y.-S. (1989) *Banking and the Promotion of Technological Development*. New York, St Martin's Press

Jessop B. (1992a) Post-Fordism and flexible specialisation: incommensurable, contradictory, complementary, or just plain different perspectives? In Ernste H., Maier V. (eds) *Regional Development and Contemporary Response: Extending Flexible Specialisation*. London, Belhaven: 25–43

Jessop B. (1992b) Fordism and post-Fordism: a critical reformulation. In Storper M., Scott A. J. (eds) *Pathways to Industrialization and Regional Development*. London, Routledge: 46–69

Jessop B. (1994) Post-Fordism and the state. In Amin A. (ed.) *Post-Fordism: A Reader.* Oxford, Blackwell: 251–79

Jewkes J., Sawers D., Stillerman R. (1969) *The Sources of Invention*, second edition. New York, W. W. Norton

Jin X.-Y., Porter A. L. (1988) Technological innovation and development: prospects for China. *IEEE Transactions on Engineering Management* 35: 258–64

Johannisson B. (1990a) Between territory and function – on the interfaces between small business, large business and communities. In Donckels R., Miettinen A. (eds) *New Findings and Perspectives in Entrepreneurship.* Aldershot, Avebury: 16–32

Johannisson B. (1990b) Community entrepreneurship – cases and conceptualization. *Entrepreneurship and Regional Development* 2: 71–88

Johannisson B. (1991) University training for entrepreneurship: Swedish approaches. *Entrepreneurship and Regional Development* 3: 67–82

Johannisson B. (1993) Designing supportive contexts for emerging enterprises. In Karlsson C., Johannisson B., Storey D. (eds) *Small Business Dynamics.* London, Routledge: 117–42

Johannisson B. (1995) Paradigms and entrepreneurial networks – some methodological challenges. *Entrepreneurship and Regional Development* 7: 215–31

Johannisson B., Alexanderson O., Nowicki K., Senneseth K. (1994) Beyond anarchy and organization: entrepreneurs in contextual networks. *Entrepreneurship and Regional Development* 6: 329–56

Johannisson B., Nilsson A. (1989) Community entrepreneurs: networking for local development. *Entrepreneurship and Regional Development* 1: 3–19

Johansson B. (1987) Information technology and the viability of spatial networks. *Papers of the Regional Science Association* 61: 51–64

Johansson B., Strömquist U. (1981) Regional rigidities in the process of economic structural adjustment. *Regional Science and Urban Economics* 11: 363–75

Johansson B., Westin L. (1987) Technical change, location, and trade. *Papers of the Regional Science Association* 62: 13–25

Johne F. A., Snelson P. A. (1988) Success factors in product innovation: a selective review of the literature. *Journal of Product Innovation Management* 5: 114–28

Johnson P. S. (1973) *Cooperative Research in Industry.* New York, John Wiley

Johnson P. S. (1975) *The Economics of Invention and Innovation.* London, Martin Robertson

Johnson S., Stabler J. C. (1991) An approach to estimating the economic impact of climate change on a regional economy. *Environment and Planning A* 23: 1197–208

Johnston W. B., Packer A. E. (1987) *Workforce 2000: Work and Workers for the Twenty-first Century.* Indianapolis, Hudson Institute

Jonash R. S. (1996) Strategic technology leveraging: making outsourcing work for you. *Research-Technology Management* 39 (2): 19–25

Jones C. I. (1995) R&D-based models of economic growth. *Journal of Political Economy* 103: 759–84

Jones M. (1996) TEC Policy failure: evidence from the Baseline Follow-up Studies. *Regional Studies* 30: 509–15

Jones-Evans D., Kirby D. A. (1995) Small technical consultancies and their client customers: an analysis in North East England. *Entrepreneurship and Regional Development* 7: 21–40

Jordan M. (1996a) Global grocer? India starts to grow its food exports. *Wall Street Journal* 13 March: A9

Jordan M. (1996b) In India, repealing reform is a tough sell: leaders decry foreign goods, but consumers love them. *Wall Street Journal* 22 May: A18

Jorgenson D. W. (1988) Productivity and economic growth in Japan and the United States. *American Economic Review* 78 (2): 217–22

Joseph R. A. (1988) Technology parks and their contribution to the development of technology-oriented complexes in Australia. *Environment and Planning C: Government and Policy* 7: 173–92

Julien P.-A. (1992) The role of local institutions in the development of industrial districts: the Canadian experience. In Pyke F., Sengenberger W. (eds) *Industrial Districts and Local Economic Regeneration*. Geneva, International Institute for Labour Studies: 197–214

Julien P.-A. (1995a) New technologies and technological information in small business. *Journal of Business Venturing* 10: 459–75

Julien P.-A. (1995b) Economic theory, entrepreneurship and new economic dynamics. In Conti S., Malecki E. J., Oinas P. (eds) *The Industrial Enterprise and Its Environment: Spatial Perspectives*. Aldershot, Avebury: 123–42

Juma C., Torori C., Kirima C. C. M. (1993) *The Adaptive Economy: Economic Crisis and Technological Innovation*. Nairobi, African Centre for Technology Studies

Jun Y. (1995) Strategic responses of Korean firms to globalization and regionalization forces. In Simon D. F. (ed.) *Corporate Strategies in the Pacific Rim: Global versus Regional Trends*. London, Routledge: 166–90

Junkerman J. (1987) Blue-sky management: the Kawasaki story. In Peet R. (ed.) *International Capitalism and Industrial Restructuring*. Boston, Allen and Unwin: 131–44

Jürgens U. (1993) National and company differences in organizing production work in the car industry. In Kogut B. (ed.) *Country Competitiveness: Technology and the Organizing of Work*. New York, Oxford University Press: 106–23

Jusenius C. L., Ledebur L. C. (1977) *Where Have All the Firms Gone? An Analysis of the New England Economy*. Washington, US Economic Development Administration

Jussawalla M. (1995) Deregulation sparks a telecommunications explosion in the Asia Pacific region. *Industrial and Corporate Change* 4: 703–10

Justman M., Teubal M. (1995) Technological infrastructure policy (TIP): creating capabilities and building markets. *Research Policy* 24: 259–81

Kaell A., Ireland D., Sadeque Z. (1995) Trade, competition policy and market access. In OECD. *New Dimensions of Market Access in a Globalising World*. Paris, Organisation for Economic Co-operation and Development: 149–68

Kagono T., Nonaka I., Sakakibara K., Okumura A. (1985) *Strategic vs. Evolutionary Management: A US–Japan Comparison of Strategy and Organization*. Amsterdam, North-Holland

Kahley W. J. (1991) Population migration in the United States: a survey of research. *Economic Review, Federal Reserve Bank of Atlanta* 76 (1): 12–21

Kaldor N. (1970) The case for regional policies. *Scottish Journal of Political Economy* 17: 337–47

Kaldor M. (1981) *The Baroque Arsenal*. New York, Hill and Wang

Kamiyama K. (1994) The typical Japanese overseas factory. In Abo T. (ed.) *Hybrid Factory: The Japanese Production System in the United States*. New York, Oxford University Press: 58–81

Kanter R. M. (1984) Variations in managerial career structures in high-technology firms: the impact of organizational characteristics on internal labor market patterns. In Osterman P. (ed.) *Internal Labor Markets*. Cambridge, MA, MIT Press: 109–31

Kanter R. M. (1994) Collaborative advantage: the art of alliances. *Harvard Business*

Review 72 (4): 96–108

Kanter R. M. (1995) *World Class: Thriving Locally in the Global Economy.* New York, Simon and Schuster

Kaplinsky R. (1984) *Automation: The Technology and Society.* London, Longman

Kaplinsky R. (1989) 'Technological revolution' and the international division of labour in manufacturing: A place for the third world? In Cooper C., Kaplinsky R. (eds) *Technology and Development in the Third Industrial Revolution.* London, Frank Cass: 5–37

Kaplinsky R. (1993) Export processing zones in the Dominican Republic: transforming manufactures into commodities. *World Development* 21: 1851–65.

Kaplinsky R. (1995a) A reply to Willmore. *World Development* 23: 537–40

Kaplinsky R. (1995b) Technique and system: the spread of Japanese management techniques to developing countries. *World Development* 23: 57–71

Karaska G. J., Linge G. J. R. (1978) Applicability of the model of the territorial production complex outside the USSR. *Papers of the Regional Science Association* 40: 149–69

Karlsson J. (1994) *World Industrial Robots 1994.* New York, United Nations and International Federation of Robotics

Kasarda J. D. (1991) Global air cargo-industrial complexes as development tools. *Economic Development Quarterly* 5: 187–96

Kash D. E. (1989) *Perpetual Innovation: The New World of Competition.* New York, Basic Books

Kassel S. (1989) *Soviet Advanced Technologies in the Era of Restructuring.* Santa Monica, CA, Rand Corporation

Kassim H. (1995) Building a workable S&T infrastructure in Malaysia. In Simon D. F. (ed.) *The Emerging Technological Trajectory of the Pacific Rim.* New York, M. E. Sharpe: 171–85

Katz J. A. (1990) Longitudinal analysis of self-employment follow-through. *Entrepreneurship and Regional Development* 2: 15–25

Katz J. M. (1982) Technology and economic development: an overview of research findings. In Syrquin M., Teitel S. (eds) *Trade, Stability, Technology, and Equity in Latin America.* London, Academic Press: 281–315

Katz J. M., Bercovich N. A. (1993) National systems of innovation supporting technical advance in industry: the case of Argentina. In Nelson R. R. (ed.) *National Innovation Systems: A Comparative Analysis.* New York, Oxford University Press: 451–75

Katz R. L. (1988) *The Information Society: An International Perspective.* New York, Praeger

Kaufman A., Gittell R., Merenda M., Naumes W., Wood C. (1994) Porter's model for geographic competitive advantage: the case of New Hampshire. *Economic Development Quarterly* 8: 43–66

Kawano E. (1993) The Japanese model of production: cooperation or coercion? In Epstein G., Graham J., Nembhard J. (eds) *Creating a New World Economy.* Philadelphia, Temple University Press: 242–57

Kawashima T., Stöhr W. (1988) Decentralized technology policy: the case of Japan. *Environment and Planning C: Government and Policy* 6: 427–39

Kay N. M. (1979) *The Innovating Firm: A Behavioural Theory of Corporate R&D.* New York, St Martin's Press

Ke S., Bergman E. M. (1995) Regional and technological determinants of company productivity growth in the late 1980s. *Regional Studies* 29: 59–71

Keck O. (1993) The national system for technical innovation in Germany. In Nelson R. R. (ed.) *National Innovation Systems: A Comparative Analysis*. New York, Oxford University Press: 115–57

Keeble D. (1967) Models of economic development. In Chorley R. J., Haggett P. (eds) *Models in Geography*. London, Methuen: 243–302

Keeble D. (1988) High-technology industry and local environments in the United Kingdom. In Aydalot P., Keeble D. (eds) *High Technology Industry and Innovative Environments: The European Experience*. London, Routledge: 65–98

Keeble D. E. (1989) High technology industry and regional development in Britain: the case of the Cambridge phenomenon. *Environment and Planning C: Government and Policy* 7: 153–72

Keeble D. (1990) Small firms, new firms and uneven development in the United Kingdom. *Area* 22: 234–45

Keeble D., Kelly T. (1986) New firms and high-technology industry in the United Kingdom: the case of computer electronics. In Keeble D., Wever E. (eds) *New Firms and Regional Development in Europe*. London, Croom Helm: 184–202

Keeble D., Tyler P. (1995) Enterprising behaviour and the urban-rural shift. *Urban Studies* 32: 975–97

Keeling D. J. (1995) Transport and the world city paradigm. In Knox P., Taylor P. J. (eds) *World Cities in a World-System*. Cambridge, Cambridge University Press: 115–31

Keen P. G. W., Cummins J. M. (1994) *Networks in Action: Business Choices and Telecommunications Decisions*. Belmont, CA, Wadsworth

Kellerman A. (1985) The evolution of service economies: a geographical perspective. *Professional Geographer* 37: 133–43

Kelley M. R. (1994) Productivity and information technology: the elusive connection. *Management Science* 40: 1406–25

Kelley M. R., Brooks H. (1989) From breakthrough to follow-through. *Issues in Science and Technology* 5 (3): 42–7

Kelley M. R., Brooks H. (1992) Diffusion of NC and CNC machine tool technologies in large and small firms. In Ayres R. U., Haywood W., Tchijov I. (eds) *Computer Integrated Manufacturing*, volume III: *Models, Case Studies, and Forecasts of Diffusion*. London, Chapman and Hall: 117–35

Kelly K., Weber J., Friend J., Atchison S., DeGeorge G., Holstein W. J. (1992) Hot spots: America's new growth regions are blossoming despite the slump. *Business Week* 19 October: 80–8

Kendrick J. W. (1977) *Understanding Productivity*. Baltimore, Johns Hopkins University Press

Kennedy C., Thirlwall A. P. (1972) Technical progress: a survey. *Economic Journal* 82: 11–72

Kennedy P. (1987) *The Rise and Fall of the Great Powers*. New York, Random House

Kennedy P. T. (1988) *African Capitalism*. Cambridge, Cambridge University Press

Kenney M. (1986) Schumpeterian innovation and entrepreneurs in capitalism: a case study of the US biotechnology industry. *Research Policy* 15: 21–31

Kenney M., Florida R. (1988) Beyond mass production: production and the labor process in Japan. *Politics and Society* 16: 121–58

Kenney M., Florida R. (1993) *Beyond Mass Production: The Japanese System and its Transfer to the US*. New York, Oxford University Press

Kenney M., Florida R. (1994a) The organization and geography of Japanese R&D: results from a survey of Japanese electronics and biotechnology firms. *Research Policy*

23: 305–22

Kenney M., Florida R. (1994b) Japanese maquiladoras: production organization and global commodity chains. *World Development* **22**: 27–44

Kenny S. (1995) Defining a national system of innovation: implications for Irish industrial development policy. *Regional Studies* **29**: 692–7

Kenworthy L. (1995) *In Search of National Economic Success: Balancing Competition and Cooperation.* Thousand Oaks, CA, Sage

Kessous J.-C., Lessard G. (1993) Industrial sector in Mali: responses to adjustment. In Helmsing A. H. J., Kolstee T. (eds) *Small Enterprises and Changing Policies.* London, Intermediate Technology Publications: 114–43

Kester A. Y. (1995) *Following the Money: US Finance in the World Economy.* Washington, National Academy Press

Kickert W. J. M. (1985) The magic word *flexibility. International Studies of Management and Organization* **14** (4): 6–31

Kidd P. T. (1994) *Agile Manufacturing: Forging New Frontiers.* Boston: Addison-Wesley

Killick T. (ed.) (1995a) *The Flexible Economy: Causes and Consequences of the Adaptability of National Economies.* London, Routledge

Killick T. (1995b) Relevance, meaning and determinants of flexibility. In Killick T. (ed.) *The Flexible Economy: Causes and Consequences of the Adaptability of National Economies.* London, Routledge: 1–33

Killick T. (1995c) Economic inflexibility in Africa: evidence and causes. In Killick T. (ed.) *The Flexible Economy: Causes and Consequences of the Adaptability of National Economies.* London, Routledge: 154–96

Kim C.-K., Curry J. (1993) Fordism, flexible specialization and agro-industrial restructuring. *Sociologia Ruralis* **33**: 61–80

Kim H. K., Lee S.-H. (1994) Commodity chains and the Korean automobile industry. In Gereffi G., Korzeniewicz M. (eds) *Commodity Chains and Global Capitalism.* Westport, CT, Praeger: 281–96

Kim K.-D. (1994) Confucianism and capitalist development in East Asia. In Sklair L. (ed.) *Capitalism and Development.* London, Routledge: 87–106

Kim L. (1980) Stages of development of industrial technology in a developing country: a model. *Research Policy* **9**: 254–77

Kim L. (1993a) South Korea. In Patel S. J. (ed.) *Technological Transformation in the Third World,* volume I: *Asia.* Aldershot, Avebury: 145–93

Kim L. (1993b) National system of industrial innovation: dynamics of capability building in Korea. In Nelson R. R. (ed.) *National Innovation Systems: A Comparative Analysis.* New York, Oxford University Press: 357–83

Kim L., Lee H. (1987) Patterns of technological change in a rapidly developing country: a synthesis. *Technovation* **6**: 261–76

Kim L., Lee J., Lee J. (1987) Korea's entry into the computer industry and its acquisition of technological capability. *Technovation* **6**: 277–93

Kim L. J., Dahlman C. J. (1992) Technology policy for industrialization: an integrative framework and Korea's experience. *Research Policy* **21**: 437–52

Kim S. (1987) Diversity in urban labor markets and agglomeration economies. *Papers of the Regional Science Association* **62**: 57–70

King A. (1982) For better and for worse: the benefits and risks of information technology. In Bjorn-Andersen N., Earl M., Holst O., Mumford E. (eds) *Information Society: For Richer, For Poorer.* Amsterdam, North-Holland: 35–56

Kinsey J. (1978) The application of growth pole theory in the Aire Métropolitaine Marsellaise. *Geoforum* **9**: 245–67

Kipnis B. A., Swyngedouw E. A. (1988a) Manufacturing plant size – toward a regional strategy. A case study in Limburg, Belgium. *Urban Studies* 25: 43–52

Kipnis B. A., Swyngedouw E. A. (1988b) Manufacturing research and development in a peripheral region: the case of Limburg, Belgium. *Professional Geographer* 40: 149–58

Kirk R. (1987) Are business services immune to the business cycle? *Growth and Change* 18 (2): 15–24

Kiser J. W. (1989) *Communist Entrepreneurs: Unknown Innovators in the Global Economy.* New York, Franklin Watts

Klein L. R., Glickman N. J. (1977) Econometric model-building at regional level. *Regional Science and Urban Economics* 7: 3–23

Kleinknecht A. (1987) *Innovation Patterns in Crisis and Prosperity.* New York, St Martin's Press

Klevorick A. K., Levin R. C., Nelson R. R., Winter S. G. (1995) On the sources and significance of interindustry differences in technological opportunities. *Research Policy* 24: 185–205

Klier T. H. (1994) The impact of lean manufacturing on sourcing relationships. *Economic Perspectives, Federal Reserve Bank of Chicago* 18 (4): 8–18

Klier T. H. (1995) The geography of lean manufacturing: recent evidence from the US auto industry. *Economic Perspectives, Federal Reserve Bank of Chicago* 19 (6): 2–16

Kline S. J., Rosenberg N. (1986) An overview of innovation. In Landau R., Rosenberg N. (eds) *The Positive Sum Strategy.* Washington, National Academy Press: 275–305

Knapp G., Huskey L. (1988) Effects of transfers on remote regional economies: the transfer economy in rural Alaska. *Growth and Change* 19 (2): 25–39

Knapp T. A., Graves P. E. (1989) On the role of amenities in models of migration and economic development. *Journal of Regional Science* 29: 71–87

Knight R. V. (1995) Knowledge-based development: policy and planning implications for cities. *Urban Studies* 32: 225–60

Knights M. (1996) Bangladeshi immigrants in Italy: from geopolitics to micropolitics. *Transactions, Institute of British Geographers* NS 21: 105–23

Knox P., Agnew J. (1994) *The Geography of the World Economy,* second edition. London, Edward Arnold

Koberg C. S., Uhlenbruck N., Sarason Y. (1996) Facilitators of organizational innovation: the role of life-cycle stage. *Journal of Business Venturing* 11: 133–49

Kodama F. (1995a) *Emerging Patterns of Innovation: Sources of Japan's Technological Edge.* Boston: Harvard Business School Press

Kodama F. (1995b) Emerging trajectory of the Pacific Rim: concepts, evidences, and new schemes. In Simon D. F. (ed.) *The Emerging Technological Trajectory of the Pacific Rim.* New York, M. E. Sharpe: 28–52

Kogut B. (1990) International sequential advantages and network flexibility. In Bartlett C. A., Doz Y., Hedlund G. (eds) *Managing the Global Firm.* London, Routledge: 47–68

Kogut B. (ed.) (1993) *Country Competitiveness: Technology and the Organizing of Work.* New York, Oxford University Press

Kogut B., Kulatilaka N. (1994) Operating flexibility, global manufacturing, and the option value of a multinational network. *Management Science* 40: 123–39

Kojima K., Ozawa T. (1984) *Japan's General Trading Companies: Merchants of Economic Development.* Paris, Organisation for Economic Co-operation and Development

Kokko A., Blomström M. (1995) Policies to encourage inflows of technology through foreign multinationals. *World Development* 23: 459–68

Kokko A., Tansini R., Zejan M. C. (1996) Local Technological capability and productivity spillovers from FDI in the Uruguayan Manufacturing sector. *Journal of Development Studies* **32**: 602–11

Komiya R. (1988) Introduction. In Komiya R., Okuno M., Suzumura K. (eds) *Industrial Policy of Japan*. Tokyo, Academic Press: 1–22

Komninos N. (1992) Science parks in Europe: flexible production, productive disintegration and R&D. In Dunford M., Kafkalas G. (eds) *Cities and Regions in the New Europe*. London, Belhaven: 86–101

Kondo K. (1995) The globalization of Fujitsu. In Simon D. F. (ed.) *Corporate Strategies in the Pacific Rim: Global versus Regional Trends*. London, Routledge: 267–90

Kono T. (1984) *Strategy and Structure of Japanese Enterprises*. London, Macmillan

Konsynski B. R., Karimi J. (1993) On the design of global information systems. In Bradley S. P., Hausman J. A., Nolan R. L. (eds) *Globalization, Technology, and Competition: The Fusion of Computers and Telecommunications in the 1990s*. Boston, Harvard Business School Press: 81–108

Kontorovich V. (1994) The future of Soviet science. *Research Policy* **23**: 113–21

Koo H. (1987) The interplay of state, social class, and world system in East Asian development: the cases of South Korea and Taiwan. In Deyo F. C. (ed.) *The Political Economy of the New Asian Industrialism*. Ithaca, NY, Cornell University Press: 165–81

Koretz G. (1995) A productivity paradox: high wages can help – or hurt. *Business Week* 10 July: 24

Korzeniewicz M. (1994) Commodity chains and marketing strategies: Nike and the global athletic footwear industry. In Gereffi G., Korzeniewicz M. (eds) *Commodity Chains and Global Capitalism*. Westport, CT, Praeger: 247–65

Korzeniewicz R. P., Martin W. (1994) The global distribution of commodity chains. In Gereffi G., Korzeniewicz M. (eds) *Commodity Chains and Global Capitalism*. Westport, CT, Praeger: 67–91

Kotkin J. (1992) *Tribes: How Race, Religion and Identity Determine Success in the New Global Economy*. New York, Random House

Kotler P., Fahey L., Jatusripitak S. (1985) *The New Competition*. Englewood Cliffs, NJ, Prentice-Hall

Kotler P., Haider D. H., Rein I. (1993) *Marketing Places: Attracting Investment, Industry, and Tourism to Cities, States, and Nations*. New York, Free Press

Kowalski J. S. (1986) Regional conflicts in Poland: spatial polarization in a centrally planned economy. *Environment and Planning A* **18**: 599–617

Kozul-Wright R. (1995) Transnational corporations and the nation state. In Michie J., Smith J. G. (eds) *Managing the Global Economy*. Oxford, Oxford University Press: 135–71

Krafcik J. F. (1988) Triumph of the lean production system. *Sloan Management Review* **30** (1): 41–52

Kresl P. K. (1995) The determinants of urban competitiveness: a survey. In Kresl P. K., Gappert G. (eds) *North American Cities and the Global Economy*. Thousand Oaks, CA, Sage: 45–68

Krikelas A. C. (1992) Why regions grow: a review of research on the economic base model. *Economic Review, Federal Reserve Bank of Atlanta* **77** (4): 16–29

Kripalani M. (1996) A traffic jam of auto makers. *Business Week* 5 August: 46–7

Kristensen P. H. (1992) Industrial districts in West Jutland, Denmark. In Pyke F., Sengenberger W. (eds) *Industrial Districts and Local Economic Regeneration*. Geneva, International Institute for Labour Studies: 122–73

Kristensen P. H. (1994) Spectator communities and entrepreneurial districts. *Entrepreneurship and Regional Development* **6**: 177–98

Kristensen P. S. (1992) Flying prototypes: production departments' direct interaction with external customers. *International Journal of Operations and Production Management* 12 (7/8): 197–213

Krogh L. C., Nicholson G. C. (1990) 3M's international experience. *Research-Technology Management* 33 (5): 23–27

Krueger A. O. (1983) *Trade and Employment in Developing Countries*, volume 3: *Synthesis and Conclusions*. Chicago, University of Chicago Press

Krueger A. O. (1990) Government failures in development. *Journal of Economic Perspectives* 4 (3): 9–23

Krueger N. F. (1995) *Prescription for Opportunity: How Communities Can Create Potential for Entrepreneurs*. Washington, Small Business Foundation of America

Krugman P. (1991) Increasing returns and economic geography. *Journal of Political Economy* 99: 483–99

Krugman P. (1992) Technology and international competition: a historical perspective. In Harris M. C., Moore G. E. (eds) *Linking Trade and Technology Policies*. Washington, National Academy Press: 13–28

Krugman P. (1994a) Competitiveness: a dangerous obsession. *Foreign Affairs* 73 (2): 28–44

Krugman P. (1994b) The fall and rise of development economics. In Rodwin L., Schön D. (eds) *Rethinking the Development Experience: Essays Provoked by the Work of Albert O. Hirschman*. Washington, Brookings Institution: 39–58

Krugman P. (1994c) The myth of Asia's miracle. *Foreign Affairs* 73 (6): 62–78

Krugman P. (1995) *Development, Geography, and Economic Theory*. Cambridge MA, MIT Press

Kuby M., Reid N. (1992) Technological change and the concentration of the US general cargo port system: 1970–88. *Economic Geography* 68: 272–89

Kuklinski A. (ed.) (1972) *Growth Poles and Growth Centres in Regional Planning*. The Hague, Mouton

Kuklinski A. (ed.) (1975) *Regional Development and Planning: International Perspectives*. Leyden, Sijthoff

Kuklinski A. (ed.) (1978) *Regional Policies in Nigeria, India, and Brazil*. The Hague, Mouton

Kuklinski A. (ed.) (1981) *Polarized Development and Regional Policies: Tribute to Jacques Boudeville*. The Hague, Mouton

Kuklinski A., Petrella R. (eds) (1972) *Growth Poles and Regional Policies*. The Hague, Mouton

Kulicke M., Krupp H. (1987) The formation, relevance and public promotion of new technology-based firms. *Technovation* 6: 47–56

Kumar N., Saqib M. (1996) Firm size, opportunities for adaptation and in-house R&D activity in developing countries: the case of Indian manufacturing. *Research Policy* 25: 713–22

Kunio Y. (1988) *The Rise of Ersatz Capitalism in South-east Asia*. Singapore, Oxford University Press

Kunzmann K. R. (1988) Military production and regional development in the Federal Republic of Germany. In Breheny M. J. (ed.) *Defence Expenditure and Regional Development*. London, Mansell: 49–66

Kutscher R. E. (1988) Structural changes of employment in the United States. In Candilis W. O. (ed.) *United States Service Industries Handbook*. New York, Praeger: 23–44

Kutscher R. E., Mark J. A. (1983) The service-producing sector: some common perceptions reviewed. *Monthly Labor Review* **106** (4): 21–4

Kuttner R. (1993) The productivity paradox: rising output, stagnant living standards. *Business Week* 8 February: 12

Kuwahara T. (1996) Technology foresight in Japan: a new approach in methodology and analysis. *STI Review* **17**: 51–70

Kyläheiko K., Miettinen A. (1995) Technology management and entrepreneurship: a critical view. In Birley S., MacMillan I. C. (eds) *International Entrepreneurship.* London, Routledge: 39–58

Lacroix R., Martin F. (1988) Government and the decentralization of R&D. *Research Policy* **17**: 363–73

Lagendijk A. (1994) The impact of internationalisation and rationalisation of production on the Spanish automobile industry, 1950–90. *Environment and Planning A* **27**: 321–43

Lagendijk A., van der Knaap B. (1995a) The impact of internationalisation on the spatial structure of automobile production in Spain. *Tijdschrift voor Economische en Sociale Geografie* **86**: 426–42

Lagendijk A., van der Knaap G. A. (1995b) The impact of foreign investments in the automobile industry on local economic development in Spain. *Area* **27**: 335–46

Lakshmanan T. R., Hua C.-I. (1987) Regional disparities in China. *International Regional Science Review* **11**: 97–104

Lakshmanan T. R., Okumura M. (1995) The nature and evolution of knowledge networks in Japanese manufacturing. *Papers in Regional Science* **74**: 63–86

Lall S. (1979) The international allocation of research by US multinationals. *Oxford Bulletin of Economics and Statistics* **41**: 313–31

Lall S. (1980) The international automotive industry and the developing world. *World Development* **8**: 789–812

Lall S. (1983) The rise of multinationals from the third world. *Third World Quarterly* **5**: 618–26

Lall S. (1985) Trade in technology by a slowly industrializing country: India. In Rosenberg N., Frischtak C. (eds) *International Technology Transfer: Concepts, Measures, and Comparisons.* New York, Praeger: 45–76

Lall S. (1990) *Building Industrial Competitiveness in Developing Countries.* Paris, Organisation for Economic Co-operation and Development

Lall S. (1994a) Industrial policy: the role of governments in promoting industrial and technological development. *UNCTAD Review.* 65–89

Lall S. (1994b) *The East Asian Miracle:* Does the bell toll for industrial strategy? *World Development* **22**: 645–54

Lall S. (1995) Industrial adaptation and technological capabilities in developing countries. In Killick T. (ed.) *The Flexible Economy: Causes and Consequences of the Adaptability of National Economies.* London, Routledge: 257–96

Lall S., Stewart F. (1996) Trade and industrial policy in Africa. *Development* June: 64–7

Lamberton D. (1994) Innovation and intellectual property. In Dodgson M., Rothwell R. (eds) *The Handbook of Industrial Innovation.* Aldershot, Edward Elgar: 301–9

Landau R., Rosenberg N. (1992) Successful commercialization in the chemical process industries. In Rosenberg N., Landau R., Mowery D.C. (eds) *Technology and the Wealth of Nations.* Stanford, Stanford University Press: 73–119

Lande P. S. (1978) The interregional comparison of production functions. *Regional Science and Urban Economics* **8**: 339–53

Lande P. S. (1982) The regional-development implications of industrial policy. In Bell M. E., Lande P. S. (eds) *Regional Dimensions of Industrial Policy.* Lexington, MA,

Lexington Books: 81–91

Lande P. S. (1994) Regional industrial structure and economic growth and instability. *Journal of Regional Science* 34: 343–60

Landes D. S. (1989) Rich country, poor country. *The New Republic* November 20: 23–7

Landesmann M. A., Abel I. (1995) The transition in Eastern Europe: the case for industrial policy. In Chang H.-J., Nolan P. (eds) *The Transformation of the Communist Economies: Against the Mainstream*, New York, St Martin's Press, 136–61

Langdale J. (1983) Competition in the United States' long-distance telecommunications industry. *Regional Studies* 17: 393–409

Langdale J. (1989) Telecommunications and international business telecommunications: the role of leased networks. *Annals of the Association of American Geographers* 79: 501–22

Landström H. (1990) Co-operation between venture capital companies and small firms. *Entrepreneurship and Regional Development* 2: 345–62

Landström H. (1992) The relationship between private investors and small firms: an agency theory approach. *Entrepreneurship and Regional Development* 4: 199–223

Landström H. (1993) Informal risk capital in Sweden and some international comparisons. *Journal of Business Venturing* 8: 525–40

Larson A. (1991) Partner networks: leveraging external ties to improve entrepreneurial performance. *Journal of Business Venturing* 6: 173–88

Larsson S. (1993) New dimensions in organizing industrial networks. *International Journal of Technology Management* 8: 39–58

Lash S., Bagguley P. (1988) Labour relations in disorganized capitalism: a five-nation comparison. *Environment and Planning D: Society and Space* 6: 321–38

Lau H.-F., Chan C.-F. (1994) The development process of the Hong Kong garment industry: a mature industry in a newly industrialized economy. In Bonacich E., Cheng L., Chinchilla N., Hamilton N., Ong P. (eds) *Global Production: The Apparel Industry in the Pacific Rim*. Philadelphia, Temple University Press: 105–125

Lawton-Smith H. (1990) Innovation and technical links: the case of advanced technology industry in Oxfordshire. *Area* 22: 125–35

Lawton-Smith H. (1991) The role of incubators in local industrial development: the cryogenics industry in Oxfordshire. *Entrepreneurship and Regional Development* 3: 175–94

Lawton-Smith H. (1996) National laboratories and regional development: case studies from the UK, France and Belgium. *Entrepreneurship and Regional Development* 8: 1–17

Leborgne D., Lipietz A. (1988) New technologies, new modes of regulation: some spatial implications. *Environment and Planning D: Society and Space* 6: 263–80

Lee C. (1995) Globalization of a Korean firm: the case of Samsung. In Simon D. F. (ed.) *Corporate Strategies in the Pacific Rim: Global versus Regional Trends*. London, Routledge: 249–66

Lee C. H. (1995) *The Economic Transformation of South Korea: Lessons for the Transition Economies*. Paris, Organisation for Economic Co-operation and Development

Lee C. H., Yamazawa I. (eds) (1990) *The Economic Development of Japan and Korea: A Parallel with Lessons*. New York, Praeger: 153–70

Lee J. (1995) Comparative advantage in manufacturing as a determinant of industrialization: the Korean case. *World Development* 23: 1195–214

Lee N., Cason J. (1994) Automobile commodity chains in the NICs: a comparison of South Korea, Mexico, and Brazil. In Gereffi G., Korzeniewicz M. (eds) *Commodity Chains and Global Capitalism*. Westport, CT, Praeger: 223–43

Leicht K. T., Jenkins J. C. (1994) Three strategies of state economic development: entrepreneurial, industrial recruitment, and deregulation policies in the American states. *Economic Development Quarterly* 8: 256–69

Leitner H. (1990) Cities in pursuit of economic growth: the local state as entrepreneur. *Political Geography Quarterly* 9: 146–70

Lele M. M. (1986) How service needs influence product strategy. *Sloan Management Review* 28 (1): 63–70

Lenz J. E. (1989) *Flexible Manufacturing: Benefits from the Low-Inventory Factory.* New York, Marcel Dekker

Leonard-Barton D. (1995) *Wellsprings of Knowledge: Building and Sustaining the Sources of Innovation.* Boston: Harvard Business School Press

Leonard-Barton D., Doyle J. L. (1996) Commercializing technology: imaginative understanding of user needs. In Rosenbloom R. S., Spencer W. J. (eds) *Engines of Innovation: US Industrial Research at the End of an Era.* Boston, Harvard Business School Press: 177–207

Leslie D. A. (1995) Global scan: the globalization of advertising agencies, concepts, and campaigns. *Economic Geography* 71: 402–26

Leslie S. W. (1980) Thomas Midgley and the politics of industrial research. *Business History Review* 54: 480–503

Leung C. K. (1993) Personal contacts, subcontracting linkages, and development in the Hong Kong–Zhujiang Delta region. *Annals of the Association of American Geographers* 83: 272–302

Leung C. K. (1996) Foreign manufacturing investment and regional industrial growth in Guangdong Province, China. *Environment and Planning A* 28: 513–36

Leus E. B. H. M., Pellenbarg P. H. (1991) Production subcontracting in the Netherlands: a survey of developments. In de Smidt M., Wever E. (eds) *Complexes, Formations and Networks.* Utrecht, Royal Dutch Geographical Society: 103–10

Leven C. L. (1964) Regional and interregional accounts in perspective. *Papers of the Regional Science Association* 13: 127–44

Leven C. L. (1985) Regional development analysis and policy. *Journal of Regional Science* 25: 569–92

Lever W. F. (1979) Industry and labour markets in Great Britain. In Hamilton F. E. I., Linge G. J. R. (eds) *Spatial Analysis, Industry and the Industrial Environment*, volume 1: *Industrial Systems.* Chichester, John Wiley: 89–114

Levine J. (1983) 3000 Sand Hill Road. *Venture* 5 (12): 74–8

Levy D., Dunning J. H. (1993) International production and sourcing: trends and issues. *STI Review* 13: 13–59

Levy J. M. (1990) *Economic Development Programs for Cities, Counties, and Towns*, second edition. New York, McGraw-Hill

Lewis H., Allison D. (1982) *The Real World War.* New York, Coward, McCann and Geoghegan

Lewis J. D. (1995) *The Connected Corporation: How Leading Companies Win through Customer–Supplier Alliances.* New York, Free Press

Lewis J. R., Williams A. M. (1987) Productive decentralization or indigenous growth? Small manufacturing enterprises and regional development in Central Portugal. *Regional Studies* 21: 343–61

Lewis P. M. (1986) The economic impact of the operation and closure of a nuclear power station. *Regional Studies* 20: 425–32

Lewis S. R. (1989) Primary exporting countries. In Chenery H., Srinivasan T. N. (eds) *Handbook of Development Economics*, volume II. Amsterdam, North-Holland:

1541–600

Leyshon A., Tickell A. (1994) Money order? The discursive construction of Bretton Woods and the making and breaking of regulatory space. *Environment and Planning A* **26**: 1861–90

Li F. (1995) *The Geography of Business Information.* Chichester, John Wiley

Liang W. W., Denny W. M. (1995) Upgrading Hong Kong's technology base. In Simon D. F. (ed.) *The Emerging Technological Trajectory of the Pacific Rim.* New York, M. E. Sharpe: 256–74

Lifton D. E., Lifton L. R. (1989) Applying the Japanese 'thin markets' strategy to industrial new product development. *International Journal of Technology Management* **4**: 177–88

Lim J. D. (1994) Restructuring of the footwear industry and the industrial adjustment of the Pusan economy. *Environment and Planning A* **26**: 567–81

Lim L. Y. C. (1980) Women workers in multinational corporations: the case of the electronics industry in Malaysia and Singapore. In Kumar K. (ed.) *Transnational Enterprises: Their Impact on Third World Societies and Cultures.* Boulder, CO, Westview Press: 109–36

Lim Y. T., Song C. H. (1996) An international comparative study of basic scientific research capacity: OECD countries, Taiwan and Korea. *Technological Forecasting and Social Change* **52**: 75–94

Lindorff D., Engardio P. (1992) Is 'the MIT of Asia' growing in Hong Kong? *Business Week* 7 December: 135

Linge G. J. R. (1991) Just-in-time: more or less flexible? *Economic Geography* **67**: 316–32

Linge G. J. R., Forbes D. K. (1990) The space economy of China. In Linge G. J. R., Forbes D. K. (eds) *China's Spatial Economy: Recent Developments and Reforms.* Oxford, Oxford University Press: 10–34

Linge G. J. R., Hamilton F. E. I. (1981) International industrial systems. In Hamilton F. E. I., Linge G. J. R. (eds) *Spatial Analysis, Industry and the Industrial Environment,* volume 2: *International Industrial Systems.* London, John Wiley: 1–117

Link A. N., Bauer L. L. (1989) *Cooperative Research in US Manufacturing.* Lexington, MA, Lexington Books

Linn R. A. (1984) Product development in the chemical industry: a description of a maturing business. *Journal of Product Innovation Management* **1**: 116–28

Lipietz A. (1986) New tendencies in the international division of labor: regimes of accumulation and modes of regulation. In Scott A. J., Storper M. (eds) *Production, Work, Territory.* Boston, Allen and Unwin: 16–40

Lipietz A. (1993) The local and the global: regional individuality or interregionalism? *Transactions, Institute of British Geographers* NS **18**: 8–18

Lipnack J., Stamps J. (1993) *The TeamNet Factor.* Essex Junction, VT, Oliver Wright

Lipparini A., Sobrero M. (1994) The glue and the pieces: entrepreneurship and innovation in small-firm networks. *Journal of Business Venturing* **9**: 125–40

List F. (Lloyd S. S., trans.) (1909 [1841]) *The National System of Political Economy.* London, Longman, Green

Littler C. R. (1988) Technology, innovation and labour-management strategies. In Urabe K., Child J., Kagono T. (eds) *Innovation and Management: International Comparisons.* Berlin, Walter de Gruyter: 337–58

Littler D. (1994) Marketing and innovation. In Dodgson M., Rothwell R. (eds) *The Handbook of Industrial Innovation.* Aldershot, Edward Elgar: 293–300

Littler D., Wilemon D. (1991) Strategic alliancing in computerized business systems.

Technovation 11: 457–73

Lloyd P. E. (1989) Research and policy review 28. Fragmenting markets and the dynamic restructuring of production: issues for spatial policy. *Environment and Planning A* 21: 429–44

Lloyd P., Meegan R. (1996) Contested governance: European exposure in the English regions. In Alden J., Boland P. (eds) *Regional Development Strategies: A European Perspective*. London, Jessica Kingsley: 55–85

Lloyd P. E., Reeve D. E. (1982) North-West England 1971–1977: a study in industrial decline and economic re-structuring. *Regional Studies* 16: 345–59

Lo F.-C., Salih K. (eds) (1978) *Growth Pole Strategy and Regional Development Policy*. Oxford, Pergamon

Lo F.-C., Salih K., Douglass M. (1981) Rural–urban transformation in Asia. In Lo F.-C. (ed.) *Rural–Urban Relations and Regional Development*. Singapore, Maruzen Asia: 7–43

Lock P. (1986) Brazil: arms for export. In Broszka M., Ohlson T. (eds) *Arms Production in the Third World*. London, Taylor and Francis: 79–104

Loftman P., Nevin B. (1996) Going for growth: prestige projects in three British cities. *Urban Studies* 33: 991–1019

Logan I. B., Mengisteab K. (1993) IMF–World Bank adjustment and structural transformation in Sub-Saharan Africa. *Economic Geography* 69: 1–24

Lorentzon S. (1993) The use of ICT at the plant of ABB at Ludvika and at the plant of Volvo at Skövde in Sweden – a regional perspective. In Bakis H., Abler R., Roche E. M. (eds) *Corporate Networks, International Telecommunications and Interdependence*. London, Belhaven: 135–60

Lorenz D. (1989) Newly industrialising countries in the world economy: NICs, SICs, NECs, EPZs or TEs? in Holtfrerich C.-L. (ed.) *Interactions in the World Economy: Perspectives from Economic History*. New York, New York University Press: 338–66

Lorenz E. H. (1989) The search for flexibility: subcontracting networks in British and French engineering. In Hirst P., Zeitlin J. (eds) *Reversing Industrial Decline? Industrial Structure and Policy in Britain and Her Competitors*. Oxford: Berg: 122–32

Lorenz E. H. (1992) Trust, community, and cooperation: toward a theory of industrial districts. In Storper M., Scott A. J. (eds) *Pathways to Industrialization and Regional Development*. London, Routledge: 195–204

Lorenzoni G., Baden-Fuller C. (1995) Creating a strategic center to manage a web of partners. *California Management Review* 37 (3): 146–63

Lorenzoni G., Ornati O. A. (1988) Constellations of firms and new ventures. *Journal of Business Venturing* 3: 41–57

Loveman G., Sengenberger W. (1991) The re-emergence of small-scale production. *Small Business Economics* 3: 1–38

Loveridge S. (1996) On the continuing popularity of industrial recruitment. *Economic Development Quarterly* 10: 151–8

Lovering J. (1988) Islands of prosperity: the spatial impact of high-technology defence industry in Britain. In Breheny M. J. (ed.) *Defence Expenditure and Regional Development*. London, Mansell: 29–48

Low B. K. H. (1996) Long-term relationship in industrial marketing: reality or rhetoric? *Industrial Marketing Management* 25: 23–35

Lubeck P. M. (1992) Malaysian industrialization, ethnic divisions, and the NIC model. In Appelbaum R. P., Henderson J. (eds) *States and Development in the Asia Pacific Rim*. Newbury Park, CA, Sage: 176–98

Luger M. I., Evans W. N. (1988) Geographic differences in production technology.

Regional Science and Urban Economics 18: 399–424

Luger M. I., Goldstein H. A. (1991) *Technology in the Garden: Research Parks and Regional Economic Development.* Chapel Hill, University of North Carolina Press

Lui T. L., Chiu S. (1994) A tale of two industries: the restructuring of Hong Kong's garment-making and electronics industries. *Environment and Planning A* 26: 53–70

Luke J. S., Ventriss C., Reed B. J., Reed C. M. (1988) *Managing Economic Development.* San Francisco, Jossey-Bass

Lund L. (1986) *Locating Corporate R&D Facilities.* Research report number 892. New York, The Conference Board

Lundvall B.-A. (1988) Innovation as an interactive process: from user–producer interaction to the national system of innovation. In Dosi G., Freeman C., Nelson R., Silverberg G., Soete L. (eds) *Technical Change and Economic Theory.* London, Pinter: 349–69

Lundvall B.-A. (ed.) (1992) *National Systems of Innovation: Towards a Theory of Innovation and Interactive Learning.* London, Pinter

Luttrell W. F. (1972) Industrial complexes and regional economic development in Canada. In Kuklinski A. (ed.) *Growth Poles and Growth Centres in Regional Planning.* The Hague, Mouton: 243–62

Lyberaki A., Smyth I. (1990) Small is small: The role and functions of small-scale industries. In van Dijk M. P., Marcussen H. S. (eds) *Industrialization in the Third World: The Need for Alternative Strategies.* London, Frank Cass: 125–45

Lynch L. M. (1993) The economics of youth training in the United States. *Economic Journal* 103: 1292–1302

Lynch R. G., Fishgold G., Blackwood D. L. (1996) The effectiveness of firm-specific state tax incentives in promoting economic development: evidence from New York State's industrial development agencies. *Economic Development Quarterly* 10: 57–68

Lynn L. H., Reddy N. M., Aram J. D. (1996) Linking technology and institutions: the innovation community framework. *Research Policy* 15: 91–106

Lyons B. R., Bailey S. (1993) Small subcontractors in UK engineering: competitiveness, dependence and problems. *Small Business Economics* 5: 101–9

Lyons D. (1995) Agglomeration economies among high technology firms in advanced production areas: the case of Denver/Boulder. *Regional Studies* 29: 265–78

Lyson T. A. (1989) *Two Sides to the Sunbelt.* New York, Praeger

MacCormack A. D., Newman L. J., Rosenfield D. B. (1994) The new dynamics of global manufacturing site location. *Sloan Management Review* 35 (4): 69–80

Macdonald R. J. (1985) Strategic alternatives in emerging industries. *Journal of Product Innovation Management* 2: 158–69

Macdonald R. J., Wang J. (1994) Time, timeliness of innovation and the emergence of industries. *Technovation* 14: 37–53

Macdonald S. (1986) Headhunting in high technology. *Technovation* 4: 233–45

Macdonald S. (1987) Towards higher high technology policy. In Brotchie J. F., Hall P., Newton P. W. (eds) *The Spatial Impact of Technological Change.* London, Croom Helm: 357–74

Macdonald S. (1992) Formal collaboration and informal information flow. *International Journal of Technology Management* 7: 49–60

Macdonald S., Williams C. (1994) The survival of the gatekeeper. *Research Policy* 23: 123–32

MacDonald S. B., Hughes J. E., Crum D. L. (1995) *New Tigers and Old Elephants.* New Brunswick, NJ, Transaction Publishers

MacDuffie J. P., Sethuraman K., Fisher M. L. (1996) Product variety and manufacturing performance: evidence from the international automotive assembly plant study. *Management Science* 42: 350–69

Macgregor B. D., Langridge R. J., Adley J., Chapman J. (1986) The development of high technology industry in Newbury district. *Regional Studies* 20: 433–47

Machalaba D. (1996) US ports are embarking on a shakeout. *Wall Street Journal* 18 October: A2

Machlup F. (1962) *The Production and Distribution of Knowledge in the United States.* Princeton, NJ, Princeton University Press

MacKay R. R. (1993) Local labour markets, regional development and human capital. *Regional Studies* 27: 783–95

MacMillan I. C., Kulow D. M., Khoylian R. (1989) Venture capitalists' involvement in their investments: extent and performance. *Journal of Business Venturing* 4: 27–47

MacMillan I. C., Siegel R., Subba Narasimha P. N. (1985) Criteria used by venture capitalists to evaluate new venture proposals. *Journal of Business Venturing* 1: 119–28

MacPherson A. (1988a) Industrial innovation in the small business sector: empirical evidence from metropolitan Toronto. *Environment and Planning A* 20: 953–71

MacPherson A. D. (1988b) New product development among small Toronto manufacturers: empirical evidence on the role of technical service linkages. *Economic Geography* 64: 62–75

MacPherson A. (1991) Interfirm information linkages in an economically disadvantaged region: an empirical perspective from metropolitan Buffalo. *Environment and Planning A* 23: 591–605

MacPherson A. (1992) Innovation, external technical linkages and small-firm commercial performance: an empirical analysis from Western New York. *Entrepreneurship and Regional Development* 4: 165–83

MacPherson A. D. (1995) Product design strategies amongst small- and medium-sized manufacturing firms: implications for export planning and regional economic development. *Entrepreneurship and Regional Development* 7: 329–48

Maddison A. (1994) Explaining the economic performance of nations. In Baumol W. J., Nelson R. R., Wolff E. N. (eds) *Convergence of Productivity: Cross-national Studies and Historical Evidence.* New York, Oxford University Press: 20–61

Magaziner I. C., Hout T. M. (1980) *Japanese Industrial Policy.* London, Policy Studies Institute

Mager N. H. (1987) *The Kondratieff Waves.* New York, Praeger

Maggi R., Haeni P. K. (1986) Spatial concentration, location and competitiveness: the case of Switzerland. *Regional Studies* 20: 141–9

Maidique M. A., Hayes R. H. (1984) The art of high-technology management. *Sloan Management Review* 25 (2): 17–31

Maidique M. A., Patch P. (1988) Corporate strategy and technological policy. In Tushman M. L., Moore W. L. (eds) *Readings in the Management of Innovation*, second edition. Cambridge, MA, Ballinger: 236–48

Maidique M. A., Zirger B. J. (1985) The new product learning cycle. *Research Policy* 14: 299–313

Maillat D. (1984) Conditions d'une strategie de développement par le bas: le cas de la région horlogère Suisse. *Revue d'Economie Régionale et Urbaine* 257–73

Maillat D. (1990) SMEs, innovation and territorial development. In Cappellin R., Nijkamp P. (eds) *The Spatial Context of Technological Development.* Aldershot, Avebury: 331–51

Maillat D. (1995) Territorial dynamic, innovative milieus and regional policy. *Entrepreneurship and Regional Development* 7: 157–65

Maillat D., Lecoq B. (1992) New technologies and transformation of regional structures in Europe: the role of the milieu. *Entrepreneurship and Regional Development* 4: 1–20

Maillat D., Lecoq B., Nemeti F., Pfister M. (1995) Technology district and innovation: the case of the Swiss Jura Arc. *Regional Studies* 29: 251–63

Maillat D., Vasserot J.-Y. (1988) Economic and territorial conditions for indigenous revival in Europe's industrial regions. In Aydalot P., Keeble D. (eds) *High Technology Industry and Innovative Environments: The European Experience*. London, Routledge: 163–83

Mair A., Florida R., Kenney M. (1988) The new geography of automobile production: Japanese transplants in North America. *Economic Geography* 64: 352–73

Majumdar B. A. (1988) Industrial policy in action: the case of the electronics industry in Japan. *Columbia Journal of World Business* 23 (3): 25–34

Malecki E. J. (1979) Locational trends in R&D by large US corporations, 1965–1977. *Economic Geography* 55: 309–23

Malecki E. J. (1980a) Corporate organization of R and D and the location of technological activities. *Regional Studies* 14: 219–34

Malecki E. J. (1980b) Dimensions of R&D location in the United States. *Research Policy* 9: 2–22

Malecki E. J. (1984) High technology and local economic development. *Journal of the American Planning Association* 50: 260–9

Malecki E. J. (1986) Research and development and the geography of high-technology complexes. In Rees J. (ed.) *Technology, Regions, and Policy*. Totowa, NJ, Rowman and Littlefield: 51–74

Malecki E. J. (1987) Hope or hyperbole? High tech and economic development. *Technology Review* 90 (7): 44–52

Malecki E. J. (1989) What about people in high technology? Some research and policy considerations. *Growth and Change* 20 (1): 67–79

Malecki E. J. (1990) New firm formation in the USA: corporate structure, venture capital, and local environment. *Entrepreneurship and Regional Development* 2: 247–65

Malecki E. J. (1994) Entrepreneurship in regional and local development. *International Regional Science Review* 16: 119–53

Malecki E. J. (1995) Culture as mediator of global and local forces. In Le Heron R., van der Knaap B. (eds) *Human Resources and Industrial Spaces*. London, John Wiley: 105–27

Malecki E. J., Bradbury S. L. (1992) R&D facilities and professional labour: labour force dynamics in high technology. *Regional Studies* 26: 123–36

Malecki E. J., Nijkamp P. (1988) Technology and regional development: some thoughts on policy. *Environment and Planning C: Government and Policy* 6: 383–99

Malecki E. J., Tödtling F. (1995) The new flexible economy: shaping regional and local institutions for global competition. In Bertuglia C. S., Fischer M. M., Preto G. (eds) *Technological Change, Economic Development and Space*. Berlin, Springer-Verlag: 276–94

Malecki E. J., Tootle D. M. (1996) The role of networks in small firm competitiveness. *International Journal of Technology Management* 11: 43–57

Malecki E. J., Varaiya P. (1986) Innovation and changes in regional structure. In Nijkamp P. (ed.) *Handbook of Regional and Urban Economics*, volume 1: *Regional Economics*. Amsterdam, North-Holland: 629–45

Malecki E. J., Veldhoen M. (1993) Network activities, information and competitiveness in small firms. *Geografiska Annaler* B75: 131–47

Malerba F. (1992a) Learning by firms and incremental technical change. *Economic Journal* **102**: 845–69

Malerba F. (1992b) The organization of the innovative process. In Rosenberg N., Landau R., Mowery D. C. (eds) *Technology and the Wealth of Nations*. Stanford, Stanford University Press: 247–78

Malerba F. (1993) The national system of innovation: Italy. In Nelson R. R. (ed.) *National Innovation Systems: A Comparative Analysis*. New York, Oxford University Press: 230–64

Malizia E. E. (1990) Economic growth and economic development: concepts and measures. *Review of Regional Studies* **20** (1): 30–6

Malmberg B. (1995) Problems of time–space co-ordination: a key to the understanding of multiplant firms. *Progress in Human Geography* **19**: 47–60

Malone T. W., Rockart J. F. (1993) How will information technology reshape organizations? Computers as coordination technology. In Bradley S. P., Hausman J. A., Nolan R. L. (eds) *Globalization, Technology, and Competition: The Fusion of Computers and Telecommunications in the 1990s*. Boston, Harvard Business School Press: 37–56

Mandel E. (1980) *Long Waves of Capitalist Development*. Cambridge, Cambridge University Press

Mangelsdorf M. E. (1993) Ground-zero training. *Inc.* **15** (2): 82–93

Mangum G., Mayall D., Nelson K. (1985) The temporary help industry: a response to the dual internal labor market. *Industrial and Labor Relations Review* **38**: 599–611

Mansell R. (1993) *The New Telecommunications: A Political Economy of Network Evolution*. London, Sage

Mansell R. (1994) Multinational organizations and international private networks: opportunities and constraints. In Steinfield C., Bauer J. M., Caby L. (eds) *Telecommunications in Transition*. London, Sage: 204–22

Mansfield E. (1988) The speed and cost of industrial innovation in Japan and the United States: external vs. internal technology. *Management Science* **34**: 1157–68

Mansfield E. (1989) The diffusion of industrial robots in Japan and the United States. *Research Policy* **18**: 183–92

Mansfield E. (1993) The diffusion of flexible manufacturing systems in Japan, Europe and the United States. *Management Science* **39**: 149–59

Mansfield E., Rapaport J., Romeo A., Villani E., Wagner S., Husic F. (1977) *The Production and Application of New Industrial Technology*. New York, Norton

Mansfield E., Teece D., Romeo A. (1979) Overseas research and development by US-based firms. *Economica* **46**: 187–96

Mansfield Y. (1990) Spatial patterns of international tourist flows: towards a theoretical framework. *Progress in Human Geography* **14**: 372–90

Mantel S. J., Rosegger G. (1987) The role of third-parties in the diffusion of innovations: a survey. In Rothwell R., Bessant J. (eds) *Innovation: Adaptation and Growth*. Amsterdam, Elsevier: 123–34

Marceau J. (1994) Clusters, chains and complexes: three approaches to innovation with a public policy perspective. In Dodgson M., Rothwell R. (eds) *The Handbook of Industrial Innovation*. Aldershot, Edward Elgar: 3–12

Marchand C. (1986) The transmission of fluctuations in a central place system. *Canadian Geographer* **30**: 249–54

Marchena Gómez M. J. (1995) New tourism trends and the future of Mediterranean Europe. *Tijdschrift voor Economische en Sociale Geografie* **86**: 21–31

Marchesnay M., Julien P.-A. (1990) The small business: as a transaction space. *Entrepreneurship and Regional Development* **2**: 267–77

Marcus A. D., Stern G., Mitchener B. (1996) Driving force: Israel is becoming high-tech frontier for the auto industry. *Wall Street Journal* 22 August: A1, A6

Marelli E. (1985) Economic policies and their effects upon regional economies. *Papers of the Regional Science Association* **58**: 127–39

Mariotti S., Mutinelli M. (1992) Diffusion of flexible automation in Italy. In Ayres R. U., Haywood W., Tchijov I. (eds) *Computer Integrated Manufacturing*, volume III: *Models, Case Studies, and Forecasts of Diffusion.* London, Chapman and Hall: 137–53

Markusen A. R. (1985) *Profit Cycles, Oligopoly, and Regional Development.* Cambridge, MA, MIT Press

Markusen A. R. (1986) Defence spending: a successful industrial policy? *International Journal of Urban and Regional Research* **10**: 105–22

Markusen A. R. (1987) *Regions: The Economics and Politics of Territory.* Totowa, NJ, Rowman and Littlefield

Markusen A. R. (1995) Interaction between regional and industrial policies: evidence from four countries. In Bruno M., Plescovic B. (eds) *Proceedings of the World Bank Annual Conference on Development Economics 1994.* Washington, World Bank: 279–98

Markusen A., Hall P., Campbell S., Dietrich S. (1991) *The Rise of the Gunbelt.* New York, Oxford University Press

Markusen A., Hall P., Glasmeier A. (1986) *High Tech America.* Boston, Allen and Unwin

Markusen A., Yudken J. (1992) *Dismantling the Cold War Economy.* New York, Basic Books

Marquis D. G. (1988) The anatomy of successful innovations. In Tushman M. L., Moore W. L. (eds) *Readings in the Management of Innovation*, second edition. Cambridge, MA, Ballinger: 79–87

Marsden D. (1993) Skill flexibility, labour market structure, training systems and competitiveness. In Foray D., Freeman C. (eds) *Technology and the Wealth of Nations: The Dynamics of Constructed Advantage.* London, Pinter: 373–88

Marshall A. (1920) *Principles of Economics.* London, Macmillan

Marshall J. N., Wood P., Daniels P. W., McKinnon A., Bachtler J., Damesick P., Thrift N., Gillespie A., Green A., Leyshon A. (1988) *Services and Uneven Development.* Oxford, Oxford University Press

Marshall M. (1987) *Long Waves of Regional Development.* New York, St Martin's Press

Martin B. (1996) Technology foresight: a review of recent government exercises. *STI Review* **17**: 15–50

Martin B. R., Irvine J. (1984) CERN: past performance and future prospects III. CERN and the future of world high-energy physics. *Research Policy* **13**: 311–42

Martin B. R., Irvine J. (1989) *Research Foresight: Priority-Setting in Science.* London, Pinter

Martin J. M. (1990) Energy and technological change: lessons from the last fifteen years. *STI Review* **7**: 9–34

Martin M. J. C. (1984) *Managing Technological Innovation and Entrepreneurship.* Reston, VA, Reston Publishing

Martin R. (1988) The political economy of Britain's north–south divide. *Transactions, Institute of British Geographers* NS **13**: 389–418

Martin R. (1989) The growth and geographical anatomy of venture capitalism in the United Kingdom. *Regional Studies* **23**: 389–403

Martin R. (1993) Remapping British regional policy: the end of the north–south divide? *Regional Studies* **27**: 797–805

Martin R. C., Miley H. W. (1983) The stability of economic base multipliers: some empirical evidence. *Review of Regional Studies* 13 (3): 18–25

Martin R. P., Holland D. (1992) Sources of output change in the US economy. *Growth and Change* 23: 446–68

Martin W. G. (ed.) (1990) *Semiperipheral States in the World-Economy*. Westport, CT, Greenwood Press

Martinelli F. (1985) Public policy and industrial development in southern Italy: anatomy of a dependent industry. *International Journal of Urban and Regional Research* 9: 47–81

Martinelli F., Schoenberger E. (1991) Oligopoly is alive and well: notes for a broader discussion of flexible accumulation. In Benko G., Dunford M. (eds) *Industrial Change and Regional Development*. London, Belhaven: 117–33

Marton K. (1986) *Multinationals, Technology, and Industrialization: Implications and Impact in Third World Countries*. Lexington, MA, Lexington Books

Mason C. M. (1985) The geography of 'successful' small firms in the United Kingdom. *Environment and Planning A* 17: 1499–513

Mason C. M., Harrison R. T. (1995) Closing the regional equity gap: the role of informal venture capital. *Small Business Economics* 7: 153–72

Mason C. M., Harrison R. T. (1996) Informal venture capital: a study of the investment process, the post-investment experience and investment performance. *Entrepreneurship and Regional Development* 8: 105–2

Mason E. S. (1982) Stages of economic growth revisited. In Kindleberger C. P., di Tella G. (eds) *Economics in the Long View: Essays in Honour of W. W. Rostow*, volume 1. New York, New York University Press: 116–40

Massey D. (1973) The basic:service categorization in planning. *Regional Studies* 7: 1–15

Massey D. (1979) A critical evaluation of industrial-location theory. In Hamilton F. E. I., Linge G. J. R. (eds) *Spatial Analysis, Industry and the Industrial Environment*, volume 1: *Industrial Systems*. London, John Wiley: 57–72

Massey D. (1995) *Spatial Divisions of Labour: Social Structures and the Geography of Production*, second edition. London, Macmillan

Massey D., Meegan R. (1982) *The Anatomy of Job Loss*. London, Methuen

Massey D., Quintas P., Wield D. (1992) *High Tech Fantasies: Science Parks in Society, Science and Space*. London, Routledge

Mayer W., Pleeter S. (1975) A theoretical justification for the use of location quotients. *Regional Science and Urban Economics* 5: 343–55

Mazzonis D. (1989) Networking cooperation and innovation among small firms in Italy: the view from the agency engaged in actions for stimulating the technological upgrading of industry. *Entrepreneurship and Regional Development* 1: 61–74

McArthur R. (1990) Replacing the concept of high technology: towards a diffusion-based approach. *Environment and Planning A* 22: 811–28

McCann P. (1995) Rethinking the economics of location and agglomeration. *Urban Studies* 32: 563–77

McCombie J. S. L. (1988a) A synoptic view of regional growth and unemployment: I – the neoclassical theory. *Urban Studies* 25: 267–81

McCombie J. S. L. (1988b) A synoptic view of regional growth and unemployment: II – the post-Keynesian theory. *Urban Studies* 25: 399–417

McCrackin B. H. (1984) Education's contribution to productivity and economic growth. *Economic Review, Federal Reserve Bank of Atlanta* 69 (10): 8–23

McCutcheon D. M., Raturi A. S., Meredith J. R. (1994) The customization–responsiveness squeeze. *Sloan Management Review* 35 (2): 89–99

McDade B. E., Malecki E. J. (1997) Entrepreneurial networking: industrial estates in Ghana. *Tijdschrift voor Economische en Sociale Geografie* **88**: (in press)

McDermott P., Taylor M. (1982) *Industrial Organisation and Location*. Cambridge, Cambridge University Press

McDonald D. W., Leahey H. S. (1985) Licensing has a role in technology strategic planning. *Research Management* **28** (1): 35–40

McDougall P. P., Shane S., Oviatt B. M. (1994) Explaining the formation of international new ventures: the limits of theories from international business research. *Journal of Business Venturing* **9**: 469–87

McDowell S. D. (1995) The decline of the license raj: Indian software export policies. *Journal of Communication* **45** (4): 25–50

McFetridge D. G. (1993) The Canadian system of industrial innovation. In Nelson R. R. (ed.) *National Innovation Systems: A Comparative Analysis*. New York, Oxford University Press: 299–323

McGrath M. E., Hoole R. W. (1992) Manufacturing's new economies of scale. *Harvard Business Review* **70** (3): 94–102

McGrath R. G., MacMillan I. C. (1992) More like each other than anyone else? A cross-cultural study of entrepreneurial perceptions. *Journal of Business Venturing* **7**: 419–29

McGrath R. G., MacMillan I. C., Scheinberg S. (1992) Elitists, risk-takers, and rugged individualists? An exploratory analysis of cultural differences between entrepreneurs and non-entrepreneurs. *Journal of Business Venturing* **7**: 115–35

McGregor A., McConnachie M. (1995) Social exclusion, urban regeneration and economic reintegration. *Urban Studies* **32**: 1587–600

McIntyre S. H. (1988) Market adaptation as a process in the product life cycle of radical innovations and high technology products. *Journal of Product Innovation Management* **5**: 140–9

McKay J., Missen G. (1995) Keeping their miracles going: questioning big firms in Korea and small firms in Taiwan. In Le Heron R., Park S. O. (eds) *The Asian Pacific Rim and Globalization*. Aldershot, Avebury: 61–85

McKee D. L. (1988) *Growth, Development, and the Service Economy in the Third World*. New York, Praeger

McKelvey M. (1991) How do national systems of innovation differ? A critical analysis of Porter, Freeman, Lundvall and Nelson. In Hodgson G. M., Screpanti E. (eds) *Rethinking Economics: Markets, Technology and Economic Evolution*. Aldershot, Edward Elgar: 117–37

McMorran R., Wallace L. (1995) Why macroeconomists and environmentalists need each other. *Finance and Development* **32** (4): 46–9

McNaughton R. B., Green M. B. (1989) Spatial patterns of Canadian venture capital investment. *Regional Studies* **23**: 9–18

McNulty J. E. (1977) A test of the time dimension in economic base analysis. *Land Economics* **53**: 359–68

McUsic M. (1987) US manufacturing: any cause for alarm? *New England Economic Review* January/February: 3–17

Melcher R. A. (1996) Manpower upgrades its resume. *Business Week* 10 June: 81–2

Mellor I., Ironside R. G. (1978) The incidence multiplier of a regional development programme. *Canadian Geographer* **22**: 225–51

Mensch G. (1979) *Stalemate in Technology: Innovations Overcome the Depression*. Cambridge, MA, Ballinger

Menzler-Hokkanen I. (1995) Multinational enterprises and technology transfer. *International Journal of Technology Management* **10**: 293–310

Mera K. (1974) Trade-off between aggregate efficiency and interregional equity: the case of Japan. *Regional and Urban Economics* **4**: 273–300

Merrifield D. B. (1994) Measurements of productivity: key to survival. *International Journal of Technology Management* **9**: 771–83

Mervis J. (1995) Reading the tea leaves in a list of major priorities. *Science* **270**: 1139–41

Metcalfe J. S. (1995) Technology systems and technology policy in an evolutionary framework. *Cambridge Journal of Economics* **19**: 25–46

Meyer D. R. (1977) Agglomeration economies and urban-industrial growth: a clarification and review of concepts. *Regional Science Perspectives* **7** (1): 80–91

Meyer J. R. (1963) Regional economics: a survey. *American Economic Review* **53**: 19–54

Meyer M. H., Utterback J. M. (1993) The product family and the dynamics of core capability. *Sloan Management Review* **34** (3): 29–47

Meyer-Krahmer F. (1985) Innovation behaviour and regional indigenous potential. *Regional Studies* **19**: 523–34

Meyer-Stamer J. (1995) Micro-level innovations and competitiveness. *World Development* **23**: 143–8

Meyers P. W., Athaide G. A. (1991) Strategic mutual learning between producing and buying firms during product innovation. *Journal of Product Innovation Management* **8**: 155–69

Meyers P. W., Wilemon D. (1989) Learning in technology development teams. *Journal of Product Innovation Management* **6**: 79–88

Michalet C.-A. (1991) Global competition and its implications for firms. In *Technology and Productivity: The Challenge for Economic Policy*. Paris, Organisation for Economic Co-operation and Development: 79–88

Micossi S., Viesti G. (1991) Japanese direct manufacturing investment in Europe. In Winters L. A., Venables A. (eds) *European Integration: Trade and Industry*. Cambridge, Cambridge University Press: 200–33

Mieskonen J. (1991) The success of FM investment: case studies from small industrial economies. *International Journal of Technology Management* **6**: 277–91

Miles I. (1988) *Home Informatics: Information Technology and the Transformation of Everyday Life*. London, Frances Pinter

Miles I. (1994) Innovation in services. In Dodgson M., Rothwell R. (eds) *The Handbook of Industrial Innovation*. Aldershot, Edward Elgar: 243–56

Miles R. E., Creed W. E. D. (1995) Organizational forms and managerial philosophies: a descriptive and analytical review. In Cummings L. L., Staw B. M. (eds) *Research in Organizational Behavior*, volume 17. Greenwich, CT, JAI Press: 333–72

Miles R. E., Snow C. C. (1994) *Fit, Failure and the Hall of Fame: How Companies Succeed or Fail*. New York: Free Press

Miller D. B., Clemons E. K., Row M. C. (1993) Information technology and the global virtual corporation. In Bradley S. P., Hausman J. A., Nolan R. L. (eds) *Globalization, Technology, and Competition: The Fusion of Computers and Telecommunications in the 1990s*. Boston, Harvard Business School Press: 283–307

Miller D. L. (1986) Mexico. In Rushing F. W., Brown C. G. (eds) *National Policies for Developing High Technology Industries: International Implications*. Boulder, CO, Westview Press: 173–99

Miller J. G., Roth A. V. (1994) A taxonomy of manufacturing strategies. *Management Science* **40**: 285–303

Miller R. (1994) Global R&D networks and large-scale innovations: the case of the automobile industry. *Research Policy* **23**: 27–46

Miller R., Coté M. (1987) *Growing the Next Silicon Valley*. Lexington, MA, Lexington

Books
Miller R., Hobday M., Leroux-Demers T., Olleros X. (1995) Innovation in complex systems industries: the case of flight simulation. *Industrial and Corporate Change* 4: 363–400

Miller R. E., Blair P. D. (1985) *Input–Output Analysis: Foundations and Extensions.* Englewood Cliffs, NJ, Prentice-Hall

Miller W. L. (1995) A broader mission for R&D. *Research-Technology Management* 38 (6): 24–36

Millson M. R., Raj, S. P., Wilemon D. (1992) A survey of major approaches for accelerating new product development. *Journal of Product Innovation Management* 9: 53–69

Mitchell G. R., Hamilton W. F. (1988) Managing R&D as a strategic option. *Research-Technology Management* 31 (3): 15–22

Mitchell K. (1995) Flexible circulation in the Pacific rim: capitalisms in cultural context. *Economic Geography* 71: 364–82

Mitchell R. (1989) Nurturing those ideas. *Business Week* 16 June: 106–18

Miwa Y. (1994) Subcontracting relationships: the automobile industry. In Imai K., Komiya R. (eds) *Business Enterprise in Japan.* Cambridge, MA, MIT Press: 141–55

Miyazaki K. (1994) Search, learning and accumulation of technological competences: the case of optoelectronics. *Industrial and Corporate Change* 3: 631–54

Mody A. (1989) *Staying in the Loop: International Alliances for Sharing Technology.* Discussion Paper 61. Washington, World Bank

Mody A., Suri R., Tatikonda M. (1995) Keeping pace with change: international competition in printed circuit board assembly. *Industrial and Corporate Change* 4: 583–613

Mody A., Wheeler D. (1987) Towards a vanishing middle: competition in the world garment industry. *World Development* 15: 1269–84

Mogee M. E. (1980) The relationship of federal support of basic research in universities to industrial innovation and productivity. In *Special Study on Economic Change*, volume 3: *Research and Innovation: Developing a Dynamic Nation.* Washington, US Government Printing Office: 257–79

Mohrman S. A., Cohen S. G. (1995) When people get out of the box: new relationships, new systems. In Howard A. (ed.) *The Changing Nature of Work.* San Francisco, Jossey-Bass: 365–410

Molina A. H. (1989) *The Social Basis of the Microelectronics Revolution.* Edinburgh, Edinburgh University Press

Molle W., Beumer L., Boeckhout I. (1989) The location of information intensive activities in the European Community. In Punset E., Sweeney G. (eds) *Information Resources and Corporate Growth.* London, Pinter: 161–72

Monkiewicz J., Maciejewicz J. (1986) *Technology Exports from the Socialist Countries.* Boulder, CO, Westview Press

Mønsted M. (1991) Flexibility and skills in small enterprises. *Entrepreneurship and Regional Development* 3: 101–10

Mønsted M. (1993) Regional network processes: networks for the service sector or development of entrepreneurs? In Karlsson C., Johannisson B., Storey D. (eds) *Small Business Dynamics.* London, Routledge: 204–22

Moomaw R. L., Williams R. (1991) Total factor productivity growth in manufacturing: further evidence from the states. *Journal of Regional Science* 31: 17–34

Moore C. L. (1975) A new look at the minimum requirements approach to regional economic analysis. *Economic Geography* 51: 350–6

Moore C. L., Jacobsen M. (1984) Minimum requirements and regional economics,

1980. *Economic Geography* **60**: 217–24

Moore F. T. (1983) *Technological Change and Industrial Development: Issues and Opportunities*. World Bank Staff Working Paper 613. Washington, World Bank

Moore J. F. (1993) Predators and prey: a new ecology of competition. *Harvard Business Review* 71 (3): 75–86

Morales A., Balkin S., Persky J. (1995) The value of benefits of a public street market: the case of Maxwell Street. *Economic Development Quarterly* 9: 304–20

Morbey G. K. (1989) R&D expenditures and profit growth. *Research-Technology Management* **32** (3): 20–3

More R. (1985) Barriers to innovation: intraorganizational dislocations. *Journal of Product Innovation Management* 2: 205–7

Morehouse W., Gupta B. (1987) India: success and failure. In Segal A. (ed.) *Learning by Doing: Science and Technology in the Developing World*. Boulder, CO, Westview Press: 189–212

Moreno Brid J. C. (1992) Structural change in Mexico's motor vehicle industry (1977–1989). In van Liemt G. (ed.) *Industry on the Move: Causes and Consequences of International Relocation in the Manufacturing Industry*. Geneva, International Labour Office: 259–78

Morgan K., Sayer A. (1985) A 'modern' industry in a 'mature' region: the remaking of management–labour relations. *International Journal of Urban and Regional Research* 9: 383–404

Morgan K., Sayer A. (1988) *Microcircuits of Capital: 'Sunrise' Industry and Uneven Development*. Cambridge, Polity Press

Moriarty B. M. (1991) Urban systems, industrial restructuring, and the spatial–temporal diffusion of manufacturing employment. *Environment and Planning A* **23**: 1571–88

Morita K., Hiraoka H. (1988) Technopolis Osaka: integrating urban functions and science. In Smilor R. W., Kozmetsky G., Gibson D. V. (eds) *Creating the Technopolis*. Cambridge, MA, Ballinger: 23–49

Morris J. L. (1988) New technologies, flexible work practices, and regional sociospatial differentiation: some observations from the United Kingdom. *Environment and Planning D: Society and Space* 6: 301–19

Morrison P. S. (1990) Segmentation theory applied to local, regional and spatial labour markets. *Progress in Human Geography* 14: 488–528

Morton O. (1995) The softwar revolution: a survey of defence technology. *The Economist* 10 June

Moseley M. J. (1974) *Growth Centres in Spatial Planning*. Oxford, Pergamon

Moss M. L. (1986) Telecommunications and the future of cities. *Land Development Studies* 3: 33–44

Moss M. L. (1987) Telecommunications, world cities, and urban policy. *Urban Studies* **24**: 534–46

Moss M. L. (1988) Telecommunications: shaping the future. In Sternlieb G., Hughes J. W. (eds) *America's New Market Geography*. New Brunswick, NJ, Center for Urban Policy Research: 255–75

Moulaert F., Djellal F. (1995) Information technology consulting firms: economies of agglomeration from a wide-area perspective. *Urban Studies* **32**: 105–22

Moulaert F., Gallouj C. (1993) The locational geography of advanced producer service firms: the limits of economies of agglomeration. *Service Industries Journal* 13: 91–106

Moulaert F., Tödtling F. (eds) (1995) The geography of advanced producer services in Europe. *Progress in Planning* 43 (2–3): 89–274

Mowery D. C. (1983a) The relationship between intrafirm and contractual forms of industrial research in American manufacturing, 1900–1940. *Explorations in Economic History* 20: 351–74

Mowery D. C. (1983b) Economic theory and government technology policy. *Policy Sciences* 16: 27–43

Mowery D. C. (1988) The diffusion of new manufacturing technologies. In Cyert R. M., Mowery D. C. (eds) *The Impact of Technological Change on Employment and Economic Growth.* Cambridge, MA, Ballinger: 481–509

Mowery D. C. (1989) Collaborative ventures between US and foreign manufacturing firms. *Research Policy* 18: 19–32

Mowery D. C. (1992) The challenges of international trade to US technology policy. In Harris M. C., Moore G. E. (eds) *Linking Trade and Technology Policies.* Washington, National Academy Press: 121–38

Mowery D. C. (1994) The changing structure of US industrial research: implications for R&D organization in the Russian Federation. *International Journal of Technology Management* 9: 547–63

Mowery D. C., Langlois R. N. (1996) Spinning off and spinning on(?): the federal government role in the development of the US computer software industry. *Research Policy* 25: 947–66

Mowery D. C., Oxley J. E. (1995) Inward technology transfer and competitiveness: the role of national innovation systems. *Cambridge Journal of Economics* 19: 67–93

Mowery D. C., Rosenberg N. (1979) The influence of market demand upon innovation: a critical review of some recent empirical studies. *Research Policy* 8: 102–53

Mowery D. C., Rosenberg N. (1989) *Technology and the Pursuit of Economic Growth.* Cambridge, Cambridge University Press

Mowery D. C., Rosenberg N. (1993) The US national innovation system. In Nelson R. R. (ed.) *National Innovation Systems: A Comparative Analysis.* New York, Oxford University Press, 29–75

Moyes A., Westhead P. (1990) Environments for new firm formation in Great Britain. *Regional Studies* 24: 123–36

Mueller F., Loveridge R. (1995) The 'second industrial divide'? The role of the large firm in the Baden-Württemberg model. *Industrial and Corporate Change* 4: 555–82

Muffatto M., Panizzolo R. (1996) Innovation and product development strategies in the Italian motorcycle industry. *Journal of Product Innovation Management* 13: 348–61

Mufson S. (1985) Don't thank us, Pepsi; we just talked with a few bean buyers. *Wall Street Journal* 17 July: 31

Mulligan G. (1987) Employment multipliers and functional types of communities: effects of public transfer payments. *Growth and Change* 18 (3): 1–11

Mulligan G. F., Fik T. J. (1994) Using dummy variables to estimate economic base multipliers. *Professional Geographer* 46: 368–78

Mulligan G. F., Gibson L. J. (1984) Regression estimates of economic base multipliers for small communities. *Economic Geography* 60: 225–37

Munday M., Morris J., Wilkinson B. (1995) Factories or warehouses? A Welsh perspective on Japanese transplant manufacturing. *Regional Studies* 29: 1–17

Murray G. C., Lott J. (1995) Have UK venture capitalists a bias against investment in new technology-based firms? *Research Policy* 24: 283–99

Murrell P. (1996) How far has the transition progressed? *Journal of Economic Perspectives* 10 (2): 25–44

Myers F. S. (1992) Japan bids for global leadership in clean industry. *Science* 256 (22

May): 1144–5

Myers M. B., Rosenbloom R. S. (1996) Rethinking the role of industrial research. In Rosenbloom R. S., Spencer W. J. (eds) *Engines of Innovation: US Industrial Research at the End of an Era.* Boston, Harvard Business School Press: 209–28

Myllyntaus T. (1990) The Finnish model of technology transfer. *Economic Development and Cultural Change* 38: 625–43

Myrdal G. (1957) *Economic Theory and Underdeveloped Regions.* London, Duckworth

Mytelka L. K. (1985) Stimulating effective technology transfer: The case of textiles in Africa. In Rosenberg N., Frischtak C. (eds) *International Technology Transfer: Concepts, Measures, and Comparisons.* New York, Praeger: 77–126

Nader J. (1994) The rise of an inventive profession: learning effects in the Midwestern harvester industry, 1850–1890. *Journal of Economic History* 54: 397–408

Nadvi K. (1994) Industrial district experiences in developing countries. In *Technological Dynamism in Industrial Districts: An Alternative Approach to Industrialization in Developing Countries?* New York, United Nations: 191–255

Nakarmi L., Shao M., Griffiths D. (1989) South Korea's new destination: the wild blue yonder. *Business Week* 11 September: 50

Narula R. (1993) Technology, international business and Porter's 'diamond': synthesizing a dynamic competitive development model. *Management International Review* 33 (special issue 2): 85–107

National Science Board (1993) *Science and Engineering Indicators 1993.* Washington, US Government Printing Office

National Science Board (1996) *Science and Engineering Indicators 1996.* Washington, US Government Printing Office

National Science Foundation (1988) Economic growth and corporate mergers dampen growth in company R&D. *Science Resources Studies Highlights* 11 March

Nau H. (1986) National policies for high technology development and trade: an international and comparative assessment. In Rushing F. W., Brown C. G. (eds) *National Policies for Developing High Technology Industries.* Boulder, CO, Westview Press: 9–29

Nayyar P. R., Bantel K. A. (1994) Competitive agility: a source of competitive advantage based on speed and variety. In Shrivastava P., Huff A., Dutton J. (eds) *Advances in Strategic Management*, volume 10A: *Resource-Based View of the Firm.* Greenwich, CT, JAI Press: 193–222

Ndegwa G. T. (1994) *What Ails African Businessmen?* Nairobi, Learners

Neff R., Holstein W. J. (1990) Mighty Mitsubishi is on the move. *Business Week* 24 September: 98–107

Nelson K. (1986) Labor demand, labor supply and the suburbanization of low-wage office work. In Scott A. J., Storper M. (eds) *Production, Work, Territory.* Boston, Allen and Unwin: 149–71

Nelson R. R. (1981) Research on productivity growth and productivity differences: dead ends and new departures. *Journal of Economic Literature* 19: 1029–64

Nelson R. R. (1984) *High-Technology Policies: A Five-Nation Comparison.* Washington, American Enterprise Institute

Nelson R. R. (1986a) Evolutionary modelling of economic change. In Stiglitz J. E., Mathewson G. F. (eds) *New Developments in the Analysis of Market Structure.* London, Macmillan: 450–71

Nelson R. R. (1986b) Incentives for entrepreneurship and supporting institutions. In Balassa B., Giersch H. (eds) *Economic Incentives.* New York, St Martin's Press: 173–87

Nelson R. R. (1987) *Understanding Technical Change as an Evolutionary Process.* Amsterdam, Elsevier

Nelson R. R. (ed.) (1993) *National Innovation Systems: A Comparative Analysis.* New York, Oxford University Press

Nelson R. R. (1994a) What has been the matter with neoclassical growth theory? In Silverberg G., Soete L. (eds) *The Economics of Growth and Technical Change.* Aldershot, Edward Elgar: 290–324

Nelson R. R. (1994b) The co-evolution of technology, industrial structure, and supporting institutions. *Industrial and Corporate Change* 3: 47–63

Nelson R. R. (1995) Recent evolutionary theorizing about economic change. *Journal of Economic Literature* 33: 48–90

Nelson R. R., Norman V. D. (1977) Technological change and factor mix over the product cycle. *Journal of Development Economics* 4: 3–24

Nelson R. R., Rosenberg N. (1993) Technical innovation and national systems. In Nelson R. R. (ed.) *National Innovation Systems: A Comparative Analysis.* New York, Oxford University Press: 3–21

Nelson R. R., Winter S. G. (1982) *An Evolutionary Theory of Economic Change.* Cambridge, MA, Harvard University Press

Nelson R. R., Wright G. (1992) The rise and fall of American technological leadership: the postwar era in historical perspective. *Journal of Economic Literature* 30: 1931–64

Nelson R. R., Wright G. (1994) The erosion of US technological leadership as a factor in postwar economic convergence. In Baumol W. J., Nelson R. R., Wolff E. N. (eds) *Convergence of Productivity: Cross-national Studies and Historical Evidence.* New York, Oxford University Press: 129–63

Nemeth R., Smith D. (1985) International trade and world-system structure: a multiple network analysis. *Review, Fernand Braudel Center for the Study of Economies, Historical Systems, and Civilizations* 8: 517–60

Nevis E. C., di Bella A. J., Gould J. M. (1995) Organizations as learning systems. *Sloan Management Review* 36 (2): 73–85

Newman R. G. (1990) The second wave arrives: Japanese strategy in the US auto parts market. *Business Horizons* 33 (4): 24–30

Newman R. G., Rhee K. A. (1990) Midwest auto transplants: Japanese investment strategies and policies. *Business Horizons* 33 (2): 63–9

Newman R. J. (1984) *Growth in the American South: Changing Regional Employment and Wage Patterns in the 1960s and 1970s.* New York, New York University Press

Nichols-Nixon C. L., Jasinski D. (1995) The blurring of industry boundaries: an explanatory model applied to telecommunications. *Industrial and Corporate Change* 4: 755–68

Nijkamp P. (1993) Towards a network of regions: the United States of Europe. *European Planning Studies* 1: 149–68

Nijkamp P., Mouwen A. (1987) Knowledge centres, information diffusion and regional development. In Brotchie J. F., Hall P., Newton P. W. (eds) *The Spatial Impact of Technological Change.* London, Croom Helm: 254–70

Nijkamp P., Rietveld P. (1986) Multiple objective decision analysis in regional economics. In Nijkamp P. (ed.) *Handbook of Regional and Urban Economics*, volume 1: *Regional Economics.* Amsterdam, North-Holland: 493–541

Nijkamp P., Rietveld P., Snickars F. (1986) Regional and multiregional economic models: a survey. In Nijkamp P. (ed.) *Handbook of Regional and Urban Economics*, volume 1: *Regional Economics.* Amsterdam, North-Holland: 257–94

Nijman J. (1996) Breaking the rules? Miami in the urban hierarchy. *Urban Geography* 17: 5–22

Niosi J. (1990) Periphery in the center: Canada in the North American economy. In

Martin W. G. (ed.) *Semiperipheral States in the World-Economy*. Westport, CT, Greenwood Press: 141–58

Niosi J., Bellon B. (1994) The global interdependence of national innovation systems: evidence, limits, and implications. *Technology in Society* **16**: 173–97

Niosi J., Bergeron M. (1992) Technical alliances in the Canadian electronics industry: an empirical analysis. *Technovation* **12**: 309–22

Niosi J., Hanel P., Fiset L. (1995) Technology transfer to developing countries through engineering firms: the Canadian experience. *World Development* **23**: 1815–24

Niosi J., Saviotti P., Bellon B., Crow M. (1993) National systems of innovation: in search of a workable concept. *Technology in Society* **15**: 207–27

Nishioka H., Takeuchi A. (1987) The development of high technology industry in Japan. In Breheny M. J., McQuaid R. W. (eds) *The Development of High Technology Industries: An International Survey*. London, Croom Helm: 262–95

Noble D. F. (1977) *America by Design: Science, Technology and the Rise of Corporate Capitalism*. New York, Alfred A. Knopf

Nolan P. (1995) Political economy and the reform of Stalinism: the Chinese puzzle. In Chang H.-J., Nolan P. (eds) *The Transformation of the Communist Economies: Against the Mainstream*. New York, St Martin's Press: 400–17

Nolan P. (1996) Large firms and industrial reform in former planned economies: the case of China. *Cambridge Journal of Economics* **20**: 1–29

Nonaka I. (1990a) Redundant, overlapping organizations: a Japanese approach to managing the innovation process. *California Management Review* **32** (3): 27–38

Nonaka I. (1990b) Managing globalization as a self-renewing process: experiences of Japanese MNCs. In Bartlett, C. A., Doz Y., Hedlund G. (eds) *Managing the Global Firm*. London, Routledge: 69–94

Nonaka I. (1994) Product development and innovation. In Imai K., Komiya R. (eds) *Business Enterprise in Japan: Views of Leading Japanese Economists*. Cambridge, MA, MIT Press: 209–21

Nonaka I., Takeuchi H. (1995) *The Knowledge-Creating Company: How Japanese Companies Create the Dynamics of Innovation*. New York: Oxford University Press

Nooteboom B. (1993) Networks and transactions: Do they connect? In Groenewegen J. (ed.) *Dynamics of the Firm: Strategies of Pricing and Organisation*. Aldershot, Edward Elgar: 9–26

Norcliffe G. B., Kotseff L. E. (1980) Local industrial complexes in Ontario. *Annals of the Association of American Geographers* **70**: 68–79

Norcliffe G., Zweerman Barschat T. (1994) Locational avoidance by nonmetropolitan industry. *Environment and Planning A* **26**: 1123–45

Nordström L. (1996) European developing regions – reality or chimera? In Alden J., Boland P. (eds) *Regional Development Strategies: A European Perspective*. London, Jessica Kingsley: 38–54

Normille D. (1994) Bright science city dreams face sober economic realities. *Science* **266**: 1176–7

Normille D. (1996) Big science is booming in Japan. *Science* **271**: 1046–8

Norton R. D., Rees J. (1979) The product cycle and the decentralization of American manufacturing. *Regional Studies* **13**: 141–51

Noss A. J. (1995) *Duikers, Cables, and Nets: A Cultural Ecology of Hunting in a Central African Forest*. Unpublished doctoral dissertation, University of Florida, Gainesville

Noyce R. N. (1982) Competition and cooperation – a prescription for the eighties. *Research Management* **25** (2): 13–17

Noyelle T. J., Stanback T. M. (1983) *The Economic Transformation of American Cities*.

Totowa, NJ, Rowman and Allenheld

Nueño P., Oosterveld J. P. (1986) The status of technology strategy in Europe. In Horwitch M. (ed.) *Technology in the Modern Corporation: A Strategic Perspective.* New York, Pergamon: 145–66

Nusbaumer J. (1987a) *The Services Economy: Lever to Growth.* Boston, Kluwer Academic

Nusbaumer J. (1987b) *Services in the Global Market.* Boston, Kluwer Academic

Nussbaum B., Bernstein A., Ehrlich E., Garland S. B., Therrien L., Hammonds K. H., Pennar K. (1988) Needed: human capital. *Business Week* 19 September: 100–41

Oakey R. P. (1981) *High Technology Industry and Industrial Location.* Aldershot, Gower

Oakey R. P. (1984) *High Technology Small Firms.* New York, St Martin's Press

Oakey R. P., Cooper S. Y. (1989) High technology industry, agglomeration and the potential for peripherally sited small firms. *Regional Studies* **23**: 347–60

Oakey R. P., O'Farrell P. N. (1992) The regional extent of computer numerically controlled (CNC) machine tool adoption and post adoption success in small British mechanical engineering firms. *Regional Studies* **26**: 163- 75

Oakey R., Rothwell R., Cooper S. (1988) *The Management of Innovation in High-Technology Small Firms.* London, Pinter

Oakey R. P., Thwaites A. T., Nash P. A. (1980) The regional distribution of innovative manufacturing establishments in Britain. *Regional Studies* **14**: 235–53

O'Brien P. (1992) The automotive industry: the permanent revolution. In van Liemt G. (ed.) *Industry on the Move: Causes and Consequences of International Relocation in the Manufacturing Industry.* Geneva, International Labour Office: 53–82

Ochel W., Wegner M. (1987) *Service Economies in Europe: Opportunities for Growth.* London, Pinter

O'Connor D. C. (1995) Technology and industrial development in the Asian NIEs: past performance and future prospects. In Simon D. F. (ed.) *The Emerging Technological Trajectory of the Pacific Rim.* New York, M. E. Sharpe: 55–80

Odagiri H. (1985) Research activity, output growth, and productivity increase in Japanese manufacturing industries. *Research Policy* **14**: 117–30

Odagiri H. (1992) *Growth through Competition, Competition through Growth: Strategic Management and the Economy in Japan.* Oxford, Clarendon Press

Odagiri H., Goto A. (1993) The Japanese system of innovation: past, present, and future. In Nelson R. R. (ed.) *National Innovation Systems: A Comparative Analysis.* New York, Oxford University Press: 76–114

Odlyzko A. M. (1996) We still need unfettered research. *Research-Technology Management* **39** (1): 9–11

OECD (1980) *Technical Change and Economic Policy.* Paris, Organisation for Economic Co-operation and Development

OECD (1981) *The Future of University Research.* Paris, Organisation for Economic Co-operation and Development

OECD (1988a) *The Newly Industrialising Countries.* Paris, Organisation for Economic Co-operation and Development

OECD (1988b) *Industrial Revival through Technology.* Paris, Organisation for Economic Co-operation and Development

OECD (1989a) *Mechanisms for Job Creation: Lessons from the United States.* Paris, Organisation for Economic Co-operation and Development

OECD (1989b) *Information Technology and New Growth Opportunities.* Paris, Organisation for Economic Co-operation and Development

OECD (1991) *Strategic Industries in a Global Economy: Policy Issues for the 1990s.* Paris,

Organisation for Economic Co-operation and Development

OECD (1992) *Technology and Productivity: The Key Relationships*. Paris, Organisation for Economic Co-operation and Development

OECD (1994) *Proposed Standard Practice for Surveys of Research and Experimental Development: Frascati Manual 1993*. Paris, Organisation for Economic Co-operation and Development

OECD (1995a) *Industry and Technology: Scoreboard of Indicators 1995*. Paris, Organisation for Economic Co-operation and Development

OECD (1995b) *Megascience Policy Issues*. Paris, Organisation for Economic Co-operation and Development

O'Farrell P. N., Hitchens D. N. M. W. (1988) The relative competitiveness and performance of small manufacturing firms in Scotland and the Mid-West of Ireland: an analysis of matched pairs. *Regional Studies* 22: 399–416

O'Farrell P. N., Hitchens D. N. M. W. (1989) The competitiveness and performance of small manufacturing firms: an analysis of matched pairs in Scotland and England. *Environment and Planning A* 21: 1241–63

O'Farrell P. N., Pickles A. R. (1989) Entrepreneurial behaviour within male work histories: a sector-specific analysis. *Environment and Planning A* 21: 311–31

Oh D., Masser I. (1995) High-tech centres and regional innovation: some case studies in the UK, Germany, Japan and Korea. In Bertuglia C. S., Fischer M. M., Preto G. (eds) *Technological Change, Economic Development and Space*. Berlin, Springer-Verlag: 295–333

Ohe T., Honjo S., Oliva M., MacMillan I. C. (1991) Entrepreneurs in Japan and Silicon Valley: a study of perceived differences. *Journal of Business Venturing* 6: 135–44

Ohlson T. (1986) The ASEAN countries: low-cost latecomers. In Broszka M., Ohlson T. (eds) *Arms Production in the Third World*. London, Taylor and Francis: 55–77

Ohmae K. (1985) *Triad Power: The Coming Shape of Global Competition*. New York, Basic Books

Ohmae K. (1995) *The End of the Nation State: The Rise of Regional Economies*. New York, Free Press

O'hUallachain B. (1984) The identification of industrial complexes. *Annals of the Association of American Geographers* 74: 420–36

O'hUallachain B. (1989) Agglomeration of services in American metropolitan areas. *Growth and Change* 20 (3): 34–49

Oinas P. (1995) Types of enterprises and local relations. In van der Knaap B., Le Heron R. (eds) *Human Resources and Industrial Spaces*. Chichester, John Wiley: 177–95

Okimoto D. I. (1989) *Between MITI and the Market: Japanese Industrial Policy for High Technology*. Stanford, CA, Stanford University Press

Okimoto D. I., Nishi Y. (1994) R&D organization in Japanese and American semiconductor firms. In Aoki M., Dore R. (eds) *The Japanese Firm: The Sources of Competitive Strength*. Oxford, Oxford University Press: 178–208

Okumura M., Yoshikawa K. (1994) Measuring horizontal inter-industrial linkages. In Johansson B., Karlsson C., Westin L. (eds) *Patterns of a Network Economy*. Berlin, Springer-Verlag: 187–204

Olfert M. R., Stabler J. C. (1994) Community level multipliers for rural development initiatives. *Growth and Change* 25: 467–86

Olleros F.-J. (1986) Emerging industries and the burnout of pioneers. *Journal of Product Innovation Management* 3: 5–18

Olleros F.-J., Macdonald R. (1988) Strategic alliances: managing complementarity to capitalize on emerging technologies. *Technovation* 7: 155–76

O'Loughlin J., Anselin L. (1996) Geo-economic competition and trade bloc formation: United States, German, and Japanese exports, 1968–1992. *Economic Geography* 72: 131–60

Oman C. (1984) *New Forms of International Investment in Developing Countries.* Paris, Organisation for Economic Co-operation and Development

Oman C. (1989) *New Forms of International Investment in Developing Countries: Mining, Petrochemicals, Automobiles, Textiles, Food.* Paris, Organisation for Economic Co-operation and Development

Oman C. (1994) *Globalisation and Regionalisation: The Challenge for Developing Countries.* Paris, Organisation for Economic Co-operation and Development

Onda M. (1988) Tsukuba science city complex and the Japanese technopolis strategy. In Smilor R. W., Kozmetsky G., Gibson D. V. (eds) *Creating the Technopolis: Linking Technology Commercialization and Economic Development.* Cambridge, MA, Ballinger: 51–68

Onida F., Malerba F. (1989) R&D cooperation between industry, universities and research organizations in Europe. *Technovation* 9: 131–95

Onkvisit S., Shaw, J. J. (1989) *Product Life Cycles and Product Management.* New York, Quorum

Oppenheim N. (1980) *Applied Models in Urban and Regional Analysis.* Englewood Cliffs, NJ, Prentice-Hall

Osborne D. (1988) *Laboratories of Democracy.* Boston, Harvard Business School Press

Osei B., Baah-Nuakoh A., Tutu K., Sowa N. K. (1993) Impact of structural adjustment on small-scale enterprises in Ghana. In Helmsing A. H. J., Kolstee T. (eds) *Small Enterprises and Changing Policies.* London, Intermediate Technology Publications: 53–70

Oshima K. (1987) The high technology gap: a view from Japan. In Pierre A. J. (ed.) *A High Technology Gap? Europe, America and Japan.* New York, Council on Foreign Relations: 88–114

Osman-Rani H., Woon T. K., Ali A. (1986) *Effective Mechanisms for the Enhancement of Technology and Skills in Malaysia.* Singapore, Institute of Southeast Asian Studies

Oster S. (1979) Industrial search for new locations: an empirical analysis. *Review of Economics and Statistics* 61: 288–92

Oster S. M. (1995) *Strategic Management for Nonprofit Organizations: Theory and Cases.* New York, Oxford University Press

Osterman P. (1988) *Employment Futures: Reorganization, Dislocation, and Public Policy.* New York, Oxford University Press

Osterman P. (1990) New technology and work organization. In Deiaco E., Hörnell E., Vickery G. (eds) *Technology and Investment: Critical Issues for the 1990s.* London, Pinter: 39–63

Ostgaard T. A., Birley S. (1994) Personal networks and firm competitive strategy – a strategic or coincidental match? *Journal of Business Venturing* 9: 281–305

Ostry S. (1990) *Governments and Corporations in a Shrinking World: Trade and Innovation Policies in the United States, Europe and Japan.* New York, Council on Foreign Relations

Ostry S., Nelson R. R. (1995) *Techno-Nationalism and Techno-Globalism: Conflict and Cooperation.* Washington, Brookings Institution

OTA (Office of Technology Assessment) (1984) *Technology, Innovation, and Regional Economic Development.* Washington, US Government Printing Office

OTA (Office of Technology Assessment) (1991) *Competing Economies: America, Europe, and the Pacific Rim.* Washington, US Government Printing Office

OTA (Office of Technology Assessment) (1993) *Defense Conversion: Redirecting R&D*. Washington, US Government Printing Office

OTA (Office of Technology Assessment) (1994) *Multinationals and the US Technology Base*. Washington, US Government Printing Office

Ó Tuathail G. (1992) 'Pearl Harbor without bombs': a critical geopolitics of the US–Japan 'FSX' debate. *Environment and Planning A* 24: 975–94

Ozawa T. (1995) Structural upgrading and concatenated integration: the vicissitudes of the Pax Americana in tandem industrialization of the Pacific Basin. In Simon D. F. (ed.) *Corporate Strategies in the Pacific Rim: Global versus Regional Trends*. London, Routledge: 215–46

Özcan G. B. (1995) Small business networks and local ties in Turkey. *Entrepreneurship and Regional Development* 7: 265–83

Pack H. (1993) Technology gaps between industrial and developing countries: Are there dividends for latecomers? In *Proceedings of the World Bank Annual Conference on Development Economics 1992*. Washington, World Bank: 283–302

Pack H. (1994) Endogenous growth theory: intellectual appeal and empirical shortcomings. *Journal of Economic Perspectives* 8 (1): 55–72

Pack H., Westphal L. E. (1986) Industrial strategy and technological change: theory versus reality. *Journal of Development Economics* 22: 87–128

Palda K. S., Pazderka B. (1982) International comparisons of R&D effort: the case of the Canadian pharmaceutical industry. *Research Policy* 11: 247–59

Panagariya A. (1995) What can we learn from China's export strategy? *Finance and Development* 32 (2): 32–5

Pandit K., Casetti E. (1989) The shifting pattern of sectoral labor allocation during development: developed versus developing countries. *Annals of the Association of American Geographers* 79: 329–44

Papaconstantinou G. (1995) Globalisation, technology and employment: characteristics and trends. *STI Review* 15: 177–235

Papadakis M. (1995) The delicate task of linking industrial R&D to national competitiveness. *Technovation* 15: 569–83

Parafina S. (1993) *Household Relations and Agricultural Decision Making in Haiti*. Unpublished MA thesis, University of Florida, Gainesville

Paris C. (1995) Demographic aspects of social change: implications for strategic housing policy. *Urban Studies* 32: 1623–43

Parisi A. J. (1989) How R&D spending pays off. *Business Week* 16 June: 177–9

Park S.-H., Chan K. S. (1989) A cross-country input–output analysis of intersectoral relationships between manufacturing and services and their employment implications. *World Development* 17: 199–212

Park S. O., Markusen A. R. (1995) Generalizing new industrial districts: a theoretical agenda and an application from a non-Western country. *Environment and Planning A* 27: 81–104

Parker J. (1995) Turn up the lights: a survey of cities. *The Economist* 29 July

Parsonage J. (1992) Southeast Asia's 'growth triangle': a subregional response to global transformation. *International Journal of Urban and Regional Research* 16: 307–17

Pascal A. H., McCall J. J. (1980) Agglomeration economies, search costs, and industrial location. *Journal of Urban Economics* 8: 383–8

Patchell J., Hayter R. (1995) Skill formation and Japanese production systems. *Tijdschrift voor Economische en Sociale Geografie* 86: 339–56

Patel P. (1995) Localised production of technology for global markets. *Cambridge Journal of Economics* 19: 141–53

Patel P., Pavitt K. (1987) Is Western Europe losing the technological race? *Research Policy* 16: 59–99

Patel P., Pavitt K. (1991) Large firms in the production of the world's technology: an important case of 'non-globalisation'. *Journal of International Business Studies* 22 (1): 1–21

Patel P., Pavitt K. (1994a) The continuing, widespread (and neglected) importance of improvements in mechanical technologies. *Research Policy* 23: 533–45

Patel P., Pavitt K. (1994b) National innovation systems: why they are important, and how they might be measured and compared. *Economics of Innovation and New Technology* 3: 77–95

Patel P., Pavitt K. (1994c) Uneven (and divergent) technological accumulation among advanced countries: evidence and a framework of explanation. *Industrial and Corporate Change* 3: 759–87

Patel S. (ed.) (1993) *Technological Transformation of the Third World* (4 volumes). Aldershot, Avebury

Patton S. G. (1985) Tourism and local economic development: factory outlets and the Reading SMSA. *Growth and Change* 16 (3): 64–74

Pavia T. M. (1991) The early stages of new product development in entrepreneurial high-tech firms. *Journal of Product Innovation Management* 8: 18–31

Pavitt K. (ed.) (1980) *Technical Innovation and British Economic Performance*. London, Macmillan

Pavitt K. (1984) Patterns of technical change: towards a taxonomy and a theory. *Research Policy* 13: 343–73

Pavitt K. (1986) 'Chips' and 'trajectories': How does the semiconductor influence the sources and directions of technical change? In MacLeod R. M. (ed.) *Technology and the Human Prospect*. London, Frances Pinter: 31–54

Pavitt K. (1993) What do firms learn from basic research? In Foray D., Freeman C. (eds) *Technology and the Wealth of Nations: The Dynamics of Constructed Advantage*. London, Pinter: 29–40

Pavitt K. (1994) Key characteristics of large innovating firms. In Dodgson M., Rothwell R. (eds) *The Handbook of Industrial Innovation*. Aldershot, Edward Elgar: 357–66

Pearce D. G. (1995) *Tourism Today: A Geographical Analysis*, second edition. London, Longman

Pearce R. D., Singh S. (1991) The overseas laboratory. In Casson M. (ed.) *Global Research Strategy and International Competitiveness*. Oxford, Blackwell: 183–212

Peattie L. (1981) *Thinking about Development*. New York, Plenum

Peck F. W., Townsend A. R. (1984) Contrasting experience of recession and spatial restructuring: British Shipbuilding, Plessey and Metal Box. *Regional Studies* 18: 319–38

Peck F., Townsend A. (1987) The impact of technological change upon the spatial pattern of UK employment within major corporations. *Regional Studies* 21: 225–39

Peck J. A. (1989) Reconceptualising the local labour market: space, segmentation and the state. *Progress in Human Geography* 13: 42–61

Peck J. (1992) Labor and agglomeration: control and flexibility in local labor markets. *Economic Geography* 68: 325–47

Peck J. (1996) *Work-Place: The Social Regulation of Labor Markets*. New York, Guilford

Peck J., Jones M. (1995) Training and Enterprise Councils: Schumpeterian workfare state, or what? *Environment and Planning A* 27: 1361–96

Peck J., Tickell A. (1994) Searching for a new institutional fix: the *after*-Fordist crisis and the global–local disorder. In Amin A. (ed.) *Post-Fordism: A Reader*. Oxford:

Blackwell: 281–315

Peck J., Tickell A. (1995) The social regulation of uneven development: 'regulatory deficit', England's South East, and the collapse of Thatcherism. *Environment and Planning A* 27: 15–40

Peck M. J., Goto A. (1981) Technology and economic growth: the case of Japan. *Research Policy* 10: 222–43

Peck M. J., Levin R. C., Goto A. (1988) Picking losers: public policy toward declining industries in Japan. In Shoven J. B. (ed.) *Government Policy towards Industry in the United States and Japan.* Cambridge, Cambridge University Press: 195–239

Pedersen P. O. (1978) Interaction between short- and long-run development in regions – the case of Denmark. *Regional Studies* 12: 683–700

Perez C. (1983) Structural change and the assimilation of new technologies in the economic and social system. *Futures* 15: 357–75

Perez C., Soete L. (1988) Catching up in technology: entry barriers and windows of opportunity. In Dosi G., Freeman C., Nelson R., Silverberg G., Soete L. (eds) *Technical Change and Economic Theory.* London, Pinter: 458–79

Perkins D. H. (1994) There are at least three models of East Asian development. *World Development* 22: 655–61

Perkins D. H., Syrquin M. (1989) Large countries: the influence of size. In Chenery H., Srinivasan T. N. (eds) *Handbook of Development Economics,* volume II. Amsterdam, North-Holland: 1691–753

Perminov S. B. (1992) Technological development and the business environment in Russia. *International Journal of Technology Management* 7: 370–6

Perrin J.-C. (1988a) New technologies, local synergies and regional policies in Europe. In Aydalot P., Keeble D. (eds) *High Technology Industry and Innovative Environments.* London, Routledge: 139–62

Perrin J.-C. (1988b) A deconcentrated technology policy – lessons from the Sophia-Antipolis experience. *Environment and Planning C: Government and Policy* 6: 415–25

Perrino A. C., Tipping J. W. (1989) Global management of technology. *Research-Technology Management* 32 (3): 12–19

Perrolle J. A. (1986) Intellectual assembly lines: the rationalization of managerial, professional, and technical work. *Computers and the Social Sciences* 2: 111–21

Perroux F. (1955) Note sur le notion de pôle de croissance. *Economie Appliquée* 8: 307–20; translation in Livingstone I. (ed.) (1971) *Economic Policy for Development.* Harmondsworth, Penguin: 278–89

Perrow C. (1992) Small-firm networks. In Nohria N., Eccles R. G. (eds) *Networks and Organizations.* Boston, Harvard Business School Press: 445–70

Persky J., Klein W. (1975) Regional capital growth and some of those other things we never talk about. *Papers of the Regional Science Association* 35: 181–90

Peters L. (1989) Academic crossroads – the US experience. *STI Review* 5: 163–93

Petersen K. (1994) The maquila revolution in Guatemala. In Bonacich E., Cheng L., Chinchilla N., Hamilton N., Ong P. (eds) *Global Production: The Apparel Industry in the Pacific Rim.* Philadelphia, Temple University Press: 268–86

Peterson T., Maremont M. (1989) Adding hustle to Europe's muscle. *Business Week* 16 June: 32–4

Petit P. (1995) Employment and technological change. In Stoneman P. (ed.) *Handbook of the Economics of Innovation and Technological Change.* Oxford, Blackwell: 366–408

Pettit S., Thompstone K. (1990) Entrepreneurial networking within rural communities – some cases from Ireland's Shannon region. In Vyakarnam S. (ed.) *When the Harvest Is In: Developing Rural Entrepreneurship.* London, Intermediate Technology

Publications: 38–60

Pezzini M. (1989) The small-firm economy's odd man out: the case of Ravenna. In Goodman E., Bamford J., Saynor P. (eds) *Small Firms and Industrial Districts in Italy*. London, Routledge: 223–38

Pfister R. L. (1976) On improving export base studies. *Regional Science Perspectives* 6 (1): 104–16

Pianta M., Evangelista R., Perani G. (1996) The dynamics of innovation and employment: an international comparison. *STI Review* 18: 67–93

Piatier A. (1984) *Barriers to Innovation*. London, Frances Pinter

Pike A. (1996) Greenfields, brownfields and industrial policy for the automobile industry in the UK. *Regional Studies* 30: 69–77

Pine B. J. (1993) *Mass Customization: The New Frontier of Business Competition*. Boston: Harvard Business School Press

Piore M. J., Lester R. K., Kofman F. M., Malek K. M. (1994) The organization of product development. *Industrial and Corporate Change* 3: 405–34

Piore M. J., Sabel C. F. (1984) *The Second Industrial Divide: Possibilities for Prosperity*. New York, Basic Books

Pisano G. P., Russo M. V., Teece D. J. (1988) Joint ventures and collaborative arrangements in the telecommunications equipment industry. In Mowery D. C. (ed.) *International Collaborative Ventures in US Manufacturing*. Cambridge, MA, Ballinger: 23–70

Pisano G. P., Shan W., Teece D. J. (1988) Joint ventures and collaboration in the biotechnology industry. In Mowery D. C. (ed.) *International Collaborative Ventures in US Manufacturing*. Cambridge, MA, Ballinger: 183–222

Pisano G., Teece D. J. (1989) Collaborative arrangements and global technology strategy. In Rosenbloom R. S., Burgelman R. A. (eds) *Research in Technological Innovation, Management and Policy*, volume 4. Greenwich, CT, JAI Press: 227–56

Pisano G. P., Wheelwright S. C. (1995) The new logic of high-tech R&D. *Harvard Business Review* 73 (5): 93–105

Plafker T. (1994) Shanghai enlists scientists to foster economic growth. *Science* 265: 866–7

Pleeter S. (1980) Methodologies of economic impact analysis: an overview. In Pleeter S. (ed.) *Economic Impact Analysis: Methodologies and Applications*. Boston, Martinus Nijhoff: 7–31

Polenske K. R. (1988) Growth pole theory and strategy reconsidered: domination, linkages, and distribution. In Higgins B., Savoie D. J. (eds) *Regional Economic Development: Essays in Honour of François Perroux*. Boston, Unwin Hyman: 91–111

Pollard J., Storper M. (1996) A tale of twelve cities: metropolitan employment change in dynamic industries in the 1980s. *Economic Geography* 72: 1–22

Poon A. (1993) *Tourism, Technology and Competitive Strategies*. Wallingford, CAB International

Popovich M. G., Buss T. F. (1989) Entrepreneurs find a niche even in rural areas. *Rural Development Perspectives* 5 (3): 11–14

Porat M. U. (1977) *The Information Economy*. Washington, US Department of Commerce, Office of Telecommunications

Port O., King R., Hampton W. J. (1988) How the new math of productivity adds up. *Business Week* 6 June: 103–14

Porter M. E. (1980) *Competitive Strategy*. New York, Free Press

Porter M. E. (1985) *Competitive Advantage*. New York, Free Press

Porter M. E. (1987) Changing patterns of international competition. In Teece D. J.

(ed.) *The Competitive Challenge*. Cambridge, MA, Ballinger: 27–57

Porter M. E. (1990) *The Competitive Advantage of Nations*. New York, Free Press

Porter M. E., Wayland R. E. (1995) Global competition and the localization of competitive advantage. In Thorelli H. (ed.) *Advances in Strategic Management*, volume 11, part A: *Integral Strategy: Concepts and Dynamics*. Greenwich, CT, JAI Press: 63–105

Porterfield S. L., Sizer M. (1995) Producer services growing quickly in rural areas, but still concentrated in urban areas. *Rural Development Perspectives* 10 (1) October: 2–8

Portes A., Castells M., Benton L. A. (eds) (1989) *The Informal Economy: Studies in Advanced and Less Developed Economies*. Baltimore, Johns Hopkins University Press

Pottier C. (1987) The location of high technology industries in France. In Breheny M. J., McQuaid R. W. (eds) *The Development of High Technology Industries: An International Survey*. London, Croom Helm: 192–222

Pottier C. (1988) Local innovation and large firm strategies in Europe. In Aydalot P., Keeble D. (eds) *High Technology Industry and Innovative Environments*. London, Routledge: 99–120

Powell W. W. (1990) Neither market nor hierarchy: network forms of organization. In Staw B. M., Cummings L. L. (eds) *Research in Organizational Behavior*, volume 12. Greenwich, CT, JAI Press: 295–336

Power T. M. (1988) *The Economic Pursuit of Quality*. New York, M. E. Sharpe

Prahalad C. K., Doz Y. L. (1981) Strategic control – The dilemma in headquarters–subsidiary relationship. In Otterbeck L. (ed.) *The Management of Headquarters–Subsidiary Relationships in Multinational Corporations*. New York, St Martin's Press: 187–203

Prahalad C. K., Doz Y., Angelmar R. (1989) Assessing the scope of innovations: a dilemma for top management. In Rosenbloom R. S., Burgelman R. A. (eds) *Research in Technological Innovation, Management and Policy*, volume 4. Greenwich, CT, JAI Press: 257–81

Prais S. J. (1988) Qualified manpower in engineering: Britain and other industrially advanced countries. *National Institute Economic Review* 127: 76–83

Prasad A. J. (1981) Licensing as an alternative to foreign investment for technology transfer. In Hawkins R. G., Prasad A. J. (eds) *Research in International Business and Finance*, volume 2: *Technology Transfer and Economic Development*. Greenwich, CT, JAI Press: 193–218

Pred A. R. (1977) *City-Systems in Advanced Economies*. London, Hutchinson

Prestowitz C. L. (1988) *Trading Places: How We Allowed Japan to Take the Lead*. New York, Basic Books

Preto G. (1995) The region as an evolutive system. In Bertuglia C. S., Fischer M. M., Preto G. (eds) *Technological Change, Economic Development and Space*. Berlin, Springer-Verlag: 257–75

Pullen M. J., Proops J. L. R. (1983) The North Staffordshire regional economy: an input–output assessment. *Regional Studies* 17: 191–200

Pulver G. C., Hustedde R. J. (1988) Regional variables that influence the allocation of venture capital: the role of banks. *Review of Regional Studies* 18 (2): 1–9

Putnam R. D. (1993) *Making Democracy Work: Civic Traditions in Modern Italy*. Princeton, NJ, Princeton University Press

Pyke F. (1992) *Industrial Development through Small-Firm Cooperation*. Geneva, International Labour Office

Pyke F. (1994) *Small Firms, Technical Services and Inter-firm Cooperation*. Geneva, International Labour Office

Pyke F., Becattini G., Sengenberger W. (eds) (1990) *Industrial Districts and Inter-firm*

Co-operation in Italy. Geneva, International Institute for Labour Studies

Pyke F., Sengenberger W. (eds) (1992) *Industrial Districts and Local Economic Regeneration.* Geneva, International Institute for Labour Studies

Quandt C. O. (1995) Manufacturing the electric vehicle: a window of technological opportunity for Southern California. *Environment and Planning A* 27: 835–62

Quéré M. (1994) Basic research inside the firm: lessons from an in-depth case study. *Research Policy* 23: 413–24

Quévreux A. (1996) Technological dynamics for the year 2010 in France (the Delphi survey approach). *STI Review* 17: 101–21

Quinn J. B. (1979) Technological innovation, entrepreneurship, and strategy. *Sloan Management Review* 20 (3): 19–30

Quinn J. B. (1992) *Intelligent Enterprise: A Knowledge and Service Based Paradigm for Industry.* New York, Free Press

Quinn J. B., Baruch J. J., Paquette P. C. (1987) Technology in services. *Scientific American* 257 (6): 50–8

Quinn J. B., Doorley T. L., Paquette P. C. (1990) Beyond products: services-based strategy. *Harvard Business Review* 68 (2): 58–68

Quinn J. B., Hilmer F. G. (1994) Strategic outsourcing. *Sloan Management Review* 35 (4): 43–55

Quintas P., Guy K. (1995) Collaborative, pre-competitive R&D and the firm. *Research Policy* 24: 325–48

Quintas P., Wield D., Massey D. (1992) Academic–industry links and innovation: questioning the science park model. *Technovation* 12: 161–75

Rachman G. (1993) Wealth in its grasp: a survey of Indonesia. 17 April

Radice H. (1995) The role of foreign direct investment in the transformation of Eastern Europe. In Chang H.-J., Nolan P. (eds) *The Transformation of the Communist Economies.* New York, St Martin's Press: 282–310

Radnor M., Kaufman S. (1988) Facing the future: the need for international technology intelligence and sourcing. In Wad A. (ed.) *Science, Technology, and Development.* Boulder, CO, Westview Press: 305–12

Rahm D., Luce T. F. (1992) Issues in the design of state science- and technology-based economic development programs: the case of Pennsylvania's Ben Franklin Partnership. *Economic Development Quarterly* 6: 41–51

Rajan A. (1987) *Services – The Second Industrial Revolution?* London, Butterworths

Ramachandran K., Ramnarayan S. (1993) Entrepreneurial orientation and networking: some Indian evidence. *Journal of Business Venturing* 8: 513–24

Ramamurti R. (1987) *State-Owned Enterprises in High Technology Industries: Studies in India and Brazil.* New York, Praeger

Ramos J. R. (1994) Employment, human resources and systemic competitiveness. In Bradford C. I. (ed.) *The New Paradigm of Systemic Competitiveness: Toward More Integrated Policies in Latin America.* Paris, Organisation for Economic Co-operation and Development: 249–69

Ranis G. (1995) Another look at the East Asian miracle. *World Bank Economic Review* 9: 509–34

Rankin L. J. (1995) The role of users in information technology standardisation. *STI Review* 16: 177–94

Ransley D. L., Rogers J. L. (1994) A consensus on best R&D practices. *Research-Technology Management* 37 (2): 19–26

Raouf A., Anjum M. F. (1995) Manufacturing systems: flexibility assessment. In Raouf A., Ben-Daya M. (eds) *Flexible Manufacturing Systems: Recent Developments.*

Amsterdam, Elsevier: 69–84

Rasiah R. (1994) Flexible production systems and local machine-tool subcontracting: electronics components transnationals in Malaysia. *Cambridge Journal of Economics* **18**: 279–98

Rausch L. M. (1995) *Asia's New High-Tech Competitors.* Washington, DC, National Science Foundation

Ray D. M. (1993) Understanding the entrepreneur: entrepreneurial attributes, experience and skills. *Entrepreneurship and Regional Development* **5**: 345–57

Ray G. F. (1969) The diffusion of new technology. *National Institute Economic Review* **48**: 40–83

Ray G. F. (1980) Innovation in the long cycle. *Lloyds Bank Review* **135**: 14–28

Ray G. F. (1984) *The Diffusion of Mature Technologies.* Cambridge, Cambridge University Press

Ray G. F. (1989) Full circle: the diffusion of technology. *Research Policy* **18**: 1–18

Reddy A. K. N. (1979) National and regional technology groups and institutions: an assessment. In Bhalla A. S. (ed.) *Towards Global Action for Appropriate Technology.* Oxford, Pergamon: 63–137

Reeder R. J., Schneider M. J., Green B. L. (1993) Attracting retirees as a rural development strategy. In Barkley D. L. (ed.) *Economic Adaptation: Alternatives for Nonmetropolitan Areas.* Boulder, CO, Westview Press: 127–44

Rees J., Briggs R., Oakey R. (1984) The adoption of new technology in the American machinery industry. *Regional Studies* **18**: 489–504

Rees J., Briggs R., Oakey R. (1986) The adoption of new technology in the American machinery industry. In Rees J. (ed.) *Technology, Regions, and Policy.* Totowa, NJ, Rowman and Littlefield: 187–217

Rees J., Lewington T. (1990) An assessment of state technology development programs. In Schmandt J., Wilson R. (eds) *Growth Policy in the Age of High Technology: The Role of Regions and States.* Boston, Unwin Hyman: 195–210

Reese P. R., Aldrich H. E. (1995) Entrepreneurial networks and business performance: a panel study of small and medium-sized firms in the Research Triangle. In Birley S., MacMillan I. C. (eds) *International Entrepreneurship.* London, Routledge: 124–44

Reich R. B. (1991) *The Work of Nations.* New York, Alfred A. Knopf

Reid G. C., Jacobsen L. R. (1988) *The Small Entrepreneurial Firm.* Aberdeen, Aberdeen University Press

Reid P. P., Schriesheim A. (eds) (1996) *Foreign Participation in US Research and Development: Asset or Liability?* Washington, National Academy Press

Reid S. D., Reid N. (1988) Public policy and promoting manufacturing under licensing. *Technovation* **7**: 401–14

Reiner T. A., Wolpert J. (1981) The nonprofit sector in the metropolitan economy. *Economic Geography* **57**: 23–33

Renaud B. M. (1973) Conflicts between national growth and regional income equality in a rapidly growing economy: the case of Korea. *Economic Development and Cultural Change* **21**: 429–45

Reve T. (1990) The firm as a nexus of internal and external contracts. In Aoki M., Gustafsson B., Williamson O. E. (eds) *The Firm as a Nexus of Treaties.* London, Sage: 133–61

Reynolds L. G. (1983) The spread of economic growth to the third world. *Journal of Economic Literature* **21**: 941–80

Reynolds P. (1994). Autonomous firm dynamics and economic growth in the United States, 1986–1990. *Regional Studies* **28**: 429–42

Reynolds P. D., Miller B., Maki W. R. (1993) Explaining regional variation in business births and deaths: U. S. 1976–88. *Small Business Economics* 7: 389–407

Reynolds P., Storey D. J., Westhead P. (1994) Cross-national comparisons of the variation in new firm formation rates. *Regional Studies* 28: 443–56

Rhee Y. W. (1990) The catalyst model of development: lessons from Bangladesh's success with garment exports. *World Development* 18: 333–46

Richardson H. W. (1971) *Urban Economics*. London, Penguin

Richardson H. W. (1972) *Input–Output and Regional Economics*. New York, John Wiley

Richardson H. W. (1973) *Regional Growth Theory*. London, Macmillan

Richardson H. W. (1985) Input–output and economic base multipliers: looking backward and forward. *Journal of Regional Science* 25: 607–61

Richardson H. W. (1988) A review of techniques for regional policy analysis. In Higgins B., Savoie D. J. (eds) *Regional Economic Development: Essays in Honour of François Perroux*. Boston, Unwin Hyman: 142–68

Riche R. W., Hecker D. E., Burgan J. U. (1983) High technology today and tomorrow: a small slice of the employment pie. *Monthly Labor Review* 106 (11): 50–8

Richter L. K. (1989) *The Politics of Tourism in Asia*. Honolulu, University of Hawaii Press

Ricklefs R. (1989) Regional variation in small firms' success is striking. *The Wall Street Journal* 12 July: B2

Riddell A. R. (1996) Globalization: emasculation or opportunity for educational planning? *World Development* 24: 1357–72

Riddle D. I. (1986) *Service-Led Growth: The Role of the Service Sector in World Development*. New York, Praeger

Riedel J. (1988) Economic development in East Asia: doing what comes naturally? In Hughes H. (ed.) *Achieving Industrialization in East Asia*. Cambridge, Cambridge University Press: 1–38

Riedle K. (1989) Demand for R&D activities and the trade off between in-house and external research: a viewpoint from industry with reference to large companies and small and medium-sized enterprises. *Technovation* 9: 213–25

Rigby D. L. (1995) Investment, capital stocks and the age of capital in US regions. *Growth and Change* 26: 524–52

Riggs H. E. (1983) *Managing High-Technology Companies*. Belmont, CA, Wadsworth

Rimmer P. J. (1994) Regional economic integration in Pacific Asia. *Environment and Planning A* 26: 1731–59

Rimmer P. J. (1995) Industrialization policy and the role of the state: newly industrializing countries. In Le Heron R., Park S. O. (eds) *The Asian Pacific Rim and Globalization*. Aldershot, Avebury: 17–36

Rink D. R., Swan J. E. (1979) Product life cycle research: a literature review. *Journal of Business Research* 7: 219–42

Rip A., Nederhof A. J. (1986) Between dirigism and laissez-faire: effects of implementing the science policy priority for biotechnology in the Netherlands. *Research Policy* 15: 253–68

Roberts E. B. (ed.) (1987) *Generating Technological Innovation*. Oxford, Oxford University Press

Roberts E. B. (1988) What we've learned: managing invention and innovation. *Research-Technology Management* 31 (1): 11–29

Roberts E. B. (1990) Evolving toward product and market-orientation: the early years of technology-based firms. *Journal of Product Innovation Management* 7: 274–87

Roberts E. B. (1991a) *Entrepreneurs in High Technology*. New York, Oxford University

Press.

Roberts E. B. (1991b) High stakes for high-tech entrepreneurs: understanding venture capital decision making. *Sloan Management Review* **32** (2): 9–20

Roberts E. B. (1995) Benchmarking the strategic management of technology – 1. *Research-Technology Management* **38** (1): 44–56

Roberts E. B., Fusfeld H. I. (1981) Staffing the innovative technology-based organization. *Sloan Management Review* **22** (3): 19–34

Roberts E. B., Wainer H. A. (1971) Some characteristics of technical entrepreneurs. *IEEE Transactions on Engineering Management* **EM-18**: 100–9

Roberts P. (1994) Sustainable regional planning. *Regional Studies* **28**: 781–7

Robertson P. L., Langlois R. N. (1995) Innovation, networks, and vertical integration. *Research Policy* **24**: 543–62

Robinson R. B. (1987) Emerging strategies in the venture capital industry. *Journal of Business Venturing* **2**: 53–77

Robinson R. D. (1988) *The International Transfer of Technology: Theory, Issues, and Practice.* Cambridge, MA, Ballinger

Robinson S. (1989) Multisectoral models. In Chenery H., Srinivasan T. N. (eds) *Handbook of Development Economics,* volume II. Amsterdam, North-Holland: 885–947

Robson M., Townsend J., Pavitt K. (1988) Sectoral patterns of production and use of innovations in the UK: 1945–1983. *Research Policy* **17**: 1–14

Rodan G. (1989) *The Political Economy of Singapore's Industrialization: National State and International Capital.* New York, St Martin's Press

Roessner J. D. (1987) Technology policy in the United States: structures and limitations. *Technovation* **5**: 229–45

Roessner J. D. (1989) Evaluation of government innovation programs: introduction. *Research Policy* **18**: 309–12

Roessner J. D., Porter A. L. (1990) Achieving technology-based competitiveness in developing countries. In Chatterji M. (ed.) *Technology Transfer in the Developing Countries.* London, Macmillan: 94–103

Roessner J. D., Porter A. L., Newman N., Cauffiel D. (1996) Anticipating the future high-tech competitiveness of nations: indicators for twenty-eight countries. *Technological Forecasting and Social Change* **51**: 133–49

Roessner J. D., Porter A. L., Xu H. (1992) National capacities to absorb and institutionalize external science and technology. *Technology Analysis and Strategic Management* **4**: 99–113

Rogers D. M. A. (1996) The challenge of fifth generation R&D. *Research-Technology Management* **39** (4): 33–41

Rogers E. M. (1986) The role of the research university in the spin-off of high-technology companies. *Technovation* **4**: 169–81

Rogers E. M., Larsen J. (1984) *Silicon Valley Fever.* New York, Basic Books

Rohwer J. (1995) *Asia Rising.* New York, Simon and Schuster

Romer P. (1990) Endogenous technical change. *Journal of Political Economy* **98**: S71–103

Romer P. (1993) Ideas and things. *The Economist* 11 September: 70–2

Romer P. (1994) The origins of endogenous growth. *Journal of Economic Perspectives* **8**: 3–22

Rommel G., Kluge J., Kempis R.-D., Diederichs R., Brück F. (1995) *Simplicity Wins: How Germany's Mid-sized Industrial Companies Succeed.* Boston, Harvard Business School Press

Romsa G., Blenman M., Nipper J. (1989) From the economic to the political: regional planning in West Germany. *Canadian Geographer* 33: 47–57

Ronayne J. (1984) *Science in Government.* Oxford, Basil Blackwell

Rondinelli D. A., Kasarda J. D. (1993) Job creation needs in third world cities. In Kasarda J. D., Parnell A. M. (eds) *Third World Cities: Problems, Policies, and Prospects.* Newbury Park, CA, Sage: 92–119

Ronstadt R. (1984) R&D abroad by US multinationals. In Stobaugh R., Wells L. T. (eds) *Technology Crossing Borders.* Boston, Harvard Business School Press: 241–64

Roobeek A. J. M. (1990) *Beyond the Technology Race: An Analysis of Technology Policy in Seven Industrial Countries.* Amsterdam, Elsevier

Rose F. (1996) Boeing to boost 737 production to more than double the rate. *Wall Street Journal* 20 June: B4

Rosenberg N. (1982) *Inside the Black Box: Technology and Economics.* Cambridge, Cambridge University Press

Rosenberg N. (1990a) Why do firms do basic research (with their own money)? *Research Policy* 19: 165–74

Rosenberg N. (1990b) Science and technology policy for the Asian NICs: lessons from economic history. In Evenson R. E., Ranis G. (eds) *Science and Technology: Lessons for Development Policy.* Boulder, CO, Westview Press: 135–55

Rosenberg N. (1991) Critical issues in science policy research. *Science and Public Policy* 18: 335–46

Rosenberg N. (1994) *Exploring the Black Box: Technology, Economics, and History.* Cambridge, Cambridge University Press

Rosenberg N., Birdzell L. E. (1986) *How the West Grew Rich: The Economic Transformation of the Industrial World.* New York, Basic Books

Rosenberg N., Landau R., Mowery D. C. (eds) (1992) *Technology and the Wealth of Nations.* Stanford, CA, Stanford University Press

Rosenberg N., Nelson R. R. (1994) American universities and technical advance in industry. *Research Policy* 23: 323–48

Rosenbloom R. S., Abernathy W. J. (1982) The climate for innovation in industry: the role of management attitudes and practices in consumer electronics. *Research Policy* 11: 209–25

Rosenbloom R. S., Christensen C. M. (1994) Technological discontinuities, organizational capabilities, and strategic commitments. *Industrial and Corporate Change* 3: 655–85

Rosenbloom R. S., Cusumano M. A. (1987) Technological pioneering and competitive advantage: the birth of the VCR industry. *California Management Review* 29 (4): 63–70

Rosenbloom R. S., Spencer W. J. (eds) (1996) *Engines of Innovation: US Industrial Research at the End of an Era.* Boston, Harvard Business School Press

Rosenfeld S. A. (1989–90) Regional development European style. *Issues in Science and Technology* 6 (2): 63–70

Rosenfeld S. A. (1992) *Competitive Manufacturing: New Strategies for Regional Development.* Piscataway, NJ, Center for Urban Policy Research Press

Rosenfeld S. A. (1995) *Industrial Strength Strategies: Regional Clusters and Public Policy,* Washington, Aspen Institute

Rosenfeld S. A. (1996) Does cooperation enhance competitiveness? Assessing the impacts of inter-firm collaboration. *Research Policy* 25: 247–63

Rosenfeld S. A., Bergman E. M. (1989) *Making Connections: After the Factories Revisited.* Research Triangle Park, NC, Southern Growth Policies Board

Rosenfeld S. A., Bergman E. M., Rubin S. (1985) *After the Factories: Changing Employment Patterns in the Rural South*. Research Triangle Park, NC, Southern Growth Policies Board

Rosenkopf L., Tushman M. L. (1994) The coevolution of technology and organization. In Baum J. A. C., Singh J. V. (eds) *Evolutionary Dynamics of Organizations*. New York, Oxford University Press: 403–24

Rosenzweig M. R. (1988) Labor markets in low-income countries. In Chenery H., Srinivasan T. N. (eds) *Handbook of Development Economics*, volume I. Amsterdam, North-Holland: 713–62

Rosenzweig P. M. (1995) International sourcing in athletic footwear: Nike and Reebok. In Bartlett C. A., Ghoshal S. (eds) *Transnational Management*, second edition. Chicago, Irwin: 170–82

Rossant J., Reed S., Griffiths D. (1989) Israel has everything it needs – except peace. *Business Week* 4 December: 54–8

Rostow W. W. (1960) *The Stages of Economic Growth: A Non-Communist Manifesto*. Cambridge, Cambridge University Press

Rothwell R. (1980) The impact of regulation on innovation: some US data. *Technological Forecasting and Social Change* 17: 7–34

Rothwell R. (1989) SMFs, inter-firm relationships and technological change. *Entrepreneurship and Regional Development* 1: 275–92

Rothwell R. (1992) Successful industrial innovation: critical factors for the 1990s. *R&D Management* 22: 221–39

Rothwell R. (1994a) Industrial innovation: success, strategy, trends. In Dodgson M., Rothwell R. (eds) *The Handbook of Industrial Innovation*. Aldershot, Edward Elgar: 33–53

Rothwell R. (1994b) Issues in user–producer relations in the innovation process: the role of government. *International Journal of Technology Management* 9: 629–49

Rothwell R., Dodgson M. (1991) External linkages and innovation in small and medium-sized enterprises. *R&D Management* 21: 125–37

Rothwell R., Dodgson M. (1994) Innovation and size of firm. In Dodgson M., Rothwell R. (eds) *The Handbook of Industrial Innovation*. Aldershot, Edward Elgar: 310–24

Rothwell R., Freeman C., Horlsey A., Jervis V. T. P., Robertson A. B., Townsend J. (1974) SAPPHO updated – Project SAPPHO phase II. *Research Policy* 3: 258–91

Rothwell R., Zegveld W. (1982) *Innovation and the Small and Medium Sized Firm*. Hingham, MA, Kluwer Nijhoff

Rothwell R., Zegveld W. (1985) *Reindustrialization and Technology*. London, Longman

Rothwell R., Zegveld W. (1988) An assessment of government innovation policies. In Roessner J. D. (ed.) *Government Innovation Policy: Design, Implementation, Evaluation*. New York, St Martin's Press: 19–35

Roure J. B., Maidique M. A. (1986) Linking prefunding factors and high-technology venture success: an exploratory study. *Journal of Business Venturing* 1: 295–306

Roussel P. A., Saad K. N., Erickson T. J. (1991) *Third Generation R&D*. Boston, Harvard Business School Press

Roy K. C. (1994) Neglected issues in technological change and rural development: an overview. In Roy K. C., Clark C. (eds) *Technological Change and Rural Development in Poor Countries*. Calcutta, Oxford University Press: 16–47

Rubalcaba-Bermejo L., Cuadrado-Roura J. R. (1995) Urban hierarchies and territorial competition in Europe: exploring the role of fairs and exhibitions. *Urban Studies* 32: 379–400

Rubenstein A. H. (1980) The role of imbedded technology in the industrial innovation process. In *Special Study on Economic Change*, volume 3: *Research and Innovation: Developing a Dynamic Nation*. Washington, US Government Printing Office: 380–414

Rubenstein A. H. (1989) *Managing Technology in the Decentralized Firm*. New York, John Wiley

Rubenstein J. M. (1992) *The Changing US Auto Industry: A Geographical Analysis*. London, Routledge

Rubenstein J. M. (1994) National content of motor vehicles. *Geographical Review* 84: 185–200

Rubin H. J. (1988) Shoot anything that flies; claim anything that falls: conversations with economic development practitioners. *Economic Development Quarterly* 2: 236–51

Rugman A. M., D'Cruz J. R. (1993) The 'double diamond' model of international competitiveness: the Canadian experience. *Management International Review* 33 (special issue 2): 17–40

Rugman A. M., Verbeke A. (1993) Foreign subsidiaries and multinational strategic management: an extension and correction of Porter's single diamond framework. *Management International Review* 33 (special issue 2): 71–84

Rullani E., Zanfei A. (1988) Area networks: telematic connections in a traditional textile district. In Antonelli C. (ed.) *New Information Technology and Industrial Change: The Italian Case*. Dordrecht, Kluwer Academic: 97–113

Rush H., Bessant J. (1992) Revolution in three-quarter time: lessons from the diffusion of advanced manufacturing technologies. *Technology Analysis and Strategic Management* 4: 3–19

Russo M. (1985) Technical change and the industrial district: the role of interfirm relations in the growth and transformation of ceramic tile production in Italy. *Research Policy* 14: 329–43

Ryans J. K., Shanklin W. L. (1986) *Guide to Marketing for Economic Development*. Columbus, OH, Publishing Horizons

Rycroft R. W., Kash D. E. (1992) Technology policy requires picking winners. *Economic Development Quarterly* 6: 227–40

Rycroft R. W., Kash D. E. (1994) Complex technology and community: implications for policy and social science. *Research Policy* 23: 613–26

Sabel C. (1982) *Work and Politics: The Division of Labor in Industry*. Cambridge, Cambridge University Press

Sabel C. (1989) Flexible specialization and the re-emergence of regional economies. In Hirst P., Zeitlin J. (eds) *Reversing Industrial Decline? Industrial Structure and Policy in Britain and Her Competitors*. Oxford: Berg: 17–70

Sabel C. F. (1992) Studied trust: building new forms of co-operation in a volatile economy. In Pyke F., Sengenberger W. (eds) *Industrial Districts and Local Economic Regeneration*. Geneva, International Institute for Labour Studies: 215–50

Sabel C. (1994) Learning by monitoring: the institutions of economic development. In Rodwin L., Schön D. (eds) *Rethinking the Development Experience: Essays Provoked by the Work of Albert Hirschman*. Washington, Brookings Institution: 231–74

Sabel C., Herrigel G., Kazis R., Deeg R. (1987) How to keep mature industries innovative. *Technology Review* 90 (3): 27–35

Sachs J. (1996) It can be done. *The Economist* 29 June: 19–21

Sadler D. (1992a) *The Global Region: Production, State Policies and Uneven Development*. Oxford, Pergamon

Sadler D. (1992b) Industrial policy of the European Community: strategic deficits and regional dilemmas. *Environment and Planning A* **24**: 1711–30

Sadler D., Swain A. (1994) State and market in eastern Europe: regional development and workplace implications of foreign direct investment in the automobile industry in Hungary. *Transactions, Institute of British Geographers* NS **19**: 387–403

Safa H. I. (1994) Export manufacturing, state policy, and women workers in the Dominican Republic. In Bonacich E., Cheng L., Chinchilla N., Hamilton N., Ong P. (eds) *Global Production: The Apparel Industry in the Pacific Rim*. Philadelphia, Temple University Press: 247–67

Sagasti F. R. (1988) Market structure and technological behavior in developing countries. In Wad A. (ed.) *Science, Technology and Development*. Boulder, CO, Westview Press: 149–68

Sagdeev R. Z. (1988) Science and *perestroika*: a long way to go. *Issues in Science and Technology* **4** (4): 48–52

Sakai K. (1990) The feudal world of Japanese manufacturing. *Harvard Business Review* **68** (6): 38–49

Sako M. (1992) *Prices, Quality, and Trust: Inter-Firm Relations in Britain and Japan*. Cambridge, Cambridge University Press

Sako M. (1994) Supplier relationships and innovation. In Dodgson M., Rothwell R. (eds) *The Handbook of Industrial Innovation*. Aldershot, Edward Elgar: 268–74

Salaff J. W. (1992) Women, the family, and the state in Hong Kong, Taiwan, and Singapore. In Appelbaum R. P., Henderson J. (eds) *States and Development in the Asia Pacific Rim*. Newbury Park, CA, Sage: 267–306

Salais R., Storper M. (1992) The four worlds of contemporary industry. *Cambridge Journal of Economics* **16**: 169–93

Salih K., Young M. L., Rasiah R. (1988) The changing face of the electronics industry in the periphery: the case of Malaysia. *International Journal of Urban and Regional Research* **12**: 375–403

Salter W. E. G. (1966) *Productivity and Technical Change*, second edition. Cambridge, Cambridge University Press

Samuels R. J. (1994) *'Rich Nation, Strong Army': National Security and the Technological Transformation of Japan*. Ithaca, NY, Cornell University Press

Samuels R. J., Whipple B. C. (1989) The FSX and Japan's strategy for aerospace. *Technology Review* **92** (7): 43–51

San G. (1991) Technology, investment and trade under economic globalisation: the case of Taiwan. In *Trade, Investment and Technology in the 1990s*. Paris, Organisation for Economic Co-operation and Development: 57–95

Sanderson S., Uzumeri M. (1995) Managing product families: the case of the Sony Walkman. *Research Policy* **24**: 761–82

Sandoval V. (1994) *Computer Integrated Manufacturing (CIM) in Japan*. Amsterdam, Elsevier

Santos M. (1979) *The Shared Space: The Two Circuits of the Urban Economy in Underdeveloped Countries*. London, Methuen

Sapienza H. J. (1992) When do venture capitalists add value? *Journal of Business Venturing* **7**: 9–27

Saporito B. (1994) The world's best cities for business. *Fortune* **130** (10) 14 November: 112–42

Sargent M., Young J. E. (1991) The entrepreneurial search for capital: a behavioral science perspective. *Entrepreneurship and Regional Development* **3**: 237–52

Sarkis J., Rasheed A. (1995) Greening the manufacturing function. *Business Horizons*

38 (5): 17–27

Sashittal H. C., Wilemon D. (1994) Integrating technology and marketing: implications for improving customer responsiveness. *International Journal of Technology Management* **9**: 691–708

Sass S. (1994) What's so special about manufacturing? *Regional Review, Federal Reserve Bank of Boston* **4** (2): 19–24

Sassen S. (1991) *The Global City: New York, London, Tokyo.* Princeton, NJ, Princeton University Press

Sassen S. (1994) *Cities in a World Economy.* Thousand Oaks, CA, Pine Forge Press

Sassen S. (1995a) The state and the global city: notes towards a conception of place-centered governance. *Competition and Change* **1**: 31–50

Sassen S. (1995b) On concentration and centrality in the global city. In Knox P., Taylor P. J. (eds) *World Cities in a World-System.* Cambridge, Cambridge University Press: 63–75

Sassen-Koob S. (1989) New York City's informal economy. In Portes A., Castells M., Benton L. A. (eds) *The Informal Economy: Studies in Advanced and Less Developed Countries.* Baltimore, Johns Hopkins University Press: 60–77

Sato K. (1978) Did technological progress accelerate in Japan? In Tsuru S. (ed.) *Economic Growth and Resources*, volume 5: *Growth and Resources Problems Related to Japan.* New York, St Martin's Press: 153–81

Saunders P. (1995) *Capitalism.* Minneapolis, University of Minnesota Press

Savoie D. J. (1986) *Regional Economic Development: Canada's Search for Solutions.* Toronto, University of Toronto Press

Saxenian A. (1983) The urban contradictions of Silicon Valley: regional growth and the restructuring of the semiconductor industry. *International Journal of Urban and Regional Research* **7**: 237–62

Saxenian A. (1994) *Regional Advantage: Culture and Competition in Silicon Valley and Route 128.* Cambridge, MA, Harvard University Press

Sayer R. A. (1985) Industry and space: a sympathetic critique of radical research. *Environment and Planning D: Society and Space* **3**: 3–29

Sayer A., Morgan K. (1986) The electronics industry and regional development in Britain. In Amin A., Goddard J. B. (eds) *Technological Change, Industrial Restructuring and Regional Development.* London, Allen and Unwin: 157–87

Sayer R., Morgan K. (1987) High technology industry and the international division of labour: the case of electronics. In Breherny M. J., McQuaid R. W. (eds) *The Development of High Technology Industries: An International Survey.* London, Croom Helm: 119–35

Sayer A., Walker R. (1992) *The New Social Economy: Reworking the Division of Labor.* Oxford, Blackwell

Schamp E. W. (1987) Technology parks and interregional competition in the Federal Republic of Germany. In van der Knaap B., Wever E. (eds) *New Technology and Regional Development.* London, Croom Helm: 119–35

Schell D. W. (1983) Entrepreneurial activity: a comparison of three North Carolina communities. In Hornaday J. A., Timmons J. A., Vesper K. H. (eds) *Frontiers of Entrepreneurship Research 1983.* Wellesley, MA, Babson College, Center for Entrepreneurial Studies: 495–518

Scherer F. M. (1982) Inter-industry technology flows in the United States. *Research Policy* **11**: 227–45

Schillinger L. (1995) Eco trip. *The New Republic* 3 July: 11–12

Schlesinger J. M. (1990) A new Nippon? MITI 'vision' for 1990s seeks a mellow Japan others shouldn't fear. *Wall Street Journal* 3 July: A1, A4

Schmenner R. W. (1982) *Making Business Location Decisions.* Englewood Cliffs, NJ, Prentice-Hall

Schmenner R. W. (1988) The merit of making things fast. *Sloan Management Review* **30** (1): 11–17

Schmenner R. W., Huber J. C., Cook R. L. (1987) Geographic differences and the location of new manufacturing facilities. *Journal of Urban Economics* **21**: 83–104

Schmitz H. (1982) Growth constraints on small-scale manufacturing in developing countries: a critical review. *World Development* **10**: 429–50

Schmitz H. (1992) Industrial districts: model and reality in Baden-Württemberg. In Pyke F., Sengenberger W. (eds) *Industrial Districts and Local Economic Regeneration.* Geneva, International Institute for Labour Studies: 87–121

Schmitz H. (1992) On the clustering of small firms. *IDS Bulletin* **23** (3): 64–8

Schmitz H., Musyck B. (1994) Industrial districts in Europe: policy lessons for developing countries? *World Development* **22**: 889–910

Schnaars S. P. (1994) *Managing Imitation Strategies.* New York, Free Press

Schoenberger E. (1986) Competition, competitive strategy, and industrial change: the case of electronic components. *Economic Geography* **62**: 321–33

Schoenberger E. (1987) Technological and organizational change in automobile production: spatial implications. *Regional Studies* **21**: 199–214

Schoenberger E. (1988) From Fordism to flexible accumulation: technology, competitive strategies, and international location. *Environment and Planning D: Society and Space* **6**: 245–62

Scholing E., Timmermann V. (1988) Why LDC growth rates differ. *World Development* **16**: 1271–84

Schumpeter J. A. (1934) *The Theory of Economic Development.* Oxford, Oxford University Press

Sciberras E. (1986) Technical innovation and international competitiveness in the television industry. In Rhodes E., Wield D. (eds) *Implementing New Technologies.* Oxford, Basil Blackwell: 177–90

Science (1995) Fertile US soil. *Science* **270** (1 December): 1445

Scott A. J. (1984) Industrial organization and the logic of intra-metropolitan location, III: a case study of the women's dress industry in the greater Los Angeles region. *Economic Geography* **60**: 3–27

Scott A. J. (1987) The semiconductor industry in South East Asia: organization, location and the international division of labour. *Regional Studies* **21**: 143–60

Scott A. J. (1988a) Flexible production systems and regional development: the rise of new industrial spaces in North America and western Europe. *International Journal of Urban and Regional Research* **12**: 171–86

Scott A. J. (1988b) *Metropolis: From the Division of Labor to Urban Form.* Berkeley, University of California Press

Scott A. J. (1988c) *New Industrial Spaces.* London, Pion

Scott A. J. (1993) *Technopolis: High-Technology Industry and Regional Development in Southern California.* Berkeley, University of California Press

Scott A. J. (1994) Variations on the theme of agglomeration and growth: the gem and jewelry industry in Los Angeles and Bangkok. *Geoforum* **25**: 249–63

Scott A. J. (1995) The geographic foundations of industrial performance. *Competition and Change* **1**: 51–66

Scott A. J. (1996a) The craft, fashion, and cultural products industries of Los Angeles: competitive dynamic and policy dilemmas in a multi-sectoral image-producing complex. *Annals of the Association of American Geographers* **86**: 306–23

Scott A. J. (1996b) Economic decline and regeneration in a regional manufacturing complex: Southern California's household furniture industry. *Entrepreneurship and Regional Development* **8**: 75–98

Scott A. J., Angel D. P. (1987) The US semiconductor industry: a locational analysis. *Environment and Planning A* **19**: 875–912

Scott A. J., Angel D. P. (1988) The global assembly-operations of US semiconductor firms: a geographical analysis. *Environment and Planning A* **20**: 1047–67

Scott A. J., Paul A. S. (1990) Collective order and economic coordination in industrial agglomerations: the technopoles of Southern California. *Environment and Planning C: Government and Policy* **8**: 179–93

Scott M. F. G. (1981) The contribution of investment to growth. *Scottish Journal of Political Economy* **28**: 211–26

Scott-Stevens S. (1987) *Foreign Consultants and Counterparts: Problems in Technology Transfer.* Boulder, CO, Westview Press

Seagrave S. (1995) *Lords of the Rim: The Invisible Empire of the Overseas Chinese.* New York, G. P. Putnam's Sons

Seers D., Schaffer B., Kiljunen M. L. (eds) (1979) *Underdeveloped Europe: Studies in Core–Periphery Relations.* Brighton, Harvester Wheatsheaf

Segal A. (ed.) (1987) *Learning by Doing: Science and Technology in the Developing World.* Boulder, CO, Westview Press

Segal L. M., Sullivan D. G. (1995) The temporary labor force. *Economic Perspectives, Federal Reserve Bank of Chicago* **19** (2): 2–19

Segal N. S. (1986) Universities and technological entrepreneurship in Britain: some implications of the Cambridge phenomenon. *Technovation* **4**: 189–204

Selya R. M. (1994) Taiwan as a service economy. *Geoforum* **25**: 305–22

Semlinger K. (1993) Small firms and outsourcing as flexibility reservoirs of large firms. In Grabher G. (ed.) *The Embedded Firm: On the Socioeconomics of Industrial Networks.* London, Routledge: 161–78

Sen A. (1979) Followers' strategy for technological development. *The Developing Economies* **17**: 506–28

Sen A. (1988) The concept of development. In Chenery H., Srinivasan T. N. (eds) *Handbook of Development Economics*, volume I. Amsterdam, North-Holland: 10–26

Sen A. (1994) Economic regress: concepts and features. In Bruno M., Pleskovic B. (eds) *Proceedings of the Annual World Bank Conference on Development Economics 1993.* Washington, World Bank: 315–33

Sengenberger W. (1993) Local development and international economic competition. *International Labour Review* **132**: 313–29

Sengenberger W., Wilkinson F. (1995) Globalization and labour standards. In Michie J., Smith J. G. (eds) *Managing the Global Economy.* Oxford, Oxford University Press: 111–34

Sengupta J. K. (1993) Growth in NICs in Asia: some tests of new growth theory. *Journal of Development Studies* **29**: 342–57

Senker J. (1985) Small high technology firms: some regional implications. *Technovation* **3**: 243–62

Senker J. (1991) Evaluating the funding of strategic science: some lessons from British experience. *Research Policy* **20**: 29–43

Senker J. (1995) Tacit knowledge and models of innovation. *Industrial and Corporate Change* **4**: 425–47

Serapio M. G. (1993) Macro–micro analyses of Japanese direct R&D investments in the US automotive and electronics industries. *Management International Review* **33**: 209–25

Sexton D. L., Bowman N. (1985) The entrepreneur: a capable executive and more. *Journal of Business Venturing* **1**: 129–40

Sforzi F. (1989) The geography of industrial districts in Italy. In Goodman E., Bamford J., Saynor P. (eds) *Small Firms and Industrial Districts in Italy*. London, Routledge: 153–73

Shachar A. (1995a) Randstad Holland: a world city? *Urban Studies* **31**: 381–400

Shachar A. (1995b) World cities in the making: the European context. In Kresl P. K., Gappert G. (eds) *North American Cities and the Global Economy*. Thousand Oaks, CA, Sage: 150–70

Shackleton J. R. (1995) *Training for Employment in Western Europe and the United States*. Aldershot, Edward Elgar

Shahidullah M. (1991) *Capacity-Building in Science and Technology in the Third World*. Boulder, CO, Westview Press

Shaiken H. (1984) *Work Transformed: Automation and Labor in the Computer Age*. New York, Holt, Rinehart and Winston

Shane S. A. (1992) Why do some societies invent more than others? *Journal of Business Venturing* **7**: 29–46

Shanklin W. L., Ryans J. K. (1984) *Marketing High Technology*. Lexington, MA, Lexington Books

Shapero A. (1984) The entrepreneurial event. In Kent C. A. (ed.) *The Environment for Entrepreneurship*. Lexington, MA, Lexington Books: 21–40

Shapero A. (1985) *Managing Professional People*. New York, Free Press

Shapero A., Hoffman C., Draheim K. P., Howell R. P. (1969) *The Role of the Financial Community in the Formation, Growth, and Effectiveness of Technical Companies: The Attitude of Commercial Loan Officers*. Austin, TX, Multi-Disciplinary Research, Inc.

Shapira P. (1990a) Helping small manufacturers modernize. *Issues in Science and Technology* **7** (1): 49–54

Shapira P. (1990b) State initiatives to modernize U.S. small and midsized manufacturers. In Bingham R. D. (ed.) *Financing Economic Development*. Newbury Park, CA, Sage: 191–209

Shapira P. (1992) Lessons from Japan: helping small manufacturers. *Issues in Science and Technology* **8** (3): 66–72

Shapira P. (1996) Modernizing small manufacturers in the United States and Japan: public technological infrastructures and strategies. In Teubal M., Foray D., Justman M., Zuscovitch E. (eds) *Technological Infrastructure Policy (TIP): An International Perspective*. Dordrecht, Kluwer Academic: 285–334

Shapira P., Roessner J. D., Barke R. (1995) New public infrastructures for small firm industrial modernization in the USA. *Entrepreneurship and Regional Development* **7**: 63–84

Sharif M. N. (1986) Measurement of technology for national development. *Technological Forecasting and Social Change* **29**: 119–72

Sharif N. (1994a) Technology change management: imperatives for developing economies. *Technological Forecasting and Social Change* **47**: 103–14

Sharif N. (1994b) Integrating business and technology strategies in developing countries. *Technological Forecasting and Social Change* **47**: 151–67

Sharp M. (1987) National policies towards biotechnology. *Technovation* **5**: 281–304

Sharp M., Shearman C. (1987) *European Technological Collaboration*. London, Routledge and Kegan Paul

Shaw B. (1991) Developing technological innovations within networks. *Entrepreneurship and Regional Development* 3: 111–28

Shaw B. (1994) User/supplier links and innovation. In Dodgson M., Rothwell R. (eds) *The Handbook of Industrial Innovation*. Aldershot, Edward Elgar: 275–84

Shaw G., Williams A. (1988) Tourism and employment: reflections on a pilot study of Looe, Cornwall. *Area* 20: 23–34

Shear J. (1994) *The Keys to the Kingdom: The FS-X Deal and the Selling of America's Future to Japan*. New York, Doubleday

Shearman C., Burrell G. (1987) The structures of industrial development. *Journal of Management Studies* 24: 325–45

Shepherd J. (1991) Entrepreneurial growth through constellations. *Journal of Business Venturing* 6: 363–73

Sherer P. M. (1996) Thailand trips in reach for new exports. *Wall Street Journal* 27 August: A8

Shinjo K. (1988) The computer industry. In Komiya R., Okuno M., Suzumura K. (eds) *Industrial Policy of Japan*. Tokyo, Academic Press: 333–65

Shmelev N., Popov V. (1989) *The Turning Point: Revitalizing the Soviet Economy*. New York, Doubleday

Short D. M., Riding A. L. (1989) Informal investors in the Ottawa-Carleton region: experiences and expectations. *Entrepreneurship and Regional Development* 1: 99–112

Short J. R., Benton L. M., Luce W. B., Walton J. (1993) Reconstructing the image of an industrial city. *Annals of the Association of American Geographers* 83: 207–24

Shove C. (1991) Key site characteristics of industrial research and development laboratories. *Economic Development Review* 9 (4): 56–64

Shrivastava P. (1995) Environmental technologies and competitive advantage. *Strategic Management Journal* 16: 183–200

Shrivastava P., Souder W. E. (1987) The strategic management of technological innovations: a review and a model. *Journal of Management Studies* 24: 25–41

Siebert H. (1969) *Regional Economic Growth: Theory and Policy*. Scranton, PA, International Textbook

Silveira M. P. W. (ed.) (1985) *Research and Development: Linkages to Production in Developing Countries*. Boulder, CO, Westview Press

Silverberg G. (1988) Modelling economic dynamics and technical change: mathematical approaches to self-organisation and evolution. In Dosi G., Freeman C., Nelson R., Silverberg G., Soete L. (eds) *Technical Change and Economic Theory*. London, Pinter: 531–59

Silverberg G. (1990) Adoption and diffusion of technology as a collective evolutionary process. In Freeman C., Soete L. (eds) *New Explorations in the Economics of Technical Change*. London, Pinter: 177–92

Silverberg G., Lehnert D. (1994) Growth fluctuations in an evolutionary model of creative destruction. In Silverberg G., Soete L. (eds) *The Economics of Growth and Technical Change*. Aldershot, Edward Elgar: 74–108

Silverberg G., Verspagen B. (1994) Learning, innovation and economic growth: a long-run model of industrial dynamics. *Industrial and Corporate Change* 3: 199–223

Simai M. (1990) *Global Power Structure, Technology and World Economy in the Late Twentieth Century*. London, Pinter

Simon D. (1995) The world city hypothesis: reflections from the periphery. In Knox P. L., Taylor P. J. (eds) *World Cities in a World-System*. Cambridge, Cambridge University Press: 132–55

Simon D. F., Rehn D. (1987) Innovation in China's semiconductor industry: the case of Shanghai. *Research Policy* **16**: 259–77

Simon D. F., Rehn D. (1988) *Technological Innovation in China.* Cambridge, MA, Ballinger

Simon D. F., Schive C. (1986) Taiwan. In Rushing F. W., Brown C. G. (eds) *National Policies for Developing High Technology Industries: International Comparisons.* Boulder, CO, Westview Press: 201–26

Simons G. R. (1993) Industrial extension and innovation. In Branscomb L. M. (ed.) *Empowering Technology.* Cambridge, MA, MIT Press: 167–201

Sinclair T., Sutcliffe C. (1988) The economic effects on destination areas of foreign involvement in the tourism industry: a Spanish application. In Goodall B., Ashworth G. (eds) *Marketing in the Tourism Industry: The Promotion of Destination Regions.* London, Croom Helm: 111–32

Singh A. (1995) The causes of fast economic growth in East Asia. *UNCTAD Review:* 91–127

Singh K. (1995) Corporate strategy in the intelligent island: the case of Singapore Telecom. *Industrial and Corporate Change* **4**: 691–702

Singh M. S. (1988) The changing role of the periphery in the international arena exemplified by Malaysia and Singapore. In Linge G. J. R. (ed.) *Peripheralisation and Industrial Change.* London, Routledge: 72–93

Singh M. S. (1995) Formation of local skills space and skills networking: the experience of the electronics and electrical sector in Penang. In van der Knaap B., Le Heron R. (eds) *Human Resources and Industrial Spaces: A Perspective on Globalization and Localization.* Chichester, John Wiley: 197–226

Singhal A., Rogers E. M. (1989) *India's Information Revolution.* New Delhi, Sage

Single A. W., Spurgeon W. M. (1996) Creating and commercializing innovation inside a skunk works. *Research-Technology Management* **39** (1): 38–41

Sisodia R. (1992) Singapore invests in the nation-corporation. *Harvard Business Review* **70** (3): 40–50

Sjölander S., Oskarsson C. (1995) Diversification: exploiting the flow of technology. A Swedish comparison. *International Journal of Technology Management* **10**: 21–30.

Sklair L. (1989) *Assembling for Development: The Maquila Industry in Mexico and the United States.* London, Unwin Hyman

Sklair L. (1994) Capitalism and development in global perspective. In Sklair L. (ed.) *Capitalism and Development.* London, Routledge: 165–85

Skoro C. L. (1988) Rankings of state business climates. *Economic Development Quarterly* **2**: 138–52

Skowronski S. (1987) Transfer of technology and international cooperation. *Technovation* **7**: 17–22

Slack B. (1993) Pawns in the game: ports in a global transportation system. *Growth and Change* **24**: 579–88

Slifko J., Rigby D. L. (1995) Industrial policy in Southern California: the production of markets, technologies, and institutional support for electric vehicles. *Environment and Planning A* **27**: 933–54

Sloan C. (1981) A good business climate: what it really means. *The New Republic* 3 January: 12–15

Smallbone D., North D., Leigh R. (1993) The use of external assistance by mature SMEs in the UK: some policy implications. *Entrepreneurship and Regional Development* **5**: 279–95

Smilor R. W., Feeser H. R. (1991) Chaos and the entrepreneurial process: patterns and policy implications for technology entrepreneurship. *Journal of Business Venturing* **6**:

165–72

Smilor R. W., Gibson D. V., Dietrich G. B. (1990) University spin-out companies: technology start-ups from UT-Austin. *Journal of Business Venturing* **5**: 63–76

Smilor R. W., Gibson D. V., Kozmetsky G. (1989) Creating the technopolis: high-technology development in Austin, Texas. *Journal of Business Venturing* **4**: 49–67

Smith A. (1996) From convergence to fragmentation: uneven regional development, industrial restructuring, and the 'transition to capitalism' in Slovakia. *Environment and Planning A* **28**: 135–56

Smith C. G. (1995) How newcomers can undermine incumbents' marketing strengths. *Business Horizons* **38** (5): 61–8

Smith D. A., Timberlake M. (1995a) Conceptualising and mapping the structure of the world system's city system. *Urban Studies* **32**: 287–302

Smith D. A., Timberlake M. (1995b) Cities in global matrices: toward mapping the world system's city system. In Knox P., Taylor P. J. (eds) *World Cities in a World-System*. Cambridge, Cambridge University Press: 79–114

Smith D. M. (1981) *Industrial Location: An Economic Geographical Analysis*, second edition. New York, John Wiley

Smith K. (1995) Interactions in knowledge systems: foundations, policy implications and empirical methods. *STI Review* **16**: 69–102

Smith K., Vidvei T. (1992) Innovation activity and innovation outputs in Norwegian industry. *STI Review* **11**: 11–33

Smith N. (1984) *Uneven Development*. Oxford, Basil Blackwell

Smith N., Dennis W. (1987) The restructuring of geographical scale: coalescence and fragmentation of the northern core region. *Economic Geography* **63**: 160–82

So A. Y., Chiu S. W. K. (1995) *East Asia and the World Economy*. Thousands Oaks, CA, Sage

Socolow R., Andrews C., Berhout F., Thomas V. (eds) (1994) *Industrial Ecology and Global Change*. Cambridge, Cambridge University Press

Soete L. (1986) Technological innovation and long waves: an inquiry into the nature and wealth of Christopher Freeman's thinking. In MacLeod R. M. (ed.) *Technology and the Human Prospect*. London, Frances Pinter: 214–38

Soete L. (1994) International competitiveness, trade and technology policies. In Granstrand O. (ed.) *Economics of Technology*. Amsterdam, North-Holland: 355–74

Soete L., Turner R. (1984) Technology diffusion and the rate of technical change. *Economic Journal* **94**: 612–23

Sokoloff K. L. (1995) Some thoughts and evidence on industrial policy: industrialization in South Korea and Mexico. In Jacoby S. M. (ed.) *The Workers of Nations*. New York, Oxford University Press: 182–200

Solow R. S. (1957) Technical change and the aggregate production function. *Review of Economics and Statistics* **39**: 312–20

Song X. M., Parry M. E. (1993) How the Japanese manage the R&D–marketing interface. *Research-Technology Management* **36** (4): 32–8

Sonneborn M., Wilemon D. (1991) R&D's contribution to strategic decision-making: rationale, content, and process. *Technovation* **11**: 267–81

Souder W. E. (1983) Organizing for modern technology and innovation: a review and synthesis. *Technovation* **2**: 27–44

Soukup W. R., Cooper A. C. (1983) Strategic response to technological change in the electronic components industry. *R&D Management* **13**: 219–30

South R. B. (1990) Transnational 'maquiladora' location. *Annals of the Association of American Geographers* **80**: 549–70

Späth B. (1992) The institutional environment and communities of small firms. *IDS Bulletin* 23 (2): 8–14

Specht P. H. (1993) Munificence and carrying capacity of the environment and organization formation. *Entrepreneurship Theory and Practice* 17: 77–86

Speiser A. P. (1988) European technology between two poles: the USA and the Far East. *International Journal of Technology Management* 3: 405–10

Spekman R. E. (1988) Strategic supplier selection: understanding long-term buyer relationships. *Business Horizons* 31 (4): 75–81

Spence A. M., Hazard H. A. (eds) (1988) *International Competitiveness*. Cambridge, MA, Ballinger

Spenner K. I. (1988) Technological change, skill requirements, and education: the case for uncertainty. In Cyert R. M., Mowery D. C. (eds) *The Impact of Technological Change on Employment and Growth*. Cambridge, MA, Ballinger: 131–84

Spilling O. R. (1991) Entrepreneurship in a cultural perspective. *Entrepreneurship and Regional Development* 3: 33–48

Spinanger D. (1992) The impact on employment and income of structural and technological changes in the clothing industry. In van Liemt G. (ed.) *Industry on the Move: Causes and Consequences of International Relocation in the Manufacturing Industry*. Geneva, International Labour Office: 83–116

Spital F. C. (1983) Gaining market share advantage in the semiconductor industry by lead time in innovation. In Rosenbloom R. S. (ed.) *Research on Innovation, Management and Policy*, volume 1. Greenwich, CT, JAI Press: 55–67

Spring W. J. (1989) New England's training systems and regional economic competitiveness. *New England Economic Indicators* second quarter: iv–ix

Spulber N. (1995) *The American Economy: The Struggle for Supremacy in the 21st Century*. Cambridge, Cambridge University Press

Sripaipan C. (1995) Technology upgrading in Thailand: a strategic perspective. In Simon D. F. (ed.) *The Emerging Technological Trajectory of the Pacific Rim*. New York, M. E. Sharpe: 147–70

Stabler J. C., Howe E. C. (1988) Service exports and regional growth in the post-industrial era. *Journal of Regional Science* 28: 303–15

Stabler J. C., Howe E. C. (1993) Services, trade, and regional structural change in Canada 1974–1984. *Review of Urban and Regional Development Studies* 5: 29–50

Stabler M. J. (1988) The image of destination regions: theoretical and empirical aspects. In Goodall B., Ashworth G. (eds) *Marketing in the Tourism Industry: The Promotion of Destination Regions*. London, Croom Helm: 133–61

Stafford H. A. (1991) Manufacturing plant closure selections within firms. *Annals of the Association of American Geographers* 81: 51–65

Stalk G., Evans P., Shulman L. E. (1992) Competing on capabilities: the new rules of corporate strategy. *Harvard Business Review* 70 (2): 57–69

Stalk G., Hout T. M. (1990) *Competing against Time: How Time-Based Competition Is Reshaping Global Markets*. New York, Free Press

Stalk G., Webber A. M. (1993) Japan's dark side of time. *Harvard Business Review* 71 (4): 93–102

Stallmann J. I., Siegel P. B. (1995) Attracting retirees as an economic development strategy: looking into the future. *Economic Development Quarterly* 9: 372–82

Stanback T. M. (1987) *Computerization and the Transformation of Employment*. Boulder, CO, Westview Press

Stanback T. M., Bearse P. J., Noyelle T. J., Karasek R. A. (1981) *Services: The New Economy*. Totowa, NJ, Allanheld, Osmun

Standing G. (1992) Alternative routes to labor flexibility. In Storper M., Scott A. J. (eds) *Pathways to Industrialization and Regional Development*. London, Routledge: 255–75

Starr C., Searl M. F., Alpert S. (1992) Energy sources: a realistic outlook. *Science* **256**: 981–7

Starr M. K., Biloski A. J. (1985) The decision to adopt new technology – effects on organizational size. In Rhodes E., Wield D. (eds) *Implementing New Technologies*. Oxford, Basil Blackwell: 303–15

Staudt E. (1994) Innovation barriers on the way from the planned to the market economy: the management of non-routine processes. *International Journal of Technology Management* **9**: 799–817

Stearns T. M., Carter N. M., Reynolds P. D., Williams M. (1995) New firm survival: industry, strategy, and location. *Journal of Business Venturing* **10**: 23–42

Steed G. P. F. (1981) International location and comparative advantage: the clothing industry and developing countries. In Hamilton F. E. I., Linge G. J. R. (eds) *Spatial Analysis, Industry and the Industrial Environment*, volume 2: *International Industrial Systems*. London, John Wiley: 265–303

Steed G. P. F. (1982) *Threshold Firms: Backing Canada's Winners*. Ottawa, Science Council of Canada

Steedman H. (1993) The economics of youth training in Germany. *Economic Journal* **103**: 1279–91

Steele L. W. (1975) *Innovation in Big Business*. New York, Elsevier

Steele L. W. (1988) What we've learned: selecting R&D programs and objectives. *Research-Technology Management* **31** (2): 17–36

Steele L. W. (1989) *Managing Technology: The Strategic View*. New York, McGraw-Hill

Steele L. W. (1991) Needed: new paradigms for R&D. *Research-Technology Management* **34** (4): 13–21

Steele P. (1995) Ecotourism: an economic analysis. *Journal of Sustainable Tourism* **3**: 29–44

Steenbakkers K. (1991) Petrochemical complexes and formations. In de Smidt M., Wever E. (eds) *Complexes, Formations and Networks*. Utrecht, Royal Dutch Geographical Society: 41–52

Steer A., Lutz E. (1993) Measuring environmentally sustainable development. *Finance and Development* **30** (4): 20–3

Steiner M. (1990) How different are regions? An evolutionary approach to regional inequality. In *Infrastructure and the Space-Economy: Essays in Honor of Rolf Funck*. Berlin, Springer-Verlag: 294–316

Steiner P. (1987) Contrasts in regional potentials: some aspects of regional economic development. *Papers of the Regional Science Association* **61**: 79–92

Stern N. (1989) The economics of development: a survey. *Economic Journal* **99**: 597–685

Stern N. (1991) The determinants of growth. *Economic Journal* **101**: 122–33

Sternberg R. (1995) Supporting peripheral economies or industrial policy in favour of industrial growth? An empirically based analysis of goal achievement of the Japanese 'Technopolis' Program. *Environment and Planning C: Government and Policy* **13**: 425–39

Sternberg R. (1996a) Government R&D expenditure and space: empirical evidence from five industrialized countries. *Research Policy* **25**: 741–58

Sternberg R. (1996b) Technology policies and the growth of regions: evidence from four countries. *Small Business Economics* **8**: 75–86

Stevens B., Andrieu M. (1991) Trade, investment and technology in a changing international environment. In *Trade, Investment and Technology in the 1990s*. Paris: Organisation for Economic Co-operation and Development: 113–25

Stevens B., Lahr M. L. (1988) Regional economic multipliers: definition, measurement, and application. *Economic Development Quarterly* **2**: 88–96

Stevens C. (1993) The environmental effects of trade. *The World Economy* **16**: 439–51

Stewart C. T., Nihei Y. (1987) *Technology Transfer and Human Factors*. Lexington, MA, Lexington Books

Stewart F. (1978) *Technology and Underdevelopment*, second edition. London, Macmillan

Stewart F. (1981) International technology transfer: issues and policy options. In Streeten P., Jolly R. (eds) *Recent Issues in World Development*. Oxford, Pergamon: 67–110

Stewart F. (1987) The case for appropriate technology: a reply to R. S. Eckaus. *Issues in Science and Technology* **3** (4): 101–9

Stewart F. (1990) Technology transfer for development. In Evenson R. E., Ranis G. (eds) *Science and Technology: Lessons for Development Policy*. Boulder, CO, Westview Press: 301–24

Stewart T. A. (1993) Welcome to the revolution. *Fortune* **128** (15) 13 December: 66–78

Stewart T. A. (1994a) Measuring company IQ. *Fortune* **129** (2) 24 January: 24

Stewart T. A. (1994b) Your company's most valuable asset: intellectual capital. *Fortune* **130** (7) 3 October: 68–74

Stewart T. A. (1995) Trying to grasp the intangible. *Fortune* **132** (7) 2 October: 157–61

Stiglitz J. E. (1987) Learning to learn, localized learning and technological progress. In Dasgupta P., Stoneman P. (eds) *Economic Policy and Industrial Performance*. Cambridge, Cambridge University Press: 125–53

Stiglitz J. E. (1991) Another century of economic science. *Economic Journal* **101**: 134–41

Stiglitz J. E. (1996) Some lessons from the East Asian miracle. *World Bank Research Observer* **11**: 151–77

Stimpson D. V., Robinson P. B., Waranusuntikule S., Zhang R. (1990) Attitudinal characteristics of entrepreneurs and non-entrepreneurs in the United States, Korea, Thailand, and the People's Republic of China. *Entrepreneurship and Regional Development* **2**: 49–55

Stobaugh R. (1985) Creating a monopoly: product innovation in petrochemicals. In Rosenbloom R. S. (ed.) *Research on Technological Innovation, Management and Policy*, volume 2. Greenwich, CT, JAI Press: 81–112

Stöhr W. (1982) Structural characteristics of peripheral areas: the relevance of the stock-in-trade variables of regional science. *Papers of the Regional Science Association* **49**: 71–84

Stöhr W. B. (1986) Regional innovation complexes. *Papers of the Regional Science Association* **59**: 29–44

Stöhr W. B. (1990) Synthesis. In Stöhr W. B. (ed.) *Global Challenge and Local Response*. London, Mansell: 1–19

Stöhr W., Pönighaus R. (1992) Towards a data-based evaluation of the Japanese technopolis policy – the effect of new technological and organizational infrastructure on urban and regional development. *Regional Studies* **26**: 605–18

Stoneman P., Kwon M.-J. (1994) The diffusion of multiple process technologies. *Economic Journal* **104**: 420–31

Stopford J., Strange S. (1991) *Rival States, Rival Firms: Competition for World Market Shares*. Cambridge, Cambridge University Press

Storey D. J. (1993) Review of *State of small business and entrepreneurship in Atlantic Canada: First annual report on small business. Small Business Economics* 5: 77–8

Storey D. J., Strange A. (1992) New players in the 'enterprise culture'? In Caley K., Chell E., Crittenden F., Mason C. (eds), *Small Enterprise Development: Policy and Practice in Action.* London, Paul Chapman: 85–95

Storper M. (1988) Big structures, small events, and large processes in economic geography. *Environment and Planning A* 20: 165–85

Storper M. (1989) Industrial policy at the crossroads: production flexibility, the region, and the state. *Environment and Planning D: Society and Space* 7: 235–43

Storper M. (1992) The limits to globalization: technology districts and international trade. *Economic Geography* 68: 60–93

Storper M. (1993) Regional 'worlds' of production: learning and innovation in the technology districts of France, Italy and the USA. *Regional Studies* 27: 433–55

Storper M. (1995a) Territorial development in the global learning economy: the challenge to developing countries. *Review of International Political Economy* 2: 394–424

Storper M. (1995b) Regional technology coalitions: an essential dimension of national technology policy. *Research Policy* 24: 895–911

Storper M., Christopherson S. (1987) Flexible specialization and regional industrial agglomerations: the case of the US motion picture industry. *Annals of the Association of American Geographers* 77: 104–17

Storper M., Harrison B. (1991) Flexibility, hierarchy and regional development: the changing structure of industrial production systems and their forms of governance in the 1990s. *Research Policy* 20: 407–22

Storper M., Scott A. J. (eds) (1992) *Pathways to Industrialization and Regional Development.* London, Routledge

Storper M., Walker R. (1984) The spatial division of labor: labor and the location of industries. In Sawers L., Tabb W. K. (eds) *Sunbelt/Snowbelt.* New York, Oxford University Press: 19–47

Storper M., Walker R. (1989) *The Capitalist Imperative: Territory, Technology, and Industrial Growth.* Oxford, Basil Blackwell

Strassoldo R. (1981) Center and periphery: socio-ecological perspectives. In Kuklinski A. (ed.) *Polarized Development and Regional Policies: Tribute to Jacques Boudeville.* The Hague, Mouton: 71–102

Stratigaki M. (1994) Women's work and informal activities in southern Europe. *Environment and Planning A* 26: 1221–34

Street J. (1992) *Politics and Technology.* New York, Guilford

Streeten P. (1980) Development ideas in historical perspective: the new interest in development. In Adelman A. (ed.) *Economic Growth and Resources,* volume 1: *National and International Policies.* New York, St Martin's Press: 56–69

Su S. (1988) Information technology as a threat and an opportunity. In Schütte H. (ed.) *Strategic Issues in Information Technology.* Maidenhead, Pergamon Infotech: 103–13

Suarez F. F., Cusumano M. A., Fine C. H. (1995) An empirical study of flexibility in manufacturing. *Sloan Management Review* 37 (1): 25–32

Suarez-Villa L. (1984) Industrial export enclaves and manufacturing change. *Papers of the Regional Science Association* 54: 89–111

Suarez-Villa L. (1989) *The Evolution of Regional Economies: Entrepreneurship and Macroeconomic Change.* New York, Praeger

Suarez-Villa L. (1991) Regional evolution and entrepreneurship: roles, eras and the space economy. *Entrepreneurship and Regional Development* 3: 335–47

Suarez-Villa L., Cuadrado-Roura J. R. (1993a) Regional economic integration and the evolution of disparities. *Papers in Regional Science* 72: 369–87

Suarez-Villa L., Cuadrado Roura J. R. (1993b) Thirty years of Spanish regional change: interregional dynamics and sectoral transformation. *International Regional Science Review* 15: 121–56

Subrahmanian K. K. (1993) India. In Patel S. J. (ed.) *Technological Transformation in the Third World*, volume I: *Asia*. Aldershot, Avebury: 59–143

Sundquist J. L. (1975) *Dispersing Population: What America Can Learn from Europe*. Washington, Brookings Institution

Suris O. (1996) Chrysler leads big three in efficiency of car factories, but all trail Japanese. *Wall Street Journal* 30 May: A2, A4

Swales J. K. (1983) A Kaldorian model of cumulative causation: regional growth with induced technical change. In Gillespie A. (ed.) *Technological Change and Regional Development*. London, Pion: 68–87

Sweeney G. P. (1985) Innovation is entrepreneur-led. In Sweeney G. (ed.) *Innovation Policies: An International Perspective*. London, Frances Pinter: 80–113

Sweeney G. P. (1987) *Innovation, Entrepreneurs and Regional Development*. New York, St Martin's Press

Sweeney G. P. (1991) Technical culture and the local dimension of entrepreneurial vitality. *Entrepreneurship and Regional Development* 3: 363–78

Sweeney G. P. (1995) *National Innovation Policy or a Regional Innovation Culture: A Reflection on the 20th Anniversary of the Six Countries Programme*. Dublin, SICA Innovation Consultants

Sweeney G. P. (1996) Learning efficiency, technological change and economic progress. *International Journal of Technology Management* 11: 5–27

Sykes H. B. (1993) Business research: a new corporate function. *Journal of Business Venturing* 8: 1–8

Syme G. J., Shaw B. J., Fenton D. M., Mueller W. S. (eds) (1989) *The Planning and Evaluation of Hallmark Events*. Aldershot, Avebury

Syrquin M. (1988) Patterns of structural change. In Chenery H., Srinivasan T. N. (eds) *Handbook of Development Economics*, volume I. Amsterdam, North-Holland: 203–73

Szakonyi R. (1989) Critical issues in long-range planning. *Research-Technology Management* 32 (3): 28–32

Takeuchi A. (1987) Two elements supporting high position of Tokyo region in the national system of Japanese machinery industry. *Geographical Reports of Tokyo Metropolitan University* 22: 129–38

Takeuchi A., Mori H. (1987) Spontaneous technological center of Japanese machinery industry in provincial area. *Report of Researches, Nippon Institute of Technology* 17 (3): 265–81

Takyi-Asiedu S. (1993) Some socio-cultural factors retarding entrepreneurial activity in sub-Saharan Africa. *Journal of Business Venturing* 8: 91–8

Tallman E. W., Wang P. (1992) Human capital investment and economic growth: new routes in theory address old questions. *Economic Review, Federal Reserve Bank of Atlanta* 77 (5): 1–12

Tam M.-Y., Persky J. (1982) Regional convergence and national inequality. *Review of Economics and Statistics* 64: 161–4

Tambunan T. (1992a) The importance of small-scale industries in Indonesia. *Tijdschrift voor Economische en Sociale Geografie* 83: 25–38

Tambunan T. (1992b) Economic development and small scale enterprises in Indonesia. *Entrepreneurship and Regional Development* 4: 85–98

Tambunan T. (1992c) The role of small firms in Indonesia. *Small Business Economics* 4:

59–77

Tambunan T. (1994) Rural small-scale industries in a developing region: sign of poverty or progress? A case study of Ciomas District, West-Java Province, Indonesia. *Entrepreneurship and Regional Development* 6: 1–13

Tan G. (1993) The next NICs of Asia. *Third World Quarterly* 14: 57–73

Tan R. R. (1995) Establishing technology transfer infrastructure as a strategy for promoting manufacturing automation in Taiwan. *Technovation* 15: 407–21

Tan T. S., Tan C. H. (1990) Role of transnational corporations in transfer of technology to Singapore. In Chatterji M. (ed.) *Technology Transfer in the Developing Countries*. London, Macmillan: 335–44

Tanaka N., Vickery G. (1993) Introduction: perspectives on globalisation. *STI Review* 13: 7–12

Tani A. (1989) International comparisons of industrial robot penetration. *Technological Forecasting and Social Change* 34: 191–210

Tannenwald R. (1996) State business tax climate: how should it be measured and how important is it? *New England Economic Review* January/February: 23–38

Tarabusi C. C. (1993) Globalisation in the pharmaceutical industry: technological change and competition in a Triad perspective. *STI Review* 13: 123–61

Tassey G. (1991) The functions of technology infrastructure in a competitive economy. *Research Policy* 20: 345–61

Tatsuno S. (1986) *The Technopolis Strategy*. New York, Prentice-Hall Press

Tatsuno S. M. (1990) *Created in Japan: From Imitators to World-Class Innovators*. New York, Harper Business

Taylor A. (1989) Why US carmakers are losing ground. *Fortune* 120 (9): 96–116

Taylor C. A. (1982) Econometric modeling of urban and other substate areas: an analysis of alternative methodologies. *Regional Science and Urban Economics* 12: 425–48

Taylor M. J. (1986) The product cycle model: a critique. *Environment and Planning A* 18: 751–61

Taylor M. J. (1987) Enterprise and the product-cycle model: conceptual ambiguities. In van der Knaap B., Wever E. (eds) *New Technology and Regional Development*. London, Croom Helm: 75–93

Taylor M. J. (1996) Industrialisation, enterprise power, and environmental change: an exploration of concepts. *Environment and Planning A* 28: 1035–51

Taylor M. J., Thrift N. J. (1982) Industrial linkage and the segmented economy: 1. some theoretical proposals. *Environment and Planning A* 14: 1601–13

Taylor P. J. (1989) *Political Geography*, second edition. London, Longman

Tchijov I. (1992) The diffusion of flexible manufacturing systems. In Ayres R. U., Haywood W., Tchijov I. (eds) *Computer Integrated Manufacturing*, volume III: *Models, Case Studies, and Forecasts of Diffusion*. London, Chapman and Hall: 197–248

Tchijov I., Sheinin R. (1989) Flexible manufacturing systems (FMS): current diffusion and main advantages. *Technological Forecasting and Social Change* 35: 277–93

Tchijov I., Sheinin R. (1992) International comparisons of FMS diffusion. In Ayres R. U., Haywood W., Tchijov I. (eds) *Computer Integrated Manufacturing*, volume III: *Models, Case Studies, and Forecasts of Diffusion*. London, Chapman and Hall: 249–62

Teece D. J. (1980) Economies of scope and the scope of the enterprise. *Journal of Economic Behavior and Organization* 1: 223–47

Teece D. J. (1981) Technology transfer and R&D activities of multinational firms: some theory and evidence. In Hawkins R. G., Prasad A. J. (eds) *Research in International Business and Finance*, volume 2: *Technology Transfer and Economic Development*.

Greenwich, CT, JAI Press: 39–74

Teece D. J. (1982) Towards an economic theory of the multiproduct firm. *Journal of Economic Behavior and Organization* 3: 39–63

Teece D. J. (1986) Profiting from technological innovation: implications for integration, collaboration, licensing and public policy. *Research Policy* 15: 285–305

Teece D. J. (1988) Technological change and the nature of the firm. In Dosi G., Freeman C., Nelson R., Silverberg G., Soete L. (eds) *Technical Change and Economic Theory*. London, Pinter: 256–81

Teece D. J. (1991) Support policies for strategic industries: impact on home economies. In OECD, *Strategic Industries in a Global Economy: Policy Issues for the 1990s*. Paris, Organisation for Economic Co-operation and Development: 35–50

Tellis G. J., Golder P. N. (1996) First to market, first to fail? Real causes of enduring market leadership. *Sloan Management Review* 37 (2): 65–75

Telscher S. (1994) Small trade and the world economy: informal vendors in Quito, Ecuador. *Economic Geography* 70: 167–87

Tenenbaum D. (1995) The greening of Costa Rica. *Technology Review* 98 (7): 42–52

Teske P., Johnson R. (1994) Moving towards an American industrial technology policy. *Policy Studies Journal* 22: 296–310

Teubal M. (1987) *Innovation Performance, Learning, and Government Policy*. Madison: University of Wisconsin Press

Thant M., Tang M., Kakazu H. (eds) (1994) *Growth Triangles in Asia: A New Approach to Regional Economic Cooperation*. Oxford, Oxford University Press

The Economist (1990) Two paths to prosperity. 14 July: 19–22

The Economist (1992) A driving force: the overseas Chinese. 18 July: 21–4

The Economist (1993) The age of the thing. 25 December: 47–51

The Economist (1994a) Going places. 19 March: 39–40

The Economist (1994b) The car makers' recovery stakes. 29 October: 73–4

The Economist (1994c) How much is that ant in the window? 30 July: 63

The Economist (1994d) Yin and yang in Asia's science cities. 21 May: 93–5

The Economist (1994e) The rise of ports like Klang. 9 April: 70–2

The Economist (1995a) Slugs or caterpillars? 2 September: 55–7

The Economist (1995b) Asia's labour pains. 26 August: 51–2

The Economist (1996a) The C-word strikes back. 1 June: 76

The Economist (1996b) The property of the mind. 27 July: 57–9

The Economist (1996c) Schindler's lift. 16 March: 71

The Economist (1996d) Single market, single-minded. 4 May: 63–4

The Economist (1996e) Back to basics in Japan. 25 May: 85–6

The Economist (1996f) Bangalore bytes. 23 March: 67

The Economist (1996g) The long drive into the Middle Kingdom. 8 June: 63–4

The Economist (1996h) Crossing the Pacific . . . and the Indian Ocean. 24 August: 51–2

The Economist (1996i) Good breeding. 18 May: 66–9

Thirlwall A. P. (1972) *Growth and Development*. Cambridge, MA, Schenkman

Thirlwall A. P. (1974) Regional economic disparities and regional policy in the Common Market. *Urban Studies* 11: 1–12

Thirlwall A. P. (1983) A plain man's guide to Kaldor's growth laws. *Journal of Post Keynesian Economics* 5: 345–58

Thomas L. G. (1994) Implicit industrial policy: the triumph of Britain and the failure of France in global pharmaceuticals. *Industrial and Corporate Change* 3: 451–89

Thomas L. J. (1983) The centralized research organization. In Brown J. K., Elvers L. M. (eds) *Research and Development: Key Issues for Management*. Report 842. New

York, The Conference Board: 30–3

Thomas M. D. (1975) Growth pole theory, technological change, and regional economic growth. *Papers of the Regional Science Association* 34: 3–25

Thomas M. D. (1986) Growth and structural change: the role of technical innovation. In Amin A., Goddard J. B. (eds) *Technological Change, Industrial Restructuring and Regional Development.* London, Allen and Unwin: 115–39

Thomas M. D. (1987) The innovation factor in the process of microeconomic industrial change: conceptual explorations. In van der Knaap B., Wever E. (eds) *New Technology and Regional Development.* London, Croom Helm: 21–44

Thomas R. J. (1994) *What Machines Can't Do: Politics and Technology in the Industrial Enterprise.* Berkeley, University of California Press

Thomas S. (1988) The development and appraisal of nuclear power. Part II. The role of technical change. *Technovation* 7: 305–39

Thompson C. (1987) Definitions of 'high technology' used by state programs in the USA: a study in variations in industrial policy under a federal system. *Environment and Planning C: Government and Policy* 5: 417–31

Thompson C. (1988a) High-technology development and recession: the local experience in the United States, 1980–1982. *Economic Development Quarterly* 2: 153–67

Thompson C. (1988b) Some problems with R&D/SE&T-based definitions of high technology industry. *Area* 20: 265–77

Thompson J. K., Rehder R. R. (1995) Nissan U.K.: a worker's paradox? *Business Horizons* 38 (1): 48–58

Thompson W. R. (1965) *A Preface to Urban Economics.* Baltimore, Johns Hopkins University Press

Thompson W. R. (1987) Policy-based analysis for local economic development. *Economic Development Quarterly* 1 (3): 203–13

Thompson W. R. (1995) Introduction: urban economics in the global age. In Kresl P. K., Gappert G. (eds) *North American Cities and the Global Economy.* Thousand Oaks, CA, Sage: 1–17

Thompson W. R., Thompson P. R. (1993) Cross-hairs targeting for industries and occupations. In Barkley D. L. (ed.) *Economic Adaptation: Alternatives for Nonmetropolitan Areas.* Boulder, CO, Westview Press: 265–86

Thomsen S. (1993) Japanese direct investment in the European Community: the product cycle revisited. *The World Economy* 16: 301–15

Thomson R. (1989) *The Path to Mechanized Shoe Production in the United States.* Chapel Hill, University of North Carolina Press

Thomson R. (ed.) (1993) *Learning and Technological Change.* New York, St Martin's Press

Thorbecke E., Koné S. (1995) The impact of stabilisation and structural adjustment programmes (SSAPs) on performance in sub-Saharan Africa. In Berthélemy J.-C. (ed.) *Whither African Economies?* Paris, Organisation for Economic Co-operation and Development: 17–56

Thorelli H. B. (1986) Networks: between markets and hierarchies. *Strategic Management Journal* 7: 37–51

Thorngren B. (1970) How do contact systems affect regional development? *Environment and Planning* 2: 409–27

Thornton D. W. (1995) *Airbus Industrie: The Politics of an International Industrial Collaboration.* New York, St Martin's Press

Thrift N. J. (1989) New times and spaces? The perils of transition models. *Environment and Planning D: Society and Space* 7: 127–9

Thurow L. (1992) *Head to Head: The Coming Economic Battle among Japan, Europe, and America*. New York, William Morrow

Thwaites A. T. (1982) Some evidence of regional variations in the introduction and diffusion of industrial products and processes within British manufacturing industry. *Regional Studies* **16**: 371–81

Thwaites A. T. (1983) The employment implications of technological change. In Gillespie A. (ed.) *Technological Change and Regional Development*. London, Pion: 36–53

Thwaites A., Alderman N. (1990) The location of R&D: retrospect and prospect. In Cappellin R., Nijkamp P. (eds) *The Spatial Context of Technological Development*. Aldershot, Avebury: 17–42

Tidd J. (1993) Technological innovation, organizational linkages and strategic degrees of freedom. *Technology Analysis and Strategic Management* **5**: 273–84

Tidd J. (1995) Development of novel products through intraorganizational and inter-organizational networks: the case of home automation. *Journal of Product Innovation Management* **12**: 307–22

Tiebout C. M. (1962) *The Community Economic Base Study*. New York, Committee for Economic Development

Time Inc. (1989) *Corporate Site Selection for New Facilities: A Study Conducted among the Largest US Companies*. New York, Time Inc.

Timmer C. P. (1988) The agricultural transformation. In Chenery H., Srinivasan T. N. (eds) *Handbook of Development Economics*, volume I. Amsterdam, North-Holland: 275–331

Tirman J. (ed.) (1984) *The Militarization of High Technology*. Cambridge, MA, Ballinger

Tisdell C. A. (1981) *Science and Technology Policy: Priorities of Governments*. London, Chapman and Hall

Toda T. (1987) The location of high-technology industry in Japan and the technopolis plan. In Brotchie J., Hall P., Newton P. W. (eds) *The Spatial Impact of Technological Change*. London, Croom Helm: 271–83

Todd D. (1992) The internationalisation of the aircraft industry: substance and myth. In van Liemt G. (ed.) *Industry on the Move: Causes and Consequences of International Relocation in the Manufacturing Industry*. Geneva, International Labour Office: 117–48

Todd D. (1994) Changing technology, economic growth and port development: the transformation of Tianjin. *Geoforum* **25**: 285–303

Todd D., Hsueh Y.-C. (1992) The industrial complex revisited: petrochemicals in Taiwan. *Geoforum* **23**: 29–40

Todd D., Simpson J. (1985) Aerospace, the state and the regions: a Canadian perspective. *Political Geography Quarterly* **4**: 111–30

Todd D., Simpson J. (1986) *The World Aircraft Industry*. London, Croom Helm

Tödtling F. (1994) The uneven landscape of innovation poles: local embeddedness and global networks. In Amin A., Thrift N. (eds) *Globalization, Institutions, and Regional Development in Europe*. Oxford, Oxford University Press: 68–90

Tödtling F. (1995) The innovation process and local environment. In Conti S., Malecki E. J., Oinas P. (eds) *The Industrial Enterprise and Its Environment: Spatial Perspectives*. Aldershot, Avebury: 171–93

Tomaney J. (1994) A new paradigm of work and technology? In Amin A. (ed.) *Post-Fordism: A Reader*. Oxford, Blackwell: 157–94

Townsend A. (1986) Spatial aspects of the growth of part-time employment in Britain.

Regional Studies **20** (4): 313–30

Townsend A. (1995) Sales of business services from a European city. *Tijdschrift voor Economische en Sociale Geografie* **86**: 443–55

Toy S. (1994) Non-dirigisme: dragging France's bureaucrats out of industry. *Business Week* 18 November: 30–2

Toye J. (1993) *Dilemmas of Development*, second edition. Oxford, Basil Blackwell

Triglia C. (1992) Italian industrial districts: neither myth nor interlude. In Pyke F., Sengenberger W. (eds) *Industrial Districts and Local Economic Regeneration*. Geneva, International Institute of Labour Studies: 33–47

Truett D. B., Truett L. J. (1994) Government policy and export performance of the Mexican automobile industry. *Growth and Change* **25**: 301–24

Trygg L. (1993) Concurrent engineering practices in selected Swedish companies: a movement or an activity of the few? *Journal of Product Innovation Management* **10**: 403–15

Tsai W. M.-H., MacMillan I. C., Low M. B. (1991) Effects of strategy and environment on corporate venture success in industrial markets. *Journal of Business Venturing* **6**: 9–28

Tsang S.-K. (1996) Against 'big bang' in economic transition: normative and positive arguments. *Cambridge Journal of Economics* **20**: 183–93

Tsipouri L. J. (1991) The transfer of technology issue revisited: some evidence from Greece. *Entrepreneurship and Regional Development* **3**: 145–57

Tsuru S. (1993) *Japan's Capitalism: Creative Defeat and Beyond*. Cambridge, Cambridge University Press

Tsuruta T. (1988) The rapid growth era. In Komiya R., Okuno M., Suzumura K. (eds) *Industrial Policy of Japan*. Tokyo, Academic Press: 49–87

Tuppen J. N., Thompson I. B. (1994) Industrial restructuring in contemporary France: spatial priorities and policies. *Progress in Planning* **42**: 99–172

Turok I. (1993) Inward investment and local linkages: how deeply embedded is 'Silicon Glen'? *Regional Studies* **27**: 401–17

Turok I., Richardson P. (1991) New firms and local economic development: evidence from West Lothian. *Regional Studies* **25**: 71–83

Tushman M. L. (1979) Managing communication networks in R&D laboratories. *Sloan Management Review* **20**: 37–49

Tushman M. L., Rosenkopf L. (1992) Organizational determinants of technological change: toward a sociology of technological evolution. In Staw B. M., Cummings L. L. (eds) *Research in Organizational Behavior*, volume 14. Greenwich, CT, JAI Press: 311–47

Twiss B., Goodridge M. (1989) *Managing Technology for Competitive Advantage*. London, Pitman

Tyebjee T. T. (1988) A typology of joint ventures: Japanese strategies in the United States. *California Management Review* **31** (1): 75–86

Tylecote A. (1995) Technological and economic long waves and their implications for employment. *New Technology, Work and Employment* **10**: 3–18

Tylecote A., Demirag I. (1992) Short-termism: culture and structures as factors in technological innovation. In Coombs R., Saviotti P., Walsh V. (eds) *Technological Change and Company Strategies*. London, Academic Press: 201–25

Udell G. G., Potter T. A. (1989) Pricing new technology. *Research-Technology Management* **32** (4): 14–18

Uekusa M. (1988) The oil crisis and after. In Komiya R., Okuno M., Suzumura K. (eds) *Industrial Policy of Japan*. Tokyo, Academic Press: 89–117

Uenohara M. (1991) A management view of Japanese corporate R&D. *Research-Technology Management* **34** (6): 17–23

Ulgado F. M. (1996) Location characteristics of manufacturing investments in the US: a comparison of American and foreign-based firms. *Management International Review* **36**: 7–26

Ul Haq M. (1995) *Reflections on Human Development.* New York, Oxford University Press

Ullman E. L., Dacey M. F. (1960) The minimum requirements approach to the urban economic base. *Papers and Proceedings of the Regional Science Association* **6**: 175–94

Ulrich K. T., Eppinger S. D. (1995) *Product Design and Development.* New York, McGraw-Hill

United Nations (1995) *World Urbanization Prospects: The 1994 Revision.* New York, United Nations

UNCTAD (1994) *World Investment Report 1994: Transnational Corporations, Employment and the Workplace.* New York, United Nations

UNCTAD (1995a) *World Investment Report 1995: Transnational Corporations and Competitiveness.* New York, United Nations

UNCTAD (1995b) *Foreign Direct Investment in Africa.* New York, United Nations

UNCTC (1982) *Transnational Corporations in International Tourism.* New York, United Nations Centre on Transnational Corporations

UNCTC (1991) *World Investment Report 1991: The Triad in Foreign Direct Investment.* New York, United Nations Centre on Transnational Corporations

UNDP (annual) *Human Development Report.* New York, United Nations

UN Office for Science and Technology (1980) Mobilizing science and technology for increasing the endogenous capabilities in developing countries. In Standke K.-H., Anandakrishnan M. (eds) *Science, Technology and Society: Needs, Challenges and Limitations.* New York, Pergamon: 476–502

Upton D. M. (1994) The management of manufacturing flexibility. *California Management Review* **36** (2): 72–89

Uribe-Echevarría F. (1993) Changing policy regimes for small-scale industries in Latin America. Lessons for Africa? In Helmsing A. J. M., Kolstee T. (eds) *Small Enterprises and Changing Policies.* London, Intermediate Technology Publications: 159–83

Urry J. (1987) Some social and spatial aspects of services. *Environment and Planning D: Society and Space* **5**: 5–26

Utterback J. M. (1987) Innovation and industrial evolution in manufacturing industries. In Guile B. R., Brooks H. (eds) *Technology and Global Industry: Companies and Nations in the World Economy.* Washington, National Academy Press: 16–48

Utterback J. M. (1994) *Mastering the Dynamics of Innovation.* Boston: Harvard Business School Press

Utterback J. M., Suárez F. F. (1993) Innovation, competition and industry structure. *Research Policy* **22**: 1–21

Uzumeri M., Sanderson S. (1995) A framework for model and product family competition. *Research Policy* **24**: 583–607

Vaessen P., Keeble D. (1995) Growth-oriented SMEs in unfavourable regional environments. *Regional Studies* **29**: 489–505

Vaessen P., Wever E. (1993) Spatial responsiveness of small firms. *Tijdschrift voor Economische en Sociale Geografie* **84**: 119–31

Vakil C. N., Brahmananda P. R. (1987) Technical knowledge and managerial capacity as limiting factors on industrial expansion in underdeveloped countries. In Robinson A. (ed.) *Economic Progress*, second edition. New York, St Martin's Press: 153–72

Valéry N. (1989) Thinking ahead: a survey of Japanese technology. *The Economist* 2 December

Valéry N. (1994) Downdraft: a survey of military aerospace. *The Economist* 3 September

Van de Ven A. (1993) The development of an infrastructure for entrepreneurship. *Journal of Business Venturing* 8: 211–30

Van de Ven A. H., Garud R. (1989) A framework for understanding the emergence of new industries. In Rosenbloom R. S., Burgelman R. A. (eds) *Research in Technological Innovation, Management and Policy*, volume 4. Greenwich, CT, JAI Press: 195–225

Van der Meer J. B. H., Calori R. (1989) Strategic management in technology-intensive industries. *International Journal of Technology Management* 4: 127–39

Van Dinteren J. H. J., Meuwissen J. A. M. (1994) Business services in the core-area of the European Union. *Tijdschrift voor Economische en Sociale Geografie* 85: 366–70

Van Duijn J. J. (1983) *The Long Wave in Economic Life*. London, George Allen and Unwin

Van Geenhuizen M., van der Knaap B. (1994) Dutch textile industry in a global economy. *Regional Studies* 28: 695–711

Van Grunsven L., Wong S.-Y., Kim W. B. (1995) State, investment and territory: regional economic zones and emerging industrial landscapes. In Le Heron R., Park S. O. (eds) *The Asian Pacific Rim and Globalization*. Aldershot, Avebury: 151–77

Van Hulst N., Olds B. (1993) On high tech snobbery. *Research Policy* 22: 455–62

Van Kooij E. (1991) Japanese subcontracting at a crossroads. *Small Business Economics* 3: 145–54

Varaiya P., Wiseman M. (1981) Investment and employment in manufacturing in US metropolitan areas 1960–1976. *Regional Science and Urban Economics* 11: 431–69

Varaldo R., Ferrucci L. (1996) The evolutionary nature of the firm within industrial districts. *European Planning Studies* 4: 27–34

Vatne E. (1995) Local resource mobilization and internationalization strategies in small and medium sized enterprises. *Environment and Planning A* 27: 63–80

Vaughan R., Pollard R. (1986) State and federal policies for high-technology development. In Rees J. (ed.) *Technology, Regions, and Policy*. Totowa, NJ, Rowman and Littlefield: 268–81

Vellas F., Bécherel L. (1995) *International Tourism: An Economic Perspective*. New York, St Martin's Press

Verbruggen H. (1992) Labour intensive manufactured exports: a direct attack on poverty. In Adriaansen W. L. M., Waardenburg J. G. (eds) *A Dual World Economy: Forty Years of Development Experience*. Oxford, Oxford University Press: 194–206

Vernon R. (1966) International investment and international trade in the product cycle. *Quarterly Journal of Economics* 80: 190–207

Vernon R. (1974) The location of economic activity. In Dunning J. H. (ed.) *Economic Analysis and the Multinational Enterprise*. New York, Praeger: 89–114

Vernon R. (1979) The product cycle in a new international environment. *Oxford Bulletin of Economics and Statistics* 41: 255–67

Vernon R. (1989) *Technological Development: The Historical Experience*. Washington: World Bank

Verspagen B. (1992) Endogenous innovation in neo-classical growth models: a survey. *Journal of Macroeconomics* 14: 631–62

Vickery G. (1988) A survey of international technology licensing. *STI Review* 4: 7–49

Vickery G. (1989) Recent developments in the consumer electronics industry. *Science Technology Industry Review* 5: 113–28

Vickery G., Blair L. (1989) *Government Policies and the Diffusion of Microelectronics*.

Paris, Organisation for Economic Co-operation and Development

Vining D. R. (1987) Review of *Regional Dynamics: Studies in Adjustment Theory. Economic Geography* **63**: 358

Volland C. S. (1987) A comprehensive theory of long wave cycles. *Technological Forecasting and Social Change* **32**: 123–45

Von Braun C.-F., Fischer H. G., Müller A. E. (1990) The need for and the issues involved in integrated R&D planning in large corporations. *International Journal of Technology Management* **5**: 559–76

Von Glinow M. A. (1988) *The New Professionals: Managing Today's High-Tech Employees.* Cambridge, MA, Ballinger

Von Hippel E. (1979) A customer-active paradigm for industrial products idea generation. In Baker M. J. (ed.) *Industrial Innovation.* London, Macmillan: 82–110

Von Hippel E. (1987) Cooperation between rivals: informal know-how trading. *Research Policy* **16**: 291–302

Von Hippel E. (1988) *The Sources of Innovation.* New York, Oxford University Press

Von Hippel E. (1994) 'Sticky information' and the locus of problem solving: implications for innovation. *Management Science* **40**: 429–39

Voss C. A. (1984) Technology push and need pull: a new perspective. *R&D Management* **14**: 147–51

Voss C. A. (1985) The need for a field study of implementation of innovations. *Journal of Product Innovation Management* **2**: 266–71

Wade R. (1990) *Governing the Market: Economic Theory and the Role of Government in East Asian Industrialization.* Princeton, NJ, Princeton University Press

Waite C. A. (1988) Service sector: its importance and prospects for the future. In Candilis W. O. (ed.) *United States Service Industries Handbook.* New York, Praeger: 1–22

Waitt G. (1994) The Republic of Korea's foreign direct investments in Australia: the chaebols down under. *Australian Geographical Studies* **32**: 191–213

Walker R. A. (1985) Technological determination and determinism: industrial growth and location. In Castells M. (ed.) *High Technology, Space, and Society.* Beverly Hills, CA, Sage: 226–64

Walker R. (1988) The geographical organization of production-systems. *Environment and Planning D: Society and Space* **6**: 377–408

Walker R., Storper M. (1981) Capital and industrial location. *Progress in Human Geography* **5**: 473–509

Walker W. B. (1980) Britain's industrial performance 1850–1950: a failure to adjust. In Pavitt K. (ed.) *Technical Innovation and British Economic Performance.* London, Macmillan: 19–37

Walker W. (1993) National innovation systems: Britain. In Nelson R. R. (ed.) *National Innovation Systems: A Comparative Analysis.* New York: Oxford University Press: 158–91

Wallerstein I. (1979) *The Capitalist World-Economy.* Cambridge, Cambridge University Press

Wallerstein I. (1994) Development: lodestar or illusion? In Sklair L. (ed.) *Capitalism and Development.* London, Routledge: 3–20

Wallerstein M. B., Mogee M. E., Schoen R. A. (eds) (1993) *Global Dimensions of Intellectual Property Rights in Science and Technology.* Washington, National Academy Press

Walsh V. (1984) Invention and innovation in the chemical industry: demand-pull or discovery-push? *Research Policy* **13**: 211–34

Walsh V. (1987) Technology, competitiveness and the special problems of small countries. *STI Review* 2: 81–133

Walsh V., Niosi J., Mustar P. (1995) Small-firm formation in biotechnology: a comparison of France, Britain and Canada. *Technovation* 15: 303–27

Walshe G. (1996) Technology foresight in the United Kingdom. *STI Review* 17: 177–88

Walters W. H. (1994) Climate and US elderly migration rates. *Papers in Regional Science* 73: 309–29

Walton R. E., Susman G. I. (1987) People policies for the new machines. *Harvard Business Review* 65 (2): 98–106

Wangwe S. M. (1993) Tanzania. In Patel S. J. (ed.) *Technological Transformation in the Third World*, volume II: *Africa*. Aldershot, Avebury: 95–142

Warf B. (1989) Telecommunications and the globalization of financial services. *Professional Geographer* 41: 257–71

Warf B. (1995) Telecommunications and the changing geographies of knowledge transmission in the late 20th century. *Urban Studies* 32: 361–78

Warndorf P. R., Merchant M. E. (1986) Development and future trends in computer-integrated manufacturing in the USA. *International Journal of Technology Management* 1: 161–78

Warner J. (1994) Stepping into the spotlight. *Business Week* 18 November: 192–3

Warner M. (1994) Innovation and training. In Dodgson M., Rothwell R. (eds) *The Handbook of Industrial Innovation*. Aldershot, Edward Elgar: 348–54

Wassmer R. W. (1994) Can local incentives alter a metropolitan city's economic development? *Urban Studies* 31: 1251–78

Watkins A. J. (1980) *The Practice of Urban Economics*. Beverly Hills, CA, Sage

Watts H. D. (1980) *The Large Industrial Enterprise*. London, Croom Helm

Watts H. D. (1981) *The Branch Plant Economy*. London, Longman

Watts H. D., Stafford H. A. (1986) Plant closures and the multiplant firm: some conceptual issues. *Progress in Human Geography* 10: 206–29

Weaver P. M. (1995) Steering the eco-transition: a material accounts approach. In Taylor M. J. (ed.) *Environmental Change: Industry, Power and Policy*. Aldershot, Avebury: 83–106

Webber M. J. (1987a) Rates of profit and interregional flows of capital. *Annals of the Association of American Geographers* 77: 63–75

Webber M. J. (1987b) Quantitative measurement of some Marxist categories. *Environment and Planning A* 19: 1303–21

Webber M., Foot S. P. H. (1988) Profitability and accumulation. *Economic Geography* 64: 335–51

Webber M., Sheppard E., Rigby D. (1992) Forms of technical change. *Environment and Planning A* 24: 1679–709

Webber M., Tonkin S. (1987) Technical changes and the rate of profit in the Canadian food industry. *Environment and Planning A* 19: 1579–96

Webber M., Tonkin S. (1988a) Technical changes and the rate of profit in the Canadian textile, knitting, and clothing industries. *Environment and Planning A* 20: 1487–505

Webber M., Tonkin S. (1988b) Technical changes and the rate of profit in the Canadian wood, furniture, and paper industries. *Environment and Planning A* 20: 1623–43

Wegener M. (1986) Transport network equilibrium and regional deconcentration. *Environment and Planning A* 18: 437–56

Weiner E., Foust D., Yang D. J. (1988) Why made-in-America is back in style. *Business Week* 7 November: 116–20

Weinstein O. (1992) High technology and flexibility. In Cooke P., Moulaert F., Swyngedouw E., Weinstein O., Wells P. (eds) *Towards Global Localization*. London: UCL Press: 19–38

Weiss C. (1990) Scientific and technological constraints to economic growth and equity. In Evenson R. E., Ranis G. (eds) *Science and Technology: Lessons for Development Policy*. Boulder, CO, Westview Press: 17–41

Weitz R. (1986) *New Roads to Development*. Westport, CT, Greenwood Press

Wells C. (1988) Brazilian multinationals. *Columbia Journal of World Business* 23 (4): 13–23

Wells P. (1987) The military scientific infrastructure and regional development. *Environment and Planning A* 19: 1631–58

West C. T. (1995) Regional economic forecasting: keeping the crystal ball rolling. *International Regional Science Review* 18: 195–200

Westhead P. (1990) Comparing rural and urban new firm formation in Wales. In Vyakarnam S. (ed.) *When the Harvest Is In: Developing Rural Entrepreneurship*. London, Intermediate Technology Publications: 232–53

Westhead P. (1995) New owner-managed businesses in rural and urban areas in Great Britain: a matched pairs comparison. *Regional Studies* 29: 367–80

Westhead P., Birley S. (1994) Environments for business deregistrations in the United Kingdom, 1987–1990. *Entrepreneurship and Regional Development* 6: 29–62

Westhead P., Moyes T. (1992) Reflections on Thatcher's Britain: evidence from new production firm registrations 1980–1988. *Entrepreneurship and Regional Development* 4: 21–56

Westney D. E. (1990) Internal and external linkages in the MNC: the case of R&D subsidiaries in Japan. In Bartlett, C. A., Doz Y., Hedlund G. (eds) *Managing the Global Firm*. London, Routledge: 279–300

Westney E. (1993) Country patterns in R&D organization: the United States and Japan. In Kogut B. (ed.) *Country Competitiveness: Technology and the Organizing of Work*. New York: Oxford University Press: 36–53

Westney D. E. (1994) The evolution of Japan's industrial research and development. In Aoki M., Dore R. (eds) *The Japanese Firm: The Sources of Competitive Strength*. Oxford, Oxford University Press, 154–77

Westney D. E., Sakakibara K. (1986) The role of Japan-based R&D in global technology strategy. In Horwitch M. (ed.) *Technology in the Modern Corporation: A Strategic Perspective*. New York, Pergamon: 145–66

Westphal L. E., Kritayakakirana K., Petchsuwan K., Sutabutr H., Yuthavong Y. (1990) The development of technological capability in manufacturing: a macroscopic approach to policy research. In Evenson R. E., Ranis G. (eds) *Science and Technology: Lessons for Development Policy*. Boulder, CO, Westview Press: 81–134

Westphal L. E., Rhee Y. W., Pursell G. (1984) Sources of technological capability in South Korea. In Fransman M., King K. (eds) *Technological Capability in the Third World*. London, Macmillan: 279–300

Westwood A. R. C. (1984) R&D linkages in a multi-industry corporation. *Research Management* 27 (3): 23–36

Wetzel W. F. (1983) Angels and risk capital. *Sloan Management Review* 24 (4): 23–34

Wetzel W. F. (1986) Informal risk capital: knowns and unknowns. In Sexton D. L., Smilor R. W. (eds) *The Art and Science of Entrepreneurship*. Cambridge, MA, Ballinger: 85–108

Wetzel W. F. (1987) The informal venture capital market: aspects of scale and market efficiency. *Journal of Business Venturing* 2: 299–313

Wheelwright S. C., Clark K. B. (1992) *Revolutionizing Product Development*. New York, Free Press

Whiston T. G. (1994) The global innovatory challenge across the twenty-first century. In Dodgson M., Rothwell R. (eds) *The Handbook of Industrial Innovation*. Aldershot, Edward Elgar: 432–42

White M., Braczyk H. J., Ghobadian A., Niebuhr J. (1988) *Small Firms' Innovation: Why Regions Differ*. London, Policy Studies Institute

Whitely R. L., Bean A. S., Russo M. J. (1996) Meet your competition: results from the 1994 IRI/CIMS annual R&D survey. *Research-Technology Management* **39** (1): 18–25

Wicker A. W., King J. C. (1988) Young and numerous: retail/service establishments in the greater Los Angeles area. In Churchill N. C., Hornaday J. A., Kirchhoff B. A., Krasner O. J., Vesper K. H. (eds) *Frontiers of Entrepreneurship Research 1987*. Wellesley, MA, Babson College, Center for Entrepreneurial Studies: 124–37

Wijnberg N. M. (1994) National systems of innovation: selection environments and selection processes. *Technology in Society* **16**: 313–20

Wild C. (1994) Issues in ecotourism. In Cooper C. P., Lockwood A. (eds) *Progress in Tourism, Recreation and Hospitality Management*. Chichester, John Wiley: 12–21

Wilkinson F. (ed.) (1981) *The Dynamics of Labour Market Segmentation*. London, Academic Press

Williams A. M., Shaw G. (eds) (1988) *Tourism and Economic Development: Western European Experience*. London, Belhaven Press

Williams A. M., Shaw G. (1995) Tourism and regional development: polarization and new forms of production in the United Kingdom. *Tijdschrift voor Economische en Sociale Geografie* **86**: 50–63

Williams C. C., Windebank J. (1994) Spatial variations in the informal sector: a review of evidence from the European Union. *Regional Studies* **28**: 819–25

Williams N. (1996) Britain's big science in a bind. *Science* **271**: 898–9

Williamson J. G. (1965) Regional inequality and the process of national development: a description of the patterns. *Economic Development and Cultural Change* **13**: 3–45

Williamson J. G. (1988) Migration and urbanization. In Chenery H., Srinivasan T. N. (eds) *Handbook of Development Economics*, volume I. Amsterdam, North-Holland: 425–65

Willingale M. C. (1984) Ship-operator port-routeing behaviour and the development process. In Hoyle B. S., Hilling D. (eds) *Seaport Systems and Spatial Change*. Chichester, John Wiley: 43–59

Willinger M., Zuscovitch E. (1988) Towards the economics of information-intensive production systems: the case of advanced materials. In Dosi G., Freeman C., Nelson R., Silverberg G., Soete L. (eds) *Technical Change and Economic Theory*. London, Pinter: 239–55

Willman P. (1987) Industrial relations issues in advanced manufacturing technology. In Wall T. D., Clegg C. W., Kemp N. J. (eds) *The Human Side of Advanced Manufacturing Technology*. New York, John Wiley: 135–51

Willmore L. (1995) Export processing zones in the Dominican Republic: a comment on Kaplinsky. *World Development* **23**: 529–35

Wilson P. A. (1992) *Exports and Local Development: Mexico's New Maquiladoras*. Austin, University of Texas Press

Wilson P. A. (1995) Embracing locality in local economic development. *Urban Studies* **32**: 645–58

Winch G. M. (1994) *Managing Production: Engineering Change and Stability*. Oxford,

Clarendon Press

Winder G. M. (1995) Before the corporation and mass production: the licensing regime in the manufacture of North American harvesting machinery, 1830–1910. *Annals of the Association of American Geographers* 85: 521–52

Wionczek M. S. (1979) Science and technology planning in LDCs. In Thomas D. B., Wionczek M. S. (eds) *Integration of Science and Technology with Development*. New York, Pergamon: 167–77

Wionczek M. S. (1993) Mexico. In Patel S. J. (ed.) *Technological Transformation in the Third World*, volume I: *Asia*. Aldershot, Avebury: 1–100

Wolch J. R., Geiger R. K. (1986) Urban restructuring and the not-for-profit sector. *Economic Geography* 62: 1–18

Wolff E. N. (1996) Technology and the demand for skills. *STI Review* 18: 95–123

Wolff G., Rigby D. L., Gauthier D., Cenzatti M. (1995) The potential impacts of an electric vehicle manufacturing complex on the Los Angeles economy. *Environment and Planning A* 27: 877–905

Wolman H., Spitzley D. (1996) The politics of local economic development. *Economic Development Quarterly* 10: 115–50

Wolman H., Stoker G. (1992) Understanding local economic development in a comparative context. *Economic Development Quarterly* 6: 406–17

Wong P.-K. (1995) Singapore's technology strategy. In Simon D. F. (ed.) *The Emerging Technological Trajectory of the Pacific Rim*. New York, M. E. Sharpe: 103–31

Wooldridge A. (1995) Big is back: a survey of multinationals. *The Economist* 24 June

Wood A. (1993) Organizing for local economic development: local economic development networks and prospecting for industry. *Environment and Planning A* 25: 1649–61

Wood A. (1994) *North–South Trade, Employment and Inequality: Changing Fortunes in a Skill-Driven World*. Oxford, Clarendon Press

Wood C. H., Kaufman A., Merenda M. (1996) How Hadco became a problem-solving supplier. *Sloan Management Review* 37 (2): 77–88

Wood S. (1988) Between Fordism and flexibility? The US car industry. In Hyman R., Streeck W. (eds) *New Technology and Industrial Relations*. Oxford, Basil Blackwell: 101–27

Woods S. (1987) *Western Europe: Technology and the Future*. Atlantic paper 63. London, Croom Helm

Woodward J. (1965) *Industrial Organization: Theory and Practice*. Oxford, Oxford University Press

World Bank (1991) *World Development Report 1991: The Challenge of Development*. New York, Oxford University Press

World Bank (1993) *The East Asian Miracle: Economic Growth and Public Policy*. New York, Oxford University Press

World Bank (1994a) *Adjustment in Africa: Reforms. Results, and the Road Ahead*. New York, Oxford University Press

World Bank (1994b) *World Development Report 1994: Infrastructure for Development*. New York, Oxford University Press

World Bank (1995a) *World Development Report 1995: Workers in an Integrating World*. Washington, World Bank

World Bank (1995b) *Bureaucrats in Business: The Economics and Politics of Government Ownership*. New York, Oxford University Press

World Bank (1996a) *Financial Flows and the Developing Countries* 3 (3): 33

World Bank (1996b) *World Development Report 1996: From Plan to Market*. New York,

Oxford University Press

Woronoff J. (1992) *Asia's 'Miracle' Economies*, second edition. New York, M. E. Sharpe

Wortmann M. (1990) Multinationals and the internationalization of R&D: new developments in German companies. *Research Policy* 19: 175–83

Yamamura K. (1987) Caveat emptor: the industrial policy of Japan. In Krugman P. R. (ed.) *Strategic Trade Policy and the New International Economics*. Cambridge, MA, MIT Press: 169–209

Yamashina H., Matsumoto K., Inoue I. (1991) Prerequisites for implementing CIM – moving towards CIM in Japan. In *Computer-Integrated Manufacturing: Perspectives for International Economic Development and Competitiveness*. Geneva, United Nations Economic Commission for Europe and Industrial Development Organization: 141–73

Yamashita S. (1995) Japan's role as a regional technological integrator and the black box phenomenon in the process of technology transfer. In Simon D. F. (ed.) *The Emerging Technological Trajectory of the Pacific Rim*. New York, M. E. Sharpe: 338–56

Yang D. J. (1989) Taiwan isn't just for cloning anymore. *Business Week* 25 September: 208–12

Yangida I. (1992) The business network: a powerful and challenging business tool. *Journal of Business Venturing* 7: 341–6

Yap L. Y. L. (1977) The attraction of cities: a review of the migration literature. *Journal of Development Economics* 4: 239–64

Yeh A. G.-O., Ng M. K. (1994) The changing role of the state in high-tech industrial development: the experience of Hong Kong. *Environment and Planning C: Government and Policy* 12: 449–72

Yeung H. W. (1994a) Critical reviews of geographical perspectives on business organizations and the organization of production: toward a network approach. *Progress in Human Geography* 18: 460–90

Yeung W.-C. H. (1994b) Hong Kong firms in the ASEAN region: transnational corporations and foreign direct investment. *Environment and Planning A* 26: 1931–56

Yonemoto K. (1986) Robotization in Japan – an examination of the socio-economic impacts. *International Journal of Technology Management* 1: 179–96

Yoshino M. Y., Rangan U. S. (1995) *Strategic Alliances: An Entrepreneurial Approach to Globalization*. Boston, Harvard Business School Press

Young R. C., Francis J. D., Young C. H. (1994a) Flexibility in small manufacturing firms and regional industrial formations. *Regional Studies* 28: 27–38

Young R. C., Francis J. D., Young C. H. (1994b) Small manufacturing firms and regional business networks. *Economic Development Quarterly* 8: 77–82

Young S., Hood N., Dunlop S. (1988) Global strategies, multinational subsidiary roles and economic impact in Scotland. *Regional Studies* 22: 487–97

Young S., Hood N., Peters E. (1994) Multinational enterprises and regional economic development. *Regional Studies* 28: 657–77

Yu S. (1995) Korea's high-technology thrust. In Simon D. F. (ed.) *The Emerging Technological Trajectory of the Pacific Rim*. New York, M. E. Sharpe: 81–102

Zangwill W. I. (1993) *Lightning Strategies for Innovation*. New York: Lexington Books

Zelinsky W. (1994) Conventionland USA: the geography of a latterday phenomenon. *Annals of the Association of American Geographers* 84: 68–86

Zhao L., Aram J. D. (1995) Networking and growth of young technology-intensive ventures in China. *Journal of Business Venturing* 10: 349–70

Ziegler J. N. (1992) Cross-national comparisons. In Alic J. A., Branscomb L. M.,

Brooks H., Carter A. B., Epstein G. L. (eds) *Beyond Spinoff: Military and Commercial Technologies in a Changing World.* Boston, Harvard Business School Press: 209–47

Zipp J. F. (1991) The quality of jobs in small business. *Economic Development Quarterly* 5: 9–22

Zuscovitch E., Cohen G. (1994) Network characteristics of technological learning: the case of the European Space Program. *Economics of Innovation and New Technology* 3: 139–60

Zysman J. (1994) How institutions create historically rooted trajectories of growth. *Industrial and Corporate Change* 3: 243–83

Index